M000095895

Real Estate Law In California

Tenth Edition

Arthur G. Bowman, A.B., M.L.A., J.D.
Author and Real Estate Educator
Member, State Bar of California and Hawaii

W. Denny Milligan, B.S., M.S., J.D.
Private Practice of Law, San Diego, California
Member, San Diego and California Bar Associations

SOUTH-WESTERN
™
THOMSON LEARNING

Australia · Canada · Mexico · Singapore · Spain · United Kingdom · United States

Real Estate Law in California, 10e
by
Arthur G. Bowman and W. Denny Milligan

COPYRIGHT © 2001 by South-Western Publishing, a division of Thomson Learning. The Thomson Learning logo is a registered trademark used herein under license.

All Rights Reserved. No part of this work covered by the copyright hereon may be reproduced or used in any form or by any means – graphic, electronic, or mechanical, including photocopying, recording, taping, or information storage and retrieval systems – without the written permission of the publisher.

Printed in the United States of America

2 3 4 03 04 05

For more information contact South-Western Publishing, 5101 Madison Road, Cincinnati, Ohio, 45227. Or you can visit our Internet site at http://www.swcollege.com

For permission to use material from this text or product contact us by
• **telephone: 1-800-730-2214**
• **fax: 1-800-730-2215**
• **web: http://www.thomsonrights.com**

ISBN

0-324-14294-3

A disinterested agency should exist to survey the body of our laws patiently and calmly and deliberately, attempting no sudden transformation, not cutting at the roots and growths of centuries, the products of a people's life in gradual evolution, but pruning and transplanting here and there with careful and loving hands.

Justice Cardozo

Contents

9   CREATION AND ENFORCEMENT OF SECURITY DEVICES, PART ONE   256

10   CREATION AND ENFORCEMENT OF SECURITY DEVICES, PART TWO   289

11   INVOLUNTARY LIENS, RECORDING, PRIORITIES, HOMESTEADS, AND TITLE INSURANCE   310

12   LIMITATIONS ON USE, INCLUDING TAX BURDEN   341

Abbreviations

Admin. Code   Administrative Code

Agr. C.   Agricultural Code

Am.Jur.2d   American Jurisprudence 2d

B. & P.   Business and Professions Code

C.   California Reports (bound volumes containing decisions of the California Supreme Court)

C.2d   California Reports, second series

C.3d   California Reports, third series

C.A.   California Appellate Reports (bound volumes containing decisions of the California Courts of Appeal)

C.A.2d   California Appellate Reports, second series

C.A.2d Supp.   California Appellate Reports, second series, supplement (cases determined in the Appellate Departments of the Superior Court)

C.A.3d   California Appellate Reports, third series

C.A.3d Supp.   California Appellate Reports, third series, supplement

Cal. Const.   California Constitution

Cal. Jur 2d.   California Jurisprudence, 2d series

C.C.   Civil Code

C.C.P.   Code of Civil Procedure

C.C. & R.s.   Covenants, Conditions, and Restrictions

C.E.B.   Continuing Education of the Bar

C.F.R.   Code of Federal Regulations

Comm. Regs.   Regulations of the California Real Estate Commissioner

Corp. C.   Corporation Code

C.R.   California Reporter (bound volumes containing decisions of both the California Supreme Court and the California Courts of Appeal)

Evid. C.   Evidence Code

Fam. Code   Family Code

F.C.R.A.   Fair Credit Reporting Act

Fed.   Federal Reporter (bound volumes containing decisions of the Federal Courts of Appeal)

Fed.2d   Federal Reporter, second series

Fed.3d   Federal Reporter, third Series

Fed. Supp.   Federal Supplement (bound volumes containing decisions of the U.S. District Courts)

Fin. C.   Financial Code

Govt. C.   Government Code

H. & S.   Health and Safety Code

Ins. C.   Insurance Code

I.R.C.   Internal Revenue Code

I.R.S   Internal Revenue Service

Lab. C.   Labor Code

L.Ed.2d   United States Supreme Court Reports, Lawyers' Edition, second series

Mil. & Vet.   Military and Veterans Code

M.L.S.   Multiple Listing Service

Ops. Cal. Atty. Gen.   Opinions of the Attorney General of California

P.2d   Pacific, second series

Pen. C.   Penal Code

Pro. C.   Probate Code

Pub. Res. C.   Public Resources Code

Ref. Book   Real Estate Reference Book

Regs.   I.R.S. Regulations

RESPA   Real Estate Settlement Procedures Act

Rest. Agency   Restatement of Agency

Rest. Torts   Restatement, Torts

Rest.2d Agency   Restatement of Agency, second series

Rest. Contracts   Restatement of Contracts

Rev. & Tax. C.   Revenue and Taxation Code (California)

S. Ct.   United States Supreme Court

Sec.   Section

Sts. & Hy. C.   Streets and Highway Code

S.W.2d   South West, second series

U.C.C.   Uniform Commercial Code

U.S.   United States Reports (bound volumes containing the decisions of the Supreme Court of the United States)

U.S.C.   United States Code

U.S.C.A.   United States Code Annotated

U.S. Const.   United States Constitution

USLW   United States Law Week

Veh. C.   Vehicle Code

Preface

In General

A number of years ago the broad expanse of California real property law, with its many special features, created a need for a book devoted exclusively to the real estate law of the state. This need was filled by the publication of the first edition of this work in 1958. The book presented complete, well-organized coverage of all basic aspects of California real estate law, intended primarily for college students and laypersons.

Objectives

As in previous editions, the main objective of this book is to acquaint all persons interested in real estate with the basic facts of California real estate law. The book deals with the law applicable to real property ownership in California—with the *practical* aspects of that law, not with theory alone. It will be helpful to all those concerned with real estate: brokers, salespeople, college students majoring in real estate, escrow and title company personnel, and the California real property owner. It will give them a better understanding of and a thorough acquaintance with the principles of real estate law in this state. The attorney will also find the discussions and practical aspects of real estate transactions—along with the hundreds of footnotes—invaluable.

Because of their scope and authoritative treatment, the previous editions of the book have had many users. Most adults in California have a vital and abiding interest in the subject of real estate. As is apparent from the many changes in the law since this book was first published, the law is a dynamic source, constantly being extended to meet the needs and requirements of modern developments in the real estate field. An understanding of the laws pertaining to real estate is essential to those engaged in any part of the industry. A basic understanding on the part of other members of the public is also desirable because it increases their awareness of the implications of our legal system in regard to their rights, duties, and obligations pertaining to real property. The present edition is an important contribution in this respect. In this new edition, the authors briefly cover what the law has been, what it presently is, and what may be anticipated in the future. It is important to understand the rationale of the law in order to be able to anticipate changes.

Ready Reference

Because of the growing number of lawsuits against sellers, brokers, and salespeople, there is an immediate need for a ready reference book within arm's reach of each licensee, to be used when the need arises. Possibly with a greater use of this text by the licensee with day-to-day problems in the field, errors and omissions insurance will decrease (because of fewer lawsuits), thus saving all licensees additional money.

Teaching Techniques and Footnotes

Because the text is designed for sophisticated brokers and others in the field as well as for the new salesperson taking a real estate law course, a compromise had to be reached. Among other things, footnotes have been placed at the end of each chapter for the broker or attorney to refer to when the need arises. However, the salesperson may wish to read only the body of the text, unhampered by any notes that previously appeared within the text page. Although the volume of cases presented in the examples is extensive, the instructor is also at liberty to pick other cases cited in the footnotes for outside reading assignments and for further discussion. And, of course, the instructor should be on the alert for cases and legislative changes that occur after the publication date.

The coverage of the book is based on the assumption that the reader will already have some basic knowledge of real estate obtained in a course on Real Estate Principles or Real Estate Practice. Describing the impact of the law on real estate ownership is the primary objective of this book.

Contents

The earlier editions of this book placed considerable emphasis on the title insurance aspects of real property ownership. Because of the inclusion of the many title aspects of real estate law in *Ogden's Revised California Real Property Law* by Arthur G. Bowman, first published in 1974, more emphasis in the book is on the brokerage aspects of real estate transactions. As a result, some of the previous material has been shortened, whereas other subjects, such as the law of contracts and agency and the duties and liabilities of the real estate licensee, have been expanded and include many practical as well as legal aspects. In addition, some tax aspects of real estate, which are included in this edition, continue to become more and more important, since learning the techniques of either saving or postponing thousands of tax dollars is desirable for anyone interested in real estate.

As will be learned in this book, the law is the foundation of all the rules relating to real property. Under all is the land, and over all is the law. A knowledge of the law is essential to guide our conduct and to allow us to be mediums for resolving conflicts or disputes between parties in a real estate transaction. As we gain an understanding of the impact of the law, we shall learn that practical considerations, rather than strict legal rights, are often determining factors.

Basically, the law is found in the California Constitution and in the statutes enacted by the legislature. Court cases, also significant, illustrate the law in action. As in previous editions, the application of the law to a particular factual situation is emphasized in this book by a discussion of many recent court cases important to the real estate field.

It should be noted that, in the interest of concision, the book often uses masculine pronouns to designate persons whose sex is not indicated. In these instances the reader should assume that the term "he," "him," or "his" is intended equally to imply "she," "her," or "hers."

Changes in the Tenth Edition

Prior editions of the book have reflected the many changes in the law based on statutory enactments and important court decisions. This new edition includes major changes in and additions to the law through the last part of 1998, with additional appropriate citations contained at the end of each chapter. Of necessity, there is an interval between the writing of a book and its publication; the reader should recognize the need to consider the impact of any later changes in the law.

At the end of each chapter are questions of the following three types: matching terms, true/false, and multiple choice. The latter, particularly, should prove of considerable value in studying for the license examination. The student is encouraged to answer the questions before checking the answers, which appear at the end of the book in "Answers to Textbook Questions."

Consideration was given to the inclusion of an outline for each chapter, but classroom experience has shown that it is more meaningful to have students create their own chapter outlines. This is encouraged since studies show that those making class outlines find it easier and more meaningful to grasp and understand the subject. A brief outline is contained in the *Instructor's Manual* as an aid for the instructor.

Coordination with DRE Guides

To present the material in the most effective manner and to afford a proper balance, the content and coverage of the previous editions were substantially revised in the fifth edition after considerable testing with attorneys and instructors throughout the state. This edition follows the presentation contained in the *Instructor's Guide* and *Student Study Guide* previously prepared by the authors for the Department of Real Estate in 1976. A different order of presentation can be used if desired, depending upon the inclination of the instructor, but the one presented here has met the test of time.

Glossary and Index

Because of the importance of the vocabulary of real estate, the book includes an extensive glossary, containing the words and phrases most frequently encountered in the law as it relates to real estate. The definitions are intended to be meaningful to the layperson having an interest in real estate, yet they retain their authoritative content.

As in previous editions, the index has been expanded to make it easier to locate a problem area at any time in the busy day of the broker or attorney, thus saving time and money. A listing in the index means the item can be found either in the body of the section referred to or in a footnote cited within that section but printed at the end of the chapter. The reader will find that many problem areas are discussed and solutions offered. The book highlights much that everyone should know about the legal aspects of real estate ownership and serves as an excellent starting point in the research of problems beyond the scope of this book.

Acknowledgments

Mr. Bowman wishes to thank Professor Robert J. Bond, Ph.D., then Chairman of the Business Department and Real Estate Coordinator, Los Angeles Valley College, Van Nuys, California, and Professor Cecilia A. Hopkins, then Chairperson of the Real Estate Department, College of San Mateo, San Mateo, California, for their work in reviewing previous editions and offering many helpful suggestions. He would also like to thank Nina J. Clifford of Cerritos College for her work in reviewing the previous edition where much valuable assistance was given by John C. Hoag, vice president and senior associate title counsel for Chicago Title Insurance Company in Los Angeles.

Mr. Milligan wishes to acknowledge the California Association of Realtors, as well as the various staff personnel at the Department of Real Estate, including the Commissioner. The suggestions of San Diego attorneys Scott Dodge (who updated the section on homesteads in Chapter 11) and Michael Dullea and Real Estate Broker Paul Vadnais are also greatly appreciated, as are those of countless Realtors, students, and instructors.

We welcome comments from our readers, as always—particularly the instructors.

Arthur G. Bowman

Denny Milligan

1

Sources of Law and Land Titles

I. INTRODUCTION

§1.1. Scope of chapter

This chapter will briefly consider the sources of law and land titles in California, and then will review the nature of property and classes of property. The chapter will conclude with a consideration of the various estates or interests in real property.

In studying the legal aspects of real estate, we shall find that the law is a dynamic force and is constantly subject to changes to meet the needs of contemporary society. As an associate justice of the California Supreme Court has observed, our crowded, computerized society creates an interdependence among its members, which inevitably brings changes in the law that governs it. The open spaces of frontier America that permitted physical and economic freedom, a laissez-faire economy, and laissez-faire law have been replaced by apartment houses, skyscrapers, and a complexity of legal rules. The very fact that people are pressed together in closely packed communities forces changes in their legal relationships.

As defined in the Civil Code, law is "a solemn expression of the will of the supreme power of the State."[1] The will of the supreme power is expressed by the state constitution and by statutes enacted by the legislature.[2] The common law of England, so far as it is not repugnant to or inconsistent with the Constitution of the United States, or the Constitution or laws of this State, is the rule on which decisions are based in all the courts of this State.[3]

As a general rule, there are no absolutes in the law. The facts and circumstances of each case are the determining factors. The vital, enduring part of the law lies in principles—starting points for reasoning—not in rules. Principles develop and change over long periods of time, while rules may vary from case to case. Principles give law the flexibility necessary to resolve conflicts.

II. REAL PROPERTY LAW AND ITS ORIGINS

§1.2. State and federal systems

In each of the states of this country, two separate systems of law are in force: state law and federal law. Federal law operates uniformly throughout the United States, with few exceptions. State law, however, may vary considerably from state to state. Each state has its own constitution, statutes, and court decisions, and it is primarily to these that we must look in determining the law that is applicable to a real estate transaction. Real property, unlike personal property, is subject to the laws of the state within which it is located, not to the laws of the domicile of the owner.

§1.3. Common law of England adopted in California

When California was admitted as a state in 1850, it adopted by statute the common law of England, not the laws of Mexico, as the law of the land. The law of real estate in the United States is based largely on the *common law* of England rather than on the civil law. The term *civil law* refers to the system of law prevailing in the countries that modeled their law after the Roman civil law. The method of the civil law, basically, is to attempt to set down at one time, by appropriate rules, just relations between all persons in all possible situations. The method of the common law, on the other hand, is to decide just relations between persons, case by case, as conflicts and disputes arise. In its earliest inception it consisted of customs and usages, and afterward of principles defined by the courts in the trial of cases that came before them. Precedent has played a basic role in the development of the common law.

§1.4. Spanish influence on California law

For a period of time California was a part of Spain, then later became a part of Mexico and was subject to the laws of those countries. Their laws were based on the civil law. Although the common law applies generally in California today, some Mexican law, which was based on Spanish law, was made the statutory law of California. This includes the community property law, a very important part of California real property law. Also, water rights in California have their origin in Mexican law. These rights were recognized in the Treaty of Guadalupe Hidalgo, by which California became a part of the United States. Full protection of all property rights of Mexicans was promised by this treaty, signed in 1848.

III. PRINCIPAL SOURCES OF THE LAW

§1.5. In general

Consideration will be given to many rules of law applicable to the ownership and transfer of real property in California, and it is important to determine the basis for these rules. To know the law applicable to real estate in California, we must look to the following principal sources: (1) the Constitution of the United States; (2) treaties; (3) laws passed by Congress; (4) federal regulations; (5) the Constitution of the State of California; (6) laws passed by the state legislature; (7) rules and regulations of state and local agencies; (8) ordinances; and (9) court decisions.

§1.6. Separation of powers

The powers of the government, both federal and state, are divided into three separate departments—legislative, executive, and judicial—and generally speaking, one department cannot exercise the functions of the others. The power to make laws is vested in the legislative department. The executive department is responsible for the administration of the laws. The judicial function is to declare the law and determine the rights of parties to a controversy before the court. The judicial branch attempts to resolve disputes or controversies between two or more persons or groups of persons. In the exercise of their jurisdiction, the courts are empowered to determine whether the legislature has exceeded its authority in enacting legislation. Thus, a measure of judicial control is placed on the powers of the legislature.

§1.7. Delegation of judicial powers

The growth of administrative law has resulted in a modification of the strict doctrine that judicial powers cannot be delegated to a nonjudicial board or officer. Such a board or officer may be invested with power to determine facts and exercise discretion. This power is judicial in nature and is termed quasi-judicial. The Real Estate Commissioner, for instance, is empowered to hold hearings and revoke licenses for causes defined by law.[4] However, an aggrieved party may still seek relief from the courts.

§1.8. Administrative law

The prohibition against the delegation of legislative power, like the companion rule that judicial power cannot be delegated, conflicts with the growing tendency to delegate to boards and officers a large measure of discretionary power that is ordinarily legislative in character. The delegation of an uncontrolled discretion is invalid. However, it is now generally established, on both the federal and state levels, that where the legislature lays down a sufficiently clear test or standard, the discretion to carry out the legislative purpose by rules and regulations may be given to a board or an officer.

§1.9. Constitutional controls

Both the national and state governments are controlled in what they can do by provisions in their respective constitutions. The fundamental difference between the two constitutions is that the Constitution of the United States is a grant of power to Congress—that is, Congress has such power as has been expressly conferred upon it—whereas the state constitution is a limitation on the power of the legislature—that is, the legislature has such powers as have not been denied to it.

Thus, unless restricted by the federal or state constitution, the state legislature has any power it chooses to exercise. This rule is emphasized in a case where the court stated that "we do not look to the Constitution to determine whether the legislature is authorized to do an act, but only to see if it is prohibited." [5]

§1.10. The Constitution of the United States

The Constitution of the United States is the supreme law of the land. Many rules of law pertaining to real property are based on provisions of the Constitution and its Amendments.

In one case, the judicial enforcement by state courts of covenants restricting the use or occupancy of real property to persons of the Caucasian race was held to violate the equal protection clause of the Fourteenth Amendment.[6] In another case,[7] California's Alien Land Law was also held to violate the equal protection clause of this amendment, which provides that "No state shall make or enforce any law which shall abridge the privileges or immunities of citizens of the United States, nor shall any state deprive any person of life, liberty, or property without due process of law; nor deny to any person within its jurisdiction the equal protection of the laws."

The exercise of the power of eminent domain is another example of the impact of the Constitution on private rights. If the federal government requires a parcel of land for one of its many functions, it cannot take the land from the owner without paying market value, because the Fifth Amendment forbids the taking of private property for public use without payment of just compensation.

§1.11. Treaties

The federal Constitution provides that treaties made under the authority of the United States are part of the supreme law of the land. A treaty, however, does not automatically supersede local laws that are inconsistent with it unless the treaty provisions are self-executing. For a treaty provision to be operative without the aid of legislation and to have the force and effect of a statute, it must appear that the framers of the treaty intended to prescribe a rule that, standing alone, would be enforceable by the courts. The Treaty of Guadalupe Hidalgo, referred to earlier, offers an example of the impact of a treaty on local property rights.

§1.12. Laws passed by Congress

Although most of the laws pertaining to real property are state laws, many federal laws are also applicable to the ownership of real property. The bankruptcy law is an example of this rule. Full power to enact bankruptcy legislation was granted to Congress by the federal Constitution. Pursuant to this grant, Congress has from time to time enacted various bankruptcy laws. For a number of years it was the view that under the provisions of the Bankruptcy Act, when a landowner is declared bankrupt, title to the land, unless exempt, automatically vests in the trustee in bankruptcy. The latter could sell the land for the purpose of obtaining funds to pay off the bankrupt's debts. This view is now debatable under various chapters of the new Bankruptcy Code. For example, title may remain in the debtor in Chapter 11 proceedings, or in the estate in Chapter 7 proceedings.

Another federal statute affecting real property is the Internal Revenue Code, various provisions of which create tax liens on property and rights to property of the person liable for the tax. The most recent major change is the 1986 Tax Reform Act, with subsequent modifications. The federal Truth in Lending Act, which applies to most loan transactions, is another example of a federal law that affects real estate transactions in California.

§1.13. Federal regulations adopted by various boards and commissions

Many federal agencies are empowered to prescribe rules and regulations necessary to carry out the provisions of laws enacted by Congress, such as the Truth in

Lending Act. Regulation Z is an example. Also, as an example, regulations have been adopted that relate to secondary financing in connection with FHA loans.

EXAMPLE When applying for a VA loan, a veteran must have the intent at the time he obtains the loan to occupy the home as his residence within a reasonable time afterward. If the veteran has no intent to do so, or if a real estate licensee (or anyone else) conspires with him to purchase the home when he has no such intent, this constitutes a false claim which carries substantial penalties.[8]

§1.14. The Constitution of the State of California

Many basic rights with respect to property are contained in the Constitution of the State of California. The state constitution that governs California was adopted at Sacramento in 1879. It has since been amended many times; however, the changes have served to keep the constitution in harmony with the demands of the constant growth and development of the state.

The constitution provides at the outset that all people have certain inalienable rights, among which are those of acquiring, possessing, and protecting property. The statutes pertaining to homesteads are based on a constitutional provision that the legislature shall, by law, protect from forced sale a certain portion of the homestead and other property of heads of families. The mechanic's lien law has as its basis a constitutional provision. Many other laws relating to property are based on provisions of the state constitution.

§1.15. State laws

A major part of the law relating to real property is contained in statutes enacted by the state legislature. Most of these statutes are now contained in numerous codes, including the Business and Professions Code, Civil Code, Code of Civil Procedure, the Probate Code, the Family Code, the Corporations Code, the Public Resources Code, Revenue & Taxation Code, and the Government Code, to name a few. The Civil Code, which sets forth most of the statutory laws relating to property rights, will be the code most frequently cited in this book. There are some 29 sets of codes, but a few statutes are still part of the general laws. The usury law, for instance, is part of the general laws. Figure 1-1 is illustrative of the legislative process.

§1.16. Rules and regulations of state and local agencies

As in the case of federal agencies, many state and local agencies are empowered to enact rules and regulations that have the force and effect of law. Thus, under the provisions of the Business and Professions Code, the Real Estate Commissioner may from time to time promulgate rules and regulations necessary for the conduct of that office and the administration and enforcement of the provisions of the Real Estate Law.

§1.17. City and county ordinances

Many ordinances affect real property, particularly the use that may be made of property. Zoning ordinances are typical examples. Ordinances may also be enacted to regulate the construction, erection, or alteration of buildings. A municipality may make and enforce reasonable regulations with reference to the location of gas tanks and the storage and use of explosive substances. Other ordinances provide for the creation of a lien in connection with the cost of removal of a substandard or unsafe structure. These are but a few of the many types of ordinances that affect the ownership and use of real property.

§1.18. Court decisions

A considerable portion of the law relating to real property is contained in the decisions of the California appellate courts. Although the courts do not make the

HOW A BILL BECOMES LAW

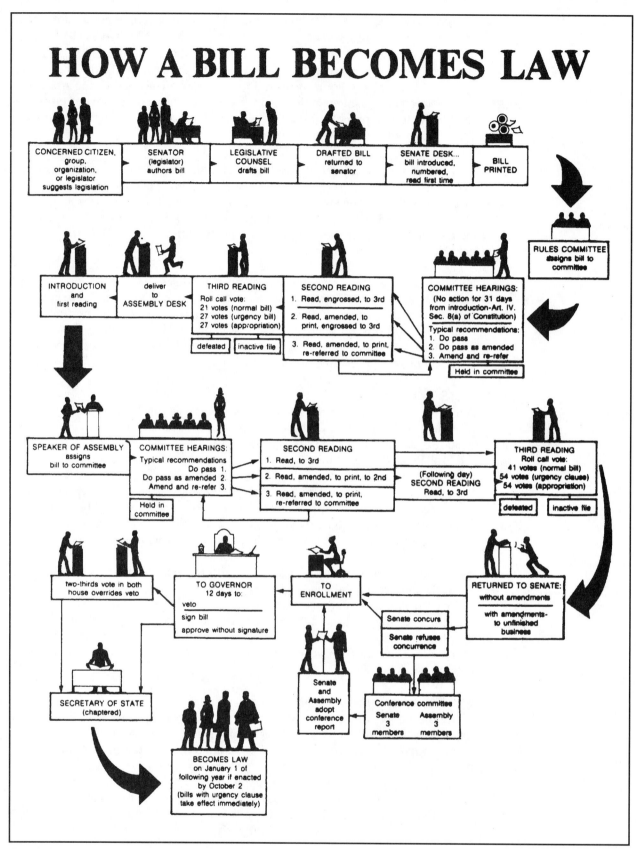

Figure 1-1
The legislative process

law—this is a function of the legislature—they do interpret the law, and it is often necessary to examine the decisions of the appellate courts to determine the meaning and effect of a law pertaining to real property. For example, the courts are sometimes called on to interpret provisions of the homestead law.

EXAMPLES
1. In an older case, the question was raised as to whether a homestead was abandoned when the husband moved from the premises to reside elsewhere. The court held that this did not constitute abandonment of the homestead.[9]

2. In another case, the court sustained the validity of a regulation of the state Agricultural Labor Relations Board granting a limited right of access to growers' premises by farm labor organizers. The court held that this did not deprive the property owners of their property rights without due process of law, stating:

> The governmental policy in favor of collective bargaining … is designed to benefit the public as a whole. It should scarcely be necessary, as we enter the last quarter of the 20th century, to reaffirm the principle that all private property is held subject to the power of the government to regulate its use for the public welfare. We do not minimize the importance of the constitutional guarantees attaching to private ownership of property; but as long as 50 years ago it was already "thoroughly established in this country that the rights preserved to the individual by these constitutional provisions are held in subordination to the rights of society. Although one owns property, he may not do with it as he pleases any more than he may act in accordance with his personal desires. As the interest of society justifies restraints upon individual conduct, so also does it justify restraints upon the use to which property may be devoted. It was not intended by these constitutional provisions to so far protect the individual in the use of his property as to enable him to use it to the detriment of society. By thus protecting individual rights, society did not part with the power to protect itself or to promote its general wellbeing. Where the interest of the individual conflicts with the interest of society, such individual interest is subordinated to the general welfare …"[10]

---

§1.19. Some applicable legal principles

To have a better understanding of the judicial process, it will be helpful to consider briefly some of the frequently encountered terms, such as *jurisdiction, venue, equity,* and *estoppel.*

Jurisdiction. Jurisdiction is essential to the validity of a judgment, order, or decree of a court. Generally, it may be said that the following are the jurisdictional requirements: (1) legal organization of the tribunal; (2) jurisdiction over the person; (3) jurisdiction over the subject matter of the action; and (4) power to grant the judgment.

A judgment may be void in whole or in part because it granted some relief that the court had no power to grant. Thus, a judgment of foreclosure without giving the right of redemption is void insofar as it bars the right of redemption.[11]

Venue. Venue is distinguished from jurisdiction in that the latter, in a strict sense, is judicial power to hear and determine a cause, whereas venue is synonymous with "place of trial" and has reference to the proper place of trial from among the courts having jurisdiction over the subject matter of an action, whether a particular county or judicial district. The Code of Civil Procedure provides that the county where the real property is situated is the proper county for the trial of certain types of actions, such as actions for recovery of real property, partition of real property, and foreclosure of liens on real property.[12] However, such actions may be transferred to another county for purposes of trial when, for instance, the convenience of witnesses and the ends of justice would be promoted by the change.[13]

Equity. The terms *equity* and *equitable rights* are frequently encountered in the field of real property law. What is their origin? In the early days of the development of the common law, there was a tendency on the part of the courts to make the system rigid and formal. If a litigant could not bring a plea for relief within the four corners of an existing remedy, relief was denied. He would then turn to the king as the fountain of justice, and if the case was meritorious, the king would intervene, through the chancellor, and give the necessary relief even though no legal remedy was available. In time this became a common procedure, and the chancellor developed a set of rules for the administration of remedies based on principles of right and justice. This system became known as equity, and the remedies as equitable remedies. Two classes of courts thus developed: law courts and equity courts. This system was brought over to colonial America, and the principles of equity are still applicable today, although only a few of the states still have separate courts for the administration of law and equity. In most states, as in California, law and equity are administered by the same court.

Statute of limitations. A statute of limitations prescribes a time within which an action must be filed. The time varies, depending on the nature of the action. For instance, an action to recover possession of real property must be commenced within five years from the time the cause of action arose,[14] whereas a personal injury suit, such as an automobile accident case, must be brought within one year.[15]

What is the purpose of a statute of limitations? It is based on the premise that if a person has a just claim, it should be asserted within a reasonable time. Stale claims are hard to prove, and defenses against them may be even harder to establish. Witnesses die, move away, or forget, or evidence otherwise becomes unavailable. The statute of limitations, like the statute of frauds, is frequently encountered in real property litigation. The statute of frauds requires that certain agreements be in writing in order to be enforceable, and is further discussed in Chapter 2.

The doctrine of laches. An unreasonable delay in asserting a claim may also be barred under the doctrine of laches. This is an equitable defense, and a court of equity will refuse relief to a party who has delayed the assertion of a claim so that granting the relief requested would work an injustice on the other party. Three elements must be present to constitute this equitable defense: (1) knowledge by the party of his right; (2) unjustified delay in asserting that right; and (3) some circumstances, such as change of position by the other party, which would make it inequitable to grant the relief requested.

Aside from these general principles, there are no hard and fast rules, and the application of the doctrine depends on the facts and circumstances of each particular case. It has been said in regard to laches that each case is a law unto itself.[16]

Estoppel. Another doctrine that applies in the field of real estate law is that of estoppel. An estoppel arises when a party, by his own declaration, act, or omission, has intentionally led another to believe a particular thing to be true and to act on such belief.[17] Although *waiver* and *estoppel* are sometimes used indiscriminately, as though possessing common elements, they rest on different legal principles.[18]

EXAMPLES
1. In one case, the court stated that for estoppel to be brought against an assertion of ownership of realty, it must be shown that (1) the party to be estopped was apprised of the true state of his title; (2) an admission was made with intent to deceive or with such culpable negligence as to amount to constructive fraud; (3) the other party was destitute not only of knowledge of the state of the title but also of means of acquiring knowledge; and (4) that the admission was relied on to his damage.[19]

2. The doctrine of estoppel has been applied in cases when a person who has an oral license to use another person's property for a limited purpose, such as a right of way, expends a considerable sum of money for its improvement without objection by the landowner, and thereafter is notified of the cancellation of the license. Under the principle of estoppel, it has been held that the license has ripened into an easement.[20]

Clean hands doctrine. The "clean hands" doctrine was expressed by the court in one case, as follows:

> *Whenever a party who, as actor, seeks to set the judicial machinery in motion and obtain some remedy, has violated conscience, or good faith, or other equitable principle in his prior conduct, then the doors of the court will be shut against him.*[21]

Maxims of jurisprudence. Over the years, a number of rules or principles have been adopted by the courts as an aid in bringing about a fair or just disposition of a controversy. In California, many of these rules have been codified. Thirty-eight of these rules, called "Maxims of Jurisprudence," are contained in the Civil Code.[22] Some of these are:

1. For every wrong there is a remedy.
2. No one should suffer by the act of another.
3. Between rights otherwise equal, the earliest is preferred.
4. The law helps the vigilant before those who sleep on their rights.
5. Interpretation must be reasonable.
6. He who comes into court must come with clean hands.
7. No one can take advantage of his wrong.
8. When one of two innocent persons must suffer, the one who caused the harm must suffer.
9. When the reason for a rule ceases, so should the rule itself.
10. The law neither does nor requires idle acts.

§1.20. Particular types of actions

It is a maxim of the law that for every wrong there is a remedy. Thus, a considerable number of court actions are available, depending upon the nature of the relief sought. Three types of action often encountered are actions for damages, for specific performance, or for rescission (discussed in Chapter 2). The following are other types of actions frequently encountered in the real estate field.

Injunction. Injunction is a type of action in which one party seeks to prevent another party from an act which, if done, could cause irreparable damage.

EXAMPLES

1. An owner of real property subject to a deed of trust allegedly in default may bring an action to enjoin a trustee's sale until the question of whether there is in fact a default can be judicially determined.
2. The owner of an easement may bring an action against the owner of the servient tenement to enjoin interference with the easement right.

Foreclosure. Foreclosure is a type of action available when there has been a default in payment of a trust deed or other lien on real property. Basically, it is an action to enforce payment of an obligation by a sale of the security.

Other types of actions. Actually, there is no limit to the various types of actions that might be brought in an effort to resolve a controversy or dispute.

EXAMPLES 1. If a party has wrongfully obtained ownership or possession of property, an action to impress a trust on the property might be brought by an aggrieved party.

2. An action might be brought on the theory of "unjust enrichment" when a party has received money or other benefit to which he is not legally entitled. It is a means by which a person can be compelled to account for that which has been received that does not belong to that person.

The objective of the law is to define rights, duties, and obligations. The courts afford a means of redress; they are a forum where conflicting interests can be resolved and where a party may be able to choose from several remedies the one most appropriate for his purposes.

Class actions. A comparatively new type of action that has been prevalent in recent times is known as a class action. In this case, the party filing the action brings it not only on his own behalf but also on behalf of all other persons in a similar situation.

EXAMPLES 1. A class action was brought to determine the validity of a due on encumbrance clause in a trust deed.[23]

2. A determination of many other rights under deeds of trust, such as interest on impound accounts, has been the subject of class actions.

IV. THE COURT STRUCTURE

§1.21. In general

Two separate systems of law are in force: federal law and state law. In certain types of proceedings, the federal courts have exclusive jurisdiction; however, in the most frequent situations, state courts have jurisdiction. Because decisions of the appellate courts are an important source of law, an understanding of the court structure and the nature of judicial proceedings is essential.

§1.22. Resort to the courts

When parties become involved in a dispute regarding property or other rights that they cannot settle amicably, it is often necessary to take the matter to court. Basically, there are two kinds of courts in the judicial system: trial courts and appellate courts. The trial court's job is to hear all the pertinent facts in the case, apply the law, and then decide in favor of one party or the other. If the losing party feels that the decision is wrong, it may be appealed to a higher court. The higher court, in announcing a decision, states the reasons for the decision and discusses the legal principles involved. Such a decision is called an *opinion*, and these opinions are published in bound volumes called *reports*, which guide the decision of similar cases in the future. The case is said to set a *precedent*, known as *stare decisis*, and as noted above, these court decisions constitute one of the chief sources of real estate law.

§1.23. Basis of court decision

California real property law stems in large part from the real estate law of England. In earlier cases, it was not uncommon for the courts to base their decisions on those older cases. In dealing with present-day problems, however, the courts must often evoke new rules without the benefit of the past. In some instances, there may not be a California case in point, but a similar case may have been decided in another state. Such a decision, although not binding on the California court, may have sufficient persuasive effect to be adopted as a rule of law in this state. What the courts attempt to do is expressed in Samuel Johnson's remark that "the law is the last result of human wisdom acting upon human experience for the benefit of the public."

The state courts in California used to consist of the Supreme Court, Courts of Appeal, a Superior Court in each county, and a Municipal Court in each judicial district. However, California voters in November, 1998 decided under Proposition 220 to consolidate Municpal Court and Superior Courts into one court effective January 1, 1999 depending on how the judges in each county voted. In virtually all of California's 58 counties (except Los Angeles and Kern Counties), it was decided to consolidate, and now there is only one trial court in most counties: the Superior Court. Because this is such a new concept, and not all counties have adopted consolidation, the former breakdown of Superior and Municipal Courts is set forth below.

§1.24. California judicial system

The foregoing brief summary of the main function of the court leads to a consideration of the court structure in this state. The state courts in California consist of the Supreme Court, Courts of Appeal, a Superior Court in each county, and a Municipal Court in each judicial district.

Municipal and Justice Courts. The state constitution requires that a Municipal Court be established in any judicial district whose population exceeds forty thousand. A district of lesser population, until the 1994 elections, had a Justice Court. There are now no Justice Courts in California. Municipal Courts are courts of limited jurisdiction; they can hear only certain types of cases in which the amount of money involved is relatively small. Most of the civil cases tried in these courts are actions for money. Actions to foreclose a mechanic's lien where the claim does not exceed $25,000 may be brought in the Municipal Courts but other types of foreclosure actions must be brought in the Superior Court. Municipal Courts now have jurisdiction over unlawful detainer actions if the total amount of damages claimed is $25,000 or less.[24] Execution sales involving real property may be had on judgments obtained in the Municipal Courts. Thus, proceedings in this court can affect *title* to real property, although questions of title to real property are otherwise beyond the jurisdiction of this lower court.

Municipal Courts include within their framework a Small Claims Court where litigants represent themselves; an attorney is not permitted to represent a party in Small Claims Court. A corporation can appear in Small Claims Court through an employee or duly appointed or elected officer or director.[25] But a corporation in Municipal or Superior Court can only appear through its attorney. A party may now bring an action in Small Claims Court whenever the amount of the claim is $5,000, depending upon the circumstances.[26]

Superior Courts. The Superior Courts are courts of general jurisdiction, and most cases involving real property originate in these courts. Actions to quiet title, actions for specific performance of a real estate contract, actions to foreclose a deed of trust, actions to enjoin the breach of a deed restriction, actions for marital dissolution, and probate proceedings are types of cases that must be brought in Superior Court. The Superior Courts also have jurisdiction to hear appeals from cases arising in Municipal Court in their respective counties.

Appellate Courts. Judgments, orders, and decrees of the Superior Court are appealable to the Courts of Appeal or to the Supreme Court of California.

The Courts of Appeal are divided into five districts with 18 divisions. Each division is autonomous, with the result that the intermediate appellate court system is not a unified structure, but is referred to as "a loose assemblage of separate tribunals." This has raised concern and a recommendation that the system be further changed in order to obtain uniform procedures.[27]

The California Supreme Court serves as the law-unifying, consistency-producing mechanism in the state judicial system. It consists of a chief justice and six associate justices. Its decisions are binding on all of the lower courts in the state. A 7-0 decision generally will have more persuasive effect when citing a case as a precedent. A close decision, such as 4-3, could go the other way if a similar case were later to come before the court, based on changing times.

All opinions of the Supreme Court are published, but since 1964, the opinions of the Courts of Appeal and Superior Court Appellate Departments are published only if they involve a new and important issue of law, a change in an established principle of law, or a matter of general public interest.

§1.25. Jurisdiction of federal courts

In several types of cases the federal courts have exclusive jurisdiction, and these proceedings sometimes affect title to real property. The federal courts have exclusive jurisdiction, for instance, over all bankruptcy cases and over all civil actions in which the United States is a party, such as a condemnation action brought by the United States government.

§1.26. Federal judicial system

Generally, the court structure of the federal system is comparable to that of the state, and consists of trial courts, intermediate courts of appeal, and the Supreme Court. Federal cases are commenced in the local United States District Court. The United States is divided into 98 districts, each with a district court. In California the state is divided into four judicial districts, known as the Northern, Eastern, Central, and Southern Districts of California. Appeals from the District Courts go to the next higher court, the Court of Appeals (formerly designated Circuit Court of Appeal). Fewer of these courts exist—just 11 in the country—and California is in the Ninth Circuit. As part of the federal judicial system there are also the Tax Court, the Court of Claims, and the Bankruptcy Court.

§1.27. United States Supreme Court

The highest court is the Supreme Court of the United States. This court is made up of nine justices, appointed for life by the President with the advice and consent of the Senate. One of the justices, designated the Chief Justice, presides over sessions of the court.

Power of judicial review. Most cases reach the Supreme Court on appeal from a lower federal court, or from a state supreme court when a question of federal law is involved. The Supreme Court has what is called "discretionary jurisdiction," that is, it can usually decide which cases to hear. If the court is of the opinion that the case at hand is of broad and general interest to the nation's welfare, it will usually grant a hearing to the parties. One of the most important functions of the court is to decide whether a state or federal law conflicts with the federal Constitution and is therefore invalid. This is known as "the power of judicial review."

How the court chooses. It is the established policy of the Supreme Court to choose "in the interest of the law, its appropriate exposition and enforcement, not in the mere interest of the litigants." If review of a case is to be had by the Supreme Court, it must be because of public interest in the questions involved.

A unanimous decision of the United States Supreme Court will generally have a much more persuasive effect than a close decision. Some of the 5-4 decisions of a few years ago are no longer precedents, with a different result being obtained in later similar cases, based on changing times and a change in the personnel of the court.

V. NATURE OF PROPERTY

§1.28. What is property?

A buyer of real property or a lender obtaining a security interest in real property, such as a beneficiary under a trust deed, will want to know what is included in the term "real estate" or "real property." He should know what besides the land itself is included in a conveyance of real property. Does a conveyance transfer the minerals, including oil and gas? Does it include water rights, easements, airspace above the surface, the right to rents, and any other thing or right?

To understand what is real property, we should first be aware of what property is. *Property* is defined as "the thing of which there may be ownership." *Ownership* is defined as "the right of one or more persons to possess and use it [property] to the exclusion of others." [28]

Things subject to ownership include the following:

1.   Property, both real and personal
2.   Inanimate things capable of appropriation or manual delivery (e.g., electricity)
3.   Domestic animals
4.   Obligations
5.   Products of labor or skill (e.g., author's book)
6.   Goodwill of a business
7.   Trademarks or signs
8.   Rights created by statutes

§1.29. Property as a "bundle of rights"

When we think of property, we generally think of the thing itself, such as an automobile, a piece of furniture, a promissory note, or a parcel of land. In a strict legal sense, however, the word does not mean the thing itself that is owned, but refers to the rights or interests that a person has in a thing, often referred to as a "bundle of rights." This bundle of rights is the exclusive right of a person to own, possess, use, enjoy, and dispose of a determinate thing, either real property or personal property, consistent with the law. This bundle of rights is called property.

§1.30. Right of disposition

The owner of property is the one who has the right of dominion over it, with rights of disposition, exclusion, and use. These rights are the chief incidents of ownership. The land may be kept as long as the owner wishes (subject, however, to the government's power of eminent domain). All or any part of it may be sold, or it may be given away. If the land is to be sold, the owner may choose the manner of its disposition and the terms of sale, because this is the exclusive right of an owner—subject, however, to the impact of the antidiscrimination laws. It may be devised to a particular person by will, the transfer becoming effective on death. The owner may create a life estate in the land or some lesser estate. He may choose to do nothing with the land during his lifetime, and upon death his property rights will pass by operation of law to other persons in accordance with the laws of succession in effect at the time of his death.

§1.31. Right of exclusion

The owner of land generally has the right to exclude others from his land.[29] No one has the right to enter on another person's land without the permission of the owner, and if he does, he may be liable to the owner for trespass. The owner, however, may give permission to others to enter on his land. A written lease may be entered into with another person for a term of years, under which the lessee would have the right to enter and take over complete possession of the property for the stated period. The owner may rent a portion of the premises to a tenant, or may give permission to another person, by the grant of either an easement or a license, to use a portion of the land for a particular purpose, such as a right of way for a driveway. Other persons may thus receive specific and separate rights in relation to the land of another. Although the owner still retains the most important proprietary rights in the land, the bundle of rights is not as large as it was originally, because other persons have acquired rights of possession in the land.

§1.32. Right of use and enjoyment
The owner has the exclusive right to use and enjoy the land. The land may be used as the owner pleases, subject, however, to the control exercised by the government over the use of the land through its power of taxation and under the police power. The owner may leave the land unimproved or may improve it. He may grow crops on the land, or may clear the land of timber. The owner may change the contour of the land or may dig all the gravel from the land and give it away, and no one can hold him liable for waste and destruction of the land. The land is his to use and enjoy to the exclusion of others.

§1.33. Limitations on right of use
Various obligations and duties imposed by law on a landowner restrict to a certain extent the use that may be made of the land, and the law in some instances may impose an affirmative duty of care. The law may require the owner to control weed growth, insects, and other pests. If the owner chooses to improve the land, he must comply with the provisions of zoning ordinances and building and safety codes. Although the owner does have the exclusive right of use, he does not have the right to an unlimited use and freedom of enjoyment. This right is subject to the paramount right of the state to control the use of land in the interest of public health, safety, morals, and welfare.

VI. CLASSES OF PROPERTY
§1.34. Real property
The Civil Code divides property into two classes: real or immovable property, and personal or movable property. *Real property* consists of land, that which is affixed to land, that which is incidental or appurtenant to land, and that which is immovable by law.[30] This is a partial definition, applicable in connection with the transfer of real property. However, for purposes of taxation, the definitions in the revenue and taxation laws of the state control whether or not they conform to definitions used for other purposes.[31]

§1.35. Property may undergo a change in class
Under the proper circumstances, real property or personal property may undergo a transformation and be changed into the other class of property. Land in place is immovable and hence is real property, but when it is severed from the earth, as, for instance, when a load of gravel or topsoil is removed from a plot of ground, it becomes movable and therefore personal property. Similarly, personal property becomes a part of the land when it is attached thereto with the intention of making it a permanent part of the land.

§1.36. Elements of real property
Under the definition contained in the Civil Code,[32] real property includes not only the ground or soil, but also things that are attached to the earth, whether by course of nature, such as trees and other vegetation, or by the hand of man, such as a house or other structure. It also includes things that are incidental to the use of land, such as an easement or right of way. It includes not only the surface of the earth, but everything under and above it. A tract of land, in legal theory, not only consists of the portion on the earth's surface, but is also like an inverted pyramid

having its apex at the center of the earth, and extending outward from the surface of the earth at its boundary lines to the periphery of the universe.

§1.37. Ownership above the surface

The doctrine of ownership of airspace is expressed in the Civil Code, which provides that "the owner of land in fee has the right to the surface and to everything permanently situated beneath or above it."[33] This doctrine, of common law origin, has been modified to meet the development and needs of air navigation. As stated in an older case, "It is ancient doctrine that common law ownership of the land extended to the periphery of the universe ... But that doctrine has no place in the modern world."[34]

Ownership of airspace today. Modern theories as to ownership of airspace are not uniform, but a rational view, based on the decision in the above-mentioned case, may be expressed as follows: The airspace is a public highway, but the landowner owns at least as much of the space above the surface as can be used and occupied in connection with his land, even though it is not occupied in a physical sense by buildings and the like. The owner has the right to prevent a use of the space by others that would interfere with his use of the land. The United States Supreme Court has held that noise, vibrations, and fear caused by constant and extremely low overflights interfered with the use of the owner's property so as to amount to a "taking," in the constitutional sense, of an air easement for which compensation must be paid.[35]

Division of airspace into strata. The division of airspace above the land into strata for purposes of ownership or use apart from the surface of the land is not uncommon in many large cities, and such division has been expressly sanctioned in several jurisdictions. Although such division was recognized in California under former law, specific recognition was given to the division of airspace in California by the adoption of the Condominium Law (discussed further in Chapter 8), including the new concept of time-sharing.

§1.38. What "land" consists of

The word *land* is defined as "the materials of the earth, whatever may be the ingredients of which it is composed, whether soil, rock or other substance,"[36] which includes oil and gas. As part of the Condominium Law, the code was amended to include "free or occupied space for an indefinite distance upwards as well as downwards, subject to limitations upon the use of airspace imposed, and rights in the use of airspace granted, by law."

§1.39. Minerals

Land includes all ores, metals, coal, and other minerals on or in the land to the center of the earth. Although in recent times there has been a modification of the doctrine of ownership above the surface, the rule of ownership to the center of the earth still applies. Minerals while they remain in place are real property; when severed from the earth, they become personal property.

Separate ownership of minerals. For purposes of ownership, land may be divided horizontally as well as vertically. For example, the owner of the land may convey the minerals to another person and retain ownership of the land, or vice versa. The minerals can be conveyed at different levels or strata beneath the surface, and the practice is not uncommon of designating horizontal spheres in mineral leases, including oil and gas leases. The grant or reservation of the minerals carries with it an implied right of entry for the purpose of extracting the minerals. To eliminate a right of entry on the surface of the land, it is common practice to convey the minerals below 500 feet beneath the surface, and to exclude specifically right of entry from the surface.

Oil and gas. Oil and gas are classified as minerals but fall into a special category. Unlike solid minerals, which are stationary, oil and gas are shifting, migratory substances that are incapable of absolute ownership as a thing in place, and must be reduced to possession before ownership becomes complete. However, the landowner owning the minerals does have an exclusive right to drill for and produce oil and gas, and to retain all such substances brought to the surface. This right may be granted by the owner separate from a grant of the surface, or may be excepted in a conveyance of the surface. When so granted or excepted it is known as a *profit à prendre*, an interest in real property in the nature of an incorporeal hereditament. An oil and gas *profit à prendre* is "essentially indistinguishable from an easement."[37]

Geothermal steam. Unless the parties otherwise intend, geothermal steam will be treated as a mineral. Provided that there is no destruction of the surface and that the parties did not agree to the contrary, extraction of the energy of geothermal steam, similar to drilling for oil, is permitted.[38]

§1.40. Water rights

General considerations. Water has a number of sources and uses. Too little or too much of it can create a variety of problems. The problem of fighting off flood waters will be considered in §14.73. A waterway as a boundary will be considered briefly in Chapter 13 in connection with land descriptions. We will be concerned here with the landowner's right to use fresh water that either borders or is found beneath the surface of his property. The principal use of water is for domestic and agricultural purposes, and sometimes it is a source of power.

Nature of water. In its natural state, water is real property; when severed from the realty and reduced to possession by being put in containers, it becomes personal property. The subject of water rights is complex, and many rules apply. Some of these rights are discussed briefly below.

Riparian water rights. The owner of land bordering on a river or other water course has no absolute ownership of the waters, but has a right, in common with others, to the reasonable use of water flowing past his land. This, in brief, is what is designated as riparian water rights.

Littoral rights. Basically, littoral rights are the rights of a landowner to the use of the water of a lake or an ocean bordering the land. They are somewhat analogous to riparian rights. Questions that may arise in connection with such lands relate to the exact location of the boundary, or to limitations in use based on rights of others, including the public, particularly as to access to the water.

Underground waters. Underground waters, such as percolating waters, were formerly regarded as part of the soil and owned absolutely by the owner of the land. However, in California the landowner has only a right in common with other owners to take a share of the water for beneficial use. The right of the overlying landowner to the percolating waters beneath his land is analogous to riparian rights.

EXAMPLE
In one case, it was stated that owners of land have a right to the use of underground waters as a supporting underground water supply available to, and for the benefit of, farming operations, and such use is a beneficial use of the underground waters.[39]

Rights of appropriators. Rights in streams and underground basins may also be appropriative. Public interest requires that there be the greatest number of beneficial uses that the water supply can yield, and surplus water may be appropriated for beneficial use subject to the rights of those who have a lawful priority. Any water not needed for the reasonable beneficial use of those having prior rights is excess or surplus water and may rightly be appropriated on privately owned land for nonoverlying use, such as devotion to public use or exportation beyond the basin watershed. As between overlying owners, their rights, like those of riparians, are correlative; each may use only a reasonable share when the water is insufficient to meet the needs of all.[40]

Ownership of land bordering on water.[41]

1. Ocean or tidal waters—to high water mark
2. Navigable stream or lake—to low water mark
3. Nonnavigable stream or lake—to middle water mark

§1.41. "Land" as including improvements

The statutory definition of land appears to exclude improvements and other fixtures on the land and appurtenant rights, thereby making land but one of the elements of real property.[42] In some cases, however, the courts have construed the word *land* alone as including improvements. The use of the word *land* has been declared synonymous with real property because of its historical, ordinary, and accepted meaning in connection with title, ownership, conveyance, or transfer by deed or inheritance, or with the exercise of the right of eminent domain, or with execution sales and redemption and similar evidences of ownership or modes of transfer.[43] Moreover, regardless of the limited statutory definition, it has been held that a conveyance of "land" transfers the land itself and all that is annexed, incidental, or appurtenant thereto.[44]

§1.42. "Land" as used in a title policy

Land is used in a limited sense in a policy of title insurance. Policies of title insurance insure title to the "land" therein described, and define the word *land* as including improvements affixed thereto that by law constitute real property. Rights in other lands, such as an appurtenant easement over land adjoining that described in the title policy, although embraced as a matter of law in the term *real property*, are not included in the coverage of the title policy unless expressly described and insured. This subject will be considered in further detail in Chapter 11.

§1.43. Things deemed affixed to land

The term *real property* includes, in addition to the land itself, that which is affixed to land. The Civil Code provides that a thing is deemed to be affixed to land when it is attached to it by roots, as in the case of trees, vines, or shrubs; or embedded in it, as in the case of walls; or permanently resting on it, as in the case of buildings; or permanently attached to what is thus permanent, as by means of cement, plaster, nails, bolts, or screws.[45] The subject of fixtures will be considered in further detail in Section VIII.

§1.44. *Fructus naturales*

Trees, shrubs, vines, and crops that are a product of nature alone, termed *fructus naturales*, are generally regarded as part of the land to which they are attached by roots, and they continue to be real property until severed, actually or constructively, at which time they become personal property. *Fructus naturales* may be owned separately from the land.

EXAMPLE Standing timber may be conveyed, or may be reserved in a conveyance, apart from the land, and the owner of the timber would have a right of removal, if not limited by the terms of the conveyance.

Transfer of "fructus naturales." An effective conveyance of growing trees and other *fructus naturales* apart from the land should, it would seem, require a writing and other formalities for the transfer of real property. However, the Civil Code provides that for purposes of sale, things attached to the land that are agreed to be severed before sale, or under contract of sale, shall be treated as goods, and governed by the rules regulating the sale of goods.[46]

§1.45. *Fructus industriales*

Grain, garden vegetables, and other growing crops that are the result of annual labor, classified as *fructus industriales* (industrial crops), may be either real property or personal property, depending on the circumstances. A growing crop of fruit on trees or vines is classed as *fructus industriales*. As between a seller and buyer of land, growing crops are a part of the land until severed or agreed to be severed, and pass to the grantee by a conveyance of the land, unless reserved in writing. As in the case of trees, a sale of growing crops may be made by the code provisions regulating the sale of goods.

§1.46. Personal property

Under the Civil Code, personal property is defined in a negative way: Every kind of property that is not real property is personal property.[47] The usual method for a transfer of tangible personal property is by a bill of sale. For a transfer of intangible personal property, such as a cause of action, an assignment is used.

§1.47. Personal property security agreements

The Uniform Commercial Code became effective in California in 1965. It established a uniform procedure for perfecting a security interest in personal property. The terms used in the Code are security agreement, security interest, and financing statements.

Among the items excluded from the operation of the Code are fixtures, oil and minerals in place, and the creation or transfer of an interest in or lien on real estate. The law has only a limited effect on land titles.

§1.48. Financing statements (Form U.C.C. 1)

Under the provisions of the Uniform Commercial Code, a security interest in personal property is perfected by the filing of a "financing statement" as follows:

1. When the collateral is equipment used in farming operations, or farm products, other than crops, or accounts or contract rights arising from or relating to the sale of farm products by a farmer, or consumer goods, then the proper place to file is the office of the county recorder in the county of the debtor's residence or, if the debtor is not a resident of this State, then in the office of the county recorder where the goods are kept. (Consumer goods are those used or bought for use primarily for personal, family, or household purposes.)[48]

2. When the collateral is crops or timber to be cut, then the proper place to file is in the office of the county recorder in the county where the land is located on which the crops are growing or to be grown, or on which the timber is standing.

3. In all other cases the proper place to file is in the office of the Secretary of State in Sacramento.

The only requirement that the description of real property appear in the financing statement is when the collateral consists of crops growing or to be grown, or timber to be cut. (See Chapter 9 for discussion on obligations secured by real and personal property.)

§1.49. Effect of filing

The filing of a financing statement is effective for five years and then expires unless a continuation statement is filed within six months before the end of the five-year period. This procedure may be repeated indefinitely.

The statement must be indexed by the filing office according to the name of the debtor. In the case of a financing statement relating to crops or timber, the statement must also be indexed in the real property index of grantors under the name of the debtor. The debtor may not necessarily be the owner of the land; he could be a lessee or a contract purchaser. If a statement relating to crops or timber is properly indexed in the office of the county recorder, and if a description of the land is included, the financing statement constitutes constructive notice thereof to any purchaser or encumbrancer of the land.

VII. IMPORTANCE OF THE DISTINCTIONS BETWEEN REAL AND PERSONAL PROPERTY

§1.50. In general

The distinction between real and personal property is an important one in considering the legal aspects. Real property is a fixed, immovable, and permanent thing, whereas personal property is readily movable from place to place, is often easily consumed or destroyed, and is regarded as something impermanent or transient. These physical contrasts in the two classes of property have resulted in different rules of law regulating their ownership.

§1.51. Real property subject to laws of state where located

Real property is exclusively subject to the laws and jurisdiction of the state within which it is located. The acquisition, disposition, and devolution of title to land in California is governed by the laws of the State of California, except in those instances when title is in the United States, or when the Constitution of the United States has granted jurisdiction to the federal government, as in the case of bankruptcy. California law controls as to form, execution, validity, and effect of instruments relating to land in this state, and determines the descent of such land to heirs or devisees of a deceased owner. Courts of the other states do not have the power to render decrees that directly affect title to land in California. A decree of distribution of real property in California made by the probate court of another state having jurisdiction over the decedent's estate by virtue of domicile of the decedent would be ineffective in California. Personal property, on the other hand, is usually regarded as situated at the domicile of its owner, regardless of the actual situs of the property, and is governed by the law of the owner's domicile.

§1.52. Method of transfer

The distinction between real and personal property is also of importance as to method of transfer. A voluntary transfer of title to real property can be made only by an instrument in writing, whereas title to personal property generally passes by delivery of possession. A written instrument may be used in connection with the transfer of personal property, such as an assignment of a claim, or a bill of sale of a chattel, but is not necessary to its validity unless required by statute.

§1.53. Requirements as to recording

The requirements as to recording form another important distinction between real and personal property. The law contemplates that instruments affecting title to real property will be recorded in a public office, so that purchasers and other persons dealing with the property may determine and rely on the ownership of the property. In the case of personal property, there are relatively few instruments that may be recorded or that give notice when recorded. Accordingly, the ownership or condition of title to personal property cannot, for the most part, be determined from the public records. Personal property security agreements constitute a main exception to this rule. Also, an abstract of judgment is now a lien on a leasehold estate with an unexpired term of more than two years. The Code of Civil Procedure lists the interests that are subject, and that are not subject, to a judgment lien on real property.[49]

§1.54. Taxation

Several cases have arisen involving the question of whether vaults and vault doors and other equipment of a bank are part of the real property and assessed as real property for tax purposes. If not real property, then such equipment would be tax exempt, because the franchise tax imposed on banks is in lieu of any tax on personal property.

EXAMPLES

1. In one case, it was held that vaults and vault doors constituted a unit for use together and that the vault doors were therefore to be considered improvements to the realty and taxable as such.[50]

2. In a later case, heavy metal safe deposit boxes were held to be personalty and not taxable. Although there was an appearance of solidity and permanence, the boxes were in fact readily movable.[51]

3. Then in another case, it was held that an electronic computer system installed in a bank was taxable as a fixture even though the bank was only a lessee of the equipment.[52]

4. In a reverse situation, it has been held that rose bushes planted by a nursery company and raised to sell as plants rather than raised for the product of the plants were not "growing crops" within the provision of the state constitution exempting growing crops from taxation, and were properly taxed as personal property.[53]

---

§1.55. Condemnation actions

When land is condemned for public use, the value of the buildings or other improvements and fixtures on the land must be considered in determining the owner's compensation. As stated in one case, if equipment is affixed to the land that is condemned, compensation for its loss will be included in the value of the property taken.[54] The Code of Civil Procedure provides that equipment designed for manufacturing or industrial purposes and installed for use in a fixed location shall be deemed a part of the realty for the purposes of condemnation, regardless of the method of installation.

§1.56. Judgment liens

The distinction between real and personal property is also important in the case of judgment liens. The term *real property* as used in connection with the lien of a judgment is taken in its technical sense, which excludes all estates that are chattels real and therefore personalty, such as an estate for years. Thus, a mere leasehold estate is not subject to such a lien,[55] although it is subject to levy under a writ of execution.

§1.57. Judicial sales

The procedures for levy upon and sale of property through court proceedings differ for real and personal property; thus it is important to know the character of the property before starting any such action or proceeding, particularly in case of execution sales and probate sales.

§1.58. Testamentary disposition

Sometimes a person wills all of his "real property" to one person, and all of his "personal property" to another, without any further identification. The Probate

Court may then be called on to determine whether a particular interest is real or personal property.

EXAMPLE   In one case, the court was required to determine the nature of an interest retained by the grantor in a deed executed in 1924 conveying to a sugar beet company a parcel of land intended to be used for agricultural purposes. The deed contained a provision that, should oil be found and drilled on the property, the grantee would pay a royalty to the grantor of one-half the income derived therefrom. The grantee did find oil at a subsequent date, and paid one-half of the income to the grantor's estate, the grantor having since died. Under the grantor's will, his daughters were given half interest in his real property, and his wife was made life tenant of a trust composed of his personal property. A question arose as to whether his retained interest in the oil royalties was real property, and thus payable to the daughters, or whether it was a personal right, which would all go to his widow. The court held it to be personal property under all the circumstances of the transaction.[56]

VIII. FIXTURES

§1.59. Nature and definition of fixtures

As we have seen, real property includes not only the land itself, but also those things that are affixed to the land. A *fixture* may be defined as a thing that was originally a chattel, but that has been attached so to land as to make it part of the land; thus it becomes real property.[57]

EXAMPLE   Lumber at a lumber yard is personal property; when it is used in the construction of a residence it becomes a part of the real property. It is not essential that the article be in actual contact with the soil itself. It may be attached to a building that is considered part of the land. A piece of plumbing, for example, may fall in this category.

The foregoing definition of a fixture is adapted primarily for determining what passes under a conveyance or mortgage of real property.

Questions of priority when goods that have not been paid for become attached to real property have been a problem in the past. To help solve the problem, the Uniform Commercial Code establishes specific rules and procedures for resolving or avoiding conflicts between security interests in fixtures and adverse real estate interests asserted by purchasers or encumbrancers of the real property.[58]

§1.60. Applicable rules

Common law rule. The general rule of the common law with respect to fixtures is that whatever is once annexed to the freehold becomes a part of it, and cannot thereafter be removed except by the person who is entitled to the inheritance.

California rule. The law of fixtures in California is essentially the same as the common law and the law prevailing generally throughout the United States.

§1.61. Trade fixtures

To encourage a tenant to be equipped with the tools and implements of his trade, articles installed by the tenant for the purpose of his trade or business are classed as trade fixtures, and as a general rule may be removed by the tenant any time during the continuance of the lease if the removal can be effected without injury to the premises, unless they have become an integral part of the premises.[59] However, for real property tax purposes the improvements include fixtures, and no exception is made in the case of trade fixtures.[60] Although most fixtures become part of the real estate, trade fixtures are personal property.

EXAMPLES Gasoline pumps and tanks sunk into the ground by the lessee of a service station; fixtures installed in a market for the purpose of conducting a soft drink stand; a shampoo bowl, dresserettes, and mirrors attached to the walls of a hotel room by the operator of a beauty parlor; a basement hardwood floor, mirrors, the woodwork of a grill room, and large plaster ornaments, all built for restaurant and café purposes and installed in a tavern; and an electric sign set in a portable frame and fastened by bolts to a fabricated steel tower on a theater.

§1.62. Tests to determine whether a thing is a fixture

In determining whether an article is a fixture, five generally recognized tests are applied, with the ultimate decision being dependent on all of the facts and circumstances of the particular case. These five tests are (1) manner of annexation; (2) character of article and adaptation to use; (3) relationship of the parties; (4) intention of the parties; and (5) agreement of the parties. These tests can be remembered by the mnemonic word MARIA.

§1.63. Manner of annexation

The first test is the manner of the article's annexation. The Civil Code[61] provides that a thing is deemed affixed to land when it is "permanently resting" on the land or "permanently attached to what is thus permanent, as by means of cement, plaster, nails, bolts or screws." This code provision is merely a rule of general guidance. A thing may be attached by means of screws but not be a fixture. Conversely, a thing may be easily removable or otherwise not attached as specified in the code and yet be a fixture, if it was intended that it remain where fastened until worn out or superseded by another article.

EXAMPLE In one situation, it was held that refrigeration equipment securely fastened to a building by bolts, nuts, and screws, with conduits and tubing interwoven in the walls, was a fixture.[62]

A building need not be physically anchored to the land to be considered realty; it may be a fixture even though it is secured to the realty by force of gravity alone.

EXAMPLE In one case, a building installed by a tenant under a lease was held to be a fixture.[63]

§1.64. Character of article and adaptation to use

The second test is the character of the article and its adaptation to the use and purpose of the realty. It must appear that the article would be essential to the ordinary and convenient use of the property to which it is annexed. An important question is whether it can be used elsewhere, or whether it was custom made for the particular building.

EXAMPLE In one case, a pipe organ, although specially installed in a residence, was held not to be a fixture.[64]

§1.65. Relationship of the parties

Other things being equal, the relationship of the parties may be the decisive factor when a dispute arises between the owner of the land and the owner of the article that has been attached to realty.

Buyer and seller. When a landowner sells his land, the law favors the buyer, and articles installed on the land will usually be regarded as fixtures and will pass to the purchaser as part of the realty. The purchaser is favored by the rule that whatever is essential for the use of the buildings will be considered a fixture, even though it may be severed without injury to the realty or to the article.

Trustor and beneficiary. As between a trustor and a beneficiary under a trust deed, the liberal rule as to what passes by deed is also applied. Moreover, if a trustor annexes fixtures to the land after the execution of the trust deed, the lien of the trust deed attaches to the fixtures as part of the land, subject, however, to intermediate rights or liens of third persons.

Landlord and tenant. When a dispute arises between a landlord and tenant, the law favors the tenant and allows him to remove almost any article he has installed in the building, in the absence of an agreement to the contrary.

§1.66. Intention of the parties

The third and often the most important test is the intention of the parties making the annexation. Was the article attached, the courts ask, with the intention of making it a permanent part of the structure? The other tests are helpful in determining the intention of the parties, and once that intention is determined, it ordinarily must govern. However, it is not the secret intention of the person installing the article that controls. The test is an objective one, and the intention may be determinable from the nature of the article, the relation of the parties, the adaptation of the article and mode of annexation, and all the surrounding circumstances.

EXAMPLES

1. In one case, carpets and drapes in an apartment building were held to be part of the realty. The manner in which the carpets were put in place was held not to be controlling, the court stating that when there is no agreement, no representation, and no basis for an estoppel as to ownership, the controlling factor should be the intention with which the installation is made. The court regarded as significant the fact that the installation was in a rental unit rather than in a private home.[65]

2. In an earlier case, the court held that carpeting was not a fixture when the carpets were in a private home.[66]

§1.67. Agreement of the parties

An agreement as to the character of the things to be affixed may be entered into permitting an article that otherwise would be a fixture to nonetheless remain personal property. An example of such an agreement is a lease giving the lessee the right, at the termination of the lease, to remove buildings and equipment installed by the lessee. Agreements may also be entered into between the landowner and the owner of the article to be affixed, such as a conditional sales agreement, under which the vendor reserves title to the article as personal property, and retains the right to remove it from the land on default in payment. Such an understanding may also be evidenced by the execution by the landowner of a security agreement to secure the purchase price of an article to be annexed to the land.

EXAMPLE The defendants leased realty to third persons under an unrecorded lease that gave the defendants a security interest in a packaging machine that had been affixed to the realty they owned, but also gave the lessees the right to remove it upon termination in the absence of default. Subsequently, the plaintiff acquired an interest in the machine as security for a loan to the lessees. The lessees defaulted and both plaintiff and defendants claimed the machine. The Supreme Court agreed that the machine was a trade fixture and held that it is subject to the rule that if mortgaged by the lessee after the machine has acquired such status, the mortgagee cannot assert a greater right against the lessor than can the lessee.[67]

Rights of third parties. Agreements that an article shall retain its personal character are valid between the parties and as to other parties with notice. Such agreements are not effective, however, after annexation has taken place, as against the rights of subsequent purchasers or mortgagees of the land for value, in good faith, and without notice of the agreement. Although the land mortgagee may prevail against the conditional sales vendor as to an article affixed *before* the mortgage is recorded, the rule is otherwise when the article is affixed to the land *after* the mortgage is recorded. In the latter case, the conditional sales vendor may exercise a right to remove the fixture unless such removal will substantially injure or diminish the value of the security.

Character of articles may be changed by agreement. The character of articles that have already been affixed to real property may also be determined by an agreement between the landowner and another party. Thus the vendor and vendee of real property may agree that articles not so annexed as to be fixtures in the eyes of the law will nevertheless pass as fixtures under a conveyance of the land. Conversely, they may agree that articles that otherwise would be fixtures are to be considered as personal property, with title to such articles remaining in the vendor of the realty.

§1.68. Illustrative cases

(1) Nursery trees planted in a nursery business for the purpose of being transplanted were held not to be affixed, and were considered to be personal property.[68] (2) A trailer used as an office at a trailer court has been held not to be a fixture.[69] (3) For tax purposes, safe deposit boxes were held not to be fixtures if they were not physically attached to the bank vault or building.[70] (4) A sign and night depository installed by a bank as lessee on the leased property were held to be so annexed to the realty as to become fixtures classifiable as real property for the purpose of taxation.[71] (5) Two cargo cranes weighing 750 tons each, installed on a wharf, were fixtures, taxed as real property.[72]

IX. ESTATES IN REAL PROPERTY

§1.69. Nature of an estate

In addition to the nature of real property and what is included in a deed or deed of trust, a buyer or lender will also be concerned with how much and what kind of an estate or interest the owner has in the property. Does he have the entire ownership? Is it unlimited or limited in its duration? What is the quality of the ownership?

The ownership interest that a person has in land is called an *estate*. This may vary in size from absolute ownership, called a "fee simple absolute," to a mere tolerated possession, called a "tenancy at sufferance." An estate in land gives the owner of such interest the right to enjoy and possess the land—now or in the future—for a period of time that may be long or short, definite or indefinite, depending on the particular interest owned.

§1.70. Not all interests are estates

Not all interests in land constitute "estates." For instance, the interest of a beneficiary under a trust deed is not an estate; it is a lien or charge on the land, but it is not considered as a segment of ownership. It is a "security" interest and is, therefore, personal property.

§1.71. Classification of estates

The word *estate* is used to express the degree, quantity, nature, duration, or extent of an interest in land. The primary classification of estates is with reference to their duration of enjoyment. The Civil Code[73] classifies estates as follows: (1) estates of inheritance or perpetual estates (called estates in fee); (2) estates for life (commonly referred to as life estates); (3) estates for years (leasehold estates); and (4) estates at will. Estates in fee and life estates are referred to as "freehold estates" since they are characteristic of the holding of a freeman under the feudal system, with the exact time of termination of the estate being unknown.

Estates are also classified in the following manner: (1) according to quality (either absolute or subject to contingencies, and either legal or equitable); (2) according to their time of enjoyment (estates entitling the holder to possession either immediately or at some time in the future, called "present" and "future interests"); or (3) with respect to the number of owners (either estates in severalty or in co-ownership, such as joint tenancy, tenancies in common, partnership interests, or the community interests of husband and wife).[74] This latter classification of estates is considered at length in Chapter 8.

Another distinction is made between possessory and nonpossessory interests. The first category includes all those interests or estates in which the holder is entitled to present possession of the property. The nonpossessory type includes those interests in which the holder's right to use the property is postponed to some future date, or the right of use is limited in nature or extent.

§1.72. Freehold estates

The uncertain duration of its existence is the characteristic that distinguishes a freehold from a nonfreehold estate. No one knows how long a fee simple estate will last, because it may be disposed of whenever the owner pleases. Since a life estate depends on the duration of a natural person's life, and is terminated only on the death of the person on whose life the estate depends—an event that is uncertain as to time—it, too, is an estate of uncertain duration. A nonfreehold estate has a certainty of duration, even though this certainty may not always be expressed in terms of a specific period of time. Because of this certainty of duration, it is a lesser estate than a fee or life estate.

§1.73. Fee estate

An estate in fee simple, also designated an *absolute tenancy*, *estate in fee*, or merely a *fee*, is the highest type of interest a person can have in land. It is potentially of indefinite duration, freely transferable, and inheritable. When we speak of A as being the owner of a parcel of land, it is generally understood that he is the fee owner; that is, he owns the land in fee or in fee simple or in fee absolute. He is an absolute owner, and as long as he obeys the law, he may do as he chooses with his land: dispose of it during his lifetime, or devise it by his last will and testament effective on his death, or do nothing with it and have it pass to his heirs at law. In California a fee simple estate is presumed to pass by a grant of real property.[75]

An estate in fee simple is a generic term, and includes an estate "in fee simple absolute" and an estate "in fee simple defeasible." The latter type, sometimes referred to as "qualified fee," creates in the grantee and his heirs an estate that can be lost or defeated by the happening of some event subsequent to the initial grant. The types that are ordinarily encountered are estates subject to a condition subsequent, such as often appears in a set of deed restrictions.

EXAMPLE A conveyance may be made on condition that the land shall not be used for certain purposes, such as the sale of intoxicating liquors, and further providing that title shall revert on breach of such condition. If there is a violation of the condition, the grantor has the right to terminate the estate granted. However, the estate is divested if, and only if, the grantor exercises his right or power of termination.

---

§1.74. Life estate

A life estate is an estate that is measured by the life of a natural person.[76] The duration of the estate may be limited to the life of the person holding it, or to the life or lives of one or more other persons.

1. A conveyance to "A for the term of his natural life," or to "A for life," creates a life estate measured by the life of the life tenant.

2. A conveyance to "A for the life of X" is a life estate measured by the life of a third person, often referred to as an *estate pur autre vie*. If A dies before X, the life estate vests in the heirs or devisees of A during the life of X.

A life estate may be created by a conveyance to the life tenant, with remainder over to some other person; or by a conveyance of a life estate only, leaving the residue of the fee estate, called a *reversion*, in the grantor; or by a conveyance of the fee, reserving a life estate to the grantor. A life estate may be created by will or by deed.

§1.75. Nature of interest of life tenant

A life tenant, unless expressly restrained, may sell, lease, encumber, or otherwise dispose of his interest, but obviously cannot create an estate that will extend beyond the duration of his life estate, unless he has been given added power to that effect.[77] The owner of the life estate has the same right of possession as an owner in fee simple, and has the right to all the rents, issues, and profits of the land accruing during the term of this life estate.[78] The owner also has certain duties and obligations, which include: (1) keeping the buildings in repair; (2) paying taxes and other annual charges; (3) paying a just proportion of extraordinary assessments; and (4) payment of interest, but not principal, on encumbrances on the land. Also, he must act reasonably with reference to the use of the land so as not to cause harm to the owners of succeeding interests.

Table 1–1
Nonfreehold Estates

	Estates for Years	Periodic Tenancy	Estates at Will	Estates at Sufferance
Characteristics	Continues for a definite period	Continues from period to period	No specified term or conditions. Original entry with permission under void contract or lease	Original entry with permission but current occupancy continues without consent
Creation	By written lease; by oral agreement if less than one year	Presumed by law; by agreement; by accepting rent at end of fixed lease term	By taking possession while negotiating a lease; under void lease	Remaining in possession at end of lease term
Duration	Definite term—computed at time lessee takes possession by days, weeks, months, or years	Indefinite term, continuing for successive periods until terminated	Statutory minimum of 30 days and notice must be given	No duration
Limitations on term	In writing it for more than one year; cannot exceed 99 years for city lots	Presumed to be month to month unless otherwise stated in writing	Acceptance of rent creates an estate for month to month or as agreed	Acceptance of rent creates an estate for month to month or as agreed
Termination	Automatically terminates at end of term	Upon 30-day notice or per lease terms	Upon 30-day notice	By notice or court action

§1.76. Nonfreehold estates

Nonfreehold estates include estates for years (usually created by a lease), periodic tenancies, and estates at will. Such a type of estate creates an interest in land, but is regarded as personal property and not real property. In the case of a leasehold estate it is referred to as a *chattel real*. The interest or estate remaining in the lessor is an estate in reversion, or simply "a reversion." The lessor is still the owner, but the estate is not possessory until the possession of the land reverts to him on termination of the leasehold estate. Leasehold estates and other types of tenancies are considered in detail in Chapter 15.

§1.77. Estates for years

An estate for years is an interest or estate in land for a certain period of time—a year, a month, or any greater or lesser period of fixed duration. Such an estate is often created by a lease, whereby the owner of an estate in land conveys the land to another person for some definite and specified period of time, usually in consideration of the payment of rent.

EXAMPLE   If A as the owner in fee simple of a parcel of land executes a ten-year lease to B, A has parted with a portion of his rights. He has given up, for a ten-year period, his right to occupy the land, and in return has received B's promise to pay rent for those ten years. B, of course, has not become the owner in fee simple, but has acquired the right to occupy the land in accordance with the provisions of the lease. B has acquired a leasehold estate in the land.

---

§1.78. Estates at will

A *tenancy at will* is defined as a tenancy created with the consent of the landlord that is to exist or continue for an indefinite period of time. It may be created by express words, or it may arise by operation of law.

EXAMPLE   In one case, it was held that a lease commencing October 1, 1943 and ending 60 days after signature of the treaty of peace on the close of the war with Germany or Japan, whichever treaty was the later, created a tenancy at will and not a tenancy for years.[79]

---

§1.79. Periodic tenancies

Periodic tenancies, created by the parties to continue for successive periods of the same length, unless sooner terminated by notice, are not expressly recognized by the California codes as a class. However, case law recognizes them as being forms of tenancy at will.

§1.80. Tenancy at sufferance

A tenancy at sufferance occurs when a tenant who was lawfully in possession remains in possession without the owner's consent after the termination of his right of occupancy. The typical example is when a lessee remains after the end of the lease.

§1.81. Future interests

An estate or interest in land, with reference to its time of enjoyment, is either a present interest or a future interest. A present interest entitles the owner to immediate possession, whereas a future interest, as the name implies, entitles the owner to possession of the property only at a time commencing in the future. Thus a future interest is classified as a nonpossessory interest. The most frequently encountered are reversions and remainders.

§1.82. Reversions

A reversion is defined as "the residue of an estate left in the grantor or his successors, commencing on the determination of a particular estate granted or devised."[80]

EXAMPLES

1. Thus, if A, owning an estate in fee simple, conveys a life estate to B, the residue of the fee simple estate that is left in A is called a reversion, so called because possession reverts to A on termination of B's lesser estate.

2. The estate of the lessor under a lease for a term of years is also referred to as a reversion.

§1.83. Remainders

When a future estate or interest in land, other than a reversion, is dependent on a precedent estate, it is called a *remainder*, and it may be created and transferred by that name.[81] Unlike a *reversion*, which is an interest left by operation of law in a grantor who conveys a lesser estate, a *remainder* is an estate created by act of the grantor in favor of some person other than the grantor. Figure 1-2 illustrates the creation of reversions and remainders in life estates.

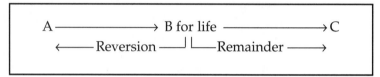

Figure 1–2 Future interests of life estates

A remainder is so called because, when the prior estate terminates, it (the remainder) "remains" away from rather than reverting to the conveyor.

EXAMPLE   A executes a deed "to B for life and upon B's death to C or his heirs."

For there to be an interest to pass in remainder, it is obvious that the particular estate that precedes the remainder must be of a lesser duration than the interest of the conveyor at the time of conveyance. Remainders are classified as vested remainders and contingent remainders.

Vested remainder. A remainder is regarded as vested if there is a person in being who would have a right, defeasible or indefeasible, to the immediate possession of the property, upon the ceasing of the intermediate or precedent interest.

EXAMPLE   Under a conveyance of land "to A for life, and on his death the remainder to B," the interest of B is a vested remainder.

Contingent remainder. A remainder is regarded as contingent if the person in whom, or the event upon which, it is limited to take effect remains uncertain.

EXAMPLE   When land is conveyed "to A for life, and the remainder to B provided B survives A," the remainder is contingent because it is dependent on an event that is uncertain, namely, the death of A during the lifetime of B.

§1.84. Transfer of remainder interests

When there is a contemplated transfer of an estate in remainder, a determination as to whether the estate is vested or contingent is essential. Remainders, contingent as well as vested, are estates in land, and pass by succession, will, or transfer, in the same manner as present interests, but the successor to a remainderman can, of course, acquire no greater interest than the remainderman had. The problem frequently arises when title is vested in a life tenant with remainder over, and a question is presented whether there are parties who presently can unite in conveying an absolute and marketable title to a purchaser.

Problem area. When title is vested in "A for life, remainder in A's children," and A presently has one child, namely, B, the interest of B is a remainder vested subject to being opened; that is, if A has other children, the class "opens up" to let in other children as remaindermen, thus decreasing B's interest to the extent necessary to allow all children of A to share equally in the remainder. A present transfer from the life tenant and B would not be sufficient to vest a marketable title in their grantee, since there is the possibility of other remaindermen.

§1.85. Doctrine of virtual representation

When title to property cannot be effectively transferred by a voluntary conveyance because of the interests of unborn or undetermined remaindermen, and it becomes necessary for the preservation of the interests of all parties that the land be sold, it has been held that the courts have inherent jurisdiction to order such sale in proceedings in which the life tenant and all living remaindermen are joined, and the unborn or undetermined interests are made parties and appear through a guardian ad litem under the doctrine of virtual representation.[82] A mortgage, exchange, or lease may also be ordered by the court under proper circumstances. A sale in partition action may also be effected, since jurisdiction over the interests of unborn or unascertained remaindermen can be obtained under the doctrine of virtual representation.

QUESTIONS

Matching Terms

Write the appropriate letter (a–j) before each statement.

a. Civil Law
b. Jurisdiction
c. Equitable
d. U.S. Constitution
e. Venue
f. Maxim
g. Laches
h. Property
i. Ownership
j. Estate

1. Between rights otherwise equal, the earliest is preferred. Maxim
2. The degree, quantity, nature, duration, or extent of an interest in land. Estate
3. Anything that may be owned. Property
4. The right to the use and enjoyment of property to the exclusion of others. Ownership
5. Power of the court to hear and determine a matter. Jurisdiction
6. Law originating in ancient Rome and applicable generally in continental Europe. Civil Law
7. Just, fair, and right; in good conscience. Equitable
8. Supreme law of the land. U.S Constitution
9. Unreasonable delay in asserting a claim. Laches
10. Relates primarily to the place of trial. Venue

True/False

Circle *T* for True or *F* for False.

T� F **11.** The law is dynamic rather than static in its force and effect.

T̳ F **12.** Real estate law is concerned primarily with rights, duties, and responsibilities.

T F̳ **13.** Like personal property, real property is always subject to the laws of the owner's domicile.

T̳ F **14.** Basically, the state legislature has such powers as have not been denied to it.

T F̳ **15.** The U.S. Constitution does not affect property rights in the state of California.

T̳ F **16.** Most laws pertaining to real property in California are laws passed by the state legislature.

T̳ F **17.** A statute of limitations prescribes a time within which an action must be filed.

T F̳ **18.** Waiver and estoppel are distinctions without a difference.

T F̳ **19.** All actions affecting real property in California are categorized as "quiet title" actions.

T̳ F **20.** The California Supreme Court consists of seven justices, including the chief justice.

Multiple Choice

Of the four choices, circle the letter representing the best answer or completion.

21. There are two classes or kinds of property: real and personal. Both have certain characteristics that are similar. Which of the following statements is *incorrect*?
    a. Real property may become personal property.
    b. Personal property may become real property.
    c. Crops may be either real or personal property.
    d. Personal property is defined as immovable property.

22. Sources of real estate law in California include
    a. State statutes.
    b. State constitution.
    c. U.S. Constitution.
    d. All of the above.

23. Sources of real estate law in California may also include
    a. Rules and regulations of federal agencies.
    b. Rules and regulations of state agencies.
    c. Court decisions.
    d. All of the above.

24. The power of a court to hear and determine a matter is known as
    a. Judicial discretion.
    b. Jurisdiction.
    c. Litigation.
    d. Venue.

25. The primary function of the courts is to
    a. Interpret and apply the law.
    b. Administer the law.
    c. Enact the law.
    d. All of the above.

26. If a cause of action on a contract is barred by lapse of time, this means that one of the following statutes is applicable:
    a. Statute of Frauds.
    b. Statute of Uses.
    c. Statute of Limitations.
    d. Statute of Descent.

27. The right to transfer and dispose of a thing or to use and possess it to the exclusion of others is known as
    a. Equitable title.
    b. Ownership.
    c. Real property.
    d. Littoral rights.

28. The right or interest that an owner of real property has is often referred to as a "bundle of rights." Which of the following best describes those rights?
    a. The right to possess and enjoy the property.
    b. The right to transfer and dispose of the property.
    c. The right to exclude others from the property.
    d. All of the above.

29. Real property may consist of
    a. Subsurface rights.
    b. Airspace.
    c. Mineral interests.
    d. Any of the above.

30. Restrictions on the right of an owner to do with his property as he pleases may be governed by
    a. Police power.
    b. Deed restrictions.
    c. Adjoining owner rights.
    d. All of the above.

31. Remainder interests in real property ordinarily relate to
    a. Undivided interests in property.
    b. Life estates.
    c. Fee simple absolute.
    d. Any of the above.

32. Real property law in California is based on
    a. State law exclusively.
    b. Federal law exclusively.
    c. Both state and federal law.
    d. None of the above.

33. An inexcusable delay in asserting a legal right is known as
    a. Laxity.
    b. Remittance.
    c. Laches.
    d. Latitude.

34. Real property ordinarily does not include
    a. Water rights.
    b. Minerals in place.
    c. Severed crops.
    d. Fixtures.

35. Personal property ordinarily includes
    a. Growing crops.
    b. Airspace.
    c. Gold or silver in place.
    d. Furniture and furnishings.

36. Which of the following tests will apply to determine whether or not a thing is a fixture?
    a. Intention of the parties.
    b. The method used to affix it to the real property.
    c. How adaptable it is to the particular property.
    d. Any of the above.

37. The owner of land in fee generally has the right to the surface and to minerals below the surface. The right can be limited by
    a. A reservation in a deed.
    b. An exception in a deed.
    c. A previous grant of the mineral estate.
    d. Any of the above.

38. Fee simple means
    a. An estate in land.
    b. Co-ownership.
    c. Ownership in severalty.
    d. Title free from liens and encumbrances.

39. An estate of inheritance or an estate for life is known as an estate
  a. Less than a freehold.
  b. Greater than a freehold.
  c. Nonfreehold.
  d. Freehold.

40. A fee simple estate has which of the following characteristics?
  a. It is of unlimited duration.
  b. It is freely inheritable.
  c. It is freely transferable.
  d. All of the above.

41. Personal property that is attached to and made a part of real property is called a
  a. Chattel real.
  b. Fixture.
  c. *Profit à prendre*.
  d. Littoral right.

42. An instrument used to secure a loan on personal property is called a
  a. Bill of sale.
  b. Trust deed.
  c. Security agreement.
  d. Bill of exchange.

43. Freehold estates include which of the following?
  a. Estate for years.
  b. Estate at will.
  c. Fee simple.
  d. All of the above.

44. An estate "to A for the life of X" does which of the following if A dies before X?
  a. Ceases to exist.
  b. Vests in the heirs or devisees of A for the life of X.
  c. Vests in X for his life.
  d. Reverts to the original grantor.

45. An interest that is dependent upon an uncertain future event is
  a. Vested.
  b. Contingent.
  c. Absolute.
  d. Unqualified.

46. Which of the following is considered an interest in real property but not an estate?
  a. Lease.
  b. Mortgage.
  c. Life estate.
  d. Fee simple qualified.

47. Things incidental or appurtenant to land are regarded as real property. Which of the following would ordinarily not be considered real property?
  a. Right of way over adjoining land.
  b. Hunting or fishing license.
  c. Party wall.
  d. Water stock in a mutual water company.

48. Jane was given real property for the term of her natural life. Which of the following statements is incorrect?
  a. Jane has a freehold estate.
  b. Jane has a fee simple estate.
  c. The duration of this estate is measured by the life of Jane.
  d. The estate can be encumbered by Jane, but not beyond her life.

49. Anthony deeded Blackacre to Baker for the life of Clay. Which of the following statements is correct?
  a. Baker holds a life estate; Anthony holds an estate in reversion.
  b. Baker holds a life estate; Clay holds an estate in remainder.
  c. Baker holds a fee simple estate; Clay holds a life estate.
  d. Clay holds a life estate; Baker holds an estate in reversion.

50. Which of the following groups of words best describes your understanding of the term *riparian rights*?
  a. Nonadjacent; reasonable.
  b. Adjacent; absolute.
  c. Reasonable; commercial.
  d. Adjacent; reasonable.

NOTES

1. C.C. 22.
2. C.C. 22.1.
3. C.C. 22.2.
4. Brecheen v. Riley (1921) 187 C. 121.
5. Fitts v. Superior Court (1936) 6 C.2d 230, 234.
6. Shelley v. Kraemer (1948) 334 U.S. 1.
7. Oyama v. State of California (1947) 332 U.S. 633.
8. 38 U.S.C. (1804); 18 U.S.C. 286, *et seq*. and 31 U.S.C. 231, *et seq.*; *see also* U.S. v. De Witt (1959) 265 Fed.2d 393.
9. Porter v. Chapman (1884) 65 C. 365.
10. Agricultural Labor Relations Board v. Superior Court (1976) 16 C.3d 392, 403.
11. Tonningsen v. Odd Fellows' Cemetery Assn. (1923) 60 C.A. 568.
12. C.C.P. 392.
13. C.C.P. 397.
14. But *see* Ateeq v. Najor (1993) 18 C.A.4th 1351.
15. C.C.P. 318, *et seq*. In professional malpractice (broker, appraiser, attorney, doctor), the statutory time period does not begin until the plaintiff discovers or should have discovered the breach of contract (Seelenfreund v. Terminix of N. Cal. Inc. [1978] 84 C.A.3d 133; Slavin v. Trout [1993] 18 C.A.4th 1536). The statute is "tolled" under certain circumstances (Gilbert Financial Corp. v. Steelform Contracting Co. [1978] 82 C.A.3d 65).
16. Esau v. Briggs (1948) 89 C.A.2d 427.
17. Evid. C. 623.
18. Altman v. McCollum (1951) 107 C.A.2d Supp. 847. While *waiver* is ordinarily a question of fact, when only one reasonable inference can be drawn, a waiver becomes a question of law (Kossler v. Palm Springs Dev. Co. [1980] 101 C.A.3d 88, 98). Waiver imports a unilateral act and its legal conse-

quences. Estoppel, on the other hand, carries a bilateral connotation: the justifiable reliance by one party on the intentional act or omission of another. Both may be equitable defenses. (*See* Morgan v. Int'l Aviation Underwriters Inc. (1967) 250 C.A.2d 176.)

19. Marks v. Bunker (1958) 165 C.A.2d 695.
20. Cooke v. Ramponi (1952) 38 C.2d 282; Stoner v. Zucker (1906) 148 C. 156.
21. Potter v. Boisvert (1953) 117 C.A.2d 688.
22. C.C. 3509, *et seq.*
23. La Sala v. American Savings and Loan Assn. (1971) 5 C.3d 864.
24. C.C.P. 86.
25. C.C.P. 116.540.
26. C.C.P. 116.220; Merco Construction Engineers Inc. v. Municipal Court (1978) 21 C.3d 724; Van Gundy v. Camelot Resorts, Inc. (1984) 152 C.A.3d Supp. 29, and *see* Houghtaling v. Superior Court (1993) 17 C.A.4th 1128 re Small Claims Court rules of evidence apply in Superior Court trial de novo re hearsay.
27. California Lawyer (April 1983), p. 13.
28. C.C. 654.
29. But *see* Agricultural Labor Relations Board v. Superior Court, §1.18, Footnote 10.
30. C.C. 658.
31. Atlantic Oil Co. v. County of Los Angeles (1968) 69 C.2d 585.
32. C.C. 658.
33. C.C. 829.
34. U.S. v. Causby (1945) 328 U.S. 256.
35. Griggs v. County of Allegheny (1962) 369 U.S. 84.
36. C.C. 659.
37. Rousselot v. Spanier (1976) 60 C.A.3d 238.
38. Goethermal Kinetics, Inc. v. Union Oil Co. (1977), 75 C.A.3d 56.
39. Trussell v. City of San Diego (1959) 172 C.A.2d 593.
40. California Water Service Co. v. Sidebotham & Son, Inc. (1964) 224 C.A.2d 715; C.C. 1415; State of California ex. rel. State Lands Commission v. Superior Court (1994) 26 C.A.4th 1390.
41. C.C. 830.
42. C.C. 650.
43. Krouser v. County of San Bernardino (1947) 29 C.2d 766.
44. Trask v. Moore (1944) 24 C.2d 365.
45. C.C. 660.
46. C.C. 658, 660.
47. C.C. 663.
48. U.C.C. 9109(1).
49. C.C.P. 697.340.
50. San Diego Trust & Savings Co. v. San Diego County (1940) 16 C.2d 142.
51. Pajaro Valley Bank v. County of Santa Cruz (1962) 207 C.A.2d 621.
52. Bank of America v. County of Los Angeles (1964) 224 C.A.2d 108.
53. Jackson & Perkins Co. of Calif. v. Stanislaus County (1959) 168 C.A.2d 559.
54. City of Beverly Hills v. Albright (1960) 184 C.A.2d 562.
55. Summerville v. Stockton Mill Co. (1904) 142 C. 529.
56. Estate of Broome (1958) 166 C.A.2d 488.
57. C.C. 660, *see also* U.C.C. 9103(1)(e) and 9313.
58. U.C.C. 9313.
59. C.C. 1019, 1025.
60. Simms v. Los Angeles County (1950) 35 C.2d 303.
61. C.C. 660.
62. Frick v. Frigidaire (1932) 119 C.A. 707.
63. Rinaldi v. Goller (1957) 48 C.A.2d 276.
64. M.P. Moller, Inc. v. Wilson (1936) 8 C.2d 31.
65. Larkin v. Cowert (1968) 263 C.A.2d 27.
66. Plough v. Petersen (1956) 140 C.A.2d 595.
67. Goldie v. Bauchett Properties (1975) 15 C.3d 307.
68. Story v. Christin (1939) 14 C.2d 592.
69. Clifford v. Epsten (1951) 106 C.A.2d 221.
70. Pajaro Valley Bank v. County of Santa Cruz (1962) 207 C.A.2d 621.
71. County of Ventura v. Channel Islands State Bank (1967) 251 C.A.2d 240.
72. Seatrain Terminals of California, Inc. v. County of Alameda (1978) 83 C.A.3d 69.
73. C.C. 761.
74. C.C. 678, 682, 688.
75. C.C. 1105.
76. Estate of Smythe (1955) 132 C.A.2d 343.
77. Holman v. Holman (1938) 25 C.A.2d 445.
78. C.C. 818; Salee v. Danere (1942) 49 C.A.2d 324.
79. National Bellas Hess v. Kalis (1951) 191 Fed.2d 739.
80. C.C. 768.
81. C.C. 769.
82. County of Los Angeles v. Winans (1910) 13 C.A. 234.

2

Contracts in General

I. INTRODUCTION

§2.1. In general

Probably no other phase of the law is as important to the parties in a real estate transaction as the law of contracts. Every transaction of any consequence almost always includes at least one contract, and often more than one. It is important, therefore, to understand the nature of contracts and to be familiar with some of the broad rules governing their creation and enforcement.

In this chapter we first review, in general, the various classifications of contracts. The essential elements are described: the offer, acceptance, and consideration. The Statute of Frauds is explained, as well as the interpretation and performance of a contract. The methods of discharging a contract are likewise outlined and the various remedies for breach of contract are summarized, including the nature of damages.

II. NATURE OF A CONTRACT

§2.2. Contracts defined

Defined simply, a *contract* is an agreement between two or more persons to do or not to do a certain thing. It is a promise or a set of promises for the breach of which the law gives a remedy, or the performance of which the law in some way recognizes a duty.[1] In every contract is an implied covenant of good faith.[2]

§2.3. Classification of contracts

Express or implied. Various terms are commonly used to classify contracts. Concerning its manner of creation, a contract may be either express or implied. In an *express contract*, the contracting parties declare the terms and manifest their intention in words, either oral or written. In an *implied contract*, their agreement is shown by acts and conduct rather than by words.

EXAMPLE   You might enter a store, pick up a magazine, wave it at the clerk at the back of the store, who nods, and leave. There is an implied contract that you will pay for the magazine later.

Bilateral or unilateral. As to the content of the agreement, a contract may be either bilateral or unilateral. A *bilateral agreement* is one in which a promise by one party (promisor) is given in exchange for a promise by the other party (promisee).

EXAMPLES   1.   "I promise to pay you $100 if you promise to install a redwood fence at the rear of my property."

2.   Another typical example is a real estate sales agreement signed by both buyer and seller.

A *unilateral agreement* is one in which one party makes a promise to induce some act or performance by the other party, but the latter can act or not as he chooses. If he does act, the party making the promise is obligated to perform.

EXAMPLES   1.   Smith offers a reward of $50 to anyone who finds and returns his lost dog. Jones finds the dog and returns it to Smith. Jones is entitled to the reward at that time.

2.   An option agreement whereby the optionor agrees to sell the optionee a parcel of real estate. If the requisites of an option are complied with (see Chapter 3), the optionor is obligated to convey the property.

3.   Open listing with a real estate broker.[3]

Executory or executed. As to the extent of performance, a contract may be executory or executed.[4] In an *executory contract*, something still remains to be done by one or both of the parties, e.g., a current, enforceable listing agreement for which some part remains to be done. In an *executed contract*, both parties have performed fully. This distinction becomes important, at times, in connection with an *oral* agreement to do an act when the law requires a *written* agreement. If such a contract has been completely executed, then it may be enforceable by court action.

Quasi-contract. A quasi-contract (sometimes called a contract implied-in-law) is not a true contract at all. It arises in a situation to prevent unjust enrichment; i.e., one should not be allowed to enrich oneself at the expense of another. Generally, a recovery requires a benefit having been received by the defendant.

EXAMPLE   Smith, under the mistaken belief he owns Blackacre, pays the taxes without the knowledge of the owner, Jones. Jones is then under the quasi-contractual duty to reimburse Smith when the error is discovered.

Valid, void, voidable, or unenforceable. As to their legal effect, contracts may be classified in different ways.

A *valid* agreement contains all the essential elements required by law, including competent parties, and is enforceable by court action.

A *void* agreement is not a contract at all; it is without any legal effect.

EXAMPLES
1. An agreement to lease property for an unlawful purpose, such as gambling, is not enforceable by either party.
2. A person under the age of 18 signs an agreement to sell property owned by him.[5] The agreement is regarded as void.
3. Likewise, restrictions in a deed based on race, color, or creed are void.

If an agreement is partially void, i.e., only part of the agreement is void and that part can be severed from the balance of the agreement, the remaining part of the agreement can be enforced.

EXAMPLE   If a person promises to pay $100,000 for the delivery of goods that include contraband as well as permitted items, the contract will not be enforced since it is tainted with illegality in its entirety. But if a separate price was set forth for each type of goods, then the valid part can be separated from the invalid part and the contract could be partially enforced.

A *voidable* contract appears to be valid and enforceable on its face, but was procured, for example, by fraud, mistake, or undue influence, and can be avoided by the innocent party if he so chooses. However, the innocent party, if he chooses, can ratify the contract by accepting the benefits. In other words, he may accept or reject it.

EXAMPLE   A contract with an incompetent person before a judicial determination of incompetency is another example of a voidable contract.[6] The guardian of the estate could avoid the contract later.

An *unenforceable contract* is one that was valid but that, for some reason, such as an undue delay in asserting rights under the contract, is not now enforceable.

§2.4. Types of real estate contracts
The types of contracts commonly used in real estate transactions include (1) the listing agreement; (2) offer to purchase and receipt for deposit; (3) escrow instruc-

tions; (4) purchase and sale agreement used in lieu of or in addition to escrow instructions; and (5) the long-term land sales contract or installment contract. A policy of title insurance is also a type of contract that is encountered in a real estate transaction. The listing agreement and offer to purchase are discussed in detail in Chapter 3.

III. ESSENTIAL ELEMENTS OF A CONTRACT

§2.5. Mutual consent

Assume a person decides to purchase an automobile, looks at several, and chooses one. Negotiations then begin between the parties. As a result, the prospective buyer promises to purchase and the seller promises to sell this automobile (bilateral contract). The initial promise is called an *offer*, and the counterpromise is the *acceptance*. Thus a contract is created, assuming the other necessary elements are present. If the parties are competent and the consent is freely given, there is a binding mutual agreement, i.e., a *meeting of the minds*.[7] The test to determine if the parties did, in fact, mutually agree is an objective one. It is not what a party secretly thought, but rather what was the reasonable meaning of the acts and words of that party. On the other hand, if *signatures* of several persons are contemplated and only one has signed, it is incomplete and not binding until the others sign.[8]

§2.6. Offer

To fully understand an offer, which creates in the offeree the power to bind the offeror in contract, other types of communications must be distinguished. Those that are only invitations to make an offer, or merely preliminary negotiations, do not create a right of acceptance so as to produce a contract. There must be a present intent to be bound if the offer is accepted.

A newspaper ad is generally an invitation to make an offer, as it does not create a reasonable belief in the mind of the reader that an intent to be contractually bound is present. Although some contracts are required to be in writing under the Statute of Frauds, which includes real estate contracts, numerous other contracts are not. Thus great care must be taken in the choice of words used when approaching a potential transaction. If a preliminary discussion is what is intended, this understanding should be set forth at the beginning. A true offer must be an intentional act *communicated* to the offeree. It must be sufficiently definite as to its terms, and the precise acts to be performed must be clearly determinable.

Certainty. An agreement to agree is not a contract (although it is sometimes referred to as an *illusory contract*).[9] A contract that provides for terms according to future mutual satisfaction of the parties is unenforceable as there is no meeting of the minds. The terms must be distinctly set forth. Since a contract will be construed against the draftor of a contract, the offer should not contain language that is vague or ambiguous. Whether a contract is ambiguous or uncertain is a question of law.[10] Further, an ambiguity may invalidate an otherwise valid contract. The following items must be covered with sufficient certainty:

1. Parties
2. Subject matter
3. Time for performance
4. Price
5. Terms

Although these items appear simple on the surface, they can give rise to serious problems.

EXAMPLE   If the buyer submits an offer on what he believes to be a 1954 MG but, in fact, is a 1964 model, the subject matter has not been clearly ascertained yet the buyer may be bound to perform if the owner accepts the offer and had made no misrepresentations. The problem would never have arisen had the buyer indicated a desire to purchase only a 1954 model.

A contract to sell for a certain price is presumed to be for cash in the absence of a provision to the contrary. Therefore, the financial terms must be specifically set forth and agreed upon. Further, especially in contracts involving the sale of real estate, the parties should be aware of who pays for what, and what obligations will be assumed.

EXAMPLE   If a loan is to be involved, are the interest rate, the points, due dates, and monthly payments set forth? Is the buyer to assume or take subject to the existing loan, or refinance? Is the seller aware that on FHA and VA loans he pays the points? Are the parties aware of the prepayment penalties involved? All of these matters must be clearly understood. Of course, if a real estate licensee is involved and he fails to disclose these items to the appropriate parties, this gives rise to a claim of negligence or fraud and misrepresentation, by act or omission to act. What about secondary financing to be carried back by the seller? Is it set forth clearly? Do the parties understand acceleration clauses? Is an option called for, or an all-inclusive note and deed of trust? If so, are precise terms set forth so that a court would enforce the contract? Quite often they are not, and the purpose for entering into the agreement has thereby been defeated.

Conditional commitment. A conditional loan commitment is not an enforceable contract, and a cause of action for promissory estoppel will not be upheld because the element of a clear and unambiguous promise is missing.[11]

Termination of offer. For a valid contract to be formed, an acceptance must occur before the offer is terminated. Termination can take place in any one of the following ways:

1. Lapse of time
2. Death or insanity of offeror or offeree
3. Revocation by offeror
4. Rejection by offeree

An offer is revoked if not accepted within the prescribed time. If no specific time is set forth, it is revoked by the lapse of a reasonable time. Upon the death or insanity of the offeror, the offer is revoked. The death or insanity of the offeree likewise terminates the offer, as an offer can be accepted only by the person to whom the offer was made. Generally, the offeror can revoke the offer before its acceptance, even though the offer is stated to be irrevocable for a specified time.[12] However, an offer can be made irrevocable if consideration is paid for such, the typical situation being an option agreement. The revocation of the offer is effective when sent to the offeree.[13] Of course, a rejection by the offeree communicated to the offeror terminates the offer. A rejection is effective upon receipt. If the offeree communicates an acceptance that arrives before his prior rejection, a contract arises.[14]

Buyer as nominee. On occasion, a potential buyer is unsure whether title will be taken in his name or in the name of someone else. On the purchase contract he will often put his name as purchaser and add the words *or nominee.* Some courts have held that such an addition destroys the instrument as a firm offer. It seems that if the offer was for all cash, the credit of any buyer is not too important. But if the agreement calls for financial terms on the part of the named purchaser, or nominee, a problem can result, thus leaving the buyer a possible way to back out of the transaction. This makes the transaction indefinite, uncertain, unilateral, and a nullity.[15] Because of the uncertainty that exists it may be better to avoid the word *nominee* completely unless a cash transaction is contemplated; even the word *assignee* can be problematical.

§2.7. Acceptance

To create a binding contract, the offer must be accepted on time and be unequivocal according to the terms of the offer.

Counteroffer. If the offer is qualified or modified by the offeree, it becomes a counteroffer.[16] The original offer is destroyed and cannot later be accepted.

EXAMPLE   In one case, a buyer added an "or more" clause in the arrangement when accepting the seller's counteroffer that provided for a second trust deed and note. The court held that the addition constituted another counteroffer.[17]

It is common in real estate transactions for the parties to alter the terms of the various offers and counteroffers by virtue of addenda or merely by interlineations. It is important, then, to determine the chronology of the modifications in order to ascertain whether the respective counteroffers have been accepted. To assure this, each change must be dated and initialed. If a number of changes are to be made in one day, the time of day should also be noted. Too often this chronology is not done. It then becomes impossible to say when, if ever, a contract was formed. The better practice is to use a counteroffer form similar to the one printed by the California Association of Realtors. Additionally, the broker must give copies of every contract and of any changes to the parties at the time the contract is signed or the changes are made, not afterward.[18]

Communication of acceptance. The acceptance of a bilateral contract must be communicated to the offeror.[19] It can be accomplished in the presence of the offeror or by other methods, but it need not be communicated in a formal way.[20] The method of communication must be in accordance with the terms of the offer or, if none, a reasonable method. In California a contract is made when the acceptance is delivered in person, or placed in the course of transmission, i.e., posted by mail[21] or by fax. Some contracts require that they be personally received by the parties or by specific agents. Generally, silence cannot constitute acceptance; however, there are a number of exceptions:

1. Complete performance
2. Silence on the part of the offerer, who intends to accept
3. Previous dealing or fiduciary relationship
4. Acceptance of the benefits by the offeree

The doing of an act in a unilateral contract constitutes acceptance by the offeree.

Signatures. Is a contract formed even though all the signatures have not been obtained? Perhaps. One line of cases hold that an agreement is valid without the signatures of all the parties *unless* there is an express intention indicated that there will be no binding contract if all parties do not sign,[22] *or* unless it involves a husband and wife and only one of them has signed the contract.[23]

Signing without reading. One who signs a contract without reading it cannot escape liability in the absence of fraud, mistake, or undue influence.[24] If a party not reading a contract signs it in reliance on the misrepresentation of the other party or agent, he is excused from performance.[25]

§2.8. Consideration

Consideration is defined as an act, forbearance, or return promise bargained for and given in exchange, giving a benefit to the promisor, or imposing a detriment on the promisee.[26] In the absence of consideration, an executory contract cannot be enforced. In a formal written agreement, consideration is presumed to have been given, although the presumption is rebuttable.[27]

Consideration must have some value, e.g., payment of money, mutual promises, transfer of property, services performed, change of status, moving from one place to another, or forbearance to sue. On the other hand, past consideration is no consideration; i.e., an act previously performed cannot be consideration for a new promise. Consideration is lacking when one performs an act which he or she is already under an obligation to perform.[28] Further, love and affection are not regarded as consideration. In an analogous situation, love and affection are often expressed as the consideration in a gift deed, but this is in fact a misstatement. It expresses the reason for the deed, but if it is truly a gift, consideration is not essential. (See §7.6.)

Whether consideration is sufficient is determined at the time it is bargained for. For an action for specific performance to be enforceable, the consideration must be *adequate*, i.e., substantially fair.[29]

To enforce a bilateral contract, both parties must have assumed a legal obligation. If one of the promises given leaves one party free to perform or not, the promise is illusory and provides no consideration; i.e., there is no mutuality of obligation. (Compare this with an option, Chapter 3.) Mutuality has particular significance in real estate transactions when there is a contingency involved.

EXAMPLES
1. Buyer and seller enter into a contract whereby buyer agrees to the purchase contingent upon obtaining specified financing. In recent times, the buyer must make a good faith attempt to satisfy this condition or else he will not be released from liability.[30]

2. An agreement conditioned upon approval of a preliminary title report (P.R.). The buyer's dissatisfaction must be genuine and not arbitrary. The test is an objective one.

3. An older case involved an agreement between buyer and seller that was subject to buyer being able to refinance a loan for $20,000 at 5 percent per annum, with a 20-year payoff. Buyer agreed to buy for $42,500 and put up $4,250 deposit. Buyer attempted unsuccessfully to obtain the loan from the bank but was advised that he could probably get it from the mortgage company that already had the loan. Buyer made no attempt to contact the mortgage company. The evidence showed, in fact, the buyer was no longer interested in the property. When buyer backed out, seller sold the house for $40,375 without a commission. The court held that buyer breached the contract and was not entitled to a full return of his deposit.[31]

Detrimental reliance. The doctrine of *detrimental reliance,*[32] which is sometimes referred to as promissory estoppel, is accepted by a majority of our courts, including California's. It is used in cases involving a gratuitous promise when there was no offer, acceptance, or consideration. If a party substantially changes his position in reliance upon a gratuitous promise, he can enforce the promise if all the following elements are present:

1. Promisor makes a gratuitous promise which should reasonably have been expected to induce action or forbearance on the part of the promisee.

2. Promisee justifiably relies on the promise.

3. Promisee is caused a substantial detriment, i.e., an economic loss.

4. Injustice can be avoided only by enforcing the promise.[33]

EXAMPLES

1. Williams makes a gratuitous promise that if his nephew, who was about to quit school, completes four years of college, he will pay him $10,000. Nephew relies on this promise and works himself through college. Williams is bound to pay the $10,000.

2. Anderson, a friend of Dunlop, gratuitously tells Dunlop that if he quits his job in New York and comes to San Diego, Anderson will give him a job at $60,000 per year for a minimum of ten years. Dunlop quits his job, sells his home, and moves his family to San Diego. Anderson will be required to fulfill the agreement under the doctrine of detrimental reliance.

3. Baker, the beneficiary of a trust deed, gratuitously promises Tompkins, the trustor, that he will not foreclose on the defaulting trust deed for one year. In reliance on this statement, Tompkins makes improvements on the property. Baker's promise is binding.

§2.9. Legal capacity

There are certain statutory limitations on the capacity of parties to enter into a contract. Those under a legal disability are minors (under age 18),[34] persons of unsound mind, intoxicated persons, and persons deprived of civil rights (convicts).[35] However, any person under the age of 18 who is, or has been, married or on active duty in the U.S. armed forces, or who has received a declaration of emancipation, can buy and sell real estate.[36]

Although a contract by a minor to purchase or sell real estate is void, in other instances it may be voidable by the minor, or he or she may ratify it. Minors cannot avoid certain contracts for the necessities of life or court-approved contracts.

§2.10. Lawful object

It is a basic rule that the contract must be legal both in its formation and in its operation. Both its consideration and its object must be lawful. The object of the contract refers to what the agreement of the parties requires them to do or not to do. When the contract has but a single object and that object is unlawful in whole or in part, the contract is void. However, if there are several distinct objects, the contract is normally valid as to those parts that are lawful, and invalid only as to the unlawful objects. The object is unlawful if it is contrary to an express provision of the law, if it is contrary to the policy of the law, or if it is otherwise contrary to good morals.[37]

EXAMPLES   Contracts in restraint of trade, to create a monopoly, or to fix prices are illegal.

IV. STATUTE OF FRAUDS

§2.11. In general

The California Statute of Frauds[38] provides that certain contracts are invalid (unenforceable) unless in writing and subscribed by the party to be charged or by his agent.

Real estate contracts that must be in writing include the following:

1. An agreement not to be performed within a year from the date of making

2. A lease for a term longer than one year

3. An agreement for the sale of an interest in real property

4. The authority of an agent of the party to be charged, to enter into an agreement for the leasing for a period longer than one year, or for the sale of real property, or an interest therein

5. An agreement authorizing or employing an agent or broker or any other person to procure, introduce, or find a purchaser or seller of real estate or a lessee or lessor, when such lease is for a period of more than one year, for compensation or commission

6. An agreement by a purchaser of real estate to pay an indebtedness secured by a mortgage or trust deed, unless the assumption of the indebtedness is specifically provided for in the deed

7. A commitment to loan money or extend credit in an amount greater than $100,000, made by a person engaged in the business of lending money, when the loan is not primarily for personal, family, or household purposes (which includes a loan secured solely by residential property consisting of one to four dwelling units)

The Statute of Frauds was first adopted in England in 1677 and became part of English common law. Later, it was introduced into this country and adopted in California. The purpose of the Statute of Frauds is to prevent perjury and dishonest conduct on the part of unscrupulous persons in attempting to prove the existence and terms of certain types of contracts. The statute is a defense only, and can be invoked only by a party to the contract, or successor in interest, or one in privity.[39]

§2.12. Note or memorandum

An oral agreement, although originally subject to the ban of the Statute of Frauds, may become enforceable if a note or memorandum is subsequently made. An oral agreement to pay a real estate broker's commission is within the Statute of Frauds. However, subsequently signed escrow instructions that provide for payment make it enforceable. The writing need not be formal. It can be a note, letter, or telegram, so long as it contains the essential requisites of a valid memorandum. The word *memorandum* implies something less than a complete contract; it functions only as evidence of the contract and need not contain every term.[40]

On the other hand, a real estate licensee is presumed to know that contracts for real estate commissions are unenforceable unless in writing and subscribed by the parties to be charged.[41] Therefore, the broker has a heavy burden in relying solely on a memorandum.

EXAMPLES

1. In one case, S, a real estate broker, and F were longtime acquaintances. F contacted S with reference to the sale of F's ranch. F declined to give S a formal listing agreement, indicating he was "not going to cheat you out of a commission." S marked down the terms, a sufficient description of the property, the amount of the commission, and the fixed termination date of the listing on the back of his business card. F initialed and dated it. F later sold the property to a person procured by S and refused to pay a commission. The court held the writing on the reverse of S's card was a sufficient memorandum. In this type of situation, the better practice is to use a properly drafted listing agreement; otherwise, inequities may result.[42]

2. In another situation, the plaintiff was working on an oral listing since the defendant assured him a signed listing would be unnecessary as his word was good. The plaintiff requested a telegram authorizing the sale, along with the terms. The defendant complied and it was accepted by the buyer. Unfortunately, the fact of employment of plaintiff by defendant was not mentioned in the telegram and defendant refused to pay a commission. The court held the writing insufficient under the Statute of Frauds.[43]

The memorandum is deemed sufficient if it shows the employment relationship between the parties; neither the amount of commission nor the specific promise to pay need be expressed. The chief element required to be shown in writing is the *fact of employment*, and that the broker to whom the commission is to be paid be named.[44]

The memorandum must be signed by the party to be charged. It need not be signed by both if a contract was intended. Hence, when two parties contract for the sale of real estate and only the seller signs, the fact that the purchaser did not is immaterial if it is the buyer who brings the action against the seller to enforce the contract. Further, the signature need not be handwritten. It can be printed, stamped, typewritten, initialed, or executed by mark, so long as it is *intended* to be the person's signature. On the other hand, the Statute of Frauds does not require the signature to be at the end of the document so long as it is found elsewhere in the instrument.[45]

When a contract is required to be in writing, the authority of an agent to enter into the contract on behalf of the principal must also be in writing. This requirement is known as the *equal dignities rule*[46]; however, an oral authority can be ratified by the principal.

§2.13. Exceptions to Statute of Frauds

The Statute of Frauds is not applicable to an executed oral agreement. Partial performance by actual possession, and making partial or full payment or substantial improvements, will likewise remove a contract from the Statute of Frauds, if the purchaser did so in reliance on the oral agreement.[47] A person may also be estopped to allege the Statute of Frauds under the equitable estoppel doctrine.

EXAMPLE A broker changed his position to his detriment by releasing the seller from his obligation to pay the commission after the buyer orally agreed to pay a commission, and as such created an equitable estoppel against the buyer from setting up the Statute of Frauds.[48]

Not applicable between brokers. Although the Statute of Frauds prevents the enforcement of an oral contract to pay a commission by a broker against a principal, it does not apply to an oral contract between brokers to share a commission.[49] However, such an oral contract is only enforceable if one of the brokers has a binding contract with the principal, and the commission has already been received.[50]

Additional exception. Although a broker cannot recover a commission under an oral contract with his principal under most circumstances, a broker may be allowed recovery for the reasonable value of his services (quantum meruit) based upon an oral agreement. This may consist of selling personal property, making a survey, locating a suitable building site, or subdividing property. However, if these services are merely *incidental* to the broker's efforts to bring about a sale of real property, the broker will not prevail.[51]

V. INTERPRETATION OF CONTRACTS

§2.14. In general

Contracts are interpreted so as to give effect to the *intention* of the parties at the time the contract was entered into. A contract may be explained by reference to the circumstances under which it was made and the matter to which it relates. If it is clear and explicit, the language of the contract will govern its interpretation.

Intention of parties. A contract will be interpreted so as to give effect to the mutual intention of the parties at the time of contracting.[52] The whole contract is to be interpreted so as to give effect to every part, if reasonably practicable, each clause helping to interpret the other; i.e., a contract is to be interpreted from the four corners of the contract, if possible. A court will not make a contract for the parties. If the terms of a document cannot be reasonably ascertained, it will be avoided. If there are several contracts relating to the same matter, between the same parties (e.g., offer to purchase and escrow instructions) and made as parts of substantially one transaction, they are to be read together.[53] Escrow instructions that are merely a customary means of consummating an underlying contract for the sale of real estate do not supplant such agreement, but merely serve to carry it into effect.[54]

The words used are to be understood in their ordinary and popular sense rather than their strict legal meaning, unless a technical meaning is intended. If technical words are used, they are to be interpreted as usually understood by persons in the profession or business to which they relate.[55] Further, a contract is interpreted according to the law and usage of the place where it is to be performed, or if no such place, where the contract was made.[56] However, the court may give effect to the intent of the parties in seeking the governing laws. In any event, a contract is interpreted in favor of the promisee.[57] When a contract is partly written and partly printed, the written parts control over the printed.[58]

§2.15. Parol evidence rule

Problems arise when the contract is ambiguous, that is, subject to more than one interpretation. Words and their meanings are extremely important in the preparation of contracts. If the written agreement is in fact ambiguous, then oral evidence is admissible to explain it. This is known as the *parol evidence rule*.[59] Parol evidence will generally be excluded in the absence of fraud or mistake; however, a court is still permitted to *interpret* the contract, or extrinsic evidence may be admitted to explain a *latent* ambiguity. Oral evidence may be used to show that the contract is not enforceable because of mistake, fraud, duress, illegality, insufficiency or failure of consideration, or incapacity of a party. Interpretations of specific types of contracts are discussed in detail in Chapter 3.

§2.16. Merger clause

Written agreements often contain a merger clause stating that the writing shall constitute the entire contract, and that there are no agreements, warranties, or representations other than those expressly mentioned. Absent fraud or other wrongful act by one of the parties, such clauses are enforceable.

§2.17. Contracts of adhesion

Under the doctrine of adhesion, a contract may be invalidated when one party in an inferior position is forced to sign or curtail or forego a service from someone who is in a superior position. Since the party of superior bargaining power not only prescribed the words, but the other party lacks the economic strength to change the language, any ambiguity in the contract is resolved against the draftor and questions of doubtful interpretation will be construed in favor of the subscribing party.[60]

VI. FREEDOM OF CONSENT

§2.18. Mistake

A mistake of fact[61] or a mistake of law may give rise to a right by one or both of the parties to a contract to a rescission. A mistake of fact is a mistake not caused by the *neglect* of a legal duty on the part of the person making the mistake.

When there is no ambiguity, and neither party is at fault, a unilateral mistake will not prevent formation of a contract; however, when there is an ambiguity known by one party who fails to explain the mistake to the innocent party, the innocent party's interpretation will prevail. Mutual mistake, when either or both parties are equally to blame, or neither is at fault, may prevent formation of a contract. Whether the mistake is material is a question of fact.

EXAMPLES

1. When a seller believes he is selling one lot and a buyer thinks he is purchasing another, a mutual mistake of fact as to the subject matter prevents creation of a contract.[62]

2. Lessee leased a structure "as is" for use as a restaurant. After the lease was executed, it was discovered that in order to comply with building code requirements, substantial remodeling of the building would have to occur. It was held that the lessee could avoid the lease.[63]

A mistake of law[64] arises and relief will be granted if the mistake is mutual, or if the mistaken party can show that the other party was aware of the mistake and did nothing to correct it. To distinguish between mistake of fact and mistake of law, it is necessary to understand that a *mistake of fact* occurs when a person understands the facts to be other than what they are; a *mistake of law* occurs when a person knows the facts but has a mistaken belief as to the legal consequences of those facts.

§2.19. Fraud and misrepresentation

These are tortious acts. They constitute defenses to a contract and invalidate any consent. They are discussed in detail in Chapter 5.

§2.20. Undue influence

Undue influence is taking an unfair advantage of another's weakness of mind, or taking a grossly oppressive and unfair advantage of another's necessities or distress.[65] The undue susceptibility to an overpersuasive influence may be the product of physical or emotional exhaustion or anguish that results in one's inability to act with unencumbered volition. Overpersuasiveness is generally accompanied by certain characteristic elements which, when simultaneously present in a significant number, characterize the persuasion as excessive.

Elements.

1. Discussion of the transaction at an unusual or inappropriate time
2. Consummation of the transaction in an unusual place
3. Insistent demand that the business be finished at once
4. Extreme emphasis on untoward consequences of delay
5. The use of multiple persuaders by the dominant side versus a single servient party
6. Absence of third-party advisers to the servient party
7. Statements that there is no time to consult financial advisers or attorneys[66]

VII. PERFORMANCE

§2.21. In general

Every party to a contract has a duty to do everything to accomplish the purpose of the contract and a duty not to do anything that interferes with the right of the other party to receive the benefits of the contract.[67]

§2.22. Statute of Limitations

The time for performance of a contract depends upon the time limitations set forth; if none are set forth, then the time for performance is within a reasonable time.[68] Further, the Statute of Limitations[69] or the doctrine of laches may be applicable. The Statute of Limitations on a written contract is four years; it is two years for an oral contract. *Laches*, an unreasonable delay in asserting a claim, is an equitable defense to prevent injustice. (See §1.19 for more detail.) The Statute of Limitations can be waived under certain circumstances or an estoppel to claim it may apply.[70]

§2.23. Tender of performance

A *tender* is an offer of performance. When properly made, a tender has the effect of placing the other party in default if he refuses to accept it. The party making the tender may then rescind, sue for damages, or sue for specific performance in certain cases. A tender must be (1) in good faith; (2) unconditional; (3) for full performance; and (4) at the proper time and place.[71] The party must tender or offer to tender his own full performance as a condition for demanding performance by the other party. No tender need be made if it would obviously be useless, e.g., when the other party repudiates the contract, gives notice of his refusal to perform, or admits inability to perform.[72] If one party is late in his performance, and no tender is made by the other party, a "time is of the essence" clause is waived. (See §2.25.) The person to whom the tender is made must specify any objections he may have at the time, or defects in form or method are waived.[73]

§2.24. Conditions and covenants

A *covenant* is a promise to perform an act or bring about an event. A covenant may be expressed or implied. For example, an implied covenant of fair dealing is ordinarily part of the contract. A *condition* is a limiting (or conditional) promise whereby the occurrence (or nonoccurrence) may excuse the promise.

EXAMPLES

1.   Suppose a buyer enters into a real estate contract conditioned upon being able to assume the existing first trust deed at the same interest rate. If, during the term of the contract, the buyer decides he can obtain better financing, he can waive that condition and proceed with the sale.

2.   Assume B agrees in writing to purchase a home, provided he or she can obtain a new loan of $160,000 at not more than 9 percent per annum, for 30 years, at no more than one and a half points, with monthly principal and interest payments not to exceed $1,287.40, with no impounds and no prepayment penalty after five years. If after diligent effort he cannot acquire such a loan, his duty to perform is excused and the seller cannot recover damages or require specific performance.[74] On the other hand, if no contingency is set forth, i.e., if B merely provided he would purchase the home, his breach of this covenant may give rise to damages and/or specific performance.

Condition precedent. A condition precedent is an act that must be performed or a particular event that must happen before a promisor's duty of performance arises under a contract.[75] The example in the previous paragraph is a condition precedent.[76]

Condition concurrent. A condition concurrent is one that is mutually dependent upon another condition and both are to be performed at the same time,[77] such as an escrow situation wherein a certain amount of money is to be placed in escrow for the transfer of title from the seller to the buyer.[78]

Condition subsequent. A condition subsequent is rare, and refers to a future event which, if it occurs, releases one or both of the parties.[79]

EXAMPLE   A purchaser of land signed a note for the balance of the price, with the provision that its payment was dependent upon performance by the vendor of a separate agreement, under which the vendor was to cultivate, plant, and care for the land for six years.[80]

Satisfaction condition. A satisfaction condition provides that performance must be satisfactory to the promisor or some third party (e.g., an all-inclusive note and trust deed conditioned upon written approval of an attorney). If the satisfaction of the promisor is the criterion, two types of contracts must be distinguished: (1) those involving fancy, taste, or judgment; and (2) those involving mechanical utility or operative fitness. In the former situation, the promisor is still bound to act in good faith, although the standard is subjective.[81] In the latter, an objective test is used.[82]

§2.25. Time is of the essence

If time is not made of the essence, some delay in performance will not necessarily defeat the contract.[83] Performance can be completed within a reasonable time. However, a "time is of the essence" (TOE) clause often does appear in real estate contracts, particularly offers to purchase, as well as escrow instructions. A contract that contains a "time is of the essence" clause means that the parties agree that it is important that performance occur at or before the time specified and not at a later time. In such a case, whether time truly is of the essence or whether it has been waived depends upon the parties' actions and the precise wording of the clause.[84] In any event, if one party wishes to invoke this clause, he must first make his full tender of performance within the time specified in the contract or express his ability and willingness to perform.[85] If there has been a waiver and one party wishes to place the other in default, he must do so by (1) giving notice that a delay will no longer be tolerated and (2) allowing the other party a reasonable time to perform.[86] See Figure 2-1 for a TOE diagram.

EXAMPLES

1. If a seller cancels an escrow after the time has elapsed without making his full tender of performance to the buyer, the seller may be held bound by and in breach of the sales contract.[87]

2. If the buyer is tardy for only a short time, with a valid reason, the court may excuse him. In one case the court noted that the buyer's failure had not been unlawful, grossly negligent, or intentional and therefore the buyer's failure had not deprived him of the right of specific performance.[88]

3. In another case, the parties had entered into an escrow in which time was of the essence. Although one time period had elapsed, the seller assured the buyer that everything was in order, that escrow would close and not to worry about it. Seller sold the property to a third party and buyer brought suit. The appellate court found that the seller was estopped from terminating the escrow.[89]

VIII. MODIFICATION OR ALTERATION

§2.26. In general

A contract may be modified[90] by the mutual consent of the parties, usually supported by further consideration. If a contract is written, it may be modified by a written agreement or by an executed oral agreement.[91] An executory modification must be supported by new consideration. On the other hand, errors in a contract can be corrected and omissions filled in without new consideration. Unless the contract otherwise expressly provides, a contract in writing may be modified by an oral agreement supported by new consideration. The Statute of Frauds is required to be satisfied if the contract as modified is within its provisions. Also, an oral contract can be altered, in writing, without new consideration. When one party signs a document containing blanks and the other, or his agent, fills them in without authority, a contract is not formed because of this unauthorized alteration.

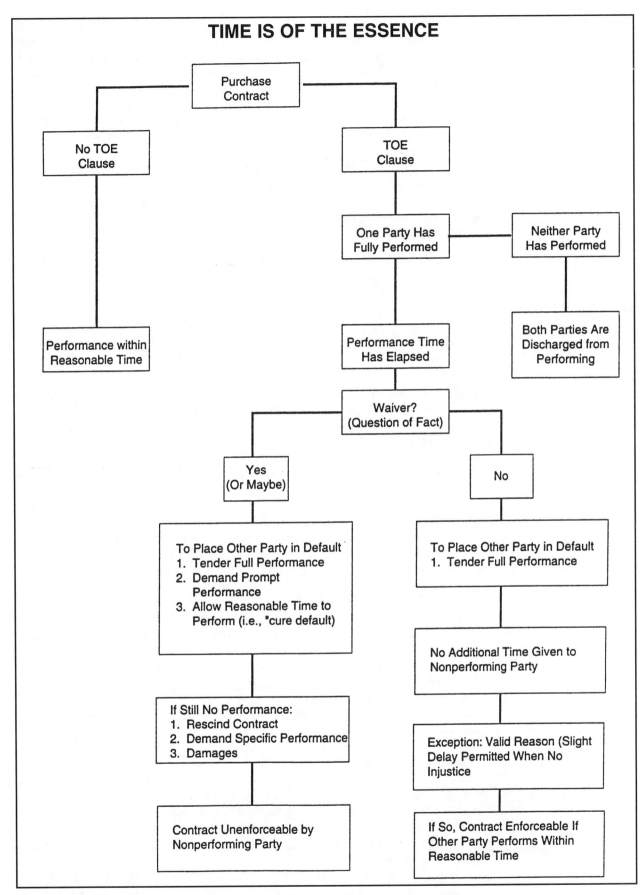

Figure 2-1
Time of the essence diagram (TOE). (© 1981 W. D. Milligan, Attorney, San Diego, California. All rights reserved.)

As far as real estate licensees are concerned, no licensee shall make or permit or allow any other person to make any addition to, deletion from, or alteration of any contract or other document, unless such is initialed and dated by all persons who have signed the original document adjacent to each addition or modification.[92] Further, a licensee shall not make or cause to be made any addition to or modification of the terms of an instrument previously signed or initialed by a party without the knowledge and consent of that party. The Real Estate Commissioner requires that no licensee solicit, accept, or execute any contract, writing, or other document relating to a real estate transaction or escrow that shall contain any blank to be filled in after signing or initialing the contract, [93] except upon certain written stipulations obtained from the party.

§2.27. Reformation
When the parties execute an agreement that does not express their understanding correctly, it may be reformed or revised, [94] either voluntarily by both parties or by appropriate court action.[95]

IX. DISCHARGE

§2.28. In general
The usual method of discharging a contract is by performance. Other methods of terminating or canceling a contract are discussed below.

§2.29. Rescission
An executory bilateral contract may be rescinded by the mutual consent of the parties.[96] The consent need not be in writing. A party may rescind unilaterally for several grounds: mistake, fraud, undue influence, duress, void consideration, breach of warranty, insanity, or illegality. Upon rescinding a contract, a party must restore everything received from the other party. Rescission is discussed further in §2.43.

§2.30. Release
An obligation is extinguished by a release given to the debtor by the creditor, upon a new consideration, or in writing.[97] A release takes effect upon its execution and delivery to the maker. The signature of the party released is not necessary, and it is immaterial that the consideration has not yet been paid. A release does not extend to claims that the creditor does not know or suspect to exist at the time of the release, but this can be waived.[98] Further, such a release is only effective as to persons connected with the transaction; it does not apply to others.[99]

§2.31. Accord and satisfaction
An *accord* is an agreement to accept, in extinction of an obligation, something different from or less than that to which the person agreeing to accept is entitled.[100] Acceptance by the creditor of the consideration of an accord (by fully performing the new obligation) extinguishes the obligation, and is called *satisfaction*.[101] A writing is not essential; it may be implied. For example, if there is an honest dispute as to an amount owed, and the debtor sends what he believes to be the total amount on the express condition that acceptance of it will constitute full payment, and the creditor accepts the amount, an accord and satisfaction are reached. If, on the other hand, there is an amount due that is undisputed, the creditor may accept the amount sent, and an accord and satisfaction will not have occurred.

§2.32. Novation
A *novation* is the substitution of a new obligation with the intent to extinguish an existing one.[102] It can be written, oral, or implied, even though the original contract is in writing. The key element is the *intent* to discharge the old contract.

EXAMPLE Assume a typical lease situation for a one-year period. Assume further that the lease has been in effect for three months and the tenant is getting transferred to another city. Even if transferred, he is still obligated on the lease, and therefore finds another person to take over the lease. If the lessor merely permits the assignment of the lease, that will not, of itself, relieve the tenant. However, if the landlord intends to relieve the lessee from any further liability, a novation takes place.

§2.33. Bankruptcy

Bankruptcy may result in a discharge of a contract on the theory of failure of consideration or anticipatory breach of contract.

§2.34. Impossibility of performance

This method and the following one, frustration of purpose, are more of an excuse for performance, although the result is the same. If a contract is *objectively* impossible to perform, it is excused. However, modern cases recognize impracticability due to excessive and unreasonable difficulty or expense.[103]

Some acceptable excuses are (1) an act of nature; [104] (2) a strike, death, or incapacity of the promisor (if it is a personal service contract); (3) operation of law; [105] (4) act of public enemy (war); (5) destruction or nonexistence of the subject matter.[106]

§2.35. Frustration of purpose (sometimes called commercial frustration)

Although frustration of purpose is sometimes confused with *impossibility of performance*, the two concepts are different. Objectively, when the purpose of a contract has been frustrated, the promisor can still perform. Under this theory, however, if the subject matter has become totally or nearly totally valueless, performance will be discharged.

Elements.

1. The event was not reasonably foreseeable.

2. There is total or near total destruction of the value of the contract.

3. The event occurred after the contract but before performance, i.e., a supervening event.

4. The main purpose of the contract was within the contemplation of the parties.

EXAMPLE In an older case, a lease was entered into after the National Defense Act, for the sole purpose of selling new automobiles. The lessee attempted to avoid the lease on the grounds of commercial frustration. However, because the lessee had other car lots and the automobile industry in general was anticipating war priorities, the lessee could have reasonably foreseen governmental restrictions. Therefore, the lessee remained liable on the lease.[107]

§2.36. Arbitration and award, and mediation

If a contract provides that disputes will be submitted to arbitration, such a promise is specifically enforceable in California.[108] In fact, if one party refuses to arbitrate, the other may obtain a court order requiring arbitration. The arbitration may result in a finding (award) that the contract is extinguished.

Mediation, a forum different from arbitration, is being used more and more to assist the parties in reaching their own resolution to a dispute. This is accomplished with the use of a trained mediator. The requirement that the parties submit to mediation is being used with growing frequency in contracts in California.

§2.37. Substantial performance

Poor construction by a contractor precludes his recovery of the balance of the contract price under the Doctrine of Substantial Performance.[109]

X. BREACH OF CONTRACT

§2.38. In general

The unjustified or unexcused failure to perform a contract, or a material part, is a *breach*. Any breach, total or partial, causing a measurable injury, gives rise to damages. A *total* breach excuses performance by the innocent party; a *partial* breach excuses performance only if the breach is *material*. A partial breach at the beginning is more likely to be considered material; whereas a partial breach after the contract has been substantially performed may not be. A breach occurs only after the nonperformance or repudiation of a covenant. The nonperformance of a condition does not result in a breach if the promisor acted in good faith. Hindrance on the part of one party is a breach giving the other party the affirmative remedies for breach.

EXAMPLE When a broker had an exclusive right to sell, and the owner wrongfully canceled the listing, the broker can recover a commission without showing he had an available purchaser.[110] On the other hand, when the injured party with knowledge of the breach continues to accept performance, such conduct may constitute a *waiver* of the breach.

---

§2.39. Anticipatory breach

A breach does not occur until the time for performance has been reached, but upon an anticipatory repudiation a total breach may take place. To constitute an anticipatory breach the promisor must manifest such intention by a clear, positive, and unequivocal refusal to perform. In such a case, the injured party may wait until time for performance and then exercise his remedies, or he may sue immediately. However, there can be no anticipatory breach of a unilateral contract or in lease situations. In unilateral contracts, the injured party has already performed and generally will not suffer unreasonable loss by waiting until the time for counterperformance. In the case of a lease, the lessor cannot sue to recover damages for the entire lease; among other things, he must mitigate damages by attempting to re-lease the property.[111]

XI. REMEDIES FOR BREACH

§2.40. In general

A material breach of contract does not automatically discharge the contract. It does, however, excuse the injured party from performing, and gives that party the election to pursue a number of remedies.

§2.41. Specific performance

The law will compel a party to perform a contract under certain circumstances.[112] The typical situation would arise when two parties enter into a binding contract to buy and sell a parcel of real estate. The seller later changes his mind and backs out. The buyer can require the seller (or vice versa) specifically to perform by selling him the property,[113] unless there is no mutuality of remedy between the parties.[114]

The following obligations will not be specifically enforced:[115]

1. An obligation to render personal service or to employ another in personal service

2. An illegal agreement

3. An agreement to procure the act or consent of the spouse of the contracting party, or a third person

4. An ambiguous agreement

5. An agreement with inadequate consideration[116]

6. An agreement not just or reasonable, or one that would create an undue hardship

7. An agreement in which assent was obtained by fraud, misrepresentation, concealment, circumvention, or unfair practice

8. An agreement in which assent was given by mistake, misapprehension, or surprise[117]

9. When a party can be adequately compensated by an award of money

A buyer can place a seller in default and obtain specific performance despite his own failure to deposit the purchase price in escrow if there has been an unwarranted repudiation by the seller and the buyer satisfies the requirements of equity. An essential basis for the equitable remedy of specific performance must be a showing by the buyer of performance, or tender of performance, or ability and willingness to perform during the contract period.[118] If the purchaser was without funds of his own, he may show he was able to perform because he made arrangements to borrow the funds, but if so, he must prove (1) that the third party was legally bound to advance the funds; and (2) that the third party had the financial ability to do so. On the other hand, specific performance may be allowed when the inability to obtain a loan is caused by the seller's repudiation.[119]

§2.42. Damages
The injured party may stand on the contract, offer to perform, and sue for damages. The various types of damages are discussed later in this chapter.

§2.43. Rescission and restitution
Rescission dissolves the contract as though it had never been made.[120] Each party then restores to the other any consideration already paid. If the action is based upon fraud, a buyer is entitled to interest, punitive damages, and reasonable expenses.[121] On the other hand, if the rescission involves the sale of a house and the buyer has gained occupancy, the buyer must pay for the reasonable rental value of the property during possession.

§2.44. Injunction
This remedy is meant to prevent irreparable damage.[122] An example of this is an action to enjoin a lender from proceeding with a trustee's sale under a trust deed for an alleged violation of a due-on-sale clause.

§2.45. Declaratory relief
A court action to determine the rights and obligations of parties to a dispute is called *declaratory relief*. This type of action is often used, along with a request for a temporary restraining order, to permit a court to determine, for example, whether or not a particular clause involves an unlawful restraint on alienation.[123]

§2.46. Remedy under land contract
Remedies under a land contract may consist of bringing an action to require the vendee either to pay the monies due under the contract or to have all his rights under the contract terminated, in which case the court may render a decree, interlocutory in nature, declaring that a default has occurred in a specified amount; fix a time in the court's discretion within which the purchaser must cure the default; and if the purchaser fails to pay the amount within the prescribed time, enter a final decree, terminating all of the vendee's rights under the contract. The vendor may also bring an action to quiet title against the vendee; or may declare a termination pursuant to the terms of the contract, which usually means compliance

with certain notice requirements. In effect, this is a forfeiture (termination) of the vendee's interest.

XII. NATURE OF DAMAGES

§2.47. In general

If there has been a breach of contract, the injured party has several types of damages available, discussed below.

§2.48. Compensatory damages

The object of damages is to compensate the party injured for what is normally lost as a result of a breach.[124]

EXAMPLES

1. Real estate broker procures a buyer for a property listed with him and the seller refuses to sell the property. The damages to the broker in such a case would be the amount of the commission.

2. The measure of damages for breach of contract to construct improvements on real property when the work is to be done on plaintiff's property is the reasonable cost to the plaintiff to finish the work in accordance with the contract.[125]

3. The developer was awarded lost profits against the contractor for delays in construction.[126]

---

§2.49. Nominal damages

When a breach causes no substantial damage or when the damage was not reasonably foreseeable, only nominal damages can be awarded.[127]

§2.50. General damages

General damages are compensatory damages. Damages for failure of a seller to convey land to a buyer,[128] and the detriment caused to a seller by a buyer's refusal to purchase land,[129] are illustrations of general damages.[130]

Buyer's and seller's measure of damages. Under the law,[131] a buyer or seller may sue the other for breach of contract under the "benefit of the bargain" rule.[132]

EXAMPLE

If the fair market value was $125,000 and the contract price was $100,000, the buyer is entitled to $25,000 for the seller's breach. If the value was only $100,000, the buyer would not be entitled to any damages.

Of course, a liquidated damage clause may alter this (see §2.56).

Damages not arising from contract. Damages for a breach of an obligation not arising from a contract (e.g., a broker's negligence, fraud, or misrepresentation) are the amount that would compensate the injured party for all detriment (including attorney's fees), proximately caused, whether anticipated or not.[133]

EXAMPLE

One defrauded in the purchase, sale, or exchange of property is entitled to recover the difference between the value of that with which he parted and the value he received, together with any additional damage arising from the particular transaction.[134]

When breach of fiduciary duty. Damages as a result of fraud between vendor and vendee are governed by different rules than in the case of breach of fiduciary duty. In the latter case, damages are measured under the broad provisions of torts in general.

EXAMPLE In one case, a brokerage firm failed to disclose that a second trust deed had an acceleration clause and the purchaser in an exchange lost the property at a foreclosure sale.[135] The court held that the "benefit of the bargain" doctrine applied and therefore the damages were the loss sustained by the purchaser: fair exchange value was $136,785.86; property was encumbered by loans totaling $81,024.02. Therefore the loss sustained was the difference between the purchase price and the encumbrances, or $55,761.84 (plus an additional expense of $500, or a total sum of $56,261.84).[136]

§2.51. Special damages
Special damages are those that arise and cause injury that is foreseeable.

EXAMPLES
1. Lost profits
2. Interest (recoverable at the legal rate of 7 percent, or up to 10 percent if set forth in the contract)[137]
3. Seller's expenses in reselling the property after the original sale fails as a result of the buyer's breach, which may also include the broker's commission[138]
4. Increase in seller's damages because of lis pendens since unable to dispose of property, pay for taxes, etc.[139]
5. Buyer's expenses for title costs and escrow expenses
6. Adverse tax consequences of contractor not completing a house within the required two-year time period.[140]

§2.52. Broker's breach of contract
If a licensee breaches a contract with his principal, the principal can bring an action against him for damages. In addition, the licensee may be found in violation of the real estate law through a disciplinary hearing.[141] In the latter event, the decision may include a stay of execution the terms of which can include an order of restitution to the injured party.[142]

§2.53. Damages for pain and suffering
Damages for emotional distress or physical suffering are possible under cases other than breach of contract, but in the case of emotional distress, are sometimes difficult to prove.[143]

§2.54. Punitive or exemplary damages
An injured party may recover damages for the sake of example and by way of punishing the defendant.[144] However, such damages are not recoverable for a breach of contract.[145] On the other hand, when the conduct constitutes a tort for fraud, punitive damages can be awarded. So long as plaintiff can show *any* damages, punitive damages can be awarded, even if the general damage amount has been offset.[146]

EXAMPLE In one case, the appellate court upheld a jury award of $215,000 in punitive damages for breach of a home construction contract in which actual damages were less than $9,000. Plaintiffs, an elderly couple, sold their home and thereafter entered into a construction contract with defendant for completion of a new home within a prescribed time in order to defer capital gains taxes. It was proven that the defendants never intended to complete the contract within the prescribed time, even though they knew of the importance of the completion date as far as the interest of the plaintiff was concerned. This amounted to fraud, which was the basis for the large award of punitive damages.[147]

§2.55. Mitigating/Minimizing damages

One injured by a breach of contract is required to act reasonably to minimize the loss. He cannot recover for harm that could have reasonably been seen and avoided.[148]

§2.56. Liquidated damages

In California, forfeiture clauses are considered to be void but liquidated damages are valid.[149] To be enforceable, the wording of a liquidated damage clause must be precise; it must be understood by the parties at the time they enter into the contract. Such a clause is designed solely for the protection of the buyer.[150] Thus, it is important to understand this area of law. In fact, it is probable that the licensee has an affirmative duty to disclose the availability of liquidated damages and explain the mechanics and effect of this remedy.

Contracts that contain liquidated damage clauses fall into the following categories:

1. A purchase (other than by an installment land contract) of four or fewer units when the buyer intends it to be an owner-occupied dwelling, provides for liquidated damages to seller if buyer fails to complete the purchase.[151] If the amount actually deposited as liquidated damages does not exceed 3 percent of the purchase price, the clause is valid unless the buyer establishes that such amount is unreasonable. If the amount actually deposited exceeds 3 percent, the clause is invalid unless the party seeking to uphold the provision establishes the reasonableness of the amount actually paid.[152] In determining the reasonableness, *both* of the following must be taken into account: (a) circumstances at the time the contract was made; and (b) the price and other terms and circumstances of the sale or contract to sell the property within six months of the buyer's default.[153]

2. A purchase (other than by an installment land contract), of (a) any non–owner occupied dwelling; (b) five or more dwelling units; or (c) any other real property (regarding liquidated damages to seller if the buyer fails to complete the purchase).[154]

3. In the case of all real property sales contracts, in order for a liquidated damage clause to be valid in favor of the seller if the buyer defaults, (a) such a clause must be separately signed or initialed by each party; (b) it must be either in ten-point bold type or eight-point red type; and (c) when the amount of the damages is made in more than one payment, each provision must satisfy conditions (a) and (b).[155] Further, the person claiming the provision is invalid must prove it was unreasonable at the time the contract was made.[156]

4. A purchase or rental of personal property or services for personal, household, or family use, or for the lease of real property for use as a dwelling (or those dependent upon the party for support). In these cases, the former liquidated damages rules apply; i.e., such a clause is void except when the actual damages are impracticable or extremely difficult to fix.[157]

5. The provisions in Paragraph 1 do not apply to any real property sales contracts.[158] In addition, specific performance remains available to the parties.[159]

§2.57. Attorney's fees

Generally, attorney's fees are not recoverable in an action.[160] However, if under a suit for *breach of contract*, the agreement provides for attorney's fees by one side but does not mention the other, a court can still award attorney's fees to the prevailing party whether or not he is the party specified in the contract.[161] Assume a lawsuit is brought for breach of contract, which contains an attorney's fee clause, and also for, say, misrepresentation. If the court finds there was a misrepresentation but no breach of contract, attorney's fees may still be awarded to the plaintiff (depending upon the circumstances).[162] If the defendant also lost on the misrepresentation cause of action, he is not the prevailing party and therefore cannot collect attorney's fees either. On the other hand, if a plaintiff, as a proximate result of defendant's tort (intentional tort and negligence), is required to prosecute or defend an action against a third party for the protection of his interest, attorney's fees are recoverable as damages.[163]

When a plaintiff voluntarily dismisses a suit, the defendant cannot collect attorney's fees from plaintiff. To allow such would encourage plaintiffs to maintain pointless litigation to avoid liability for fees.[164]

QUESTIONS

Matching Terms

a. Mutual assent
b. Consideration
c. Acceptance
d. Void
e. Illusory
f. Promise
g. Tender
h. Novation
i. Breach
j. Mitigate

1. Having no legal force or binding effect. Void
2. An offer of performance. Tender
3. Agreement between two or more persons to do or not to do something. Promise
4. Unexcused failure to perform a contract. Breach
5. Meeting of the minds. Mutual Assent
6. Substitution of a new obligation with intent to extinguish an existing one. Novation
7. To minimize or lessen damages. Mitigate
8. Anything of value. Consideration
9. Vague; uncertain. Illusory
10. Compliance by offeree with terms and conditions of an offer. Acceptance

True/False

T F 11. There is an implied covenant of good faith in every contract.
T F 12. In an implied contract, the agreement is evidenced by acts and conduct, rather than by words.
T F 13. In an executed contract, one party has performed but the other has not.
T F 14. The acceptance of a bilateral contract must generally be communicated to the offeror.
T F 15. For a contract to be valid, both its consideration and its object must be lawful.
T F 16. The Statute of Limitations requires certain types of contracts to be in writing in order to be enforceable.
T F 17. Ordinarily, a unilateral mistake will render a contract invalid.
T F 18. A "time is of the essence" clause in a contract contemplates dilatory performance.
T F 19. Undue influence may have the same effect on enforceability of a contract as fraud and deceit.

T F 20. As a basic rule, contracts will be interpreted so as to effect the intention of the parties at the time the contract was entered into.

Multiple Choice

21. The statute that requires certain types of contracts to be in writing to be enforceable is known as the
   a. Statute of Frauds.
   b. Statute of Limitations.
   c. Statute of Uses.
   d. Statute of Descent.
22. Which of the following is ordinarily not essential to the validity of a contract?
   a. Meeting of the minds.
   b. Disinterested witness.
   c. Mutual assent.
   d. Absence of duress.
23. All contracts are either
   a. Oral or written, when expressed.
   b. Unilateral or bilateral.
   c. Legal or illegal.
   d. All of the above.
24. A contract to be valid requires
   a. A promise.
   b. Consideration.
   c. Lawful purpose.
   d. All of the above.
25. Consideration for a contract can be in the form of
   a. Services.
   b. Money.
   c. Promise.
   d. Any of the above.
26. Of the following words, which one does not belong with the others?
   a. Offer.
   b. Acceptance.
   c. Abatement.
   d. Rejection.
27. A "time is of the essence" clause in a contract
   a. Means that the time of performance is immaterial.

b. Renders the contract unenforceable.

c. Makes the contract uncertain.

d. Contemplates a punctual performance.

28. The competency of a party to execute a valid contract is dependent upon

    a. Age.

    b. Soundness of mind.

    c. Mental capacity.

    d. All of the above.

29. An agreement that requires one of the parties to commit an illegal act but for adequate consideration is

    a. Void.

    b. Voidable.

    c. Valid.

    d. Enforceable.

30. For a contract to be valid, the parties must be capable of contracting. Persons who are not fully capable of contracting include

    a. Minors.

    b. Intoxicated persons.

    c. Persons of unsound mind.

    d. Any of the above.

31. Illegal consideration or purpose includes

    a. Wagers on the outcome of an election.

    b. Agreement to lease premises for the sale of narcotics.

    c. Agreement to commit a criminal act.

    d. Any of the above.

32. A contract for the sale of land made by a person under 18 years of age is

    a. Void.

    b. Voidable.

    c. Illegal.

    d. Enforceable.

33. An example of a void contract is one that is

    a. Not in writing.

    b. Not valid.

    c. Difficult to perform.

    d. Induced by fraud.

34. An offer may be terminated by

    a. Lapse of time.

    b. Revocation by offeror.

    c. Rejection by offeree.

    d. Any of the above.

35. The substitution of a new obligation with the intent to extinguish an existing one is known as

    a. Novation.

    b. Discharge by breach.

    c. Rescission.

    d. Any of the above.

36. The word *rescinded* means

    a. Altered.

    b. Terminated.

    c. Substituted.

    d. Subordinated.

37. A contract may be discharged by

    a. Performance.

    b. Impossibility of performance.

    c. Agreement between the parties.

    d. Any of the above.

38. A contract must be definite and certain in its terms. If the precise acts to be done are not clearly ascertainable, a contract may not have been formed. Which of the following would render a contract of questionable validity?

    a. Buyer to obtain a loan, but amount, interest rate, and terms not specified.

    b. Seller to subordinate to a construction loan for a commercial building.

    c. Buyer may withdraw at any time prior to close of escrow.

    d. Any of the above.

39. Undue influence means taking any fraudulent or unfair advantage of another person's

    a. Weakness of mind.

    b. Distress.

    c. Dire necessity.

    d. Any of the above.

40. A person agreed in writing to pay $1,000 to John Brown for legal services. John Brown performed the legal services satisfactorily, but was not licensed to practice law. John Brown is entitled to collect

    a. $1,000.

    b. Nothing.

    c. Reasonable value of the service.

    d. $500.

41. Which of the following are examples of contracts calling for acts that are contrary to public policy?

    a. Acts that tend to obstruct the administration of justice.

    b. Acts in restraint of trade.

    c. Acts that impair the legislative process.

    d. Any of the above.

42. Which of the following is considered to be a bilateral contract?

    a. A promise for an act.

    b. A promise for a promise.

    c. Two contracts are combined into one.

    d. None of the above.

43. A contract between an adult and a minor can be set aside by

    a. The adult.

    b. Either party.

    c. The minor.

    d. Neither party.

44. Which of the following contracts do not have to be in writing to be enforceable?

    a. Agreement between broker and owner to pay a commission on sale of real property.

    b. Contract between brokers to share a commission.

c. Option to buy unimproved real property.

d. All of the above.

45. Which of the following statements is true?

    a. A minor's contract is voidable by either party.

    b. Courts never consider inadequacy of consideration a valid defense.

    c. Past consideration is not a sufficient consideration.

    d. A valid contract can be enforced at any time.

46. When a minor disaffirms a contract of purchase, he is required to return the article received. This is known as the

    a. Right to full performance.

    b. Right to partial performance.

    c. Duty of restitution.

    d. Duty of retribution.

47. The right to disaffirm a contract made by a minor may be made

    a. Only during minority.

    b. At any time after attaining the age of majority.

    c. Within a reasonable time after attaining the age of majority.

    d. There is no right to disaffirm if the minor was of ordinary intelligence.

48. The requirement of consideration is satisfied by

    a. A promise exchanged for an act.

    b. A promise exchanged for a forbearance to act.

    c. A promise exchanged for a promise.

    d. Any of the above.

49. For an offer to be legally effective, it must

    a. Be communicated.

    b. Manifest an intent to contract.

    c. Be sufficiently definite and certain.

    d. All of the above.

50. A rejection of an offer by the offeree is effective

    a. As soon as made.

    b. As soon as mailed to the offeror.

    c. When received by the offeror.

    d. None of the above.

NOTES

1. C.C. 1427 1428.
2. Jacobs v. Freeman (1980) 104 C.A.3d 177; Moreland Dev. Co. v. Gladstone Holmes, Inc. (1982) 135 C.A.3d. 973.
3. Baumgartner v. Meek (1954) 126 C.A.2d 505.
4. C.C. 1661.
5. C.C. 33. However, an emancipated minor can buy and sell real estate (C.C. 63).
6. C.C. 39.
7. C.C. 1550.
8. Nakasukasa v. Wade (1954) 128 C.A.2d 86; Angell v. Rowland (1978) 85 C.A.3d. 536; *see also*, Conditions & Covenants, infra. But a party who has signed a written contract may be compelled to specifically perform, though the other party has not signed it, if the latter has performed, or offers to perform on his part and the case is otherwise proper for enforcing specific performance (C.C. 3388; Ellis v. Mihelis [1963] 60 C.2d 206,

215-216). Neither husband nor wife is obligated to perform if only one signs a contract to sell (Andrade Dev. Co. v. Martin [1982] 138 C.A.3d 330; C.C. 5127). *See also* footnote 76.

9. *See* Myers v. Gager (1959) 175 C.A.2d 314, 323. But *see* Moreland Dev. Co. v. Gladstone Holmes, Inc. (1982) 135 C.A.3d 973.
10. Michel & Pfeffer v. Oceanside Properties, Inc. (1976) 61 C.A.3d 433.
11. Laks v. Coast Federal Savings and Loan (1976) 60 C.A.3d 885.
12. Roth v. Moeller (1921) 185 C. 415, 419.
13. C.C. 1587.
14. Rest. Contracts 39.
15. Rivadell, Inc. v. Razo (1963) 215 C.A.2d 614, 625; concluding that the word *nominee* is synonymous with the word *assignee*. But a contrary decision is Born v. Koop (1962) 200 C.A.2d 519 and JMR, Inc. v. Hedderly (1968) 261 C.A.2d 144. *See also* Cisco v. Van Le (1943) 60 C.A.2d 575; Ott v. Nome S & L. (1958) 265 Fed.2d 643.
16. C.C. 1585; Krasley v. Sup. Court (1980) 101 C.A.3d 425; *see* Sabo v. Fasano (1984) 154 C.A.3d 502; *see also* §3.50 and Figure 3-3.
17. Born v. Koop (1962) 200 C.A.2d 519.
18. Comm. Regs. 2902; B. & P. 10142.
19. C.C. 1565, 1581.
20. But *see* Carr v. Lauritson (1940) 41 C.A.2d 31.
21. C.C. 1583.
22. Angell v. Rowlands (1978) 85 C.A.3d 536, 540.
23. *See* Andrade Dev. Co. v. Martin (1982) 138 C.A.3d 330.
24. Grene v. Taft Realty Co. (1929) 101 C.A. 343, 345.
25. Wyatt v. Union Mortgage Co. (1979) 24 C.3d 773, 783.
26. C.C. 1605.
27. C.C. 1614; Evid. C. 622.
28. Louisville Title Inc. Co. v. Surety Title & Guaranty Co. (1976) 60 C.A.2d 781, 791.
29. C.C. 3391.
30. Mattei v. Hopper (1958) 51 C.2d 119. *See also* Wilson v. Lewis (1980) 106 C.A.3d 809 re postdated check as failure of consideration.
31. Fry v. Elkins (1958) 162 C.A.2d 256.
32. Rest. Contracts 90.
33. *See* Thomas v. International Alliance of Stage Employees (1965) 232 C.A.2d 446, 454; Munoz v. Kaiser Steel Corp. (1984) 156 C.A.3d 965.
34. C.C. 33; *see* footnote 5.
35. C.C. 1556; Pen. C. 2600.
36. C.C. 62. Mil & Vet 986.10. A veteran under age 21 is deemed to be of the age of majority when contracting for the purchase of a house or farm from the Department of Veteran Affairs.
37. But *see* Calwood Structures Inc. v. Herskovic (1980) 105 C.A.3d 519, 522 which stated: "Sometimes the forfeiture resulting from unenforceability is disproportionately harsh considering the nature of the illegality."
38. C.C. 1624, as amended in 1988. But *see* Fisher v. Parrons (1963) 213 C.A. 2d 829 and a contrary case, Bed, Bath & Beyond of La Jolla Inc. v. La Jolla Village Square Venture Partners (1997) 52 C.A. 4th 867.
39. Bumb v. Bennett (1958) 51 C.2d 294; O'Banian v. Paradiso (1964) 61 C.2d 559.
40. Kerner v. Hughes Tool Co. (1976) 56 C.A.3d 924.
41. Krog v. Baur (1941) 46 C.A.2d 801, 804.
42. Seck v. Foulks (1972) 25 C.A.3d 556.
43. Franklin v. Hansen (1963) 59 C.2d 570; *see also* Paulsen v. Leadbetter (1968) 267 C.A.2d 148; Ira Garsen Realty Co. v. Avedon (1960) 246 C.A.2d 624.19.
44. Barcelon v. Cortese (1968) 263 C.A.2d 517, 525.
45. Marks v. McCarty Corp. (1949) 33 C.2d 814.
46. C.C. 1624(c); C.C. 1624(d); Burge v. Dixon (1984) 152 C.A.3d 1120; C.C. 2309, 2933.

47. But *see* Phillippe v. Shappell Ind. (1987) 43 C.3d 1247. Also, the statute of frauds is not a bar predicated on fraudulent misrepresentation. Ballou v. Master Properties No. 6 (1987) 189 C.A.3d 65. *See also* Sutton v. Warner (1993) 12 C.A.4th 415 re past performance and substantial improvements.

48. Le Blond v. Wolfe (1948) 83 C.A.2d 282; *see also* Owens v. Foundation for Ocean Research (1980) 107 C.A.3d 179 re equitable estoppel; Hughes v. Morrison (1984) 160 C.A.3d 103.

49. Grant v. Marinell (1980) 112 C.A.3d 617, 619; Goossen v. Adair (1960) 185 C.A.2d 810. *See* Phillippe v. Shappell (1987) 43 C.3d 1247, when defendant, although a broker, was acting as a principal.

50. Daft v. Enos (1957) 155 C.A.2d 315, 317. There is an additional exception when a principal requests over the telephone, e.g., that his agent sign his name.

51. Owens v. National Container Corp. of Calif. (1952) 115 C.A.2d 21; Carey v. Cusack (1966) 245 C.A.2d 57.

52. C.C. 1636.

53. C.C. 1642.

54. Katemis v. Westerlind (1953) 120 C.A.2d 537, 542.

55. C.C. 1645.

56. C.C. 1646; C.C.P. 1857; Larwin-So. Cal. Inc. v. JGB Investment Co. (1980) 101 C.A.3d 626, 635.

57. C.C. 1649, 1654; Sands v. E.I.C., Inc. (1980) 118 C.A.3d 231.

58. C.C. 1651; C.C.P. 1862.

59. C.C.P. 1856; Beggerly v. Gbur (1980) 112 C.A.3d 180; EPA Real Estate Partnership v. Kang (1992) 12 C.A. 4th 171.

60. Space v. Omnibus (1974) 44 C.A.3d 970; *see also* Bondanza v. Peninsula Hospital and Medical Center (1979) 23 C.3d 260; *see* C.C. 1670.5 re unconscionable contract. The case of Speare v. Omnibus Industries (1975) 44 C.A.3d 970, contains the following interesting observation: Contracts of adhesion, most of which are editorial nightmares, proliferate. There is dark suspicion that the same people who prepare these prepare income tax forms and directions as to how to put together packaged Christmas toys.

61. C.C. 1577.

62. Bareld v. Price (1871) 40 C. 535.

63. Williams v. Puccinelli (1965) 236 C.A.2d 512; Wright v. Lowe (1956) 140 C.A.2d 891, 896.

64. C.C. 1578.

65. C.C. 1575; Crowley v. Katleman (1993) 21 C.A. 4th 1081.

66. Odorizzi v. Bloomfield School Dist. (1966) 246 C.A.2d 123, 133; Channell v. Anthony (1976) 58 C.A.3d 290.

67. Corson v. BMI (1979) 87 C.A.3d 422.

68. C.C. 1657.

69. C.C.P. 337. *See also*, Loken v. Century 21 Award Properties (1995) 36 C.A. 4th 263, C.C. 2079.4, C.C. 1102 et seq.

70. C.C.P. 337; Slavin v. Trout (1993) 18 C.A. 4th 1536; Buescher v. Lastar (1976) 61 C.A.3d 73.

71. C.C. 1486-1487; Ateeq v. Najor (1993) 15 C.A. 4th 1351; Gaffney v. Downey S & L (1988) 200 C.A.3d 1154.

72. C.C. 1440, 1511, 1515.

73. C.C.P. 2076.

74. That is, if the condition cannot occur, neither party is in breach. Bennett v. Carlson (1963) 213 C.A.2d 307. A seller is not required to incur the expense of a termite inspection report while the transaction is contingent on the buyer obtaining a loan commitment, unless the contract expressly requires it (Fogarty v. Saathoff [1982] 128 C.A.3d 780). On the other hand, a contracting party can waive provisions placed in a contract solely for his benefit (Reeder v. Longo [1982] 131 C.A.3d 291).

75. C.C. 1436; Comm. Regs. 2785(a)(8).

76. Another example occurs when an agreement signed by a husband is not to become effective until the signature of the wife is obtained. Fugate v. Cook (1965) 236 C.A.2d 700; Tamimi v. Bettencourt (1960) 243 C.A.2d 377; Davinroy v. Thompson (1959) 169 C.A.2d 63; Spade v. Cossette (1952) 110 C.A.2d 782; but *see* Wilks v. Vencill (1947) 30 C.2d 104, 107.

77. C.C. 1437.

78. Kossler v. Palm Springs Developers Ltd. (1980) 101 C.A.3d 88, 96—neither party can place the other in default without first performing or tendering his own performance with the ability to perform.

79. C.C. 1438.

80. Ebbert v. Mercantile Trust Co. (1931) 213 C. 496.

81. Larwin-So. Cal. Inc. v. JGB Investment Co. (1980) 101 C.A.3d 626, 640; Jacobs v. Freeman (1980) 104 C.A.3d 177; Converse v. Fong (1984) 159 C.A.3d 86.

82. Kadner v. Shields (1971) 20 C.A.3d 251.

83. Fowler v. Ross (1983) 142 C.A.3d 472; Henry v. Sharma (1984) 154 C.A.3d 1665.

84. *See,* e.g., Lifton v. Harshman (1947) 80 C.A.2d 422, 433, 434; Pence v. Brown (1960) 186 C.A.2d 425; Andover Land Co. v. Huffman (1968) 264 C.A.2d 87.

85. Pittman v. Canham (1992) 2 C.A. 4th 556; Am-Cal. Investment Co. v. Sharlyn Est. Inc. (1967) 255 C.A.2d 526, 539; Fogarty v. Saathoff (1982) 128 C.A.3d 78; Landis v. Bloomquist (1967) 257 C.A.2d 533.

86. Pence v. Brown, supra at 428 429; Kossler v. Palm Springs Dev. Co. (1980) 101 C.A.3d 88, 98; but *see* contra Altadena Escrow Corp. v. Beebe (1960) 181 C.A.2d 743.

87. Diamond v. Huenergardt (1959) 175 C.A.2d 214; but *see* Fogarty v. Saathoff (1982) 128 C.A.3d 78.

88. Williams Plumbing Co. v. Sinsley (1975) 53 C.A.3d 1027; *see also* C.C. 3275 and Katemis v. Westerlind (1953) 120 C.A.2d 537, wherein time could be extended by a broker for 30 more days and buyer was late, and it caused seller no loss; Stratton v. Tejani (1982) 137 C.A.3d. 758; *see* Fowler v. Ross (1983) 142 C.A.3d 472.

89. McCown v. Spencer (1970) 8 C.A.3d 216.

90. C.C. 1697.

91. C.C. 1698; Coldwell, Banker & Co. v. Pepper Tree Office Center Assoc. (1980) 106 C.A.3d 272, 280; Beggerly v. Gbur (1980) 112 C.A.3d 180; Louison v. Yohanan (1981) 117 C.A.3d 258; Sanders Const. Co. v. San Joaquin First Federal S & L (1982) 136 C.A.3d 387 re construction and lease of a building.

92. Comm. Regs. 2901.

93. Comm. Regs. 2900.

94. C.C. 3399, 3401.

95. La Mancha Development Corp. v. Sheegog (1978) 78 C.A.3d 9.

96. C.C. 1689.

97. C.C. 1541.

98. C.C. 1542.

99. Leof v. City of San Mateo (1980) 104 C.A.3d 398.

100. C.C. 1521.

101. C.C. 1523.

102. C.C. 1530, 1531.

103. Christian v. Superior Court (1937) 9 C.2d 526; *see also* Autry v. Republic Productions (1947) 30 C.2d 144 for distinction between impossibility of performance and frustration of purpose.

104. C.C. 1511(2).

105. C.C. 1511(1).

106. C.C. 1597.

107. Lloyd v. Murphy (1944) 25 C.2d 48. Waegemann v. Montgomery Ward and Co. (1983) (9th Cir.) 713 Fed.2d 452.

108. C.C.P. 1828, *et seq.*

109. Tolstoy Construction Co. v. Minter (1978) 78 C.A.3d 665.

110. Blank v. Borden (1974) 11 C.A.3d 963.

111. Johnson v. Compton (1955) 135 C.A.2d 683.

112. C.C. 3384, *et seq.*, 3387; *see also* §2.25; if contingency is not met by the buyer, seller may not be required to specifically perform; *see* Barnes v. Chamberlain (1983) 147 C.A.3d 762.

113. And can restrain the seller from allowing another to move into the house buyer had agreed to purchase (Grey v. Webb [1979] 97 C.A.3d 232). Converse v. Fong (1984) 159 C.A.3d 86. If the buyer sues, he should be careful not to cancel the escrow except under strict procedures; otherwise, his case may be dismissed (Cohen v. Shearer [1980] 108 C.A.3d 939). *See also* Bleecher v. Conte (1981) 29 C.3d 345. A buyer can get additional compensation for the difference between what the interest note would have been at the time of the original transaction and what it was at the time of trial, i.e., put the parties in the position they would have been in had the sale taken place then (Hutton v. Gliksberg [1982] 128 C.A.3d 240; but *see* Erich v. Granoff [1982] 109 C.A.3d 920, 927, 932).

114. Landis v. Bloomquist (1967) 257 C.A.2d 533.

115. C.C. 3390 3391.

116. Which is determined at the time the contract was made (Berkeley Lawn Bowling Club v. City of Berkeley [1974] 42 C.A.3d 280, 291).

117. Paratose v. Perry (1966) 239 C.A.2d 384.

118. Cockrill v. Boas (1931) 213 C. 490, 492; C.C. 1439, 3392; Henry v. Sharma (1984) 154 C.A.3d 665; Stevens Group Fund IV v. Sobrato Dev. Co. (1991) 1 C.A. 4th 886.

119. Am-Cal. Investment Co. v. Sharlyn Est. Inc. (1967) 255 C.A.2d 526, 539 540; D-K Investment Corp v. Sutten (1971) 19 C.A.3d 537, 546; Stratton v. Tejani (1982) 139 C.A.3d 204; *see* Hutton v. Gliksberg (1982) 128 C.A.3d 240.

120. *See* §2.29. Since 1961, rescission is unilateral, and under a restitution cause of action, a party does have a right to a jury (Paulerena v. Superior Court [1965] 231 C.A.2d 906, 913; Runyon v. Pacific Air Ind., Inc. [1970] 2 C.3d 304). A contract can be rescinded for duress or economic compulsion (IMO Dev. Corp. v. Dow Corning Corp. [1982] 135 C.A.3d 451).

121. C.C. 1692.

122. C.C. 3420.

123. C.C. 711.

124. C.C. 3300, 3358. If in conflict with C.C. 3306 and 3307, the latter sections will prevail (C.C.P. 1859); Al-Susry v. Nilsen Farms Mini-Market Inc. (1994) 24 C.A. 4th 641.

125. Walker v. Signal Companies, Inc. (1978) 84 C.A.3d 982, 993.

126. Burnett & Doty Development Co. v. Phillips (1978) 84 C.A.3d 584.

127. C.C. 3360. Nominal damages can be an "insignificant amount." They can also be the basis for an award of punitive damages (Civic Western Corp. v. Zila Ind. [1977] 66 C.A.3d, 1, 19).

128. C.C. 3306.

129. C.C. 3307.

130. A lesser degree of certainty is necessary for an action for damages than for specific performance (Yackey v. Pacifica Dev. Co. [1979] 99 C.A.3d 776, 784).

131. C.C. 3306, 3307.

132. Smith v. Mady (1983) 146 C.A.3d 129.

133. C.C. 3333; Overgaard v. Johnson (1977) 63 C.A.3d 821; *see also* C.C. 1709, and §5.20, *et seq.*; and C.C. 3334 wrongful occupation of real estate.

134. C.C. 3343; Stout v. Turney (1978) 22 C.3d 718. This is known as the "out-of-pocket-loss" rule; Cory v. Villa Properties (1986) 180 C.A.3d 592.

135. Pepitone v. Russo (1976) 64 C.A.3d 685; Walters v. Marler (1978) 83 C.A.3d 1, 24 (and recovery of attorney's fees); Liodas v. Sahadi (1977) 19 C.3d 278; C.C. 2224, 2237.

136. Loss of future profits or other damages may also be recoverable under C.C. 3333 and 1709.

137. C.C. 3287; in an action not arising out of breach of contract, interest may be given in the discretion of the jury (C.C. 3288; Pepitone v. Russo [1977] 64 C.A.3d 685, 690). For a case on prejudgment interest, *see* Chesapeake Industries, Inc. v. Togova Enterprises, Inc. (1983) 149 C.A.3d 901.

138. *See* Barton v. White Oak Realty, Inc. (1969) 271 C.A.2d 579.

139. Yackey v. Pacica Development Co. (1979) 99 C.A.3d 776.

140. Walker v. Signal Co. Inc. (1978) 84 C.A.3d 982, 993.

141. *See* §5.44, *et seq.*

142. Govt. Code 11519.

143. Emotional distress from financial injury (Jarchow v. Transamerica Title Ins. Co. (1975) 48 C.A.3d 917); *see also* Godfrey v. Steinpress (1982) 128 C.A.3d 154 re broker's fraud by concealment of termite report showing repairs would have exceeded the value of the house, as causing intentional infliction of emotional distress; *see* Young v. Bank of America (1983) 141 C.A.3d 108 re treble damages for callous and willful action of bank concerning a Visa card.

144. C.C. 3294, which includes malice, i.e., a conscious disregard of the rights of others; C.C. 3295 re Protective Order; Sasson v. Katash (1983) 146 C.A.3d 119. However, the plaintiff must produce evidence of the defendant's financial condition before punitive damages can be awarded Adams v. Murakami (1991) 54 C. 3d 105.

145. But punitive damages may be awarded when a defendant fraudulently induces a plaintiff to enter into a contract (Walker v. Signal Co. Inc. [1978] 84 C.A.3d 982, 996).

146. Esparza v. Specht (1976) 55 C.A.3d 1.

147. Walker v. Signal Co. Inc. (1978) 84 C.A.3d 982.

148. 1 Witkin, *Summary of Law* (8th ed.) p. 567.

149. C.C. 1671, *et seq.*; *see* Chapter 3, Figure 3-2(b), paragraph 12; Zlotoff v. Tucker (1984) 154 C.A.3d 988.

150. Guthman v. Moss (1984) 150 C.A.3d 501.

151. C.C. 1675(a) and (b).

152. C.C. 1675(c) and (d).

153. C.C. 1675(e); *see also* Freeman v. Rector (1951) 37 C.2d 16.

154. C.C. 1676; *see also* Bleecher v. Conte (1981) 29 C.3d 345.

155. C.C. 1677, 1678; Guthman v. Moss (1984) 150 C.A.3d 501.

156. C.C. 1671(b), 1676; Hong v. Somerset Associates (1984) 161 C.A.3d 111.

157. C.C. 1671(c) and (d).

158. C.C. 1681.

159. C.C. 1680.

160. C.C.P. 1021. However, attorney's fees can be awarded if a statute permits in a limited number of circumstances (e.g., C.C. 789.12; C.C.P. 1021.6 for implied indemnity; for part of damages re a conservation easement, *see* §14.26; C.C. 3306a re quiet title action; C.C.P. 1021.5 re attorney's fees to the successful party affecting the public interest if [a] significant benefit to the public; [b] financial burden on private enforcement make it appropriate; [c] such fees should not be paid out of recovery; C.C.P. 1038 re case not brought in good faith. *See also* D'Amico v. Board of Medical Examiners [1974] 11 C.3d 1, 25; Coalition for L.A. County etc. Investment v. Board of Supervisors [1978] 76 C.A.3d 241 re substantial benefit rule; Save El Toro Assn. v. Days [1979] 98 C.A.3d 544). *See also* Moe v. Transamerica Title Insurance Co. (1971) 21 C.A.3d 289, 303.

161. C.C. 1717 and C.C. 1717.5; Palmer v. Shawback (1993) 17 C.A. 4th 296; Beneficial Standard Properties, Inc v. Scharps (1977) 67 C.A.3d 227; Reynolds Metals Co. v. Alperson (1979) 25 C.3d 124, 129; but *see* contra Carol-Randolph Anaheim Inc. v. Moore (1978) 78 C.A.3d 477 and Sain v. Silvestre (1978) 78 C.A.3d 461, 476. Attorney's fees under C.C. 1717(a) are fixed by the courts and can be claimed only as costs of suit (*see also* C. Herzog v. Riel [1979] 99 C.A.3d Supp. 12). *See* La Pietra v. Freed (1979) 87 C.A.3d 1025 re prevailing party in arbitration hearing; Jerard v. Salter (1956) 196 C.A.2d 840, 848; C.C.P. 1284.2; Cecil v. Bank of America (1956) 142 C.A.2d 249; Saucedo v. Mercury S & L (1980) 111 C.A.3d 309; Lewis v. Alpha Beta (1983) 141 C.A.3d 29 (tenant's exclusive right to sell liquor in shopping center); Jones v. Drain (1983) 149 C.A.3d 484 (even if not a party to a contract, can collect under

C.C. 1717); but *see* Super 7 Motel Assoc. v. Wang (1993) 16 C.A. 4th 541 (broker not entitled to attorney's fees even if sued by buyer as attorney's fees clause is only between buyer and seller); Sweat v. Hollister (1995) 37 C.A. 4th 603; Reynolds Metals Co. v. Alperson [1979] 25 C.3d 124, 129); Stegman v. Bank of America (1984) 156 C.A.3d 843 (nonassuming grantee under a trust deed is not entitled to attorney's fees). Effective January 1, 1984, when a contract provides for attorney's fees, such provision is construed as applying to the entire contract, unless each party was represented by counsel in the negotiations and execution of the contract, and the fact of that representation is specified in the contract (C.C. 1717, as amended); Milman v. Shukhat (1994) 22 C.A. 4th 538.

162. Lerner v. Ward (1993) 13 C.A. 4th 155; Xuerbe v. Marcus & Millichap, Inc. (1992) 3 C.A. 4th 338; C.C. 1021; Pederson v. Kennedy (1982) 128 C.A.3d 976; McKenzie v. Kaiser-Aetra (1976) 55 C.A.3d 84. The judge (not the jury) determines the amount of attorney's fees to be awarded, but it must first be determined who is the prevailing party (Mabee v. Nurseryland Garden Centers, Inc. [1979] 88 C.A.3d 420, 424; C.C. 1717[b][1]). *See* Manier v. Anaheim Business Center Company (1984) 161 C.A.3d 503: In a suit for specific performance by a buyer based upon a purchase contract to buy real estate, the court found there was no contract as handwritten changes to the initial offer had not been initialed by plaintiff (buyer). Seller requested attorney's fees as he was the prevailing party under C.C. 1717. Buyer argued that because no contract, C.C. 1717 did not apply. The court held that the prevailing party is entitled to attorney's fees whether or not the contract was enforceable. For a case when neither party was the prevailing party, *see* Naseer v. Superior Court (1984) 156 C.A.3d 52. In Gray v. Don Miller & Associates, Inc. (1984) 35 C.3d 498, the buyer was allowed to recover attorney's fees from a negligent broker in a specific performance action (*see also* Manning v. Sifford [1980] 111 C.A.3d 7).

163. Prentice v. North American Title Guaranty Corp. (1963) 59 C.2d 618; Doris v. Air Technical Industries, Inc. (1978) 22 C.3d 1, 7, limiting the Prentice case to exceptional circumstances ; UMET Trust v. Santa Monica Medical Investment Company (1983) 140 C.A.3d 864, 871 re exceptional circumstances definition; Glendale Federal Savings & Loan v. Marina View Heights Development Inc. (1977) 66 C.A.3d 101, 149; De La Hoya v. Slim's Gun Shop (1978) 80 C.A.3d Supp 6; Pederson v. Kennedy (1982) 128 C.A.3d 976; *see also* Margolin v. Regional Planning Commission (1982) 134 C.A.3d 999 re attorney's fees on private attorney general theory; Taranow v. Brokstein (1982), 135 C.A.3d 662 (a contract permitting attorney's fees incurred in a lawsuit may be used to recover attorney's fees in an arbitration proceeding, but the contract must require disputes to be submitted to arbitration). For computation of attorney's fees, *see* Press v. Lucky Stores, Inc. (1982) 138 C.A.3d 61; Leaf v. City of San Mateo (1984) 150 C.A.3d 484 (an attorney representing himself is entitled to recover attorney's fees, if fees would otherwise be awarded); C.C. 3333, 1709; Walters v. Marler (1978) 83 C.A.3d 130 (overruled in part by Gray v. Don Miller & Associates, Inc. [1984] 35 C.3d 498); Pepitone v. Russo (1976) 64 C.A.3d 685, 688 689 (but *see* Pederson v. Kennedy, Footnote 162); Real Property Services Corp. v. City of Pasadena (1994) 25 C.A. 4th 375; Super 7 Motel Assoc. v. Wang (1993) 16 C.A. 4th 541; Sweat v. Hollister (1995) 37 C.A. 4th 603.

164. *See* C.C. 1717(b)(2); International Industries, Inc. v. Olen (1978) 21 C.3d 218 (4 3 decision). This case also held (at page 224) that contractual provisions for attorney fees will not be inflexibly enforced and that the form of the judgment is not necessarily controlling, but must give way to equitable considerations. But defendant is entitled to costs if plaintiff voluntarily dismisses a case (C.C.P. 1031, 1032[b]); attorney can now get fee for referring a case to an expert attorney (Moran v. Harris [1982] 130 C.A.3d 872).

3

Real Estate Contracts and Their Use

I. INTRODUCTION

§3.1. In general

In Chapter 2 we discussed contracts in general. In this chapter we describe and dissect the most frequently encountered real estate contracts: the listing agreement, the offer to purchase, and the option contract. Revocation of these types of contracts is outlined, and rights to compensation are explained. The real estate licensee should remember that it is required by law to retain, for three years, *all* listings, offers to purchase, canceled checks, trust records, and all other real estate documents.[1]

II. LISTING AGREEMENTS

§3.2. In general

A contract of employment is essential to the creation of the broker–client relationship. Under the Statute of Frauds it must be in writing and subscribed by the party to be charged, otherwise it is unenforceable.[2] Of course, the agreement must contain the necessary elements sufficient to satisfy the Statute of Frauds. This type of contract authorizes a broker to solicit an offer to purchase on the terms set forth in the agreement or on the terms acceptable to the owner. A listing that provides that the broker promises to use "due diligence" is a *bilateral* contract. If the broker does not exercise due diligence, the seller may revoke. Ordinarily, an exclusive agency or exclusive right to sell falls into this category. A listing such as an open listing that does not expressly obligate the broker to a specified performance is regarded as a *unilateral* contract; thus, a commission is payable only upon the performance of the act by the first broker in producing a buyer ready, willing, and able to purchase.[3]

§3.3. Authority to take listing

In one case, a question arose as to whether a salesperson who took a listing from the seller was required to have written authority from the broker to take such a listing. The court held that written authority was not essential in such cases.[4]

§3.4. Contract of employment

The authority given brokers is governed by the terms of their contracts. The forms often used are ones approved by the California Association of Realtors or used by local real estate boards. A *listing*, defined briefly, is a contract of employment between a principal and an agent. The agent holding a listing is bound by the rules of law applying to the agency relationship and owes certain obligations to the principal. Although the written agreement employing a broker to sell real estate is usually called a listing, it need not be entitled "Listing." The most commonly used form is captioned "Authorization to Sell," but there is really no such document as a "standard" listing agreement (see Figure 3-1).

Essential requirements of contract of employment. It is essential that the contract, whatever its designation, be complete in all of its terms. It must have all the essential elements of a valid contract: competent parties, a lawful object, a meeting of the minds, a sufficient consideration, and a proper description of the property involved. An approved form of listing agreement, when properly filled out and duly executed by the person employing the broker, accomplishes the purpose and is sufficient evidence in writing of the contract of employment.

Terms. Consent to a contract must be free, mutual, and communicated.[5] In order to be assured that the sellers understand what they are signing, the terms must be carefully set forth and explained.

CALIFORNIA ASSOCIATION OF REALTORS®

EXCLUSIVE AUTHORIZATION AND RIGHT TO SELL

1. **EXCLUSIVE RIGHT TO SELL:** _____ ("Seller") hereby employs and grants _____ ("Broker") the exclusive and irrevocable right, commencing on (date) _____ and expiring at 11:59 P.M. on (date) _____ ("Listing Period") to sell or exchange the real property in the City of _____, County of _____, California, described as: _____ ("Property").

2. **TERMS OF SALE:**
   A. **LIST PRICE:** The listing price shall be _____
   _____ ($ _____).
   B. **PERSONAL PROPERTY:** The following items of personal property are included in the above price: _____
   _____
   _____

   C. **ADDITIONAL TERMS:** _____
   _____

3. **MULTIPLE LISTING SERVICE:** Information about this listing ☐ will, ☐ will not, be provided to a multiple listing service ("MLS") of Broker's selection and all terms of the transaction, including, if applicable, financing will be provided to the MLS for publication, dissemination and use by persons and entities on terms approved by the MLS. Seller authorizes Broker to comply with all applicable MLS rules.

4. **TITLE:** Seller warrants that Seller and no other persons have title to the Property, except as follows: _____
   _____

5. **COMPENSATION TO BROKER:**
   Notice: The amount or rate of real estate commissions is not fixed by law. They are set by each Broker individually and may be negotiable between Seller and Broker.
   A. Seller agrees to pay to Broker as compensation for services irrespective of agency relationship(s), either ☐ _____ percent of the listing price (or if a sales contract is entered into, of the sales price), or ☐ $ _____, AND _____ as follows:
      1. If Broker, Seller, cooperating broker, or any other person, produces a buyer(s) who offers to purchase the Property on the above price and terms, or on any price and terms acceptable to Seller during the Listing Period, or any extension;
      2. If within _____ calendar days after expiration of the Listing Period or any extension, the Property is sold, conveyed, leased, or otherwise transferred to anyone with whom Broker or a cooperating broker has had negotiations, provided that Broker gives Seller, prior to or within **5 calendar days** after expiration of the Listing Period or any extension, a written notice with the name(s) of the prospective purchaser(s);
      3. If, without Broker's prior written consent, the Property is withdrawn from sale, conveyed, leased, rented, otherwise transferred, or made unmarketable by a voluntary act of Seller during the Listing Period, or any extension.
   B. If completion of the sale is prevented by a party to the transaction other than Seller, then compensation due under paragraph 5A shall be payable only if and when Seller collects damages by suit, settlement, or otherwise, and then in an amount equal to the lesser of one-half of the damages recovered or the above compensation, after first deducting title and escrow expenses and the expenses of collection, if any.
   C. In addition, Seller agrees to pay: _____
      _____
   D. Broker is authorized to cooperate with other brokers, and divide with other brokers the above compensation in any manner acceptable to Broker;
   E. Seller hereby irrevocably assigns to Broker the above compensation from Seller's funds and proceeds in escrow.
   F. Seller warrants that Seller has no obligation to pay compensation to any other broker regarding the transfer of the Property except: _____
      _____
      If the Property is sold to anyone listed above during the time Seller is obligated to compensate another broker: (a) Broker is not entitled to compensation under this Agreement and (b) Broker is not obligated to represent Seller with respect to such transaction.

6. **BROKER'S AND SELLER'S DUTIES:** Broker agrees to exercise reasonable effort and due diligence to achieve the purposes of this Agreement, and is authorized to advertise and market the Property in any medium selected by Broker. Seller agrees to consider offers presented by Broker, and to act in good faith toward accomplishing the sale of the Property. Seller further agrees, regardless of responsibility, to indemnify, defend and hold Broker harmless from all claims, disputes, litigation, judgments and attorney's fees arising from any incorrect information supplied by Seller, whether contained in any document, omitted therefrom, or otherwise, or from any material facts which Seller knows but fails to disclose.

7. **AGENCY RELATIONSHIPS:** Broker shall act as the agent for Seller in any resulting transaction. Depending upon the circumstances, it may be necessary or appropriate for Broker to act as an agent for both Seller and buyer, exchange party, or one or more additional parties ("Buyer"). Broker shall, as soon as practicable, disclose to Seller any election to act as a dual agent representing both Seller and Buyer. If a Buyer is procured directly by Broker or an associate licensee in Broker's firm, Seller hereby consents to Broker acting as a dual agent for Seller and such Buyer. In the event of an exchange, Seller hereby consents to Broker collecting compensation from additional parties for services rendered, provided there is disclosure to all parties of such agency and compensation. Seller understands that Broker may have or obtain listings on other properties, and that potential buyers may consider, make offers on, or purchase through Broker, property the same as or similar to Seller's Property. Seller consents to Broker's representation of sellers and buyers of other properties before, during, and after the expiration of this Agreement.

8. **DEPOSIT:** Broker is authorized to accept and hold on Seller's behalf a deposit to be applied toward the sales price.

Seller and Broker acknowledge receipt of copy of this page, which constitutes Page 1 of _____ Pages.
Seller's Initials (_____) (_____)   Broker's Initials (_____) (_____)

THIS FORM HAS BEEN APPROVED BY THE CALIFORNIA ASSOCIATION OF REALTORS® (C.A.R.). NO REPRESENTATION IS MADE AS TO THE LEGAL VALIDITY OR ADEQUACY OF ANY PROVISION IN ANY SPECIFIC TRANSACTION. A REAL ESTATE BROKER IS THE PERSON QUALIFIED TO ADVISE ON REAL ESTATE TRANSACTIONS. IF YOU DESIRE LEGAL OR TAX ADVICE, CONSULT AN APPROPRIATE PROFESSIONAL.

The copyright laws of the United States (Title 17 U.S. Code) forbid the unauthorized reproduction of this form, or any portion thereof, by photocopy machine or any other means, including facsimile or computerized formats. Copyright © 1998, CALIFORNIA ASSOCIATION OF REALTORS®, INC. ALL RIGHTS RESERVED.

Published and Distributed by:
REAL ESTATE BUSINESS SERVICES, INC.
a subsidiary of the CALIFORNIA ASSOCIATION OF REALTORS®
525 South Virgil Avenue, Los Angeles, California 90020
PRINT DATE

REVISED 10/97

OFFICE USE ONLY
Reviewed by Broker or Designee _____
Date _____

EQUAL HOUSING OPPORTUNITY

EXCLUSIVE AUTHORIZATION AND RIGHT TO SELL (A-14 PAGE 1 OF 2)

Figure 3-1
Example of an "Authorization to Sell" form

Property Address: _____

9. **LOCKBOX:**
   A. A lockbox is designed to hold a key to the Property to permit access to the Property by Broker, cooperating brokers, MLS participants, their authorized licensees and representatives, and accompanied prospective buyers.
   B. Broker, cooperating brokers, MLS and Associations/Boards of REALTORS® are **not** insurers against theft, loss, vandalism, or damage attributed to the use of a lockbox. Seller is advised to verify the existence of, or obtain, appropriate insurance through Seller's own insurance broker.
   C. (If checked:) ☐ Seller authorizes Broker to install a lockbox. If Seller does not occupy the Property, Seller shall be responsible for obtaining occupant(s)' written permission for use of a lockbox.

10. **SIGN:** (If checked:) ☐ Seller authorizes Broker to install a FOR SALE/SOLD sign on the Property.

11. **DISPUTE RESOLUTION:**
    A. **MEDIATION:** Seller and Broker agree to mediate any dispute or claim arising between them out of this Agreement, or any resulting transaction, before resorting to arbitration or court action, subject to paragraph 11C below. Mediation fees, if any, shall be divided equally among the parties involved. If any party commences an action based on a dispute or claim to which this paragraph applies, without first attempting to resolve the matter through mediation, then that party shall not be entitled to recover attorney's fees, even if they would otherwise be available to that party in any such action. THIS MEDIATION PROVISION APPLIES WHETHER OR NOT THE ARBITRATION PROVISION IS INITIALED.
    B. **ARBITRATION OF DISPUTES: Seller and Broker agree that any dispute or claim in Law or equity arising between them regarding the obligation to pay compensation under this Agreement, which is not settled through mediation, shall be decided by neutral, binding arbitration, subject to paragraph 11C below. The arbitrator shall be a retired judge or justice, or an attorney with at least five years of residential real estate experience, unless the parties mutually agree to a different arbitrator, who shall render an award in accordance with substantive California Law. In all other respects, the arbitration shall be conducted in accordance with Part III, Title 9 of the California Code of Civil Procedure. Judgment upon the award of the arbitrator(s) may be entered in any court having jurisdiction. The parties shall have the right to discovery in accordance with Code of Civil Procedure §1283.05.**

    "NOTICE: BY INITIALING IN THE SPACE BELOW YOU ARE AGREEING TO HAVE ANY DISPUTE ARISING OUT OF THE MATTERS INCLUDED IN THE 'ARBITRATION OF DISPUTES' PROVISION DECIDED BY NEUTRAL ARBITRATION AS PROVIDED BY CALIFORNIA LAW AND YOU ARE GIVING UP ANY RIGHTS YOU MIGHT POSSESS TO HAVE THE DISPUTE LITIGATED IN A COURT OR JURY TRIAL. BY INITIALING IN THE SPACE BELOW YOU ARE GIVING UP YOUR JUDICIAL RIGHTS TO DISCOVERY AND APPEAL, UNLESS THOSE RIGHTS ARE SPECIFICALLY INCLUDED IN THE 'ARBITRATION OF DISPUTES' PROVISION. IF YOU REFUSE TO SUBMIT TO ARBITRATION AFTER AGREEING TO THIS PROVISION, YOU MAY BE COMPELLED TO ARBITRATE UNDER THE AUTHORITY OF THE CALIFORNIA CODE OF CIVIL PROCEDURE. YOUR AGREEMENT TO THIS ARBITRATION PROVISION IS VOLUNTARY."

    "WE HAVE READ AND UNDERSTAND THE FOREGOING AND AGREE TO SUBMIT DISPUTES ARISING OUT OF THE MATTERS INCLUDED IN THE 'ARBITRATION OF DISPUTES' PROVISION TO NEUTRAL ARBITRATION."   Seller's Initials ____/____   Broker's Initials ____/____

    C. **EXCLUSIONS FROM MEDIATION AND ARBITRATION:** The following matters are excluded from Mediation and Arbitration hereunder: (a) A judicial or non-judicial foreclosure or other action or proceeding to enforce a deed of trust, mortgage, or installment land sale contract as defined in Civil Code §2985; (b) An unlawful detainer action; (c) The filing or enforcement of a mechanic's lien; (d) Any matter which is within the jurisdiction of a probate, small claims, or bankruptcy court; and (e) An action for bodily injury or wrongful death, or for latent or patent defects to which Code of Civil Procedure §337.1 or §337.15 applies. The filing of a court action to enable the recording of a notice of pending action, for order of attachment, receivership, injunction, or other provisional remedies, shall not constitute a violation of the mediation and arbitration provisions.

12. **EQUAL HOUSING OPPORTUNITY:** The Property is offered in compliance with federal, state, and local anti-discrimination laws.

13. **ATTORNEY'S FEES:** In any action, proceeding, or arbitration between Seller and Broker regarding the obligation to pay compensation under this Agreement, the prevailing Seller or Broker shall be entitled to reasonable attorney's fees and costs, except as provided in paragraph 11A.

14. **ADDITIONAL TERMS:** _____
    _____
    _____

15. **ENTIRE CONTRACT:** All prior discussions, negotiations, and agreements between the parties concerning the subject matter of this Agreement are superseded by this Agreement, which constitutes the entire contract and a complete and exclusive expression of their agreement, and may not be contradicted by evidence of any prior agreement or contemporaneous oral agreement. This Agreement and any supplement, addendum, or modification, including any photocopy or facsimile, may be executed in counterparts.

Seller warrants that Seller is the owner of the Property or has the authority to execute this contract. Seller acknowledges that Seller has read and understands this Agreement, and has received a copy.

Seller _____ Date _____   Seller _____ Date _____

Address _____   Address _____

City _____ State _____ Zip _____   City _____ State _____ Zip _____

This form is available for use by the entire real estate industry. It is not intended to identify the user as a REALTOR®. REALTOR® is a registered collective membership mark which may be used only by members of the NATIONAL ASSOCIATION OF REALTORS® who subscribe to its Code of Ethics.
PRINT DATE

Page 2 of _____ Pages.

REVISED 10/97

OFFICE USE ONLY
Reviewed by Broker
or Designee _____
Date _____

EQUAL HOUSING OPPORTUNITY

EXCLUSIVE AUTHORIZATION AND RIGHT TO SELL (A-14 PAGE 2 OF 2)

Figure 3-1 (Cont.)
Example of an "Authorization to Sell" form

EXAMPLE If the sellers agree to sell FHA or VA, do they know they will be paying the points, and how many? If the new loan is to be conventional, do the sellers know there may be a prepayment penalty, particularly if the buyer does not refinance with the sellers' lender? Do the sellers appreciate the tax consequences of this sale, i.e., should it be an installment sale, or if income property, should the property be exchanged up or down? Are the sellers carrying back a note and trust deed (sometimes referred to as "soft money")? If so, is there to be a prepayment penalty clause or a prohibition against prepayment (in an installment sale)?[6] Do the sellers appreciate the potential costs of obtaining a structural pest clearance in the event the structure is infested with termites or there is dry rot?[7] All these items, and others, must be explained to and understood by the sellers.

Principal entitled to copy of contract. Whatever the form of the contract of employment, whether a listing agreement or some other agreement, the broker *must* deliver to his customer or client a copy of the document that the latter has signed or initialed.[8] Further, a listing agreement, as well as any other real estate contract, prepared by a salesperson, that would materially affect the parties, must be reviewed and initialed by the broker within five working days.[9]

Listing agreement does not compel a sale. The usual contract creating the relationship of brokerage authorizes the broker to find a purchaser, but this does not obligate the owner to sell. The language employed may recite that the broker is authorized to sell, but this means that he is authorized only to find a purchaser. It does not bind the owner to sell and convey. However, if the seller chooses not to sell after a buyer has been procured by the broker, the broker's right to a commission is unaffected.

§3.5. A listing is a personal service contract
An exclusive listing is an agreement between a real estate broker and client, and therefore cannot be transferred to another broker without the client's express consent. In fact, if it is assigned to another broker with the client's permission, a new listing with the new broker should be drafted and the old one properly canceled.[10]

§3.6. Types of listings
Various kinds of listing agreements are in common use, the ones most frequently encountered being the open listing, exclusive agency listing, and exclusive right to sell listing.[11] Other types that may be encountered are the net listing, option listing, multiple listing, oral listing, and buyer's listing.

§3.7. Open listing
An open listing is a written memorandum signed by the party to be charged—in most cases the seller of the property—authorizing the broker to act as agent for the sale of designated property. Usually there is no time limit to the employment.[12] By the use of an open listing, the seller may employ a number of brokers, each of whom will have an equal opportunity to earn a commission. Under such listing, a commission is payable only to the broker who first procures a buyer who is ready, willing, and able to buy, pursuant to the terms of the listing or pursuant to other terms acceptable to the seller. The sale of the property by any one of the brokers, or by the seller, terminates the open listing of all other brokers.[13]

Another type of listing form should not be utilized to create an open listing by scratching out certain words.

EXAMPLE In one case, Marks contacted the seller regarding the property, but was informed that the seller had given an open listing to a number of other brokers. Marks mailed a printed exclusive listing to the seller but had altered the form by printing the words "Open Listing" at the top and crossing out the word "exclusive" from the body of the listing where it appeared twice. However, the language appearing later in the listing, whereby the seller agreed to pay the agent a 5 percent commission whether the property was sold by the agent or by someone else, including the owner, was not stricken! Thereafter, the property was sold by another broker and Marks sued the seller for his commission, but lost. The Real Estate Commissioner then brought disciplinary action against Marks, and Marks appealed to the court. It was held that the attempted fraudulent enforcement of such a listing constituted grounds for the revocation of the broker's license.[14]

§3.8. Exclusive agency listing

If an exclusive agency listing, the broker is designated as the *exclusive agent*, and the broker named in the listing is entitled to a commission even if the property is sold by another broker. However, since such a listing refers only to sales by "agents," the owner may sell the property himself without being liable for payment of a commission.

§3.9. Exclusive right to sell listing

The exclusive right to sell listing goes one step further than the exclusive agency listing. It not only makes the broker the sole agent of the owner for the sale of the property, but provides that the broker will receive a commission if the property is sold by the named broker, by the seller, or by anyone else within the prescribed time. Even if a sale is made through the owner's efforts, the owner must pay a commission to the broker. In such a case, the broker need not show that he was the procuring cause of the sale.[15]

§3.10. Termination date

The exclusive right and the exclusive agency types of listing must be for a definite term and contain a specified date of termination. If the contract does not provide for a definite termination date, the broker is subject to a penalty of revocation or suspension of his license.[16]

EXAMPLE In one situation, Houston executed a written agreement with Babcock giving an exclusive right to sell lots in a tract. The agreement lacked a definite termination date. At the time Houston terminated Babcock's services there were seven lots in escrow containing authorizations to pay real estate commissions. These authorizations were then revoked. The trial court found that Babcock was unaware that the law required a definite termination date on an exclusive listing until after he was discharged. However, it held that Houston was not liable for the commissions because the contract contained no definite termination date. The appellate court reversed, holding that if (1) the broker had fully performed his services; (2) the seller was not prejudiced; and (3) the seller would otherwise be unjustly enriched—then the broker should be permitted to recover his commissions as to the lots in escrow.[17]

In other words, the lack of a definite termination date makes such a contract *voidable*.[18] On the other hand, the Real Estate Commissioner may bring disciplinary action against the broker for violation of the Real Estate Law. Although recommended, the *actual* date of termination need not be set forth in order to collect a commission.

EXAMPLE In one case, the parties signed an exclusive agency listing indicating that the authorization to sell "is to continue in full force and effect for a period of 90 days hereof, and thereafter until revoked by me in writing, but to terminate automatically six months after end of listing period." After the expiration of the ninety-day period, but within the six-month period, the defendant exchanged his property through another broker and did not pay the plaintiff any commission. The court held that the contract had a definite date of final and complete termination, i.e., it ended automatically six months after the end of the listing period.[19]

The Real Estate Commissioner has shed some light on the situation wherein a broker extended a listing agreement because the property was off the market for several weeks as a result of a deal that fell through. He stated:

> *The Real Estate Law provides for disciplinary action against the licensee who claims, demands or receives compensation under an exclusive listing agreement which does not contain a "definite, specified date of final and complete termination."*
>
> *It has long been DRE's position that an exclusive listing contract which provides for an extension of the listing pegged to the possible cancellation of an escrow for sale of real property does not satisfy Section 10176(f) and therefore that, if a licensee claimed a commission under such a listing agreement, he would be subject to disciplinary action against his license.*
>
> *If, however, the clause in the listing were to include an alternative fixed date certain for termination, it is the DRE's position that the clause would be enforceable and would not be a basis for disciplinary action. In referring to an alternative fixed date certain for termination, I have in mind a contractual clause along the following lines:*
>
> > *"If the property is placed into escrow and escrow is subsequently canceled, this agreement shall terminate on the later of the termination dates set forth above or 30 days from the date that escrow is canceled provided, however, that in no event shall this agreement terminate later than _____" (the blank should be completed by insertion of a calendar date or a specified number of days after the original termination date set forth in the agreement).*[20]

§3.11. Net listing

In a net listing, the compensation to the broker is not definitely stated. Such a listing entitles the broker to receive as compensation all proceeds acquired from the sale in excess of the selling price fixed by the seller. If the property is sold for the sum specified for the seller's account or for less, the broker does not receive any compensation. If the property sells for more than the price fixed by the seller, the broker is entitled to retain the surplus. Although net listings are legal and have been held enforceable, their use is generally frowned on, as they often give rise to a claim of unfairness.[21]

Duty to disclose selling price. The law provides for revocation or suspension of a license if the broker fails to disclose the amount of his compensation in connection with a net listing. This must be done before or at the time the principal binds himself to the transaction.[22]

§3.12. Option listing

An option listing gives the broker an option to purchase the property. When exercising the option, the broker is in a fiduciary position and must make disclosure of all outstanding offers and other material information in his possession. As stated in an older case, when a broker is employed to find a purchaser for the property of a principal and is given an option, running concurrently with the agency, to purchase the property, he cannot, when pursuing his own interests, ignore those of the principal, and he will not be permitted to enjoy the fruits of an advantage taken of a fiduciary relation, whose dominant characteristic is the confidence reposed by one person in another.[23] Were the rule otherwise, the broker would be tempted to wait until he had arranged for a profitable resale of the property to a third party, and then exercise the option.

Duty to disclose amount of profit. Under the Real Estate Law, a license may be revoked or suspended if the broker fails to disclose the full amount of the profit before exercising the option. This disclosure must be in writing, and the written consent of the seller must be obtained approving the amount of the profit.[24]

§3.13. Multiple listing

A *multiple listing* is the name commonly applied to a service by realty boards to their members. The types of listings that can be placed on an M.L.S. were codified in 1983.[25] A *multiple listing* service is defined as an organized real estate listing service conducted by a group of brokers, usually members of a real estate board. The brokers pool their exclusive right to sell listings by furnishing such listings to the multiple organization, which distributes the listing to all members of the group who then have an equal opportunity to sell the listed properties. The listing broker is responsible for the truth of all statements in the listing of which he had knowledge or reasonably should have had knowledge.[26] In the event of a sale, the brokerage commission is divided in agreed proportions between the listing broker and the member of the board who effected the sale. If the listing broker sells the property, he is entitled to the commission in its entirety.

It would seem that because of the extensive exposure a given property would have by being placed on the M.L.S., a broker could be held in breach of his fiduciary duty not to do so in many instances unless the seller specifically—and knowingly—agreed to the contrary. In some situations a seller may prefer that only one brokerage house have the responsibility for showing the property because of the concern of theft (however slight that may be). There could also be the problem of misinformation being given to the potential buyer by increasing the number of people who are permitted to show the property, thus increasing the legal exposure of the seller for this misinformation.

Multiple listing services have come under attack in past years, generally for violations of restraint of trade. It has been determined, for example, that an M.L.S. may not refuse membership to part-time licensees or those who wish to join the board who sponsors the M.L.S.[27] But an M.L.S. can restrict membership to real estate licensees, i.e., it need not be open to the public.[28] In fact, real estate brokers have sufficient effect on interstate commerce to establish federal jurisdiction for private antitrust action.[29] In one case it was held that the Board of Realtors is not liable for antitrust violation when individual member brokers refuse to show low-commission properties.[30]

Elements of Restraint of Trade

1. Formation and operation of a conspiracy
2. Illegal acts done pursuant thereto
3. Damages caused by such acts[31]

It is an antitrust violation for new tract brokers to require new home purchasers to list their old homes with the new tract broker as a condition to buying a new home.[32]

§3.14. Oral listing (or back pocket listing)

Despite numerous warnings by other brokers against the use of oral listings, some licensees continue to use them. Not only are those listings unenforceable under the Statute of Frauds, but also their use may be construed by others as being unprofessional and can certainly give rise to hard feelings.

EXAMPLE Assume a not too infrequent situation wherein broker A has an oral listing. Broker A advertises the property for sale and broker B calls him. Not wanting B to realize that the listing is only an "oral open" listing, A conceals this fact from B, but does agree to share the commission if B sells the property. B diligently works on the listing, believing in good faith that a valid listing exists, only to find out later, after considerable time, that his efforts were fruitless. Fair play dictates that this type of listing not be used without full disclosure to other licensees.

§3.15. Buyer's listing

A growing number of brokers, particularly in the investment end of real estate sales, obtain written listings with buyers and solely represent these buyers.[33] The commission is worked out in a number of ways: Either (1) the buyer pays the commission at an hourly rate; or (2) the sales price is reduced by one-half of the commission and the buyer pays the broker a like amount; or (3) the buyer's broker shares a portion of the selling broker's commission. In any event, to avoid dual agency problems, the buyer's broker *must* be sure to disclose to the seller and his principal that the broker is solely representing the buyer, even though he may receive a portion of the commission.[34]

§3.16. Right to contact seller while listing in effect

There appears to be no prohibition against a broker contacting a seller who has given an open listing to another broker in order to obtain his own open listing. Should the second broker obtain an exclusive listing on the same property, the first broker's open listing would then cease if the seller notified him of a cancellation. However, the actions on the part of the second broker may constitute an intentional interference with an existing contract, which gives rise to damages by the first broker against the second for the amount of the commission he would have earned.[35]

What about one broker contacting a seller who has exclusively listed a property with another broker during the period of the listing? Some boards and M.L.S.' rules prohibit their members from contacting the seller until the listing has *expired*.[36] On the other hand, if the second broker does not demean the first broker and does not attempt to induce the seller to breach the existing contract, does a board have the right to prohibit this action?[37] This question has not been resolved in the courts, but it may be determined that to prohibit such contact with the seller may be a restraint of trade that prohibits free competition.

III. REVOCATION OF AUTHORITY

§3.17. In general

In the absence of a contract to the contrary, a broker is not entitled to compensation for his services when his principal in good faith revokes his authority before the broker has earned the commission by procuring a purchaser. Accordingly, if the principal's agreement to pay a commission is unilateral, or if he has not contracted to employ the broker for any particular length of time, the principal can without liability terminate the employment at any time before the broker fully performs.[38] The broker is not entitled to reimbursement for expenses incurred in attempting to make a sale unless expressly agreed to by the principal.

§3.18. When revocation of employment is not permitted

If the broker has expended time and effort to sell the property and is in the midst of negotiations that are approaching success, the principal cannot, without incurring liability, terminate the broker's employment with the purpose of enjoying the fruits of the broker's efforts and thereby avoiding the payment of a commission. In such a case, performance may be said to be prevented by the principal's wrongful acts, and the broker will be entitled to the commission. The seller's repudiation will relieve a broker of further performance or tender of performance.

EXAMPLES

1. Property was withdrawn from sale in violation of an exclusive and irrevocable listing for a fixed term. In such case, the broker is entitled to a commission.[39]

2. An action was brought for a broker's commission under an exclusive agency listing. The listing was for five months, but the defendant rescinded the agreement in three months. A few days later, the defendant accepted an offer from another broker. The trial court found that the broker did not present to the defendant any offers and made only a token attempt to advertise the property for sale. The court concluded, as a matter of law, that the defendant had good cause for the revocation of the agency agreement.[40]

   The court in the above case reasoned that the consideration in an exclusive agency or exclusive right to sell contract is the promise of the broker, express or implied, to make a diligent effort to find a buyer. A principal is privileged to discharge, before the time fixed by the contract of employment, an agent who fails to perform a material part of the promised service. The right to rescind for a partial failure of consideration may be exercised although there has been a partial performance by the party against whom the right is exercised. The right to rescind exists after the broker has had a reasonable time to exercise diligence and has failed to do so.[41]

   If a broker is performing services under an exclusive contract, the broker is entitled to a commission when the owner (1) takes the property off the market; (2) gives a lease with an option to purchase; (3) exchanges the property; (4) enters into a contract to sell; or (5) otherwise wrongfully deprives the broker of the opportunity to make a sale during the term of the agreement.[42]

3. An action was brought for compensation under an exclusive right to sell contract and the broker was allowed his full commission as provided for in a withdrawal from sale clause. The clause provided that "if said property is withdrawn from sale, transferred, conveyed, leased with the consent of an agent, or made unmarketable by [the owner's] voluntary act during the term hereof or any extension thereof, the agent would receive six percent of the price of the property."[43]

IV. RIGHT TO COMPENSATION

§3.19. In general

Brokers are customarily paid on a commission basis. A commission is defined as an agent's compensation for performing the duties of the agency. In real estate practice, this is generally a percentage of the selling price, or a percentage of rentals, or the like. The amount or rate of the commission that a broker may charge is not fixed by law, but is a matter of contract between the parties, and may be any amount agreed on.[44]

In response to a widespread belief that commissions were preset, the Real Estate Law requires that any printed or form agreement or modification that establishes or is intended to establish compensation to be paid a licensee for the sale of four or fewer residential units or for the sale of a mobile home shall contain the following statement in not less than ten-point boldface type immediately preceding any provision relating to compensation:

> *Notice: The amount or rate of real estate commissions is not fixed by law. They are set by each broker individually and may be negotiable between the seller and broker.*[45]

The amount of compensation shall not be preprinted in any such agreement.

Although a violation of this section could result in disciplinary action against the licensee (and thus affect any commissions to be paid), it would not affect the validity of a transfer of title to the real property.

Years ago, 5 percent was the prevailing rate of commission payable to a broker on a sale of residential property. An increase to 6 percent has been in effect in most areas in recent years, although some brokers charge less. If no amount has been fixed in the agreement, it will be presumed that the customary commission payable in the area was intended. It should be remembered that an agreement between brokers in a given area to maintain a commission at a set level constitutes *price fixing*, which is against California and federal laws.

Splitting the commission. Splitting a commission between brokers is not uncommon. This is the customary practice in a multiple listing, whereby the commission is split between the listing broker and the selling broker. However, the commission cannot be split with an unlicensed person.

EXAMPLE A lawyer not licensed as a real estate broker or salesperson cannot recover a share of a real estate broker's commission if the compensation is not paid to the lawyer solely for services rendered in his capacity as a lawyer.[46]

§3.20. Exclusion from a commission

Sometimes, when a listing is taken, a seller will inform the licensee that there is a prospective buyer with whom the seller has been negotiating. In such event, a seller will often want to exclude the broker from a commission if the sale is consummated with the particular person. To avoid a problem, a clause can readily be inserted on the seller's copy of the listing containing the following words:

> *Owner shall not be obligated to pay a commission to agent in the event of sale, exchange, option to buy, or lease to _____.*

EXAMPLE A Tennessee case has held that a broker is not entitled to a commission under an exclusive listing agreement on the sale of a home to a buyer who was shown the house by the seller prior to the execution of the exclusive listing, even though the buyer entered into an executory contract to purchase the house before the end of the listing period and completed the purchase during the safety period.[47]

§3.21. Seller may pay two commissions

In addition, a further problem can arise in a situation when one broker's listing has just expired and the seller is listing with another broker. What can occur is that the second broker may show the property to a buyer who was first shown the property by the first broker. Does this mean that the seller may have to pay two commissions? Since that possibility could occur, the second broker must be careful to explain the problem to the seller.[48] Some listing agreements provide against this possibility by indicating that the seller is not obligated to the first broker if a valid listing agreement with another broker is entered into during the "safety clause" period and a sale is made.[49]

§3.22. Computation of commission

The computation of the amount of commission due a broker on a sale of real property is based on the total price paid, disregarding the amount of the encumbrances on the property. If property is listed at a given amount but sold at a greater price, the broker will be entitled to the same rate of commission on the higher price as provided for at the lower price.[50]

§3.23. Written contract and license essential

Before a broker can maintain an action to recover a commission for selling land, the broker must allege and prove that he was a duly licensed real estate broker at the time the services were performed,[51] and that he was employed under a contract in writing.[52]

EXAMPLE　In one case, the main issue was whether a licensed real estate broker may assert equitable estoppel against a Statute of Frauds defense in an action by the broker to recover a real estate commission. The court decided against the broker. The court concluded that a licensed real estate broker cannot invoke equitable estoppel to avoid the Statute of Frauds unless the broker shows actual fraud.[53]

An unfortunate result can occur in the case when an unlicensed person obtains a listing and agrees with a cooperating broker to share a commission. Even though the lister cannot legally collect a commission, can the selling broker do so? It may be possible under equitable principles.[54]

Branch office license not required. In one case, the trial court denied a licensed real estate broker recovery of commissions for obtaining leases for the defendants. It appeared that the plaintiff was not licensed to do business at the address from which the brokerage services were rendered and that, although he had complied with the fictitious name statute, he was not licensed as a broker in the fictitious name under which such services were performed. The Court of Appeal reversed the judgment of the trial court with directions to enter judgment for the plaintiff. The court pointed out that the Business and Professions Code, prohibiting a real estate broker from recovering commissions without alleging and proving that the broker was a duly licensed real estate broker, contains no requirement that the broker prove that he had a branch office license for the branch office from which the services were performed or a fictitious name license authorizing the use of the fictitious name under which his services were rendered. It then noted that the statutory purpose of the licensing law was to protect the public from the perils incident to dealing with incompetent or untrustworthy real estate practitioners, and it concluded that such purpose was satisfied by proof of a valid real estate broker's license.[55]

Effect of sale of stock. The sale of corporate stock without a securities license does not prevent a real estate broker from obtaining a commission in a real estate sale wherein the stock sale was only an incidental part of the transaction.[56]

§3.24. When commission is earned

As a general rule, a commission is earned when the broker has procured a buyer who is ready, willing, and able to buy the property on the exact terms of the listing agreement or any other terms acceptable to the seller. In such event, the broker is usually entitled to a commission regardless of whether the sale is ever consummated. Proof that a buyer is ready, willing, and able can only be shown by a contract binding him to purchase the property.[57]

EXAMPLES　The following two cases illustrate the rights of the parties when the contract of sale is subject to a contingency:

1.　An action was brought by the broker to recover a commission. The contract of sale was contingent on the buyer's ability to obtain a loan, a provision inserted at the buyer's request. Before the time for closing of the escrow, the seller repudiated the contract. In the meantime, the buyer waived the condition. In this resulting action, the seller contended that he was not liable because the buyer's obligation to perform was not unconditional. However, the court held that since the condition had been inserted at the request of and for the protection of the buyer, who had waived the requirement, the condition was accordingly fulfilled, and the broker was entitled to his commission. Judgment for the broker was confirmed on appeal.[58]

2. An action was brought to recover a real estate commission on a sale of a parcel of Marin County property for $87,000. The purchase contract contained the following provision: "Balance of the purchase price is to be paid as follows: Subject to buyers assuming an existing loan of approximately $58,000 secured by a First Trust Deed bearing 6 percent interest."

    The buyers deposited cash in the escrow for the difference between the first trust deed and the amount of the sale. It was thereafter discovered that the first trust deed contained a due-on-sale clause. The beneficiary was unwilling to waive his right to declare the entire balance due on a transfer of the property, so the escrow failed to close. The court held that no commission was payable, stating that when a contract for the sale of real property is conditional, the broker's commission is not earned if the condition is not performed.[59]

The ability of the buyer is judged in terms of financial ability to purchase the property. The buyer need not have all the money in his immediate possession or to his credit at the bank. The buyer is only required to be able to command the necessary funds to close the transaction within the prescribed time.[60]

§3.25. Asking price

Ordinarily, the price at which a broker is authorized to sell property is considered merely an asking price to guide the broker in negotiations with prospective purchasers. If the broker procures a purchaser willing to pay a lower price, the owner cannot deprive the broker of a commission by conducting the final negotiations and selling at a lower figure to the purchaser procured by the broker.[61]

§3.26. Procuring cause

In other than exclusive listing situations, the broker must be the procuring cause of the sale.[62] *Procuring cause* is defined as the cause originating a series of events that, without break in their continuity, result in the accomplishment of the prime object of the employment.[63] The word *procure* does not necessarily imply the formal consummation of an agreement. In its broadest sense, the word means to prevail on, induce, or persuade a person to do something. The originating cause, which ultimately leads to the conclusion of the transaction, is held to be the procuring cause. A broker has earned a commission when he has performed such services as constitute the proximate and efficient cause of a sale.[64] (See Figure 3-2.)

What or who is the procuring cause is a question of fact to be determined from all the circumstances of each specific case.[65] What constitutes a "break in the chain of events" is likewise a question of fact.[66] In other words, there is no clear-cut answer to this perplexing problem. The elements of good faith and fair dealing, as in any agreement, are applicable in these types of cases.

Determination as to procuring cause. Open listings have frequently given rise to disputes over who was the procuring cause of a sale. To entitle the broker to a commission, the sale must, of course, be the direct or proximate result of the acts performed by the broker. However, the broker is not personally obliged to bring the buyer and the seller to an agreement. Whether the broker was the motivating force that caused the principal to execute a sales agreement with the buyer is a question of fact, to be determined from all the circumstances of the case.

EXAMPLE   A finding by the trial court that the broker was the procuring cause of the sale of ranch property was sustained by evidence that the buyer had no thought of buying the ranch before the broker's salesman contacted him; that his interest was so

PROCURING CAUSE

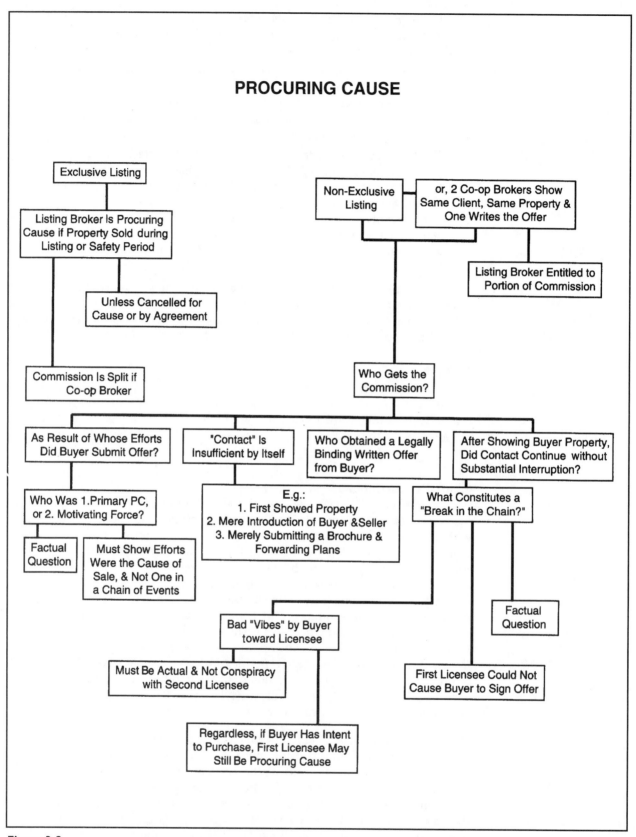

Figure 3-2

Procuring cause: He who shakes the tree gets the fruit. (All rights reserved by Denny Milligan.)

much aroused that he promised "to look at it"; and that such interest did not subside, although the sale was consummated directly between the seller and buyer after the buyer had gone out to look at the property by himself.[67]

Good faith break in the chain of events. The broker must be the effective cause of bringing the parties together; the negotiations that the broker commences must continue *without substantial interruption*; and they must conclude with agreement between the parties. If there is a good faith break in the continuity of causation of these negotiations, the broker is not the procuring cause.[68] In the last case the appellate court, citing the trial court, stated:

> *In those brokerage commission cases, the cause is usually … a mental condition or interest created in another person's mind that becomes a motivating force that causes him to act, and the motivating force continues without cessation, until it brings about the consummation of the act, and the person who created such interest in the other person's mind that resulted in the act is said to be the procuring cause of the act.*[69]

What constitutes a sufficient break in the chain? It is not enough that the broker contributed directly or indirectly to the sale. He must set in motion a chain of events which, without break in their continuity, cause the buyer and seller to come to terms as the proximate result of his peculiar activities. It is not controlling that the broker may have first called it to the buyer's attention.

Merely putting a prospective purchaser on the track of property that is on the market will not suffice to entitle the broker to the commission contracted for, and even though a broker opens negotiations for the sale of the property, he will not be entitled to a commission if he finally fails in his efforts, without fault or interference of *the owner* [or other licensee], to induce a prospective purchaser to buy or make an offer to buy, notwithstanding that the owner may subsequently, either personally or through the instrumentality of other brokers, sell the property to the same individual, at the same price and upon the terms at which the property was originally offered for sale.[70]

Burden of proof. The broker must prove that the sale was the direct and proximate result of *his efforts*. If more than one party has contributed to the culmination of the sale, the broker must prove that his activities and efforts were a *predominant contributing cause*.[71] A broker is entitled to the commission for effecting a sale only when it affirmatively appears that the purchaser, *as the result of the broker's efforts*, was induced to buy the property, or that a prospective purchaser was ready, willing, and able to buy upon the terms and at the price specified by the owner.[72]

Mere introduction is insufficient. Merely introducing the principal to a party who comes to an agreement with the principal after the termination of the agency, but who is not ready, willing, and able to consummate the transaction during the life of the agency, is in itself insufficient to entitle the broker to a commission.[73] A broker is not entitled to the commission merely because he made efforts to sell and first caused the property to be called to the attention of the person who subsequently made the purchase.[74]

Not contingent upon written offer. A broker is the procuring cause if he finds a purchaser who is ready, willing, and able to buy the property on the stated terms and obtains a valid contract. On the other hand, the broker, unable to secure a written offer, may still be considered the procuring cause if through *the broker's efforts* a "meeting of the minds" between buyer and seller occurs.[75]

1. If the offeror presented by broker A decides not to enter into a contract, but is thereafter induced by broker B or another person to enter into a contract with substantially the same terms that he originally declined, broker A is not entitled to a commission under the theory that A is the procuring cause of the sale. On the other hand, broker A is the procuring cause of the sale if he negotiated a meeting of the minds of offeror and offeree notwithstanding the fact that the written contract for the sale of the property is executed through negotiations by broker B.[76]

2. If a broker introduces a prospective buyer to the seller, and thereafter abandons the employment with the seller, or the buyer is unwilling to accept the terms of the seller, or the buyer ceases to make further endeavors to negotiate a deal, the broker will not be entitled to a commission if the seller later renews negotiations either directly with the buyer or through the use of another broker and effects a sale without the efforts of the first broker.[77]

As the reader can readily see, this area of the law can be confusing and difficult at best. Although some real estate boards have set up a definition to be used, that definition may not be a legally binding one. In any event, a policy determination, such as the following, used in part by some boards, may be appropriate:

> As to matters within the jurisdiction and authority of this Board, the licensee who first obtains an offer to purchase or escrow instructions executed by buyer and seller is presumed to be the procuring cause and entitled to the commission. This presumption may be rebutted by evidence of lack of fair play on the part of the other licensee.

§3.27. Safety clause

Listing forms in general use contain a provision by which the owner agrees to pay the broker the commission if a sale is made within a specified time after the termination of the listing to a person to whom the broker has shown the property during the listing term.[78] Generally, it is required that the broker notify the owner of the names of these persons either prior to the expiration of the listing period or shortly thereafter. It is suggested that this notice be given to the owner in writing.

EXAMPLES 1. One case involved the broker's right to a commission on a sale consummated after termination of his employment. The contract gave the broker an exclusive right to sell certain real property during a specified term (June 16 to July 16, 1952), or within 30 days thereafter to a person with whom the broker had "negotiated for a sale" during the specified term. A salesman employed by the broker held an interview with a prospective buyer in the broker's office on July 11, 1952. During the conference, for an hour or more, the salesman discussed the property with the prospect, informing him that the property would be good clover ground, was easily leveled, and so forth. The salesman offered to show the property to the prospect, but the prospect said he preferred to go alone. The salesman thereupon made a diagram showing the location of the property. Three days later the salesman phoned the prospect, who said he wanted more information regarding the description, water, taxes, and so on. The next day the salesman went to Merced, obtained the information, telephoned the information to the prospect, and gave him the name of the owner. The prospect stated he was debating between this property and another parcel. Within a week the salesman telephoned the prospect, who said he was still waiting to make up his mind. Within the 30-day period the prospect purchased the property through another broker with whom the owner had listed the property. The original broker claimed he was entitled to a commission, but the seller refused to pay.

An action was filed and recovery allowed. The main question raised pertained to the meaning of the words "negotiated for a sale." The court stated that *negotiation*, when used in a contract such as the one in question, means that "the efforts of the broker to interest a prospect must have proceeded to the point where the prospect would be considered a likely purchaser."[79]

2. In another case, it was held that when an agreement provides that a real estate broker's commission is to be paid if the property is sold within a specified period to a person whose name is furnished the owner by the broker, and the property is sold by the owner to such party during the prescribed period, it is immaterial that the agent was not the procuring cause of the sale.[80]

3. In the absence of an express intention of the parties, a commission will not be allowed during the safety clause time period unless the broker's activities had at least some connection with the final sale of the property. The fact that a party saw a "For Sale" sign, learned the termination date of the listing, and did not purchase the property until one day after the listing period expired, does not entitle the original broker to a commission.[81]

4. A fourth case held that a real estate broker was the primary procuring cause of the sale of real property and thus entitled to a commission when, although the sale was made after the seller's contract with the broker had been terminated, the listing agreement provided that the commission would be paid if the property was sold within one year after the termination to a prospect procured by the broker before such termination, and the buyer, although not personally procured by the broker, was the brother of the person procured by the broker, and the evidence showed that the property was actually purchased for the benefit of such person.[82]

§3.28. Cooperating broker's right to a commission

When a listing calls for the use of other real estate licensees, an agency relationship may be established between the cooperating licensees and the seller. Therefore, it would seem that if (1) the "co-op" broker procures a ready, willing, and able buyer; (2) the seller refuses to consummate the transaction; and (3) the listing broker refuses to sue for the commission, then the co-op broker should be able to collect his portion of the commission directly from the seller. Although a Superior Court Appellate Department for Los Angeles County held the co-op broker could not do so,[83] a District Court of Appeals said the broker could if he also brought the listing broker in as a party defendant; however a more recent case held the co-op broker under the facts of that case lacked standing to sue.[84] Logic and fairness dictate that if the seller knew and agreed to the use of co-op brokers, then the co-op broker should have the right to sue for and collect a commission in the event the seller wrongfully defaults. In any event, it is desirable that the listing agreement specifically provide for such a contingency.

§3.29. Extension of listing by oral agreement

Merely because a seller permits a broker to continue with a prospective buyer's representative after the termination of the listing does not extend the listing. By this act the seller is merely waiving the time element as to that particular buyer.[85] However, the waiver lasts no longer than the time during which the owner encourages the broker to render services and is diligently complying with the owner's request.[86]

EXAMPLES

1. In one case, it was held that when an owner of realty, after expiration of the time limit in a listing contract within which a broker was to sell the property, encouraged the broker to continue his efforts to find a purchaser, and the broker did so with the owner's knowledge and approval, with the result that

a purchaser was produced to whom the owner sold the property, the time limit in the contract was waived and the broker was entitled to his commission. The owner raised as a defense the fact that the agreement extending the time was not in writing and was therefore unenforceable, but the court held that a provision in a written agreement limiting time for performance may be waived orally.[87]

2.   When evidence supported the finding that the vendor stated to the escrow officer that a delay of a few days beyond the date specified for payment of purchase money in the escrow agreement would make no difference, and the statement was repeated by the escrow officer to purchaser who relied thereon in obtaining purchase money and was ready, willing, and able to pay, the vendor waived time for performance and was estopped to set up the Statute of Frauds against the purchaser to defeat an oral extension of time.[88]

As to the authority of a broker to extend the time period of a listing or purchase contract without notice to the parties, or otherwise, such would probably be treated as "overreaching." It can be used to the detriment of either or both buyer and seller and should be avoided. To use such a clause in a contract that contains a time of the essence clause renders the clause meaningless. The Department of Real Estate recommends against the use of this type of extension clause.[89]

§3.30. "No deal—no commission" agreements

Contracts may expressly provide that no commission is payable unless a completed sale is made. This is known as a "no deal—no commission" arrangement. The right of brokers to recover commissions must be measured of necessity by the terms of their contracts. If the seller and broker contract that no commission shall be considered earned until the happening of a specified event or contingency, or until certain terms and conditions are complied with, the commission will not be deemed earned unless the event, contingency, or condition occurs. Such contracts are not the usual ones between a seller and broker, however, and to create such a contract the courts have held that the terms must be clear and unequivocal. It has also been held in such cases that if the seller's refusal to complete the transaction is arbitrary and without legal cause, or in bad faith, the broker will be entitled to a commission.[90]

§3.31. Agreement for commission contained in a purchase agreement

When the only agreement to pay a broker a commission is contained in a purchase agreement between the buyer and seller, it has been held that the broker's right to a commission depends on performance of the provisions contained in the contract. If the buyer refuses to perform, or if the agreement is canceled or rescinded, the broker is not entitled to recover a commission.[91]

EXAMPLE   When the broker's right to a commission is based solely on a purchase contract executed by the seller, the prospective purchaser, and the broker (the broker having been employed under an oral agreement), the right to a commission is not defeated as a matter of law by the failure of the parties actually to consummate the sale. This is a question of fact in each case. The court stated: "Such a three-party writing may unequivocally specify, or where uncertain may be construed or shown by extrinsic evidence to mean, that the broker has fully performed the duties of his employment and earned the commission by having obtained a buyer ready, able, and willing to proceed with a purchase in accord with those terms of the writing." When the purchase agreement can be so interpreted, the sale itself need never be consummated to entitle the broker to the commission.[92]

§3.32. Agreement for commission evidenced by escrow instructions

In one case, it was held that the requirement that a contract with a broker to sell real property be in writing is satisfied by evidence that the buyers signed escrow instructions providing for payment of a commission out of monies deposited in escrow, and that the sellers signed similar instructions.[93] However, if the escrow is not consummated, e.g., because of a mutual rescission of buyer and seller, or because buyer breaches the contract, the commission does not become due.[94]

§3.33. Payment of commission from escrow funds

Sometimes a broker who has earned a commission pursuant to the listing agreement is the motivating cause in setting up escrow instructions that provide for payment of commissions out of the "escrow proceeds" or at the "close of escrow." If the sale is not consummated, there will, of course, be no "escrow proceeds" or "close of escrow," and therefore no commission. In such a case, the broker may be estopped from relying on the listing agreement because of his acquiescence in the subsequent agreement for payment of commission in the escrow.[95] The escrow instructions should merely fix the *time* for payment and not adversely affect the obligation to pay a commission already earned.

§3.34. Recovery of commission from a defaulting buyer

Although in the past the courts have generally refused a recovery of a commission from a defaulting buyer, that is beginning to change. It would seem that if the buyer solicits a broker to find property, and the broker does so and is to receive a commission from the seller but the buyer refuses to perform, without a valid reason, the buyer should become liable to the broker for a breach of his implied promise.[96] Also, if a prospective buyer employs a broker, the broker will earn a commission from the buyer when he produces a ready, willing, and able seller for the buyer.[97] On the other hand, if there is no pre-existing relationship between the buyer and broker, the courts have refused to find the existence of an implied promise and have denied the broker a commission upon the buyer's default. To protect the broker, a clause could be added to the purchase contract, signed by all parties, that in the event of the buyer's default without cause, the buyer will pay the broker's commission.

§3.35. Commission payable though seller not obligated to perform

One case raised a question as to whether the broker was entitled to a commission when the seller was not obligated to sell to the buyer because of inadequacy of consideration. The seller had entered into a contract with a buyer obtained by the broker, based on the terms of the seller. The seller thereafter decided not to go through with the deal because he considered the selling price inadequate. The buyer brought an action against the seller for specific performance, but because the purchase price was in fact inadequate, the court refused to compel the seller to perform. The seller in turn refused to pay the broker his commission. In the resulting action by the broker, the court held that the seller was still liable to the broker for the commission, even though the seller could not be compelled to perform the contract with the buyer. However, the court pointed out that if the broker had been aware that the selling price was inadequate, he would not have been entitled to the commission.[98]

§3.36. Interference with prospective economic advantage

In one case, it was held that a person, sued for maliciously inducing a *third person* to breach an oral contract with a broker to pay a commission, cannot defend on the ground that the contract was unenforceable under the Statute of Frauds.[99]

The California Supreme Court later held that the mere fact the prospective economic relationship has not attained the dignity of a legally enforceable agreement does not permit third parties to interfere with performance. A prospective purchaser may not induce a seller bound under an oral agreement to breach the agreement and sell to him at a price that necessarily excludes the broker.[100]

The elements of this tort are as follows:

1. An economic relationship between broker and vendor or broker and vendee containing the probability of future economic benefit to the broker

2. Knowledge by the defendant of the existence of the relationship

3. Intentional acts on the part of the defendant designed to disrupt the relationship[101]

4. Actual disruption of the relationship

5. Damages to the plaintiff proximately caused by the acts of the defendant

A defendant may have certain affirmative defenses to such an act, namely, privilege[102] or justification,[103] such as free competition.

§3.37. Finder's fee

An agreement to pay compensation for finding and introducing a person interested in purchasing realty is not within the purview of the real estate licensing acts. This is true when the finder's *only* act is to introduce the prospective buyer, leaving sale negotiations with the seller.[104] The finder's lack of a broker's or salesperson's real estate license does not render the agreement unenforceable.[105] However, an agreement to pay a finder's fee may have to be in writing to be enforceable under many situations.[106]

EXAMPLE   A case involved payment of a finder's fee for obtaining financing for a proposed shopping center construction project. A defense to the action was based on the plaintiff's failure to possess a real estate broker's license. The court ruled that the evidence showed that the plaintiff's services had been restricted to those of a finder, for which no license was required.[107]

The line between introduction and further activity is a narrow one, involving a question of fact as to whether the finder has exceeded the mere act of introduction. As a caution, the licensee should always know exactly the extent of the finder's involvement in the transaction to be protected from potential violation if an unlawful compensation is paid.

Payment of finder's fee by or to a salesperson. Under the Real Estate Law,[108] it is unlawful for any licensed real estate salesperson or broker to *pay* any compensation *directly* to another salesperson or to a broker acting in the capacity of a salesperson. The compensation must be paid through the employing broker. To supplement this, it is equally unlawful for any salesperson to *accept* any compensation except through the employing broker. Therefore, even as to finder's fees between two salespeople, the compensation must be paid through the broker.[109]

In distinguishing when a licensee is acting in the capacity of a finder or middleman, the courts have declared that a broker acts as an agent when there is confided in the broker the power to act on behalf of the parties and to exercise discretion, skill, and judgment; whereas a middleman possesses none of these prerogatives and earns a commission simply by bringing the parties together.[110] As to whether a salesperson can pay a finder's fee to a nonlicensee directly, the law is silent. The better practice, though, is to have the broker pay the finder directly.

Finder not an agent. If a person is performing acts *only* as a finder, that person is not an *agent* in the strict sense of the word. In that regard, in one case it was determined that the person is under no legal duty to inform the seller that the offer that was presented came from the finder's mother.[111]

Violations. It is clear that if a broker *hires* a nonlicensee to perform acts for which a license is required, the broker has violated the law. It is equally against the law for a broker to *pay* a nonlicensee (even though he has not employed such a person) any compensation if the nonlicensee has solicited potential buyers or sellers for the licensee, by virtue of telephone or door-to-door solicitation. The marginal area involves the "hostess" who works in a subdivision and (1) takes the prospect to the house; and (2) gives them a brochure, but explains nothing or gives no verbal information. Anything beyond this would surely be construed to be a violation.

Referral programs. The Department of Real Estate discourages the involvement of real estate licensees in referral programs utilizing the services of unlicensed persons, feeling that the risk of "crossing the line" is too great to justify the use of any such program. To assist licensees, the Department of Real Estate presented and responded to two questions frequently asked regarding finder's fees.[112]

Q. Is it okay for a licensee to offer a partial refund of a commission to a property owner as an inducement to obtain a listing?

A. It is not a violation of the Real Estate Law or of any of the general laws of the state if a licensee rebates a portion of his commission to a principal in the transaction. Section 10137 of the Real Estate Law makes it unlawful for a real estate broker to compensate any person who is not licensed as a broker or a salesman for performing any acts for which a real estate license is required. A principal in a real estate transaction is not performing acts for which a license is required. Hence, there is no violation of the law if the fee paid by the licensee is simply a refund or a reduced commission.[113]

Q. Is it legal for a licensee to agree to pay a finder's fee to a third party for referring a listing prospect to the licensee?

A. In determining whether the payment of a fee by a licensee to an unlicensed person in a real estate sales transaction is an unlawful payment of commission or a finder's fee, it is necessary to look to the acts for which the unlicensed person is being compensated. If the payment to the unlicensed person is for the simple act of introducing the two parties to a real estate transaction or for the introduction of a prospective seller or buyer of real property to the real estate licensee, there is no requirement that the payee be licensed. If, on the other hand, the unlicensed person solicits prospective buyers or sellers, or if he enters into any of the negotiations toward consummation of the transaction, the payment of compensation to him would appear to constitute a violation of Section 10137 and 10138 by the licensee and a violation of Section 10139 by the recipient of the compensation.

RESPA. In 1976, the Real Estate Settlement Procedures Act (RESPA) became effective. It provides that no one may pay anything of value to a referring nonlicensee when there is an original federally related first trust deed involving four or fewer units. A violation constitutes a misdemeanor, which could result in a fine of up to $10,000 and/or one year in jail.[114]

Although many do not feel Congress intended to outlaw payment of finder's fees, both licensee and finder should be wary of this area until more clearly defined rules or court cases appear.

In any event, RESPA does not apply to second trust deeds or other junior liens, private lenders, assumptions or taking subject to, installment land contracts, or loans involving the purchase of investment property.

§3.38. Disclosing compensation from a lender

It is a substantial misrepresentation for a real estate licensee, who is acting as an agent, to fail to disclose to the principal the form, amount, and source of compensation that he has received or expects to receive from a lender in connection with obtaining financing for the transaction.[115]

V. PROBATE SALES

§3.39. In general

Property of an estate may be sold, encumbered, leased, or exchanged under prescribed conditions, and the services of a real estate broker may be utilized. Proceedings to effect a sale of real property occur frequently. When a sale of property of the estate is necessary for the purpose of paying debts, legacies, family allowance, or expenses of administration, or when it is to the advantage, benefit, and best interests of the estate and those interested therein that any property of the estate be sold, the representative may sell the same, either at public auction or private sale, using his discretion as to which property to sell first, subject to a prescribed order of resort if the decedent died testate.

The Probate Code contains many sections relating to probate sales that are referred to in the footnotes for this chapter. Most references to the Probate Code have changed since the 1987 and subsequent overhaul of the Probate Code by the Law Revision Commission. Although the sections have been renumbered, much of the content remains the same.

§3.40. Contract with real estate broker

Before proceeding with a sale, the representative may enter into a contract with a real estate broker or brokers to secure a purchaser for the estate; this contract may provide for the payment of a commission out of the proceeds of the sale.

Under the Probate Code,[116] an exclusive right to sell may be granted if, prior to the execution of the contract, the executor or administrator obtains the permission of the court, showing an advantage and necessity to the estate. Failure to follow such a procedure can result in additional problems for the broker.[117]

When the sale is confirmed to such purchaser, the contract with the broker is binding and valid as against the estate for an amount to be allowed by the court. The code provides that no personal liability shall attach to the representative, and no liability shall be incurred by the estate unless an actual sale is made and confirmed by the court. An exclusive agency agreement would not be enforceable against the estate unless the broker was the procuring cause of a sale.[118]

§3.41. Notice of sale

Unless notice of sale is waived in the will, it is necessary to give notice of sale for the period and in the manner prescribed. By advertising property for sale, the representative is not bound to accept the highest bid received, since the advertising for bids is not an offer but rather an invitation to make an offer. The representative may call for higher bids or may postpone the sale from time to time. The price offered at a private sale must be at least 90 percent of the appraised value of the real property to be sold.

§3.42. Confirmation of sale

When a bid is accepted it is subject to confirmation by the court. A return of sale and petition for confirmation is fixed and set for hearing. At the hearing, if it appears to the court that good reason existed for the sale, that the sale was legally made and fairly conducted, and that the sum bid is not disproportionate to the value, the court may confirm the sale and direct the execution of a conveyance. Before confirming the sale, the court asks if there are any higher bids. If an increased bid in the requisite amount is made in open court, the court in its discretion may accept such bid and confirm the sale to the new bidder, or it may order a new sale. The court may also postpone the hearing, at which time it may receive additional bids and accept a higher bid. The Probate Code provides that if a sale returned for confirmation is on credit and a higher offer is made to the court, either for cash or credit, or if such sale returned is for cash, and a higher offer is made to the court on credit, such higher offer shall be considered *only* if the personal representative informs the court that the offer is acceptable before confirmation of the sale.

§3.43. Commission payable

If a commission is payable, the order of confirmation must so provide; if this is not done, a commission cannot be recovered.

Commission payable to original broker. The Probate Code provides that in the case of a sale on an increased bid in open court made to a purchaser not procured by the broker holding the listing, the court shall allow a commission on the full amount for which the sale is confirmed, with one-half the commission on the original bid to be paid to the broker whose bid is returned to the court for confirmation, and the balance of the commission payable to the broker who obtains the new purchaser to whom the sale is confirmed. If the successful bidder is not produced by a bona fide agent, then the broker holding the listing is allowed a full commission on the amount of the original bid. Since 1983, the court can give consideration to any agreement between the listing broker and co-op broker whose bid was returned for court confirmation.[119]

Determining compensation to broker on increased bid. If the sale is confirmed to a new bidder on a sale in open court, the court is empowered to fix a reasonable compensation for the services of the broker procuring the successful bidder. However, the compensation of the broker producing the successful bidder shall be one-half of the amount of the bid in the original return and all the compensation on the difference between the original bid and the amount for which the sale is confirmed.[120]

EXAMPLE   In one case it was held that in the absence of a listing agreement with the estate, a broker whose client is outbid at a court confirmation hearing is not entitled to a commission.[121]

---

§3.44. Deed by representative

After confirmation of the sale, and when the terms of the sale have been met, the representative executes a deed, which must refer to the order confirming sale, and a certified copy of the order is recorded in the county recorder's office together with the deed.

§3.45. Sale to representative prohibited

Except when the will of the decedent or a contract in writing made during the lifetime of the decedent so permits, the representative is prohibited from purchasing any property of the estate, or any claim against the estate, or being interested in any such purchase, directly or indirectly.[122] A transaction in violation of this rule is voidable at the instance of the heirs or other parties interested in the estate. The rule applies regardless of adequacy of consideration, lack of actual fraudulent intent, or apparent regularity of the proceedings. If a prohibited sale is made to a person who is acting for the representative and the property is resold to a bona fide purchaser for value and without notice of the representative's interest, it is probable that such purchaser's title would not be set aside. But if the interest of the representative is disclosed by the record chain of title, as when the probate sale is made to a third party who then, or shortly thereafter, conveys to the representative individually, or to the spouse of the representative, it would appear that a subsequent purchaser would be charged with notice of the possible invalidity of the sale.

§3.46. Effect of death on prior listing

In one case, the trial court entered judgment in favor of a real estate broker and against an executor for a commission based on the amount received by the executor from the sale of the decedent's property. The broker was the transferee of an exclusive authorization and right to sell listing given by the deceased to another broker, and the sale was made by the executor during the term specified in the written agreement. The transaction was consummated independently of any efforts by the broker. The Court of Appeals reversed the judgment of the trial court, holding that the listing terminated by operation of law on the death of the property owner, with no contractual liability under the agreement devolving on the executor.[123]

§3.47. Breach of duty

Selling probate property to a relative or friend is a breach of duty that can cause a broker's license to be revoked.

EXAMPLE   A broker's license was revoked in connection with a probate sale. The broker received a commission in the sale but concealed from the court that the ostensible purchaser was his brother-in-law and that the real purchaser was a corporation in which the broker had an interest.[124]

---

§3.48. Broker as principal

Whether a commission can be collected by a broker in a probate sale, while acting as a principal, even when full disclosure is made, has not been clearly articulated by the courts. The cases are in conflict.[125]

VI. REAL ESTATE PURCHASE CONTRACT AND RECEIPT FOR DEPOSIT

§3.49. In general

In California, brokers generally use a purchase contract when accepting earnest money to bind an offer for the purchase of property. This contract is one of the most important instruments used in a real estate transaction. The purchase contract not only constitutes a receipt for a deposit by the prospective purchaser, but when duly executed by the buyer and seller, it also constitutes a *contract* for the purchase and sale of real property.[126] In addition to being a contract between the seller and buyer, it also evidences the agreement between the seller and the broker for the payment of a specified sum as a commission.

§3.50. Contract rules apply

The elementary concepts of contract law are applicable to the purchase contract.[127] Of particular significance are the elements of offer and acceptance. In the ordinary transaction, when the buyer signs the purchase contract, this constitutes an offer by the buyer. This offer may be revoked at any time before communication of the seller's acceptance. If the seller accepts the buyer's offer and communicates the acceptance to the buyer, a binding contract arises. If the seller makes a counteroffer,[128] a binding contract does not come into being until the buyer's subsequent acceptance is communicated to the seller. For an acceptance to result in the formation of a binding contract, it must be made in the exact terms set forth in the offer. Forms of the "Residential Purchase Agreement and Receipt for Deposit," and "Counter Offer" published by the California Association of Realtors appear as Figures 3-3 and 3-4.

CALIFORNIA
ASSOCIATION
OF REALTORS®

RESIDENTIAL PURCHASE AGREEMENT
(AND RECEIPT FOR DEPOSIT)
For Use With Single Family Residential Property — Attached or Detached

Date:_____, at _____, California,
Received From _____ ("Buyer"),
A Deposit Of _____ Dollars $ _____, toward the
Purchase Price Of _____ Dollars $ _____,
For Purchase Of Property Situated In _____, County Of _____
California, Described As _____ ("Property").

1. **FINANCING:** Obtaining the loans below **is a contingency** of this Agreement. Buyer shall act diligently and in good faith to obtain the designated loans. Obtaining deposit, down payment and closing costs **is not a contingency.**
   A. **BUYER'S DEPOSIT** shall be held uncashed until Acceptance and then deposited within **3 business days** after .. $ _____
   Acceptance or ☐ _____, ☐ with Escrow Holder,
   ☐ into Broker's trust account, or ☐ _____, by ☐ Personal Check, ☐ Cashier's Check,
   ☐ Cash, or ☐ _____
   B. **INCREASED DEPOSIT** shall be deposited with _____ .. $ _____
   within ____ Days After Acceptance, or ☐ _____
   C. **FIRST LOAN IN THE AMOUNT OF** .... $ _____
   NEW First Deed of Trust in favor of LENDER, encumbering the Property, securing a note payable at maximum
   interest of _____% fixed rate, or _____% initial adjustable rate with a maximum interest rate cap of
   _____%, balance due in _____ years. Buyer shall pay loan fees/points not to exceed _____.
      ☐ FHA ☐ VA: Seller shall pay (i) _____% discount points, (ii) other fees not allowed to be paid by Buyer,
      not to exceed $_____, and (iii) the cost of lender required repairs not otherwise provided for in
      this Agreement, not to exceed $ _____.
   D. **ADDITIONAL FINANCING TERMS:** _____ .. $ _____
      _____
      ☐ seller financing, (C.A.R. Form SFA-14); ☐ junior or assumed financing, (C.A.R. Form PAA-14, paragraph 5)
   E. **BALANCE OF PURCHASE PRICE** (not including costs of obtaining loans and other closing costs) to be deposited .. $ _____
   with escrow holder within sufficient time to close escrow.
   F. **TOTAL PURCHASE PRICE** .... $ _____
   G. **LOAN CONTINGENCY** shall remain in effect until the designated loans are funded (or ☐ _____ **Days** After Acceptance, by which time Buyer
   shall give Seller written notice of Buyer's election to cancel this Agreement if Buyer is unable to obtain the designated loans. If Buyer does not
   give Seller such notice, the contingency of obtaining the designated loans shall be removed by the method specified in paragraph 16B.)
   H. **LOAN APPLICATIONS; PREQUALIFICATION: For NEW financing,** within 5 (or ☐ _____) **Days** After Acceptance, Buyer shall provide Seller
   a letter from lender or mortgage loan broker stating that, based on a review of Buyer's written application and credit report, Buyer is prequalified
   for the NEW loan indicated above. If Buyer fails to provide such letter within that time, Seller may cancel this Agreement in writing.
   I. ☐ **APPRAISAL CONTINGENCY:** (If checked) This Agreement is contingent upon Property appraising at no less than the specified total
   purchase price. If there is a loan contingency, the appraisal contingency shall remain in effect until the loan contingency is removed,
   otherwise, the appraisal contingency shall be removed within 10 (or ☐ _____) **Days** After Acceptance.
   J. **ALL CASH OFFER:** If this is an all cash offer, Buyer shall, within 5 (or ☐ _____) **Days** After Acceptance, provide Seller written verification
   of sufficient funds to close this transaction. Seller may cancel this Agreement in writing within **5 Days** After: (i) time to provide verification
   expires, if Buyer fails to provide verification; or **(ii)** receipt of verification, if Seller reasonably disapproves it.
2. **ESCROW:** Close Of Escrow shall occur _____ **Days** After Acceptance (or ☐ on _____ (date)). Buyer and Seller shall deliver signed
   escrow instructions consistent with this Agreement ☐ within _____ **Days** After Acceptance, ☐ at least _____ **Days** before Close Of Escrow,
   or ☐ _____. Seller shall deliver possession and occupancy of the Property to Buyer at _____ AM/PM, ☐ on
   the date of Close Of Escrow, ☐ no later than _____ **Days** After date of Close Of Escrow, or ☐ _____
   _____. Property shall be vacant, unless otherwise agreed in writing. If transfer of title and
   possession do not occur at the same time, Buyer and Seller are advised to (a) consult with their insurance advisors, and (b) enter into a written
   occupancy agreement. The omission from escrow instructions of any provision in this Agreement shall not constitute a waiver of that provision.
3. **OCCUPANCY:** Buyer ☐ does, ☐ does not, intend to occupy Property as Buyer's primary residence.
4. **ALLOCATION OF COSTS:** (Check boxes which apply. If needed, insert additional instructions in blank lines.)
   GOVERNMENTAL TRANSFER FEES:
   A. ☐ Buyer ☐ Seller shall pay County transfer tax or transfer fee. _____
   B. ☐ Buyer ☐ Seller shall pay City transfer tax or transfer fee. _____
   TITLE AND ESCROW COSTS:
   C. ☐ Buyer ☐ Seller shall pay for **owner's** title insurance policy, issued by _____ company.
   (Buyer shall pay for any title insurance policy insuring Buyer's **Lender,** unless otherwise agreed.)
   D. ☐ Buyer ☐ Seller shall pay escrow fee. _____ Escrow holder shall be _____
   SEWER/SEPTIC/WELL COSTS:
   E. ☐ Buyer ☐ Seller shall pay for sewer connection, if required by Law prior to Close Of Escrow. _____
   F. ☐ Buyer ☐ Seller shall pay to have septic or private sewage disposal system inspected. _____
   G. ☐ Buyer ☐ Seller shall pay to have wells tested for water quality, potability, productivity, and recovery rate. _____
   OTHER COSTS:
   H. ☐ Buyer ☐ Seller shall pay Homeowners' Association transfer fees. _____
   I. ☐ Buyer ☐ Seller shall pay Homeowners' Association document preparation fees. _____
   J. ☐ Buyer ☐ Seller shall pay for zone disclosure reports. _____
   K. ☐ Buyer ☐ Seller shall pay for Smoke Detector installation and/or Water Heater bracing. _____
   Seller, prior to close of escrow, shall provide Buyer a written statement of compliance in accordance with state and local Law, unless exempt.
   L. ☐ Buyer ☐ Seller shall pay the cost of compliance with any other minimum mandatory government retrofit standards and inspections required
   as a condition of closing escrow under any Law. _____
   M. ☐ Buyer ☐ Seller shall pay the cost of a one-year home warranty plan, issued by _____,
   with the following optional coverage: _____. Policy cost not to exceed $ _____.
   PEST CONTROL REPORT:
   N. ☐ Buyer ☐ Seller shall pay for the Pest Control Report ("Report"), which, within the time specified in paragraph 16, shall be prepared by
   _____, a registered structural pest control company.
   O. **(1)** Buyer shall have the right to disapprove the Report as specified in paragraph 16, UNLESS any box in 4 O (2) is checked below
   OR **(2)** (Applies if any box is checked below)
      (a) ☐ Buyer ☐ Seller shall pay for work recommended to correct conditions described in the Report as **"Section 1."**
      (b) ☐ Buyer ☐ Seller shall pay for work recommended to correct conditions described in the Report as **"Section 2,"** unless waived by Buyer

Buyer and Seller acknowledge receipt of copy of this page, which constitutes Page 1 of _____ Pages.

Buyer's Initials (_____) (_____)   Seller's Initials (_____) (_____)

THIS FORM HAS BEEN APPROVED BY THE CALIFORNIA ASSOCIATION OF REALTORS® (C.A.R.). NO REPRESENTATION IS MADE AS TO THE LEGAL VALIDITY OR
ADEQUACY OF ANY PROVISION IN ANY SPECIFIC TRANSACTION. A REAL ESTATE BROKER IS THE PERSON QUALIFIED TO ADVISE ON REAL ESTATE
TRANSACTIONS. IF YOU DESIRE LEGAL OR TAX ADVICE, CONSULT AN APPROPRIATE PROFESSIONAL.
The copyright laws of the United States (Title 17 U.S. Code) forbid the unauthorized reproduction of this form, or any portion thereof, by
photocopy machine or any other means, including facsimile or computerized formats. Copyright © 1991-1998, CALIFORNIA ASSOCIATION OF
REALTORS®, INC. ALL RIGHTS RESERVED.

Published and Distributed by:
REAL ESTATE BUSINESS SERVICES, INC.
a subsidiary of the CALIFORNIA ASSOCIATION OF REALTORS®
525 South Virgil Avenue, Los Angeles, California 90020
PRINT DATE

REVISED 4/98

OFFICE USE ONLY
Reviewed by Broker
or Designee _____
Date _____

EQUAL HOUSING OPPORTUNITY

RESIDENTIAL PURCHASE AGREEMENT AND RECEIPT FOR DEPOSIT (RPA-14 PAGE 1 OF 5)

Figure 3-3
Residential Purchase Agreement and Receipt for Deposit

5. **PEST CONTROL TERMS:** If a Report is prepared pursuant to paragraph 4N:
   A. The Report shall cover the main building and attached structures and, if checked: ☐ detached garages and carports, ☐ detached decks, ☐ the following other structures on the Property: _____.
   B. If Property is a unit in a condominium, planned development, or residential stock cooperative, the Report shall cover only the separate interest and any exclusive-use areas being transferred, and shall not cover common areas, unless otherwise agreed.
   C. If inspection of inaccessible areas is recommended in the Report, Buyer has the option, within 5 Days After receipt of the Report, either to accept and approve the Report by the method specified in paragraph 16B, or to request in writing that further inspection be made. If upon further inspection no infestation or infection is found in the inaccessible areas, the cost of the inspection, entry, and closing of those areas shall be paid for by Buyer. If upon further inspection infestation or infection is found in the inaccessible areas, the cost of inspection, entry, and closing of those areas shall be paid for by the party so designated in paragraph 4O(2)a. If no party is so designated, then cost shall be paid by Buyer.
   D. If no infestation or infection by wood destroying pests or organisms is found in the Report, or upon completion of required corrective work, a written Pest Control Certification shall be issued. Certification shall be issued prior to Close Of Escrow, unless otherwise agreed in writing.
   E. Inspections, corrective work and Pest Control Certification in this paragraph refers only to the presence or absence of wood destroying pests or organisms, and does not include the condition of roof coverings. Read paragraphs 9 and 12 concerning roof coverings.
   F. Nothing in paragraph 5 shall relieve Seller of the obligation to repair or replace shower pans and shower enclosures due to leaks, if required by paragraph 9B(3). Water test of shower pans on upper level units may not be performed unless the owners of property below the shower consent.

6. **TRANSFER DISCLOSURE STATEMENT; NATURAL HAZARD DISCLOSURES;SUBSEQUENT DISCLOSURES; MELLO-ROOS NOTICE:**
   A. Within the time specified in paragraph 16A(1), if required by law, a Real Estate Transfer Disclosure Statement ("TDS") and Natural Hazard Disclosure Statement ("NHD") (or substituted disclosure) shall be completed and delivered to Buyer, who shall return signed copies to Seller.
   B. In the event Seller, prior to Close Of Escrow, becomes aware of adverse conditions materially affecting the Property, or any material inaccuracy in disclosures, information, or representations previously provided to Buyer (including those made in a TDS) of which Buyer is otherwise unaware, Seller shall promptly provide a subsequent or amended disclosure, in writing, covering those items, **except for those conditions and material inaccuracies disclosed in reports obtained by Buyer.**
   C. Seller shall (i) make a good faith effort to obtain a disclosure notice from any local agencies which levy a special tax on the Property pursuant to the Mello-Roos Community Facilities Act; and (ii) promptly deliver to Buyer any such notice made available by those agencies.
   D. If the TDS, the NHD (or substituted disclosure), the Mello-Roos disclosure notice, or a subsequent or amended disclosure is delivered to Buyer after the offer is signed, Buyer shall have the right to terminate this Agreement within **3 days** after delivery in person, or **5 days** after delivery by deposit in the mail, by giving written notice of termination to Seller or Seller's agent.

7. **DISCLOSURES:** Within the time specified in paragraph 16A(1), Seller, shall (i) if required by law, disclose if Property is located in any zone identified in 7A; (ii) if required by law, provide Buyer with the disclosures and other information identified in 7B, and, (iii) if applicable, take the actions specified in 7C. Buyer shall then, within the time specified in paragraph 16, investigate the disclosures and information, and other information provided to Buyer, and provide written notice to Seller of any item disapproved.
   A. **ZONE DISCLOSURES:** Special Flood Hazard Areas; Potential Flooding (Inundation) Areas; Very High Fire Hazard Zones; State Fire Responsibility Areas; Earthquake Fault Zones; Seismic Hazard Zones; or any other federal, state, or locally designated zone for which disclosure is required by Law.
   B. **PROPERTY DISCLOSURES AND PUBLICATIONS:** Lead-Based Paint Disclosures and pamphlet; Earthquake Guides (and disclosures), Environmental Hazards Booklet, and Energy Efficiency Booklet (when published).
   C. ☐ (If checked:) **CONDOMINIUM/COMMON INTEREST SUBDIVISION:** Property is a unit in a condominium, planned development, or other common interest subdivision. Seller shall request from the Homeowners' Association ("HOA"), and upon receipt provide to Buyer: copies of covenants, conditions, and restrictions; articles of incorporation, by-laws, and other governing documents; statement regarding limited enforceability of age restrictions, if applicable; copies of most current financial documents distributed; statement indicating current regular, special and emergency dues and assessments, any unpaid assessment, any additional amounts due from Seller or Property, any approved changes to regular, special or emergency dues or assessments; preliminary list of defects, if any; any written notice of settlement regarding common area defects; and any pending or anticipated claims or litigation by or against the HOA; any other documents required by Law; a statement containing the location and number of designated parking and storage spaces; and copies of the most recent 12 months of HOA minutes for regular and special meetings, if available.
   D. **NOTICE OF VIOLATION:** If, prior to Close Of Escrow, Seller receives notice or is made aware of any notice filed or issued against the Property, for violations of any Laws, Seller shall immediately notify Buyer in writing.

8. **TITLE AND VESTING:**
   A. Within the time specified in paragraph 16A, Buyer shall be provided a current preliminary (title) report (which is only an offer by the title insurer to issue a policy of title insurance, and may not contain every item affecting title). Buyer shall, within the time specified in paragraph 16A(2), provide written notice to Seller of any items reasonably disapproved.
   B. At Close Of Escrow, Buyer shall receive a grant deed conveying title (or, for stock cooperative or long-term lease, an assignment of stock certificate or of seller's interest), including oil, mineral and water rights, if currently owned by Seller. Title shall be subject to all encumbrances, easements, covenants, conditions, restrictions, rights, and other matters which are of record or disclosed to Buyer prior to Close Of Escrow, unless disapproved in writing by Buyer within the time specified in paragraph 16A(2). However, title shall not be subject to any liens against the Property, except for those specified in the Agreement. Buyer shall receive an ALTA-R owner's title insurance policy, if reasonably available. If not, Buyer shall receive a standard coverage owner's policy (e.g. CLTA or ALTA with regional exceptions). Title shall vest as designated in Buyer's escrow instructions. The title company, at Buyer's request, can provide information about availability, desirability, and cost of various title insurance coverages. THE MANNER OF TAKING TITLE MAY HAVE SIGNIFICANT LEGAL AND TAX CONSEQUENCES.

9. **CONDITION OF PROPERTY:**
   A. **EXCEPT AS SPECIFIED IN THIS AGREEMENT, Property is sold "AS IS," WITHOUT WARRANTY, in its PRESENT physical condition.**
   B. (IF CHECKED) SELLER WARRANTS THAT AT THE **TIME POSSESSION IS MADE AVAILABLE TO BUYER:**
      ☐ (1) Roof shall be free of leaks KNOWN to Seller or DISCOVERED during escrow.
      ☐ (2) Built-in appliances (including free-standing oven and range, if included in sale), heating, air conditioning, electrical, mechanical, water, sewer, and pool/spa systems, if any, shall be repaired, if KNOWN by Seller to be inoperative or DISCOVERED to be so during escrow. (Well system is not warranted by this paragraph. Well system is covered by paragraphs 4G, 12 and 16.)
      ☐ (3) Plumbing systems, shower pans, and shower enclosures shall be free of leaks KNOWN to Seller or DISCOVERED during escrow.
      ☐ (4) All fire, safety, and structural defects in chimneys and fireplaces KNOWN to Seller or DISCOVERED during escrow shall be repaired.
      ☐ (5) Septic system, if any, shall be repaired, if KNOWN by Seller to be inoperative, or DISCOVERED to be so during escrow.
      ☐ (6) All broken or cracked glass, torn existing window and door screens, and multi-pane windows with broken seals, shall be replaced.
      ☐ (7) All debris and all personal property not included in the sale shall be removed.
      ☐ (8) _____
   C. **PROPERTY MAINTENANCE:** Unless otherwise agreed, Property, including pool, spa, landscaping and grounds, is to be maintained in substantially the same condition as on the date of Acceptance.
   D. **INSPECTIONS AND DISCLOSURES:** Items discovered in Buyer's Inspections which are not covered by paragraph 9B, shall be governed by the procedure in paragraphs 12 and 16. Buyer retains the right to disapprove the condition of the Property based upon items discovered in Buyer's Inspections. Disclosures in the TDS and items discovered in Buyer's Inspections do NOT eliminate Seller's obligations under paragraph 9B, unless specifically agreed in writing. WHETHER OR NOT SELLER WARRANTS ANY ASPECT OF THE PROPERTY, SELLER IS OBLIGATED TO DISCLOSE KNOWN MATERIAL FACTS, AND TO MAKE OTHER DISCLOSURES REQUIRED BY LAW

Buyer and Seller acknowledge receipt of copy of this page, which constitutes Page 2 of _____ Pages.

Buyer's Initials (_____) (_____)   Seller's Initials (_____) (_____)

REVISED 4/98

OFFICE USE ONLY
Reviewed by Broker or Designee _____
Date _____

EQUAL HOUSING OPPORTUNITY

RESIDENTIAL PURCHASE AGREEMENT AND RECEIPT FOR DEPOSIT (RPA-14 PAGE 2 OF 5)

Figure 3-3 (Cont.)
Residential Purchase Agreement and Receipt for Deposit

Property Address: _____ Date: _____

10. **FIXTURES:** All EXISTING fixtures and fittings that are attached to the Property, or for which special openings have been made, are INCLUDED IN THE PURCHASE PRICE (unless excluded below), and shall be transferred free of liens and "AS IS," unless specifically warranted. Fixtures shall include, but are not limited to, existing electrical, mechanical, lighting, plumbing and heating fixtures, fireplace inserts, solar systems, built-in appliances, window and door screens, awnings, shutters, window coverings, attached floor coverings, television antennas, satellite dishes and related equipment, private integrated telephone systems, air coolers/conditioners, pool/spa equipment, garage door openers/remote controls, attached fireplace equipment, mailbox, in-ground landscaping, including trees/shrubs, and (if owned by Seller) water softeners, water purifiers and security systems/alarms, and _____.
FIXTURES EXCLUDED: _____.

11. **PERSONAL PROPERTY:** The following items of personal property, free of liens and "AS IS," unless specifically warranted, are INCLUDED IN THE PURCHASE PRICE: _____.

12. **BUYER'S INVESTIGATION OF PROPERTY CONDITION:** Buyer's Acceptance of the condition of the Property is a contingency of this Agreement, as specified in this paragraph and paragraph 16. Buyer shall have the right, at Buyer's expense, to conduct inspections, investigations, tests, surveys, and other studies ("Inspections"), including the right to inspect for lead-based paint and other lead hazards. No Inspections shall be made by any governmental building or zoning inspector, or government employee, without Seller's prior written consent, unless required by Law. Property improvements may not be built according to codes or in compliance with current Law, or have had permits issued. Buyer shall, within the time specified in Paragraph 16A(2), complete these Inspections and notify Seller in writing of any items reasonably disapproved. Seller shall make Property available for all Inspections. Buyer shall: keep Property free and clear of liens; indemnify and hold Seller harmless from all liability, claims, demands, damages and costs; and repair all damages arising from Inspections. Buyer shall carry, or Buyer shall require anyone acting on Buyer's behalf to carry, policies of liability, worker's compensation, and other applicable insurance, defending and protecting Seller from liability for any injuries to persons or property occurring during any work done on the Property at Buyer's direction, prior to Close Of Escrow. Seller is advised that certain protections may be afforded Seller by recording a notice of non-responsibility for work done on the Property at Buyer's direction. At Seller's request, Buyer shall give Seller, at no cost, complete copies of all Inspection reports obtained by Buyer concerning the Property. Seller shall have water, gas, and electricity on for Buyer's Inspections, and through the date possession is made available to Buyer.

13. **FINAL WALK-THROUGH; VERIFICATION OF CONDITION:** Buyer shall have the right to make a final inspection of the Property within **5 (or ☐ _____) Days** prior to Close Of Escrow, NOT AS A CONTINGENCY OF THE SALE, but solely to confirm that Repairs have been completed as agreed in writing, and that Seller has complied with Seller's other obligations.

14. **PRORATIONS AND PROPERTY TAXES:** Unless otherwise agreed in writing, real property taxes and assessments, interest, rents, HOA regular, special, and emergency dues and assessments imposed prior to Close of Escrow, premiums on insurance assumed by Buyer, payments on bonds and assessments assumed by Buyer, and payments on Mello-Roos and other Special Assessment District bonds and assessments which are now a lien shall be PAID CURRENT and prorated between Buyer and Seller as of Close Of Escrow. Prorated payments on Mello-Roos and other Special Assessment District bonds and assessments and HOA special assessments that are now a lien but not yet due, shall be assumed by Buyer WITHOUT CREDIT toward the purchase price. Property will be reassessed upon change of ownership. Any supplemental tax bills shall be paid as follows: **(1)** For periods after Close Of Escrow, by Buyer; and, **(2)** For periods prior to Close Of Escrow, by Seller. TAX BILLS ISSUED AFTER CLOSE OF ESCROW SHALL BE HANDLED DIRECTLY BETWEEN BUYER AND SELLER. Exceptions: _____.

15. **SALE OF BUYER'S PROPERTY:**
A. This Agreement is NOT contingent upon the sale of Buyer's property, unless paragraph 15B is checked.
OR B. ☐ (If checked) This Agreement IS CONTINGENT on the Close Of Escrow of Buyer's property, described as (address) _____
_____ ("Buyer's Property"), which is
(if checked) ☐ listed for sale with _____ Company, and/or
(if checked) ☐ in Escrow No. _____ with _____ Escrow Holder, scheduled to
Close Escrow on _____ (date). Buyer shall deliver to Seller, within **5 Days** After Seller's request, a copy of the contract for the sale of Buyer's Property, escrow instructions, and all amendments and modifications thereto. If Buyer's Property does not close escrow by the date specified for Close Of Escrow in this paragraph, then either Seller or Buyer may cancel this Agreement in writing.
After Acceptance:
(1) (Applies UNLESS (2) is checked): Seller SHALL have the right to continue to offer the Property for sale. If Seller accepts another written offer, Seller shall give Buyer written notice to **(I)** remove this contingency in writing, **(II)** provide written verification of sufficient funds to close escrow on this sale without the sale of Buyer's Property, and **(III)** comply with the following additional requirement(s) _____
_____.
If Buyer fails to complete those actions within **72 (or ☐____) hours** After receipt of such notice, Seller may cancel this Agreement in writing.
OR ☐ **(2) (APPLIES ONLY IF CHECKED:)** Seller SHALL NOT have the right to continue to offer the Property for sale, except for back-up offers.

16. **TIME PERIODS/DISAPPROVAL RIGHTS/REMOVAL OF CONTINGENCIES/CANCELLATION RIGHTS:**
A. **TIME PERIODS:** The following time periods shall apply, unless changed by mutual **written** agreement:
(1) SELLER HAS: 5 (or ☐ _____) Days After Acceptance to, as applicable, order, request or complete, and **2 Days** After receipt (or completion) to provide to Buyer all reports, disclosures, and information for which Seller is responsible under paragraphs 4, 6, 7, and 8.
(2) BUYER HAS: (a) 10 (or ☐ _____) Days After Acceptance to complete all Inspections, investigations and review of reports and other applicable information for which Buyer is responsible,(including Inspections for lead-based paint and other lead hazards under paragraph 12), with an additional **7 Days** to complete geologic Inspections. WITHIN THIS TIME, Buyer must either disapprove in writing any items, (including, if applicable, the pest control Report under paragraph 4O(1)) which are unacceptable to Buyer, or remove any contingency or disapproval right associated with that item by the active or passive method, as specified below; **(b) 5 (or ☐ _____) Days** After receipt of **(I)** each of the items in paragraph 16A(1); and **(II)** notice of code and legal violations under paragraph 7D, to either disapprove in writing any items which are unacceptable to Buyer, or to remove any contingency or disapproval right associated with that item, by the active or passive method, as specified below.
(3) SELLER'S RESPONSE TO BUYER'S DISAPPROVALS: Seller shall have **5 (or ☐ _____) Days** After receipt of Buyer's written notice of items reasonably disapproved, to respond in writing. If Seller refuses or is unable to make repairs to, or correct, any items reasonably disapproved by Buyer, or if Seller does not respond within the time period specified, Buyer shall have **5 (or ☐ _____) Days** After receipt of Seller's response, or after the expiration of the time for Seller to respond, whichever occurs first, to cancel this Agreement in writing.
B. **ACTIVE OR PASSIVE REMOVAL OF BUYER'S CONTINGENCIES:**
(1) ☐ **ACTIVE METHOD (APPLIES IF CHECKED):** If Buyer does not give Seller written notice of items reasonably disapproved, removal of contingencies or disapproval right, or notice of cancellation within the time periods specified, Seller shall have the right to cancel this Agreement by giving written notice to Buyer.
(2) PASSIVE METHOD (Applies UNLESS Active Method is checked): If Buyer does not give Seller written notice of items reasonably disapproved, or of removal of contingencies or disapproval right, or notice of cancellation within the time periods specified, Buyer shall be deemed to have removed and waived any contingency or disapproval right, or the right to cancel, associated with that item.
C. **EFFECT OF CONTINGENCY REMOVAL:** If Buyer removes any contingency or cancellation right by the active or passive method, as applicable, Buyer shall conclusively be deemed to have: **(1)** Completed all Inspections, investigations, and review of reports and other applicable information and disclosures pertaining to that contingency or cancellation right; **(2)** Elected to proceed with the transaction; and, **(3)** Assumed all liability, responsibility, and expense for repairs or corrections pertaining to that contingency or cancellation right, or for inability to obtain financing if the contingency pertains to financing, except for items which Seller has agreed in writing to repair or correct.

Buyer and Seller acknowledge receipt of copy of this page, which constitutes Page 3 of _____ Pages.
Buyer's Initials (_____) (_____)   Seller's Initials (_____) (_____)

REVISED 4/98

┌─ OFFICE USE ONLY ─┐
Reviewed by Broker
or Designee _____
Date _____
└────────────────┘

EQUAL HOUSING OPPORTUNITY

Figure 3-3 *(Cont.)*
Residential Purchase Agreement and Receipt for Deposit

D. **CANCELLATION OF SALE/ESCROW; RETURN OF DEPOSITS:** If Buyer or Seller gives written NOTICE OF CANCELLATION pursuant to rights duly exercised under the terms of this Agreement, Buyer and Seller agree to sign mutual instructions to cancel the sale and escrow and release deposits, less fees and costs, to the party entitled to the funds. Fees and costs may be payable to service providers and vendors for services and products provided during escrow. Release of funds will require mutual, signed release instructions from both Buyer and Seller, judicial decision, or arbitration award. **A party may be subject to a civil penalty of up to $1,000 for refusal to sign such instructions, if no good faith dispute exists as to who is entitled to the deposited funds (Civil Code §1057.3).**

17. **REPAIRS:** Repairs under this Agreement shall be completed prior to Close Of Escrow, unless otherwise agreed in writing. Work to be performed at Seller's expense may be performed by Seller or through others, provided that work complies with applicable laws, including governmental permit, inspection, and approval requirements. Repairs shall be performed in a skillful manner with materials of quality comparable to existing materials. It is understood that exact restoration of appearance or cosmetic items following all Repairs may not be possible.

18. **WITHHOLDING TAXES:** Seller and Buyer agree to execute and deliver any instrument, affidavit, statement, or instruction reasonably necessary to comply with federal (FIRPTA) and California withholding Laws, if required (such as C.A.R. Forms AS-11 and AB-11).

19. **KEYS:** At the time possession is made available to Buyer, Seller shall provide keys and/or means to operate all Property locks, mailboxes, security systems, alarms, and garage door openers. If the Property is a unit in a condominium or subdivision, Buyer may be required to pay a deposit to the HOA to obtain keys to accessible HOA facilities.

20. **LIQUIDATED DAMAGES: If Buyer fails to complete this purchase by reason of any default of Buyer, Seller shall retain, as liquidated damages for breach of contract, the deposit actually paid. However, if the Property is a dwelling with no more than four units, one of which Buyer intends to occupy, then the amount retained shall be no more than 3% of the purchase price. Any excess shall be returned to Buyer. Buyer and Seller shall also sign a separate liquidated damages provision for any increased deposit. (C.A.R. Form RID-11 shall fulfill this requirement.)**   Buyer's Initials _____/_____   Seller's Initials _____/_____

21. **DISPUTE RESOLUTION:**

    A. **MEDIATION:** Buyer and Seller agree to mediate any dispute or claim arising between them out of this Agreement, or any resulting transaction, before resorting to arbitration or court action, subject to paragraphs 21C and D below. Mediation fees, if any, shall be divided equally among the parties involved. If any party commences an action based on a dispute or claim to which this paragraph applies, without first attempting to resolve the matter through mediation, then that party shall not be entitled to recover attorney's fees, even if they would otherwise be available to that party in any such action. THIS MEDIATION PROVISION APPLIES WHETHER OR NOT THE ARBITRATION PROVISION IS INITIALED.

    B. **ARBITRATION OF DISPUTES: Buyer and Seller agree that any dispute or claim in Law or equity arising between them out of this Agreement or any resulting transaction, which is not settled through mediation, shall be decided by neutral, binding arbitration, subject to paragraphs 21C and D below. The arbitrator shall be a retired judge or justice, or an attorney with at least 5 years of residential real estate law experience, unless the parties mutually agree to a different arbitrator, who shall render an award in accordance with substantive California Law. In all other respects, the arbitration shall be conducted in accordance with Part III, Title 9 of the California Code of Civil Procedure. Judgment upon the award of the arbitrator(s) may be entered in any court having jurisdiction. The parties shall have the right to discovery in accordance with Code of Civil Procedure §1283.05.**

    "NOTICE: BY INITIALING IN THE SPACE BELOW YOU ARE AGREEING TO HAVE ANY DISPUTE ARISING OUT OF THE MATTERS INCLUDED IN THE 'ARBITRATION OF DISPUTES' PROVISION DECIDED BY NEUTRAL ARBITRATION AS PROVIDED BY CALIFORNIA LAW AND YOU ARE GIVING UP ANY RIGHTS YOU MIGHT POSSESS TO HAVE THE DISPUTE LITIGATED IN A COURT OR JURY TRIAL. BY INITIALING IN THE SPACE BELOW YOU ARE GIVING UP YOUR JUDICIAL RIGHTS TO DISCOVERY AND APPEAL, UNLESS THOSE RIGHTS ARE SPECIFICALLY INCLUDED IN THE 'ARBITRATION OF DISPUTES' PROVISION. IF YOU REFUSE TO SUBMIT TO ARBITRATION AFTER AGREEING TO THIS PROVISION, YOU MAY BE COMPELLED TO ARBITRATE UNDER THE AUTHORITY OF THE CALIFORNIA CODE OF CIVIL PROCEDURE. YOUR AGREEMENT TO THIS ARBITRATION PROVISION IS VOLUNTARY."

    "WE HAVE READ AND UNDERSTAND THE FOREGOING AND AGREE TO SUBMIT DISPUTES ARISING OUT OF THE MATTERS INCLUDED IN THE 'ARBITRATION OF DISPUTES' PROVISION TO NEUTRAL ARBITRATION."   Buyer's Initials _____/_____   Seller's Initials _____/_____

    C. **EXCLUSIONS FROM MEDIATION AND ARBITRATION:** The following matters are excluded from Mediation and Arbitration: **(a)** A judicial or non-judicial foreclosure or other action or proceeding to enforce a deed of trust, mortgage, or installment land sale contract as defined in Civil Code §2985; **(b)** An unlawful detainer action; **(c)** The filing or enforcement of a mechanic's lien; **(d)** Any matter which is within the jurisdiction of a probate, small claims, or bankruptcy court; and **(e)** An action for bodily injury or wrongful death, or for latent or patent defects to which Code of Civil Procedure §337.1 or §337.15 applies. The filing of a court action to enable the recording of a notice of pending action, for order of attachment, receivership, injunction, or other provisional remedies, shall not constitute a violation of the mediation and arbitration provisions.

    D. **BROKERS:** Buyer and Seller agree to mediate and arbitrate disputes or claims involving either or both Brokers, provided either or both Brokers shall have agreed to such mediation or arbitration, prior to or within a reasonable time after the dispute or claim is presented to Brokers. Any election by either or both Brokers to participate in mediation or arbitration shall not result in Brokers being deemed parties to the Agreement.

22. **DEFINITIONS:** As used in this Agreement:

    A. **"Acceptance"** means the time the offer or final counter offer is accepted in writing by the other party, in accordance with this Agreement or the terms of the final counter offer.

    B. **"Agreement"** means the terms and conditions of this Residential Purchase Agreement and any counter offer.

    C. **"Days"** means calendar days, unless otherwise required by Law.

    D. **"Days After . ."** means the specified number of calendar days after the occurrence of the event specified, not counting the calendar date on which the specified event occurs.

    E. **"Close Of Escrow"** means the date the grant deed, or other evidence of transfer of title, is recorded.

    F. **"Law"** means any law, code, statute, ordinance, regulation, or rule, which is adopted by a controlling city, county, state or federal legislative or judicial body or agency.

    G. **"Repairs"** means any repairs, alterations, replacements, or modifications, (including pest control work) of the Property.

    H. **"Pest Control Certification"** means a written statement made by a registered structural pest control company that on the date of inspection or re-inspection, the Property is "free" or is "now free" of "evidence of active infestation in the visible and accessible areas".

    I. **Section 1** means infestation or infection which is evident. **Section 2** means present conditions likely to lead to infestation or infection.

    J. **Singular and Plural** terms each include the other, when appropriate.

    K. **C.A.R. Form** means the specific form referenced, or another comparable form agreed to by the parties.

23. **MULTIPLE LISTING SERVICE ("MLS"):** Brokers are authorized to report the terms of this transaction to any MLS, to be published and disseminated to persons and entities authorized to use the information, on terms approved by the MLS.

Buyer and Seller acknowledge receipt of copy of this page, which constitutes Page 4 of _____ Pages.

Buyer's Initials (_____) (_____)   Seller's Initials (_____) (_____)

OFFICE USE ONLY
Reviewed by Broker
or Designee _____
Date _____

REVISED 4/98

RESIDENTIAL PURCHASE AGREEMENT AND RECEIPT FOR DEPOSIT (RPA-14 PAGE 4 OF 5)

Figure 3-3 *(Cont.)*
Residential Purchase Agreement and Receipt for Deposit

Property Address: _____ Date: _____

24. **EQUAL HOUSING OPPORTUNITY:** The Property is sold in compliance with federal, state, and local anti-discrimination Laws.
25. **ATTORNEY'S FEES:** In any action, proceeding, or arbitration between Buyer and Seller arising out of this Agreement, the prevailing Buyer or Seller shall be entitled to reasonable attorney's fees and costs from the non-prevailing Buyer or Seller, except as provided in paragraph 21A.
26. **SELECTION OF SERVICE PROVIDERS:** If Brokers give Buyer or Seller referrals to persons, vendors, or service or product providers ("Providers"), Brokers do not guarantee the performance of any of those Providers. Buyer and Seller may select ANY Providers of their own choosing.
27. **TIME OF ESSENCE; ENTIRE CONTRACT; CHANGES:** Time is of the essence. All understandings between the parties are incorporated in this Agreement. Its terms are intended by the parties as a final, complete, and exclusive expression of their agreement with respect to its subject matter, and may not be contradicted by evidence of any prior agreement or contemporaneous oral agreement. **This Agreement may not be extended, amended, modified, altered, or changed, except in writing signed by Buyer and Seller.**
28. **OTHER TERMS AND CONDITIONS,** including ATTACHED SUPPLEMENTS:
    ☑ Buyer Inspection Advisory (C.A.R. Form BIA-14) _____
    ☐ Purchase Agreement Addendum (C.A.R. Form PAA-14 paragraph numbers: _____ , _____
    _____
    _____
    _____
29. **AGENCY CONFIRMATION:** The following agency relationships are hereby confirmed for this transaction:
    Listing Agent: _____ (Print Firm Name) is the agent of (check one):
    ☐ the Seller exclusively; or ☐ both the Buyer and Seller.
    Selling Agent: _____ (Print Firm Name) (if not same as Listing Agent) is the agent of (check one):
    ☐ the Buyer exclusively; or ☐ the Seller exclusively; or ☐ both the Buyer and Seller.
    Real Estate Brokers are not parties to the Agreement between Buyer and Seller.
30. **OFFER:** This is an offer to purchase the Property on the above terms and conditions. All paragraphs with spaces for initials by Buyer and Seller are incorporated in this Agreement only if initialed by all parties. If at least one but not all parties initial, a counter offer is required until agreement is reached. Unless Acceptance of Offer is signed by Seller, and a signed copy delivered in person, by mail, or facsimile, and personally received by Buyer, or by _____, who is authorized to receive it, by (date) _____, at _____ AM/PM, the offer shall be deemed revoked and the deposit shall be returned. Buyer has read and acknowledges receipt of a copy of the offer and agrees to the above confirmation of agency relationships. If this offer is accepted and Buyer subsequently defaults, Buyer may be responsible for payment of Brokers' compensation. This Agreement and any supplement, addendum, or modification, including any photocopy or facsimile, may be signed in two or more counterparts, all of which shall constitute one and the same writing.

Buyer and Seller acknowledge and agree that Brokers: (a) Do not decide what price Buyer should pay or Seller should accept; (b) Do not guarantee the condition of the Property; (c) Shall not be responsible for defects that are not known to Broker(s) and are not visually observable in reasonably accessible areas of the Property; (d) Do not guarantee the performance or Repairs of others who have provided services or products to Buyer or Seller; (e) Cannot identify Property boundary lines; (f) Cannot verify inspection reports, square footage or representations of others; (g) Cannot provide legal or tax advice; (h) Will not provide other advice or information that exceeds the knowledge, education and experience required to obtain a real estate license. Buyer and Seller agree that they will seek legal, tax, insurance, and other desired assistance from appropriate professionals.

BUYER _____ BUYER _____

31. **BROKER COMPENSATION:** Seller agrees to pay compensation for services as follows:
    _____ , to _____ , Broker, and
    _____ , to _____ , Broker,
    payable: **(a)** On recordation of the deed or other evidence of title; or **(b)** If completion of sale is prevented by default of Seller, upon Seller's default; or, **(c)** If completion of sale is prevented by default of Buyer, only if and when Seller collects damages from Buyer, by suit or otherwise, and then in an amount equal to one-half of the damages recovered, but not to exceed the above compensation, after first deducting title and escrow expenses and the expenses of collection, if any. Seller hereby irrevocably assigns to Brokers such compensation from Seller's proceeds, and irrevocably instructs Escrow Holder to disburse those funds to Brokers at close of escrow. Commission instructions can be amended or revoked only with the written consent of Brokers. In any action, proceeding or arbitration relating to the payment of such compensation, the prevailing party shall be entitled to reasonable attorney's fees and costs, except as provided in paragraph 21A.
32. **ACCEPTANCE OF OFFER:** Seller warrants that Seller is the owner of this Property, or has the authority to execute this Agreement. Seller accepts the above offer, agrees to sell the Property on the above terms and conditions, and agrees to the above confirmation of agency relationships. Seller has read and acknowledges receipt of a copy of this Agreement, and authorizes Broker to deliver a signed copy to Buyer.

If checked: ☐ SUBJECT TO ATTACHED COUNTER OFFER, DATED _____.

SELLER_____ Date _____

SELLER_____ Date _____

(_____/_____) **ACKNOWLEDGMENT OF RECEIPT:** Buyer or authorized agent acknowledges receipt of signed Acceptance on (date) _____,
(Initials)   at _____ AM/PM.

Agency relationships are confirmed as above. Real Estate Brokers are not parties to the Agreement between Buyer and Seller.
Receipt for deposit is acknowledged:
Real Estate Broker (Selling Firm Name) _____ By _____ Date _____
Address _____ Telephone _____ Fax _____
Real Estate Broker (Listing Firm Name) _____ By _____ Date _____
Address _____ Telephone _____ Fax _____

This form is available for use by the entire real estate industry. It is not intended to identify the user as a REALTOR®. REALTOR® is a registered collective membership mark which may be used only by members of the NATIONAL ASSOCIATION OF REALTORS® who subscribe to its Code of Ethics.

REVISED 4/98

Page 5 of _____ Pages.

┌─ OFFICE USE ONLY ─┐
Reviewed by Broker
or Designee _____
Date _____
└──────────────────┘

RESIDENTIAL PURCHASE AGREEMENT AND RECEIPT FOR DEPOSIT (RPA-14 PAGE 5 OF 5)

Figure 3-3 (Cont.)
Residential Purchase Agreement and Receipt for Deposit

CALIFORNIA
ASSOCIATION
OF REALTORS®

COUNTER OFFER   No. _____

(For use by Seller or Buyer. May be used for Multiple Counter.)

This is a counter offer to the: ☐ Offer, ☐ Counter Offer, ☐ Other _____, dated _____,
regarding (property address): _____
between _____, "Buyer," and _____, "Seller."

1. **TERMS:** The terms and conditions of the above referenced document are **accepted subject to the following:**
   A. **Paragraphs in the purchase contract (offer) which require initials by all parties, but are not initialed by all parties, are excluded from the final agreement unless specifically referenced for inclusion in paragraph 1C of this or another Counter Offer.**
   B. **Unless otherwise specified in writing, down payment and loan amount(s) will be adjusted in the same proportion as in the original offer.**
   C. _____
   _____
   _____
   _____
   _____
   _____
   _____
   _____
   _____
   _____
   _____
   _____
   _____
   _____
   _____
   _____
   _____
   _____
   _____
   _____
   _____

   D. **The following attached supplements are incorporated in this Counter Offer:**
   ☐ _____   ☐ _____
   ☐ _____   ☐ _____

2. ☐ **(If Checked:) MULTIPLE COUNTER OFFER:** Seller is making a Counter Offer(s) to another prospective buyer(s) on terms which may or may not be the same as in this Counter Offer. Acceptance of this Counter Offer by Buyer shall **not** be binding unless and until it is subsequently re-signed by Seller in paragraph 7 below. Prior to the completion of all of these events, Buyer and Seller shall have no duties or obligations for the purchase or sale of the Property.

3. **RIGHT TO ACCEPT OTHER OFFERS:** Seller reserves the right to continue to offer the Property for sale or for other transaction, and to accept any other offer at any time prior to communication of acceptance, as described in paragraph 4. Seller's acceptance of another offer prior to Buyer's acceptance and communication of acceptance of this Counter Offer shall revoke this Counter Offer.

4. **EXPIRATION:** Unless acceptance of this Counter Offer is signed by the person receiving it, and communication of acceptance is made by delivering a signed copy in person, by mail, or by facsimile which is personally received, to the person making this Counter Offer or to _____, by 5:00 PM on the third calendar day after this Counter Offer is written (or, if checked, ☐ date: _____, time _____ AM/PM), this Counter Offer shall be deemed revoked and the deposit shall be returned to Buyer. This Counter Offer may be executed in counterparts.

   As the person(s) making this Counter Offer on the terms above, receipt of a copy is acknowledged.

   _____ Date: _____ Time: _____ AM/PM

   _____ Date: _____ Time: _____ AM/PM

5. **ACCEPTANCE:** I/WE accept the above Counter Offer (if checked: ☐ **SUBJECT TO THE ATTACHED COUNTER OFFER**) and acknowledge receipt of a copy.

   _____ Date: _____ Time: _____ AM/PM

   _____ Date: _____ Time: _____ AM/PM

6. **ACKNOWLEDGMENT OF RECEIPT:** Receipt of signed acceptance on (date) _____, at _____ AM/PM, by the maker of the Counter Offer, or other person designated in paragraph 4, is acknowledged.   (_____/_____) (Initials)

7. | **MULTIPLE COUNTER OFFER SIGNATURE LINE:** (Paragraph 7 applies only if paragraph 2 is checked.) By signing below, Seller accepts this Multiple Counter Offer, and creates a binding contract. (NOTE TO SELLER: Do NOT sign in this paragraph until after Buyer signs the acceptance in paragraph 5, and returns to Seller for re-signing.)

   _____ Date: _____ Time: _____ AM/PM

   _____ Date: _____ Time: _____ AM/PM

THIS FORM HAS BEEN APPROVED BY THE CALIFORNIA ASSOCIATION OF REALTORS® (C.A.R.). NO REPRESENTATION IS MADE AS TO THE LEGAL VALIDITY OR ADEQUACY OF ANY PROVISION IN ANY SPECIFIC TRANSACTION. A REAL ESTATE BROKER IS THE PERSON QUALIFIED TO ADVISE ON REAL ESTATE TRANSACTIONS. IF YOU DESIRE LEGAL OR TAX ADVICE, CONSULT AN APPROPRIATE PROFESSIONAL.

This form is available for use by the entire real estate industry. It is not intended to identify the user as a REALTOR®. REALTOR® is a registered collective membership mark which may be used only by members of the NATIONAL ASSOCIATION OF REALTORS® who subscribe to its Code of Ethics.

The copyright laws of the United States (17 U.S. Code) forbid the unauthorized reproduction of this form by any means, including facsimile or computerized formats.
Copyright © 1986-1997, CALIFORNIA ASSOCIATION OF REALTORS®

Published and Distributed by:
REAL ESTATE BUSINESS SERVICES, INC.
a subsidiary of the CALIFORNIA ASSOCIATION OF REALTORS®
525 South Virgil Avenue, Los Angeles, California 90020

Page _____ of _____ Pages.

OFFICE USE ONLY
Reviewed by Broker
or Designee _____
Date _____

EQUAL HOUSING OPPORTUNITY

COUNTER OFFER (CO-14 PAGE 1 OF 1) REVISED 9/95

Figure 3-4
Counter Offer

§3.51. Purchase contract should evidence all terms of contract

In the preparation of a purchase contract, all the basic provisions of the contract of sale and purchase should be set forth, with nothing left for further determination in the escrow agreement or otherwise, including arrangements for financing. If the buyer must obtain financing before being unconditionally obligated to purchase the seller's property, the contract should so state. It should further specify the amount of the loan the buyer needs, the duration of the loan, the rate of interest, the amount of monthly payments, including principal and interest, the conditions of prepayment, if any, and the total loan charges and fees that the buyer is willing to incur. Provision should be made as to the disposition of the matter if the buyer is unable to obtain such a loan.[129]

§3.52. All conditions should be specified

If the purchase and sale are contingent on the happening of some other event or condition, the purchase contract should spell out the contingency with certainty and clarity. If the buyer must sell property that he presently owns before being obligated to purchase the seller's property, the contract should so recite. It should specify what is to happen to the deposit money in the event the buyer is unable to sell his property under the designated terms within the specified time. The contract should further contain a complete understanding among the buyer, the seller, and the broker as to the return of the deposit in the event the buyer's offer is not accepted.

Filling in blanks on a preprinted offer to purchase form by a real estate licensee is permitted by law, but the drafting of contracts or complicated additions to contracts may constitute the unlawful practice of law. Use of boilerplate provisions can be dangerous. For example, if clauses are overreaching, such as giving the broker the right to extend time for performance at his option, they may not be binding and can certainly give rise to problems. A form that contains an incomplete blank can subject the licensee to disciplinary measures.[130]

A basic minimum checklist on financing is (1) amount of increased deposit, if any;[131] (2) amount of total cash down payment; (3) when down payment is to be paid; (4) maximum amount of loan or loans; (5) maximum length of loans in terms of time; (6) balloon payment, if any; (7) maximum rate of interest on each loan; (8) amount of periodic payments and mode of payment (monthly, quarterly, etc.); (9) whether payments include principal and interest or PITI; (10) prepayment charges, if any; (11) loan charges, if any, set-up charges, assumption fees, and points; (12) specific clauses used in FHA or VA loans; (13) whether or not sale is conditional upon buyer's ability to obtain a specified loan within a period of time; (14) whether loan can be assumed or can be taken "subject to."[132]

§3.53. Disposition of deposit

The listing agreement may authorize the broker to accept a deposit from the purchaser. The seller becomes entitled to the deposit when the seller accepts the purchaser procured by the broker. The deposit money does not belong to the broker, and the broker is not entitled to retain custody of it.[133] Normally, the authority of the broker is only to produce a purchaser who is willing to contract with the seller on the prescribed terms. The broker, solely by virtue of employment as a broker, has no authority to accept a deposit. If the purchaser pays money to a broker who is not authorized to accept a deposit, the broker holds the deposit as the agent of the purchaser and not the seller, and the risk of loss is on the purchaser. However, if the listing agreement gives the broker the authority to accept a deposit, as it often does, he holds it as the agent of the seller.[134]

In any event, the law requires earnest money to be deposited within a certain time[135] unless the seller and buyer are informed and agree that the broker hold the deposit for a specified time.

Although a postdated check or promissory note can be accepted, the licensee must obtain the seller's permission or else the licensee is in violation of the Real Estate Law.[136] A postdated check is at best a promissory note and, as such, might influence the seller's decision to accept the offer.[137] In any event, it is not good practice to accept either because of the potential difficulty in collection if it becomes necessary. But the decision is that of the seller, not the licensee.

Deposit money must be kept separate. Since the deposit money does not belong to the broker in any event, it is a basic rule that it must not be commingled with his own funds. This is not only a general principle of agency—a violation of this rule subjects the broker to disciplinary action by the Real Estate Commissioner. Further, if earnest money is deposited in escrow with the buyer's instructions and the conditions of the instructions are not complied with, the buyer retains ownership of the money.[138]

§3.54. Forfeiture of deposit

Purchase contracts often provide for a forfeiture of the deposit if the buyer defaults.[139] When the contract provides that the seller shall pay the broker one-half (or some other proportion, not exceeding the full amount of the commission) of the buyer's deposit in the event of a default by the buyer, the broker is, of course, entitled to a share of such deposit if the buyer refuses to perform and the seller elects to declare a forfeiture.

§3.55. Who selects termite or escrow company

The selection of an escrow agent in a real estate transaction is one of the terms of the contract subject to the meeting of the minds of the principals to the transaction. It is, however, not generally a critical term of the contract to either principal. As a consequence, it is not unusual for this decision to be made by an agent in the transaction with the consent of the principals.

There is nothing inherently wrong if the agent is the one who decides. Problems may develop, however, when the licensee loses sight of the fact that the decision is his to make only if the principals have declined to express a choice, having been given an opportunity to do so. If the licensee erroneously believes that he has a vested, legal right to select the escrow holder, it can easily lead to a conscious or unconscious overreaching on his part.

EXAMPLE An example of overreaching is the listing agreement containing a fine-print provision under which the owner purports to agree to the use of an escrow agent selected in advance by the listing broker.

Such a provision—often overlooked by the owner when he or she signs the listing—may cause problems later when a buyer wants a particular escrow company. It could cause a transaction to fail if the buyer and seller cannot agree on the escrow company. The same holds true in selecting a termite company (licensed pest control company).

The Real Estate Commissioner recognizes that many licensees pride themselves on offering full service—including an escrow service—to their clients. Clearly a plan or arrangement that contemplates providing such full service to the parties to a transaction is not per se illegal, unethical, or improper. However, it may become objectionable—and conceivably the basis for disciplinary action by the department—if it usurps or ignores the rights of one or both of the principals, including the right to choose a mutually acceptable escrow holder or termite company.[140]

§3.56. Possession usually determines risk of loss

The purchaser is not entitled to possession of the land unless he is given the right of possession under the contract, or unless the seller places the purchaser in possession.[141] The question of risk of loss usually depends on right of possession. The problem of who should bear the loss if the property is materially damaged, as by fire, without fault on the part of either party, after the execution of the contract but before execution of the deed, was for many years a perplexing one in California. However, the Uniform Vendor and Purchaser Risk Act provides, in effect, that transfer of possession is determinative of the question of risk of loss, "unless the contract expressly provides otherwise."[142] Under this code provision, if the possession has been transferred, the risk of loss is on the purchaser; if possession has not been transferred, the risk of loss is on the seller.

EXAMPLE   In one case, it was held that under the terms of the contract, the buyer must stand the loss when the property was severely damaged by flood after the purchase agreement was fully executed and delivered.[143]

---

§3.57. Attorney's fees
In the C.A.R. form, the prevailing party is entitled to reasonable attorney's fees and costs.[144] The word *party* in this instance refers to buyer and seller. However, the last paragraph of the C.A.R. form relating to acceptance also refers to attorney's fees to the prevailing party in an action between seller and broker. Many other listing agreements do not include an attorney's fees clause, the absence of which could be detrimental to the buyer or seller.[145]

VII. OPTION AS A CONTRACT RIGHT IN LAND
§3.58. In general
An *option* is defined as a contract by which the owner of property invests another person with the *right* to purchase such property at a stipulated sum within a specified period of time, but without imposing any *obligation* to purchase. The distinguishing characteristic of an option is the initial lack of mutuality of enforcement. The owner of the land, called the optionor, binds himself to sell if the purchaser, called the optionee, elects to accept the offer, but the optionee is not bound to buy, and may reject the offer contained in the option. However, the exercise of the right to purchase by the optionee will give rise to a mutually binding contract of sale, and the interest acquired is said to relate back to the time of giving the option so as to cut off intervening rights acquired with knowledge of the existence of the option.[146] A purchaser from the optionor with notice of the option would take title subject to the right of the optionee to exercise his right and require a conveyance of the land.

§3.59. Assignment of option
Generally, the rights of the optionee under an option to purchase are assignable. Options to purchase are often contained in a lease, and such an option ordinarily passes with an assignment of the lease, even though the option is not specifically mentioned in the assignment.

§3.60. Termination of option
An option terminates on expiration of the specified time within which the optionee may accept or exercise a right to purchase. However, for title insurance purposes a recorded option is not ignored solely on the basis of the expiration of the specified time, as the option may have been extended or its exercise may have been prevented by acts of the optionor.

The Civil Code provides that a recorded instrument creating an option to purchase real property ceases to be constructive notice within six months after the option has expired by its terms or by operation of law, when no conveyance, contract, or other instrument has been recorded showing that the option has been exercised or extended.[147]

§3.61. Right to revoke an option

An option to purchase, unless supported by a sufficient consideration, is revocable by the optionor at any time before the optionee exercises a right to purchase, but an option to purchase that is supported by a sufficient consideration is irrevocable for its duration. In the latter case, the death of the optionor does not impair the right of the optionee to exercise his right to purchase within the period allowed, unless the death of the optionor renders impossible the performance of a condition precedent to the right to purchase.

It has been held that any consideration for the option, however small, is sufficient to render an option binding on the optionor.[148] However, the consideration for the sale must be adequate for the optionee to obtain specific performance.

§3.62. Necessity for writing

The California Supreme Court has held that a contract between a contemplated purchaser and a broker, employing the broker to obtain an option for the purchase of real property, comes within the Statute of Frauds and must be in writing.[149]

§3.63. Option compared with preemption right

An option to purchase is distinguishable from a *right of preemption*, or right of first refusal. An option creates in the optionee a power to compel the owner of the property to sell it at a stipulated price whether or not the owner is willing to part with ownership at that time. On the other hand, a preemption does not give the party having such right the power to compel an unwilling owner to sell; it merely requires the owner, *when and if he decides to sell*, to offer the property first to the person entitled to the preemption at the stipulated price. On receiving such an offer, the preemptioner may then elect whether to buy. If he decides not to buy, then the owner of the property may sell to anyone. Sometimes a prospective buyer of the property merely triggers the right of the preemptionee when the owner desires to sell, and a person making an offer for the property has no assurance that he will be able to obtain the property, even though the owner is willing to sell it to him at the offering price. In any such situation, the prospective buyer should be informed of the right of first refusal in favor of another party.[150]

QUESTIONS

Matching Terms

a. Commission
b. Confirmation
c. Co-op broker
d. Listing agreement
e. Exclusive
f. Fiduciary listing
g. Exclusive right to sell listing
h. Net listing
i. Liquidated
j. Exclusive agency

1. Authority given to one person only. Exclusive
2. Listing agreement that obligates owner to pay a commission even if he makes the sale. Exclusive Right to sell listing
3. Relationship of broker to client. Fiduciary listing
4. Broker entitled to proceeds of sale in excess of a stated amount. Net Listing
5. Broker's compensation for performing the duties of his agency. Commission
6. Broker who effects a sale for another broker having a listing. Co-op broker
7. Listing agreement that allows owner to sell without payment of a commission. Exclusive Agency

8. Agreed-to amount as damages in the event of a breach of contract. liquidated
9. Contract of employment between seller of real property and broker. Listing agreement
10. Court approval of a probate sale. Confirmation

True/False

T (F) 11. A preemptive right and an option are identical rights.

T (F) 12. In an open listing, it is not necessary that the broker be the procuring cause in order to be entitled to a commission.

(T) F 13. In an exclusive listing, it is necessary to have a specified date of termination.

(T) F 14. A broker must have a valid real estate license in order to be entitled to a commission.

(T) F 15. Ordinarily, an exclusive agency listing is a bilateral contract.

T (F) 16. Once an owner lists property with a broker, he is compelled to sell if the broker procures a buyer ready, willing, and able to buy the property.

T F **17.** An option listing gives the broker the right to buy the property under prescribed conditions.

T F **18.** The amount or rate of commission that a broker can charge is fixed by law.

T F **19.** Under an exclusive agency listing, a broker has a duty to make a diligent effort to find a buyer.

T F **20.** To be enforceable, an option agreement must be supported by consideration.

Multiple Choice

21. The broker–client relationship is ordinarily created by the
   a. Escrow instructions.
   b. Deposit receipt.
   c. Listing agreement.
   d. Land sales contract.

22. If the buyer procured by the broker offers to buy at less than the asking price and seller accepts,
   a. A commission is payable on the selling price.
   b. No commission is payable.
   c. A commission is payable on the asking price.
   d. None of the above.

23. A listing agreement that entitles a broker to all proceeds in excess of the seller's asking price is called
   a. An open listing.
   b. An option listing.
   c. A net listing.
   d. A multiple listing.

24. A listing agreement that gives the broker the right to buy the property is called
   a. An exclusive right to sell.
   b. An option listing.
   c. A multiple listing.
   d. An open-end listing.

25. As compared with a contract, the distinguishing characteristic of an option is the initial lack of
   a. Mutuality of enforcement.
   b. Consideration.
   c. Meeting of the minds.
   d. Mutual assent.

26. An option is
   a. Valid without consideration.
   b. Valid if the consideration is $10 or more, although it is not delivered.
   c. Valid if the consideration is delivered, even if less than $10.
   d. Not valid if the delivered consideration is substantially less than market value of the property.

27. An oral option to buy a parcel of real property is
   a. Enforceable for a reasonable period, not

exceeding six months.
   b. Unenforceable.
   c. Contrary to the Statute of Limitations.
   d. Enforceable if the consideration is adequate.

28. A right of first refusal is sometimes given to a third party by a landowner. This right is also called a preemptive right. The person having such a right
   a. Can compel the owner to sell the land to him at the market price whenever he chooses to buy.
   b. Has the same right as the holder of an option to buy.
   c. Has the right to buy at a specified price if the landowner chooses to sell.
   d. All of the above.

29. A listing broker received 40 percent of the total 6 percent commission from the sale of a $100,000 house. The salesperson was to receive 50 percent of what the broker received. The salesperson would be entitled to receive
   a. $2,400.
   b. $1,200.
   c. $3,000.
   d. $1,500.

30. If an owner enters into an exclusive right to sell listing and thereafter sells the property through his own efforts during the time of the listing,
   a. The broker is entitled to a full commission.
   b. The broker is entitled to half of his commission.
   c. No commission is payable.
   d. The sale is unenforceable.

31. If an owner enters into a net listing and thereafter the broker procures a buyer for the property for the net asking price,
   a. The broker is entitled to a finder's fee.
   b. The sale is invalid.
   c. The broker is entitled to a reasonable commission.
   d. No commission is payable.

32. Broker Smith took a listing, after which the owner-principal sold directly to a friend in the neighborhood. To assure herself of a commission, under what type of listing should Smith have contracted?
   a. Net.
   b. Open.
   c. Exclusive agency.
   d. Exclusive right to sell.

33. The amount of commission payable on a sale of real property is based on
   a. Total price paid.
   b. Total price paid, less encumbrances.
   c. Total price paid, less cost of sale.
   d. Listing price, regardless of amount of sale.

34. If a broker agrees to act under an oral listing, the responsibility of the broker, when compared with an agreement in writing, is
    a. More.
    b. Less.
    c. The same.
    d. None.
35. The legal relationship between a seller and his real estate broker is that of
    a. Principal and agent.
    b. Attorney and client.
    c. Lender and borrower.
    d. Dominant and servient tenement.
36. A real estate broker is under a duty to use which of the following in the performance of his duties?
    a. Care.
    b. Skill.
    c. Diligence.
    d. All of the above.
37. The broker ordinarily has earned his commission at such time as
    a. The listing agreement is signed.
    b. The transaction is accepted by an escrow agent.
    c. The property comes out of escrow free and clear.
    d. He procures a buyer ready, willing, and able to perform on the seller's terms.
38. Real property subject to a $90,000 encumbrance is listed with a broker at $242,500 but is sold for $241,000. The broker's commission is based on
    a. $242,500.
    b. $242,500 less amount of the encumbrance.
    c. $241,000.
    d. $241,000 less amount of the encumbrance.
39. If an owner enters into an exclusive agency listing and thereafter sells the property through his own efforts,
    a. No commission is payable.
    b. The broker is entitled to 50 percent of his commission.
    c. The broker is entitled to a full commission.
    d. The broker is entitled to his expenses.
40. The amount of the commission payable is ordinarily based on
    a. Statutory limitations.
    b. Agreement of the parties.
    c. Rules and regulations of the Real Estate Commissioner.
    d. The asking price as set forth in the listing.
41. A purchase contract and receipt for deposit when executed by a prospective buyer is basically an
    a. Offer.
    b. Acceptance.
    c. Option.
    d. Implied contract.

42. For a purchase contract to be effective as a contract, it must be
    a. Signed only by the buyer.
    b. Signed by the buyer and seller.
    c. Signed only by the broker.
    d. Approved by the escrow holder.
43. In an open listing, if more than one broker procures a buyer,
    a. The broker who first procures a buyer acceptable to the seller is entitled to a commission.
    b. Each broker is entitled to a commission.
    c. The commission is divided between the brokers.
    d. No commission is payable.
44. Procuring cause means
    a. Introducing a prospect to the seller when no sale results.
    b. Obtaining a list of two or more likely prospects.
    c. The cause of originating a series of events that leads to a sale.
    d. None of the above.
45. A ready and willing buyer means one willing to enter into
    a. An option agreement.
    b. An unconditional agreement of purchase.
    c. A qualified agreement of purchase.
    d. A right of first refusal agreement.
46. An able buyer means one
    a. Who is financially able.
    b. Having the ability to obtain the necessary funds.
    c. Having the ability to obtain the necessary financing.
    d. Any of the above.
47. A listing agreement between a property owner and a real estate broker is ordinarily terminated if
    a. Either party dies.
    b. The owner becomes bankrupt.
    c. The property is destroyed by fire.
    d. Any of the above.
48. A listing with one broker as the only agent for the sale of real property, but which allows the owner to sell without payment of a commission, is an example of an
    a. Open listing.
    b. Exclusive agency.
    c. Option listing.
    d. Exclusive right to sell.
49. In a net listing the amount payable as a commission is
    a. Ascertainable when the listing is signed.
    b. Due when the listing is signed.
    c. Not ascertainable until a sale is made.
    d. Subject to approval by the Real Estate Commission.

50. An open listing is one that is
  a. Exclusive.
  b. Nonexclusive.
  c. Irrevocable by the owner.
  d. For a limited duration, not exceeding three months.

NOTES

1. B. & P. 10148.
2. Tamini v. Bettencourt (1960) 243 C.A.2d 377.
3. Baumgartner v. Meek (1954) 126 C.A.2d 565.
4. Oaks v. Brahs (1955) 132 C.A.2d 182.
5. C.C. 1565. Further, the agreement cannot be a "tying agreement," i.e., it cannot be tied to "I'll sell you this house if you list your other house with me." As a broker, that's a violation of the Federal Sherman Act and Clayton Act.
6. See §9.47.
7. See "Q and A on Pest Control Certification," *California Association of Realtors* magazine (December 1975).
8. B. & P. 10142.
9. Comm. Regs. 2725.
10. Knipe v. Barkdull (1963) 222 C.A.2d 547, 551; 1 Witkin, Summary of California Law (9th ed.), Contracts section 921-953.
11. See C.C. 1086B1090; for a new type of listing with Cal-Vet, see Mil & Vet 987.785.
12. There is no reason why an open listing could not contain a specified termination date; in such event, the owner's right to terminate would be restricted.
13. Edens v. Stoddard (1954) 126 C.A.2d 56.
14. Marks v. Watson (1952) 112 C.A.2d 196.
15. Leonard v. Fallas (1954) 51 C.A.2d 649; for a case explaining the difference between an exclusive agency and exclusive right to sell, see Strout Western Realty v. Gregoire (1950) 101 C.A.2d 215. See also the case of Metzenbaum v. R.O.S. Associates (1986) 188 C.A.3d 202.
16. B. & P. 10176(f); see also Figure 3B1, Paragraph 1.
17. Babcock v. Houston (1973) 33 C.A.3d 858; Summers v. Freeman (1954) 128 C.A.2d 828.
18. If an exclusive listing has no definite termination date and the seller cancels the listing, the lack of a definite date will be a defense in an action for a prospective commission. Dale v. Palmer (1951) 106 C.A.2d 663, 667B668; see also Nichols v. Boswell-Alliance Const. Corp. (1960) 181 C.A.2d 584.
19. Lowe v. Lloyd (1949) 93 C.A.2d 684; see also Nystrom v. 1st National Bank of Fresno (1978) 81 C.A.3d 759.
20. "Commissioner's Column," *California Association of Realtors* magazine (August 1978).
21. Sierra Pacific Ind. v. Carter (1980) 104 C.A.3d 519; Grandi v. Watson (1951) 107 C.A.2d 395; Comm. Regs. 2785(a)(1).
22. B. & P. 10176(g).
23. Curry v. King (1907) 6 C.A. 568.
24. B. & P. 10176(h).
25. C.C. 1086B1090.
26. C.C. 1088.
27. Marin County Board of Realtors v. Paulssan (1976) 16 C.3d 920; Glendale Board of Realtors v. Hounsell (1977) 72 C.A.3d 210; see also Feldman v. Sacramento Board of Realtors (1981) 119 C.A.3d 739; People v. N.A.R. (1981) 120 C.A.3d 459; United M.L.S. Inc. v. Bernstein (1982) 134 C.A.3d 486.
28. Derish v. San Mateo Burlingame Board of Realtors (1982) 136 C.A.3d 534.
29. McLain v. Real Estate Board (1980) 48 USLW 4063.
30. Supermarket Homes, Inc. v. San Fernando Valley Board of Realtors (9th Cir. 1986) 786 F2d 1400.
31. Saxer v. Philip Morris Inc. (1975) 34 C.A.3d 7; Chicago Title Insurance Co. v. Great Western Financial Corp. (1968) 69 C.2d 305. Real estate is subject to the Federal Sherman Anti-Trust Act and the California Cartwright Act; see 15 U.S.C. 1B7; U.S. v. N.A.R.E.B (1950) 339 U.S. 485; B. & P. 16700B16758.
32. See Siegel v. Chicken Delight, Inc. (9th Cir, 1971) 448 Fed.2d 43, 47; Claussen v. Weller (1983) 145 C.A.3d 27; MacManus v. A. E. Realty Partners (1983) 146 C.A.3d 275; B. & P. 16720; C.C.2295.
33. Broker who contracts with a buyer is liable for breach if he fails to perform. Barr v. Rhoades (1969) 274 C.A.2d 852.
34. See Rest.2d Agency §13b.
35. See N.A.R.'s "Standards of Practice" 21-5, 21-6, 21-7.
36. See N.A.R.'s "Standards of Practice" 21-3, 21-5, but see 21B8.
37. See Eltolad Music Co. Inc. v. April Music Inc. (1983) 139 C.A.3d 697.
38. Tetrick v. Sloan (1959) 170 C.A.2d 540.
39. Baumgartner v. Meek (1954) 126 C.A.2d 505; E.H. Boly & Son, Inc. v. Schneider (1975) 525 Fed.2d 20; McAlinden v. Nelson (1953) 121 C.A. 21136.
40. Coleman v. Mora (1968) 263 C.A.2d 137.
41. The key, however, is to *in fact* revoke the listing for lack of due diligence; otherwise it may be a defense in an action by a broker for his commission. Carlsen v. Zane (1968) 261 C.A.2d 399; Whitney Inv. Co. v. Westview Development Co. (1969) 273 C.A.2d 594.
42. Coleman v. Mora, *supra*, 145; see also Figure 3-1, paragraph 5.
43. Blank v. Borden (1974) 11 C.3d 963; see also Never v. King (1969) 276 C.A.2d 461.
44. Greenwood & Co. Real Estate v. C-D Investment Co. (1993) 23 C.A. 4th 447. Comm. Regs. 2785. For antitrust violations, see Footnote 30 and People v. N.A.R. (1981) 120 C.A.3d 459, 472; see also Figure 3-1, paragraph 5. Some brokers are paying 100 percent commissions to their salespeople and in return the salespeople pay for office space, phone, stationery, use of secretary, etc. Each broker considering this concept, however, should carefully consider the actual liability to him for an act of negligence, misrepresentation, or fraud by the salespeople working under this concept.
45. B. & P. 10147.5.
46. Provisor v. Haas Realty, Inc. (1967) 256 C.A.2d 850.
47. Parker v. Compton (1973) 511 S.W.2d 708. On the other hand, the first broker is entitled to a commission even though the seller sent a "termination letter" to the first broker and then hired the second broker who sold the property (Century 21 Butler Realty v. Vasquez [1995] 41 C.A. 4th 888.
48. Delbon v. Brazil (1955) 134 C.A.2d 461.
49. See "Safety clause," §3.27.
50. But caveat Carlsen v. Zane (1968) 261 C.A.2d 399.
51. Cline v. Yamaga (1979) 97 C.A.3d 239; B. & P. 10136. But see Bernasconi Commercial Real Estate v. Omni Health Plan Inc. (1995) 35 C.A. 4th 1644.
52. B. & P. 10136; see Tatterson v. Standard Realty Co. (1927) 81 C.A. 23, 29; Firpo v. Murph (1925) 72 C.A. 249, 253; Davis v. Chipman (1930) 210 C. 609, 623; Koeberle v. Hotchkiss (1935) 8 C.A.2d 634, 641; Greenwood & Co. Real Estate—see C-D Inv. Co. (1993) 23 C.A. 4th 447; Friddle v. Epstein (1993) 16 C.A. 4th 1649.
53. Phillippe v. Shappell Ind., Inc. (1987) 43 C. 3d 1247; MGW, Inc. v. Fredricks Dev. Corp. (1992) 5 C.A. 4th 92 re oral brokers' commissions and punitive damages based on conspiracy and interference with prospective economic advantage; American Ind'l Ent., Inc. v. FDIC, 3 Fed. 3d 1263.
54. See Norwood v. Judd (1949) 93 C.A.2d 276; but see Richardson v. Roberts (1962) 210 C.A.2d 603.
55. Schantz v. Ellsworth (1971) 19 C.A.3d 289; B. & P. 10136.
56. Weber v. Jorgensen (1971) 16 C.A.3d 74; see also Lyons v. Stevenson (1977) 65 C.A.3d 595.

57. Martin v. Culver Enterprises, Inc. (1966) 239 C.A.2d 925, 929; *see also* Masin v. Drain (1984) 150 C.A.3d 714.

58. Wesley N. Taylor Co. v. Russell (1961) 194 C.A.2d 816.

59. Kopf v. Milan (1963) 60 C.2d 600; *see also* the Florida case of Falovitch v. Adrienne Realty (1977) 345 So.2d 839.

60. Baber v. Pappas (1929) 97 C.A. 534, 536; Kaufman v. Nilan (1962) 207 C.A.2d 1, 8B9.

61. Palmtog v. Danielson (1947) 30 C.2d 517, 521; Rest. Agency 447(b).

62. Even with exclusive listings, there may be two or more co-op brokers both claiming a portion of the commission, since each claims she is the procuring cause. Since this is the more typical case, and since these matters are often determined by arbitration through a real estate board, these cases are not appealed to the courts. Therefore, there are currently no California cases on this particular point.

63. Rose v. Hunter (1957) 155 C.A.2d 319.

64. Justice v. Ackerman (1960) 183 C.A.2d 649; Kuhl Corp. v. Sullivan (1993) 13 C.A. 4th 1589.

65. E. A. Strout Western Realty Agency, Inc. v. Lewis (1967) 255 C.A.2d 254.

66. Vidler v. De Bel (1954) 125 C.A.2d 325; William E. David & Co. v. Smith (1967) 256 C.A.2d 552. For further discussion *see* Milligan, "Procuring Cause Revisited," *San Diego Realtor* magazine (Dec., 1990).

67. Oaks v. Brahs (1955) 132 C.A.2d 182.

68. Real Estate Sales Transactions, C.E.B., p. 167 California.

69. Oaks v. Brahs, supra 184.

70. Nelson v. Meyer (1959) 122 C.A.2d 438, 446; *see also* Hughes v. Morrison (1984) 160 C.A.3d 103.

71. Pacific Improvement Co. (1922) 57 C.A. 1 Sessions v.

72. Cone v. Keil (1912) 18 C.A. 675, 679.

73. Tetrick v. Sloan (1959) 170 C.A.2d 540, 545.

74. Augustine v. Trucco (1954) 124 C.A.2d 229, 237. To be entitled to a commission, a broker must "do something more than merely show the property and make unsuccessful efforts wholly unconnected with and to no extent traceable to the subsequent sale." Wright v. Kimbrough (1921) 52 C.A. 42, 46.

75. Dicta from Buckaloo v. Johnson (1975) 14 C.3d 815, 820B821.

76. California Department of Real Estate's *Reference Book* (1980), p. 193.

77. Baird v. Madson (1943) 57 C.A.2d 465 474B475; *see also* Coldwell Banker & Co. v. Pepper Tree Office Center Assoc. (1980) 106 C.A.3d 272, 278 (submitting a brochure to a prospective tenant's broker and forwarding floor plans does not constitute procuring cause).

78. *See* Figure 3B1, paragraph 3(b).

79. Delbon v. Brazil (1955) 134 C.A.2d 461.

80. Leonard v. Fallas (1959) 51 C.2d 649.

81. Simank Realty Inc. v. DeMarco (1970) 6 C.A.3d 610.

82. E. A. Strout Western Realty Agency, Inc. v. Lewis (1967) 255 C.A.2d 254; Anthony v. Enzler (1976) 61 C.A.2d 872. The safety clause is not intended to apply to the situation in which the seller lists with another broker who sells the property to a buyer shown the property by the first broker. Cramer v. Guenio (1976) 331 So.2d 550.

83. Goodwin v. Glick (1956) 139 C.A.2d Supp. 936.

84. Smith v. Wright (1961) 188 C.A.2d 790; Masin v. Drain (1984) 150 C.A.3d 714; Colbaugh v. Hartline (1994) 29 C.A. 4th 1516.

85. Love v. Gulgas (1948) 87 C.A.2d 608, 618.

86. Augustine v. Trucco (1954) 124 C.A.2d 229, 239; Kraemer v. Smith (1960) 179 C.A.2d 52; Lewis v. Fappiano (1957) 150 C.A.2d 252.

87. Filante v. Kikendall (1955) 134 C.A.2d 695.

88. Wilsen v. Bidwell (1948) 88 C.A.2d 832.

89. "Commissioner's Question Box," *California Association of Realtors* magazine (December 1977).

90. Swanson v. Thurber (1955) 132 C.A.2d 171.

91. Lawrence Block Co. v. Palston (1954) 123 C.A.2d 300.

92. Collins v. Vickter Manor, Inc. (1957) 47 C.2d 875.

93. Martin v. Chernabaeff (1954) 124 C.A.2d 648.

94. Paulson v. Leadbetter (1968) 267 C.A.2d 148.

95. Cochran v. Ellsworth (1954) 126 C.A.2d 429.

96. *See* Chan v. Tsang (1991) 1 C.A. 4th 1578; Donnellon v. Rocks (1972) 22 C.A.3d 925; E. H. Boly & Son, Inc. v. Schneider (1975) 525 Fed.2d 20; Higson v. Montgomery Ward & Co. (1968) 263 C.A.2d 333; Brown v. Watt (1967) 256 C.A.2d 44.

97. Allen v. Gindling (1955) 136 C.A.2d 21, 28.

98. Austin v. Richards (1956) 146 C.A.2d 436.

99. Zimmerman v. Bank of America (1961) 191 C.A.2d 55; MGW Inc. v. Fredericks Dev. Corp. (1992) 5 C.A. 4th 92.

100. Buckaloo v. Johnson (1975) 14 C.3d 815, 827; N.A.R.'s "Standards of Practice," 21B5, 21B6, 21B7, 21B8.

101. Petrich v. Nurseryland Garden Centers, Inc. (1983) 140 C.A.3d 243.

102. Including unfair competition, Lowell v. Mother's Cake & Cookie Co. (1978) 79 C.A.3d 13; *see also* Rest. Torts 768, 769, re brokers.

103. For a Negligent Interference with a Contractual Relationship, *see* Chamelean Engineering Corp. v. Air Dynamics Inc. (1980) 101 C.A.3d 418; J'Aire Corp. v. Gregory (1979) 24 C.3d 799. For Civil Conspiracy to Interfere with a Contractual Relationship, *see* Owens v. Foundation for Ocean Research (1980) 107 C.A.3d 179, 185; *see also* Wyatt v. Union Mortgage Co. (1979) 24 C.3d 773. For Interference with Business Relationship, *see* Herzog v. "A" Company, Inc. (1982) 138 C.A.3d 656.

104. Zolk v. General Exploration Co. (1980) 105 C.A.3d 786; Preach v. Monter Rainbow (1993) 12 C.A. 4th 1441.

105. Porter v. Cirod, Inc. (1966) 242 C.A.2d 761. However, whether the individual performs one act or many, if he performs an act for which a real estate license is required and has no license, he violates the real estate law. Shaffer v. Beinhorn (1923) 190 C. 569.

106. C.C. 1624; Hasehian v. Krotz (1969) 268 C.A.2d 314. But *see* contra, Grant v. Marinell (1980) 112 C.A.3d 617, which held that C.C. 1624 bars oral finder's fees between brokers and buyers (and sellers). It is not a bar to a third-party finder who is neither a buyer nor a seller, and it is not a bar to an oral contract between brokers to share a commission. However, an oral finder's fee between a seller and an unlicensed finder must be in writing (Tenzer v. Superscope, Inc. [1983] 148 C.A.3d 430). But *see* Stoll v. Shuff (1994) 21 C.A. 4th 22.

107. Tyrone v. Kelley (1970) 9 C.3d 1.

108. B. & P. 10137.

109. *See* Chapter 4, §4.18, Compensation of Salesperson.

110. Williams v. Kinsey (1946) 74 C.A.2d 583, 596.

111. Smith v. Howard (1958) 158 C.A.2d 343.

112. Real Estate Bulletin (Spring 1976 & Fall 1991).

113. *See also* 34 Ops. Cal. Atty. Gen. 146 (1959). A broker may also advertise or offer a discount or credit against a commission to a buyer (Williams v. Kinsey [1946] 74 C.A.2d 583).

114. 24 C.F.R. 3500.14; 12 U.S.C. 2601-2617. For exemptions, *see* 12 U.S.C. 2607.

115. Comm. Regs. 2904.

116. Pro. C. 760.

117. Estate of Cattalini (1979) 97 C.A.3d 366. On the importance of obtaining prior court approval, *see* Estate of Ross (1980) 101 C.A.3d 895.

118. *See* Jorgensen, "New Probate Listing Form Now Available from C.A.R.," *California Association of Realtors* magazine (January 1975).

119. Pro. C. 10161. In one case, an order confirming sale was amended to provide for the commission, but the heirs

appealed, questioning the jurisdiction of the court to amend the order. The appellate court held that the probate court has exclusive jurisdiction to adjust brokers' claims, and ruled in favor of the broker—Estate of Efird (1955) 130 C.A.2d 227; Estate of Hughes (1935) 3 C.A.2d 551; Estate of Brown (1987) 193 C.A.3d 1612. Even though a broker is not properly licensed at the time he procures the buyer, if he is licensed at the time of confirmation, he is entitled to the commission—Estate of Lopez (1992) 8 C.A. 4th 317.

120. Pro. C. 10165. In the situation in which one broker has a listing, another broker brings in an offer that causes a confirmation hearing, and yet another broker's client overbids at the hearing, the courts appear to be in somewhat of a quandary since the Probate Code does not specifically cover this situation. *See also* Melikian, et al.. v. Aquila, Ltd. (1998) 63 C.A.4th 1364.

121. Simonini v. Passalacqua (1986) 180 C.A. 3d 400.

122. Pro. C. 9880.

123. Charles v. Webster Real Estate v. Rickard (1971) 21 C.A.3d 612.

124. Whitehead v. Gordon (1969) 2 C.A.3d 659; *see also* Batson v. Strehlow (1968) 68 C.2d 662.

125. Commission allowed: Estate of Baldwin (1973) 34 C.A.3d 596; Estate of Leventhal (1980) 105 C.A.3d 691. Commission not allowed: Estate of Toy (1977) 72 C.A.3d 392; Estate of Mitchell (1942) 20 C.2d 48.

126. Meyer v. Benko (1976) 55 C.A.3d 937.

127. *See* Figure 3-3 for C.A.R.'s latest form of purchase contract. Although no "form" is best for everyone, for the sake of consistency and a better understanding by all, in an effort to alleviate existing confusion the C.A.R. Purchase Contract should be considered in most situations. It is suggested that it and the Counter Offer form be discussed in detail. If there is more than one counteroffer, the seller should be sure to reject, in writing, the one or ones he does not want before accepting another.

128. *See* Figure 3-4 for C.A.R.'s Counter Offer form.

129. It is important to always use the latest edition of the C.A.R. purchase contract form.

130. Comm. Regs. 2900.

131. *See* Figure 3-3(a), paragraph 1.

132. Be wary of due-on-sale clause, discussed in §9.45.

133. Holloway v. Thiele (1953) 116 C.A.2d 68; Hogg v. Real Estate Comm. (1942) 54 C.A.2d 712.

134. *See* Figure 3-1.

135. Comm. Regs. 2832; *see* §4.41 for further details.

136. de St. Germain v. Watson (1950) 95 C.A.2d 862; *see also* Wilson v. Lewis (1980) 106 C.A.3d 802, 808.

137. *See* Wilson v. Lewis (1980) 106 C.A.3d 802.

138. Vineland Homes Inc. v. Barish (1956) 138 C.A.2d 747.

139. *See* Figure 3-3(b). Paragraph 20 is also important since the liquidated damage law makes a distinction between a one to four owner-occupied dwelling and nonresidential property (*see* §2.56).

140. Real Estate Bulletin, Dept. of Real Estate (Summer 1975); *see also* C.C. 2995; "Principal, Not Broker, Selects Escrow Agent," *California Association of Realtors* magazine (January 1973).

141. *See* Figure 3-3.

142. C.C. 1662; Dixon v. Salvation Army (1983) 142 C.A.3d 463.

143. Tinker v. McLellan (1958) 165 C.A.2d 291. Since buyers and sellers, landlords and tenants, and other parties can have separate insurable interests in the same property, it behooves each to obtain insurance. *See* Long v. Keller (1980) 104 C.A.3d 312, in which a lessee did not have insurance.

144. *See* Figure 3-3, paragraph 25; *see also* §2.57.

145. For example, *see* Citizens Savings & Loan v. Khoury (1978) 84 C.A.3d 244.

146. Erich v. Granoff (1980) 109 C.A.3d 920.

147. C.C. 884.010.

148. Kowal v. Day (1971) 20 C.A.2d 720; C.C. 3391.

149. Pacific Southwest Development Corporation v. Western Pacific Railroad Co. (1956) 47 C.2d 62. The "writing" can be the original lease of which the option is a part; therefore, it may not be necessary for the tenant to exercise the option in writing (Ripani v. Liberty Loan Corp. [1979] 95 C.A.3d 603).

150. *See* Rollins v. Stokes (1981) 123 C.A.3d 701.

4

Law of Agency and Regulation of Real Estate Agents

I. INTRODUCTION

§4.1. Scope of chapter

In this chapter, the general law of agency is considered as well as the agency relationship between a real estate licensee and the seller or buyer. *Agency* is defined, the authority of agents is listed, and the termination of agency is outlined. The broker–salesperson relationship is differentiated, and the role of the Department of Real Estate is set forth. The duties placed upon real estate licensees are constantly growing as the real estate field attains a professional status. Duties and liabilities of the real estate licensee are the subjects of Chapter 5, including the problem area of dual representation.

§4.2. Principal and agent

Most real estate transactions today use the services of a real estate broker. The real estate broker is ordinarily an *agent*, and the relationship between the broker and the person represented is substantially governed by the same general legal principles that apply to any agency relationship.

An agent is a person who represents another, called a *principal*, in dealing with third persons; such a relationship is called an *agency*. An agent acts for and in the place of the principal for the purpose of bringing him into legal relations with third persons. As is pointed out later, an agent is distinguished from a servant, an employee, or an independent contractor.

§4.3. Broker defined

Although a broker is an agent, the term *broker* is somewhat less inclusive than the term *agent*. The term *broker* generally applies to an agent who, for a commission or brokerage fee, acts as a negotiator or intermediary between the principal and third persons in connection with the acquisition of contractual rights, or the sale or purchase of property, real or personal, when the custody of the property is not entrusted to him for the purpose of discharging the agency. A broker is distinguished from a *middleman* or *finder* in that a broker helps bring about a meeting of the minds, whereas a middleman or finder merely introduces the parties and leaves the negotiations to them.[1]

II. THE AGENCY RELATIONSHIP

§4.4. In general

In most real estate transactions, the agency relationship is used in at least two situations. First, a *real estate broker* is employed as an agent for the owner of real property for the purpose of finding a buyer. Second, the services of an *escrow agent* are ordinarily used to consummate the transaction. The subject of escrows is considered further in Chapter 6.

§4.5. Agency defined

An *agency* is the relationship between a *principal* and an *agent* whereby the agent represents or acts on behalf of the principal in dealings with a third party.[2] From this simple relationship, a vast body of rules of law has emerged, governing the rights and duties of principal, agent, and third party. Agency is often referred to as a *triangular relationship*. In the ordinary sales transaction, the broker is the agent for the seller (the principal) in dealing with a third party, the buyer.

Special agency. The agency is not a general agency, however. The broker is a *special agent*, authorized to perform for a principal only in a particular transaction. That he is authorized to act in a number of transactions affecting various parcels of real property does not make the broker a general agent if he is given only limited authority in each transaction. As a general rule, the acts of a special agent do not bind the principal unless strictly within the authority conferred.

As described in Chapter 5, a broker's duties and responsibilities are not confined to the relationship with his principal. He also has certain responsibilities to the buyer or other parties to the transaction. The licensee is subject to regulation by the Real Estate Commissioner and also to laws of wider application, such as the Fair Housing Laws.

A real estate broker frequently uses the services of a salesperson. The salesperson is strictly the agent of the broker and cannot contract in his own name or accept money for services from any person other than the broker under whom he is licensed.[3] The broker is authorized to deal with the public and can contract in his own name, collect money, and perform other services within the scope of the contract between himself and his principal.

§4.6. Creation of agency

Anyone who has the capacity to contract may appoint an agent and any person may be an agent.[4] Although the relationship of principal and agent can be created in other ways, such as by ratification[5] or by estoppel, it is normally created by express contract. When it is created in this way, the basic principles of contract law apply. However, consideration is not always essential to the creation of an agency. One may gratuitously undertake to act as an agent and will be held to certain obligations of an ordinary agent on the assumption of these duties.[6] Generally, however, there is a contract, and consideration must be present in some form. It occurs in *unilateral* form when the principal signs a listing agreement promising compensation for services by the agent, and the agent thereafter renders the service requested. It may also be in *bilateral* form when, for instance, the broker enters into a counterpromise to "use due diligence" in finding a purchaser. The ultimate effect will, of course, depend on the specific type of agency contract used.

An agency relationship can be established even though a broker is acting under an oral contract of employment, for example, an oral open listing agreement. Such a relationship can be implied from the acts of the parties. Although a broker is ordinarily the agent of the seller who employs him, the broker may, without realizing it, act as agent of either buyer or seller or both at any stage of a particular transaction. If a broker contacts a potential buyer, or vice versa, to purchase real estate, writes up an offer, and takes it to the seller, the broker represents the buyer.[7] Depending upon what statements were made to the seller, the broker may also represent the seller at the same time. Thus a broker stands in a precarious position at all times. For example, whom does the broker represent if he presents a counteroffer to the buyer in the above situation?

The listing broker clearly represents the seller, to whom the broker owes a fiduciary duty to act in the highest good faith. Generally speaking, a salesperson in the listing broker's own office, or a cooperating licensee, likewise represents the seller in the absence of a clear indication to the contrary. There is a strong inference that a broker represents the person who pays the commission—although this inference can be rebutted. As to whom a real estate licensee represents and at what particular time, this is a gray area of the law. The salesperson should always be careful in this regard.

§4.7. Forms of agency agreements

A *listing agreement* between a broker and an owner of real property is a form of agency agreement.[8] The usual contract creating the relationship of broker and client authorizes the broker to find a purchaser. Although the agreement is referred to as an authorization to sell, this does not ordinarily mean that the broker can enter into a binding contract of sale with the purchaser; he is authorized merely to find a purchaser.

Another form of agency agreement is a *power of attorney*. This is in the form of a written instrument giving authority to an agent to act on behalf of a principal, either as a general agent or as a limited agent. The agent acting under such a grant of authority is called an attorney-in-fact. This form is considered in Chapter 7.

§4.8. Fiduciary duty

The duties and liabilities of real estate licensees to their principals and third parties are discussed in detail in Chapter 5. Suffice it to say at this point that the agent owes a definite *loyalty* to his principal, creating a fiduciary relationship that the law compares to that of a trustee and beneficiary under a trust.[9] To further analogize, the duty owed is similar to that between an attorney and client, or guardian and ward, or one spouse and the other spouse.

§4.9. Authority of agent

Once the agency relationship is created, the authority of the agent is to do everything necessary, proper, or usual in the ordinary course of business for the purpose of the agency, and to make representations as to facts involved in the transaction in which he is engaged. The authority of an agent may be actual or ostensible. *Actual authority* is that which the principal intentionally confers on the agent.[10] *Ostensible* authority is that which the principal intentionally or by want of ordinary care causes or allows third persons to believe the agent possesses.[11] Ostensible agency is also referred to as agency by estoppel. The acts or declarations of the agent alone do not establish ostensible authority. However, when the principal knows that the agent presents himself as clothed with certain authority which he does not have, and the principal remains silent, such conduct on the part of the principal may sometimes give rise to liability.

Emergency broadens authority. An agent has expanded authority in an emergency, including the power to disobey instructions when it is clearly in the interest of the principal and when there is no time to obtain instructions from the principal.[12]

Restrictions on authority. An agent can never have the authority, either actual or ostensible, to do an act that is—and is known or suspected to be by the person with whom the agent deals—a fraud upon the principal,[13] nor may an agent be authorized to perform an act to which the principal is bound to give his personal attention.[14]

Oral authorization (Equal Dignities Rule). An oral authorization is sufficient except that an authority required by law to be in writing can only be given by an instrument in writing.[15]

EXAMPLE In a husband–wife situation, one spouse does not have the power to bind the other to buy or sell real estate unless the authority to do so is written.[16] On the other hand, an oral request of a principal to have his name signed by his agent in or out of his presence (e.g., authority given over the phone) is an exception to this rule.[17]

Duty to ascertain agent's authority. A principal is not liable for the acts of the agent beyond the scope of his actual or ostensible authority. A third person who knowingly deals with an agent is under a duty to ascertain the scope of the agency.[18] If, for example, the agent acts beyond his authority, the third party cannot hold the principal. One case held, however, that "when an agent on behalf of the principal performs an unauthorized act, if the principal has put the agent in a position to mislead innocent parties, the principal is responsible to the latter."[19]

§4.10. Delegation of authority

Unless specifically forbidden by the principal, the powers of an agent can be delegated to another person in any of the following situations, and in no others:[20]

1. When the act is purely mechanical
2. When it is such as the agent cannot, and the subagent can, lawfully perform
3. When it is the common practice
4. When the delegation is specifically authorized

III. REAL ESTATE BROKER AS SPECIAL AGENT

§4.11. In general

A *real estate broker* is a person who, for compensation or expectation of compensation, carries out negotiations on behalf of a principal with respect to real property or business opportunities.[21] A broker includes one who

1. Sells or offers to sell, buys or offers to buy, solicits prospective sellers or purchasers, solicits or obtains listings or negotiates the purchase, sale, or exchange of real property, business opportunities, mobile homes,[22] or securities

2. Leases or rents or offers to lease or rent, or places for rent, or solicits listings of places for rent, or solicits prospective tenants, or negotiates the sale, purchase, or exchange of leases on real property or on a business opportunity, or collects rents therefrom

3. Solicits borrowers or lenders for or negotiates loans or collects payments or performs services for borrowers or lenders or note owners in connection with loans secured by liens on real property or business opportunities[23]

4. Sells or offers to sell, buys or offers to buy, or exchanges or offers to exchange a real property sales contract, or promissory note secured by a lien on real property, or a business opportunity, and performs services for the holders thereof

A person must also have a real estate license if he or she engages, as a principal, in the business of buying, selling, or exchanging eight or more real property sales contracts (installment land contracts)[24] or promissory notes during a calendar year.[25] However, if a person purchases, sells, or exchanges for his own account as an investment, and does not receive compensation, he is not a real estate broker within the meaning of the law.[26]

Penalties. It is a misdemeanor, punishable by a fine not exceeding $100 for each offense, to pay a commission or any compensation to an unlicensed person for performing acts for which a real estate license is required.[27] Further, any person acting as a broker or salesperson without a license shall be punished by a fine of up to $1,000 and/or six months in custody, or if a corporation, by a fine up to $10,000.[28] On the other hand, it is not a violation of the Real Estate Law if a broker advertises that if a buyer or seller brings an ad to the broker's office, and either lists with her or purchases real estate through her, the broker will agree to allow the seller credit of $50 on the commission under the listing, or credit the buyer with $50 on account of the purchase price.[29]

§4.12. Advance fee rental agents

An advance fee rental agent is a person who engages in the business of supplying prospective tenants with listings of residential real properties for tenancy pursuant to an arrangement under which the prospective tenants are required to pay a fee in advance of or contemporaneously with the supplying of the listings.[30]

Prior to the acceptance of a fee from a prospective tenant, an advance fee rental agent is required to provide the prospective tenant with a written contract containing certain information required by the Commissioner.[31]

EXAMPLE In one case, plaintiff operated a property rental data service. He actively solicited landlords, for free, and charged prospective tenants $15 for a pamphlet that described the apartment unit. The court held that plaintiff was required to hold a broker's license.[32]

§4.13. Exclusions

The following are not required to obtain a real estate broker's or salesperson's license:

1. Anyone dealing with his or her own property

2. Any regular officer of a corporation or general partner of a partnership, with respect to real estate owned by the corporation or partnership[33]

3. Anyone holding a duly executed power of attorney from the owner with respect to the real estate[34]

4. An attorney at law in rendering legal service to a client

5. A receiver, trustee in bankruptcy, or any person acting under order of any court

6. A trustee selling under a trust deed

7. Banks, savings and loans, industrial loan corporations, pension trusts, credit unions, or insurance companies[35]

8. A lender making a loan guaranteed by the federal government

9. Resident manager of an apartment, hotel, motel, trailer park, or the employees of the manager[36]

10. A stenographer, bookkeeper, receptionist, telephone operator, or other clerical help while performing those functions[37]

The above exemptions are not applicable to a person who uses them to evade the provisions of the licensing act.

Attorney engaging in real estate sales must have real estate license. Although an attorney, performing his duties as an attorney, need not have a real estate license in order to assist clients in real estate matters, he must have a real estate license if engaged in the practice of real estate and if expecting to receive a commission.

EXAMPLE In one case, the defendant broker was employed to sell a parcel of real estate. A prospective buyer was shown the property but wanted his lawyer to check it out first. In the course of the transaction, although the evidence was conflicting, the broker maintained that the plaintiff wanted half of the commission or else he would "blow the deal." When the escrow instructions were drafted, the defendant asked the plaintiff for the number of his broker's license. Upon learning he had none, the defendant refused to pay him any commission. The court held that the plaintiff was not entitled to any commission. If the defendant had paid an unlicensed person a real estate commission, he would have been violating the real estate law that expressly forbids such payment.[38]

§4.14. Out-of-state brokers

To sell real estate legally in California for another person, or recover a commission whether the land is located within or without California, the broker must be licensed *in* California. In fact, every nonresident applicant for a California real estate license must file with the Real Estate Commissioner an irrevocable consent to allow service of summons to be made on the Secretary of State.[39] However, a California broker may pay a commission to a broker from another state.[40] As far as recovery of a commission is concerned, a problem may exist.

EXAMPLE Assume a broker in Arizona, not licensed as a broker in California, lists a parcel of real estate located in California. Assume further that the contract was signed by the parties in Arizona, but the seller resides in California. Will the Arizona broker be permitted to recover a commission in California if suit is brought in California against the seller? That question has not been answered. However, it would seem safer for the Arizona broker to sue in Arizona (the place where the contract was signed), obtain judgment, and enforce it in California through the full faith and credit clause of the U.S. Constitution. It would appear that the same rationale would hold true if the case involved a California broker dealing with out-of-state property.[41]

The better practice may be to list the property with a broker in the state where the property is located on a previously agreed-upon commission split.

§4.15. Cooperating brokers

The general rule is that the listing broker can delegate duties to a co-op broker unless the principal forbids him from doing so. Actually, custom dictates that a listing broker cooperate with other brokers rather than monopolize the listing. When brokers cooperate, the principal obtains the most exposure and thus can more readily market his property, which is what the listing broker is hired to do. It is highly improbable that a broker can perform his duty to use his "best efforts" and not cooperate with other brokers. In fact, the National Association of Realtors' Code of Ethics, Article 22, states in part, "In the sale of property which is exclusively listed with a Realtor, the Realtor shall utilize the services of other brokers upon mutually agreed upon terms when it is in the best interest of the client."[42]

When a principal approves the use of a cooperating broker (through a Multiple Listing Service or otherwise), the cooperating broker represents the principal in the same manner as does the listing broker.[43] That is, although the law is somewhat unclear, when a cooperating broker is so endorsed by the principal, the listing broker is not responsible to third parties for the acts of the cooperating broker. On the other hand, if an agent utilizes a cooperating broker without authority from the principal, the cooperating broker is his agent and the principal has no connection with the cooperating broker.[44]

It should be borne in mind, however, that if a cooperating broker is authorized by the seller, the broker will be liable to the seller for any misrepresentations made by him to a buyer *even though the cooperating broker has never met the seller!*[45]

Interesting agency questions arise regarding real estate *exchanges* when all parties are represented by different brokers. Is each broker the agent of his principal and the other broker's principal because he is a cooperating broker? At present, there is little case law to help. The answer probably lies in the examination of individual fact situations, but will remain problematical for all brokers until determined.

IV. RELATIONSHIP BETWEEN BROKER AND SALESPERSON

§4.16. In general

A *real estate salesperson* is one who, for compensation, is employed by a *real estate broker* to perform the acts for which a real estate license is required.[46] A salesperson, to the same extent as the broker, is subject to the obligations arising out of the fiduciary relationship between broker and principal. A broker may nonetheless work for another broker and still keep his broker's license. He does not need to add the new broker's name to his license; only the change of address to the new broker's address is necessary.

Although perhaps liable for a salesperson's tort under the doctrine of respondeat superior, the broker is not responsible for punitive damages when the broker neither directed nor ratified the act. [47]

§4.17. Salesperson's and broker's licenses

A salesperson's license is issued for a four-year term. It remains in the possession of the employing broker until it is canceled, transferred, or inactivated, and it must be available for inspection by the Real Estate Commissioner.[48] It need not be displayed. The broker must notify the Commissioner in writing of a new salesperson within five days, and again when he is terminated within ten days.[49] If a salesperson is discharged for a violation of the Real Estate Law, the broker must forthwith file a written statement with the Commissioner.[50] A person's license cannot be lent to anyone else; one also cannot reproduce it or permit it to be used for any unlawful purpose.[51]

A broker acting as a salesperson may perform licensed activities at any office of the employing broker without having to obtain a branch office license.[52] Every licensee is required to maintain on file with the Commissioner his principal place of business and residence address and the address of the business where most of his activities occur. In addition, the broker must inform the Commissioner of each branch office.[53] A real estate licensee can refer to his or her status as: salesman, saleswoman, or salesperson.[54]

§4.18. Compensation of salesperson

Although salespeople are usually compensated by way of an agreed-upon percentage of the commissions received, there are some brokers who pay their salespeople salaries in lieu of commissions. In any event, a salesperson cannot contract for compensation from third parties in his own name; it must be on behalf of the employing broker. Further, no real estate salesperson may be employed by or accept compensation from any person other than the broker under whom he is licensed.[55] However, the direct payment to a salesperson, e.g., from a builder, as a "finder's fee" for introducing a prospective purchaser to the builder without performing any other act, is permissible. It is the Commissioner's view that since the mere act of introduction does not require a real estate license, then payment of a fee directly to the salesperson would not be a violation of the Real Estate Law; however, the D.R.E. takes a very narrow view of this.[56] On the other hand, special compensation from a cooperating broker to another broker's salesperson *must* be paid through the salesperson's broker.[57]

§4.19. Review of agreements

All real estate agreements prepared or signed by a salesperson that would materially affect the rights or duties of the parties to a transaction are required to be reviewed by the broker.[58]

§4.20. Broker-salesperson agreement

It is now mandatory that every broker have a written agreement with each of his salespeople, whether licensed as a salesperson or broker. The agreement must be dated and signed by the parties and cover the material aspects of the relationship between the parties, including supervision, duties, and compensation. The broker no longer needs to retain a copy for three years, but must have such an agreement. The retention time period is now left up to the broker.[59] It has been held that a written employment contract between a broker and salesperson may not be modified by subsequent oral agreement unless new consideration is given.[60]

A form of Broker-Associate Licensee Contract, published by the California Association of Realtors, appears as Figure 4-1. This is an independent contractor form.

EXAMPLE A real estate salesperson worked for a developer to sell his homes. The contract between them provided for a commission of 6.5 percent of the sales price for obtaining a fully executed contract that closed escrow, and a second commission

CALIFORNIA ASSOCIATION OF REALTORS®

BROKER-ASSOCIATE LICENSEE CONTRACT
(Independent-Contractor)

THIS AGREEMENT, made this _____ day of _____, 19_____ by and between
_____
_____ (hereinafter "Broker") and
_____ (hereinafter "Associate Licensee").
IN CONSIDERATION of the respective representations and covenants herein, Broker and Associate Licensee agree and contract as follows:

1. **BROKER:** Broker represents that he/she/it is duly licensed as a real estate broker by the State of California, ☐ doing business as _____
_____ (Firm name), ☐ a sole proprietorship, ☐ a partnership, ☐ a corporation.
Broker is a member of the _____ Board(s)/Association(s) of REALTORS7, and a Participant in the
_____ multiple listing service(s).

2. **ASSOCIATE LICENSEE:** Associate Licensee represents that, (a) he/she is duly licensed by the State of California as a ☐ real estate broker, ☐ real estate salesperson, and (b) he/she has not used any other names within the past five years except _____
_____. Broker shall keep his/her/its license current during the term of this agreement. Associate Licensee shall keep his/her license current during the term of this agreement, including satisfying all applicable continuing education and provisional license requirements.

3. **LISTING AND SALES ACTIVITIES:** Broker shall make available to Associate Licensee, equally with other licensees associated with Broker, all current listings in Broker's office, except any listing which Broker may choose to place in the exclusive servicing of Associate Licensee or one or more other specific licensees associated with Broker. Associate Licensee shall not be required to accept or service any particular listing or prospective listing offered by Broker, or to see or service particular parties. Broker shall not restrict Associate Licensee's activities to particular geographical areas. Broker shall not, except to the extent required by law, direct or limit Associate Licensee's activities as to hours, leads, open houses, opportunity or floor time, production, prospects, sales meetings, schedule, inventory, time off, vacation, or similar activities. In compliance with Commissioner's Regulation 2780, et seq. (Title 10, California Code of Regulations, §2780, et seq.), Broker and Associate Licensee shall at all times be familiar with, all applicable federal, California and local anti-discrimination laws.

4. **BROKER SUPERVISION:**
   (a) Associate Licensee shall submit for Broker's review:
   i. All documents which may have a material effect upon the rights and duties of principals in a transaction, within 24 hours after preparing, signing, or receiving same. Broker may exercise this review responsibility through another licensee provided the Broker and the designated licensee have complied with Commissioner's Regulation 2725 (Title 10, California Code of Regulations, §2725).
   ii. Any documents or other items connected with a transaction pursuant to this agreement, in the possession of or available to Associate Licensee, (i) immediately upon request by Broker or Broker's designated licensee, and/or (ii) as provided in Broker's Office Policy Manual, if any.
   iii. All documents associated with any real estate transaction in which Associate Licensee is a principal.
   (b) In addition, without affecting Associate Licensee's status, Broker shall have the right to direct Associate Licensee's actions to the extent required by law, and Associate Licensee shall comply with such directions. All trust funds shall be handled in compliance with Business and Professions Code §10145, and other applicable laws.

5. **OFFICE FACILITIES:** Broker shall make available for Associate Licensee's use, along with other licensees associated with Broker, the facilities of the real estate office operated by Broker at _____
and the facilities of any other office locations made available by Broker pursuant to this agreement.

6. **ASSOCIATE LICENSEE'S REPORT:** Associate Licensee shall work diligently and with his/her best efforts, (a) To sell, exchange, lease, or rent properties listed with Broker or other cooperating Brokers, (b) To solicit additional listings, clients, and customers, and (c) To otherwise promote the business of serving the public in real estate transactions to the end that Broker and Associate Licensee may derive the greatest benefit possible, in accordance with law.

7. **UNLAWFUL ACTS:** Associate Licensee shall not commit any act for which the Real Estate Commissioner of the State of California is authorized to restrict, suspend, or revoke Associates Licensee's license or impose other discipline, under California Business and Professions Code Sections 10176 or 10177 or other provisions of law.

8. **LISTING COMMISSIONS:** Commissions shall be charged to parties who desire to enter into listing agreements and other contracts for services requiring a real estate license, with Broker.
   ☐ as shown in "Exhibit A" attached which is incorporated as a part of this agreement by reference, or
   ☐ as follows: _____
   _____
   _____
   Any proposed deviation from that schedule must be reviewed and approved in advance by Broker. Any permanent change in commission schedule shall be disseminated by Broker to Associate Licensee.

9. **COMPENSATION TO ASSOCIATE LICENSEE:** Associate Licensee shall receive a share of commissions which are actually collected by Broker, on listings and other contracts for services requiring a real estate license which are solicited and obtained by Associate Licensee, and on transactions of which Associate Licensee's activities are the procuring cause,
   ☐ as shown in "Exhibit B" attached which is incorporated as a part of this agreement by reference, or
   ☐ as follows: _____
   _____
   _____
   _____
   _____
   The above commissions may be varied by written agreement between Broker and Associate Licensee before completion of any particular transaction. Expenses which must be paid from commissions, or are incurred in the attempt to collect commissions, shall be paid by Broker and Associate Licensee in the same proportion as set forth for the division of commissions.

10. **DIVIDING COMPENSATION WITH OTHER LICENSEES IN OFFICE:** If Associate Licensee and one or more other licensees associated with Broker both participate on the same side (either listing or selling) of a transaction, the commission allocated to their combined activities shall be divided by Broker and paid to them according to the written agreement between them which shall be furnished in advance to Broker.

11. **COMMISSIONS PAID TO BROKER:** All commission will be received by Broker. Associate Licensee's share of commissions shall be paid to him/her, after deduction of offsets, immediately upon collection by Broker or as soon thereafter as practicable, except as otherwise provided in (a) Paragraph 9, above, (b) Broker's Office Policy Manual, or (c) A Separate written agreement between Broker and Associate Licensee. Broker may impound in Broker's account Associate Licensee's share of commissions on transactions in which there is a known or pending claim against Broker and/or Associate Licensee, until such claim is resolved.

12. **UNCOLLECTED COMMISSIONS:** Neither Broker nor Associate Licensee shall be liable to the other for any portion of commissions not collected. Associate Licensee shall not be entitled to any advance payment from Broker upon future commissions.

THIS FORM HAS BEEN APPROVED BY THE CALIFORNIA ASSOCIATION OF REALTORS® (C.A.R.). NO REPRESENTATION IS MADE AS TO THE LEGAL VALIDITY OR ADEQUACY OF ANY PROVISION IN ANY SPECIFIC TRANSACTION. A REAL ESTATE BROKER IS THE PERSON QUALIFIED TO ADVISE ON REAL ESTATE TRANSACTIONS. IF YOU DESIRE LEGAL OR TAX ADVICE, CONSULT AN APPROPRIATE PROFESSIONAL.
This form is available for use by the entire real estate industry. It is not intended to identify the user as a REALTOR®. REALTOR® is a registered collective membership mark which may be used only by members of the NATIONAL ASSOCIATION OF REALTORS® who subscribe to its Code of Ethics.
The copyright laws of the United States (17 U.S. Code) forbid the unauthorized reproduction of this form by any means, including facsimile or computerized formats.
Copyright © 1990-1997, CALIFORNIA ASSOCIATION OF REALTORS®

Published and Distributed by:
REAL ESTATE BUSINESS SERVICES, INC.
a subsidiary of the CALIFORNIA ASSOCIATION OF REALTORS®
525 South Virgil Avenue, Los Angeles, California 90020

┌─ OFFICE USE ONLY ─┐
Reviewed by Broker
or Designee _____
Date _____
└────────────────┘

EQUAL HOUSING OPPORTUNITY

FORM I-14 REVISED 1990

Figure 4-1
Broker-Associate Licensee Contract

13. **ASSOCIATE LICENSEE EXPENSES; OFFSETS:** Associate Licensee shall provide and pay for all professional licenses, supplies, services, and other items required in connection with Associate Licensee's activities under this agreement, or any listing or transaction, without reimbursement from Broker except as required by law. If Broker elects to advance funds to pay expenses or liabilities of Associate Licensee shall pay to Broker the full amount advanced on demand, or Broker may deduct the full amount advanced from commissions payable to Associate Licensee on any transaction without notice.

14. **INDEPENDENT CONTRACTOR RELATIONSHIP:** Broker and Associate Licensee intend that, to the maximum extent permissible by law, **(a)** This agreement does not constitute a hiring or employment agreement by either party, **(b)** Broker and Associate Licensee are independent contracting parties with respect to all services rendered under this agreement or in any resulting transactions, **(c)** Associate Licensee's only remuneration shall be his.her proportional share, if any, of commissions collected by Broker, **(d)** Associate Licensee retains sole and absolute discretion and judgment in the methods, techniques, and procedures to be used in soliciting and obtaining listings, sales, exchanges, leases, rentals, or other transactions, and in carrying out Associate Licensee's selling and soliciting activities, except as required by law or in Broker's Office Policy Manual, **(e)** Associate Licensee is under the control of Broker as to the results of Associate Licensee's work only, and not as to the means by which those results are accomplished except as required by law, or in Broker's Office Policy Manual, if any, **(f)** This Agreement shall not be construed as a partnership, **(g)** Associate Licensee has no authority to bind Broker by any promise or representation unless specifically authorized by Broker in writing, **(h)** Broker shall not be liable for any obligation or liability incurred by Associate Licensee, **(i)** Associate Licensee shall not be treated as an employee with respects to services performed as a real estate agent, for state and federal tax purposes, and **(j)** The fact the Broker may carry worker compensation insurance for his/her/its own benefit and for the mutual benefit of Broker and licensees associated with Broker, including Associate Licensee, shall not create or inference of employment.

15. **LISTING AND OTHER AGREEMENTS PROPERTY OF BROKER:** All listings of property, and all agreements for performance of licensed acts, and all acts or actions required a real estate license which are taken or performed in connection with this agreement, shall be taken and performed in the name of Broker. All listings shall be submitted to Broker within 24 hours after receipt by Associate Licensee. Associate Licensee agrees to and does hereby contribute all right and title to such listings to Broker for the benefit and use of Broker, Associate Licensee, and other licensees associated with Broker.

16. **TERMINATION OF RELATIONSHIP:** Broker or Associate Licensee may terminate their relationship under this agreement at any time, on 24 hours written notice, with or without cause. Even after termination, this agreement shall govern all disputes and claims between Broker and Associate Licensee connected with their relationship under this agreement, including obligations and liabilities arising from existing and completed listings, transactions, and services.

17. **COMMISSIONS AFTER TERMINATION AND OFFSET:** If this agreement is terminated while Associate Licensee has listings or pending transactions that require further work normally rendered by Associate Licensee, Broker shall make arrangements with another licensee associated with Broker to perform the required work, or shall perform the work him/herself. The licensee performing the work shall be reasonably compensated for completing work on those listings or transactions, and such reasonable compensation shall be deducted from Associate Licensee's share of commissions. Except for such offset, Associate Licensee shall receive his/her regular share of commissions on such sales or other transactions, if actually collected by Broker, after deduction of any other amounts or offsets provided in this agreement.

18. **ARBITRATION OF DISPUTES:** All disputes or claims between Associate Licensee and other licensee(s) associated with Broker, or between Associate Licensee and Broker, arising from or connected in any way with this agreement, which cannot be adjusted between the parties involved, shall be submitted to the Board of REALTORS® of which all such disputing parties are members for arbitration pursuant to the provisions of its Bylaws, as may be amended from time to time, which are incorporated as a part of this agreement by reference. If the Bylaws of the Board do not cover arbitration of the dispute, or if the Board declines jurisdiction over the dispute, then arbitration shall be pursuant to the rules of the American Arbitration Association, as may be amended from time to time, which are incorporated as a part of this agreement by reference. The Federal Arbitration Act, Title 9, U.S. Code, Section 1, et seq., shall govern this agreement.

19. **PROPRIETARY INFORMATION AND FILES:** Associate Licensee shall not use to his/her own advantage, or the advantage of any other person, business, or entity, except as specified provided in this agreement, either during Associate Licensee;s association with Broker or thereafter, any information gained for or from the business or files of Broker. All files and documents pertaining to listings and transactions are the property of Broker and shall be delivered to Broker by Associate Licensee immediately upon request or upon termination of their relationship under this agreement.

20. **INDEMNITY AND HOLD HARMLESS:** All claims, demands, liabilities, judgments, and arbitration awards, including costs and attorney's fees, to which Broker is subjected by reason of any action taken or omitted by Associate Licensee in connection with services rendered or to be rendered pursuant to this agreement, shall be:

☐ Paid in full by Associate Licensee, who hereby agrees to indemnify and hold harmless Broker for all such sums, or

☐ Other: _____
_____
_____

Associate Licensee shall pay to Broker the full amount due by him/her demand, or Broker may deduct the full amount due by Associate Licensee from commissions due on any transaction without notice.

21. **ADDITIONAL PROVISIONS:** _____
_____
_____

22. **DEFINITIONS:** As used in this agreement, the following terms have the meanings indicated:
   (a) "Listing" means an agreement with a property owner or other party to locate a buyer, exchange party, lessee, or other party to a transaction involving real property, a mobile home, or other property or transaction which may be brokered by a real estate licensee, or an agreement with a party to locate or negotiate for any such property or transaction.
   (b) "Commission means compensation for acts requiring a real estate license, regardless of whether calculated as a percentage of transaction price, flat fee, hourly rate, or in any other manner.
   (c) "Transaction" means a sale, exchange, lease, or rental of real property, a business opportunity, or a mobile home which may lawfully be brokered by a real estate licensee, or a loan secured by any property of those types.
   (d) "Associate Licensee" means the real estate broker or real estate salesperson licensed by the State of California and rendering the services set forth herein for Associate Licensee.

23. **NOTICES:** All notices under this agreement shall be in writing. Notices may be delivered personally, or by certified U.S. mail, postage prepaid, or by facsimile, to the parties at the addresses noted below. Either party may designate a new address for purposes of this agreement by giving notice to the other party. Notices mailed shall be deemed received as of 5:00 P.M. on the second business day following the date of mailing.

24. **ATTORNEY FEES:** In any action, proceeding, or arbitration between Broker and Associate Licensee arising from or related to this agreement, the prevailing party shall, in the discretion of the court or arbitrator, be entitled to reasonable attorney fees in addition to other appropriate relief.

25. **ENTIRE AGREEMENT; MODIFICATION:** All prior agreements between the parties concerning their relationship as Broker and Associate Licensee are incorporated in this agreement, which constitutes the entire contract. Its terms are intended by the parties as a final and complete expression of their agreement with respect to its subject matter, and may not be contradicted by evidence of any prior agreement or contemporaneous oral agreement. This agreement may not be amended, modified, altered, or changed in any respect whatsoever except by a further agreement in writing duly executed by Broker and Associate Licensee.

BROKER: **ASSOCIATE LICENSEE:**

_____   _____
(Signature)   (Signature)

_____   _____
(Name Printed)   (Name Printed)

_____   _____
(Address)   (Address)

_____   _____
(City, State, Zip)   (City, State, Zip)

_____   _____
(Telephone)   (Fax)   (Telephone)   (Fax)

NOTE: (1) Broker and Associate Licensee should each receive an executed copy of this agreement.

(2) Attach commission schedules Exhibits A and B if applicable.

Figure 4-1 (*Cont.*)
Broker-Associate Licensee Contract

of 3.5 percent for servicing the contract through close of escrow. The contract further provided that the salesperson would be entitled to both commissions upon termination of the employment if escrow were closed before termination. The salesperson resigned before close of escrow on one transaction and demanded the additional 3.5 percent of the commission.

The court held that the salesperson was in an equal bargaining position and did not have to accept the agreement when first employed. Therefore, the contract was not a contract of adhesion. The additional commission of 3.5 percent was an incentive for salespeople to remain on the job until escrow closed. To allow salespeople to receive the 3.5 percent would necessitate other salespeople to service the transaction without pay. Therefore, the salesperson is not entitled to the additional 3.5 percent.[61]

§4.21. Salesperson acting as principal

When a salesperson who owns real estate sells it, what obligation does he have to notify his broker? Does he have to pay the broker a commission? The law requires that when a salesperson enters into an agreement, as a principal, to buy or sell real estate, business opportunity, or mobile home, he shall make a written disclosure of the fact to the supervising broker within five days from the execution of the agreement or before consummation of the transaction, whichever occurs first.[62] As to any possible commission to be paid to the broker, that depends upon the agreement between the broker and salesperson. In any event, the broker–salesperson agreement should spell out any commission the broker will receive, if any, on the sale of any or all property bought or sold by a salesperson.

§4.22. Employee versus independent contractor

It is common practice in real estate to refer to a salesperson as an independent contractor.[63] However, what the parties call this relationship is not determinative. The test of whether a salesperson is an independent contractor or employee is the *right of control* the broker has over the salesperson. Since the broker is required by law to supervise his salespeople (which was further clarified by the Department of Real Estate in 1997), the law imposes the *responsibility* for control on him. The duty to supervise includes the obligation to review, oversee, inspect, and manage documents that may have a material effect upon the rights or obligations of a party to the transaction, and the obligation to supervise regarding the handling of trust funds and advertising.[64] Therefore, it is probable that in some instances a salesperson is an employee and not an independent contractor.[65] In fact, as between a broker and a third person, a salesperson is an agent and not an independent contractor as a matter of law, if the salesperson is acting within the scope of his employment.[66] For the broker to avoid potential damage brought against him for the negligence of his salespeople, it would be advisable for the broker to carry public liability insurance on all salespeople as well as office personnel. It is also advisable that the broker be named as coinsured on a saleperson's automobile coverage and be notified in the event of cancellation of such insurance. Although generally an employer is not liable to a third person for the negligence of the employee going to and coming from work, there are exceptions to that rule. One of those exceptions is the outside salesperson who is involved in both office work and field work.[67]

Definition. An employee acts when, how, and in the manner prescribed by the employer. The employee is "every person in the service of an employer under any appointment or contract of hire or apprenticeship, express or implied, oral or written, whether lawfully or unlawfully employed."[68] An *independent contractor* is "any person who renders service for a specified recompense for a specified result, under the control of his principal *as to the result of his work only* and not as to the means by which such result is accomplished."[69]

Worker's compensation. Whether or not a real estate salesperson will be treated as an employee or independent contractor under the Worker's Compensation Act has not been definitely established; however, generally he *will* be considered an employee.[70] It is therefore advisable for the broker to carry Worker's Compensation Insurance on all salespeople. In fact, if an employer is not so insured, he is subject to a fine of $300 and/or six months in custody.[71]

California State Unemployment Insurance. Ordinarily, a real estate salesperson is compensated by virtue of a commission. In that event, the broker is not required to withhold for unemployment; however, to be exempt, the licensee must be remunerated *solely* by way of commission, and there must be a written contract between the salesperson and broker that provides that "the salesperson will not be treated as an employee for state tax purposes."[72]

Federal Income Tax Withholding and Social Security Tax. If a licensee is truly an independent contractor, the broker is not required to withhold. If the licensee is an employee, these taxes must be withheld even though the employee is paid in the form of a commission. According to the Internal Revenue Service, if a licensee is subject to the details and means by which the result is accomplished, as well as the result itself, an employer–employee relationship exists. It is not necessary that the broker *actually* exercise control. Beginning in 1983, a qualified real estate agent is not to be treated as an employee of the broker; therefore, the broker is not required to withhold.[73] Now, in order to comply with the law, to qualify for independent contractor status, specific state and federal requirements must be met. Among these are a written contract between the independent contractor and the broker expressly stating that the independent contractor will not be treated as an employee for state and federal tax purposes pursuant to the services performed.[74]

Minimum Wage Law. When a broker and salesperson enter into a written independent contractor contract whereby the salesperson is to be paid by commission, and when there is minimal control over the salesperson, for purposes of the minimum wage law, the salesperson will usually not be treated as an employee and therefore will not be entitled to the minimum wage.[75]

This area is cloudy at best. One may think an independent contractor relationship exists when, in fact, an employer–employee relationship does. It is prudent to consult an attorney for advice regarding the particular situation.

§4.23. Trade secrets

A trade secret may consist of any formula, pattern, device, or compilation of information that is used in one's business and that gives one an opportunity to obtain an advantage over competitors who do not know or use it. Although the nature of a trade secret is somewhat nebulous, a characteristic common to those secrets that have found protection from disclosure and use by the courts is the need for their continued use by the former employer in order to maintain a competitive advantage over others.[76]

A broker must allege that his real estate listings are trade secrets and necessary for the continued operation of his business, or that the use of this information by a former employee would result in a loss of patronage by those persons who gave the listings.

One case held that

> There is no certainty that a sale will follow a listing, or that another listing will follow, or even that the seller or buyer will have need for the further services of the broker. Further patronage of the broker by the buyer or seller of real property will ordinarily depend on whether the broker can satisfy the buyer or seller that it will adequately service them in buying or selling their properties under satisfactory financial terms…. A former employee has the right to engage in a com-

petitive business for himself and to enter into competition with his former employer, provided such competition is fairly and legally constructed.... This right may be limited by the employee himself upon entering into an employment contract....

V. TERMINATION OF AGENCY

§4.24. In general

The parties may agree to terminate an agency, the principal may revoke it, or the agent may renounce it.[77] An agency or employment is also terminated by expiration of a specified term, extinction of the subject matter, or death or incapacity of either the principal or agent. Incapacity on the part of the agent is a valid ground for termination, as well as a discharge of the agent by the principal for cause. If in the case of an open listing, for example, the agency contract provides that it is to remain in effect until written notice is given, the agency continues until the notice of revocation is received; however, when a broker–client relationship appears from the terms of the contract to have been created for an indefinite period of time, there is a presumption in favor of the relationship.[78]

§4.25. Agency coupled with an interest

Unless an agency is coupled with an interest, it can be terminated by the principal at any time prior to the actual execution of the agency by the agent. The power on the part of the principal to revoke should be distinguished from the right to do so. That is, if a principal wrongfully terminates an agent, this may give rise to damages.

If the agency is created for the benefit of the agent or a third person, the principal may not terminate the relationship at will. Consequently, it is *irrevocable* by the principal and will not be terminated by the death or incapacity of the principal.[79] A mere statement in the contract that the agency is irrevocable or coupled with an interest is ineffective. Further, in an ordinary agency listing, even though the agent incidentally may benefit by receiving a commission, it does not make the contract one "coupled with an interest."

VI. ADMINISTRATIVE REGULATIONS

§4.26. In general

Real estate brokers are regulated by the provisions of the Real Estate Law for the purposes, among others, of raising the standards of the profession and requiring its members to act fairly and ethically with their clients. A primary function of the law is to allow only those persons who are honest, truthful, and reputable to operate as brokers or salespersons. The enactment of the Real Estate Law is within the general power of the state to regulate any occupation whose members should be specially qualified. Good moral character on the part of persons engaged in the real estate profession may reasonably be required as a safeguard to the public.

§4.27. Department of Real Estate

The California Department of Real Estate was created by legislative act in 1917. It was the first act of this nature to become law in the United States and has served as a pattern for similar legislation in many other states. The enactment was sponsored by real estate brokers who felt that reasonable regulation of persons engaged in the business of real estate would benefit the public and help to create and maintain higher professional and ethical standards. Although the first law was declared unconstitutional, another law was enacted in 1919 which, with subsequent amendments, has been in force since that date. The jurisdiction of the Department of Real Estate extends not only to the issuance of licenses but also to their suspension or revocation, and also includes the regulation of the sale of subdivisions in addition to other activities.

§4.28. Real Estate Advisory Commission

The Real Estate Commissioner, appointed by the governor for a four-year term, is the chief officer of the Department of Real Estate, and is chairman of the Real Estate Advisory Commission, composed of ten members. Six members are required by law to be experienced in the real estate business. Four are public members. The commission is authorized to inquire into the needs of real estate licensees, to confer and advise with the governor and other state officers on real estate matters, and to pass on the claims of equivalent experience or educational qualification made by applicants for the broker's license who have not been engaged actively full time as real estate salespersons in California for two years.[80]

§4.29. Duties of Real Estate Commissioner

The Real Estate Commissioner is charged with the enforcement of the Real Estate Law, and in this connection has full power to regulate and control the issuance, suspension, and revocation of all licenses under that law, and to perform all other acts and duties provided in the law and necessary for its enforcement. The Commissioner is empowered to promulgate necessary rules and regulations for the administration and enforcement of the law and for the conduct of his office. These regulations have the same effect as the Real Estate Law and become a part of the California Administrative Code. One of the Commissioner's most important functions is the licensing of real estate brokers and salespersons.

§4.30. Real estate licenses

Under the provisions of the Real Estate Law, it is unlawful for any person to engage in the business of, act in the capacity of, or advertise or assume to act as a real estate broker or salesperson without first obtaining a license from the Department of Real Estate.[81]

All licenses issued by the Real Estate Commissioner are for a term of four years. A broker or salesperson's license may be renewed every four years on proper application, payment of the required fee, and furnishing proof as to the educational requirement,[82] unless it has been revoked as a disciplinary measure.

Real estate broker's license. The applicant for a real estate broker's license must (1) be at least 18 years old; (2) have had previous experience and education as required by law; (3) evidence a reputation for honesty and truthfulness; (4) complete certain college courses; and (5) pass the examination.[83] The Real Estate Law requires that every applicant for a real estate broker license must either have been actively engaged as a real estate salesperson for at least two years during the five years immediately preceding the application, or prove to the satisfaction of the Real Estate Advisory Commission that he or she has had general real estate experience that would be the equivalent of two years of full-time experience as a salesperson. As an alternative means of qualification, the applicant may show graduation from an accredited four-year university or college and completion of the required real estate courses.

Effective January 1, 1986, the applicant must have completed eight classes of three semester-units each or the quarter equivalent thereof in college-level courses in (1) legal aspects of real estate; (2) real estate practice; (3) real estate finance; (4) real estate appraisal; (5) real estate economics or accounting; and (6) three of the following: real estate principles, business law, property management, real estate office administration, escrows, advanced legal aspects of real estate, advanced real estate finance, or advanced real estate appraisal.[84] If an applicant completes both real estate economics and accounting, only two courses listed in group (6) are required.

Real estate salesperson's license. The applicant for a real estate salesperson's license must (1) be at least 18 years old; (2) have the application for license signed by the licensed broker who is to employ the applicant when qualified by examination (if the license is to be issued on an inactive basis, no broker signature is required); (3) be of good reputation for honesty and truthfulness; (4) pass an examination as required, and (5) pass a real estate principles course and within 18 months thereafter pass two other real estate courses.[85]

Qualifications of applicants for a license. Applicants for a real estate license show, by written examination, an appropriate knowledge of the English language, including reading, writing, and spelling, and of arithmetic common to real estate and business opportunity practices; an understanding of the principles of real estate and business opportunity conveyancing, the general purposes and general legal effects of deeds, mortgages, land contracts of sale and leases, agency contracts and purchase contracts, and of the elementary principles of land economics and appraisals; and a general and fair understanding of the obligations between principal and agent, of the principles of real estate practice and the canons of business ethics pertaining thereto, as well as pertinent provisions of the California Real Estate Law, including the regulation of subdivided lands.[86]

Licensing of corporations and partnerships. The provision of the law requiring brokers to be licensed applies to corporations and partnerships as well as to individuals. However, the law was amended in 1968 to eliminate a partnership license. Partnerships can exist in the real estate business, but all members of a partnership performing activities calling for a license must be licensed individually as brokers.[87]

If a partner in a real estate brokerage operation is a nonlicensee and will not be performing acts for which a license is required, the partner need not have a real estate license.[88] If an unlicensed partner is entitled by agreement to share in the commission earned and received by the partnership, he will be taxed on his share as ordinary income, but he cannot sue for the commission if it is not paid.[89]

A corporation can be licensed as a real estate broker, but only if at least one officer is a duly qualified real estate broker.[90] In fact, a broker can be the designated officer for any number of licensed real estate corporations.[91]

If the qualified officer of the corporation wishes to transact business as an individual or for another firm, he must secure a separate license.[92] If for any reason there is no remaining officer licensed to transact business on behalf of the corporation, the license of the corporation is automatically canceled. Upon the qualifying of another officer or officers, the license of the corporation will be reinstated with payment of the proper fee.[93]

A salesperson cannot be a majority shareholder, director, or officer. However, these provisions do not apply in the case of a corporation licensed to act through an individual real estate broker who is an officer and director of a corporation and who has the responsibility to supervise the performance of acts for which a real estate license is required by those real estate salespersons who are shareholders, officers, or directors of the corporation.[94] In other words, a salesperson may now be a majority shareholder, officer, or director provided the designated broker for the corporation is also a director and officer and is in a position to exercise supervision over the salesperson. A certified copy of any resolution of the board of directors assigning responsibility over the licensed salespeople in the corporation must be filed with the Real Estate Commissioner within five days after adoption.[95]

Suspension of license. For a violation of the Real Estate Law, the Commissioner may deny, suspend, or revoke the license of any officer or agent acting under a corporate real estate license without revoking the license of the corporation.[96] If the corporate real estate license is revoked or suspended, the licenses of *all* officers to act as brokers on behalf of the corporation are automatically revoked. If disciplinary action is not expressly imposed against the individual officer as well as the corporation, the supervision or termination shall be without prejudice to the right of that individual to obtain another real estate broker license.[97]

§4.31. Business and branch office

A licensee must have a definite place of business;[98] however, if the broker is a member of a partnership, he may operate from a branch office without obtaining an individual branch office license, provided one of the member's broker's license is at the location.[99] The Commissioner must be notified of any change of address. There is no longer a fee for doing so.

Business license. Local municipalities often require that each broker obtain a business license. Occasionally doing business in a particular location may not require such a license or the need to pay a tax.

EXAMPLES
1. A broker filed an action for declaratory relief and an injunction contending a license tax ordinance should not be applicable to him. His only office was in a neighboring city and he only occasionally did business in the defendant city. The court granted him summary judgment declaring the ordinance void as to this broker.[100]

2. No license fee for the privilege of auctioning real estate may be collected from any real estate auctioneer whose business is limited exclusively to auctioning real estate, except by the city in which the auctioneer has a permanent place of business.[101]

---

§4.32. Fictitious business names

If a broker is to engage in the real estate business under a fictitious firm name, that fictitious name must appear on the broker's license in accordance with the rules and regulations of the Real Estate Commissioner.[102] Other rules and regulations pertain to branch offices, signs and license display, and many other related matters.

§4.33. Business opportunity

A real estate license is required for a person to engage in the sale of business opportunities. Such persons are defined in terms of acts similar to those performed by real estate brokers, but with reference to *business opportunities.* This term means and includes business, business opportunity, and goodwill of an existing business. The primary distinction between the business of real estate brokerage and that of business opportunity brokerage lies in the respective subject matters.[103] The term *real estate* as used in the Real Estate Law is regarded as synonymous with *real property.* Thus, an equity in real estate under a contract of purchase is included within the scope of real estate brokerage. The sale of a business opportunity, however, involves the sale of personal property, and the rules and laws governing the transfer of chattels generally apply.

§4.34. Mineral, oil, and gas brokers

Mineral, oil, and gas brokers are also subject to regulations under the Real Estate Law [104] and are required to obtain a mineral, oil, and gas license from the Department of Real Estate. The law defines mineral, oil, and gas property as land used for, intended to be used for, or concerning which representations are made with respect to the mining of minerals or the extraction of oil and gas therefrom. This law differs from the law affecting real estate brokers in one important respect: It has a special provision requiring that each licensee maintain with the Real Estate Commissioner a bond in the penal sum of $5,000.

Exception from license requirements. The sections of the code requiring mineral, oil, and gas operators to obtain a license make an exception of licensed real estate brokers who engage in the sale, lease, or exchange of real property or an interest therein in those cases in which the transfer of mineral, oil, or gas property is *purely incidental* to the sale, lease, or exchange of real property.

EXAMPLE If the property to be conveyed, leased, or exchanged is primarily of agricultural value, the fact that it may have some incidental oil and gas or mineral value does not require the broker to hold a mineral, oil, and gas license. Many real estate brokers specialize in the sale of orchards and other types of agricultural property in the San Joaquin and Sacramento valleys. This property may also have some mineral value. If the latter is incidental to the agricultural value, the broker is regarded as engaged in a real estate transaction rather than in a transaction in mineral, gas, or oil property. Further, the law provides that a real estate broker who occasionally makes a transfer of mineral, oil, or gas property as an incident to his real estate business may secure a permit for such transaction from the Real Estate Commissioner without having to obtain a license. No more than ten such permits may be issued by the Commissioner in any fiscal year to any one licensee.

§4.35. Mortgage loan brokers

It has been a longtime requirement of the Real Estate Law that the person who negotiates a loan on real property for another and for a compensation must be licensed as a real estate broker or salesperson. In 1955, because of complaints of hidden charges and excessive commissions exacted by some brokers, the legislature passed the Real Property Loan Brokerage Law. The law became inadequate to cope with objectionable practices, however, and the legislature enacted a new law, which is regarded as the most comprehensive and stringent mortgage loan legislation in California history. It also established a new classification for real estate brokers engaged in the sale of real estate securities, namely Real Property Securities Dealers, and established controls on such dealers' operations.[105]

In 1963 additional provisions were added, extending the coverage to conservatorship and liquidation proceedings and to the treatment of merchandising of out-of-state subdivision properties under the securities sections of the Real Estate Law.[106]

EXAMPLES
1. In a recent case it was held that a mortgage loan broker is liable to the lender for the fraud or negligence of an independent property appraiser it hires to appraise property.[107] This rationale can readily be carried through to any broker who does not verify the competence of any individual contractor he hires to assist in a real estate transaction, whether it be, for example, an appraiser, contractor, or termite inspector.

2. In another case, it was held that a purchaser who exchanged 24 promissory notes secured by second trust deeds for real property worth $80,000 was engaged in the business of selling real property securities within the meaning, and in violation, of the Real Property Securities Dealer's Act.[108]

3. A mortgage loan broker is customarily the borrower's agent. As such, the principal can justifiably rely on his oral representations. In a recent case, plaintiffs were persons of modest means and limited experience in financial affairs. They retained a broker to negotiate complex loan transactions. Defendants were sued for breach of fiduciary duty, civil conspiracy, misleading television commercials, and misrepresentation about terms. The television ads contained terms that were not available. Defendants used "bait and switch" tactics and charged late penalties that were not due. Defendants were found liable for $25,000 plus $200,000 punitive damages.[109]

4. Another case presented facts that mortgage loan brokers are prohibited from placing any funds for investment, from whatever source, unless they are secured by a lien on real estate. The court also held that mortgage loan brokers are not permitted to issue unsecured notes in exchange for payoff funds.[110]

5. A mortgage loan broker cannot use broker-controlled funds in a real estate transaction without the express written consent of the borrower. Broker-controlled

funds are funds owned by the broker, or funds owned by a person related to a broker, or funds in which the broker has a 10 percent ownership interest.[111]

§4.36. Application of corporate securities law

In 1955 the law was amended to clarify the uncertain situation with respect to jurisdiction of the Department of Real Estate and the Department of Corporations over persons selling promissory notes secured by a lien on real property. It is now specifically provided that the Corporate Securities Law does not apply to the sale of any security (other than an interest in a real estate development) the issuance of which is subject to authorization by the Real Estate Commissioner, or of a promissory note secured by a lien on real property that is not one of a series of notes secured by interests in the same real property.[112]

§4.37. Franchising

The Franchise Investment Law was enacted in 1970 to regulate the sale of franchises.[113] Before the enactment of this law, the sale of franchises in California was subject only to very limited regulation. Essentially, the law is a modified disclosure law designed to provide a prospective purchaser with full and adequate disclosure of all material terms of the franchise agreement.

The word *franchise* as used in the law[114] means a contract or agreement between two or more persons by which

1. A franchisee is granted the right to engage in the business of offering, selling, or distributing goods or services under a marketing plan or system prescribed in substantial part by a franchisor.

2. The operation of the franchisee's business pursuant to such plan or system is substantially associated with the franchisor's trademark, service mark, trade name, logotype, advertising, or other commercial symbol designating the franchisor or its affiliate.

3. The franchisee is required to pay, directly or indirectly, a franchise fee.

The intent of the law is to compel a franchisor to furnish a prospective franchisee with sufficient information to enable him to make an intelligent decision regarding the franchise being offered. The law provides that a franchisor who proposes to offer or sell a franchise must register such sale with the Corporation Commissioner. A person licensed as a real estate broker or real estate salesperson is authorized to sell franchise interests.

EXAMPLE

In 1978, the United States Supreme Court affirmed a judgment of the United States District Court of Nevada which had upheld a regulation of the Nevada Real Estate Advisory Commission requiring that not less than 50 percent of the surface area of an advertisement of a broker using a franchise name be devoted to the broker's own name as opposed to the franchised trade name or logo type. In reaching its decision, the Nevada District Court concluded that the 50:50 advertising rule constituted a "legitimate means to the legitimate and important end of insuring that the public realizes it is doing business with an independent broker and not a national firm when it buys or sells real estate in Nevada."

Franchised brokers in California should make it clear in their advertising that they are independent firms so as not to create an impression in the mind of a reader of the advertisement that services and benefits of a giant nationwide organization will be available to him if he engages the services of the local franchisee.[115]

§4.38. Activities of Department in aid of licensees

Although the service of the Department of Real Estate is basically that of protecting the public as a licensing and law enforcement agent, it endeavors to conduct its affairs so as to be of material assistance to its licensees and to encourage a high level of ethical and professional standards. The Commissioner publishes a *Real Estate Reference Book* and a quarterly *Real Estate Bulletin* to all licensed brokers and salespersons to keep them informed of the latest administrative provisions and also of current practices in real estate and allied activities. The *Reference Book* sets forth the requirements to be met in obtaining a license and contains valuable study suggestions for the real estate license requirements. The *Bulletin* outlines items of current interest.

§4.39. Advertising

Under the Real Estate Law, a licensee may not publish in any newspaper or periodical, or by mail, any matter that does not describe that the licensee is performing acts for which a real estate license is required. Further, a mortgage loan broker must put in any advertisement that he is a "Real Estate Broker—California Department of Real Estate."[116] Further, an advertisement under the name of the salesperson may be permitted with the permission of the employing broker.[117] The Commissioner allows, as sufficient, the use of the terms *broker*, *agent*, or *Realtor*, or their abbreviations.[118] But it is grounds for suspension or revocation of a license to use willfully the term *Realtor* or any trade name of which a licensee is not a member.[119] It is a misdemeanor for any person to place or maintain upon any property in which one has no interest or right or possession, any sign or advertisement that advertises anything that is to be or has been sold, without the consent of the owner, lessee, or person in possession before such sign is placed upon the property.[120]

May a real estate licensee advertise the sale of his own real estate without disclosing he is a licensee? Under California law the licensee may do so; however, if a "bait and switch" tactic is used, a violation has occurred.[121] On the other hand, if an agency relationship is created, i.e., a listing contract, then the fact that the seller is a licensee should be disclosed in the advertisement. In any event, even though the Real Estate Law does not require a licensee, when acting as a principal, to disclose at any time that he is a licensee in the offer to purchase or the escrow instructions, the better practice is to do so, to avoid a future claim of unfair dealing.

§4.40. Solicitation at residence

It is unlawful for a person to solicit a sale or offer a sale of goods or services at a residence, in person or on the phone, without *clearly* revealing at the time, and before making any other statement or asking any other question (except a greeting), that the purpose of the contact is to effect a sale, by doing all of the following:

1. Identify the solicitor
2. Identify the trade name
3. Identify the kind of goods or services
4. If in person, show or display an identification that states the solicitor's name, trade name, and address

It is unlawful, in soliciting, to use any plan, scheme, or ruse that misrepresents one's true status or mission. For an intentional violation, a person bound to a contract is entitled to damages of two times the amount of the sales price up to $250, whichever is greater, but in no case less than $50.[122]

§4.41. Trust funds

Definition. Trust funds are money or things of value received by the broker or salesperson on behalf of the principal or any other person in the performance of any acts for which a real estate license is required, and not belonging to the broker but being held for the benefit of others.[123] If the licensee receives a deposit, personal check, or cash, these are trust funds. The same holds true for a check made payable to an escrow company, a title company, or a broker, as well as a promissory note made payable to the seller, or a pink slip to an automobile. Commingling of trust funds is a violation of the Real Estate Law.[124]

Initial requirements. Upon receipt of trust funds, received on behalf of the principal, they must be placed in one of the following:

1. A neutral escrow depository (licensed escrow corporation)
2. The hands of the principal
3. A trust account[125]

These funds must be placed no later than three business days following receipt, unless otherwise designated by the buyer, in writing, with the approval of the seller.[126] Funds received by the licensee must be maintained for the benefit of the offeror (buyer), until acceptance of the offer.[127] When acting as a principal, the licensee must place the funds in a neutral escrow.[128]

A record of *all* trust funds must be maintained,[129] which is required to be kept for three years.[130] In addition, the broker is required to keep a *separate* record for each transaction, accounting for all funds that have been deposited and maintained, according to sound accounting principles.[131]

Although a trust account is not required to be kept if no trust funds are ever received, it is good practice to do so. If a trust account is kept,[132] it must designate the broker as the trustee, and all such funds must provide for withdrawal without previous notice.[133] However, a broker can deposit trust funds into an interest-bearing account for payment of a client's taxes and property assessments on a one- to four-family residence, if the amount is insured by an agency of the federal government.[134]

Trust funds cannot be withdrawn except upon the signature of the broker or by at least one of the following when authorized in writing by the broker:

1. A salesperson licensed with the broker
2. An unlicensed employee of the broker with fidelity bond coverage at least equal to the maximum amount of trust funds to which an employee has access at any time[135]

This regulation is in no way intended to limit the responsibility or liability of a broker or the broker-officer of a corporate broker license. A broker may not disburse, or cause to be disbursed, any trust funds without the prior written consent of every principal who is an owner of the funds in the account if the disbursement will reduce the balance of funds to an amount less than the existing aggregate trust fund liability of the broker to all owners of the funds.[136]

It is difficult to abstain from having any of the broker's own funds in a trust account, if one is maintained, but there are restrictions against this. Since banks sometimes have service charges, out of necessity, the broker should keep some of his own money in the account to cover this contingency. The better practice, however, is to have the bank charge the broker's office or general account for the trust account service charges. The Real Estate Commissioner allows the broker to leave up to $200 of his own funds in the account for the purpose of covering service charges. Earned commissions may remain in the trust account for a period not to exceed 30 days.

Trust funds cannot be used as offset. Sometimes when a licensee thinks he has money due him either from his broker or a third party, he attempts to withhold trust funds as an offset against the alleged debt. Even if the licensee has a valid claim, trust funds may *not* be used. Disciplinary action can be taken against the licensee under these circumstances.

EXAMPLE   A property owner owed the broker $1,000 and had signed a personal note for this amount. The note was overdue. The owner listed his property with the broker and the broker obtained an offer with a $1,000 deposit, which he placed in his trust account. The escrow instructions called for a portion of the $1,000 in order to close. The broker refused to release the money on the theory that the owner owed him this money and he could use it as an offset. This is not so. Even though the owner did owe the money and there was no dispute about this indebtedness, it was separate and apart from the trust funds involved in the transaction. The broker should have turned the entire $1,000 over to the escrow agent as instructed by the seller. To collect on the note, the broker's recourse would be action in the civil courts.[137]

§4.42. Antidiscrimination laws

Discrimination is prohibited by both federal and state laws and cases. In 1968, in *Jones v. Mayer*, the Supreme Court of the United States held that a provision of the Civil Rights Statute enacted by Congress in 1866[138] bars all racial discrimination, private as well as public, in the sale or rental of property. In addition, Title VIII of the 1968 Federal Open Housing Law provides for a maximum penalty of $1,000 plus attorney's fees. Title VIII further requires licensees to display at their place of business an Equal Housing Opportunity poster.[139] In California a broker has a duty to take reasonable steps to be aware of and familiarize his salespeople with the federal and state laws relating to the prohibition of discrimination.[140]

Two significant antidiscrimination laws in California are the Unruh Act and the Rumford Act. The Unruh Act provides for civil action against persons conducting business establishments, by aggrieved persons claiming discrimination on account of sex, color, race, religion, ancestry, or national origin.[141] The business of a real estate broker is subject to the requirements of the Unruh Act. Therefore, the real estate broker, as an operator of a business, is prohibited from withholding services or discriminating in any way on account of sex, race, color, religion, or national origin.

EXAMPLE   In one case, the brokers tried to talk the plaintiff (who was black) out of purchasing a property, saying it was sold when, in fact, it was not. In a later case, a mortgage broker was held liable for damages for race discrimination for failure to obtain a loan for a black couple in a mostly white area.[142]

The Unruh Act specifically provides as follows:

> *All persons within the jurisdiction of this state are free and equal, and no matter what their sex, race, color, religion, ancestry, or national origin are entitled to the full and equal accommodations, advantages, facilities, privileges, or services in all business establishments of every kind whatsoever. This section shall not be construed to confer any right or privilege on a person which is conditioned or limited by law or which is applicable alike to persons of every sex, color, race, religion, ancestry, or national origin.*[143]

Penalties for a violation of the Unruh Act are also provided as follows:

> *Whoever denies, or who bids or invites such denial, or whoever makes any discrimination, distinction or restriction on account of sex, color, race, religion, ancestry, or national origin, contrary to the provisions of Section 51 of this code is liable for each and every such offense for the actual damages, and $250 in addition thereto, suffered by any person denied the rights provided in Section 51 of this Code.*[144]

An additional penalty is the possible revocation or suspension of a real estate license.[145]

The Rumford Act empowers the State Fair Employment Practices Commission (F.E.P.C.) to act against discrimination in both publicly assisted and private housing accommodations under specified conditions.[146] The Act states in part: "The practice of discrimination because of race, color, religion, sex, marital status, national origin or ancestry in housing accommodations is declared to be against public policy."[147] This also includes discrimination by a real estate licensee on the basis of a person being physically handicapped.[148]

The Rumford Act has had a somewhat stormy history. An amendment to the state constitution repealing the act was approved by the electorate in 1964, but the amendment was subsequently declared unconstitutional. Thus the Rumford Act is still in effect as amended.[149]

In other words, no one may refuse to sell, lease, or rent to another because of race, color, sex, religion, ancestry, or national origin, and a real estate licensee may not do so regardless of his or her principal's directions.[150] Likewise, "block busting" (panic selling) is prohibited for a real estate licensee.[151]

It has been determined by the California Attorney General that race, creed, or color is not a "material fact" that need be disclosed, even at the request of the owner.[152] On the other hand, a licensee's response to an inquiry from a prospective buyer as to the ethnic composition of various areas that is *factual* and in *good faith* does not violate the Rumford Fair Housing Act.[153] However, a violation would occur if the broker either has the intent to aid in a plan to keep neighborhoods segregated or to make differing responses based on the race of the prospective purchaser. Further, *volunteering* information that a particular neighborhood does or does not have minority residents would subject a licensee to revocation or suspension of his real estate license.

EXAMPLE In one case, it was held that both the broker and seller may be guilty of discrimination, but a broker who in good faith does all within his power to serve a member of a racial minority is not liable if the broker's failure to complete the transaction is due solely to the owner's refusal to sell because of the buyer's race or color.[154]

Brokers are urged to consider carefully their individual office guidelines and procedures to see if any could be regarded as discriminatory.

Here are a few examples of discriminatory practices to be avoided:

1. Showing properties only in a specific ethnic or racially oriented neighborhood unless the prospect has particularly requested to see that area

2. Accepting a listing from an owner in which the broker agrees to prequalify all prospects according to the owner's discriminatory ideas about what type of buyer will be good for the neighborhood

3. Refusing to perform licensed activities or refusing or failing to cooperate with or assist another real estate licensee in performing licensed activities for prospects because of prospect's race, color, sex, religion, ancestry, physical handicap, or national origination

4. Discrimination because of race, color, sex, religion, ancestry, physical handicap, or national origination by use of waiting lists, processing certain applications more slowly than others, or hindering the obtaining of financing.[155]

§4.43. Real Estate Recovery Fund

The purpose of the Real Estate Recovery Fund is to further education and research in real estate with a reserve of $400,000[156] (Education and Research Account), to allow recovery, up to prescribed amounts, on the grounds of fraud, misrepresentation, deceit, or conversion of trust funds[157] (Recovery Account). On the Recovery Account it is required to be shown that the claimant has made all reasonable searches to ascertain whether the licensee possesses real or personal property or other assets that could be applied to satisfy the debt.

Right to recover from fund.

EXAMPLES   1.   A husband and wife recovered a joint judgment against a real estate salesperson in a case involving the turning over of community property to the salesperson on the basis of his false and fraudulent misrepresentations. They filed an application for an award from the Real Estate Fund. The order of the trial court awarded each of them the statutory maximum from the fund. On appeal, it was held that there could be only a single recovery from the fund for a cause of action to recover damages for loss of community property, and that it was improper to award both husband and wife the maximum amount.[158]

2.   After recovering a judgment against a real estate broker for damages for fraud and treble damages for conversion of an advance fee, the plaintiff applied for satisfaction of the judgment from the Real Estate Fund. The trial court directed payment of the entire judgment from the fund. On appeal, it was held that recovery from the fund is limited to "actual and direct loss," and, therefore, treble damages were not payable. The court reasoned that had the legislature intended exemplary or punitive damages to be included in an award against the fund, it could simply have called for payment of the judgment, rather than limiting payment to "actual and direct loss."[159]

On the other hand, recovery of interest[160] and costs is permitted.[161] Further, if there is more than one claimant in the same transaction against the same licensee there can be no priority given; all will receive a pro rata share.[162]

Suspension of license. If the Commissioner is required to pay from the fund in settlement of a claim or satisfaction of judgment against a broker or salesperson, the license is automatically suspended and is not reinstated until the person has paid, in full, plus interest at the prevailing rate, the amount paid from the fund. A discharge in bankruptcy does not relieve a person from those penalties.[163]

No right to recover from fund.

EXAMPLES   1.   Conduct constituting breach of fiduciary duty is not a basis for recovery from the fund; neither is a loan to a real estate licensee for his personal use; and neither is the direct hiring of a salesperson (rather than a broker) to act as a nonresident apartment manager.[164]

2.   No right to recover punitive damages or attorney's fees.[165]

3.   If the licensee is acting as a principal, there is no right of recovery.[166]

4.   The fund is only liable for a loss. If the aggrieved person receives a tax benefit by a reduction in his tax liability, the fund is only liable for damages less the tax savings.[167]

VII. PROFESSIONAL STATUS OF THE BROKER

§4.44. What is a professional?

The word *professional* has several meanings. The one we are concerned with is "a person practicing a profession, especially a learned or skilled profession." The word *profession* is defined as an occupation requiring advanced education and training.

Historically, the word *profession* related to the three learned professions: theology, law, and medicine. Today, however, the word is used to describe a calling "in which one professes to have acquired some special knowledge, used by way either of *instructing, guiding,* or *advising* others, or of *serving* them in some art."

§4.45. Continuing education
The concept of a professional in the real estate field encompasses strict adherence to ethical principles, a concern for education beyond training, and performance of a public service that leads to a good public image. In this regard, in addition to the basic educational requirements, licensees are required to successfully complete 45 hours of "continuing educational" courses every four years before the renewal of the license. Three hours must relate to ethics, and three hours must relate to the law of agency; further, beginning in 1995, there are additional requirements added from year to year that the reader should verify.[168]

§4.46. High standards of real estate practice required
As in other professions, those engaged in real estate activities should have regard for more than the law as contained in statutes, rules, and regulations; professional courtesy and ethics require additional consideration. It is said that the person who tries only to stay on the border of the law will at some time step across. The course of conduct set forth in the Real Estate Law and the rules and regulations prescribed pursuant thereto *must* be followed by a broker.

A broker should also observe a rule of conduct to maintain the high standards of real estate practice and the respect that the public has for any profession requiring the exercise of the highest degree of skill, competence, honesty, and integrity.

Figure 4-2 is illustrative of reminder information contained in the publications of the California Department of Real Estate.

§4.47. Real estate boards
A National Association of Real Estate Boards was formed in 1908. The national association and its constituent boards and state associations form a composite organization of brokers whose object has been to forward the interests of brokers, disseminate education, and raise the standards of real estate practice and the esteem in which brokers are held in the community. To this end, a Code of Ethics was formulated and adopted which, as recommended by the Real Estate Commissioner, should be scrupulously observed.

In 1972 the name of the association was changed to National Association of Realtors.

§4.48. Realtor
The Code of Ethics uses the word *Realtor*, which is not a synonym for *real estate broker*. It is the distinctive and exclusive designation for those within the membership of the national association, and its exclusive use has been upheld by the courts. Every Realtor has pledged that he will observe and abide by the Code of Ethics promulgated by the national association and adopted by his board to govern real estate practice of members of the board, and has manifested good business character.

§4.49. Realtist
In 1947 a national organization composed predominantly of black real estate brokers, known as the National Association of Real Estate Brokers, was formed in Miami, Florida, and its members adopted the name *Realtist*. The organization now has local boards in the principal cities of 40 states. The California Association of Real Estate Brokers, organized in 1955, has four board affiliates in Oakland, Sacramento, Los Angeles, and San Diego. A Realtist must be a member of a local board as well as of the national organization. Both nationally and locally, Realtists are working for better housing for the communities they serve. In many cases, individuals are both Realtors and Realtists by virtue of voluntary dual membership.

TEST YOUR KNOWLEDGE

Broker, who represented seller, received a check from buyer payable to broker's order in the sum of $1,000 deposit toward purchase offer of $10,000 property listed by broker.

Which of the following is consistent with broker's legal responsibility?

I. Endorse the check and give it to seller.

II. Deposit the check in broker's personal bank account and send his (broker's) personal check for $1,000 to seller.

III. Deposit check in trust fund account and advise seller of deposit and offer.

IV. Endorse check and forward to escrow account.

V. Hold check until seller accepts offer.

Select one:

(a) I only, (b) III only, (c) both I and III, but not II, (d) I, II, and III, (e) IV, (f) V.

Answer below.

ANSWER:
(b) is correct answer. I is incorrect because seller hasn't accepted. II is violation of law. III (b) is correct answer because check drawn on trust account is buyer's money until acceptance by seller. IV is incorrect because escrow not appropriate until acceptance. V is incorrect because buyer did not instruct broker to hold check and possibility that check is invalid. Of course, the best procedure would be to ask buyer for instruction pertinent to his check.

Figure 4-2[169]

§4.50. California Association of Realtors

The pioneer real estate organizations in California were the San Diego Realty Board, organized in 1887, and the San Jose Real Estate Board, founded in 1890. Others followed in the 1900s. In 1905 the California Real Estate Association was formed at Los Angeles; it now comprises over 200 local real estate boards throughout the state, and also individual members from communities that do not have a local board. In 1974 the name was changed to the California Association of Realtors. The objects and purposes of the California Association of Realtors are set forth in its constitution:

1. To unite its members
2. To promote high standards
3. To safeguard the land-buying public
4. To foster legislation for the benefit and protection of real estate
5. To cooperate in the economic growth and development of the state

The objectives and ideals of the association have accomplished a great deal in the advancement of the real estate profession and the service afforded by it to the public.

To fill a long-standing need, a Legal Services Plan was adopted by the Association in 1978, making legal services readily available to members. The objectives of this plan are fourfold:

1. To enable members to offer better service by promptly giving them the legal advice they might need, either by phone, by written opinion, or in person
2. To implement a program of preventive law
3. To reduce the cost of legal services
4. To make legal advice so easily accessible that it will be utilized by 100 percent of the membership whenever a need arises[170]

A word of caution, however: There is no substitute for a broker or salesperson having his own local attorney. In some instances when the licensee contacts, by phone, some sort of attorney information hotline, not enough information is given concerning a particular situation and therefore misinformation is received. Further, the person giving the advice may not be a real estate attorney competent to give adequate advice.

QUESTIONS

Matching Terms

a. Agent
b. Gratuitous
c. Fictitious
d. Realtor
e. Trust funds
f. Agency
g. Negligence
h. Principal
i. Delegation
j. Real estate broker

1. Relationship in which one person acts on behalf of another, either special or general. Agency
2. Special agent. Real Estate Broker
3. One who authorizes another person to act on his behalf. Principal
4. Failure to use ordinary care. Negligence
5. Transfer of authority or duties from one person to another. Delegation
6. Any person empowered to act by and on behalf of a principal. Agent
7. An agent who acts without compensation. Gratuitous

8. Member of National Association of Realtors. Realtor
9. Money in the hands of one person that is held for the benefit of another. Trust Funds
10. Name assumed by a business for purposes of convenience. Fictitious

True/False

T (F) 11. Basically, there is no difference between an agent and an employee.

T (F) 12. Basically, there is no difference between an agent and an independent contractor.

(T) F 13. The agency relationship, upon performance by the agent, generally involves a triangular relationship.

T (F) 14. Like any contract, consideration is always essential to the creation of an agency relationship.

T F **15.** Anyone who has capacity to contract may appoint an agent to act on his behalf.

T F **16.** Any act that a person can lawfully perform can be done by his duly appointed agent.

T F **17.** The authority of an agent may be either actual or ostensible.

T F **18.** The law requires that every real estate broker have a written agreement with each salesperson covering their relationship.

T F **19.** An agency relationship may be terminated by agreement, by revocation, or by renunciation.

T F **20.** Once issued in accordance with the law, a broker's license is not subject to revocation.

Multiple Choice

21. A real estate broker is under a duty to use the following in the performance of his duties:
   a. Care.
   b. Skill.
   c. Diligence.
   d. All of the above.

22. A listing agreement between a property owner and a real estate broker is ordinarily terminated if
   a. Either party dies.
   b. The owner becomes bankrupt.
   c. The property is destroyed by fire.
   d. Any of the above.

23. Which of the following is an advantage to a homeowner in retaining a broker to sell his house?
   a. Assistance in determining selling price.
   b. More contact with potential buyers.
   c. Assistance in obtaining necessary financing.
   d. All of the above.

24. An agency may be created by
   a. Appointment.
   b. Ratification.
   c. Estoppel.
   d. Any of the above.

25. Agencies may be classified as either
   a. Express or implied.
   b. Actual or ostensible.
   c. General or special.
   d. All of the above.

26. The chief officer of the State Department of Real Estate is the
   a. Corporations Commission.
   b. Savings and Loan Commission.
   c. Real Estate Commissioner.
   d. Deputy Attorney General.

27. The relationship of a real estate broker and his principal is
   a. Confidential.
   b. Fiduciary.

c. One of trust.
   d. All of the above.

28. A real estate salesperson
   a. Must be licensed by the Department of Real Estate.
   b. Must be licensed by the Division of Corporations if employed by a partnership or corporation.
   c. Need not be licensed if he has a college degree plus two years' experience.
   d. Need not be licensed if he is employed by a licensed broker.

29. A salesperson's license must be
   a. On file at the broker's principal office.
   b. Carried by the salesperson.
   c. Filed with the county clerk.
   d. Filed with the county recorder.

30. The licensing requirements of the Real Estate Law apply to
   a. Any person acting under a power of attorney.
   b. A trustee selling real property under a deed of trust in default.
   c. Anyone dealing with his or her own property.
   d. Mineral, oil, and gas brokers.

31. An oral agreement to sell a parcel of real property for a commission is
   a. Illegal.
   b. Void.
   c. Unenforceable.
   d. Enforceable if the amount of commission is reasonable.

32. A real estate salesperson may accept compensation from
   a. Buyer.
   b. Seller.
   c. The broker for whom he is employed.
   d. Any of the parties he has assisted.

33. A real estate broker who employs salespersons must execute a written agreement with each salesperson showing
   a. Amount and type of supervision to be exercised by the broker.
   b. Duties of the parties.
   c. Compensation to be paid.
   d. All of the above.

34. The real estate license requirements include which of the following?
   a. Application.
   b. Qualification.
   c. Examination.
   d. All of the above.

35. A corporation can be licensed as a real estate broker provided
   a. All of the officers of the corporation are licensed brokers.

b. At least one officer of the corporation is a licensed broker.

c. A majority of the officers of the corporation are licensed brokers.

d. None of the above.

36. The Real Estate Law provides that applicants for a real estate salesperson's license must

a. Be at least 18 years of age.

b. Be of good reputation for honesty and truthfulness.

c. Have an appropriate knowledge of the English language.

d. All of the above.

37. The Real Estate Law provides that an applicant for a real estate salesperson's license must be

a. At least 18 years of age.

b. Residents of California for two years.

c. Citizens of the United States.

d. All of the above.

38. At the time a listing agreement is executed, a copy must be

a. Delivered to the principal.

b. Forwarded to the Department of Real Estate.

c. Posted on the property.

d. All of the above.

39. The broker–client relationship is ordinarily created by

a. The deposit receipt.

b. A trust declaration.

c. The listing agreement.

d. The escrow instructions.

40. Basically, rights under listing agreements are governed primarily by the law of

a. Agency.

b. Tort.

c. Contracts.

d. Trusts.

41. A Realtor is

a. Anyone licensed by the Department of Real Estate.

b. A member of a local real estate board.

c. Any real estate business partnership.

d. Any of the above.

42. Which of the following has a meaning comparable to *fiduciary*?

a. Guarantor.

b. Pecuniary.

c. Trustee.

d. Mercenary.

43. An oral agreement between brokers for a division of commissions is

a. Invalid.

b. Contrary to public policy.

c. Valid.

d. Unenforceable.

44. If a broker who is a notary takes an acknowledgment, he

a. Need not require the person to appear before him personally if known by an associate.

b. Need not keep a separate notarial record.

c. Must use due care in ascertaining the identity of the person.

d. Is not subject to discipline by the Real Estate Commissioner for carelessness as a notary.

45. A real estate licensee in his duties as a licensee is required to exercise

a. Skill.

b. Care.

c. Good faith.

d. All of the above.

46. The Real Estate Recovery Fund is intended to

a. Protect the public when dealing with real estate licensees.

b. Assure payment of a broker's commission.

c. Relieve the broker of personal liability.

d. Do all of the above.

47. The objects and purposes of C.A.R. include which of the following?

a. To unite its members.

b. To promote high standards.

c. To safeguard the land-buying public.

d. All of the above.

48. The word *ethics* as it relates to licensees means

a. High standards.

b. Good conscience.

c. Integrity.

d. All of the above.

49. The number of college-level real estate courses presently required for a salesperson's initial license is

a. One.

b. Two.

c. Three.

d. None.

50. The number of college-level real estate courses presently required for a broker's license is

a. Two.

b. Four.

c. Six.

d. Eight.

NOTES

1. McConnell v. Cowan (1955) 44 C.2d 805.

2. C.C. 2295, *et seq.*

3. B. & P. 10137. Under the doctrine of respondeat superior, a broker is liable for the acts of his salespeople. Garton v. Title Ins. & Trust Co. (1980) 106 C.A.3d 365; Kahn v. Gordon (1967) 249 C.A.2d 722; Walter v. Marler (1978) 83 C.A.3d 1; *see also* §4.16, or 5.33. A broker can also be liable for punitive damages if the broker had adverse knowledge of the unfitness of the salesperson (C.C. 3294[b]). Settling a case with an

employee does not release the employer under the doctrine of respondeat superior (Mayhugh v. County of Orange [1983] 141 C.A.3d 737).

4. C.C. 2296.
5. C.C. 2307, 2310 2314.
6. Rodes v. Shannon (1963) 222 C.A.2d 721; Beeler v. Western American Finance Co. (1962) 201 C.A.2d 702.
7. Wright v. Lowe (1956) 140 C.A.2d 891, 896-897.
8. Charles V. Webster Real Estate v. Rickard (1971) 21 C.A.3d 612.
9. C.C. 2228, *et seq.*; Rest. Agency 13.
10. C.C. 2299, 2316.
11. C.C. 2300, 2317.
12. C.C. 2320.
13. C.C. 2306.
14. C.C. 2304.
15. C.C. 2309.
16. O'Banion v. Paradiso (1964) 61 C.2d 559; C.C. 5127.
17. Murphy v. Munson (1949) 95 C.A.2d 306, 312; Kadota Fig Assoc. v. Case-Swayne Co. (1946) 73 C.A.2d 815. Further, an exception exists when the principal is estopped to deny liability for the act of his agent. Higson v. Montgomery Ward & Co. (1968) 263 C.A.2d 333, 342.
18. Mudgett v. Day (1859) 12 C.139; 2 Cal. Jur. 2d, Agency 44; 3 Am. Jur.2d, Agency 320, pp. 676-678.
19. Eamoe v. Big Bear Land & Water Co. (1950) 98 C.A.2d 370, 374. To avoid personal liability on a contract negotiated on his principal's behalf, an agent must disclose the agency and the identity of the principal, regardless of whether the third person might have known that the agent was acting in a representative capacity. It is not the third person's duty to seek out the identification of the principal (W. W. Leasing Unlimited v. Commercial Standard Title Insurance Company [1983] 149 C.A.3d 792).
20. C.C. 2349. This includes selling time-share interests. *See* "Commissioner's Forum," *California Real Estate* magazine (October 1980); Cal-Am Corp. v. D.R.E. (1980) 104 C.A.3d 453.
21. B. & P. 10131, *et seq.*; see footnote 24.
22. Mobile homes can be converted to real estate and sold by a real estate licensee, even if they are less than one year old, if certain requirements are met. H. & S. 10551.
23. Brokers can now make or arrange loans under the Consumer Finance Lenders Law without being separately licensed. Fin. C. 24055, 24466.
24. *See* B. & P. 10029; C.C. 2985.
25. B. & P. 10131.1. "Sale," "resale," and "exchange" include every disposition of any interest in a real property sales contract or promissory note secured directly or collaterally by a lien on real property. Although this does not apply to renegotiation of a loan by a broker, it does apply if he has a direct or indirect monetary interest as a party (B. & P. 10230). Also query B. & P. 10231, 10231.2 re requirements of broker to submit information to D.R.E. before soliciting funds. For further new criteria under B. & P. 10131 or 10131.1, *see* B. & P. 10232, 10232.1-10232.5.
26. 32 Ops. Cal. Atty. Gen. 210.
27. B. & P. 10138.
28. B. & P. 10139.
29. 34 Ops. Cal. Atty. Gen. 146 (1959).
30. Comm. Regs. 2850, 2851 re corporate bond.
31. Comm. Regs. 2852, 2853
32. Rees v. D.R.E. (1978) 76 C.A.3d 286; *see also* Anderson v. D.R.E. (1979) 93 C.A.3d 696, which held that such a regulation infringed on plaintiff's freedom of commercial speech by imposing overly restrictive requirements for licensure; B. & P. 10167, *et seq.*
33. B. & P. 10133(c).
34. 18 Ops. Cal. Atty. Gen. 200 (1951); Richardson v. Roberts (1962) 210 C.A.2d 603, 607; Riley v. Chambers (1919) 181 C. 589; Hayter v. Fulmor (1944) 66 C.A.2d 554. According to the Attorney General, the power must be a general power of attorney to be exempt and recorded.
35. B. & P. 10133.1.
36. B. & P. 10131.01.
37. B. & P. 10133.2. As to what functions assistants are allowed to do, *see San Diego Realtor* magazine (March 1994).
38. Provisor v. Haas Realty, Inc. (1967) 256 C.A.2d 850; *see also* Davis v. Chipman (1930) 210 C. 609, 618-619.
39. B. & P. 10151.5 But *see* two Delaware cases: Coyle v. Peoples (1975) 349 A.2d 870; Trainer v. Deemer (1933) 35 Del. 396.
40. B. & P. 10137. The listing broker is responsible (and therefore liable if not paid) for withholding 30 percent of taxes for a foreign broker selling property in the U.S. and collecting a commission through the listing broker. I.R.C. 1441.
41. Cochran v. Ellsworth (1954) 126 C.A.2d 429; Hayter v. Fulmor (1944) 66 C.A.2d 554, 559. Since state laws differ, brokers should always be careful; *see* University Financing Consultants, Inc. v. Barouche (1983) 148 C.A.3d 1165.
42. Comm. Regs. 2785(c)(8); N.A.R.'s Code of Ethics, Article 6.
43. C.C. 2351.
44. C.C.2350; *see also* C.C. 2027, which states that a subagent of an agent is not responsible to the principal. See also Kroeber v. Hurlbert (1940) 38 C.A.2d 261.
45. Kruse v. Miller (1956) 143 C.A.2d 656; Johnston v. Seargeants (1957) 152 C.A.2d 180.
46. B. & P. 10132. See People v. Asuncion (1984) 152 C.A.3d 422; Grand v. Griesinger (1958) 160 C.A.2d 397 in which the licenses of two salespeople were revoked when they completely controlled the operation of rental agencies under agreements granting brokers a percentage of the profits.
47. Agareval v. Johnson (1978) 81 C.A.3d 513, 526. But *see* Alhino v. Starr (1980) 112 C.A.3d 158, 174; and C.R.E.L. Inc. v. Wallace (1993) 18 C.A. 4th 1575. *See also* §4.5, 5.32. However, the broker may have a cause of action against the salesperson for equitable indemnity; *see* Valley Title Insurance Co. v. Superior Court (1981) 124 C.A.3rd 867.
48. B. & P. 10160. The license must be retained at the main business office of the broker.
49. B. & P. 10161.8(a) & (b); Comm. Regs. 2752.
50. B. & P. 10178.
51. B. & P. 119.
52. Comm. Regs. 2728.5. A broker-salesperson still has a broker status for licensing purposes. He does not transfer a license as does a salesperson; he merely changes business addresses. He does not need the signature of the employing broker.
53. Comm. Regs. 2715.
54. B. & P. 11017, subsequently repealed.
55. Tatterson v. Standard Realty (1927) 81 C.A. 23; Galbavy v. Clevelin Realty Corp. (1943) 58 C.A.2d Supp. 903. If a corporation is wholly owned by a salesperson, the Department of Real Estate has concluded that it is not a violation of B. & P. 10137 for a broker to pay commissions earned by a salesperson to a corporation in accordance with the salesperson's instructions to the broker (*Real Estate Bulletin* [Fall 1980]). *See* Beggerly v. Gbur (1980) 112 C.A.3d 180 re a salesperson not being able to collect a commission from his broker because it was not covered in the broker-salesperson agreement.
56. "Commissioner's Column," *California Real Estate* (October 1977).
57. "Commissioner's Column," *California Real Estate* (July 1978).
58. Comm. Regs. 2725.
59. Comm. Regs. 2726.
60. Marani v. Jackson (1986) 183 C.A.3d 695.
61. Chretian v. Donald L. Bren Co. (1984) 151 C.A.3d 385.

62. Comm. Regs. 2727. If a broker wishes to hire another broker to take over his business for a few months, it is necessary to transfer all salespeople's licenses to the assuming broker. "Commissioner's Forum," *California Real Estate* (August 1979).

63. *See* Figures 4 1(a) and 4 1(b) for the California Association of Realtors Independent Contractor Form. California Association of Realtors also has an Employee Agreement Form. Many local governments have enacted statutes requiring independent contractors to have their own business licenses. Failure to have such can be cause to have a license revoked or suspended. Comm. Regs. 2910(7).

64. B. & P. 10177(h); Comm. Regs. 2725. Supervisory duties include as appropriate: the establishment of policies, rules, procedures and systems to review, oversee, inspect, and manage, (a) real estate transactions, (b) documents that materially effect the rights and obligations of the parties, (c) filing, storage, and maintenance of these documents, (d) handling of trust funds, (e) advertising, (f) familiarizing salespeople with discrimination laws, (g) keeping records and reports of salespeople.

65. Resnik v. Anderson and Miles (1980) 109 C.A.3d 569, 573. A salesperson's relationship with his broker cannot be classified as an independent contractor relationship insofar as the labor commissioner is concerned.

66. Gipson v. Davis Realty Co. (1963) 215 C.A.2d 190; 59 Ops. Cal. Atty. Gen. 369 (1976); B. & P. 10032. In fact, even if a salesperson is deemed to be an independent contractor, the employer may still be liable. Gonzales V.R.J. v. Norick Construction Co. (1977) 70 C.A.3d 131. When a negligent act is committed by an employee of the independent contractor, however, the employer of the independent contractor is not responsible. Smith v. Lucky Stores (1976) 61 C.A.3d 826. But *see* Castro v. State of California (1980) 114 C.A.3d 503 re Peculiar Risk Doctrine. Errors and omissions insurance should be carefully considered for the broker and all the salespeople. It is even possible to pass on a ratable share of such insurance to the salespeople, but there is a contrary view. "Errors and Omissions," *San Diego Realtor* (April 1979).

67. Hinman v. Westinghouse Electric Co. (1970) 2 C.3d 956.

68. Lab. C. 3351.

69. Lab. C. 3353; *see also* "Independent Contractor Relationship," *California Real Estate* (January 1976); Foss v. Anthony Industries (1983) 139 C.A.3d 794.

70. Payne v. White House Properties, Inc. (1980) 112 C.A.3d 465, 471; but this case held in this particular circumstance that the salesperson was not an employee for worker's compensation purposes; Grubb and Ellis v. Spengler (1983) 143 C.A.3d 890; Aschwanden v. Worker's Comp. Appeals Bd. (1991) 230 C.A. 3d 130.

71. Lab. C. 3700, *et seq.*, 3710.2. *See* "Worker's Compensation—Yes or No," *California Real Estate* (January 1976); "The Whys and Wherefores of Worker's Compensation Insurance," *California Real Estate* (December 1975); *see also* Lab. C. 2750.5 re rebuttable presumption that a worker is an employee. Although not resolved by the courts, it is the position of the State Dept. of Labor that real estate salespeople are employees for worker's compensation purposes. Whether a person is an independent contractor or an employee for worker's compensation is an issue to be decided upon the facts of each case (Brown v. Industrial Accident Commission [1917] 174 C. 457; Payne v. White House Properties, Inc. [1980] 112 C.A.3d 465, 470).

72. *See* Calif. Emp. Stab. Comm. v. Morris (1946) 28 C.2d 812. It is the existence of the right of control, not the exercise of it that is critical (Robinson v. George [1940] 16 C.2d 238). The mere fact that both parties may have mistakenly believed that they were entering into the relationship of principal and independent contractor is not binding (Max Grant v. Director of Benet Payments [1977] 71 C.A.3d 647). For factors that are considered in determining whether there is an employment relationship, *see* Tieburg v. California Unemployment Insurance Appeals Board (1970) 2 C.3d 943, 950.

73. Tax Equity and Fiscal Responsibility Act of 1982, §269 amended; I.R.C. 3508. *See also* California Unemployment Insurance Code §650 and 13004.1. Also a broker must periodically file an information form (1099) with federal government and comparable form (599) with the state.

74. Grubb and Ellis v. Spengler (1983) 143 C.A.3d 890, 896.

75. Grubb and Ellis v. Spengler, *supra.*

76. California Francisco Investment Corp. v. Urionis (1971) 14 C.A.3d 318; Gordon Termite Control v. Terrones (1978) 84 C.A. 3d 176; Greenly v. Cooper (1978) 77 C.A.3d 382.

77. C.C. 2355, 2356.

78. Walter v. Libby (1945) 72 C.A.2d 138, 141.

79. Rest. Agency 138. The essentials are (1) to secure performance of a duty; or (2) to protect a title, legal or equitable; (3) the power must be given when the duty or title is created; or (4) it must be for consideration. *See also* Pacific Lankmark Hotel, Ltd. v. Marriott Hotels, Inc. (1993) 19 C.A. 4th 615.

80. B. & P. 10050, *et seq.*

81. B. & P. 10000, *et seq.*

82. B. & P. 10170, *et seq.*; Comm. Regs. 3005, *et seq.*

83. B. & P. 10150.6, 10152, 10153; Comm. Regs. 2720. For definition of *dishonesty*, *see* Hogg v. Real Estate Commissioner (1942) 54 C.A.2d 712. An applicant who is not a resident of California is eligible to be licensed in California if the applicant's state allows reciprocity (B. & P. 10151.5).

84. B. & P. 10153.2.

85. B. & P. 10153.3, 10153.4.

86. B. & P. 10153.

87. B. & P. 10137.1.

88. "Commissioner's Forum," *California Real Estate* (November 1979).

89. Neil v. U.S. (1951) 112 Fed. Supp. 870; *see also Real Estate Bulletin* (Fall 1980).

90. B. & P. 10159; Comm. Regs. 2740.

91. "Commissioner's Forum," *California Real Estate* (August 1979).

92. Comm. Regs. 2740.

93. Comm. Regs. 2744. Since a salesperson must be a natural person employed by a broker, the Department of Real Estate does not issue a salesperson's license to a corporation (*Real Estate Bulletin* [Fall 1980]).

94. B. & P. 10159.2; "Commissioner's Column," *California Real Estate* (March 1979). The Commissioner does not permit a salesperson to evade the requirement of a broker's supervision through the hiring of a dummy broker for a corporation owned wholly or in part by a salesperson (*Real Estate Bulletin* [Fall 1980]). A broker does not have to be chief executive officer so long as the broker is a supervising broker and an officer-director.

95. B. & P. 10159.2(c); Comm. Regs. 2743.

96. B. & P. 10180.

97. Comm. Regs. 2745.

98. B. & P. 10162 and notify the Commissioner of every branch office (B. & P. 10163) and current residence address (Comm. Regs. 2715).

99. Comm. Regs. 2728.

100. Brabant v. City of South Gate (1977) 66 C.A.3d 764.

101. B. & P. 16002.1.

102. Comm. Regs. 2731 2733; B. & P. 17900, *et seq.*

103. B. & P. 10250, *et seq.*, subsequently repealed.

104. B. & P. 10500, *et seq*; Comm. Regs. 2960.

105. B. & P. 10240, *et seq.*, 10245 (and retain records for four years); Comm. Regs. 2340, *et seq. See also* §9.4; B. & P. 10237.

106. B. & P. 10249.2.

107. Barry v. Raskov (1991) 232 C.A. 3d 447.

108. Harvey v. Davis (1968) 69 C.2d 362. Regarding advertising, *see* B. & P. 10232, 10232.1–10232.5, 10236, 10237.2.
109. Wyatt v. Union Mortgage Co. (1979) 24 C.3d 773.
110. Milner v. Fox (1980) 102 C.A.3d 567; B. & P. 10231, 10231.1.
111. Comm. Regs. 2845, 2840 re new Disclosure Statement.
112. Corp. C. 25100. *See also* §13.51, *et seq.*
113. Corp. C. 31000, *et seq.*; Comm. Regs. 2785(b)(9).
114. Corp. C. 31005.
115. *Real Estate Bulletin* (Spring 1980).
116. B. & P. 10140.6. Under Comm. Regs. 2847, a broker may voluntarily submit advertising for approval.
117. Former Comm. Regs. 2770 was repealed in 1996. Review of advertising is now up to the broker under Regs. 2725.
118. Comm. Regs. 2770.1.
119. B. & P. 10177(e).
120. Pen. C. 556.1.
121. B. & P. 12024.6. False and misleading advertisements are fraudulent. It is better to avoid subjective words (many adjectives) in ads. Advertising a "view" when none can be guaranteed is misleading. For subdivision criteria, *see* Comm. Regs. 2799.1 which prohibits "free" items to induce a purchaser, unless it is without condition.
122. B. & P. 17500.3, *et seq.* As a prerequisite, the aggrieved party must write the solicitor and request a termination of the contract and all the money returned. A reasonable time for the return and cancellation is 20 business days from the date of the demand. *See also* C.C. 1689.5, *et seq.*; B. & P. 7159.
123. *Reference Book*, Dept. of Real Estate.
124. B. & P. 10176(e); Comm. Regs. 2835.
125. B. & P. 10145; Comm. Regs. 2951.
126. Comm. Regs. 2832. Under this regulation the broker may be able to hold the deposit uncashed if certain conditions are met.
127. Savage v. Moyer (1949) 33 C.2d 548; Sarten v. Pomatto (1961) 192 C.A.2d 288; *see* §5.16.
128. B. & P. 10145.
129. Comm. Regs. 2831 and 2831.1. But if a trust fund check is made payable to third parties (e.g., escrow) and is not more than $1,000, the broker need not comply with this.
130. B. & P. 10148. Further, the Commissioner requires the written permission of all licensees, upon renewal of their licenses, to examine all real estate broker's records maintained in a financial institution.
131. Comm. Regs. 2831.1.
132. Comm. Regs. 2831 re trust fund record; Comm. Regs. 2831.1 re separate record for each beneficiary and transaction.
133. Comm. Regs. 2832. and 2835 (regarding commingling).
134. B. & P. 10145; Comm. Regs. 2830.1.
135. Comm. Regs. 2834.
136. Comm. Regs. 2832.1, and 2833.
137. *Real Estate Bulletin* (Fall 1975).
138. Now 42 U.S.C. 1982; Havens Realty Corp, et al. v. Coleman et al. (1982) 102 S. Ct. 1114.
139. Section 804–866. It is known as the HUD Fair Housing Poster.
140. Comm. Regs. 2725; *see also* Gladstone Realtors v. Bellwood (1979) 99 S. Ct. 1601.
141. C.C. 51, 52.
142. Wagner v. O'Bannon (1969) 274 C.A.2d 121; Green v. Rancho Santa Margarita Mortgage Co. (1994) 28 C.A. 4th 686.
143. C.C. 51.
144. C.C. 52.
145. Comm. Regs. 2780.
146. H. & S. 35700-35744; 56 Ops. Cal. Atty. Gen. 546 (1973).
147. H. & S. 35700; *see also* Comm. Regs. 2780.
148. Comm. Regs. 2780–2781.
149. Mulkey v. Reitman (1966) 64 C.2d 529.
150. B. & P. 125.6; Comm. Regs. 2780.
151. B. & P. 10177(1).
152. 53 Ops. Cal. Atty. Gen. 196.
153. 58 Ops. Cal. Atty. Gen. 154.
154. Vargas v. Hampson (1962) 57 C.2d 479.
155. *Real Estate Bulletin* (Spring 1980).
156. B. & P. 10450.6. Liability of the fund shall not exceed $100,000 for any one licen*see*. B. & P. 10474(c); Deas v. Knapp (1981) 29 C.3d 69; Deas v. Knapp (1982) 129 C.A.3d 443; Stuart v. D.R.E. (1983) 148 C.A.3d 1.
157. B. & P. 10450.6.
158. Wolff v. Hoaglund (1970) 11 C.A.3d 227. To qualify for the fund, a person must prove the elements under B. & P. 10471–10472, among other things, that the aggrieved party was not the spouse of the debtor, and the debtor must have been licensed at the time of the wrong. Powers v. Fox (1979) 96 C.A.3d 440; Buccella v. Mayo (1980) 102 C.A.3d 315. The fund is not available if a licensee is selling his own home and committed fraud, since a seller is not required to be licensed. Robinson v. Murphy (1979) 96 C.A.3d 163; Froid v. Fox (1982) 132 C.A.3d 832: The court held that recovery from the fund is offset by the defrauded investor's tax benefits received. *See also* Booth v. Robinson (1983) 147 C.A.3d 371. Recovery from the Fund includes negligent misrepresentation (Andrepart v. Meeker (1984) 158 C.A.3d 878; Vinci v. Edmonds (1986) 185 C.A.3d 1251; Dierenfiled v. Stabaile (1988) 198 C.A.3d 126.
159. Circle Oaks Sales Co. Inc. v. Smith (1971) 16 C.A.3d 682. The fund is not available re a fraud practiced by one broker upon another licensee. Middlesteadt v. Karpe (1975) 52 C.A.3d 297. The amount a person could otherwise recover from the fund is reduced by the amount of federal tax write-offs obtained (Froid v. Fox [1982] 132 C.A.3d 832). For what steps the D.R.E. will go to so as not to pay people who are defrauded, *see* Gray v. Fox (1984) 151 C.A.3d 482. Recovery from the fund does not include attorney's fees under B. & P. 10471 (Acebo v. Real Estate Education, Research and Recovery Fund [1984] 155 C.A.3d 907).
160. Including postjudgment interest.
161. Nordahl v. Dept. of Real Estate (1975) 48 C.A.3d 657; Antonio v. Hempel (1977) 71 C.A.3d 128. However, total recovery (including costs) cannot exceed the statutory limit (Deas v. Knapp [1981] 29 C.3d 69).
162. Shirai v. Karpe (1976) 57 C.A.3d 276; B. & P. 10474, *et seq.*
163. B. & P. 10475; Rodriquez v. DRE (1996) 51 C.A. 4th 1289.
164. Merrield v. Edmonds (1983) 146 C.A.3d 336, 341.
165. Acebo v. Real Estate Education, Research and Recovery Fund (1984) 155 C.A.3d 907.
166. McCaughey v. Fox (1979) 94 C.A.3d 645; Robinson v. Murphy (1979) 96 C.A.3d 763; Wallace v. Onate (1992) 2 C.A. 4th 549.
167. Froid v. Fox (1982) 132 C.A.3d 832.
168. B. & P. 10170, *et seq.*; B. & P. 10153.7, 10171.1, 10171.3; Comm. Regs. 3005-3013. B. & P. 10170.8. The 45 hours of continuing education does not apply to a person who has been licensed 30 years in good standing and is 70 years of age. B. & P. 10171.1. Three hours of continuing education must be a course in ethics, professional conduct, and legal aspects of real estate. *See also* B. & P. 10170.4(c) re claim of equivalency. If a broker is licensed both as an individual and as an officer of a corporation, the Department of Real Estate looks to the renewal of the individual license as the date for completion of the continuing education requirements. Under B. & P. 10171.1, a person who was licensed only as an officer of a corporate broker must satisfy the requirements before renewal of that license and before being eligible for issuance of a license in an individual capacity or as the licensed officer of a different corporation (*California Real Estate* magazine [July 1982]).
169. *Real Estate Bulletin* (Winter 1975).
170. *California Real Estate* magazine (October 1978).

5

Duties and Liabilities of Licensees

131

I. INTRODUCTION

§5.1. In general

The responsibilities of a real estate licensee and the duties owed, both to the principal and to the buyer, are many and varied. A breach of these duties may give rise not only to disciplinary measures brought by the Real Estate Commissioner,[1] but also to a lawsuit for damages by the injured party, as well as by a real estate board's ethical panel if the licensee is a member of a local board. These duties and the consequences of a breach are described in detail in this chapter. What constitutes a secret profit, the duty to keep the principal fully informed, and the need to use care, skill, and diligence are explained. What comprises fraud and deceit, misrepresentation, and negligence are also analyzed. Possible criminal action is discussed, as is the unlawful practice of law. With consumer protection laws and litigant groups constantly on the increase, it is essential that the licensee be thoroughly acquainted with these aspects of the Real Estate Law.

§5.2. Fiduciary duty

As discussed in Chapter 4, a fiduciary relationship exists when there is a special confidence placed in one who, in equity and good conscience, is bound to act in good faith and with due regard to the interests of the principal. As a fiduciary, a real estate agent is under an obligation to give diligent and faithful service to the principal. The principal and broker do not deal at arm's length, but are engaged to deal fairly with one another.[2] In fact, implied in every contract between broker and client is a covenant of good faith and fair dealing. This covenant includes the duty of the broker to do everything the contract presupposes will be done to accomplish its purpose.[3]

Disciplinary measures can be brought against the agent even if the principal has suffered no injury. The lack of injury or absence of intention to act in a fraudulent manner will not excuse the act, but may mitigate the penalty imposed. Further, the agent, for a violation, will be required to return all of the profits.[4] It is a fundamental rule that the licensee, similar to a trustee, is bound to act in the highest good faith and may not obtain any advantage over the principal by the slightest misrepresentation, concealment, duress, or adverse pressure of any kind.[5]

The Real Estate Law was enacted for the protection of the public and for the purpose of insuring that real estate licensees will be honest, truthful, and of good reputation. Therefore, a licensee who violates the law will not be insulated from the consequences of unlawful actions simply because the other party suffers no pecuniary loss. "Regardless of the lack of pecuniary damage to the principal, the licensee has demonstrated a lack of integrity."[6]

§5.3. Broker acting as principal

Although as a general rule the licensee must have been acting as an agent in a real estate transaction before he will be disciplined for misconduct, that is not always the case.[7]

EXAMPLE   A licensed real estate broker was the owner of an apartment house located in Southern California. He decided to sell the apartment house and gave an exclusive listing to an independent broker. In furnishing this broker with information to complete the listing agreement, the owner-broker described the real property as an 18-unit apartment house. He knew that the property was approved by the local building department for only 14 units and failed to disclose this information to the listing broker and to the buyer that the listing broker procured for the property. Shortly after taking possession of the apartment house, the buyer discovered that 4 of the 18 units were illegal and complained to the Department of Real Estate. An accusation was filed against the owner-broker alleging fraud and dishonest dealing as a principal in the transaction. At the hearing on the accusation, the

Administrative Law Judge found that the owner-broker's conduct in the transaction was prompted by the desire to induce the buyer to purchase the property at a price that a 14-unit apartment house would not have commanded. The Administrative Law Judge concluded that the actions and omissions of the owner-broker constituted dishonest dealing. The Real Estate Commissioner adopted the Proposed Decision calling for a 60-day suspension of the owner-broker's license even though he was a principal in the transaction.[8]

On the other hand, nothing prevents a broker from acting on his own behalf provided he makes a full, complete, and honest disclosure of the truth of the transaction.[9]

II. DUTIES AND LIABILITIES TO PRINCIPAL

§5.4. Disclosure and nondisclosure

Of paramount importance is the duty of an agent to make a full and complete disclosure of all "material facts" that might influence the principal.[10] The agent must exercise ordinary care to communicate to the principal knowledge acquired in the course of the agency with respect to material facts.[11]

A broker is not liable for a mere mistake in judgment that does not result from a failure to know that which a person of ordinary prudence under similar circumstances would know.[12] However, the burden of proof is on the broker to show he acted with the utmost good faith.[13]

EXAMPLES

1. This includes the price that can be obtained, the possibility of a sale at a higher price, dealing with the property in another fashion, the tax consequences of a sale or an exchange, that the property would be more saleable if improvements were made, and all other matters that a disinterested and skillful agent would think relevant.[14]

2. If after taking a listing, the broker, upon checking more "comps," determines that the listing price is too low, the broker must immediately inform the seller.[15]

3. The agent might also realize that selling a mountain cabin may produce more profit for the principal if it were subdivided by virtue of a T.S.O. (time-sharing ownership) concept, even though the sale may take considerably longer to complete and the broker might have to become more educated as to this concept. If that is the case, the seller must be notified and at least have the opportunity to reject the idea.[16]

4. The failure of a broker (representing all sides in an exchange) to disclose that a second trust deed had an acceleration clause is an undeniable breach of fiduciary duty for nondisclosure of a material fact and it constitutes fraud.[17]

5. An action was taken by a seller (who took back a trust deed in an installment sale) against a broker and an attorney for fraud and negligence for failure to inform the seller of a purchaser's default at the time it occurred, and seller's right to foreclose at that time.[18]

6. An agent has no authority to accept a promissory note as a down payment without permission of the principal.[19]

§5.5. Nondisclosure of tax consequences

The area of tax consequences involves a precarious area for the licensee as it may tread on the expertise of a qualified C.P.A. or qualified real estate or tax attorney. On the other hand, some tax areas are widely known to real estate agents in general. If the matter of concern fits into this area, the licensee can furnish information to the principal and, at the same time, urge that he consult his accountant or a competent attorney. Of course, the tax consequences of holding title should *never* be discussed with the parties; not only may that constitute the unlawful practice of law, but also the consequential damages resulting from misinformation given could be extreme.[20]

EXAMPLES

1. It is a well-known fact that under the tax laws if the seller sells his residence and, within a period of 24 months, purchases a more expensive home, he can delay payment of a capital gains tax.[21] However, this type of transaction should not be confused with the sale or exchange of income-producing property. If a set of apartments is sold and another, larger set is then purchased, the seller has incurred an immediate capital gain. To alleviate the tax, an exchange must occur.[22]

2. Until 1998, the tax laws allowed senior citizens at least 55 years of age to elect to exclude up to $125,000 of gain realized on the sale of a principal residence, which must have been owned and occupied for at least three of the five years immediately prior to the sale. The exclusion was available only once in a lifetime. Under the new law, there is no age requirement and the exclusion is not limited to a one-time use. Further, there is no taxable capital gain if the gain is less than $500,000 for a married couple and $250,000 for a single taxpayer. Be sure to check with your CPA for more details.[23]

The law does not require that one who is fully informed as to the facts have independent advice, nor is it necessary that one who is competent need assistance in forming it. The primary consideration is whether the consent was given competently, voluntarily, and with a clear understanding of the material facts that would reasonably have influenced the principal's judgment. In reviewing transactions between agent and principal, if the proof shows that the principal received no independent advice, the courts will invariably give careful consideration to that fact.[24]

§5.6. Duty not to compete

Unless otherwise agreed upon, an agent is subject to a duty not to compete with his principal concerning the subject matter of the agency.

EXAMPLE

One case involved an action by a seller against a broker to recover secret profits and commission. The seller had given the broker an exclusive listing and the broker had procured a buyer. During escrow, the buyer informed the broker that she could not complete the purchase and was willing to take $1,200 and forfeit the balance of the $6,200 deposit. The broker did not inform the seller, but instead opened up another escrow between broker and buyer, wherein the broker would purchase the property from the buyer for $5,000 less than what the buyer was buying it from the seller. The broker testified that he had told the seller, but the seller denied such knowledge. The court held that the broker withheld vital information from the seller. An agent is required to exercise the highest degree of good faith toward his principal and may not obtain an advantage by misrepresentation, deceit, or concealment. The broker was required to return the secret profit plus the commission.[25]

§5.7. Purchase of principal's property

The listing broker may not purchase the principal's property, directly or indirectly, without fully disclosing his interest. This rule includes a purchase by the broker's spouse or by an entity in which the agent has an interest, for example, a corporation. It is also possible that there will be a violation if the agent fails to disclose to the principal that the buyer is a relative of the broker, or that a close personal relationship exists between them, even if the broker does not acquire an interest in the property.

EXAMPLES

1. A broker, while acting as agent, sold the property of Adams to his (the broker's) wife for the sum of $150,000 without disclosing that she was the buyer. The property had been listed with him at that figure, under a net listing. The wife purchased the property for $150,000, which included a $5,000 commission to the broker. Sometime thereafter, the wife resold the property for $160,000. Action was brought for the secret profit. The appellate court held that the relationship of principal and agent is a fiduciary one. The agent is bound to exercise utmost good faith and honesty. The burden is cast upon the agent to prove that he acted with the utmost good will toward his principal and that he make a full disclosure prior to the transaction. If the agent makes a secret profit, the principal may recover such profit.

   The general principle that denies the agent the right, without the knowledge or consent of the principal, to become the purchaser of property that he is employed to sell, precludes the agent from selling or conveying to the agent's spouse, to a corporation in which the agent has a large concealed interest, indirectly to himself in the name of a third person, and even to a clerk of the agent who is engaged in the affairs of the vendor relating to the sale of the land. The sale to the agent's wife is the same as a sale to himself.[26]

2. In another case, the broker, on the purchase of land through an estate, did not fully reveal that he and his wife were the sole owners of the entity that was buying the property. At the trial, the broker attempted to claim that he was acting as "middleman" or "finder" in the transaction and deserved the fee he had received. The court ordered the return of the fee by the broker, saying that it is manifest that the broker violated his fiduciary duties as a real estate agent by failing to fully disclose all the material facts of the transaction and by becoming "an undisclosed purchaser of his principal's property." Although the respondent had been compensated for acting as a broker or agent, he was in fact acting as a principal. As far as probate sales are concerned, the law makes no provisions for compensation of "finders." [27]

3. In a third case, a broker's license was revoked in connection with a probate sale. The broker had received a commission in the sale, but concealed from the court that the ostensible purchaser was his brother-in-law and that the real purchaser was a corporation in which the broker had an interest.[28]

4. S listed his property with broker E's company, Rem Realty Company. E executed a contract to purchase the property, describing himself as a real estate broker but not disclosing that he was in fact Rem Realty Company. He also collected a commission. S was not informed that the purchaser was her broker. The court held that E owed S the duty of full disclosure. E's license was suspended for six months.[29]

The disclosure rule applies when the agent occupies a fiduciary relationship with the principal. If the agent is dealing at arm's length with the seller, and not in a present or past fiduciary relationship, no disclosure is necessary. In fact, it is permissible for an agent to purchase his principal's property, so long as full disclosure is made, even though the agent will still obtain a commission. On the other hand, an agent who learns of material facts during the listing, which he fails to disclose, cannot wait until the expiration of the agreement and then purchase the property.

§5.8. Submit all offers

When a licensee learns of an offer on a principal's property, his duty is to submit the offer in a timely fashion. For example, assume a co-op broker telephones and indicates he has an offer and asks when it can be presented. If the seller is available or will be available later that day, the offer should be presented then. Some authorities hold that an offer should be presented whether it is written or oral. "The duty of the agent to communicate an offer to the principal is the same whether the offer be written or oral."[30] If, in the instance of an oral offer, the listing broker is informed by a reliable co-op broker of its existence, it would seem incumbent on the listing broker to inform the seller of this fact and give the cooperating broker a reasonable period of time within which to have the oral offer put in written form. Further, if a second offer is presented to the listing broker before the first is actually presented to the principal, the two offers should be presented either at the same time, or else one after the other, the seller being made aware of both.[31]

Although some authorities may disagree, others maintain that, in a proper case, an offer should be presented to the principal *even if another offer has been accepted*. In that instance, the licensee must inform the "backup" offeror of its status, must not induce the principal to breach the offer already accepted, and should have the principal contact a real estate attorney if he has any questions. Since a fair number of offers do "fall out of escrow," considering or even accepting contingent backup offers is not uncommon. On the other hand, the broker, to avoid potential problems, could add to the listing agreement (prior to it being signed, of course) that the seller will refuse to accept any backup offers.[32] However, it is suggested that the seller definitely be made aware of such an added provision.

What if an offer is so low that a licensee knows the seller would not accept it; must it still be submitted? Yes, unless otherwise agreed. The licensee can protect himself by having the seller sign an agreement that the broker need not submit an offer below a certain minimum price.

EXAMPLES

1. Plaintiff listed real property with a broker. The property was to be condemned for a right of way in approximately five years, and was listed for $15,000 on the broker's advice. Thereafter, the broker opened an escrow giving his own name as prospective purchaser of the property, and began preliminary negotiations with the prospective condemnor without the knowledge of the plaintiff. Within a few months thereafter, the broker twice submitted offers from one Martin, a personal friend of the broker and a licensed real estate salesperson, whom the broker had sponsored for licensure. The plaintiff accepted a $13,000 offer by Martin, and Martin signed escrow instructions under which the broker would take title to the property. The deal was consummated for $13,000, but the broker indicated a purchase price of $40,000 through documentary transfer stamps. Within a year, the state commenced condemnation action and the broker asserted a fair market value of the property of $105,000. The plaintiff learned of the broker's acquisition of the property and the condemnation negotiations between the state and the broker. He brought suit against the broker.

    The court held that a real estate agent has a duty to disclose to the principal all offers to buy the property in addition to the offer accepted, and must refrain from a dual representation in a sale transaction without full disclosure to both principals. When the acts of an agent have been questioned by the principal to whom the agent has a fiduciary duty, the burden is upon the agent to prove that he acted with the utmost good faith toward the principal, including making a full disclosure of all facts relating to the transaction. As a fiduciary, the broker should have undertaken on behalf of the plaintiff the acts that he undertook for his own account. Moreover, the broker was under a duty to disclose to the plaintiff his personal and professional relationship with the offeror, and the fact that the broker himself was to be the actual purchaser of the property.[33]

2. Judgment was obtained against a broker who did not disclose a $17,000 offer in preference to a $13,000 offer. The court stated that it is obviously a breach of a real estate broker's duty for failing to disclose to his client an offer to buy the client's property listed for sale with the broker.[34]

The Commissioner has also added his comments to this topic:

Q. If, at the time a written offer is presented to a seller by a broker, having knowledge that a more advantageous offer is about to be submitted, should he so advise the seller?

A. Yes. As agent he has a responsibility to disclose to the client any information of which he has knowledge that might be of assistance to the client in determining whether to accept or reject the offer.

Q. If, prior to presenting a written offer, a listing broker or salesperson received a second written offer for the same property, must he present the first offer and allow the seller to either accept or reject that offer before presenting the second offer?

A. No. An agent has a duty to make a timely presentation of offers to his principal, but if a second offer is received by the agent before he has presented the first offer to his principal, then both offers should be presented at the same time. This allows the seller, to whom the listing agent has a fiduciary obligation, to accept the offer that he considers the more favorable.[35]

§5.9. Listing overpriced properties

Some sellers are unrealistic in their belief as to market value for their properties. Obviously if the price is too high, the chance of sale is remote. Therefore, the seller should be told at the time the listing is taken of the *realistic* market value. If the seller insists on listing at too high a price, the broker can and probably should decline to take the listing.

Sometimes, in order to get a listing (or to assure that another licensee does not), a broker may deliberately appraise a property in excess of its reasonable market value, the end result being that the property is not sold, or it is sold for the true market value. This clearly is a breach of fiduciary duty and, if it is proven, the licensee will be disciplined.[36]

§5.10. Seller will accept less

A problem occurs frequently toward the end of a listing, when the licensee informs a prospective purchaser that the seller will accept an amount less than the listed price. It is fraud against the seller for a broker to tell a prospective buyer that the seller will accept less than the listing price.[37] Without express permission to do so, the agent is breaching his duty to the principal. However, a fine gray thread runs throughout this problem—that is, the valid exercise of the broker's authority to negotiate a sale. In any event, the licensee is under an obligation to tell the principal if he has so informed a prospective buyer. It is far better for the broker to receive a reduced listing price in writing.

Along these same lines, at least in past years, some M.L.S.'s require that the sales price and other information be reported to the board, which then publishes the information to all members, when an offer is first accepted but before escrow closes. This requisite is clearly a violation of a broker's fiduciary duty if the broker complies, and it is unreasonable for the M.L.S. to require it. The information should not be disclosed until *after* escrow closes, because a number of transactions never become completed, and the entire board membership would thus be made aware of what price the seller would accept, and on what terms.

§5.11. Failure to disclose may constitute grand theft

Sellers should be aware that a small number of licensees may, in fact, steal from them.

EXAMPLE The defendants, Mr. and Mrs. Barker, were convicted of grand theft. The victim owned real property and asked Mr. Barker, a real estate broker with whom he had previously dealt, for his opinion regarding an offer he had received of $25 per acre. Barker said the property was worth $50 an acre. Later, Barker told the seller that it was worth only $35 to $40 per acre. Subsequently, Barker told Marsh, a prospective buyer, that the property could be bought for $50 per acre. Marsh offered $45 and gave Barker a $500 deposit. Barker then told the seller he was unable to find anyone who would pay more than $25 per acre, and the seller agreed to sell.

The seller accepted an offer from Mrs. MacDonald (really Mrs. Barker) at $25 per acre, and at the same time the MacDonald-Marsh escrow was opened. Neither the seller nor Marsh knew that Mrs. MacDonald was in fact Mrs. Barker. After escrow closed, Marsh confronted Barker with a handwriting expert's opinion that Mrs. MacDonald and Mrs. Barker were the same person. Barker denied this, saying Mrs. MacDonald was a real person living in Michigan.

The court held that Barker was under a duty to disclose to the seller. Barker and Mrs. Barker knowingly and designedly, by false pretenses, defrauded the seller of the difference between the sum they intended to pay and the amount Marsh had offered.[38]

§5.12. Ownership or interest in escrow or title company

Does the Department of Real Estate frown on a licensee owning an interest in an escrow or title corporation or a lending institution? No, so long as full disclosure of this fact is made to all parties.[39] On the other hand, it has come to the attention of the Real Estate Commissioner's office that some licensees who have an interest in such corporations are refusing to present offers when the offer designates an escrow company other than their own. This act is a violation of the Real Estate Law.[40]

§5.13. Secret profits

The licensee is liable to his principal for *any* secret profit or other benefit received. He will not be permitted to retain *anything* from the transaction unless he fully discloses the benefit he will receive and obtains the principal's approval. The cases involving violations are significant in number.

EXAMPLES

1. Option and net listings are legally permissible;[41] however, they are not encouraged as they are subject to abuse. For example, an unscrupulous agent may take an option listing at lower than market value, not properly advertise it in the newspaper or M.L.S., purchase the property, and then resell it at a higher price. In an attempt to alleviate the problem, the Real Estate Law requires that the agent disclose to the principal, in writing, the full amount of the selling price and the profit realized or to be gained by the agent, and that the agent obtain the principal's written consent approving such profit prior to or coincident with the signing of the agreement to sell.[42]

2. A broker acting as a principal in obtaining an option to purchase real estate need not disclose the profit to the seller. Further, it has been held that a good faith net listing is the one exception to the duty of full disclosure of a broker's profits. In one case, the plaintiffs employed the defendant, a real estate broker, to sell their property. The plaintiffs told the defendant that they wanted $37,500 "net to them." The trial court found that the plaintiffs had not been influenced by the defendant in determining the selling price, but had arrived at their own independent judgment; that the defendant had at no time made any false, willful, or fraudulent representations; and that there had been no breach of fiduciary duty on the part of the defendant. In fact, the plaintiffs told the defendant that he should not ask much more above $37,500 because they thought that a higher price might kill the sale. The appellate court stated that when an owner authorizes a net sale

with the understanding that the agent shall be entitled to any excess thereafter as a commission or shall look to the purchaser for the payment, the agent may, without violating any trust relationship, purchase the property on his own account or act as the agent for others in acquiring it.[43] On the other hand, since the court did not discuss the duty of a licensee to disclose what he believes the actual market to be, then net listings should still be discouraged.

3. Realtor had listed homes and arranged FHA or VA loans through a lender. The lender paid Realtor an amount equal to the loan origination fee as consideration for placing the loan with them. Realtor never informed the various sellers of this compensation. The Real Estate Commissioner charged Realtor with taking secret profits. The court held that there was no violation, since the loan fee received was not a profit under the seller's listing agreements.[44]

§5.14. Dual representation

It is a basic rule that an agent may not act for more than one party to a transaction without the full consent of all parties.[45] The rationale for this rule is that the interests are obviously adverse. The fact that one principal had knowledge is insufficient. The fact that a broker's commission was paid by one party does not necessarily make that broker the exclusive agent of the party.[46] Not disclosing that a broker represents opposing parties is acting in a fraudulent manner. The agent will not be entitled to a commission, and if the contract is still executory, the principals may repudiate.[47] Figure 5-1 is a diagram showing the dual agency relationship and conflict of interest problems.

Because of a potential conflict of interest, an agent *must* fully disclose to each party all the facts that the agent knows will reasonably affect the principal's judgment in consenting to a dual agency (e.g., one of the parties and the broker are good friends).[48] In fact, the transaction can be avoided by the nonconsenting principal without showing that he suffered actual loss as a result of the undisclosed dual agency.[49] Also, in a dual agency, the agent is under no duty to disclose to one principal confidential information given to him by the other.[50] In order to eliminate *any* claim of an unknown dual agency, it should be specifically set forth in writing in the listing agreement and in the purchase contract *and* separately initialed by the respective parties so they are aware that it exists. On the other hand, if a cooperating broker wants to solely represent the buyer and not the seller (but still receive a portion of the commission), this too should be disclosed in writing, severing any agency relationship the broker may have with the seller and indicating that all his fiduciary duty is owed to the buyer. A potential conflict of interest should therefore be avoided.

Prior to 1987, there were sharp differences within the real estate community as to whether dual agency is a problem and, if so, what should be done about it. There was also no uniformity regarding what constitutes a dual agency. The California Association of Realtors proposed legislation designed to educate buyers and sellers about the agency relationship. The Department of Real Estate also recognized that there was a need for clarification in the law. Because of the uncertainty in the minds of a considerable number of people in the profession, steps were taken to eliminate confusion and create more specific guidelines by the sponsorship and enactment of legislation that requires a disclosure regarding real estate agency relationships[51] (see Figure 5-2). Although this does not necessarily eliminate the dual agency problems, it at least assists the buyer and seller if they will read and understand the agency disclosure form.

What about the situation in which a broker represents all parties to an exchange? The broker is clearly the agent of all parties and owes each the duty of utmost fairness and honesty and acts in a fiduciary capacity to all. How can a broker ethically represent all parties to an exchange when all sides are diametrically

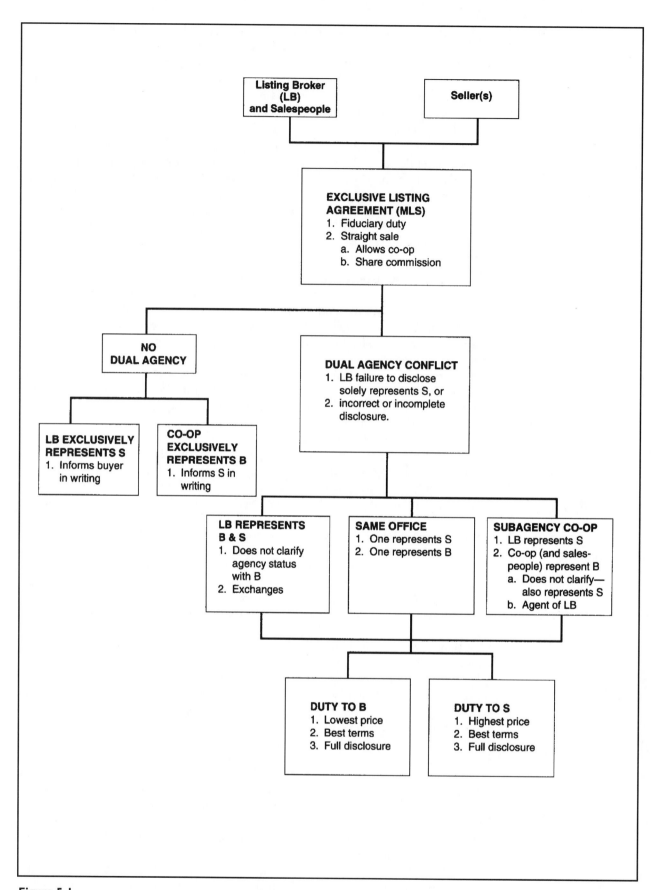

Figure 5-1

The dual agency relationship. (© 1981 W. D. Milligan, Attorney, San Diego, California. All rights reserved.)

CALIFORNIA ASSOCIATION OF REALTORS®

DISCLOSURE REGARDING
REAL ESTATE AGENCY RELATIONSHIPS
(As required by the Civil Code)

When you enter into a discussion with a real estate agent regarding a real estate transaction, you should from the outset understand what type of agency relationship or representation you wish to have with the agent in the transaction.

SELLER'S AGENT

A Seller's agent under a listing agreement with the Seller acts as the agent for the Seller only. A Seller's agent or a subagent of that agent has the following affirmative obligations:
To the Seller:
    A Fiduciary duty of utmost care, integrity, honesty, and loyalty in dealings with the Seller.
To the Buyer and the Seller:
    (a) Diligent exercise of reasonable skill and care in performance of the agent's duties.
    (b) A duty of honest and fair dealing and good faith.
    (c) A duty to disclose all facts known to the agent materially affecting the value or desirability of the property that are not known to, or within the diligent attention and observation of, the parties.

An agent is not obligated to reveal to either party any confidential information obtained from the other party that does not involve the affirmative duties set forth above.

BUYER'S AGENT

A selling agent can, with a Buyer's consent, agree to act as agent for the Buyer only. In these situations, the agent is not the Seller's agent, even if by agreement the agent may receive compensation for services rendered, either in full or in part from the Seller. An agent acting only for a Buyer has the following affirmative obligations:
To the Buyer:
    A fiduciary duty of utmost care, integrity, honesty, and loyalty in dealings with the Buyer.
To the Buyer and the Seller:
    (a) Diligent exercise of reasonable skill and care in performance of the agent's duties.
    (b) A duty of honest and fair dealing and good faith.
    (c) A duty to disclose all facts known to the agent materially affecting the value or desirability of the property that are not known to, or within the diligent attention and observation of, the parties.

An agent is not obligated to reveal to either party any confidential information obtained from the other party that does not involve the affirmative duties set forth above.

AGENT REPRESENTING BOTH SELLER & BUYER

A real estate agent, either acting directly or through one or more associate licensees can legally be the agent of both the Seller and the Buyer in a transaction, but only with the knowledge and consent of both the Seller and the Buyer.

In a dual agency situation, the agent has the following affirmative obligations to both the Seller and the Buyer:
    (a) A fiduciary duty of utmost care, integrity, honest and loyalty in the dealings with either Seller or the Buyer.
    (b) Other duties to the Seller and the Buyer as stated above in their respective sections.

In representing both Seller and Buyer, the agent may not, without the express permission of the respective party, disclose to the other party that the Seller will accept a price less than the listing price or that the Buyer will pay a price greater than the price offered.

The above duties of the agent in a real estate transaction do not relieve a Seller or Buyer from the responsibility to protect his or her own interests. You should carefully read all agreements to assure that they adequately express your understanding of the transaction. A real estate agent is a person qualified to advise about real estate. If legal or tax advice is desired, consult a competent professional.

Throughout your real property transaction you may receive more than one disclosure form, depending upon the number of agents assisting in the transaction. The law requires each agent with whom you have more than a casual relationship to present you with this disclosure form. You should read its contents each time it is presented to you, considering the relationship between you and the real estate agent in your specific transaction.

This disclosure form includes the provisions of Sections 2079.13 to 2079.24, inclusive, of the Civil Code set forth on the reverse hereof. Read it carefully.

I/WE ACKNOWLEDGE RECEIPT OF A COPY OF THIS DISCLOSURE.

BUYER/SELLER _____ Date _____ Time _____ AM/PM

BUYER/SELLER _____ Date _____ Time _____ AM/PM

AGENT _____ By _____ Date _____
          (Please Print)   (Associate Licensee or Broker-Signature)

> This Disclosure form must be provided in a listing, sale, exchange, installment land contract, or lease over one year, if the transaction involves one-to-four dwelling residential property, including a mobile home, as follows:
> (a) From a Listing Agent to a Seller: Prior to entering into the listing.
> (b) From an Agent selling a property he/she has listed to a Buyer: Prior to the Buyer's execution of the offer.
> (c) From a Selling Agent to a Buyer: Prior to the Buyer's execution of the offer.
> (d) From a Selling Agent (in a cooperating real estate firm) to a Seller: Prior to presentation of the offer to the Seller.
>
> It is not necessary or required to confirm an agency relationship using a separate Confirmation form if the agency confirmation portion of the Real Estate Purchase Contract is properly completed in full. However, it is still necessary to use this Disclosure form.

THIS FORM HAS BEEN APPROVED BY THE CALIFORNIA ASSOCIATION OF REALTORS® (C.A.R.). NO REPRESENTATION IS MADE AS TO THE LEGAL VALIDITY OR ADEQUACY OF ANY PROVISION IN ANY SPECIFIC TRANSACTION. A REAL ESTATE BROKER IS THE PERSON QUALIFIED TO ADVISE ON REAL ESTATE TRANSACTIONS. IF YOU DESIRE LEGAL OR TAX ADVICE, CONSULT AN APPROPRIATE PROFESSIONAL.

This form is available for use by the entire real estate industry. It is not intended to identify the user as a REALTOR®. REALTOR® is a registered collective membership mark which may be used only by members of the NATIONAL ASSOCIATION OF REALTORS® who subscribe to its Code of Ethics.

The copyright laws of the United States (17 U.S. Code) forbid the unauthorized reproduction of this form by any means, including facsimile or computerized formats. Copyright © 1987-1997, CALIFORNIA ASSOCIATION OF REALTORS®

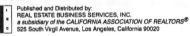

Published and Distributed by:
REAL ESTATE BUSINESS SERVICES, INC.
a subsidiary of the CALIFORNIA ASSOCIATION OF REALTORS®
525 South Virgil Avenue, Los Angeles, California 90020

┌─ OFFICE USE ONLY ─┐
Reviewed by Broker
or Designee _____
Date _____

FORM AD-14 REVISED 10/95

Figure 5-2
Disclosure Regarding Real Estate Agency Relationships

CHAPTER 2 OF TITLE 9 OF PART 4 OF DIVISION 3 OF THE CIVIL CODE

2079.13 As used in Sections 2079.14 to 2079.24, inclusive, the following terms have the following meanings:

(a) "Agent" means a person acting under provisions of tile 9 (commencing with Section 2295) in a real property transaction, and includes a person who is licensed as a real estate broker under Chapter 3 (commencing with Section 10130) of Part 1 of Division 4 of the Business and Professions Code, and under whose license a listing is executed or an offer to purchase is obtained.

(b) "Associate licensee" means a person who is licensed as a real broker or salesperson under Chapter 3 (commencing with Section 10130) of Part 1 of Division 4 of the Business and Professions Code and who is either licensed under a broker or has entered into a written contract with a broker to act as the broker's agent in connection with acts requiring a real estate license and to function under the broker's supervision in the capacity of an associate licensee.

The agent in the real property transaction bears responsibility for his or her associate licensees who perform as agents of the agent. When an associate licensee owes a duty to any principal, or to any buyer or seller who is not a principal, in a real property transaction, that duty is equivalent to the duty owed to that party by the broker for whom the associate licensee functions.

(c) "Buyer" means a transferee in a real property transaction, and includes a person who executes an offer to purchase real property from a seller through an agent, or who seeks the services of an agent in more than a casual, transitory, or preliminary manner, with the object of entering into a real property transaction. "Buyer" includes vendee or lessee.

(d) "Dual agent" means an agent acting, either directly or through an associate licensee, as agent for both the seller and the buyer in a real property transaction.

(e) "Listing agreement" means a contract between an owner of real property and an agent, by which the agent has been authorized to sell the real property or to find or obtain a buyer.

(f) "Listing agent" means a person who has obtained a listing of real property to act as an agent for compensation.

(g) "Listing price" is the amount expressed in dollars specified in the listing for which the seller is willing to sell the real property through the listing agent.

(h) "Offering price" is the amount expressed in dollars specified in an offer to purchase for which the buyer is willing to buy the real property.

(i) "Offer to purchase" means a written contract executed by a buyer acting through a selling agent which becomes the contract for the sale of the real property upon acceptance by the seller.

(j) "Real property" means any estate specified by subdivision (1) or (2) of Section 761 in property which constitutes or is improved with one to four dwelling units, any leasehold in this type of property exceeding one year's duration, and mobilehomes, when offered for sale or sold through an agent pursuant to the authority contained in Section 10131.6 of the Business and Professions Code.

(k) "Real property transaction" means a transaction for the sale of real property in which an agent is employed by one or more of the principals to act in that transaction, and includes a listing or an offer to purchase.

(l) "Sell," "sale," or "sold" refers to a transaction for the transfer of real property from the seller to the buyer, and includes exchanges of real property between the seller and buyer, transactions for the creation of a real property sales contract within the meaning of Section 2985, and transactions for the creation of a leasehold exceeding one year's duration.

(m) "Seller" means the transferor in a real property transaction, and includes an owner who lists real property with an agent, whether or not a transfer results, or who receives an offer to purchase real property of which he or she is the owner from an agent on behalf of another. "Seller" includes both a vendor and a lessor.

(n) "Selling agent" means a listing agent who acts alone, or an agent who acts in cooperation with a listing agent, and who sells or finds and obtains a buyer for the real property, or an agent who locates property for a buyer or who finds a buyer for a property for which no listing exists and presents an offer to purchase to the seller.

(o) "Subagent" means a person to whom an agent delegates agency powers as provided in Article 5 (commencing with Section 2349) of Chapter 1 of Title 9. However, "subagent" does not include an associate licensee who is acting under the supervision of an agent in a real property transaction.

2079.14 Listing agents and selling agents shall provide the seller and buyer in a real property transaction with a copy of the disclosure form specified in Section 2079.16. and, except as provided in subdivision (c), shall obtain a signed acknowledgement of receipt from that seller or buyer, except as provided in this section or Section 2079.15, as follows:

(a) The listing agent, if any, shall provide the disclosure form to the seller prior to entering into the listing agreement.

(b) The selling agent shall provide the disclosure form to the seller as soon as practicable prior to presenting the seller with an offer to purchase, unless the selling agent previously provided the seller with a copy of the disclosure form pursuant to subdivision (a).

(c) Where the selling agent does not deal on a face-to-face basis with the seller, the disclosure form prepared by the selling agent may be furnished to the seller (and acknowledgement of receipt obtained for the selling agent from the seller) by the listing agent, or the selling agent may deliver the disclosure form by certified mail addressed to the seller at his or her last known address, in which case no signed acknowledgement of receipt is required.

(d) The selling agent shall provide the disclosure form to the buyer as soon as practicable prior to execution of the buyer's offer to purchase, except that if the offer to purchase is not prepared by the selling agent, the selling agent shall present the disclosure form to the buyer not later than the next business day after the selling agent receives the offer to purchase from the buyer.

2079.15 In any circumstance in which the seller or buyer refuses to sign an acknowledgement of receipt pursuant to Section 2079.14, the agent, or an associate licensee acting for an agent, shall set forth, sign, and date a written declaration of the facts of the refusal.

2079.17 (a) As soon as practicable, the selling agent shall disclose to the buyer and seller whether the selling agent is acting in the real property transaction exclusively as the buyer's agent, exclusively as the seller's agent, or as a dual agent representing both the buyer and the seller. This relationship shall be confirmed in the contract to purchase and sell real property or in a separate writing executed or acknowledged by the seller, the buyer, and the selling agent prior to or coincident with execution of that contract by the buyer and the seller, respectively.

(b) As soon as practicable, the listing agent shall disclose to the seller whether the listing agent is acting in the real property transaction exclusively as the seller's agent, or as a dual agent representing both the buyer and seller. This relationship shall be confirmed in the contract to purchase and sell real property or in a separate writing executed or acknowledged by the seller and the listing agent prior to or coincident with the execution of that contract by the seller.

(c) The confirmation required by subdivisions (a) and (b) shall be in the following form.

_____ is the agent of (check one):   _____ is the agent of (check one):
(Name of Listing Agent)   (Name of Selling Agent if not the same as the Listing Agent)

☐ the seller exclusively; or   ☐ the buyer exclusively; or

☐ both the buyer and seller.   ☐ the seller exclusively; or

                                                                                            ☐ both the buyer and seller.

(d) The disclosures and confirmation required by this section shall be in addition to the disclosure required by Section 2079. 14.

2079.18 No selling agent in a real property transaction may act as an agent for the buyer only, when the selling agent is also acting as the listing agent in the transaction.

2079.19 The payment of compensation or the obligation to pay compensation to an agent by the seller or buyer is not necessarily determinative of a particular agency relationship between an agent and the seller or buyer. A listing agent and a selling agent may agree to share any compensation or commission paid, or any right to any compensation or commission for which an obligation arises as the result of a real estate transaction, and the terms of any such agreement shall not necessarily be determinative of a particular relationship.

2079.20 Nothing in this article prevents an agent from selecting, as a condition of the agent's employment, a specific form of agency relationship not specifically prohibited by this article if the requirements of Section 2079.14 and Section 2079.17 are complied with.

2079.21 A dual agent shall not disclose to the buyer that the seller is willing to sell the property at a price less than the listing price, without the express written consent of the seller. A dual agent shall not disclose to the seller that the buyer is willing to pay a price greater than the offering price, without the express written consent of the buyer.

This section does not alter in any way the duty or responsibility of a dual agent to any principal with respect to confidential information other than price.

2079.22 Nothing in this article precludes a listing agent from also being a selling agent, and the combination of these functions in one agent does not, of itself, make that agent a dual agent.

2079.23 A contract between the principal and agent may be modified or altered to change the agency relationship at any time before the performance of the act which is the object of the agency with the written consent of the parties to the agency relationship.

2079.24 Nothing in this article shall be construed to either diminish the duty of disclosure owed buyers and sellers by agents and their associate licensees, subagents, and employees or to relieve agents and their associate licensees, subagents, and employees from liability for their conduct in connection with acts governed by this article or for any breach of a fiduciary duty or a duty of disclosure.

Figure 5-2 (Cont.)
Disclosure Regarding Real Estate Agency Relationships

opposed? The owner who wishes to exchange upward wants to obtain the real estate for as little as possible, while the owners in the other positions want as high a price as possible. Thus a built-in conflict of interest results. The same rationale holds true when one broker represents both a buyer and a seller in a direct sale.

EXAMPLES

1. A licensed broker obtained an exclusive listing on ranch property, which was advertised for sale. Prospective purchasers contacted the broker and gave him an exclusive listing on their home, inserting a provision that the cash proceeds from the sale of their home were to be applied to the purchase of the ranch. Subsequently, without the knowledge of buyer or seller, the broker acted as the agent of each, and collected a commission on the sale of the house and the sale of the ranch.

   Judgment against the broker was affirmed. Notwithstanding the fact that he acted as agent of and received a commission from the sellers of the ranch, he prevented the sellers from securing the full price offered for the ranch by the purchasers by demanding and receiving a commission from the purchasers.[52]

2. It is a breach of duty for a licensee to reveal confidential information received from a client to others, e.g., that the seller is about to go into foreclosure, allowing other people to purchase the property at a reduced price or purchase a note from the beneficiary at a discount.[53]

---

§5.15. Duty to use care, skill, and diligence

The real estate licensee is presumed to have superior knowledge and skills in the real estate field, and is under an obligation to exercise greater care and skill than the ordinary person. He will therefore be held to a higher standard of care.[54] He is further liable for negligence or incompetence in the performance of his duties.[55] The real estate law is designed "to protect the public not only from the conniving real estate salesperson but also from the uninformed, negligent, or unknowledgeable salesperson."[56]

The skill required includes an ordinary professional knowledge concerning the title and natural characteristics of the property the broker is selling.[57] Further, unless otherwise agreed, a paid agent is subject to a duty to the principal to act with standard care and with skill that is standard in the locality for the kind of work that the agent is employed to perform and, in addition, to exercise any special skill that he has.[58]

Because the broker is charged with superior knowledge, he has a duty either to make an investigation of any matter pertaining to the agency of which he does not have sufficient knowledge to allow him to make reliable recommendations, or to disclose to the client the fact that he lacks such knowledge.[59] In fact, in one case it was determined that there is a duty to refer a given situation to a specialist if the licensee does not have adequate experience to handle it.[60]

EXAMPLES

1. The plaintiff, Wilson, contacted a broker to assist him in purchasing a ranch. The broker examined an expired listing and showed the property to Wilson. Wilson asked if there were any other encumbrances on the property except the existing first trust deed. The broker said there were none, although he did not have a current title report. Rather than purchase at that time, Wilson leased with an option to buy and moved onto the property. He then learned of a second trust deed.

   The court held that had the broker advised Wilson to obtain a title search it would have disclosed the second trust deed. Instead, the broker told Wilson that there were no other encumbrances except the first trust deed, without seeking to ascertain the true facts. The broker, as agent of Wilson, was required to exercise reasonable skill and ordinary diligence and not to act negligently.[61]

2. Homeowners consistently complain because licensees have left business cards stuck on doors and mailboxes to show they had called. The concern is understandable because the cards draw attention to the fact that the owner may not be at home, and thus the property is left susceptible to burglars. Another problem area that bears noting is the negligence on the part of some individuals in the M.L.S. who fail to put the key back in the lock box, or leave the door unlocked. On at least one occasion, a note was made on a listing published in an M.L.S. that the key was "under front door mat." Such acts can give rise to liability for any loss occasioned by this type of negligence or exercise of poor judgment.

3. More homes are becoming burglarized every year, some of which contain lockboxes. It therefore seems incumbent upon the licensee to inform the seller of this problem in order to give the seller the option of having a lockbox or not. Although not using a lockbox creates more time consumption on the part of the licensee, the problem should be dealt with.

§5.16. Duty to account

The broker is accountable to his principal for all money or other property received from or on behalf of the principal.[62] The licensee is obligated to render an account upon demand.

EXAMPLES

1. Broker returned a deposit to the buyer without authorization from the seller, when the offer to purchase authorized the seller to retain the sum deposited in the event of a repudiation of the contract by the buyer. The court held that the broker was bound to account to his principal and is liable therefore, as the money the broker received belongs to the principal, the seller.[63]

2. When a seller's broker has no authority to accept a deposit from a prospective purchaser, but he does so, he is acting as agent for the purchaser and not the seller. This rule does not apply, however, when the evidence supports a conclusion that such a broker actually had authority to receive a deposit on behalf of the seller.[64]

3. In an older case, the defendant selling broker, T, was a member of an M.L.S. with whom S had listed his property. The listing agreement made the listing and selling brokers coagents of S, and authorized the selling broker to accept and hold a deposit from a buyer. T found a buyer, B. B signed the offer to purchase, which contained a liquidated damage clause. B's husband was overseas at the time and she could not obtain financing without his signature. T returned B's deposit. In an action by S against T for damages, the court held that there was no question but that under the listing and purchase contract T was S's agent to receive a deposit. T maintained that the sale was conditional upon financing, hence he received the money as B's agent. However, the purchase contract did not state that financing was a contingency. Since the offer was drawn by T, it was construed "most strongly against him." T had no right to return the deposit to B, and was therefore liable in damages to S. "In the absence of special circumstances, moneys received by one in the capacity of agent are not his, and the law implies a promise to pay them to the principal on demand."[65]

4. B received $1,000 from H as deposit on an offer to purchase a piece of real estate. B deposited the money into his trust account but withdrew it the same day. He commingled and converted it for his own use without the knowledge and consent of H. B's explanation for his conduct was that he was using his trust account as a personal account to avoid possible attachment of the account as a result of a civil litigation in which he was involved. By immediately cashing the check, he felt that H would be less likely to renege on his offer. Although B had been a broker for 18 years, without prior

disciplinary record, the court held against him, stating: "Among the qualifications of a real estate broker is a full understanding of the essential duties and obligations between principal and agent, the principles of real estate practice and the canons of business ethics."[66]

§5.17. Fraud, deceit, and misrepresentation

The law regards *all* acts of the agent or subagent as *fraudulent* if they are in violation of the agent's fiduciary duty.[67] It has been held that an *oral* contract by a principal authorizing a broker to act as his agent and find a buyer for his property, under which the broker receives confidential information, is sufficient to create a fiduciary relationship between the parties.[68]

Although the terms are quite often used interchangeably, there is a difference between fraud and deceit. *Actual fraud*[69] arises only out of a contract, while *deceit*[70] arises out of an obligation toward every person. However, the elements are substantially the same. The elements of fraud are as follows:

1. An affirmative representation or concealment of a material fact when under a duty to disclose

2. If based upon a representation, that it was false and the party *knew* of its falsity

3. If based on concealment, that it was done with the *intent* to induce the injured party to enter into the transaction

4. The injured party *relied* on the representation or lack of knowledge of the concealment

5. That the party was *induced* to enter into the transaction

6. That as a result, the party was damaged[71]

Fraud includes (1) intentional fraud; (2) negligent fraud (negligent misrepresentation); (3) concealment; and (4) promissory fraud (promise made without any intention of performing). Intentional, negligent, or promissory fraud often involves a broker *and* seller relationship; while intentional or negligent fraud or concealment generally involves a broker or seller dealing with a prospective purchaser. The elements of negligent fraud—hereinafter called "misrepresentation"— are basically the same as actual fraud, except that rather than misstating *intentionally* or concealing, the party does not have sufficient information to justify the statement made.

EXAMPLES

1. A widow in her seventies sued the defendant, a broker, for fraud and misrepresentation. The defendant represented her in an exchange of her property, which netted her $400 per month, for a 42-unit apartment complex that the defendant told her would net between $700 and $900 per month. The defendant did not verify the expense and maintenance statement, or the alleged vacancy allowance. The defendant also told the plaintiff that there were only three to four vacancies but that the building could easily run at 100 percent occupancy, and assured the plaintiff that the "building had been excellently maintained and that if the property did not suit her it could easily be resold." The defendant had based his $700 to $900 net income per month on a 100 percent occupancy. By the time the plaintiff took possession, she discovered that a large number of apartments had leaks, there were maintenance problems with drapes and carpets, and she had difficulty with tenants who had not been evicted for nonpayment of rent. The resident manager received a $100 a month apartment rent-free and was reimbursed for some painting and maintenance. The manager normally collected only about $4,200 per month—far short of the $5,136 set forth on the broker's statement. Since the trust deed payments were $4,044, there was never enough income

to meet fixed and maintenance expenses. The plaintiff lost the property in a foreclosure sale. (In this resulting action, the plaintiff lost in the trial court but the case was reversed on appeal, since the trial court committed prejudicial error in failing to instruct the jury on the fiduciary duties of a broker, negligence, misrepresentation, fraud, and other instructions.)[72]

2. A seller sued the buyer, the brokers, and the salespeople for fraud and negligence. The plaintiff owned a home operated as a rest home, free of encumbrances and valued at $127,000, but listed for $135,000. The buyers owned a skid row building encumbered with a first trust deed of $169,000. Through their brokers, the plaintiffs sold their home to the buyers, for which they received $10,000 in cash, $10,000 for the furniture, and a promissory note and second trust deed for $117,500 on the buyer's property. Later, the buyers defaulted on the first trust deed on the skid row property and the plaintiffs lost their $117,500.

    The plaintiffs testified that there was a close friendship with one of the defendant's salespeople and they had full confidence and trust in two others who had assisted. The plaintiffs relied on their statements that: (1) the buyer's property was worth $895,000 (although it was worth only $85,000 according to expert testimony); (2) the second trust deed of $117,500 was ample security; and (3) the buyer was a wealthy businessman.

    The court held that the statements of the agents were not mere statements of opinion. The agents were speaking as experienced operators in real estate. As agents of the plaintiffs, it was necessary for them to investigate the value of the buyer's property, which the plaintiffs reasonably believed they had done. Under the circumstances, the plaintiffs had no obligation to make an independent investigation. (The court went on to say, "It would be a good guess that if the Sphinx is ever sold for its replacement costs, less depreciation, the seller will be a man named Jack Casey"—who was the buyer, the defendant in this action.)[73]

§5.18. Cooperating broker owes fiduciary duty to seller

There are a number of cases concerning cooperating brokers' duties.

EXAMPLES
1. One case involved the issue of whether or not the defendants, cooperating brokers, breached a fiduciary duty to the plaintiffs. The plaintiffs had listed their property with a real estate broker. The defendants and the listing broker advertised the property for sale. In April 1969, the defendants brought an offer to the plaintiffs that was accepted, but the transaction was never consummated. In May 1969, the defendants discovered that on June 30, 1965, the plaintiffs' property had been sold to the state for nonpayment of delinquent taxes, with the right of redemption for five years. The plaintiffs maintained they were unaware of the sale. The defendants did not inform the plaintiffs, and concealed this fact from them until after the five-year redemption period expired. In August 1971, the defendants purchased the property for the minimum requested bid of $7,500.

    The court held that there was an agency relationship established by stating that whenever the acts or omissions of a broker cause injury in a real estate transaction, there is a compelling reason to find him an agent. As a footnote, the court mentioned that under the form of M.L.S. agreements used in many areas, a broker on the multiple listing is by virtue of the agreement an agent of the seller.[74]

2. The sellers of real property brought an action based on fraud against the cooperating real estate broker when the broker, in showing the property to prospective purchasers, represented falsely that the residence was not built

on a filled lot. The purchasers bought in reliance on such representation, and later brought an action against the sellers for rescission. The purchasers prevailed in the rescission action. The sellers then brought this action against the co-op broker and recovered judgment. It was held that the co-op broker violated his duty to his principals by not informing them of the representations he had made to the purchasers that the lot was not a filled lot, and thereby perpetrated a fraud on the confidence bestowed on him by the sellers.[75]

Fact versus opinion. The elements of fraud and misrepresentation ordinarily include an affirmation of fact, not of mere opinion. Despite this general rule, misrepresentation of opinion is actionable in many situations, and particularly when the agent is clothed with a real estate license, his badge of authority, which advertises that he possesses superior knowledge or special information regarding real property. A statement by an agent to his buyer that a certain lot is an excellent investment and will increase in value, when there is no solid basis in fact, may be actionable because he is presumed to have superior knowledge and what he thought was opinion may well be affirmation of fact. The same statement made by a layman, on the other hand, may be treated as opinion.

Predictions as to future events by a third party are generally deemed opinions and are not actionable fraud. However, there are three recognized exceptions: (1) when a party holds himself out to be specially qualified and the other party reasonably relies on this superior knowledge; (2) when the opinion is by a fiduciary or other trusted person; and (3) when a party states his opinion as an existing fact that justifies a belief in the truth of the opinion.[76] Another example is a representation by the seller of a motel that a buyer could keep it rented all the time, which reasonably implies knowledge of past full occupancy.[77] Generally, a private person is not entitled to rely on the opinion of another private person concerning the future decisions of a public body.

§5.19. Concurrent duties

Since most real estate transactions are handled through an escrow company, few real estate licensees are affected by the law that requires a broker to disclose the sales price. There is a chance that the law may apply under isolated circumstances, so licensees should be aware of the law. In essence, the law requires that within a month after the close of a real estate transaction, the broker must give a written statement to the buyer and seller as to the purchase price and, if the property was exchanged, the amount of the money added, if any. If the transaction was closed through escrow and escrow issues a closing statement, this is deemed compliance. If the transaction does not close through escrow, the broker must, within one week, cause any trust deeds to be recorded, or deliver to the beneficiary a written recommendation that it is to be recorded forthwith, unless written instructions not to record are received from the beneficiary.[78]

§5.20. Corporate agent or officer liable for intentional tort

All persons who are shown to have participated in an intentional tort are liable for the full amount of the damages suffered even though the corporation may also be liable.[79] Therefore a licensee working for a real estate corporation can also be held liable if he participates in a fraud or other intentional tort, such as an intentional interference with a contractual relationship.

Action by the qualifying broker of a real estate corporation must be regarded as an action by the corporation and not by the broker as an individual. Thus, as an agent of the corporation, the qualifying broker owes a duty to supervise the salesperson. For a breach of such duty, he can be liable to the salesperson (and the corporation) in an action for indemnification. Having no contractual relationship with a seller or buyer, the qualifying broker cannot be personally liable (unless he participated, e.g., in a fraud).[80]

III. DUTIES AND LIABILITIES TO THIRD PARTIES

§5.21. In general

In California the real estate licensee is required to deal fairly and honestly with all parties and not act in a negligent manner.[81] The ancient rule of caveat emptor ("let the buyer beware") has little application in today's complicated market. The buyer cannot be charged with knowledge of what is hidden under the carpeting, under the floors, or behind the walls.

The seller's agent is under the same duty as the seller to disclose to the buyer facts materially affecting the value or desirability of the property that are known or should be known with the exercise of reasonable diligence. For a fraudulent act, the agent is jointly and severally liable with the seller for the full amount of damages suffered by the buyer.

Although it is currently lawful for a licensee to represent both a buyer and a seller (if full disclosure is made), such representation is hazardous. From the standpoint of the buyer, it is sometimes best to use the services of a competent broker who does not have the listing and who will represent the buyer, thus avoiding any dual representation conflict of interest problems.

§5.22. Fraud and misrepresentation

Fraud and misrepresentation between broker and principal were discussed earlier in this chapter. Fraud applies equally to the buyer.

EXAMPLES

1. If an agent informs a prospective purchaser that the house has copper piping, when in fact it is galvanized, the statement is either fraudulent, if the licensee knows, or misrepresentation, if he merely took the word of the seller without verifying. Intent versus a careless act is the difference.

2. Other common examples would be a statement that the house has hardwood floors under the carpeting, when the floors are really plywood or concrete; an assertion that the home has 1,800 square feet when it actually has only 1,650 (remember, the garage is not counted in determining the square footage); representations as to income and vacancy factor; and compliance with building codes. In a newer case, the agent breached his fiduciary duty and committed constructive fraud by making false representations to the buyer that the property was more than one acre in size and that it could be subdivided, when, in fact, both statements were false. (Further, the court awarded the buyer the broader "benefit of the bargain" measure of damages rather than the "out of pocket" loss.)[82]

3. In December 1968, R suggested that plaintiff consider purchasing an 11-unit apartment. In order to induce plaintiff to purchase, R, acting as agent for Quality Properties, and the owner, Roach, made representations, orally and in writing, that the apartment would be worth $140,000 only if rents were raised; that rents were understated; and that R could raise rents. With the increased rents and with existing expenses, the building would be worth $140,000. Plaintiff would have net spendable income of $500 per month; the property would show a principal build-up or equity build-up, would be a good investment, and would show a 30 percent return on $15,000 down, as well as a net spendable income.

   Plaintiff put $15,000 down and the balance of $125,000 in an all-inclusive trust deed. Before close of escrow, R represented she would manage the building free of charge for one year. At close of escrow, every unit was occupied. R sent notices to increase the rent. R had not previously consulted with the tenants. Sixty days later, 65 percent of the units were vacated. No new tenants could be secured at existing rents or under the new rent schedule. Rents then were not sufficient to meet either operating expenses or payments of principal on the trust deed.

In 1969 plaintiff discharged R. In the next few months, plaintiff was requested to pay money out of his own pocket.

Plaintiff elected not to rescind, but instead, from July 1969 to December 1971, rented the building furnished (unfurnished when purchased) to a flight school for its students. In February 1972, plaintiff surrendered possession by a deed in lieu of foreclosure, to Roach, for a total loss to plaintiff of approximately $42,000, and brought suit against defendants for fraud.

Defendants moved for a nonsuit in the Superior Court, which was granted under an older case that stated that a plaintiff waives his right to seek damages for fraud if, after he discovers the fraud, he makes a new agreement with the other party to the original contract, and such new agreement results in a compromise and adjustment of plaintiff's rights under the original contract and thereby supersedes the original contract.

The District Court of Appeals reversed the case in favor of plaintiff. Plaintiffs' new agreement was not with the defendants, but with the flight school. This new agreement did not affect the old one, or the defendants.[83]

4.   In a recent case, it was held that for purposes of recovery for fraud under Civil Code 3343, the buyer was entitled to summary judgment against the seller even though the buyer knew, prior to close of escrow, that the home was not designed by a famous architect—which was one of the main purposes for the purchase. Whether this case is good law is questionable.[84]

§5.23. Constructive fraud

When one broker reads, for example, the listing appearing in the M.L.S., he may reasonably be able to rely on it. If he does, and the buyer is damaged, the cooperating broker may nevertheless be liable under the theory of constructive fraud. Constructive fraud[85] consists in any of the following:

1.   Any breach of duty that, without an actually fraudulent intent, gains an advantage to the person in fault, or anyone claiming under him by misleading another to his prejudice, or to the prejudice of anyone claiming under him.[86]

2.   Any such act or omission as the law specially declares to be fraudulent, without respect to actual fraud

Actual fraud is always a question of fact to be determined by the trier of fact.[87] *Constructive fraud* exists when conduct, though not actually fraudulent, has all the consequences and all the legal effects of actual fraud.[88] Constructive fraud comprises all acts, omissions, and concealments involving a breach of equitable duty, trust, or confidence, and resulting in damage to another; it exists in cases in which conduct, although not actually fraudulent, ought to be so treated—that is, as a constructive or quasi-fraud.[89]

EXAMPLES   1.   A vendor of land, representing a frontage to be 80 feet, without any actual fraudulent intent, was guilty of constructive fraud when the frontage was only 77 feet.[90]

2.   If the broker is merely the innocent conduit of the seller's fraud, he may be innocent of actual fraud, but he may be guilty of constructive fraud, if he passes on the misstatements as true without investigating them himself.[91]

§5.24. Duty to disclose

The area of disclosure continues to grow. Licensees now have a duty not only to disclose, but also to investigate and to explain. In fact, on a one- to four-dwelling unit, the law requires the seller and the seller's broker to accurately complete a Real Estate Transfer Disclosure Statement for the buyer.[92] See Figure 5-3 for a form of "Real Estate Transfer Disclosure Statement" published by the California Association of Realtors. To eliminate any later claim that the buyer was not informed of a defect, it is recommended that the seller, in every instance, disclose in writing all aspects that materially affect the value or desirability of the property being sold.

EXAMPLES

1. In the landmark case of Easton v. Strassburger, the court held that a listing broker owes a duty of due care to a buyer to conduct a reasonably competent and diligent inspection of a residential property in order to discover defects for the benefit of the buyer. This duty does not include just what the broker knew, but what should have been known. The court stated that to hold otherwise would not only reward the unskilled broker for his own incompetence, but also might provide the unscrupulous broker the means to protect himself at the expense of the inexperienced and unwary who rely on him (but beware of the two-year statute of limitations.[93]

2. A buyer purchased a home not knowing that, ten years before, a woman and her four children had been murdered in the home. The seller and real estate agents knew the event emotionally affected the market value and did not disclose the murders to the buyer. In fact, the agent had asked the neighbors not to mention the murders to the purchaser. The court held that the murders were of sufficient materiality to impose a duty on the seller and his agents to disclose it.[94]

3. In a recent 1997 case, B purchased a home in a planned development. S did not disclose that the project was involved in a pending lawsuit affecting the property. The homeowner association did know about the suit, but there was no proof that either the buyer's or seller's brokers knew of the lawsuit. B discovered the suit after close of escrow and sued S and both brokers. Held: Upon visual inspection there was no showing of any defects and the home inspection report also showed no defects. Under both statutory and nonstatutory theories, the brokers are not liable. According to this case, brokers' duties do not involve inspections (1) of areas that are reasonably and normally inaccessible, (2) of areas that are offsite or of public records or permits, and (3) of more than the unit offered for sale. Of course if it is proven that the brokers knew of the lawsuit, then they have a duty to disclose.[95]

4. Assume a prospective buyer asks, "Does the house have termites?" and the broker says, "Here's a termite report stating the house is free from infestation." If the agent has seen a previous (or subsequent) report that discloses termites and dry rot that have not been corrected, his duty is to disclose this to the buyer.[96]

---

§5.25. Concealment

Actual concealment should be distinguished from *nondisclosure*.

Concealment. Concealment is a term of art that includes mere nondisclosure when a party has a duty to disclose. Actual concealment occurs when the seller fixes up his property by hiding defects. His action constitutes actionable fraud.

EXAMPLE Plastering and painting over structural defects or paneling a wall or room in an effort to hide holes brought about by termite infestation.

CALIFORNIA
ASSOCIATION
OF REALTORS®

REAL ESTATE TRANSFER DISCLOSURE STATEMENT
(CALIFORNIA CIVIL CODE 1102, ET SEQ.)

THIS DISCLOSURE STATEMENT CONCERNS THE REAL PROPERTY SITUATED IN THE CITY OF _____
_____, COUNTY OF _____, STATE OF CALIFORNIA,
DESCRIBED AS _____.
THIS STATEMENT IS A DISCLOSURE OF THE CONDITION OF THE ABOVE DESCRIBED PROPERTY IN COMPLIANCE
WITH SECTION 1102 OF THE CIVIL CODE AS OF _____, 19 _____. IT IS NOT A WARRANTY
OF ANY KIND BY THE SELLER(S) OR ANY AGENT(S) REPRESENTING ANY PRINCIPAL(S) IN THIS TRANSACTION,
AND IS NOT A SUBSTITUTE FOR ANY INSPECTIONS OR WARRANTIES THE PRINCIPAL(S) MAY WISH TO OBTAIN.

I
COORDINATION WITH OTHER DISCLOSURE FORMS

This Real Estate Transfer Disclosure Statement is made pursuant to Section 1102 of the Civil Code. Other statutes require disclosures, depending upon the details of the particular real estate transaction (for example: special study zone and purchase-money liens on residential property).

Substituted Disclosures: The following disclosures have or will be made in connection with this real estate transfer, and are intended to satisfy the disclosure obligations on this form, where the subject matter is the same:

☐ Inspection reports completed pursuant to the contract of sale or receipt for deposit.

☐ Additional inspection reports or disclosures:_____
_____

II
SELLER'S INFORMATION

The Seller discloses the following information with the knowledge that even though this is not a warranty, prospective Buyers may rely on this information in deciding whether and on what terms to purchase the subject property. Seller hereby authorizes any agent(s) representing any principal(s) in this transaction to provide a copy of this statement to any person or entity in connection with any actual or anticipated sale of the property.

THE FOLLOWING ARE REPRESENTATIONS MADE BY THE SELLER(S) AND ARE NOT THE REPRESENTATIONS OF THE AGENT(S), IF ANY. THIS INFORMATION IS A DISCLOSURE AND IS NOT INTENDED TO BE PART OF ANY CONTRACT BETWEEN THE BUYER AND SELLER.

Seller ☐ is ☐ is not occupying the property.

A. The subject property has the items checked below (read across):

☐ Range	☐ Oven	☐ Microwave
☐ Dishwasher	☐ Trash Compactor	☐ Garbage Disposal
☐ Washer/Dryer Hookups		☐ Rain Gutters
☐ Burglar Alarms	☐ Smoke Detector(s)	☐ Fire Alarm
☐ T.V. Antenna	☐ Satellite Dish	☐ Intercom
☐ Central Heating	☐ Central Air Conditioning	☐ Evaporator Cooler(s)
☐ Wall/Window Air Conditioning	☐ Sprinklers	☐ Public Sewer System
☐ Septic Tank	☐ Sump Pump	☐ Water Softener
☐ Patio/Decking	☐ Built-in Barbecue	☐ Gazebo
☐ Sauna		
☐ Hot Tub ☐ Locking Safety Cover*	☐ Pool ☐ Child Resistant Barrier*	☐ Spa ☐ Locking Safety Cover*
☐ Security Gate(s)	☐ Automatic Garage Door Opener(s)*	☐ Number Remote Controls _____
Garage: ☐ Attached	☐ Not Attached	☐ Carport
Pool/Spa Heater: ☐ Gas	☐ Solar	☐ Electric
Water Heater: ☐ Gas	☐ Water Heater Anchored, Braced, or Strapped*	
Water Supply: ☐ City	☐ Well	☐ Private Utility or
Gas Supply: ☐ Utility	☐ Bottled	Other _____
☐ Window Screens	☐ Window Security Bars ☐ Quick Release Mechanism on Bedroom Windows*	

Exhaust Fan(s) in _____ 220 Volt Wiring in _____ Fireplace(s) in _____
☐ Gas Starter _____ ☐ Roof(s): Type: _____ Age: _____ (approx.)
☐ Other: _____

Are there, to the best of your (Seller's) knowledge, any of the above that are not in operating condition? ☐ Yes ☐ No. If yes, then describe. (Attach additional sheets if necessary.): _____
_____

B. Are you (Seller) aware of any significant defects/malfunctions in any of the following? ☐ Yes ☐ No. If yes, check appropriate space(s) below.
☐ Interior Walls ☐ Ceilings ☐ Floors ☐ Exterior Walls ☐ Insulation ☐ Roof(s) ☐ Windows ☐ Doors ☐ Foundation ☐ Slab(s)
☐ Driveways ☐ Sidewalks ☐ Walls/Fences ☐ Electrical Systems ☐ Plumbing/Sewers/Septics ☐ Other Structural Components
(Describe: _____
_____)
If any of the above is checked, explain. (Attach additional sheets if necessary): _____
_____

*This garage door opener or child resistant pool barrier may not be in compliance with the safety standards relating to automatic reversing devices as set forth in Chapter 12.5 (commencing with Section 19890) of Part 3 of Division 13 of, or with the pool safety standards of Article 2.5 (commencing with Section 115920) of Chapter 5 of Part 10 of Division 104 of, the Health and Safety Code. The water heater may not be anchored, braced, or strapped in accordance with Section 19211 of the Health and Safety Code. Window security bars may not have quick release mechanisms in compliance with the 1995 Edition of the California Building Standards Code.

Buyer and Seller acknowledge receipt of copy of this page, which constitutes Page 1 of 2 Pages.
Buyer's Initials (_____) (_____)   Seller's Initials (_____) (_____)

The copyright laws of the United States (17 U.S. Code) forbid the unauthorized reproduction of this form by any means, including facsimile or computerized formats.
Copyright © 1990-1997, CALIFORNIA ASSOCIATION OF REALTORS®. In compliance with Civil Code Section 1102.6 Effective July 1, 1997.

Published and Distributed by:
REAL ESTATE BUSINESS SERVICES, INC.
a subsidiary of the CALIFORNIA ASSOCIATION OF REALTORS®
525 South Virgil Avenue, Los Angeles, California 90020

┌─ OFFICE USE ONLY ─┐
Reviewed by Broker
or Designee _____
Date _____

EQUAL HOUSING OPPORTUNITY

REAL ESTATE TRANSFER DISCLOSURE STATMENT (TDS-14 PAGE 1 OF 2) REVISED 3/97

Figure 5-3
Real Estate Transfer Disclosure Statement

Subject Property Address: _____ Date _____

C. Are you (Seller) aware of any of the following:

1. Substances, materials, or products which may be an environmental hazard such as, but not limited to, asbestos, formaldehyde, radon gas, lead-based paint, fuel or chemical storage tanks, and contaminated soil or water on the subject property .... ☐ Yes ☐ No
2. Features of the property shared in common with adjoining landowners, such as walls, fences, and driveways, whose use or responsibility for maintenance may have an effect on the subject property .... ☐ Yes ☐ No
3. Any encroachments, easements or similar matters that may affect your interest in the subject property .... ☐ Yes ☐ No
4. Room additions, structural modifications, or other alterations or repairs made without necessary permits................... ☐ Yes ☐ No
5. Room additions, structural modifications, or other alterations or repairs not in compliance with building codes............... ☐ Yes ☐ No
6. Fill (compacted or otherwise) on the property or any portion thereof............................... ☐ Yes ☐ No
7. Any settling from any cause, or slippage, sliding, or other soil problems .... ☐ Yes ☐ No
8. Flooding, drainage or grading problems .... ☐ Yes ☐ No
9. Major damage to the property or any of the structures from fire, earthquake, floods, or landslides .... ☐ Yes ☐ No
10. Any zoning violations, nonconforming uses, violations of "setback" requirements.......................... ☐ Yes ☐ No
11. Neighborhood noise problems or other nuisances .... ☐ Yes ☐ No
12. CC&R's or other deed restrictions or obligations .... ☐ Yes ☐ No
13. Homeowners' Association which has any authority over the subject property .... ☐ Yes ☐ No
14. Any "common area" (facilities such as pools, tennis courts, walkways, or other areas co-owned in undivided interest with others).. ☐ Yes ☐ No
15. Any notices of abatement or citations against the property .... ☐ Yes ☐ No
16. Any lawsuits by or against the seller threatening to or affecting this real property, including any lawsuits alleging a defect or deficiency in this real property or "common areas" (facilities such as pools, tennis courts, walkways, or other areas, co-owned in undivided interest with others).. ☐ Yes ☐ No

If the answer to any of these is yes, explain. (Attach additional sheets if necessary.): _____
_____
_____

Seller certifies that the information herein is true and correct to the best of the Seller's knowledge as of the date signed by the Seller.

Seller _____ Date _____

Seller _____ Date _____

III
AGENT'S INSPECTION DISCLOSURE

(To be completed only if the Seller is represented by an agent in this transaction.)

THE UNDERSIGNED, BASED ON THE ABOVE INQUIRY OF THE SELLER(S) AS TO THE CONDITION OF THE PROPERTY AND BASED ON A REASONABLY COMPETENT AND DILIGENT VISUAL INSPECTION OF THE ACCESSIBLE AREAS OF THE PROPERTY IN CONJUNCTION WITH THAT INQUIRY, STATES THE FOLLOWING:

☐ Agent notes no items for disclosure.
☐ Agent notes the following items: _____
_____
_____
_____

Agent (Broker Representing Seller)_____ By _____ Date _____
           (Please Print)   (Associate Licensee or Broker Signature)

IV
AGENT'S INSPECTION DISCLOSURE

(To be completed only if the agent who has obtained the offer is other than the agent above.)

THE UNDERSIGNED, BASED ON A REASONABLY COMPETENT AND DILIGENT VISUAL INSPECTION OF THE ACCESSIBLE AREAS OF THE PROPERTY, STATES THE FOLLOWING:

☐ Agent notes no items for disclosure.
☐ Agent notes the following items: _____
_____
_____

Agent (Broker Obtaining the Offer)_____ By _____ Date _____
           (Please Print)   (Associate Licensee or Broker Signature)

V

BUYER(S) AND SELLER(S) MAY WISH TO OBTAIN PROFESSIONAL ADVICE AND/OR INSPECTIONS OF THE PROPERTY AND TO PROVIDE FOR APPROPRIATE PROVISIONS IN A CONTRACT BETWEEN BUYER AND SELLER(S) WITH RESPECT TO ANY ADVICE/INSPECTIONS/DEFECTS.

I/WE ACKNOWLEDGE RECEIPT OF A COPY OF THIS STATEMENT.

Seller _____ Date _____ Buyer _____ Date _____

Seller _____ Date _____ Buyer _____ Date _____

Agent (Broker Representing Seller) _____ By _____ Date _____
                                            (Associate Licensee or Broker Signature)

Agent (Broker Obtaining the Offer) _____ By _____ Date _____
                                            (Associate Licensee or Broker Signature)

SECTION 1102.3 OF THE CIVIL CODE PROVIDES A BUYER WITH THE RIGHT TO RESCIND A PURCHASE CONTRACT FOR AT LEAST THREE DAYS AFTER THE DELIVERY OF THIS DISCLOSURE IF DELIVERY OCCURS AFTER THE SIGNING OF AN OFFER TO PURCHASE. IF YOU WISH TO RESCIND THE CONTRACT, YOU MUST ACT WITHIN THE PRESCRIBED PERIOD.

A REAL ESTATE BROKER IS QUALIFIED TO ADVISE ON REAL ESTATE. IF YOU DESIRE LEGAL ADVICE, CONSULT YOUR ATTORNEY.

This form is available for use by the entire real estate industry. It is not intended to identify the user as a REALTOR®. REALTOR® is a registered collective membership mark which may be used only by members of the NATIONAL ASSOCIATION OF REALTORS® who subscribe to its Code of Ethics.

PRINT DATE

OFFICE USE ONLY
Reviewed by Broker or Designee _____
Date _____

EQUAL HOUSING OPPORTUNITY

Page 2 of 2 Pages.

Figure 5-3 (Cont.)
Real Estate Transfer Disclosure Statement

SELLER DISCLOSURE OBLIGATIONS
UNDER CIVIL CODE SECTION 1102, ET SEQ.

A transferor (seller) of real property (including a residential stock cooperative) containing 1-to-4 residential units must, unless exempt, supply a transferee (buyer) with a completed Real Estate Transfer Disclosure Statement in the form prescribed in Civil Code §1102.6. This requirement applies to transfers of real property by sale, exchange, installment land sale contract, as defined in Civil Code §2985, lease with an option to purchase, any other option to purchase, or ground lease coupled with improvements.

EXEMPTED TRANSFERS: Summary of exempted transfers (Civil Code §1102.2) where a Real Estate Transfer Disclosure Statement is **not** required:

a. Transfers requiring a public report pursuant to §11018.1 of the Business & Professions Code and transfers which are made without a public report pursuant to §11010.4 of the Business & Professions Code.
b. Transfers pursuant to court order (such as probate sales, sales by a bankruptcy trustee, etc.).
c. Transfers by foreclosure or trustee's sale (including a deed in lieu of foreclosure) and a transfer by a beneficiary who has acquired the property by foreclosure or deed in lieu of foreclosure.
d. Transfers by a fiduciary in the course of the administration of a decedent's estate, guardianship, conservatorship, or trust.
e. Transfers from one co-owner to one or more other co-owners.
f. Transfers made to a spouse or to a direct blood relative.
g. Transfers between spouses in connection with a dissolution of marriage or similar proceeding.
h. Transfers by the State Controller pursuant to the Unclaimed Property Law.
i. Transfers as a result of failure to pay property taxes.
j. Transfers or exchanges to or from any governmental entity.

Figure 5-3 (Cont.)
Real Estate Transfer Disclosure Statement

Nondisclosure. Nondisclosure exists when a seller or agent knows of a material fact that would affect the value, but fails to disclose. In many situations, merely because the buyer does not inquire will not relieve the seller or broker from liability to the buyer. The test appears to be as follows: (1) Are the material facts known to the seller or agent; and (2) could the prospective buyer have determined the defect upon a casual observation of the premises?

EXAMPLES

1. A seller who learns that a previous statement has become false because of a change in circumstances has a duty to correct the statement and disclose the change to the buyer before close of escrow.[97]

2. Plaintiffs bought a condominium on the representation of brokers that they were luxurious condominiums and had outstanding investment potential. In fact, it was alleged, the construction was substandard and in violation of the minimum requirements of the Uniform Building Code. The court held that the alleged statements are statements of opinion and ordinarily do not constitute fraud. If, however, one advances an opinion that one does not honestly believe, then an action for affirmative fraud will lie.[98]

3. When seller's agents represented that a proposed sale would be submitted to (and subject to) the board of directors for approval, they should have disclosed that such submission was subject to prior approval of one of the members of the board. The failure to disclose this qualifying fact constitutes actionable misrepresentation.[99]

"Puffing" versus misrepresentation. Because the real estate licensee is presumed to have superior knowledge, his statements are more likely to be construed as statements of fact. However, the agent may offer his opinion, such as, "This is the best buy in town." The determining factor is: Would a reasonable person have relied on the statement? [100]

§5.26. Earthquake faults (Special Studies Zone Act)
Since January 1, 1975, the Public Resources Code,[101] known as the Alquist-Priolo Special Studies Zones Act, imposes a special duty upon the agent for a seller of

real property—or upon the seller if the seller is acting without an agent—to disclose to a prospective buyer the fact that the property is located within a Special Studies Zone, if that is the case. These Special Studies Zones have been delineated by the State Geologist, and are areas identified by the California Division of Mines and Geology as containing potentially active earthquake faults.[102] They are narrow strips of land (ordinarily one-quarter mile or less in width) along potentially and recently active traces of well-defined faults in the earth's surface.

EXAMPLE A real estate broker in Northern California, acting as agent of the seller, negotiated the sale of real property in a Special Studies Zone along the San Andreas fault. The broker, however, did not advise the buyer that the property was located in a Special Studies Zone.

An Accusation was filed against the licensee and the evidence introduced at the administrative hearing established the following facts:

1. The real property was within such a zone.

2. The house was one of several relatively new residences built by a reputable builder subsequent to the effective date of the Alquist-Priolo Special Studies Zones Act.

3. Broker had no idea that the property was located in this zone, although he knew that some properties located in hills in the surrounding community were within the zone; and

4. Had buyer known the property was so situated, buyer would not have purchased it.

The Administrative Law Judge found a basis for disciplinary action against the broker.

After having been served with the Accusation, the broker obtained a map delineating the Special Studies Zones in the area in which he conducted most of his real estate business as a means to prevent a recurrence of the violation.[103]

When dealing with a seller and a property outside of their usual business areas, agents must also exercise care to determine if the property is in a Special Studies Zone. Most cities and counties affected by these zones are able to supply copies of maps indicating which particular properties are within a zone. These Special Studies Zones maps may also be examined at any office of the California Division of Mines and Geology.

More legislative action along the lines of the Alquist-Priolo Act can be anticipated as agencies of government seek new ways to minimize the loss of life and property from earthquakes.

§5.27. Importance of disclosure

In a pertinent case, it was held that deceit may be negative and facts not known by the buyer or within the reach of his or her diligent attention must be disclosed to the buyer by the seller, and the representing broker, if they materially affect the desirability of the property, and if the broker is aware that the facts are unknown to the buyer. The court referred to nondisclosure as "negative fraud" and did not excuse the broker because of an "as is" provision in the purchase contract.[104] It is not necessary that there be a contractual relationship between agent and buyer.

A reasonably prudent buyer of real estate has every right to rescind a contract when the agent by his mere silence has allowed the transaction to be closed without properly informing the buyer. The agent who is not aware of public and private restrictions and controls such as zoning, setbacks, four-family use in a single-family dwelling zone, safety and health regulations, freeway condemnations, school districts, and a variety of other restrictions has not properly performed his obligation to the buyer despite the premise that the buyer is also presumed to know the law and the transaction into which he entered.

Whenever the agent or seller knows the circumstances under which the buyer is buying, he has a duty to disclose matters that would change the course of the transaction. The physical condition of the premises and other relevant information must be fully, not partially, disclosed. The ultimate conclusion for all agents and sellers to follow is that full disclosure must be made whenever elementary fair conduct demands it. It should be noted that actionable nondisclosure includes improvements that were added without a building permit or in violation of building codes.[105] A neighbor's noisy activity, amounting to a nuisance, must also be disclosed.[106]

No matter what is said or not said in a real estate transaction, whether intentional, reckless, careless, or nondisclosure through silence, the buyer must of course have believed it to be true and must have relied upon it. The so-called test of reliance—that which a reasonable, prudent person would do—is no longer reliable, since the courts today apply many subjective standards in assessing the buyer's experience and knowledge.

§5.28. Disclaimers

An "as is" clause or other such provision will not relieve a seller or agent from a fraudulent act.[107] Further, it will not shield a seller from the fraudulent acts of his agent of which he has knowledge. Generally an "as is" clause means that the buyer takes the property in the condition visible to or observable by him.[108] In other words, if from a reasonable inspection a buyer should be expected to observe a defect, he will be charged with notice; otherwise the broker or seller has a duty to inform him of the defect.

EXAMPLES 1. L's complaint against S and his broker, B, alleged, in part, that S failed to inform L that the apartment units were illegally built and that the building had been placed for condemnation, that neither S nor B informed L of such information, and that as a result of such nondisclosure L was damaged.

Among other items, the purchase contract contained language stating that L bought the premises "in its present state and condition." One of the provisions was that "No representations, warranties of any kind or character have been made by any party hereto, or their representatives, which are not herein expressed." L's case was based upon nondisclosure rather than active concealment occurring between the parties not in a confidential relationship.

The court noted that, "The principle is fundamental that deceit may be negative as well as affirmative; it may consist of suppression of that which is one's duty to declare as well as of the declaration of that which is false." The court declared that:

> It is now settled in California that where the seller knows of facts materially affecting the value or desirability of the property, which are known or accessible only to him and also knows that such facts are not known to, or within the reach of, the diligent attention and observation of the buyer, the seller is under a duty to disclose them to the buyer.... The real estate agent or broker representing the seller is a party to the business transaction. In most instances he has a personal interest in it and derives a profit from it. Where such agent or broker possesses, along with the seller, requisite knowledge ... whether he acquires it from, or independently of, his principal, he is under the same duty of disclosure ... and if no disclosure is made ... such agent or broker becomes jointly and severally liable with the seller for the full amount of the damages.[109]

A provision in a contract that the buyer takes the property in the condition in which it is, or "as is," does not confer on the seller a general immunity from liability for fraud. To be more precise, the court stated that, "We are of the opinion that, generally speaking, such a provision means that the buyer takes the property in a condition *visible to or observable by him.*"

2. A seller who advertises a property as a "fixer upper" and offers it for sale on an "as is" basis is not thereby relieved of an affirmative duty to disclose all material facts to a purchaser when the purchaser cannot reasonably ascertain those facts for himself. Failure to make such disclosure constitutes actual fraud.

   The seller, a licensed real estate broker, bought a residential property that was the subject of an order for noncompliance with county codes because of an illegal room and other violations. The broker advertised the property for sale as a "fixer upper" to be sold "as is."

   At the time of sale the broker also caused the escrow instructions to refer to the "as is" condition of the property and a disclaimer of any warranties "as to any condition having to do with city regulations or zoning or any other municipal conditions applying to the subject property." However, seller failed to inform the buyer or the real estate agent who accompanied the buyer about the noncompliance order.

   After the sale the buyer learned about the order and, after considerable expense and delay, was able to correct the defects and get electrical and water services. When the buyer complained, seller offered to rescind the purchase but refused to compensate the buyer for time and expenses incurred in making the required building code corrections. The buyer complained to DRE.

   An investigation by DRE led to the filing of an Accusation. After hearing the case, the Administrative Law Judge recommended a 45-day license suspension on each count. The Commissioner declined to accept the proposed decision and instead revoked the broker's license, with a right to a restricted license under terms and conditions after 45 days from the effective date.

   The broker petitioned for a writ of mandate in Superior Court. The petition was heard and denied. The broker then appealed. The Court of Appeal said that the seller's verbal and written disclaimers did not constitute effective notice, which "entails more than elliptical obfuscation."

   The Court held that the seller's offer to rescind the purchase but not compensate the buyer for incurred expenses was "at best an excessively dubious factor in mitigation" and that DRE "acted well within its discretion" in revoking the broker's license.[110]

3. Plaintiff bought a home "as is" and agreed to waive a termite clearance, but claimed that seller represented that the house was in good condition and fit for occupancy. In fact, it was termite-ridden and decayed by dry rot. The court held that the mere fact that the buyer agreed to waive a termite clearance does not establish that he knew the house was infested with termites and that he was willing to accept it in that condition.[111]

4. An agreement between buyer and seller containing an exculpatory clause shielding the seller from the representations by the seller's agent that are outside the agent's authority will shield an innocent seller from liability resulting from intentional misrepresentation by the agent allowing the buyer to rescind. Of course, the broker is still liable to the buyer for fraud.[112] If the misrepresentation is merely negligent, the seller may still be liable if the buyer suffers damages.[113] In the latter instance, the seller has a right of indemnity against the broker.[114]

5. Another caveat that appears in numerous set-up sheets is worded thus:

The above statements are based upon information from sources deemed reliable and which we believe to be correct, but we cannot assume responsibility for errors or omissions therein.

Such a statement will excuse an innocent misrepresentation or misstatement of facts, but will not protect one from making an intentional false statement.[115] The broker, therefore, has a duty to determine factors that would materially affect the property and disclose these facts to the prospective buyer. Failure to do so constitutes fraud.

§5.29. Cooperating broker liability
Liability is not limited just to the listing broker.

EXAMPLES 1. In one case, two of the defendant broker's salespeople received a listing from Granberg. He had informed the salespeople that the property was partly R-1 zoned and partly C-2. When the listing was signed, the zoning space was blank, but when it was turned in to the M.L.S. it showed a C-2 only. A co-op broker was contacted by a prospective buyer to be shown some C-2 property. Among others, the co-op broker showed the buyer Granberg's property, not knowing of any error on the listing. As is often the case, the M.L.S. form was shown to the buyer. Neither the buyer nor the co-op broker had contact with Granberg. When the buyer bought the property and discovered the R-1 zoning, he contacted Granberg, who agreed to rescind and paid the buyer his expenses. Granberg then brought suit against the listing broker, his salespeople, and the co-op broker. The jury found against the listing broker and for the co-op broker, who was clearly not to blame. This decision was upheld on appeal, the court holding that:

> *The law is well settled that representations made to one person with the intention that they will be repeated to another and acted upon by him and which are repeated to and acted upon to his injury gives the person so acting the same right of relief as if the representations had been made to him directly.*[116]

2. In another case, a co-op broker brought suit against a seller for a commission allegedly due her, failing to mention the number of fraudulent statements she had made to the seller and the listing broker as to an exchange in which the co-op broker had the listing. False representations had been made by the co-op broker as to vacancies, market value, and conditions. The seller cross-complained against the co-op broker, alone, and won. In that case, the faultless listing broker was not even brought into the suit other than as a witness for the seller. The court held that the co-op broker was the agent of the seller and "as such owed them the duty to make full and fair disclosure." Real estate brokers are under a duty to deal fairly with all parties and be well informed on current market conditions. A representation concerning income is a representation of fact. Reliance on the opinion of an agent is justifiable. Even one under no duty to speak as to a matter, if he undertakes to do so, must make a full and fair disclosure.[117]

§5.30. Intent not necessary
Actual intent to deceive is not essential in all cases.

EXAMPLE In one case, N's license was suspended by the Commissioner and he appealed the decision. N owned a subdivision and was selling the various lots. B, a potential buyer, inquired about an old house next to the one B wished to purchase. N told B that the house would be torn down and replaced with a modern home. After B bought the adjacent home, N used the old house as his real estate office instead of tearing it down. The court upheld the Commissioner, stating:

> To be actionable deceit, the representations need not be made with knowledge of actual falsity, but need only be an assertion, as a fact, of which is not true by one who has no reasonable ground for believing it to be true ... [the] intent to induce [another] to alter their position can be inferred from the fact that he made the representation with knowledge that [the injured party] would act in reliance thereon.... The intent which is essential is the intent to induce another party to enter into the contract.[118]

§5.31. False promise
False promises can result in disciplinary proceedings against a licensee.

EXAMPLE   Disciplinary proceedings were instituted against a broker based on the following facts: B had made false promises, and in arranging for loans failed to disclose and concealed from X (the buyer) that a $500 bonus was being charged to X. If X had known of this, X would not have signed the agreement. B also was found to have commingled and converted a total of $3,000 by not immediately placing these funds in trust or in an escrow account or in the hands of the seller. Instead, he did not account for these funds to X for one month. Further, B convinced X to assume a G.I. loan and a second trust deed to be paid off in monthly installments and the balance in six months. X told B that he could not pay it off in six months, but B said, "Go ahead and make these payments, and by that time you will have enough equity in your house and I can 'G.I.' it and everything will be paid off." B's license was revoked.[119]

§5.32. Fraud as to rents
Misinformation as to rents can be actionable fraud.

EXAMPLE   A was looking for income property and saw an ad in a newspaper for 27 units. The manager gave A a prospectus containing information regarding income, taxes, number of units that were leased, etc. The manager told A that the complex "is all filled up and everybody has a one-year lease." A bought the apartments. The leases did not reflect the fact that all but one tenant had been given two or three months' free rent. A testified she did not know of the concessions until two months after escrow closed. The defendant admitted he knew of the rent concessions.

The court determined that the leases as drawn reflected a scheme of giving rent concessions to inflate the rentals above their true market value so that a higher price could be obtained for the apartment building. The court also stated that, in its broadest sense, the concept of fraud embraces anything that is intended to deceive. This includes statements, acts, concealment, and omissions involving a breach of legal or equitable duty, trust, or confidence which results in injury to one who justifiably relies thereon.[120]

§5.33. Negligence
A broker is liable not only for his own negligence, but also for the negligence of his salespeople under the doctrine of respondeat superior.[121]

EXAMPLES   1.   In an action for personal injuries sustained by a lessee of a dwelling house as the result of a fall down a flight of basement stairs, a judgment for $65,700 in favor of the plaintiff was affirmed by the California Supreme Court against all defendants, namely: (1) the owner of the real property (lessor); (2) the real estate salesperson who showed the house to the plaintiff and negotiated the lease; and (3) the real estate broker.

The plaintiff had assumed the door was a closet door; it actually led directly to the basement. Plaintiff had not been cautioned about the door, which was one of several leading from an entry hall. Plaintiff sued the owners on the basis of common law principles of landlord and tenant negligence law: that they were liable for failure to warn plaintiff of the known latent danger (concealed hazard) behind the basement door, the precipitous stairway becoming a veritable trap causing plaintiff's injuries. Plaintiff's claim against the Realtors rested on their voluntarily undertaking to show her the house and on their negligence in failing to warn her of the existence of the doorway, the stairs, and the basement.

The court stated that the case, as far as the real estate agents were concerned, was one admittedly without exact precedent, but the court was satisfied that, having affirmatively undertaken to show the house to the plaintiff in the regular course of their business, with the purpose of earning a commission if she decided to rent it, the defendants were under a duty of care to warn her of a concealed danger in the premises of which they were aware and from which her injury might be reasonably foreseen if she did become a tenant.[122]

2.   In 1970 W hired defendant to make a survey and divide real estate into two separate parcels. When W hired defendant he told defendant he wanted the property divided so that the house, retaining wall, and driveway would be contained on one parcel. Defendant erred so that the division resulted in part of the retaining wall and driveway being located on the other parcel. In 1971 plaintiff purchased the property. Plaintiff then entered into a contract to sell the vacant lot and discovered defendant's error. Plaintiff paid the buyer of the vacant lot $5,000 and his attorney's fees, and the buyer gave plaintiff an easement. Plaintiff sued defendant to recover these damages.

The court held that the absence of privity of contract does not bar an action for the negligent performance of a contract. Defendant, when he prepared his report, could reasonably have anticipated that it would be used and relied upon by persons such as plaintiff.[123]

3.   Plaintiff listed his Tahoe cabin with a broker. Defendant made an offer, plaintiff to take two notes back on two pieces of property. Broker (also a defendant) informed plaintiff that the maker of the note was a "financially substantial individual" and was a building contractor. Plaintiff accepted $2,000 and a $12,000 note made by the contractor, who was allegedly financially substantial. On the date plaintiff signed escrow instructions, the contractor recorded a deed conveying the property in question to defendant. Plaintiffs were never advised. Escrow closed and title insurance was issued by First American Title, which did not disclose the reconveyance back to defendant.

Plaintiffs learned a few months later of the contractor reconveying as they were in default. (In effect, by contractor reconveying property back to defendant, plaintiff had no security whatsoever, which is what they bargained for, and therefore were out $12,000.)

Plaintiff won the case against defendant for fraud and misrepresentation and against broker for negligent misrepresentation, for $12,360 and $2,000 punitive damages and costs, and against First American Title for negligence in not checking title before escrow closed, as plaintiff would not have proceeded with the transaction had plaintiff known of the reconveyance back to defendant.[124]

§5.34. Broker competing with buyer

The broker's role in a real estate transaction is to bring together a prospective purchaser and the seller of real estate, to their mutual advantage. On rare occasions the broker is personally interested in the real estate, and would like to purchase it for his own account.

EXAMPLE An Idaho case points out the problems brokers may create if they compete with a prospective purchaser. Tifft was a real estate broker and offered certain property to a prospective purchaser, Funk. The purchaser executed an offer on certain terms and conditions which the broker delivered to the seller. While the seller was considering the offer, the broker decided he would like to buy the property for his own account. He contacted the seller and subsequently made an offer to purchase it himself, on better terms than those offered by Funk.

The seller agreed to accept the better terms and sold the property to the broker. When the prospective purchaser discovered these facts he filed suit against the real estate broker, contending he had breached his obligation to the public.

The court held that the real estate broker had breached his duty to deal honestly and fairly with the general public and not take advantage of prospective purchasers. The court pointed out that Idaho's License Act imposed a duty on real estate licensees to treat all parties to the real estate transaction fairly. The broker breached his duty when he outbid the buyer without notice to the buyer before the seller accepted the broker's offer. Broker was held to be the constructive trustee of the buyer.

Many authorities in the past have held that the broker's only duty was to the seller, to obtain the best price and terms possible. Such cases have previously held that the broker owed little duty to the prospective purchaser since the broker was working only for the seller.

The present court contended that its ruling was a logical extension of the Truth in Lending Act that imposed upon real estate brokers certain obligations to the public. The Interstate Land Full Disclosure Act is similar legislation that requires the broker to protect the public at large. The court found that reading all these statutes together created a duty on the part of the real estate broker to treat a prospective purchaser fairly in such transactions.[125]

A broker should never purchase his own listing without revealing to both buyer and seller the full facts involved and giving the prospective purchaser an opportunity to purchase. Even with full disclosure, the purchase of one's own listing creates many legal problems.

§5.35. Other types of misrepresentation

Other types of false representation that have been held actionable include the following:

1. Misrepresentations as to freedom of a building from termites[126]
2. Misrepresentations as to deed restrictions[127]
3. Misrepresentations as to tenantable condition of residential property[128]
4. Misrepresentations as to income or that the business was profitable[129]
5. Concealment of the fact that there was an encroachment on a state right of way[130]
6. Failure to disclose an engineer's report on hillside property[131]
7. Misrepresentations as to the water supply[132]
8. Misrepresentations as to compliance with building code requirements[133]
9. Misrepresentation as to zoning[134]
10. Fraudulent representation as to acreage[135]
11. Filled land misrepresentation[136]
12. Misrepresentation to prospective purchaser of a secured promissory note with respect to fair market value of property without a reasonable basis[137]
13. Misrepresentation that a house was located within a particular school district

14. Putting net taxes on analysis sheet rather than gross taxes (i.e., deducting exemptions)

15. Broker's opinion that the purchaser would have an enforceable access easement[138]

16. Misrepresentation that a buyer's view would be protected[139]

17. Misrepresentation by a broker to the prospective buyer that the seller had accepted buyer's offer and buyer expended funds in reliance on the representation[140]

18. Misrepresentation by a loan broker as to the value of property securing a loan purchased by an investor

19. Material misrepresentation about the property after the execution of a purchase agreement, but before consummation of the sale, is actionable.

§5.36. Secret profits
Under the Real Estate Law, a licensee has a duty to be honest and truthful. If this duty is violated, he may be obliged to give up his secret profits to the buyer.

EXAMPLE   In one case, the broker was found to have violated numerous acts that constitute fraud. At W's request, broker T undertook to look for property that might be of interest to W. Defendant D, also a broker, told T that he was the exclusive agent for Sunset Oil Company and he had several acres for sale. When T mentioned that another broker, X, had a For Sale sign on the property, D replied that Sunset had taken the property away from X. T then submitted an offer to D at 4,000 per acre. D promised to take the offer to Sunset. Later, D told T that Sunset had refused the offer and would not take less than $5,000 per acre. W made the offer at $5,000 per acre. At D's direction, T inserted in the offer a provision for payment by Sunset of 10 percent commission, which T and D agreed to divide equally. T informed W of this and W agreed. Subsequently, D informed T that Sunset had accepted W's offer. Some questions arose in escrow about the transaction, but D explained them satisfactorily to T.

After he had purchased the property, W learned that D had never been given a listing by Sunset and had never presented or intended to present W's offers. Instead, D had presented his own offer of $4,000 and Sunset accepted. D falsely represented to W that the least Sunset would take was $5,000 per acre for the property, resulting in a $1,000 per acre profit for D. All the reasons D gave for the unusual handling of the sale were fabrications. D never disclosed W's offer to Sunset until after the escrow papers were signed. All of the money D received from W he used to pay Sunset. W sued D for fraud and won.

The court held that there was no evidence of agency or other fiduciary relationship between W and D, but public policy does not permit one to take advantage of one's own wrong. As a broker, D had the duty to be honest and truthful in his dealings.

D clearly violated this duty. Through fraudulent misrepresentation, he received money from W that W would have otherwise had. Thus, D is an involuntary trustee for the benefit of W on the secret profit of $1,000 per acre. The facts did not sustain a judgment on a theory of tort as there was no fiduciary duty owed to W; they were sufficient to uphold recovery under the quasi-contractual theory of unjust enrichment.[141]

---

§5.37. Implied warranties on sale of property
Recent cases have imposed a greater liability on the seller with respect to the condition of the land and improvements, particularly in the case of newly subdivided lands.

EXAMPLES

1. In one case, a seller was held liable to the buyer for defects when a house was built on unstable ground.[142]

2. An action for damages resulted from earth movement under the plaintiff's lot and house. The plaintiff was the original purchaser in a subdivision, and brought his action against the tract developer and a soil engineering company engaged by the developer in connection with cutting, filling, and grading operations. The plaintiff recovered a judgment for damages.[143]

3. In another case, it was held that a subsequent purchaser of a tract house could recover damages in an action against the original subdivider based on negligence in the installment of a radiant heating system. The court applied the products liability rule, stating:

   > We think, in terms of today's society, there are no meaningful distinctions between Eichler's mass production and sale of homes and the mass production and sale of automobiles and that the pertinent overriding policy considerations are the same. Law, as an instrument of justice, has infinite capacity for growth to meet changing needs and mores. Nowhere is this better illustrated than in the recent developments in the field of product liability. The law should be based on current concepts of what is right and just and the judiciary should be alert to the never-ending need for keeping legal principles abreast of the times. Ancient distinctions that make no sense in today's society and that tend to discredit the law should be readily rejected.[144]

4. The doctrine of strict liability was extended to the sale of a manufactured building lot (a lot created by cutting, filling, grading, compacting, and the like).[145]

5. Breach of warranty applies under third-party beneficiary principles, and tolling the statute of limitations as to negligence.[146]

6. Doctrine of implied warranty of quality and fitness applies to the sale of newly constructed real property improvements,[147] including condominiums.

---

§5.38. Ordinances requiring disclosures

The Government Code provides a means of affording further protection to a buyer of residential property. The code provides as follows:

> A city by ordinance may provide that prior to the sale or exchange of any residential building, the owner or his authorized agent shall obtain from the city a report of the residential building record showing the regularly authorized use, occupancy, and zoning classifications of such property.[148]

A number of cities have enacted ordinances pursuant to the foregoing code section. A real estate broker should be knowledgeable as to any such ordinances in his area of operation.

IV. UNLAWFUL PRACTICE OF LAW

§5.39. In general

No person shall practice law in California unless he or she is an active member of the State Bar Association. To do so constitutes a misdemeanor.[149] Practicing law includes dispensing legal advice and counsel, and preparation of legal instruments and contracts by which legal rights are secured.[150] Unfortunately, what constitutes the unlawful practice of law has not been clearly articulated, but the licensee must at all times be vitally concerned with this problem area.

The main purpose for the rule is to protect the public. Over the years the definition of what constitutes the practice of law has been modified, particularly with the increase in literacy and the simplification of many documents that traditionally were hand-tailored by an attorney for use in a particular transaction, but are now available as printed forms requiring only a little preparation. In an attempt to resolve the problem of what services should be performed only by a licensed attorney and what services, although historically constituting the practice of law, could be performed by laypersons, treaties were entered into between the State Bar of California and such organizations as the California Bankers Association, the California Land Title Association, the Escrow Institute of California, automobile associations, insurance claims adjusters, and entertainment agencies. Such treaties have been revoked primarily because of concerns expressed by the U.S. Department of Justice about possible anticompetitive effects of the agreements. A solution is the issuance of "unauthorized law practice" opinions of the State Bar that are binding unless overruled by the State Supreme Court. In any case, the best guide is found in opinions expressed by the appellate courts in actual cases that establish precedents.

Even though laypersons might be qualified to express an opinion in a real estate problem, prudence dictates that the services of an attorney be utilized because of the responsibilities involved. The consequences of a real estate licensee engaging in the unlawful practice of law can be severe, including possible fine, damages claimed by an injured party, and possible loss of license.

§5.40. Crime
In an older case, a real estate licensee was found guilty of practicing law without a license. The court stated that if the

> *defendant had only been called upon to perform and had only undertaken to perform the clerical services of filling in the blanks ... in accordance with information furnished him by the parties, or had merely acted as a scrivener to record the stated agreement ... he would not have been guilty of practicing law without a license.*[151]

§5.41. Negligence
In addition to the fact that the licensee is prohibited from practicing law unless properly licensed, if the licensee does so in a negligent manner, he can also be held liable for damages.

EXAMPLES

1. In one case, the defendant broker was held liable for negligently drafting a promissory note with monthly payments insufficient to pay the interest.[152]

2. A notary was found liable for negligently drafting a will. He thought affixing his signature as a notary public was sufficient, rather than the required signatures of two witnesses.[153]

If the licensee is also a Realtor or Realtor-Associate, a violation of the Code of Ethics would occur if he wrongfully practiced law. Article 17 of the Code of Ethics states, "The Realtor shall not engage in activities that constitute the unauthorized practice of law and shall recommend that legal counsel be obtained when the interest of any party to the transaction requires it."

§5.42. Guidelines
There is no simple solution for the licensee. It is difficult to practice real estate without walking into the often gray area of practicing law as well. An important factor is common sense. For example, is the instrument simple or standardized? Did the draftsmen charge a fee for drafting or giving advice? Was the drafting incidental to the transaction? In other words, the more complicated the transaction, the more likely it will be construed as practicing law.

One answer is not just to suggest that in every transaction both the buyer and seller should contact separate qualified real estate attorneys, but to insist upon it. Otherwise, the potential financial and emotional ramifications are extreme.

§5.43. A word of caution

The Department of Real Estate has set forth a caveat in the *Reference Book*. It says:

> *The intelligent real estate broker is first to recognize that "a man who is his own lawyer has a fool for a client." Law is a complex, highly technical profession, requiring years of preparation and constant study and research. Often what appears to be a minor difficulty is in fact a massive iceberg of concealed hazards. Only competent lawyers are qualified to counsel brokers and their clients on legal problems. Indeed, under the Business and Professions Code, the practice of law by persons who are not members of the State Bar is specifically prohibited.*
>
> *The term "to practice law" and equivalent expressions are not confined to appearances in court. They include legal advice and counsel and the preparation of legal instruments by which such legal rights are secured. It has been held, for example, that the selection and preparation of a mortgage or deed of trust by a broker in an independent loan transaction in which a fee was charged was the unlawful practice of law, even though only one transaction was involved.*

Thus, the broker jeopardizes his position and reputation and does a disservice to his customers when he wanders deliberately or inadvertently into the unlicensed practice of law. The preceding discussion is clearly not intended to encourage such folly, but it will equip the careful reader with a fund of background information vital to his daily activities, and it will help him to recognize when a lawyer should be consulted or recommended.

V. DISCIPLINARY PROCEEDINGS

§5.44. In general

Disciplinary hearings are conducted by virtue of the Administrative Procedures Act.[154] Although there are numerous sections of the law whereby a licensee can have his license suspended or revoked, of particular significance are two sections of the Business and Professions Code,[155] which include such acts as the following:

1. Misrepresentation
2. False promise
3. Divided agency without knowledge or consent of all parties
4. Commingling funds
5. Not having definite termination date on exclusive listing
6. Secret profits
7. Dishonest dealing
8. Obtaining real estate license by fraud[156]
9. Conviction of felony or crime involving moral turpitude
10. False advertising
11. Negligence or incompetence
12. Lack of reasonable supervision of salespeople[157]
13. Violation of restricted license
14. Violation of franchise law
15. Disregarding provisions of the Real Estate Law or Commissioner's Regulations (e.g., illegal subdivision)[158]

In addition, when a final judgment is obtained in a civil action against a real estate licensee upon the ground of fraud or misrepresentation with reference to any transaction for which a license is required, the Real Estate Commissioner may, after a hearing, suspend or revoke the license of the licensee. Further, the Commissioner can discipline a licensee for a violation of the Real Estate Law whether an act was willful or unintentional.[159]

The accusation against the licensee must be brought within three years after occurrence; however, in a case of fraud, misrepresentation, or false promise, the accusation must be filed within one year from the date of discovery or three years after the occurrence, whichever is later, but in no event more than ten years.[160]

§5.45. Crime involving moral turpitude

A conviction or plea of guilty or nolo contendere[161] to any felony is sufficient grounds for suspension or revocation whether it involves moral turpitude or not.[162] The question then remains which misdemeanors involve moral turpitude. The California Supreme Court has held that a plea of guilty to contributing to the delinquency of a minor, which involved registering as a sex offender, constitutes moral turpitude per se.[163]

The crime must be substantially related to the qualifications, functions, or duties of the business or profession.[164]

§5.46. Administrative adjudication

A hearing to determine whether a license should be revoked, suspended, limited, or conditioned is initiated by filing a written Accusation. To determine whether a license should be issued or renewed, the Real Estate Commissioner files a Statement of Issues. Upon proper notice, a hearing is held by a hearing officer (Law Judge). The Law Judge rules on the admissions and exclusions of evidence, but the rules of evidence need not be technically followed. The burden of proof is on the Department of Real Estate for a suspension or revocation, but is placed on the applicant if the proceeding is to establish the requisites for obtaining a license. The standard of proof is a "convincing proof to a reasonable certainty."[165]

The decision may include a stay of execution, the terms of which can include an order of restitution to the injured party.[166]

If the respondent is dissatisfied with the decision, he may seek judicial review. However, all conflicts in the evidence are resolved in favor of the prevailing party. The Commissioner's order denying reinstatement of a license must state the reasons for denial.[167]

§5.47. Effect of suspension of license

For a violation of the Real Estate Law, a licensee may have his license suspended or revoked. If a broker's license is suspended, all the broker's rights and privileges are likewise suspended during the period. In addition, all the licenses of the salespeople working under the broker become inoperative, and therefore all transactions of the salespeople cannot be processed during the period of suspension. A commission may be paid, if it has already been earned, i.e., if only ministerial acts and duties are all that remain in order to close an existing transaction. Executory contracts such as exclusive listings are rendered voidable at the option of the principal.[168]

VI. REALTOR'S CODE OF ETHICS AND ARBITRATION OF DISPUTES

§5.48. Code of Ethics

A real estate broker or salesperson who is not a member of a real estate board is not obligated to abide by the National Association of Realtors' Code of Ethics or to arbitrate disputes with other licensees. However, by becoming a member of a local real estate board, the licensee is obliged to do so. In fact, by belonging to a local real estate board, one generally also joins the California Association of Realtors and the National Association of Realtors as well.

What does *ethics* mean? The California Department of Real Estate *Reference Book* sets forth the following:

> *The word [ethics] comes from the Greek word "ethos" which means moral custom, use and character. Ethics is usually expressed as a set of principles or values—a standard of conduct by which the individual guides his own behavior and judges that of others. It refers then to our conduct, socially and in business, and in attitudes toward others. Whenever one person who has the status of being an expert or knowing a great deal more about a field than others, assumes the duty of directing the business, health, investment, or general well-being of another upon a fee basis, there is vested in such person a high degree of confidence and trust. When one takes advantage of this position of trust to the detriment of another party solely for the purpose of one's own gain, we say that he is unethical.*
>
> *Professional courtesy and ethics should not stop at those things which have been sanctioned by law. The individual who tries only to stay on the border of the law, inevitably, at some time, steps across. The course of ethical conduct set forth in the Real Estate Law is that which a licensee must observe.*[169]

The various sections of the Code of Ethics are interpreted according to the facts of a particular case by the hearing panel. To be sure, each Realtor or Realtor-Associate should be well acquainted with the Code of Ethics, as well as the procedural aspects of both ethics hearings and arbitration hearings.[170]

In addition, board counsel should be present at every ethics hearing and any arbitration when another attorney is present, in order to assure protection for the board as well as the member.

§5.49. Disciplinary hearings

When a board member is charged with an ethical violation or a violation of the rules and regulations, the member must be adequately notified of the charges in order to be able to defend himself. Failure to be properly notified will cause the decision to be set aside for violation of due process of law.[171] Unfortunately, some boards are unfamiliar with the procedures for conducting these types of hearings. However, a growing number of boards are following the Objectives of the California Association of Realtors regarding ethics and arbitration, which include the following:

1. To provide a procedure that will be upheld by courts
2. To eliminate haphazard methods that frequently result in confusion and dissatisfaction
3. To clothe the disciplinary body with dignity that will demand respect by those brought before it

Discipline. For a violation, a member may be suspended from membership for up to one year, his membership may be revoked, or he may receive a letter of censure. Because of the potential penalties involved, the procedural aspects must be more closely adhered to in ethics hearings than in arbitration hearings.

§5.50. Arbitration and mediation hearings

Arbitration is an acceptable substitute and is generally less expensive than the judicial process if it is conducted fairly and impartially. Such hearings are favored by the courts, and the statutes are liberally construed.[172] Board members are required to arbitrate with other members when the dispute involves the "real estate business," usually involving a commission. Clients or former clients of members may also have a right to arbitrate a real estate dispute with a member. As between members from different boards, the California Association of Realtors has set up an Interboard Arbitration Procedure. If a member refuses to arbitrate, a court will require him to do so. On the other hand, a board can refuse to arbitrate if the matter is too complex.[173]

The hearing procedures are somewhat analogous to an ethics hearing, but perhaps somewhat more relaxed. Be that as it may, because a member may lose a partial or total commission amounting to hundreds, if not thousands, of dollars, the hearing must be conducted with all fairness, with only qualified individuals sitting on the tribunal. The prevailing party may enforce the award like a judgment in any competent court in California or in federal court.[174]

Mediation is a growing method of resolving disputes, often between a real estate licensee and the seller or buyer. Such hearings can result in quick, inexpensive resolution of a problem, but usually only if (1) the mediator is properly trained, and (2) the parties enter the mediation with the *intent* to resolve it. Although real estate boards may have a mediation panel, many buyers and sellers may be reluctant to mediate before such a mediator. It is suggested that the better practice is to have a trained, outside mediator, qualified in real estate matters.

§5.51 Use of computers for complying with due diligence

We are definitely in the computer age and are using computers more and more. It is much easier nowadays to check on comps, obtain property profiles and ages of properties, and get other pertinent information on-line than it was in previous years. Some title companies are now allowing brokers access to this information, which includes access to a county's recordings. For example, Commonwealth Title Company's Web page, with this information, is: **http://www.niteowl.net.** The user will have to contact Commonwealth to obtain a password and have the proper software installed (which is free), but the access provided can certainly assist the broker. Other title companies likely have similar Web pages with the same type of assistance.

QUESTIONS

Matching Terms

a. Constructive
b. Disclaimer
c. Discipline
d. Breach
e. Caveat emptor
f. Collusion
g. Commingling
h. Fraud
i. Latent
j. Patent

1. Failure to perform a duty. Breach
2. Two or more persons working together to cheat or defraud another person. Collusion
3. Deception, deceit, or trickery. Fraud
4. Improper mixing of clients' funds with one's own. Commingling
5. Readily seen; obvious. Patent
6. Inferred or implied. Constructive
7. Denial of responsibility or liability. Disclaimer
8. Hidden from view; not apparent. Latent
9. Let the buyer beware. Caveat emptor
10. To impose a penalty upon. Discipline

True/False

T F 11. Every contract between a real estate broker and client is a covenant of good faith and fair dealing.
T F 12. A real estate broker does not owe a duty to anyone except his principal.
T F 13. In order for fraud to occur, there must be something spoken or written.
T F 14. Disciplinary proceedings cannot be brought against a licensee unless damages to a client have resulted from a wrongful act.
T F 15. A broker cannot be a principal in a real estate transaction.
T F 16. Generally, knowledge of the agent will be imputed to the principal.
T F 17. Good faith is always a requirement in dealings between a broker and the client.
T F 18. A real estate agent may not represent both parties to a transaction without the written consent of each.
T F 19. A real estate broker has a duty to use care, skill, and diligence in the discharge of his duties.
T F 20. There can be liability for fraud and deceit even though the buyer agrees to take the property "as is."

Multiple Choice

21. A real estate agent is under a duty to
   a. Remain loyal to the principal.

b. Use reasonable care in handling the principal's interest.

c. Maintain a trust fund account when he accepts funds on behalf of his principal.

d. All of the above.

22. The doctrine of "caveat emptor"

a. Has limited application today.

b. Is applicable in California to encourage land sales.

c. Will protect a real estate agent in all cases.

d. Will afford a defense to a broker who misinforms a buyer.

23. If a husband and wife are buying a home and are not familiar with ownership methods in California, the broker should advise

a. Joint tenancy.

b. Tenancy in common.

c. Community property.

d. None of the above.

24. If a broker makes a secret profit at the expense of his client, he is

a. Not liable if more than six months elapse before discovery.

b. Not liable if the profit does not exceed 5 percent.

c. Subject to disciplinary action by the Department of Real Estate.

d. None of the above.

25. Patent defects in the condition of premises mean that defects are

a. Obvious.

b. Hidden.

c. Concealed.

d. Not readily discoverable.

26. If a salesperson misinforms a buyer as to deed restrictions

a. There is no liability if the restrictions are a matter of record.

b. The salesperson and broker may both be liable for damages.

c. The broker and not the salesperson is liable to the buyer.

d. The seller and not the broker is liable to the buyer.

27. The liability of a broker may extend to

a. Misstatements as to area.

b. Misrepresentation as to income from the property sold.

c. Concealment of defects unlikely to be discovered by the buyer.

d. All of the above.

28. If a broker buys his client's property through a dummy, he is

a. Relieved of any liability if the sale is for the asking price.

b. Subject to disciplinary proceedings.

c. Protected by the doctrine of "caveat emptor."

d. All of the above.

29. A real estate broker obtained a listing on a property for $100,000. Knowing that the property was worth $120,000, the broker had a third party buy it for him at the listing price. Under these circumstances the broker is liable on the theory of

a. Double agency.

b. Secret profit.

c. Commingling.

d. Dilatory action.

30. If a seller insisted on listing at a price substantially higher than market value, the broker should

a. List at any price the seller desired.

b. List at a lower price, representing actual market value.

c. Decline to take the listing.

d. None of the above.

31. Latent defects in the condition of premises means that defects are

a. Apparent.

b. Obvious.

c. Readily discoverable.

d. Concealed.

32. Ethics in real estate practice is derived from

a. Tradition.

b. Professional association codes.

c. Regulations issued by the Real Estate Commissioner.

d. Any of the above.

33. A real estate broker is permitted to give legal advice to a buyer if

a. The broker has enough experience and is licensed as a broker.

b. The broker has taken a course in real estate law.

c. He is requested to do so by his principal.

d. None of the above.

34. Wrongful acts of a licensee can result in

a. Suspension of license.

b. Revocation of license.

c. A but not b.

d. Either a or b.

35. Wrongful acts of a licensee can result in

a. Suspension of license.

b. Loss of membership in C.A.R.

c. Liability for damages in a civil action.

d. Any of the above.

36. Crimes involving moral turpitude include which of the following?

a. Contributing to the delinquency of a minor.

b. Driving while intoxicated.

c. Assault and battery.

d. Any of the above.

37. An Accusation is the basis for an administrative hearing to determine if a real estate license should be
    a. Revoked.
    b. Suspended.
    c. Limited.
    d. Any of the above.
38. The standard of proof in an administrative hearing before a hearing officer to determine whether a real estate license should be revoked or suspended is
    a. "Convincing proof to a reasonable certainty."
    b. "Beyond a reasonable doubt."
    c. "A preponderance of evidence."
    d. "Slight evidence if creditable."
39. If a broker is charged with "conversion," this means
    a. Commingling client's funds with his own.
    b. Misappropriating client's funds.
    c. Misrepresenting facts.
    d. Failing to disclose material facts about the property known to him.
40. A real estate broker misrepresents to the buyer the income from the property being sold, which information is relied upon by the buyer. Upon discovery of the true facts, after close of escrow, the buyer sues the seller for fraud and deceit. Which of the following statements is correct?
    a. Seller is not liable since he did not personally misrepresent the facts.
    b. Seller has no liability after title passes.
    c. Seller is liable but has recourse against the broker.
    d. Seller is liable and has no recourse against the broker.
41. Duties of a real estate broker to his client include
    a. Advising buyers how to take title.
    b. Preparation of any complicated agreements needed to close the transaction.
    c. Overstating the price the seller paid for the property.
    d. None of the above.
42. Renewal real estate licenses are issued for a period of
    a. Two years.
    b. Three years.
    c. Four years.
    d. Indefinite duration.
43. Grounds for disciplinary action against a real estate licensee include
    a. Negligence.
    b. False advertising.
    c. Secret profits.
    d. Any of the above.
44. Grounds for disciplinary action against a real estate licensee also include

    a. Not having termination date on an exclusive listing.
    b. Commingling funds.
    c. Failure to maintain trust records.
    d. Any of the above.
45. Breach of duty by a broker to his client can result in
    a. Action for damages.
    b. Loss of commission.
    c. Loss of license.
    d. All of the above.
46. If a salesperson is negligent in showing property to a prospective buyer, and as a proximate cause of the negligence the buyer's prospect is injured,
    a. Only the salesperson is liable for damages.
    b. Only the broker is liable for damages.
    c. Both the salesperson and broker may be liable for damages.
    d. Neither broker nor salesperson is liable if there is no sale.
47. Matters that must be disclosed to a prospective buyer if known to the seller include
    a. Imminent eminent domain proceedings.
    b. Probable zoning change.
    c. Unrecorded easements.
    d. Any of the above.
48. Fraud includes
    a. Intentional misstatements.
    b. Careless misstatements.
    c. Silence when there is a duty to speak.
    d. All of the above.
49. Persons who owe a fiduciary duty include
    a. Salespersons.
    b. Brokers.
    c. Cooperating brokers.
    d. All of the above.
50. Grounds for revocation or suspension of a real estate license include
    a. Violation of antidiscrimination laws.
    b. Violation of Code of Ethics.
    c. Violation of franchise law.
    d. All of the above.

NOTES

1. *See* B & P 10176 & 10177.
2. Woodbridge Realty v. Plymouth Dev. Co. (1955) 130 C.A.2d 270, 281. In establishing a cause of action against a broker, the seller must set forth a fiduciary duty and a breach thereof. Crocker Anglo National Bank v. Kushman (1964) 224 C.A.2d 490.
3. Colwell Co. v. Hubert (1967) 248 C.A.2d 567, 576. Attorneys are often accused by licensees of "blowing a deal." When a transaction falls through, it is often as a result of the licensee's negligence or nondisclosure of a material fact. Assisting a buyer or a seller should be a team effort between the licensee and attorney, both with the thought of what is *best* for the principal. By so doing, many of the current problems will be alleviated.

4. Sierra Pac. Ind. v. Carter (1980) 104 C.A.3d 579. One case held that "by misconduct, breach of conduct or willful disregard, in a material respect, of an obligation imposed upon him by the law of agency he may forfeit his right to compensation." Baird v. Mattsen (1943) 57 C.A.2d 465, 475-476. But another case held that when a broker is negligent in the performance of his duties, but there is no disloyalty, fraud, or bad faith, the broker is not deprived of all rights to compensation. Tackett v. Croanquist (1966) 244 C.A.2d 572, 578.

5. Timmeson v. Forest E. Olson Inc. (1970) 6 C.A.3d 860, 871. Broker loaning money to a buyer is a material fact that must be disclosed. Bay Shores Homes, Inc. v. San Diego Trust & Savings Bank (1969) 276 C.A.2d 108. Unlike a buyer alleging fraud against a seller, damages being limited by the out-of-pocket rule available to buyers (C.C. 3343), principals alleging fraud or breach of a fiduciary duty short of fraud against brokers can recover the entire amount of damages proximately caused by the breach of duty, whether or not anticipated. C.C. 3333.

6. Buckley v. Savage (1960) 184 C.A.2d 18; Rattray v. Scudder (1946) 48 C.2d 214; Mensel v. Salka (1960) 179 C.A.2d 612.

7. Katz v. DRE (1979) 96 C.A.3d 895; Buckley v. Savage (1960) 184 C.A.2d 18; Grand v. Griesinger (1958) 160 C.A.2d 397; but see Schmig v. Keisen (1922) 189 C. 596.

8. Real Estate Bulletin (Summer 1976); "Commissioner's Forum," California Real Estate magazine (January/February, 1994)

9. Bate v. Marsteller (1959) 175 C.A.2d 577, 580; Bell v. Watson (1957) 148 C.A.2d 684.

10. C.C. 2020; Quistgard v. Derby (1952) 114 C.A.2d 271. Broker can't collect commission from seller if broker has misrepresented the value of the property.

11. Checker v. Beckman & Co. (1972) 28 C.A.3d 5.

12. Checker v. Beckman, supra, 16.

13. Wilson v. Lewis (1980) 106 C.A.3d 802, 806.

14. See, e.g., Fisher v. Losey (1947) 78 C.A.2d 121; Klein v. Commissioner, T.C. Memo 1993-491—No valid Starker exchange; see also In re Exchanged Titlis Inc., 159 B.R. 308—re bankrupt accommodator on Starker exchange.

15. Jorgensen v. Beach 'N' Bay Realty, Inc. (1981) 125 C.A.3d 155. See Brady v. Carmen (1960) 179 C.A.2d 63, 71.

16. See §8.80 for more details.

17. Pepitone v. Russo (1976) 64 C.A.3d 685.

18. Brown v. Critcheld (1980) 100 C.A.3d 858.

19. de St. Germain v. Watson (1950) 95 C.A.2d 862.

20. See Estate of Anderson (1983) 149 C.A.3d 336; see Chapter 9 for more details; see also "Ordinances requiring disclosures," §5.38. The licensee is better off to recommend a C.P.A. or competent attorney to a buyer or seller.

21. I.R.C. 1034. See also Carleton v. Tortosa (1993) 14 C.A. 4th 745 when broker found not liable for not informing client that IRC 1031 exchange would save capital gains taxes. This case is questionable law, in the author's view, and should be looked at only with the facts set forth in that case.

22. I.R.C. 1031. For a delayed exchange, see Starker v. U.S. (9th Cir. 1979) 602 Fed.2d 1341, and Private Letter Ruling 7938087. There may be substantial tax savings if property is sold via an installment sale under I.R.C. 453. Therefore, the licensee should know the fundamentals of installment sales in order to assist his clients.

23. I.R.C. 121. If a husband and wife are planning to divorce, it may be better for them to get the divorce and then divide the residence as separate property before selling it. Each may then be able to claim the $250,000 exclusion. I.R.C. 121(d)(6). For another potential problem, see I.R.C. 483 re Imputed Interest. See also Rev. Rul. 82-1.

24. Stevens v. Hutton (9145) 71 C.A.2d 676; Santos v. Wing (1961) 197 C.A.2d 678.

25. Menzel v. Salka (1960) 179 C.A.2d 612.

26. See, e.g., Adams v. Herman (1951) 106 C.A.2d 92.

27. Batson v. Strehlow (1968) 68 C.2d 662.

28. Whitehead v. Gordon (1969) 2 C.A.3d 659; Sierra Pacific v. Carter (1980) 104 C.A.3d 579; Abell v. Watson (1957) 155 C.A.2d 158.

29. Estrin v. Watson (1957) 150 C.A.2d 107.

30. Duin v. Security First National Bank (1955) 132 C.A.2d Supp. 904, 906. Improperly submitting competing offers (Comm. Regs. 2785[a][6]).

31. Further, under N.A.R.'s "Standards of Practice," Article 7, "The Realtor shall receive and shall transmit all offers on a specified property to the owner for his decision, whether such offers are received from a prospective purchaser or another broker." See also Milligan, "Presentation (Multiple) Offers: Revisited," San Diego Realtor (January 1981).

32. Comm. Regs. 2785(a)(5).

33. Smith v. Zak (1971) 20 C.A.3d 785.

34. Simone v. McKee (1956) 142 C.A.2d 307.

35. "Commissioners Question Box," California Real Estate (May 1975).

36. Real Estate Bulletin (Fall, 1977).

37. Bate v. Marsteller (1965) 232 C.A.2d 605; Tackett v. Croanquist (1966) 244 C.A.2d 512.

38. People v. Barker (1960) 53 C.2d 539; People v. Shirley (1978) 78 C.A.3d 424, 439.

39. Real Estate Bulletin (Spring 1974).

40. B. & P. 10177.4; C.C. 2995 re real estate developers.

41. See §3.11 and §3.12.

42. B. & P. 10176(g) and (h). See also McPhersen v. R. E. Commissioner (1958) 162 C.A.2d 751; Gray v. Fox (1984) 151 C.A.3d 482. Cooperating broker (who was sharing the commission) allegedly was purchasing the property for himself. However, he was double-escrowing the property and reselling at a higher price.

43. Pascal v. Cotton (1962) 205 C.A.2d 597; Allen v. Dailey (1970) 92 C.A. 308; see also Sierra Pacic Ind. v. Carter (1980) 104 C.A.3d 579.

44. Rylander v. Karpe (1976) 60 C.A.3d 317; Ornamental & Structural Steel, Inc. v. B.B.G., Inc. 20 Ariz. App. 16; B. & P. 10176(g). But see Comm. Regs. 2904, which states that a licensee who acts as an agent for either party is guilty of substantial misrepresentation if he receives or anticipates receiving compensation from a lender in connection with securing financing for the transaction, by failing to disclose to both parties the amount and source of compensation. For illegal kickbacks re escrow, pest control, and title companies, see B. & P. 10177.4, Fin. C. 17420, B. & P. 8640. Broker must disclose compensation from company offering home service contracts. "Commissioner's Column," California Real Estate (January 1978).

45. Culver & Assoc. v. Jaoudi Ind. (1991) 1 C.A. 4th 300; B. & P. 10176(d); C.C. 1090, 2232. Neither principal is liable for commission unless both know of the dual representation. McConnell v. Cowan (1955) 44 C.2d 805; Rhoades v. Savage (1963) 219 C.A.2d 294. See Milligan, "Dual agency," San Diego Realtor (April 1981). For a classic case on a violation of dual agency, see Jorgensen v. Beach 'N' Bay Realty, Inc. (1981) 125 C.A.3d 155: The seller's brokers listed her property. Broker brought an offer for $200,000. Seller wanted $5,000 more, but broker told her she might lose the deal if she didn't accept. Before close of escrow, broker had a listing with the buyer to resell, and did resell the property at a substantially higher price and failed to disclose this to seller. Broker also failed to disclose that the buyers were "investors," and told the seller that the buyers would be moving into the house, which they had no intention of doing. The court held that there was a

breach of fiduciary duty (the dual agency relationship was disclosed), and that there was a failure to exercise reasonable care in setting the sales price of the residence. *See also* the case of Gray v. Fox (1984) 151 C.A.3d 482.

46. Bonaccorso v. Kaplan (1963) 218 C.A.2d 63, 68.

47. Standard Realty & Dev. Co. v. Ferrera (1957) 151 C.A.2d 514, 516.

48. Darrow v. Robert A. Klein (1931) 111 C.A. 310; Wilson v. Lowe (1980) 106 C.A.3d 802.

49. Vice v. Thacker (1947) 20 C.2d 84. When a buyer dictates the terms to the broker's salesperson, which were not the suggestions of the seller, the broker and the salesperson are the agents of the buyer in transmitting the offer to the seller (Wright v. Lowe [1956] 140 C.A.2d 891).

50. Rest.2d Agency, 392 com. b. But *see* Jorgensen v. Beach 'N' Bay Realty, Inc. (1981) 125 C.A.3d 155.

51. C.C. 2373, *et seq.*

52. Ohanesian v. Watson (1953) 118 C.A.2d 386; Foreman and Clark Corp. v. Fallon (1971) 3 C.3d 875; Ford v. Cournale (1974) 36 C.A.3d 172; Wolfe v. Price (1966) 244 C.A.2d 165; Sands v. Eagle Oil & Rening Company (1948) 83 C.A.3d 312; Skoop v. Weaver (1976) 16 C.3d 432. In the latter case the court stated that "there is a compelling reason to find a real estate agent to be an agent whenever his acts or omissions cause injury in a real estate transaction."

53. Beeler v. West American Finance Co. (1962) 201 C.A.2d 702, 706.

54. Richards Realty Co. v. R. E. Commissioner (1956) 144 C.A.2d 357. *See* Li v. Yellow Cab Co. (1975) 13 C.3d 804 re comparative negligence. An agent has the duty to use reasonable skill and diligence, and if the duty is violated, the agent is liable for any loss the principal sustains as a result of the agent's negligence (Kerivan v. Title Insurance & Trust Company [1983] 147 C.A.3d 225, 230).

55. B. & P. 10177(g); C.C. 2020. This would include, e.g., informing a VA seller to obtain a "Release from Liability"; otherwise, the veteran seller is liable for payment in the event of default by the purchaser. Although the release does not automatically restore the G.I. loan entitlement, it should be checked into if the seller wishes to again utilize his VA benefits.

56. Handeland v. DRE (1976) 58 C.A.3d 513, 518.

57. Brady v. Carmen (1960) 179 C.A.2d 63, 68; Colpe Investment Co. v. Seeley & Co. (1933) 132 C.A.2d 16,19.

58. Rest.2d Agency 379.

59. Schoenberg v. Romike Prop. (1967) 251 C.A.2d 154, 162; C.C. 2020.

60. Horne v. Peckham (1979) 97 C.A.3d 404; Comm Regs. 2785(b)(6).

61. Wilson v. Hisey (1957) 147 C.A.2d 443; *see also* Eamoe v. Big Bear Land & Water Co. (1950) 98 C.A.2d 370, wherein an agent erroneously sold the wrong lot to the buyer.

62. Pro. C. 16440(a); Pro. C. 16420 (remedies for breach of trust).

63. Lyon v. Giannoni (1959) 168 C.A.2d 336; Comm Regs. 1785(a)(10). *See also,* C.C. 1057.3.

64. Sarten v. Pomatto (1961) 192 C.A.2d 288.

65. Holloway v. Thiele (1953) 116 C.A.2d 68; Hogg v. Real Estate Commissioner (1942) 54 C.A.2d 712.

66. Brown v. Gordon (1966) 240 C.A.2d 659.

67. C.C. 2234.

68. Beeler v. Western American Finance Co. (1962) 201 C.A.2d 702.

69. C.C. 1572.

70. C.C. 1710.

71. *See* Walters v. Marler (1978) 83 C.A.3d 1, 17 for elements of negligent misrepresentation. *See also* Glendale Federal Savings & Loan v. Marina View Heights Development Co. (1977) 66 C.A.3d 101.

72. Ford v. Cournale (1974) 36 C.A.3d 172.

73. Schoenberg v. Romike Properties (1967) 251 C.A.2d 154; *see also* Banville v. Schmidt (1974) 37 C.A.3d 92. Fraud can also be alleged against former owners and even subsequent purchasers (Geernaert v. Mitchell [1995] 31 C.A. 4th 601).

74. Skopp v. Weaver (1976) 16 C.3d 432.

75. Kruse v. Miller (1956) 143 C.A.2d 656.

76. Borba v. Thomas (1977) 70 C.A.3d 144.

77. Daniels v. Oldenburg (1950) 100 C.A.2d 724.

78. B. & P. 10141; B. & P. 10141.5.

79. Golden v. Anderson (1967) 256 C.A.2d 714, 719-720.

80. Walters v. Marler, et al. (1978) 83 C.A.3d 1, 35.

81. B. & P. 10176(a), (b), (c), (d), (i); B. & P. 10177(c), (f), (g), (h), (j), (l).

82. Salahutdin v. Valley of California, Inc. (1994) 24 C.A. 4th 555. *See also* C.C. 1709, 3333 & 3343.

83. Smith v. Roach (1975) 53 C.A.3d 893. *See also* Schmidt v. Mesmer (1897) 116 C.261, and Bogdasanan v. Grogan (1948) 31 C.2d 744, which distinguished and disapproved the Schmidt case. Further, a person uttering a misrepresentation is liable only to those in whom he intended to induce reliance. Bell v. Renaldo (1975) 51 C.A.3d 779. A broker must disclose fraudulent acts of his principal to the buyer. Willig v. Golde (1946) 75 C.A.2d 809.

84. Jue v. Smisor (1994) 23 C.A. 4th 312.

85. C.C. 1573.

86. Breach of duty arises out of a confidential or fiduciary relationship. Odorizzi v. Bloomfield School District (1966) 246. C.A.2d 533.

87. C.C. 1574.

88. Agair v. Shaeffer (1965) 232 C.A.2d 513.

89. Efron v. Kalmanovitz (1969) 226 C.A.2d 546.

90. De Bairos v. Barlin (1920) 46 C.A. 665; Hayter v. Fulmor (1949) 92 C.A.2d 392, 398.

91. Saporta v. Barbageleta (1963) C.A.2d 463; Schoenberg v. Benna (1967) 251 C.A.2d 154; Wilbur v. Wilson (1960) 170 C.A.2d 314.

92. C.C. 1102 *et seq.*; Wilson v. C-21, Great Western Realty (1993) 15 C.A. 4th 298 (licensee not required to inspect foundation for lack of "J" bolts, even though neighbor suggested the possibility of potential problems); Brosie v. Sparks (1993) 17 C.A. 4th 1756 (TDS is not a part of the contract and may not give rise to a claim against the licensee if it contains inaccuracies); Jue v. Smiser (1994) 23 C.A. 4th 312. Plaintiff owner lost her home at a foreclosure sale, at which was purchased by defendant—her broker—who acted as a foreclosure consultant. Held: in favor of plaintiff who got her home back—and was awarded her attorney's fees and treble damages (Onofrio v. Rice [1997] 55 C.A. 4th 413).

93. Easton v. Strassburger (1984) 152 C.A.3d 90. The seller is bound to disclose facts not within the diligent attention of the buyer. Murray v. Haden (1989) 211 C.A. 3d 311; Vaill v. Edmonds (1991) 4 C.A. 4th 247—when buyer sees evidence of erosion and evidence of a geological fault, the broker is not negligent or incompetent. Moradzadeh v. Antonio (1992) 5 C.A. 4th 1289—lessor of commercial property has a duty to disclose to the prospective tenant material facts affecting the value or desirability of the property. Alexander v. McKnight (1992) 7 C.A. 4th 973—seller is obligated to disclose to prospective buyers that the neighbors are tormentors and openly hostile; Brasier v. Sparks (1993) 17 C.A. 4th 1756. Buist v. C. Dudley De Velbiss (1960) 180 C.A.2d 325. Fraud or dishonest dealings, within the meaning of B. & P. 10176, includes *failure* of a licensee to *disclose* to a prospective buyer requesting his services, that such licensee will not show or negotiate real estate that is for sale because of his intention to negotiate a sale with a buyer who will provide the licensee with greater com-

pensation. Comm. Regs. 2706. For two-year statute of limitations, *see* C.C. 2079.4; Sweat v. Hollister (1995) 37 C.A. 4th 603.

94. Reed v. King (1983) 145 C.A.3d 261.

95. Padgett v. Phariss (1997) 54 C.A. 4th 1270; Shapiro v. Sutherland (1998) 60 C.A. 4th 666. If a buyer asks how many square feet a particular house has, the broker is obligated either to say he does not know (and he should know) or else tell him the truth. If he attempts to avoid or evade the question by saying, "The seller says it has 1,800," and the broker knows that it has only 1,700 square feet, his actions are fraudulent—Mills v. Hellinger (1950) 100 C.A.2d 482; William v. Marshall (1951) 37 C.2d 445; Salahutdin v. Valley of California, Inc. (1994) 24 C.A. 4th 555.

96. Orlando v. Berkely (1963) 220 C.A.2d 224. Comm. Regs. 2903 states that a licensee has a duty to disclose to all purchasers, sellers, or parties to an exchange all knowledge he may have of any infestation of any wood-destroying organisms or any structural defects.

97. Alexander Groswird v. Hayne Investment, Inc. (1982) 133 C.A.3d 624.

98. Cooper v. Jevne (1976) 56 C.A.3d 860; Barnhouse v. City of Pinole (1982) 133 C.A.3d 171.

99. Jacobs v. Freeman (1980) 104 C.A.3d 177.

100. Mere statements of opinion about probable potential income from property usually do not constitute fraud. Pacesetter Homes Inc. v. Brodkin (1970) 5 C.A.3d 206.

101. Pub. Res. C. 2621.9.

102. The *California Real Estate* magazine (November 1975) contains an article on the impact of this law in real estate transactions. *See also* §12.48.

103. *Real Estate Bulletin* (Spring 1980).

104. Lingsch v. Savage (1963) 213 C.A.2d 729; Cooper v. Jerne (1976) 56 C.A.3d 860.

105. Barder v. McClung (1949) 93 C.A.2d 692; Curran v. Heslop (1953) 115 C.A. 2d 476.

106. Shapiro v. Sutherland (1998) 60 C.A.4th 666.

107. C.C. 1668; *see also* Milligan, "The Dangers of the As Is Clause," *California Real Estate* magazine (June 1978); Prichard v. Reitz (1986) 178 C.A.3d 465.

108. Lingsch v. Savage (1963) 213 C.A.2d 729; Shapiro v. Hu (1986) 188 C.A.3d 324, wherein the court held that an "as is" clause relieves seller of responsibility of liability for defects that were not intentionally concealed. *See also* Wilson v. Century 21 Great Western Realty (1993) 15 C.A. 4th 298 (re C.C. 1102, *et seq.* and C.C. 1668). But *see* Loughrin v. Superior Court (1993) 15 C.A. 4th 1188.

109. Lingsch v. Savage, supra.

110. Katz v. DRE (1979) 96 C.A.3d 895; Rothstein v. Janss Investment Co. (1941) 45 C.A.2d 64.

111. Orlando v. Berkeley (1963) 220 C.A.2d 224.

112. Speck v. Wylie (1934) 1 C.2d 625, 626, 628; Kett v. Graeser (1966) 241 C.A.2d 571.

113. Eamoe v. Big Bear Land & Water Co. (1950) 98 C.A.2d 370, 372-374.

114. Walsh v. Hooker & Fay (1963) 212 C.A.2d 450, 462. Broker can also be indemnified by the seller. Gardner v. Murphy (1975) 54 C.A.3d 164. For partial indemnification, *see* American Motorcycle Assn. v. Superior Court (1978) 20 C.3d 578.

115. Podlasky v. Price (1948) 87 C.A.2d 151. An integration clause stating "There are no oral agreements not contained herein" will not necessarily protect a defendant. Southern California, etc. Assemblies of God v. Shepherd of Hills, etc. Church (1978) 77 C.A.3d 951. A statement in the purchase contract that buyer is aware of certain clearly *specified* (spelled out in the agreement) conditions and accepts the property in such condition might minimize the risk to the seller and broker.

116. Granberg v. Turnham (1958) 166 C.A.2d 390.

117. Hale v. Wolfson (1969) 276 C.A.2d 285.

118. Nichandros v. Real Estate Division (1960) 181 C.A.2d 179.

119. Bell v. Watson (1957) 148 C.A.2d 684.

120. Ach v. Finkelstein (1968) 264 C.A.2d 667.

121. 59 Ops. Cal. Atty. Gen. 369 (1976). *See also* §4.5, §4.16; Easton v. Strassburger (1984) 152 C.A.3d 90.

122. Merrill v. Buck (1964) 58 C.2d 552.

123. Kent v. Bartlett (1975) 49 C.A.3d 724.

124. Banville v. Schmidt (1974) 37 C.A.3d 92; Black v. Sherasen, Hammill & Co. (1968) 266 C.A.2d 362.

125. Funk v. Tifft (1975) 515 Fed.2d 23. This fact situation could have been decided on the theory of Interference with a Prospective Economic Advantage; *see* §3.36.

126. Wice v. Schilling (1954) 124 C.A.2d 735.

127. Evans v. Rancho Royale Hotel Co. (1952) 114 C.A.2d 503.

128. Unger v. Compau (1956) 142 C.A.2d 722.

129. Leary v. Baker (1953) 119 C.A.2d 106; Eatwell v. Beck (1953) 41 C.2d 128.

130. Kallgren v. Steele (1955) 131 C.A.2d 43.

131. Gilbert v. Corlett (1959) 171 C.A.2d 116.

132. Crawford v. Nastos (1960) 182 C.A.2d 659.

133. Curran v. Heslop (1953) 115 C.A.2d 476; Milmoe v. Dixon (1950) 101 C.A.2d 257. As stated by the court in the last-cited case, a party who makes an inspection of the property does not forfeit his right to rely on the representations or concealment of the seller as to matters of a technical nature, or as to facts not determinable by the exercise of reasonable diligence in the inspection.

134. Carroll v. Gova (1979) 98 C.A.3d 892; Wilbur v. Wilson (1960) 179 C.A.2d 314.

135. Jue v. Smiser (1994) 23 C.A. 4th 312; Salahutdin v. Valley of California Inc. (1994) 24 C.A. 4th 555.

136. Clauser v. Tayler (1941) 44 C.A.2d 453.

137. Comm. Regs. 2785(a)(12).

138. Southern California etc. Assemblies of God v. Shepherd of Hills, etc. Church (1978) 77 C.A.3d 951.

139. Cohen v. S and S Construction Co. (1984) 151 C.A.3d 941.

140. Gray v. Don Miller and Associates (1984) 35 C.3d 498.

141. Ward v. Taggert (1959) 51 C.2d 736.

142. Sweeney v. Stone (1968) 265 C.A.2d 693.

143. Oakes v. McCarthy Co. (1968) 267 C.A.2d 231.

144. Kriegler v. Eichler Homes, Inc. (1969) 269 C.A.2d 224.

145. Avner v. Longridge Estates (1969) 272 C.A.2d 607.

146. Gilbert Financial Corp. v. Steelform Const. Co. (1978) 82 C.A.3d 65; C.C. 1735; Eden v. Van Time (1978) 83 C.A.3d 879. *See also* express warranty case wherein R-1 zoning was claimed, but it was really R-2, and no building permit had been obtained. Szabo v. Superior Court (1978) 84 C.A.3d 839.

147. Pollard v. Saxe, et al. (1974) 12 C.3d 374; Siders v. Scholl (1987) 188 C.A.3d 1217.

148. Govt. C. 38780.

149. B. & P. 6125, 6126.

150. Agran v. Shapiro (1954) 127 C.A.2d Supp. 807; Abar v. Rogue (1981) 124 C.A.3d 862; Drake v. Superior Court (1994) 21 C.A. 4th 1826.

151. People v. Sipper (1943) 61 C.A.2d Supp. 844.

152. Engebrecht v. Shelton (1945) 69 C.A.2d 151.

153. Biakanja v. Irving (1958) 49 C.2d 647.

154. Govt. C. 10500, *et seq.*

155. 10176, 10177.

156. *See* Madrid v. DRE (1984) 150 C.A.3d 816.

157. Unfortunately, there appear to be no reported cases defining *reasonable supervision*. Presumably it depends on each particular fact situation.

158. Manning v. Fox (1984) 151 C.A.3d 531.

159. Handeland v. DRE (1976) 58 C.A.3d 513; CREL Inc. v. Wallace (1993) 18 C.A. 4th 1575.
160. B. & P. 10101.
161. If conviction is based on nolo contendere, the Law Judge need not find whether the underlying acts were actually committed. Arneson v. Fox (1980) 28 C.3d 440.
162. Watkins v. Real Estate Commissioner (1960) 182 C.A.2d 397; Jennings v. Karpe (1974) 36 C.A.3d 709.
163. In re Duggan (1976) 17 C.A.3d 416.
164. Brandt v. Fox (1979) 90 C.A.3d 737 (defendant's felony was for distributing cocaine). *See also* Pieri v. Fox (1979) 96 C.A.3d 802; Gold v. Fox (1979) 98 C.A.3d 167; B. & P. 475, 480, 490, 726, 727, 2902, 2910, 2946, 2960.
165. Realty Projects, Inc. v. Smith (1973) 32 C.A.3d 204. For a more thorough explanation, *see* Milligan, "Real Estate Commissioner's Disciplinary Proceedings," *California Real Estate* (March 1976). *See also* Norman I. Krug Real Estate Investments, Inc. v. Praszker (1994) 22 C.A. 4th 1814, a case in which one broker tried to avoid disciplinary action by stipulating to a reversal of a judgment; it didn't work.
166. Govt. C. 11519. Real Estate Commissioner's action for injunction and claim for restitution on behalf of injured party; *see* B. & P. 10081.
167. Crandell v. Fox (1978) 86 C.A.3d 760.
168. 25 Ops. Cal. Atty. Gen. 43 (1955); C.C. 2355; C.C. 1689.
169. (1979-1980) p. 56.
170. For a detailed analysis, *see* Milligan, *An Original Guidebook on Real Estate Ethics and Arbitration, A Procedures and Forms Manual* (1976), 165 pages. *See also* Williams v. Inglewood Board of Realtors (1963) 219 C.A.2d 479.
171. Cunningham v. Burbank Board of Realtors (1968) 262 C.A.2d 211.
172. United Multiple Listing Service, Inc. v. Bernstein (1982) 134 C.A.3d 486 (requirement that member of M.L.S. arbitrate commission disputes is a reasonable membership rule).
173. Berke v. Hecht (1989) 208 C.A.3d 463.
174. *See* Milligan,"Real Estate Ethics and Arbitration Procedures," *California Real Estate* (June 1976). *See also* Comm. Regs. 2785(c)(9).

Acquisition and Alienation of Title

I. INTRODUCTION

§6.1. In general

There are many different methods of acquisition and transfer of title to real property. The Civil Code provides that property may be acquired in the following ways: (1) by occupancy; (2) by accession; (3) by transfer; (4) by will; or (5) by succession.[1] This list is not exclusive, however. The following specific methods by which title may be acquired or transferred are considered in this chapter, without reference to the code classification: (1) adverse possession; (2) condemnation; (3) dedication; (4) accession; (5) wills and succession, including transfers in trust; (6) escheat; (7) involuntary alienation; (8) title by estoppel; (9) abandonment; and (10) forfeiture. The subject of transfers by deed is considered in detail in Chapter 7, along with a discussion of the utilization of escrow in real estate transactions.

As we have already seen, the law of real property is governed by the laws of the state in which the real property is located. The domicile of the owner does not necessarily determine the applicable law. When an owner of real property located in California is deceased or missing, California law applies, even though the owner's residence is in another state. Questions often arise about the applicable procedure to effect a sale or other disposition of such person's property. The procedure is covered by various provisions of the Probate Code, and is a method of transfer of title frequently encountered in dealing with real property.

II. ADVERSE POSSESSION

§6.2. In general

Adverse possession is a means of acquiring title to real property after a lapse of time, based on continued possession and payment of taxes. In California the occupancy of land for any period of time confers a title that prevails against all except the state and persons having a better title.[2] If the occupant maintains adverse possession of the land for the period of time that the owner is given to bring an action for recovery of the land, namely five years, the occupant acquires title by adverse possession, which is declared by the Civil Code to be sufficient against all; except that property interests dedicated to a public use by a public utility, or dedicated to or owned by the state or any public entity, are not subject to adverse possession.[3] A new title is created in the adverse possessor, and the title of the record owner is lost.

Usually the property that is acquired by adverse possession is a small parcel that has for all intents been abandoned by the record owner, or the record owner is a nonresident or is deceased and the heirs either are not aware of the property or are not interested in it. One justification for the theory of title by adverse possession is that it restores the property to the tax rolls and the property is maintained in better condition by the claimant.[4]

§6.3. Necessity for quiet title decree

Although it has been said that no title can be better or more absolute than that acquired by adverse possession,[5] such a title is not considered a marketable title, that is, a title free from reasonable doubt and fairly deducible from the record that a purchaser can be compelled to accept, until the title is established by judicial proceedings against the record owner. An action to quiet title is the type of proceeding undertaken to establish the title.[6] On the recordation of a certified copy of a decree quieting title, the adverse possessor's title becomes a matter of public record. Another method is to obtain a quitclaim deed from the record owner in order to avoid a suit to quiet title.

§6.4. Elements of adverse possession

The essential elements of adverse possession are as follows:

1. The possession must be by actual occupation and must be open and notorious, that is, the circumstances of possession must be such as to constitute reasonable notice to the record owner.

2. Possession must be hostile[7] to the true owner's title, that is, not permissive, and must be exclusive.

3. Possession must be held under either a claim of right or a color of title.

4. Possession must be continuous and uninterrupted for a minimum of five years.

5. The claimant must have paid all taxes levied and assessed during the five-year period.[8]

§6.5. Occupancy of land

The person taking possession does not actually have to reside on the property. Under specified conditions, it is possible to acquire title to vacant land by adverse possession. Use of the land for the ordinary purposes for which it is adapted, such as for agriculture, is sufficient. Personal occupation is not essential; possession may be by a tenant of the person claiming by adverse possession.

§6.6. Claim of right and color of title

Adverse possession may be based on either a claim of right or color of title.

Under a *claim of right*, the claimant enters as an intruder and remains such as against the true owner, without any bona fide belief, necessarily, in his title.

Possession under *color of title* is based on some written instrument, judgment, or decree of court that gives an appearance of title, but that is not good title in fact.

EXAMPLE A deed that describes the land and on its face purports to pass the title, but fails to do so because of a want of title in the person executing the deed, or because the deed is voidable. If the claim is based on color of title, actual possession of all of the land claimed is not mandatory if part of the land is occupied under such circumstances as to constitute constructive possession of the whole area.

Advantage of color of title. When a claim is supported by color of title, there is a marked difference in the extent and character of the possession that will establish an adverse title. For example, the required showing of actual occupation is less exacting, and the land is deemed to have been actually occupied not only when it has been cultivated, improved, or enclosed, but also when it has been used for other purposes, such as for pasturage or for any ordinary use of the occupant. Furthermore, if a part of the tract of land claimed under color of title is actually occupied, that is, lived on in good faith by the claimant, his possession is considered to extend to the whole tract. Thus the claimant is deemed to be in constructive possession of the entire land described in the color of title, although it is not in his actual possession in the sense that he is physically occupying or using all of it.

When the claim is based on a claim of right, the land is deemed to have been possessed and occupied only if it has been protected by a substantial enclosure or has been usually cultivated or improved. Only the land actually so occupied is deemed to have been held and claimed adversely.

§6.7. Acts breaking continuity of possession

The requisite continuity of possession by the adverse claimant may be broken at any time during the five-year period by such acts as a re-entry into possession by the true owner, or the commencement of an action of ejectment or to quiet title by the true owner, or by acts on the part of the occupant that recognize the superior title of the true owner, such as the adverse claimant's taking a lease from the true owner.

§6.8. Tacking on possession

An adverse claimant does not have to depend solely on his own possession to establish title by adverse possession. The claimant may tack on or add his possession to that of a prior adverse holder to complete the adverse period when there is privity of estate between the two persons, as in the case of a claimant who enters into possession under a conveyance from a prior adverse possessor.

§6.9. Payment of taxes

It is not essential that taxes be paid on time by the adverse claimant. It has been held that a redemption of land sold for delinquent taxes, made in good faith by an adverse claimant while in possession, is a payment of taxes that satisfies the rule.[9] The adverse possessor may be able to claim ownership when he satisfied the legal requirements, including payment of taxes, even though the record owner also pays the taxes. However, it has been held that if the taxes are only assessed to the record owner, the adverse claimant must pay the taxes first. If the owner pays first, the claimant cannot establish his title even though he does pay the taxes.[10]

§6.10. Limitations on doctrine of adverse possession

There are various exceptions and limitations placed on the doctrine of title by adverse possession. Title by adverse possession cannot be acquired to property devoted to public use, and this rule has been extended by statute to include property owned by certain government bodies and agencies in a proprietary capacity, and to include property interests dedicated to a public use by a public utility, or dedicated to or owned by the state or any other public entity.

EXAMPLE   In one case, it was held that although a party could not take title by adverse possession to property owned by a public entity, he could take title as against any private party having rights in the same property, such as the owner of the underlying fee when the surface was used for street purposes. In this case, the defendant took possession of the north half of the street. Defendant's property abutted the street on the south. After the street was abandoned by the county, the defendant was declared to be the owner of both the north and the south halves of the street.[11]

Owner under disability. Owners under certain disabilities, such as minority or insanity, are protected from claims of adverse title by statutory provisions to the effect that the duration of the disability, not to exceed 20 years, is not computed as part of the period prescribed for acquiring adverse title.[12] Under these provisions, title by adverse possession cannot be established against an owner who is a minor, unless the adverse possession continues until the expiration of five years after the minor attains his majority. The exemption applies, however, only to disabilities existing at the inception of adverse possession. Accordingly, when adverse possession commences against a legal owner not under a disability, the running of the statute is not interrupted by the subsequent adjudication of insanity of the legal owner, or by the death of the legal owner and the descent of the land to a person under a disability.

Limitations based on extent of title claimed. Another limitation arises from the general rule that the extent of the title acquired by adverse possession depends on the extent of the denial of title in the legal owner. When a separation of the ownership of the land and the ownership of the minerals has occurred, the possession by the owner of the surface is not considered adverse to the owner of the minerals, and cannot be the basis of an adverse title to the minerals interest.[13]

EXAMPLE   In one case it was held that adverse possession against a life tenant is not adverse to the remaindermen, who do not have a right of possession until the termination of the life estate, at which time the statute begins to run against them.[14]

III. CONDEMNATION (EMINENT DOMAIN)

§6.11. In general

Real property may be acquired in condemnation proceedings through the exercise of the power of *eminent domain*, which is the sovereign right of the state to take private property for public use on the payment of just compensation.[15]

Whether the owner wants to part with the title is immaterial. Also, the owner cannot set his price. A fair valuation, based on an appraisal, is paid. If the condemning authority and the owner cannot agree on the price, the owner is entitled to a jury trial on the issue.[16]

In another type of condemnation, an owner is not entitled to compensation for the value of the property taken. An example of this type of case is when the condemnation occurs in the exercise of the police power. For instance, an unsafe building might be condemned under the provisions of the Health and Safety Code in the exercise of the police power.

In most cases when a condemnation action is filed in the exercise of the power of eminent domain, the question for determination by the court is the amount of damages. At times, however, the main question is whether the taking is, in fact, for a public purpose.

Recent court cases have expanded the scope of eminent domain, and the acquisition of property for community redevelopment is now one of the leading uses of eminent domain in California. Redevelopment agencies have been able to use their eminent domain powers to further projects by private developers. A primary justification is to eliminate blight. But this does not mean that each particular property must be blighted. A redevelopment agency may use eminent domain to acquire individual properties that are not themselves blighted but are located in a blighted area.[17] Even though some of the purposes, such as shopping centers, condominiums, or industrial parks, do not appear to be public in nature, the rationale is that as long as the community benefits as a whole, the fact that there is also benefit to a private developer is not determinative.[18]

Although there might not be comparable situations in other states, a case originating in Hawaii under its Land Reform Act, first enacted in the 1960s and held to be constitutional by the United States Supreme Court on May 30, 1984, could cause expansion of the doctrine to other areas where there is ownership of large parcels of land by only a few owners, without the possibility of homeowners acquiring more than a leasehold estate. Under the provisions of the Land Reform Act, if the majority of householders having long-term leases in an area of at least five acres indicated to the state a desire to purchase a fee title, the state would enter into negotiations with the lessor on their behalf. If negotiations failed, the state could condemn the land and then convey it to the householders for a consideration. The Supreme Court in its opinion concluded that a state may use its condemnation powers to transfer property from one private owner to another as long as the aim is a broad public benefit.[19]

§6.12. Statutory provisions

Various statutes have been enacted in this state authorizing the exercise of the power of eminent domain through special proceedings in the Superior Court in the county in which the real property is located. These statutes prescribe (1) who may exercise the right, that is, cities, counties, the state, and other government agencies, as well as corporations and individuals in charge of a public use, such as a public utility or a privately owned school; (2) the purpose for which land may be condemned, that is, for streets, railroads, drainage, water supply and irrigation, utilities, off-street parking, airports, schools, public buildings and grounds, and the like; (3) the nature of the right or interest acquired, whether fee or easement; (4) the property that may be taken, that is, either private property, or public property if already dedicated; (5) the requisite steps in the proceedings, that is, the filing of a complaint, issuance of summons, and so on. Under prescribed conditions, an order for immediate possession may be obtained.

The Code of Civil Procedure authorizes not only the acquisition of property for a designated public use, but also any interest in other property necessary to that use, such as a buffer area adjacent to an airport where jet noise and fumes have become of increasing concern.[20]

§6.13. The United States may also condemn land

The power of eminent domain may also be exercised by the federal government, and various federal statutes authorize agencies of the government to acquire property for the United States by condemnation proceedings brought in the local United States District Court.

Because of the impact of the exercise of the power of eminent domain on a vast number of people in recent years and the relocation problems that have arisen, a new concept was adopted with the enactment of a federal law entitled Uniform Relocation Assistance and Real Property Acquisition Policies Act of 1970. The law applies to all direct federal and federally aided programs involving some 18 federal agencies and more than 50 different programs they administer. It has been estimated that approximately 200,000 families, persons, businesses, farms, and others throughout the United States are displaced annually. The fair and equitable treatment of such relocatees has become a major concern of local, state, and federal agencies.

§6.14. Condition for exercise of right

Whether the land is taken by an instrumentality of the state or by the United States, two conditions must apply: (1) the taking must be for a public use; and (2) just compensation, measured by the fair market value of the property, must be paid to the property owner. Also, when the taking is a portion only of the owner's land, the owner may be entitled to damages for loss of value of the portion not taken. This is referred to as severance damages. In a partial taking in eminent domain, the value of the benefit conferred on the portion not taken is offset against or deducted from severance damages. However, if the benefit is greater than the severance damages, the benefit is not deducted from the value of the portion taken.

EXAMPLES
1. One case presented an unusual situation involving severance damages. The state needed only .65 acre of farmland, but was permitted to condemn an additional 54 acres that would be landlocked to avoid payment of excessive severance damages.[21] Subsequently, a law was enacted that restricts the acquisition of physical remnants if the owner proves that the public entity has a reasonable, practical, and economically sound means to prevent the property from becoming a remnant.[22]

2. In another case, the Supreme Court denied recovery for the loss of goodwill, but by legislative enactment, loss of goodwill is now an element of recoverable damages under prescribed conditions.[23]

---

§6.15. Condemnation by private school

One case raised a question as to whether the taking of property by a private school for school purposes constituted a public use. The court held that it did. Even though the school was a private college, it was open to the public and was contributing to public education.[24]

§6.16. Condemnation by private individual

The Civil Code provides that any person under prescribed conditions may maintain an action to acquire property by eminent domain; thus, a private individual may maintain such an action if the use is of a benefit to the public.[25] This right was recognized in one case involving an action to condemn a right of way for a sewer line over adjoining land used for residential purposes.[26] However, a private person must allege and prove that he proposes to devote the property to public use and it must appear that he is authorized to devote the property to public use.[27]

§6.17. Replacement housing

The Government Code provides for relocation assistance to persons displaced because of the acquisition of real property by a public entity for public use.[28] These provisions include moving expenses and additional payments to cover the replacement cost of a dwelling.

In 1971 guidelines for public entities were adopted to encourage acquisition by agreement with an owner rather than by litigation.[29]

§6.18. Whether fee or easement condemned

When the fee title to land is condemned for a particular public use, the general rule is that the former owner retains no reversionary or other interest, and such use may be changed or abandoned. Following proper abandonment, the land can be disposed of by the government agency in any manner provided by law, without limitations as to any rights of the former owner. When an easement only is condemned, however, the title to the underlying fee remains in the landowner, and on abandonment of the public use, the original owner or his or her successor owns the land, free of public use.

§6.19. Inverse condemnation

Sometimes public works are undertaken with resulting damage to private property, but no condemnation action is filed by the public body. In such a situation, the property owner may initiate an action himself to recover damages. Such an action is referred to as an *inverse condemnation* action.

EXAMPLE   In one case the plaintiff recovered $30,000 against BART for inverse condemnation. BART had excavated a sidewalk area adjacent to the plaintiff's property, resulting in withdrawal of lateral support so that the building settled and cracked.[30]

---

§6.20. Effect on deed restrictions

Property owners may be compensated for violation of deed restrictions when a lot within their subdivision is condemned.

EXAMPLE   In one case it was held that a building restriction enforceable by other owners in a subdivision constitutes property within the meaning of the eminent domain provisions of the California constitution, and such owners were entitled to compensation when a lot in the subdivision was taken for a public purpose (electricity substation) prohibited by the deed restrictions. This overruled previous cases holding that deed restrictions were not a property interest.[31]

IV. DEDICATION

§6.21. In general

As we shall see, easements may be acquired by dedication. Fee title may also be acquired in such a manner. *Dedication* is defined as the devotion of land to a public use by an unequivocal act of the fee owner manifesting an intention that the land shall be accepted and used for such public purpose.

EXAMPLE   A conveyance of land to a city for park purposes.

---

§6.22. Nature of interest created whether fee or easement

The nature of the interest created in the public by statutory dedication is usually specified by statute, the Subdivision Map Act providing, for instance, that a dedication shall convey an easement when a public body can condemn for such purpose only an easement, but in all other cases said dedication shall convey a fee simple estate subject to the terms of the dedication. Other map acts, including the Subdivision Map Act, do not specify which particular interest is conferred by dedication. It has been stated, however, that the public acquires the same rights in property by dedication as by condemnation.[32] In applying this rule, it has been held that the dedication of a park vested the fee title in the government agency. It is doubtful, though, that in all cases the fee title acquired by dedication, which normally is a donation, is the same as the fee title acquired by condemnation, which requires the payment of compensation for the value of the land taken.

§6.23. Limitation on use of land acquired by dedication

When the fee title to land is condemned for a public use, the public body may, as a rule, thereafter abandon such use and devote the land to another use. But the fee acquired by dedication may be considered to be a qualified or determinable fee, with the original owner retaining an interest in the nature of a possibility of reverter on abandonment of the dedicated public use. This would appear to preclude the public body from diverting such use, or from leasing or otherwise disposing of the land for purposes inconsistent with the dedication use.[33]

§6.24. Dedication of public lands

A public body, as well as a private owner, may dedicate its land for a particular use. Thus, a city council may pass a resolution declaring a certain area of city-owned lands to be a public park. By dedicating lands owned in fee to park use, a city does not purport to deprive itself of the power to change the use and devote the land to another purpose.[34]

Change in use of dedicated lands. The last cited case involved the right or power of the city to extend a street through West Lake Park, the land having been owned in fee by the city and dedicated as a public park. The court pointed out the distinction between cases in which land has been donated to a city for park purposes and cases in which land owned by a city has been dedicated by the city to such uses, and stated that the city is only dedicating its own property to a different public use from that to which it had been previously subjected. The court upheld the right of a municipality to thus meet changing conditions and the right of the city to use a portion of the park lands for street purposes.

§6.25. Subsurface use of park property

The subsurface of land dedicated for park purposes can be used for other purposes, provided the surface use is not changed.

EXAMPLE   One case involved the subsurface use of Union Square Park as a public automobile garage and parking station. In upholding the right of the city to make such use of the park, the court stated that there was nothing in the terms of the original grant of Union Square that would deprive the City and County of San Francisco of the right to change the character of the use of the land so long as the contemplated use was not inconsistent with enjoyment by the public of the land for park purposes.[35]

§6.26. Implied dedication

In 1970 the California Supreme Court ruled in two cases that evidence of use of privately owned shorelands by the public for over five years with the owner's knowledge, without asking or receiving permission, and without objection by anyone, established an implied dedication of an easement to the public.[36] These cases have had far-reaching consequences and have resulted in legislative action in an attempt to resolve the conflict between the rights of private owners and the rights of the public.

EXAMPLES

1. In one of these cases, it was proved that the public had regularly used certain oceanfront lots for parking, for beach access, and for water recreation for over five years preceding commencement of the action. The owners had full knowledge of these activities but made no significant objection. Members of the public who fished on the property were never asked or told to leave. The city beautified and improved the property, oiled the parking areas, installed safety devices, and spent substantial sums to prevent erosion. The trial court held that as a consequence of these facts, the plaintiff's fee interest was subject to an easement in the city for itself and on behalf of the public to use the property for public recreation. The trial court's decision was affirmed by the Supreme Court.

2. The trial court in the second case denied an injunction to prevent the landowners from interfering with public use of Navarro Beach and its access road as it passed through their property. The plaintiffs at the trial showed continuous use of the beach and roadway by the public, whose members neither requested nor received permission, for over a hundred years, for picnicking, swimming, fishing, and other recreation. The prior owners knew of and did not interfere with such use. After the defendants acquired title to the property, they put up No Trespassing signs and tried to prevent public access by blocking the road. The trial court's decision was reversed on appeal, and the public use could continue.

The law was amended in 1971 to provide, among other things, that subject to specified exceptions, no use of private real property by the public made after the effective date of the section shall ever "ripen to confer upon the public or any government body or unit a vested right to continue to make such use permanently," unless an express written irrevocable offer of dedication to such use has been made.[37] The exceptions relate to use by a government agency of private lands when such entity has expended public funds on improvements on the land, and to coastal property unless the owner has taken specified steps to prevent the public from obtaining rights, such as posting signs on the property, publishing a notice in a newspaper, or recording a notice in the county recorder's office.

§6.27. Subdivision dedication

As a condition for approval of a subdivision, the developer may be required to dedicate a portion of the land for park purposes or pay an additional fee in lieu thereof.

EXAMPLE

In one case, the court sustained the constitutionality of the Business and Professions Code[38] authorizing a requirement of a dedication of land, or in lieu of land payment of a fee, for park or recreational purposes, as a condition for approval by a city or county of a subdivision map.[39]

V. ACCESSION

§6.28. In general

Accession as a method of acquisition of title may occur by annexation, by accretion, or by reliction. Accession literally means "adding to."

§6.29. Annexation

Annexation occurs when a person affixes his property to the land of another, without an agreement permitting him to remove it. The thing so affixed belongs to the owner of the land, unless the landowner requires its removal.

§6.30. Innocent improver of land

What is the rule when an improvement may have been installed by a stranger or a trespasser? Formerly, California followed the common law rule under which things affixed to land by a stranger or trespasser, without an agreement permitting removal, belonged to the owner of the land. Under this rule, the intention of the person making the improvement did not control, and many persons, under a mistake as to the location of their property, materially improved another person's land without any recourse when the mistake was discovered. This harsh rule, however, was held inapplicable in cases when the improvements were made by a public service corporation or a public agency, or when the improvements were made by a person under a mistaken belief of ownership and the real owner, having notice of the error and the work, made no effort to prevent continuance of the work.[40]

Statutory rule. The strict rule as to ownership of things mistakenly affixed to another person's land was modified by statutory enactment. The Civil Code provides that a person who affixes improvements to the land of another, in good faith and erroneously believing, because of a mistake of law or fact, that he has a right to do so, may remove the improvement on payment of all damages proximately resulting from the affixing and removal of such improvements. Such payment is required to be made to the owner of the land and to any other person having an interest in the land who acquired such interest for value in reliance on such improvements.[41]

The Code of Civil Procedure defines a good faith improver and gives such person, when existing forms of relief are inadequate, relief for improvements made on the land of another in the mistaken belief that the improver owns the land.[42]

§6.31. Accretion and reliction

Acquisition of title by accession may also be in the form of *accretion*, which is defined as the process of gradual and imperceptible addition to land bordering on a river or stream, caused by the action of the water in washing up sand, earth, and other materials.[43] The land formed as the result of accretion is called *alluvion*. Accession also includes land that has been covered by water but that has become uncovered by the gradual recession of the water. This latter process is known as *reliction*. The added land becomes the property of the owner of the land to which it is added. The same rule applies to land fronting on the ocean.

§6.32. Accretion distinguished from avulsion

Accretion is to be distinguished from *avulsion*, which occurs when a river or stream, navigable or nonnavigable, by sudden violence carries away a part of the bank of the river or stream, and bears it to the opposite bank or to another part of the same bank. In such case, the owner of the part carried away may reclaim it within one year after the owner of the land to which it has been united takes possession thereof.

EXAMPLE
One case involved a claim of right to property along the Russian River, which had changed its course 1,500 feet easterly of its original position in 1850. It was held that the change in the course of the river was not by imperceptible degrees but rather by a sudden change resulting from the effect of flood waters, and the doctrine of avulsion rather than accretion therefore controlled.[44]

---

§6.33. Alluvion must be created by natural causes

For land to be alluvion it must be created by natural causes. It has been held that land created by an addition resulting from any cause whatsoever other than natural causes is not the property of the adjoining or upland owner.[45] In a controversy between the state or its grantees and the upland owner, artificial accretions (so-called) belong to the state or its grantees as the owner of the tidelands.

§6.34. Waterline boundary descriptions

Under the doctrine that alluvion formed by accretion to land having a waterline boundary belongs to the owner as part of his land, a conveyance of the land by a description calling for a waterline boundary will ordinarily carry title to any alluvion formed before the conveyance, unless a different intent is expressed in the grant. This conclusion results from the rule that when a waterline is the boundary of a given parcel, that line, no matter how it shifts, remains the boundary.

VI. WILLS AND SUCCESSION

§6.35. In general

When a person dies, title to his real property vests in the deceased's heirs or devisees. The law permits a person to make a will disposing of his estate to other persons on his death (that is, to make testamentary disposition). In the absence of a will, the estate passes by succession to the deceased's heirs as designated by the laws of succession in effect at the time of death.

EXAMPLE   Husband and wife (both had children by former marriages) left all their property to the other with an oral agreement that when both died, the property would be divided among all the children. Husband predeceased wife, and when wife died her will left all the property to her son. The court found that an oral contract existed and that all the property should be divided among the children.[46] This case is an example of why testators should not have oral agreements. Undoubtedly, a lot of money was spent on attorney's fees after the couple's deaths, which would have been avoided had the couple spent a nominal sum for attorney's fees and set forth their agreement in writing in their wills.

Probate proceedings are ordinarily required so that the heirs or devisees obtain marketable title to the property of the deceased.[47] The main purpose of probate proceedings is to collect the assets of the estate of the decedent, pay the debts and taxes that may be due, and determine the persons to whom the balance of the estate is to be distributed. Probate can be avoided by the use of a living trust (discussed in §6.52).

§6.36. Characteristics of a valid will

A *will* is an instrument by which a natural person disposes of his or her property, effective upon death. An essential characteristic of a will is that it operates only on the death of the maker of the will. Up to the time of death, the will is said to be ambulatory, and no rights of the maker in his property are divested by execution of the will, and no rights vest in the beneficiaries under the will until the death of the maker.

§6.37. Terminology

The maker of the will, whether a man or a woman, is called the *testator*. When a person dies leaving a will, he or she is said to die *testate*; if he or she dies without leaving a will, the person is said to die *intestate*. The personal representative of a person who dies leaving a will is the *executor*. If no will is left, the representative is called the *administrator*.

A will may be amended or changed by a *codicil*.

§6.38. Gifts by will

A *devise* is a gift of real property by will. The one who takes such property is called a *devisee*. A *bequest* is a gift of personal property by will. A *legacy* is also a gift of personal property by will, but it usually denotes a gift of money. The recipient of a gift of personal property by a will is called a *legatee*.

§6.39. Types of wills

Three types of wills have heretofore been valid in California: a witnessed will, a holographic will, and a nuncupative will.

Witnessed will. The witnessed will, sometimes designated as a formal will, is one in writing, signed at the end by the testator, and witnessed by at least two attesting witnesses, who must sign at the testator's request and in his presence and to whom the testator declares the instrument to be his will.[48] Witnessed wills are ordinarily drafted by attorneys, since extreme care is required in their preparation. They are valid only if executed according to the strict policy of the law.

Holographic will. A holographic will is one written and signed by the hand of the testator, and it need not be witnessed.[49] Its use is recommended only when the time factor or other circumstances do not permit the execution of a formal will. The principal objection to such wills is that they often fail to carry out the testator's intention and are more apt to result in litigation than a formal will. Formerly, if a holographic will was not *entirely* handwritten, dated, and signed by the testator, the testator's wishes might not be carried out, and he would be declared to have died intestate. However, a California Supreme Court case held that some typewritten or preprinted words may appear in the will even if they are intended to be part of the will, although not essential to it.[50] As a result, a holographic will does not now have to be written entirely in the testator's handwriting, provided it is signed by the testator and the material provisions are in the handwriting of the testator. If no date is on the will, it is still effective; however, another will signed and dated may make it ineffective and an expensive lawsuit could be instituted to determine which will was the most recent.[51]

Nuncupative will. A nuncupative will, sometimes designated as an oral will, was a will that requires no writing, but could be made only by persons in military service in actual contemplation, fear, or peril of death, or by persons in expectation of immediate death from an injury received the same day. Such a will could dispose of personal property only, and not exceeding $1,000 in value.[52] The provisions allowing noncupative wills were repealed effective 1983.

§6.40. Who can make a will

By statutory provision, every person of sound mind, over the age of 18, may dispose of his or her property by will.[53] The right to dispose of property by will is entirely statutory. Such right is actually a statutory privilege that may be enlarged, diminished, or abolished by the legislature, subject to rights that may have become vested before legislative changes.

Traditionally over the years, wills have been prepared by attorneys. Because of escalating attorney's fees or for other reasons, many persons failed to make wills or attempted to handle them themselves by use of holographic wills, which in many cases was an invitation to litigation. Effective January 1, 1983, the legislature, with the endorsement of the State Bar, approved the nation's first form of statutory will and a statutory will with a trust. Forms have been published and distributed by the State Bar of California. The purpose of the legislation is to make the will process simpler and less costly for consumers. It was not intended that the new forms be solely a do-it-yourself, fill-in-the-blanks process that would eliminate the need for a lawyer, but it was intended to reduce the costs of obtaining legal services. On the other hand, because a will does not avoid the expensive aspects of a probate upon death, it is essential that each person consult with an attorney concerning a living trust in addition to a will.

§6.41. Limitations on right to dispose of property by will

Several limitations have been placed on the right of disposition of property by will, including rights of pretermitted heirs (forgotten children), rights arising from a subsequent marriage, special rights of the family, restrictions on subscribing witnesses,[54] and restrictions on persons who have willfully and intentionally caused the death of the decedent or have caused such death in the perpetration of specified crimes, including arson, robbery, rape, or mayhem.[55]

§6.42. Laws of succession

When a person dies without leaving a will, his estate is distributed to his heirs at law. The provisions of the Probate Code that designate the persons to whom the court shall order distribution of the property of such decedent are known as the statutes of succession.

Heirs are relatives of the decedent, but not all relatives are heirs; their status depends on the closeness of the relationship.[56] Heirs are divided into classes starting with the immediate family (spouse and children) and extending to the most distant relatives. When there is a surviving member of one class, members of later classes of heirs do not take under the laws of succession.

When the decedent was a married person, it is necessary to determine whether the property is separate or community, as different rules are applicable.

Community property. On the death of one of the spouses, one-half of the community property belongs to the surviving spouse, and the other half is subject to testamentary disposition irrespective of the number of children.[57] If there is no will, all the community property goes to the surviving spouse.

Separate property. When there is no will, separate property passes in accordance with the following:[58]

1. One-half to surviving spouse; one-half to child if only one child

2. One-third to surviving spouse; two-thirds equally to children when more than one child

3. If no surviving spouse, equally to children (if child is deceased leaving issue, that share goes to his or her issue)

4. If no children, one-half to surviving spouse; one-half to decedent's parents

5. If no surviving spouse, parent, child, or grandchild, then to sisters or brothers; if none, then to nephews, nieces, aunts, uncles, cousins, etc. If the decedent leaves no relative entitled to take the estate under the laws of succession, then the estate escheats to the State of California.

Careful consideration should be given to the consequences if a person decides not to make a will disposing of his property. A will can effect a saving in estate and death taxes, as well as costs and attorney's fees for the guardianship of a minor.

EXAMPLES

1. If a husband dies and leaves a wife and two children, and no will, only one-third of his separate property goes to his wife, while two-thirds goes to the children. Since the surviving spouse receives all of the community property, this may be adequate or it may not!

2. As to any property going to the minor children, a guardianship will be required with annual accountings through the court, plus attorney's fees, which might have been avoided if there had been proper tax and estate planning.

---

§6.43. Tax considerations

There are a number of reasons to make a will. For instance, testator can appoint a guardian for the children if the other spouse is predeceased, with a waiver of a guardian's bond that may be more costly than to have had a will drawn. Perhaps equally important, however, are tax considerations.

Property acquired from a decedent receives a new tax basis (stepped-up or stepped-down) to reflect fair market value at the applicable valuation date.[59] This new basis applies to the surviving spouse's one-half of the community property as well as the one-half that is included in the decedent's gross estate.[60] Therefore, it may be advantageous to hold title to real property as community property rather than in joint tenancy if it is owned by husband and wife.[61]

Substantial tax savings may accrue to a husband and wife if a living trust or testamentary trust is properly drafted.[62] As with other laws, tax laws are subject to frequent legislative changes, so it is essential that one's will be reviewed periodically.

VII. TRANSFERS IN TRUST

§6.44. In general

Real property is often acquired in a trust, either a *testamentary trust*, i.e., one created by will, or an *inter vivos trust*, i.e., one created and effective during the lifetime of the trustor, commonly referred to as a living trust. In this section, we consider some of the rules applicable to the ownership and transfer of property held in a trust.

§6.45. Classification of trusts

The Civil Code formerly divided trusts into two classes: (1) *voluntary trusts*, which arise out of a personal confidence reposed in, and voluntarily accepted by, one person for the benefit of another; and (2) *involuntary trusts*, which are trusts created by operation of law. In lieu of the Civil Code provisions, the Probate Code was amended, effective in 1987, to define the word *trust* and to create a new Trust Law Division.[63]

A basic classification of trusts regards them as (1) *express trusts*, which arise as the result of an express declaration of trust or some other external expression of intent to create the trust; (2) *resulting trusts*, in which the intention to create a trust is implied by law from certain acts of the parties; and (3) *constructive trusts*, in which a trust is imposed by law, not to effectuate intention but to redress a wrong or prevent unjust enrichment.

A *trust* may be defined as a fiduciary arrangement by which an owner of property, referred to as the *settlor* or trustor, transfers title to the property, called the *corpus* of the trust, with the intention that it be held and administered by the transferee, called the *trustee*, for the benefit of another person or persons, called the *beneficiary*.

In every trust arrangement there is a division of ownership of the corpus into a legal title and into an equitable title. Legal title is held by the trustee who is also responsible for the management and control of the trust. The equitable title is held by the beneficiary who is entitled to the benefits resulting from the management and control and who has a right to enforce the trust.

§6.46. Express trusts

An express trust in land must be evidenced by a writing that indicates with reasonable certainty the intention of the trustor to create a trust, as well as the subject matter, purpose, and beneficiary of the trust. An express trust is usually created by a formal declaration of trust, or by a deed reciting that title is to be held in trust. As mentioned above, trusts may also be created by last will and testament.

Validity of trust. Of primary concern in title examination is the question of the validity of a trust affecting title to real property. In the case of testamentary trusts, the problem is only of temporary concern, since the validity of the testamentary trust will be determined by a decree of distribution in the probate proceedings; this decree, when it becomes final (beyond attack in the proceedings), is deemed to be conclusive.

Essential requirements of a valid trust. Before approving the acts of the trustee under other types of trusts, however, the title examiner needs to determine whether the trust in question is valid. In a valid express trust, it is essential that there be the following: (1) a trustee; (2) an estate conveyed to him; (3) a beneficiary; (4) a lawful purpose; and (5) a valid term. It has been held that while a court of equity will, in certain instances, make good the absence of the first requisite, if the second or third be lacking, or if the fourth or fifth is illegal, the trust itself must fail.[64] An exception is made in the case of gifts for charitable purposes. Such trusts are usually created by will, and the courts sometimes sustain the validity of such a trust even though all of the requisites of a valid private trust are lacking.

Who may act as trustee. Any person, including a corporation, having capacity to take and hold title to property may be the trustee. The settlor may be the trustee, or one of several beneficiaries may be the trustee. A sole beneficiary can be one of several trustees, but ordinarily the sole beneficiary cannot be the sole trustee, because the trust would be extinguished by merger of the legal and equitable estates.

Appointment of trustee by the court. A trust will not be allowed to fail for want of a trustee. Under the provisions of the Probate Code, when there is no appointed trustee, or when all of the trustees are deceased, renounce the trust, or are discharged, the court may appoint one or more successor trustees.[65] The court may also appoint a trustee to fill a vacancy when the trust instrument does not provide a method of appointment.[66]

Who may be the beneficiary. Anyone capable of taking an interest in property, including a minor or an incompetent person, may be a beneficiary. The trustor may be a beneficiary under any trust other than a spendthrift trust.[67]

Term of trust. A private trust must be for a lawful term. Case law has interpreted this as referring to the common law rule against perpetuities, which is concerned with remoteness of vesting and which was recently amended in California. The permitted term has been lives in being plus 21 years. Heretofore, a private trust was void in its inception if by any possibility it could endure beyond the express limitations prescribed by the state constitution and statutes. Under the Probate Code, interests that fall within the rule against perpetuities are to be liberally construed to give effect to the general intent of the creator in favor of not finding any interest void or voidable. An interest is valid if it must vest, if at all, within 90 years after creation.[68]

Trust purpose. The purpose of the trust must be legal, and it must be definite. Under the provisions of the Probate Code, a trust can be created for any purpose for which persons may lawfully contract.[69]

Trusts other than express trusts recognized. In addition to express trusts, other types are recognized in California. Two of these are resulting trusts and constructive trusts.

§6.47. Resulting trusts
A *resulting trust* arises when a transfer of property is made under circumstances that raise an inference that the transferee was not intended to have the beneficial interest in the property.

EXAMPLES   1.   When A conveys land to B in trust, but the trust is void for lack of a valid purpose or for some other reason, B will be deemed to hold the legal title under a resulting trust in favor of A or A's successors.

2. Another example is when A pays the consideration for purchase of a parcel of land and has the title taken in the name of B, without any intention that B have the beneficial interest.

§6.48. Constructive trusts

Constructive trusts are imposed by law when a person holding title is under an equitable duty to convey it to another person because his retention of title is wrongful. Fraud, mistake, undue influence, duress, and breach of a confidential relationship are wrongful acts that may raise a constructive trust.

EXAMPLE One case involved a situation in which a wife had conveyed property to her husband on his representations that on her death he would convey the property to her children by a previous marriage. The husband thereafter repudiated his agreement. The court held that a constructive trust could be enforced in favor of the children.[70]

§6.49. Powers of the trustee

When the ownership of real property is vested in a trustee, the powers of the trustee to deal with the property are of vital concern. A trustee has only such powers as are expressly given him under the terms of the trust, and such as are necessarily implied to enable him to carry out the objects and purposes of the trust.

§6.50. Acts that may be authorized

For title purposes, the terms of the trust are strictly construed. If the act to be insured is not expressly authorized, or would not be supported by implied powers, special proceedings to raise a new or additional power may be appropriate. A court of equity has power to direct or permit a trustee to deviate from the terms of the trust for the purpose of saving the estate from serious loss or destruction and carrying out the purposes of the trust.

Power of sale. With respect to the power of sale, a trustee can sell property if a power of sale is conferred in specific words, or if such sale is necessary or appropriate to enable the trustee to carry out the purposes of the trust, unless such sale is forbidden under the terms of the trust or it appears that the property was to be retained in specie in the trust. An authorization to the trustee to dispose of property, or to invest and reinvest, may confer a power of sale. Power to sell does not authorize a sale on credit as a general rule, but the taking of a purchase money encumbrance may be justified under proper circumstances.

Power to exchange property. A power of sale does not authorize an exchange of the trust property for other property, unless the trustee could properly purchase the property taken in exchange. A power to sell and dispose of property, however, may include power to exchange.

Encumbrances by trustee. Although a power to mortgage may be implied by the terms of the trust or as necessary to carry out the purposes of the trust, it is not assumed, at least for title insurance purposes, that a trustee has power to mortgage unless such power is expressly conferred by the terms of the trust. Power to mortgage or otherwise encumber, or to mortgage and hypothecate, is regarded as sufficient to give the trustee power to execute a deed of trust.

Power to lease. Power to lease is not necessarily implied from the power to sell or power to dispose of land. However, even though the trust instrument does not expressly authorize a lease, such power is sometimes regarded as implied from the purposes of the trust, or as justified by the trustee's duty to keep the land productive.

§6.51. When individual ownership is presumed

Sometimes an instrument runs in favor of a person "as trustee" without designating a trust or disclosing any beneficiaries. In such cases, there is a presumption that the title held is free from trust by virtue of the provisions of the Probate Code.[71] If an interest in real property is conveyed by an instrument in writing to a person in trust, or when such person is designated trustee or "as trustee," and no beneficiary is indicated or named in the instrument, it is presumed that such person holds the interest in his individual right and free from any trust. Such presumption is conclusive as to any undisclosed beneficiary and the original grantor or trustor and anyone claiming under them in favor of the purchaser or encumbrancer in good faith and for a valuable consideration, when the instrument is recorded in the office of the county recorder where the land is situated.

§6.52. Living and testamentary trusts

When a trust is created by will, a special jurisdiction, created and limited by statute, arises in the probate court. The Probate Code confers jurisdiction on the probate court to administer testamentary trusts. Without such a statute, jurisdiction to administer testamentary trusts would remain exclusively in the superior court sitting as a court of equity.[72]

With probate fees and expenses what they are, there is an ongoing need for people to consider the advisability of placing their assets into a living trust in order to avoid the cost of probate. As an example, if an estate totals $300,000 (this includes fair market value of the property, not the equity), the probate fees could be over $14,000 under present rules. Most of this could have gone to children or grandchildren if the assets were in a living trust. There are advantages and disadvantages, which should be reviewed with an attorney.[73]

§6.53. Transactions by a testamentary trustee

Upon distribution, title passes to the trustee, and he or she may deal with the property as authorized by the trust. If real property is being sold by the trustee, it is necessary to determine that the trustee has the power of sale. This rule also applies to other transactions the trustee may enter into, including mortgages, trust deeds, leases, exchanges, and so forth. Also, it is necessary to determine from the proceedings that the trust by its terms has not terminated. An examination of the file may disclose that the trustee is still acting of record, but this may not be relied on because of an event actually occurring that would terminate the trust on the death of the beneficiary, for instance, or on a child attaining a designated age that entitles him to the trust estate. Often, off-record proof is required to establish that the event of termination has not in fact occurred, and that the trust is still legally in effect.

§6.54. Duties of trustee

In all matters connected with the trust, the trustee is bound to act in the highest good faith toward the beneficiary, and may not obtain any advantage over the latter by the slightest misrepresentation, concealment, threat, or adverse pressure of any kind.[74] The trustee must not use or deal with the trust property for his personal profit, or for any other purpose not connected with the trust.

Prudent man rule. California has adopted a standard for investments made by fiduciaries that is commonly called the "prudent man rule." In making investments, a trustee is expected to exercise the judgment and care, under the circumstances then prevailing, that persons of prudence, discretion, and intelligence exercise in the management of their own affairs, not in regard to speculation, but in regard to the permanent disposition of their funds considering the probable income as well as the probable safety of their capital.

VIII. ESCHEAT

§6.55. In general

Title by *escheat* is the method by which title to property reverts to the state as the original owner. If a person owning property dies without leaving a will and without heirs, title to the property escheats to the State of California.[75] Formerly, under the Alien Land Law, the property acquired by an alien ineligible to citizenship also escheated to the State of California. However, this law was repealed many years ago.

§6.56. Escheats are not favored

Escheats are not favored, and unless there is an express provision therefor, the right of the state to have property escheat to it does not exist. Escheat for lack of known heirs is not automatic in California. There is a presumption that every decedent left heirs, and a proceeding is required to declare judicially the fact of escheat.[76] However, a nonresident who becomes entitled to property by succession must appear and demand possession within five years from the time of succession or his rights are barred and the property shall be escheated.[77]

IX. INVOLUNTARY ALIENATION

§6.57. In general

Transfer of title to real property normally occurs by virtue of the voluntary act of the owner, evidenced by a deed transferring his interest to another party. However, in a variety of situations an owner may be divested of his title by virtue of court proceedings, such as an action to quiet title, a foreclosure action, or an execution sale following a judgment for money. Also, a bankruptcy proceeding will cause transfer of title by operation of law. Execution sales and sales in proceedings to foreclose involuntary liens, such as federal tax liens, are considered in Chapter 11.

§6.58. Bankruptcy proceedings

A *bankruptcy proceeding* is one initiated in a United States District Court under the federal Bankruptcy Code,[78] whereby an insolvent debtor may be adjudged bankrupt by the court, which thereupon takes possession of his property, administers it in accordance with the provisions of the bankruptcy law, and distributes whatever assets there may be proportionately among the creditors in accordance with their respective rights.

Vesting of title in trustee in bankruptcy. A petition for adjudication may be filed either by the debtor or by the requisite number of creditors. The petition is referred by the court to a Bankruptcy Judge, who is authorized to make orders and decrees, subject to a right of appeal to the court. A trustee is appointed by the judge, and on his qualification, the trustee, under former law, is vested by operation of law with all of the bankrupt's property (subject to certain exemptions), as of the date of filing of the petition. Under the 1978 Bankruptcy Code, it is not entirely clear whether title to the debtor's real property vests in the debtor, the trustee (as it did under the former Bankruptcy Act), or the estate. A reasonable view is that title to the debtor's real property in proceedings under Chapters 7, 11, 12, or 13 vests in the *estate* and revests in the debtor at discharge or conclusion of the bankruptcy proceedings.

Exempt property. Title to property that is exempt by state law, such as the Homestead Law, remains in the bankrupt, awaiting the legal formality of having it appraised and set apart to him. When property is properly claimed as exempt, an order is obtained setting it apart to the bankrupt, and a certified copy recorded. Title to such property thereupon vests in the bankrupt, free from the effect of the bankruptcy proceedings.

Valid liens not affected. Outstanding valid liens on real property of the bankrupt existing before the adjudication are not disturbed by the bankruptcy proceedings, and title to the property passes to the trustee subject to such liens. The trustee, however, has the right to contest their validity by appropriate proceedings. Such contest may be made on the ground that the lien was fraudulently obtained; that it involved a preference; or that it was obtained within four months of bankruptcy and is void under the Bankruptcy Code. The lien may also be avoided on any other proper ground, such as lack of consideration.[79]

Effect on power of sale under a trust deed. When the power of sale under a trust deed is to be exercised on property passing to a trustee in bankruptcy, it is necessary that leave of the bankruptcy court be first obtained to effect a valid sale by the trustee under the trust deed.

Sale of property by trustee in bankruptcy. Subject to approval of the court, the trustee in bankruptcy may effect a sale of the bankrupt's property acquired by the trustee by virtue of the bankruptcy.

X. TITLE BY ESTOPPEL
§6.59. In general
Title to real property may pass by an equitable estoppel if justice requires that this be done. The principle of *equitable estoppel* that is sometimes applied in cases involving title to real property is this: When the true owner permits another person to appear either as the owner of the property or as having full power of disposition over it, an innocent third party who is led into dealing with the apparent owner will be protected by a court of equity against the claims of the true owner whose conduct made the fraud possible.[80]

XI. ABANDONMENT
§6.60. In general
Title by abandonment and title by forfeiture, strictly speaking, are not methods of transferring title from one person to another, but they do result in the extinguishment of a right or interest in favor of another, and are frequently encountered in title work.

§6.61. Nature of abandonment
Abandonment consists of a voluntary giving up of a thing by the owner because he no longer desires to possess it or to assert any right or dominion over it. It is the relinquishment of a right, the giving up of something to which one is entitled.

§6.62. Property subject to abandonment
As a general rule, personal property may be abandoned by the owner, but as to real property, a fee title ordinarily cannot be divested by abandonment. However, in a unique case in which a portion of a concrete foundation slid onto adjoining land as the result of an earthquake, such portion of the foundation was found to be abandoned, so that the owner of the adjoining land was justified in making use of it.[81] This principle might be of importance in hilly areas where the surface of lots tends to creep downward. As to other rights in real property, the general rule is that easements, licenses, mining claims, and other rights regarded as incorporeal hereditaments may be divested by abandonment. Thus, an ordinary lease of land for years is a chattel real, which is personal property, and as such is capable of abandonment.

In 1968 the California Supreme Court held that the exclusive and perpetual privilege of drilling for oil and gas in California is a profit à prendre, an incorporeal hereditament, and is subject to abandonment. The court pointed out that the rulings in previous cases that a fee interest in real property cannot be abandoned are explainable upon an analysis of the particular facts involved. In these cases, the court concerned itself with title to corporeal real property. In this latest case, the court decided that incorporeal interests, as distinguished from corporeal ones, may be abandoned, whatever their life, whether limited or unlimited in time, whether "fee" or for a term, and whether perpetual or restricted.[82]

§6.63. Land contract

The interest of the vendee under a land sales contract may be abandoned. As stated in one case, under the common law any title to an interest in land other than a fee simple estate may be abandoned, hence equitable rights in land may be abandoned.[83]

XII. FORFEITURE

§6.64. Nature of forfeiture

A *forfeiture* is a divestiture or loss of property without compensation in consequence of a default. A forfeiture is distinct from an abandonment in that a forfeiture arises from the operation of facts and circumstances independent of any question of intent, whereas an intention to part with ownership is a necessary element of abandonment.

§6.65. Property subject to forfeiture

Fee title may be lost by virtue of a breach of a condition in a deed, or the leasehold estate of a lessee may be lost by breach of a condition of the lease, or the interest of a contract buyer may be extinguished for breach of the conditions of the land sales contract. Although a breach of a condition on which an estate is granted gives the grantor or lessor a right to terminate or forfeit the estate, the breach of condition does not alone terminate the estate. It is necessary for the grantor or lessor or his successors to enter the estate or bring an action for recovery of possession or do some other act equivalent to entry. Forfeitures are not favored by the courts but are sometimes permitted.

QUESTIONS

Matching Terms

a. Accretion
b. Alienation
c. Alluvion
d. Devise
e. Ambulatory
f. Escheat
g. Eminent domain
h. Bankruptcy
i. Reliction
j. Dedication

1. Subject to change.
2. An example of transfer of title by operation of law.
3. Reversion of title to the state.
4. Donation of land for a public purpose.
5. Opposite of acquisition.
6. Gradual recession of water from the usual water mark.
7. Addition to property by natural causes over a prolonged period of time.
8. A gift of real property by will.
9. Power of the government to acquire property for a public purpose.
10. Soil deposited by accretion.

True/False

T F 11. Just compensation for the taking of land for a public purpose generally means market value.

T F 12. Inverse condemnation is not recognized in California.

T F 13. Accretion, reliction, and annexation are all examples of title by accession.

T F 14. Private corporations do not have the power to condemn property, even if for a public purpose.

T F 15. Only an easement can be acquired by dedication, not the fee.

T F 16. Everyone has the right to make a will.

T F 17. Escheats are favored in the law.

T F 18. An owner can use reasonable force to throw off an adverse possessor from the owner's real property.

T F 19. Dedication of property can result only from express words.

T F 20. All heirs are relatives, but not all relatives are heirs.

Multiple Choice

21. Alienation expresses a meaning most completely opposite to
    a. Acceleration.
    b. Acquisition.
    c. Amortization.
    d. Transfer.
22. Escheat is a legal term meaning
    a. Property subject to a mortgage has been released.
    b. A fraudulent act has been committed.
    c. Property has reverted to the state.
    d. An agent's license has been revoked.
23. Involuntary alienation means
    a. An estate cannot be transferred without the express consent of the owner.
    b. Aliens cannot own estates in fee simple in California.
    c. Ownership of property may be transferred by operation of law.
    d. A transfer of title cannot be effected except by deed.
24. The power of eminent domain may be exercised by
    a. Cities.
    b. Counties.
    c. The state.
    d. Any of the above.
25. Land may be acquired by the government in eminent domain proceedings for
    a. Any purpose.
    b. Public purpose.
    c. Private purpose.
    d. None of the above.
26. Examples of transfer of title by involuntary alienation include
    a. Bankruptcy.
    b. Foreclosure sale.
    c. Execution sale.
    d. Any of the above.
27. Trusts may be classified as
    a. Voluntary.
    b. Constructive.
    c. Resulting.
    d. Any of the above.
28. A valid private trust must include
    a. Lawful term.
    b. Trust estate.
    c. Beneficiary.
    d. All of the above.
29. The minimum period for obtaining title by adverse possession in California is
    a. Three years.

    b. Five years.
    c. Seven years.
    d. Ten years.
30. Possession under a claim of adverse possession must be
    a. Open and notorious.
    b. Continuous for the required time.
    c. Hostile.
    d. All of the above.
31. An execution sale is a form of
    a. Transfer by operation of law.
    b. Testamentary disposition.
    c. Voluntary alienation.
    d. Transfer by estoppel.
32. A bankruptcy proceeding is an example of
    a. Voluntary alienation.
    b. Involuntary alienation.
    c. Transfer by escheat.
    d. Transfer by devise.
33. A will is a method of disposition of property effective when
    a. Executed.
    b. The maker dies.
    c. It is amended.
    d. A decree of distribution is entered.
34. The person making a will is called the
    a. Testator.
    b. Trustee.
    c. Administrator.
    d. Executor.
35. Probate proceedings are under the jurisdiction of the
    a. U.S. District Court.
    b. Superior Court.
    c. Municipal Court.
    d. Tax Court.
36. Acquisition of property by its incorporation with other property is known as
    a. Accession.
    b. Succession.
    c. Rescission.
    d. Commingling.
37. The process of gradual and imperceptible addition to land bordering on a stream is called
    a. Avulsion.
    b. Reliction.
    c. Accretion.
    d. Alluvion.
38. A voluntary conveyance of land to a city "for park purposes" is an example of title by
    a. Dedication.
    b. Escheat.
    c. Estoppel.
    d. Eminent domain.
39. If an owner of real property dies leaving a will, but without heirs, his property

a. Escheats to the state where the property is located.
b. Escheats to the United States.
c. Vests in the devisees.
d. Escheats to the state of the owner's domicile.

40. If a person dies intestate, this indicates that he died
a. Without heirs.
b. Without leaving property.
c. Without survivors.
d. Without a will.

41. Regarding a probate sale, which one of the following statements doesn't apply?
a. It must be for the highest and best offer.
b. It must be sold for cash.
c. The sale must be approved by the court.
d. A commission to a broker may be payable.

42. Ownership under a claim of adverse possession, once established, is ordinarily evidenced by a
a. Commissioner's deed.
b. Sheriff's deed.
c. Certificate of sale.
d. Decree quieting title.

43. The sudden tearing away of land by the action of flood waters is called
a. Avulsion.
b. Alluvion.
c. Reversion.
d. Riparian.

44. Eminent domain has a meaning similar to
a. Foreclosure.
b. Escheat.
c. Condemnation.
d. Dedication.

45. In exercising the power of eminent domain, the government is subject to two limitations, i.e., the taking must be for a public use, and the owner is entitled to payment of just compensation. Which of the following would be considered in determining the amount of just compensation?
a. Value of land.
b. Value of improvements.
c. Severance damages.
d. All of the above.

46. Which of the following statements is correct?
a. Title by adverse possession cannot be acquired to public property.
b. "Tacking-on" is not permissible; claimant must have personally been in possession.
c. Payment of taxes must be made on time each year.
d. A tenant can acquire title by adverse possession as long as he pays rent.

47. For a private trust to be valid there must be a
a. Valid term.
b. Lawful purpose.

c. Trust estate.
d. All of the above.

48. A trust created by will is called a
a. Living trust.
b. Testamentary trust.
c. Resulting trust.
d. Constructive trust.

49. Property may be subject to forfeiture by breach of conditions in a
a. Deed restriction.
b. Lease.
c. Contract of sale.
d. Any of the above.

50. Which of the following interests in real property can be abandoned?
a. Incorporeal interest.
b. Vendee's interest under a land sales contract.
c. Tenant's interest under a lease.
d. Any of the above.

NOTES

1. C.C. 1000.
2. C.C. 1006.
3. C.C. 1007.
4. Sorensen v. Costa (1948) 32 C.2d 453.
5. Woodward v. Faris (1895) 109 C.12.
6. C.C.P. 760.020; C.C.1006, 2931a; Murray v. Murray (1994) 26 C.A. 4th 1062.
7. Hostility may be established when the occupancy or use occurred by mistake (Gilardi v. Hallam [1981] 30 C.3d 317); Mesnick v. Caton (1986) 183 C.A.3d 1248; *see also* Buic v. Buic (1992) 5 C.A. 4th 1600; California Maryland Funding Inc. v. Lowe (1995) 37 C.A. 4th 1798.
8. West v. Evans (1946) 29 C.2d 414; *see also* Estate of Williams (1977) 73 C.A.3d 141; Tobin v. Stevens (1988) 204 C.A.3d 945; Marriage of Keener (1994) 26 C.A. 4th 186.
9. Warden v. Bailey (1933) 133 C.A. 383; *see also* Winchell v. Lampert (1956) 146 C.A.2d 575; Gilardi v. Hallam (1981) 30 C.3d 317.
10. Carpenter v. Lewis (1897) 119 C.18.
11. Abar v. Rogers (1972) 23 C.A.3d 506.
12. C.C.P. 328, 352.
13. Foss v. Central Pacic Railroad Co. (1935) 9 C.A.2d 117.
14. Thompson v. Pacific Electric Railway Co. (1928) 203 C.578.
15. C.C.P. 1230.010, *et seq.*; San Diego County Water Authority v. Mireiter (1993) 18 C.A. 4th 1808.
16. *See* Redevelopment Agency v. First Christian Church (1983) 140 C.A.3d 690.
17. H. S. 33031, *et seq.*
18. Huntington Park Redev. Agency v. Duncan (1983) 142 C.A.3d 17.
19. Hawaii Housing Authority v. Midkiff (1984) 104 S. Ct. 2321.
20. C.C.P. 1240.110.
21. People ex rel. Dept. of Public Works v. Superior Court (1968) 68 C.2d 206.
22. C.C.P. 1240.410; City of San Diego v. Newmann (1993) 6 C. 4th 738.
23. Community Redevelopment v. Abrams (1975) 15 C.3d 813; C.C.P. 1263.510.
24. University of Southern California v. Robbins (1934) 1 C.A.2d 523.
25. C.C. 1001.

26. Lingg v. Garvotti (1955) 45 C.2d 20.
27. People v. Okan (1958) 159 C.A.2d 456.
28. Govt. C. 7260.
29. Govt. C. 7267, *et seq.*
30. Holtz v. San Francisco BART (1976) C.3d 648.
31. Southern California Edison Co. v. Bourgerie (1973) 9 C.3d 169.
32. Washington Boulevard Beach Co. v. City of Los Angeles (1940) 38 C.A.2d 135.
33. Hall v. Fairchild-Gilmore-Wilton Co. (1924) 66 C.A.615.
34. Spinks v. City of Los Angeles (1934) 220 C.366.
35. City and County of San Francisco v. Lanares (1940) 16 C.2d 441.
36. Gion v. City of Santa Cruz and Dietz v. King (1970) 2 C.3d 29; *see also* County of Los Angeles v. Berkeley (1979) 88 C.A.3d 551; City of Long Beach v. Dougherty (1977) 75 C.A.3d 952; County of Orange v. Chandler-Sherman Corp. (1976) 54 C.A.3d 571.
37. C.C. 1009.
38. B. & P. 11546.
39. Associated Home Builders v. City of Walnut Creek (1971) 4 C.3d 633.
40. Burrow v. Carley (1930) 210 C.95.
41. C.C. 1013.5.
42. C.C.P. 871.1, *et seq.*
43. C.C. 1014.
44. Butts v. Cummings (1953) 117 C.A.2d 432.
45. Carpenter v. City of Santa Monica (1944) 63 C.A.2d 772; Los Angeles Athletic Club v. City of Santa Monica (1944) 63 C.A.2d 795; State of California ex. rel. State Labor Commission v. Superior Court (1993) 21 C.A. 4th 38.
46. Halper v. Froula (1983) 148 C.A.3d 1000; Hensley v. Superior Ct. (1987) 193 C.A.3d 341; Juran v. Epstein (1994) 23 C.A. 4th 882. A third-party beneficiary may have no right to sue (Kalmanovitz v. Bitting [1996] 43 C.A. 4th 311).
47. Probate can be avoided under certain circumstances, e.g., a living trust; *see* §6.44 and Chapter 8 for more details.
48. Pro. C. 6110.
49. Pro. C. 6111.
50. Estate of Helman (1973) 33 C.A.3d 109; Estate of Rudolph (1980) 112 C.A.3d 81.
51. Pro. C. 6110, 6111.
52. This was formerly Pro. C. 54, 55, now repealed.
53. Pro. C. 6100, 6101.
54. *See*, e.g., Estate of Parsons (1980) 103 C.A.3d 384; Pro. C. 282.
55. Pro. C. 6560, 6120, 6570-6573; *see also* Estate of Ladd (1980) 91 C.A.3d 219.
56. Unadopted children are not "issue"; Estate of Davis (1980) 107 C.A.3d 93. An "equitable adoption," however, can occur. Estate of Wilson (1980) 111 C.A.3d 242; Estate of Bauer (1980) 111 C.A.3d 554. In Estate of Reedy (1993) 18 C.A. 4th 769, it was held that children of a biological daughter can be heirs of their biological grandfather, even though the biological mother can not, under Probate Code 6408.
57. Pro. C. 100, 6101.
58. Pro. C. 101, 102, 6400 *et seq.*
59. Date of death or alternative date (I.R.C. 1014).
60. I.R.C. 1014(b)(6).
61. *See* Chapter 8 for more details.
62. Discussed in sec. 6.44, *et seq.* The reader should be aware that these laws are subject to ongoing changes, particularly as to the tax aspects.
63. Pro. C. 82, 15001 *et seq.* In the creation of a voluntary trust there are many legal, title, tax, and practical considerations requiring the advice of an expert.
64. In re Walkerly (1895) 108 C. 627.
65. Pro. C. 15660.
66. Pro. C. 15660.
67. Bixby v. Hotchkis (1943) 58 C.A.2d 445.
68. Pro. C. 21205.
69. Pro. C. 15203.
70. Allen v. Meyers (1936) 5 C.2d 311; *see also* Estate of Arallo (1980) 106 C.A.3d 669.
71. Pro. C. 18103.
72. Pro. C. 17301.
73. *See* Estate of Heggstad (1993) 16 C.A. 4th 943; Estate of Wernicke (1993) 16 C.A. 4th 1069.
74. Pro. C. 16002; Estate of Pitzer (1984) 155 C.A.3d 979.
75. Pro. C. 6800.
76. Estate of Roach (1888) 76 C. 297; C.C.P. 1410, 1420.
77. Roten-Oeschger v. Flournoy (1977) 72 C.A.3d 254.
78. 11 U.S.C. 101 *et seq.*
79. 11 U.S.C. 548.
80. Davis v. Davis (1864) 26 C. 23; Butler v. Woodburn (1942) 19 C.2d 420.
81. Kafka v. Bozio (1923) 191 C. 746.
82. Gerhard v. Stephens (1968) 68 C.2d 864.
83. Carden v. Carden (1959) 167 C.A.2d 202.

7

Transfers by Deed, and the Use of Escrow

OVERVIEW

I. INTRODUCTION

§7.1. In general

The most prevalent method of transfer or conveyance of title to real property today is by deed. The word *title* has been defined as the evidence of ownership, that is, the method by which an owner's right to property is established or evidenced. It is in this sense that one speaks of "examining the title"—examining the instruments and acts of record that evidence the ownership of real property. In another sense, the word *title* denotes the result of operative facts and not the facts themselves, and in this sense *title* simply means ownership. It is the title that is transferred, which means not only the physical object but also all rights that pertain to its ownership.

The first portion of this chapter considers in detail many of the rules that are applicable to transfers of title by deed, including a discussion of acknowledgments, and transfers under a power of attorney.

The consummation of a real estate transaction is usually handled through the agency of an escrow holder, with the preparation, execution, and delivery of the deed handled through escrow. This chapter concludes with a brief consideration of the nature of escrow and the escrow procedure.

§7.2. Transfer at common law

Under the early English common law, ownership of real property was transferred by delivery of possession, called livery of seizin. This transfer was effected by a delivery of the land itself or something symbolic of the land: a twig, a stone, or a handful of dirt. Another method of transfer was by a statement, usually made before witnesses in view of the land, to the effect that possession was transferred, followed by entry by the new owner. No written instrument was required in these early transfers, hence there was no recording system. This mode of transferring land was sufficient for the needs during those times, because ownership was notorious and transfer was seldom made except in descent from father to son.

§7.3. Requirement of recording

Although recordation of a deed (and of many other types of instruments) is not a requisite of validity, recording is ordinarily done to give notice of record to third parties of rights under such instrument. To obtain the benefits of title insurance, recording is a requirement, and most deeds are in fact recorded.

Many rules are applicable to the recordation of a document; these are considered further in Chapter 11.

II. DEEDS

§7.4. In general

As mentioned above, the most familiar method of transfer is by deed. The word *transfer* is defined in the Civil Code as an act of the parties, or of the law, by which title to property is conveyed from one living person to another.[1] The term includes voluntary transfers (by act of the parties) and involuntary transfers (by act of the law). A *voluntary transfer* is the type primarily considered in a discussion of deeds, although an *involuntary transfer*, such as an execution sale or a foreclosure sale, also involves the execution of a deed.

§7.5. Definition of a deed

Briefly, a *deed* is a written instrument, executed and delivered, by which the title to real property is transferred from one person, called the *grantor*, to another person, called the *grantee*.

§7.6. Types of deeds

The two types of deeds in general use in California are the grant deed and the quitclaim deed. Warranty deeds are rarely used in California, although such deeds are permissible; they are widely used in the Eastern and Midwestern states. In *warranty deeds*, the warranties are defined in explicit terms. For instance, the grantor expressly covenants (agrees) that he has "lawful authority to sell," and that "the real estate is free from all encumbrances," and that he will "defend the title against the just and lawful claims of all persons."

Other designations are given to deeds, usually in connection with court proceedings, such as a sheriff's deed, a commissioner's deed, an executor's deed, a trustee's deed, or a tax deed. A *sheriff's deed* is one given to the purchaser at an execution sale after the time for redemption has expired. A *commissioner's deed* is one given by a court-appointed official, called a commissioner, in court proceedings to effect a sale of property, such as an action to foreclose a trust deed by judicial foreclosure in lieu of a trustee's sale. These types of deeds customarily are in the form of quitclaim deeds.

A *gift deed* involves no monetary or other consideration. Sometimes the consideration is designated as "love and affection." Actually, as between adult competent parties, a deed can be made without any consideration whatsoever. "Love and affection" might be the reason, but "consideration" in the legal sense is really unnecessary. In fact, the words *for a valuable consideration* found in most deeds is superfluous language. A gift deed can be either a grant deed or a quitclaim deed. That a deed is given without consideration may give rise to litigation. For instance, a gift deed, if made to defraud creditors or for other wrongful purposes, can be avoided by the defrauded party. Also, whether there was consideration for a deed would be important in connection with the rights of a second grantee who recorded his deed first, when the owner executed more than one deed to the same property in favor of different grantees. In connection with gift deeds another matter of concern is the fact that there may be substantial gift tax consequences for any type of gift, i.e., a transfer of title without consideration.[2]

Trust deeds are commonly used in California, but they are not primarily for the purpose of conveying a title from one person to another; they are used to create a lien on real property. A form of deed called a *reconveyance deed* may be used to convey the title from the trustee to the trustor when the debt secured by the deed has been paid.

§7.7. Form of deed

Any form of written instrument, otherwise sufficient, that contains apt words of conveyance, such as *grant, transfer,* or *convey,* is sufficient to pass title to land in California. There is no fixed and absolute form. Statutory provisions authorize the conveyance of real property by means of a simple form of deed. A form of grant deed in common use appears at Figure 7-1. This statutory form of grant deed is characterized by the word *grant* in its operative words of conveyance.

For a *quitclaim deed*, the operative words *remise, release,* and *quitclaim,* or merely *quitclaim,* are substituted for grant.

A form of quitclaim deed in common use appears at Figure 7-2. It is an individual form and shows the individual acknowledgment form.

In the sale of real property, a grant deed is ordinarily used. Although a quitclaim deed can be used to transfer a fee title, in the ordinary sales transaction the buyer would want a grant deed. Quitclaim deeds are used in a variety of situations. For example, one might be used in a transfer of title from one spouse to the other in connection with marital dissolution proceedings. A quitclaim deed can also be used to clear a cloud on the title or to relinquish any interest a person might have in a parcel of real estate. Also, a quitclaim deed is used for the purpose of relinquishing an interest less than the fee, such as an easement or a right to enforce deed restrictions. An example of a recital included in a quitclaim deed given to release an easement is:

> *This deed is given for the purpose of quitclaiming and conveying to the grantee herein, all right, title and interest of the grantor in and to all rights of way, ease-*

RECORDING REQUESTED BY

AND WHEN RECORDED MAIL THIS DEED AND, UNLESS OTHERWISE
SHOWN BELOW, MAIL TAX STATEMENT TO:

Name

Street
Address

City &
State
Zip

Title Order No. _____ Escrow No. _____

T 355 Legal (2-94)

SPACE ABOVE THIS LINE FOR RECORDER'S USE

Grant Deed

THE UNDERSIGNED GRANTOR(s) DECLARE(s)

DOCUMENTARY TRANSFER TAX IS $ _____

☐ _____ unincorporated area ☐ City of _____

Parcel No. _____

☐ computed on full value of interest or property conveyed, or

☐ computed on full value less value of liens or encumbrances remaining at time of sale, and

FOR A VALUABLE CONSIDERATION, receipt of which is hereby acknowledged,

hereby GRANT(S) to

the following described real property in the

county of   , state of California:

Dated _____

STATE OF CALIFORNIA
COUNTY OF _____ } S.S.

On _____ before me,

_____

a Notary Public in and for said County and State, personally appeared

_____

personally known to me (or proved to me on the basis of satisfactory
evidence) to be the person(s) whose name(s) is/are subscribed to the
within instrument and acknowledged to me that he/she/they executed
the same in his/her/their authorized capacity(ies), and that by his/her/their
signature(s) on the instrument the person(s), or the entity upon behalf
of which the person(s) acted, executed the instrument.

WITNESS my hand and official seal

Signature _____

(This area for official notarial seal)

Figure 7–1
Grant deed.

Name

Street
Address

City &
State
Zip

Title Order No. _____ Escrow No. _____

SPACE ABOVE THIS LINE FOR RECORDER'S USE

T 360 LEGAL (1-94)

Quitclaim Deed

THE UNDERSIGNED GRANTOR(s) DECLARE(s)
DOCUMENTARY TRANSFER TAX IS $ _____
☐ _____ unincorporated area ☐ City of _____
Parcel No. _____
☐ computed on full value of property conveyed, or
☐ computed on full value less value of liens or encumbrances remaining at time of sale, and

FOR A VALUABLE CONSIDERATION, receipt of which is hereby acknowledged,

hereby REMISE, RELEASE AND FOREVER QUITCLAIM to

the following described real property in the
county of   , state of California:

Dated _____

STATE OF CALIFORNIA
COUNTY OF _____ } S.S.
On _____ before me,
_____
a Notary Public in and for said County and State, personally appeared
_____
_____
personally known to me (or proved to me on the basis of satisfactory
evidence) to be the person(s) whose name(s) is/are subscribed to the
within instrument and acknowledged to me that he/she/they executed
the same in his/her/their authorized capacity(ies), and that by his/her/their
signature(s) on the instrument the person(s), or the entity upon behalf
of which the person(s) acted, executed the instrument.

WITNESS my hand and official seal

Signature _____

(This area for official notarial seal)

Figure 7-2
Quitclaim deed.

ments, and rights reserved in the deed from _____ to _____, recorded in Book _____, Page _____, Official Records, _____ County.

§7.8. Distinction between grant deed and quitclaim deed

There are two main distinctions between a grant deed and a quitclaim deed: (1) A grant deed contains implied covenants or warranties; and (2) the doctrine of after-acquired title applies when a grant deed is issued.

§7.9. Implied warranties in grant deeds

The Civil Code provides that from the use of the word *grant* in any conveyance by which a fee estate is passed, the following covenants and none other, on the part of the grantor and his heirs, are implied, unless restrained by express terms in the conveyance:

1. *"That previous to the time of the execution of such conveyance, the grantor has not conveyed the same estate, or any right, title or interest therein, to any person other than the grantee."*

2. *"That such estate is at the time of the execution of such conveyance free from encumbrances done, made, or suffered by the grantor, or any person claiming under him."*[3]

This simply means that the grantor warrants that he has not previously conveyed or presently encumbered the property. It is not a warranty that it is not encumbered; however, it should be pointed out that knowingly recording a false grant deed is a felony.[4]

§7.10. Doctrine of after-acquired title

A grant deed also conveys any after-acquired title of the grantor, unless a different intent is expressed.[5] A quitclaim deed, however, transfers only such interest as the grantor may have at the time the conveyance is executed.

§7.11. Requisites of a deed

The requisites of a valid deed in California are (1) a competent grantor; (2) a grantee capable of holding title; (3) a sufficient description of the property; (4) operative words of conveyance; (5) due execution by the grantor; (6) delivery; and (7) acceptance.

Nonessential matters. Generally, a consideration is not necessary to the validity of a voluntary transfer. A date is not essential, nor is an acknowledgment essential to the validity of the deed, although acknowledgment is a prerequisite to the recording of a deed. A deed need not be recorded to be valid as between the parties and as against third parties having notice of the conveyance. It is a common practice to record deeds, and recordation of a deed is essential, of course, for title insurance purposes. Since 1965 the name and address where the tax statement is to be mailed must be disclosed on the deed as a condition for recording.[6] However, failure to note any such name and address does not affect the notice otherwise imparted by recording.

§7.12. What interests may be conveyed by a deed

Generally, any interest in real property, whether present or future, vested or contingent, may be conveyed by deed.[7] However, under the provisions of the Civil Code, a mere possibility, not coupled with an interest, cannot be transferred. This exception is declaratory of the common law rule that a mere possibility of an interest, such as the expectancy of an heir apparent in the estate of a living ancestor, was not an interest capable of passing by conveyance or assignment. The rule in equity was different, though, and in California the courts have often enforced conveyance of the prospective interest of an heir against his share of the estate after it devolved on him, and have recognized other transfers of expectations or interests to be acquired in the future, provided they were fairly made and for an adequate consideration, and not contrary to public policy.

§7.13. Effect of lack of consideration

Although consideration is not essential to the validity of a deed as between the parties, lack of consideration is of material concern when rights of third persons may be adversely affected by the conveyance.[8] For instance, a conveyance by a grantor who is or will be rendered insolvent by such a conveyance is fraudulent as to creditors, without regard to the grantor's actual intent, if the conveyance is made without a fair consideration. Such a conveyance may be set aside by a creditor in an appropriate proceeding.

§7.14. When consideration is required

The general rule that consideration is not essential to the validity of a deed applies only to voluntary conveyances by private individuals. It does not apply in the case of conveyances by public officials of government-owned property, nor does it apply in the case of deeds by administrators, executors, guardians, trustees, receivers, and similar representatives, or in the case of a deed by an attorney-in-fact under a power of attorney. Also, under title company rules, a deed in lieu of foreclosure of a trust deed must be evidenced by a consideration, either the cancellation of the debt if the grantor is personally liable, or by a monetary consideration paid to the grantor if he is not personally liable for the debt. Also, a deed without sufficient consideration may be a fraud against creditors.[9]

§7.15. Date is desirable

Although a date is not essential, it is customary and desirable for a deed to recite the date of its execution. Under the provisions of the Civil Code, a deed is presumed to have been delivered at its date.[10] The date of a conveyance may be of evidentiary value in determining priority between conflicting grants, or when rights of third persons, such as creditors levying a writ of attachment or execution, are involved.

§7.16. Designation of grantor

The deed must designate a grantor, whose name must appear in the body of the deed, or the grantor must be otherwise so described as to be identified, for example, "I, the undersigned, do hereby grant to _____." A deed signed and acknowledged by persons named in the body of the deed as grantors, and by other persons as well, is not the deed of those not named as grantors. This rule has its origin in the fact that deeds in earlier periods of time were not signed but were sealed, and identification of the grantor was therefore required in the body of the deed.

§7.17. Name variance

As between the grantor and grantee, a conveyance executed by the true owner under any name may be sufficient. However, a conveyance in which the name of the grantor materially differs from the name under which the record title is held does not impart constructive notice to subsequent purchasers or encumbrancers. Accordingly, substantial identity between the name of the grantor in the deed and the record owner should be insisted on by the grantee. Identity problems often arise in connection with the use of initials or the use of abbreviations, derivations, and nicknames, and special rules apply in determining whether a name variance will affect marketability of title or prevent the recorded instrument from imparting constructive notice.

§7.18. Title taken under an assumed name

A person may assume any name when purchasing property, and if the name assumed is other than his legal name, a conveyance by him under such assumed name will pass good title. For purposes of giving good notice on the records, the conveyance must be made in the assumed name. A difficulty is sometimes encountered in connection with the statement of identity required by a title company when the person taking title under an assumed name has insufficient proof that he is in fact one and the same person.

§7.19. Change of name of owner

The phrase *who acquired title as* immediately following the name of the grantor is often noted in deeds. This expression results from the rule that when the grantor has had a change of name, both names must appear in the caption of the deed. The Civil Code provides that any person in whom the title to real property is vested, who shall afterward, from any cause, have his or her name changed, must, in any conveyance of real property so held, set forth the name in which he or she derived title to the real property.[11] Any conveyance, though recorded, that does not comply with the foregoing requirement does not impart constructive notice to subsequent purchasers and encumbrancers, although it is valid as between the parties and those having notice.

When change of name occurs. A change of name may result in various ways and is frequently encountered in title work. A person may change his name by court proceedings, or by the assumption of a new name without resort to legal proceedings, or, in the case of a woman, by marriage. A corporation may change its name by amendment of its articles of incorporation. Whether the change of name is by court proceedings or otherwise, or whether the owner is a natural person or a corporation, the requirement that reference in a conveyance be made to the name under which title was acquired is considered mandatory.

§7.20. Proceedings to establish identity

Sometimes the record title to real property is vested in a decedent under a name substantially different from the name under which probate proceedings are filed. An example is that of a married woman who acquired title in her maiden name but whose estate was administered under her married name. Under such circumstances, the title of a purchaser at a probate sale or of a distributee or the successor in interest is technically unmarketable. Unless corrective measures are undertaken in the probate proceedings, it may be necessary to obtain a decree in a civil action establishing identity under the provisions of the Code of Civil Procedure.[12]

§7.21. Designation of grantee

A deed must designate a grantee to whom the title passes. The *grantee* must be named or designated in such a way as to be determinable, and must be a person in being, either natural or artificial, capable of taking title. It has been held that a deed to a dead person is void. However, an exception to this rule is made in the case of a government patent in favor of a deceased patentee, under which title inures to his grantee, assigns, or heirs. Infants and insane or incompetent persons may be grantees.

§7.22. Certainty as to grantee

A grantee must be named or designated in such a way that the grantee can be determined with certainty. For instance, a deed to "A or B" has been held to be void for uncertainty.[13] However, under some circumstances, such a deed might be considered sufficient to convey the grantor's interest, on the theory that such designation of the grantees was ineffective to create an intended joint tenancy but nonetheless transferred the grantor's interest.

A deed to a vague group, such as the "inhabitants" of a town, is usually considered insufficient, except in the case of the dedication of an easement for a public purpose. Sometimes it is desired to have a deed made in favor of a large number of grantees without naming them, for reasons of expediency, as in the case of a quitclaim deed to all of the owners of lots in a specified tract for the purpose of relinquishing a general easement where time does not permit a search of the records to learn the identity of all of the owners. Such a quitclaim deed usually designates the grantees as "the record owners of all lots of Tract in severalty and upon the same tenure as their respective interests appear of record." The designation of the grantees in this manner is sufficient, since a means of identifying them is given, that is, by an examination of the records.

§7.23. Minors and incompetent persons as grantees

As stated previously, minors and incompetent persons may acquire title to real property, and ownership by such persons is not uncommon. Guardianship proceedings are not essential for the purpose of acquiring title, but are necessary for the purpose of conveying, encumbering, leasing, or otherwise dealing with the ward's property. Where guardianship proceedings are in effect, a transfer should not be made to the guardian, but should be made to the minor or to the incompetent person, with the status disclosed, as follows: "to Jane Doe, an incompetent person," or "to Jane Doe, a minor."

Minors. Minors are all persons under 18 years of age. As a general rule, deeds by minors are regarded as void.[14]

§7.24. Deeds to heirs

A deed that purports to convey a present interest to the "heirs" of a living person is technically void for uncertainty, since living persons do not have heirs. However, such a deed might be sustained on proof that the grantor intended to convey title to the children of the person named. A deed to the "heirs of John Doe, deceased" is sufficient, since the persons who are to take title can be determined with certainty by the Probate Court in appropriate proceedings.

§7.25. Deeds to organizations

Generally, a grantee, if not a natural person, must be a legal entity capable of holding title, such as a corporation or a partnership, or must be otherwise authorized to acquire and transfer property. Generally, since 1970, any form of association can acquire title and convey in the name of the association if the association does in fact exist. However, in the case of a joint venture, it is not considered capable of acquiring or conveying title in the joint venture name. Ownership of title is with the joint venturers, who should be named. If joint venturers are married, proof that a married joint venturer's interest in the joint venture is separate property must be given to a title insurer. Otherwise, the spouse of the joint venturer must join in any conveyance of the property.

§7.26. Sufficient description essential

A deed must contain a description sufficient to identify the land conveyed. The description is considered adequate if a competent surveyor can take the deed and locate the land on the ground from the description contained therein. The subject of descriptions is considered in detail in Chapter 13.

§7.27. Execution of a deed

A deed must be *executed* (signed) by the grantor, or by his attorney-in-fact acting pursuant to written authorization. Usually a grantor writes his name in ink in longhand. However, signatures in pencil or typed or by hand printing have been held to be sufficient, although such methods are not recommended. Signatures by mark are valid. Also, the grantor's name may be written for him by another person at the grantor's request and in his presence. The grantor may also adopt and ratify a signature made by another person without previous authority.

§7.28. Signature by mark

The Civil Code provides that a signature includes a mark, when the person cannot write, if the name is written near the mark by a person who writes his own name as witness, with two witnesses necessary to have the document acknowledged.[15] Physical weakness that prevents a person from writing his name, or inability to write legibly, is sufficient reason for execution by mark. An instrument executed by mark need not affirmatively state that one of the witnesses wrote the person's name; it is sufficient if it can be established that such is the fact. However, it is the usual practice to include such a statement.

Procedure for executing deed by mark. Execution of a deed by mark is done in the following manner: The grantor makes his mark before two witnesses, one of whom writes the grantor's name near the mark. The witnesses then sign as such, and the grantor acknowledges execution. The standard form for such execution is as follows:

John Doe, being unable to write, made his mark in my presence, and I signed his name at his request and in his presence.

John X Doe

Additional Witness:

Persons who may witness signature by mark. If one spouse signs by mark, the other spouse may act as a witness, but it is preferable to have a disinterested party as a witness. The notary who takes the acknowledgment may be the additional witness. The acknowledgment is by the grantor, not the witness. This is distinguishable from a case in which a witness form of acknowledgment is used. (This form is discussed later in this chapter.)

§7.29. Signature in foreign language

Persons who cannot write their names in English may either sign by mark or sign in a foreign language. If the signature is in a foreign language it should be witnessed, and the witness should sign a statement as follows: "Witness to the signature of A. B., whose name is written in Chinese."

§7.30. Delivery of a deed

A deed is not an effective transfer of real property until it has been delivered. *Delivery* is the act, however evidenced, by which the deed takes effect and passes title. Delivery is not merely a transfer of the physical possession of the deed, such as the act of handing the deed to the grantee. Whether there has been a delivery is a question of intention. The grantor must intend that title pass before there is a legal delivery. Anything that clearly manifests the intention of the grantor that his deed shall presently become operative and effectual, that he divests control over it, and that the grantee has become the owner, constitutes sufficient delivery.

Presumptions as to delivery. Certain presumptions apply in California that are of evidentiary value in determining whether there has been a delivery, but these presumptions are rebuttable, that is, they are not conclusive:

1.   If a deed is found in the possession of the grantee, there is a presumption of delivery.

2.   Finding the deed in the possession of the grantor raises a presumption of nondelivery.

3.   Recordation of a deed raises a presumption of delivery, unless the deed is not recorded until after the death of the grantor.

Evidence of delivery. The best evidence of delivery is the act of handing the deed to the grantee, but manual delivery is not essential. Even though the deed is not handed to the grantee, it is deemed to be constructively delivered to him when, by agreement of the parties, it is understood to be delivered and the grantee is entitled to immediate delivery, or when it is delivered by the grantor to a third party for the benefit of the grantee, and the latter's assent is shown or may be presumed.

EXAMPLE   The grantor executed a deed in favor of the grantee with intent to pass title, but retained possession of the deed for safekeeping. Delivery was held to be sufficient under these facts.[16]

Manual delivery. Manual delivery does not in and of itself prove legal delivery.

EXAMPLE   When A hands a deed to B with the request not to record the deed until A's death, and with the understanding that it is to be returned to A if B dies first, A and B both believing that a deed is not effective until recorded, there is no delivery; however, when A hands a deed to B with the intent to pass title, but with an oral request not to record the deed until after A's death, valid delivery has occurred.

Manual delivery not always legal delivery. Another case relating to manual delivery involved a husband who, under pressure from his wife to execute a deed, signed and handed a deed to his wife, saying: "I will sign the deed, but it won't benefit you any, for it is not acknowledged." The husband's belief that the deed would be of no effect unless acknowledged, although erroneous, evidenced his lack of intention to pass title, and it was held that valid delivery had not occurred.[17] It is quite easy, however, to see the evidentiary problems in a case such as this in that the husband's testimony that there was no intent may not be believed. Thus, another reason to contact a real estate attorney before the problem arises.

Time of delivery. To be effective, a deed must be delivered to the grantee during the grantor's lifetime. A deed cannot be used to take the place of a will.

EXAMPLES
1. One case involved a situation in which husband and wife each signed a deed in favor of the other, and placed the two deeds in a safe deposit box with the understanding that on the death of one, the survivor would record the deed in his or her favor and destroy the other deed. It was held that the survivor could not take title, since there was no effective delivery during the grantor's lifetime.[18]
2. Another case held that the inclusion of a deed in a trunk to which both the grantor and grantee had access was not a valid delivery.[19]

Delivery into escrow—when title passes. As will be seen later in this chapter, escrows are customarily used in the closing of a real estate transaction, with a deed in completed form deposited in escrow some time prior to closing. When all of the conditions of escrow have been satisfied within the time frame required, title passes to the grantee, even though there has been no physical delivery of the deed to him. This is true even if the grantor has died, provided the following has occurred:

1. Escrow instructions have been signed.
2. The grantor has signed and acknowledged the deed.
3. The conditions of escrow have been met.

Conditional delivery. A deed cannot be effectively delivered to a grantee conditionally. If a grantor makes a deed, intending to divest himself of the title, and delivers it to the grantee on an oral condition that the grantee perform some act, such as the payment of money, the grantee will take title absolutely.[20] However, oral conditions on delivery should be carefully considered as bearing on lack of intent to deliver, or on possible fraud that may result in an action to avoid the deed. A deed may be handed to a third party for delivery to the grantee on performance of some act or the occurrence of some event. The usual escrow arrangement is an example of delivery to a third party on condition.

Effect of redelivery. When a deed has been delivered with intent to pass title, a subsequent redelivery of the deed to the grantor, or the destruction or cancellation of the deed, does not operate in itself to retransfer the title to the grantor.[21]

§7.31. Conditions in deeds (restraints on alienation)

Conditions affecting use or transfer are sometimes imposed in deeds. These conditions will be deemed void if they violate the Civil Code, which provides that "conditions restraining alienation, when repugnant to the interest created, are void."[22] This section invalidates any restraint, however short, if it is repugnant to the grant. A conveyance of the fee with the condition that the grantee cannot sell or dispose of the property to specified persons, or for a specified period of time, is regarded as an unlawful restraint, void in its inception. In such a case, the grant is valid, but the condition is void and of no effect.

§7.32. Acceptance of the deed

Ordinarily, a deed cannot be given effect unless there is an acceptance by the grantee. In some cases, acceptance is presumed, as in the case of a beneficial conveyance to a person incapable of consenting—a deed to an infant or an incompetent person, for instance. Acceptance may be presumed when a beneficial conveyance is irrevocably delivered to a custodian for delivery to the grantee on the grantor's death, even though the grantee has no knowledge of the deed until after the death of the grantor.

However, this doctrine will not be applied when intervening rights of third parties are involved.

What constitutes acceptance. Acceptance of a deed may be shown by acts, words, or conduct of the grantee indicating an intention to accept, such as the retention of the deed, execution of an encumbrance on the property, recordation of the deed, or other acts of ownership.

Acceptance by government agency. Deeds or grants conveying real property or any interest therein to a California political corporation or government agency, for public purposes, are not entitled to be recorded unless the consent of the grantee is evidenced therein by a resolution or certificate of acceptance.[23] This rule doesn't apply, however, in the case of a deed to the United States of America or an agency thereof.

§7.33. Effect of lack of acceptance

As a general rule, there must be acceptance during the grantor's lifetime.

EXAMPLE
In one case, A and B were joint tenants, and A executed a deed of his interest to his grandson, to be delivered by A's son to the grantee on the death of A, the grandson having no knowledge of the deed until delivered to him after A's death. It was held that the deed was not effective because there was no acceptance by the grantee during the grantor's lifetime, and title therefore vested in B as surviving joint tenant.[24] This case has been strongly criticized.[25]

§7.34. Documentary transfer tax

After the repeal of the federal law requiring internal revenue stamps, California enacted a law that provided for a documentary stamp tax on conveyances at the rate of $.55 for each $500 consideration or fractional part thereof. Later, the California law was amended to eliminate the need for stamps, with payment of the tax to be made at the time of recording. Presently, the law requires that every document subject to tax that is submitted for recordation must show on its face the amount of tax due and the incorporated or unincorporated location of the real property described in the document, provided that, if requested, the amount of tax due may be shown on a separate paper instead of on the document itself.

§7.35. Recitals in deeds
It is not uncommon for deeds to specify with particularity the matters subject to which the grantee is to take, such as easements, covenants, conditions and restrictions, taxes, and assessments. Also, various special recitals may be incorporated in a deed to explain its purpose, or the interest of the parties and their intent, or to incorporate therein portions of other documents of record.

§7.36. Exceptions and reservations
Exceptions and reservations are also not uncommon in deeds. Technically, an *exception* withdraws a part of the thing described as granted (for example, A grants to B lot 1 of tract X, except the south half thereof), whereas a *reservation* creates some right or privilege for the benefit of the grantor in the land described that did not exist independently before the grant (for example, A grants Blackacre, reserving an easement over the west 20 feet thereof). However, today the terms are used interchangeably in conveyancing.

Reservations or exceptions in favor of a third party. For a considerable period of time in California, the rule was followed that reservations or exceptions in a deed in favor of a stranger were invalid. In a 1972 case, the California Supreme Court rejected this rule. Pointing out that the rule in question was based on feudal considerations and that it could operate to frustrate the grantor's intent and produce an inequitable result, the court declared that the common law rule was no longer the law in this state. The court further reasoned that balancing of equities and policy considerations might warrant application of the old common law rule to presently existing deeds in some cases, but that in the case before it, the balance fell in favor of giving effect to the grantor's intent.[26]

§7.37. Status of the parties
Although showing the status of the grantor or grantee in a deed is not essential to its validity, it is desirable and it is usually done. The status of the parties to a conveyance is given to indicate marriage, age, competency to deal with the property, or relation with others. When the parties are acting in a fiduciary capacity, status should always be shown, thus: (1) "as executor"; (2) "as administrator"; (3) "as trustee"; and so on.

§7.38. Conveyance in favor of decedent's estate
When it is necessary to prepare instruments to vest real or personal property in a decedent's estate subject to administration, the following designations are used: (1) for real property, the deed is in favor of "the heirs or devisees of John Doe, deceased, subject to administration of his estate"; (2) for personal property, such as a note secured by a trust deed, the transfer is made "to A, as executor of the will of John Doe, deceased, subject to administration of his estate," or "to A, as administrator of the estate of John Doe, deceased, subject to administration of his estate." A deed should not be made in favor of "the estate of" a deceased person, because an estate is not an entity capable of holding title. However, such a deed might be given effect, depending on the circumstances.

§7.39. Tenancy of title
The tenancy of title of the grantee or grantees should also be set forth in the deed, although failure to disclose the tenancy will not invalidate the deed. Tenancy of

title refers to the manner of holding title. It is shown immediately after the status of the grantee, and is designated in the following manner: (1) "as his (or her) separate property"; (2) "as joint tenants"; (3) "as community property"; or (4) "as tenants in common"; and so on. In the case of a tenancy in common, the fractional interest of each tenant is ordinarily shown.

§7.40. Effect of apparent invalidity

As noted above, conveyances are considered void if deficient in certain respects. Even though the defects appear on the face of the instrument, this does not mean that the instrument can be disregarded in title work. As a general rule of title practice, all instruments of record are reflected in title reports and policies unless they have been judicially construed to be invalid in proceedings binding on all the parties. An instrument apparently void on its face may be given some effect by the courts on the basis of intention of the parties, or on equitable principles. A deed executed by an attorney-in-fact in his name instead of in the name of his principal is said to be void, but such a deed has been sustained in equity as an agreement to convey by the principal.[27] Under other circumstances, a party may be estopped to assert the invalidity of a deed.

§7.41. Void deeds

The following deeds have been held to be void and pass no title even in favor of innocent purchasers: (1) a forged deed; (2) a deed from a person whose incapacity has been judicially determined; (3) a deed from a person entirely without understanding; (4) a deed from a minor; (5) a deed executed in blank, when the grantee's name is inserted without the grantor's authorization or consent; (6) a deed materially altered in escrow without the knowledge or consent of the grantor; and (7) an undelivered deed, such as a deed stolen from the grantor or a deed delivered by an escrow holder in violation of the grantor's instructions. A deed to a fictitious person is also void. However, as we learned earlier, a deed to an actual person by a name that he has assumed for the purpose of taking title is valid. A distinction is thus made between a fictitious person and a fictitious name. Another type of void deed is one purely testamentary in character, that is, a deed not intended by the grantor to become operative until after his death.

§7.42. Voidable deeds

The following types of deeds are not considered to be void, but are voidable, and pass title subject to being set aside in appropriate proceedings: (1) a deed procured through fraud, mistake, undue influence, duress, or menace; and (2) a deed by a person of unsound mind whose incapacity has not been judicially determined. As a general rule, a bona fide purchaser for value from the grantee in the voidable deed obtains title good as against the original grantor.

III. ACKNOWLEDGMENTS

§7.43. In general

Before a deed (or most other instruments) can be recorded, its execution must be acknowledged by the person executing it, or proved by a subscribing witness or by proof of the handwriting,[28] and the acknowledgment or proof certified as provided by law.[29] An *acknowledgment* is a formal declaration, made before an officer designated by statute, by the person who has executed an instrument, that he did in fact execute the instrument. Proof of an acknowledgment is evidenced by a certificate made by the officer before whom the acknowledgment is made. There are many rules that must be complied with that are intended to assure that the document is in fact genuine. This is particularly important for a title insurer, since the insurance does cover the genuineness of the documents in the chain of title.

Purpose of an acknowledgment. The main purposes of an acknowledgment are to entitle the instrument to be recorded and thus impart constructive notice of its contents, and to obviate proof of execution of the instrument if it is to be offered in evidence in judicial proceedings.

Who may acknowledge. Under recording laws, the phrase "person executing the instrument" means the person whose property rights are transferred, encumbered, or otherwise affected, such as the grantor in a deed, the vendor in a contract of sale, or the lessor in a lease. When two or more persons execute an instrument by which property rights are affected, such instrument is entitled to be recorded if acknowledged by any one of such persons.

Persons authorized to take acknowledgments. The Civil Code designates the persons who are authorized to take acknowledgments, classifying them as to acknowledgments taken within the State of California, outside the state but within the United States, outside the United States, and by officers of the United States Armed Services.[30] Most acknowledgments are taken before a notary public, who must affix the seal to the certificate of acknowledgment.

§7.44. Notaries public

Notary public seals. Notaries public in California are required to have a seal on which must appear the name of the notary, the words "Notary Public," the State Seal, the date on which the notary's commission expires, and the county in which the notary has his principal place of business. If the notary transfers his principal place of business to a different county than that shown on the seal, he must have the seal altered to indicate the change. Notaries may use a rubber-stamp seal. All notaries who are appointed or reappointed must use a seal that legibly reproduces under photographic methods the required elements of a notarial seal.

Statewide jurisdiction of notaries. Notaries public in California have statewide jurisdiction.[31]

Appointment of notaries. The California Secretary of State is authorized to appoint and commission notaries public in such numbers as are deemed necessary for the public convenience. The term of office is four years. A notary must file a bond in the amount of $10,000 and take, subscribe, and file his oath of office in the office of the county clerk of the county within which the notary's principal place of business is maintained. He must also pass a written and proctored examination; and first-time applicants must be fingerprinted.

§7.45. Records

The notary must keep a sequential journal containing specified information, including (1) date, time, and type of each official act; (2) character of instrument acknowledged; (3) signature of each person whose signature is being acknowledged; (4) nature of information used to verify the identity of the signator; and (5) fee charged, if any. When requested, and upon payment of $.30 per page, a notary must provide any person with a certified copy of any page from the journal.[32] In California, in the transfer of a deed, the grantor's fingerprint is also taken.

§7.46. Certificate of acknowledgment

Form of certificate of acknowledgment. For several years the Civil Code prescribed various forms of the certificate of acknowledgment for use by individuals, corporations, partnerships, attorneys-in-fact, and so on. In 1990 the legislature amended the law to establish one form for general use for the acknowledgement of an instrument taken within this state, with the capacity of the person signing the document indicated at the signature point. Figure 7-3 is the form now used.[33]

```
┌─────────────────────────────────────────────────────────────┐
│                                                               │
│   STATE OF CALIFORNIA                                    ⎱     │
│   COUNTY OF _____    ⎰ S.S.│
│                                                               │
│   On _____ before me,│
│                                                               │
│   _____ │
│   a Notary Public in and for said County and State, personally appeared│
│                                                               │
│   _____ │
│                                                               │
│   _____ │
│   personally known to me (or proved to me on the basis of satisfactory│
│   evidence) to be the person(s) whose name(s) is/are subscribed to the within│
│   instrument and acknowledged to me that he/she/they executed the same in│
│   his/her/their authorized capacity(ies), and that by his/her/their signature(s) on│
│   the instrument the person(s), or the entity upon behalf of which the│
│   person(s) acted, executed the instrument.                   │
│                                                               │
│   WITNESS my hand and official seal                           │
│                                                               │
│   Signature _____ │
│                                                               │
└─────────────────────────────────────────────────────────────┘
```

Figure 7–3
Certificate of Acknowledgment.

Acknowledgments taken outside the state. Any certificate of acknowledgement taken in another place is sufficient in this state if it is taken in accordance with the laws of the place where the acknowledgement is made.[34] In such cases, there should be attached a certificate of the clerk of the court of record of the county or district where the acknowledgment is taken to the effect that the officer taking it was authorized by law to do so, and that the officer's signature is true and genuine. The certificate of the clerk is known as a Certificate of Authenticity and Conformity.

Acknowledgment taken outside the United States. A certificate of acknowledgment taken outside the United States by a foreign notary public must be authenticated by a United States resident consular officer or a judge of a foreign court of record. However, as to countries that have adapted the Hague Convention, in lieu of authentication by a consular officer, an executed certificate, called an "Apostille," may be used.

Invalid acknowledgments.

1.   Acknowledgments taken by a party in interest are invalid.

2.   An acknowledgment taken by a party directly interested, such as the grantee in the deed or the mortgagee in a mortgage, is void.

3.   When a corporation executes an instrument, an employee or officer of the corporation may take the acknowledgment if he is not personally interested and if he does not execute the instrument as an officer of the corporation.

4.   As a general rule, a husband or wife should not take the other's acknowledgment of a deed or other instrument.

Effect of lack of acknowledgment. Failure to acknowledge an instrument does not necessarily prevent its recordation or admissibility in evidence. The Civil Code specifies several alternative methods of proving the execution of instruments, each of which has the same effect as acknowledgment unless acknowledgment is an essential requirement to the validity of an instrument, such as a Declaration of Homestead. Proof of the execution of an instrument, including a deed, may be made either (1) by a subscribing witness, that is, a witness whose name is subscribed to an instrument as a witness and who states under oath the facts of execution and identity;[35] (2) by proof of handwriting, that is, proof by a person who is well acquainted with the grantor's signature when the grantor and the subscribing witness, if any, are nonresident, or are dead, or cannot be located;[36] or (3) by court decree, that is, any person interested under an instrument may bring an action in court to have it proved.

Curative acts. If defects occur in the certificate of acknowledgment, they are deemed to be cured after one year from date of recordation. The Civil Code provides that all instruments impart constructive notice after one year from the time they have been recorded, notwithstanding any defect or omission in the certificate or the absence of such certificate.[37] This is known as a Curative Act, and although it does not cure the absence of acknowledgment of an instrument whose validity depends on acknowledgment, it apparently will cure any defect in the form of the certificate of acknowledgment when the instrument has been acknowledged before a proper officer.

§7.47. Responsibility of person taking acknowledgment

The person taking an acknowledgment assumes considerable responsibility for his act. He must know, or have satisfactory proof on the oath or affirmation of a credible witness known to him, that the person making the acknowledgment is in fact the individual who is described and who executed the instrument. Both the notary public and the surety on his bond are liable for the notary's misconduct or his negligence, as where the notary acknowledges the signature on a forged instrument. In two cases decided in 1970, the liability of notaries who acknowledged signatures on a forged deed was reaffirmed.

EXAMPLES
1. In the first of these two cases, the notary relied solely on an introduction by his law associate for identification of the parties signing the deed. The court held that this was not enough, stating that personal knowledge is not acquired merely through the introduction of another person. The court quoted from an earlier Supreme Court case as follows:

    > *It is not enough that the person be introduced to the notary by a responsible person. If that were enough there would be no purpose in requiring the oath, for such person could always furnish the introduction. This point has been often decided, although sufficiently obvious from the statute. To take an acknowledgment upon such introduction without the oath is negligence sufficient to render the notary liable in case the certificate turns out to be untrue.*[38]

2. In another case, a notary was held liable to a purchaser of accounts receivable for negligently acknowledging a forged signature on a guaranty agreement.[39]

IV. TRANSFERS BY ATTORNEYS-IN-FACT

§7.48. In general

An attorney-in-fact may be vested with certain powers of an owner, including authority to sell and convey real property, and conveyances by an attorney-in-fact are not uncommon. A *power of attorney* is defined as an instrument in writing whereby one person, designated as the principal, authorizes another person, designated as the attorney-in-fact, to act for him as his agent. The powers granted are determined by the express terms of the instrument itself; they are not implied, except as may be necessary to carry out the powers expressly granted.

Formerly, a power of attorney ended if the principal became mentally incapacitated. California has adopted the Uniform Durable Power of Attorney Act,[40] which provides for a *durable power of attorney*. Such a power isn't affected by the principal's subsequent incapacity. Also, a so-called springing power of attorney can now be used which doesn't take effect until the principal is no longer able to handle his own affairs.

§7.49. Special or general powers

The power of attorney may be *special*, limiting the agent to a particular or specific act, such as a power of attorney to convey a particular parcel of real property; or the power may be *general*, authorizing the agent to transact all business on behalf of the principal. Under the provisions of a general power of attorney, the agent may transfer and convey any property of the principal, subject to limitations otherwise applying, such as a homestead.

§7.50. Limitations of general words

General words in a power of attorney are limited and controlled by particular terms. Thus, when the authority to perform specific acts is given, and general words are also employed, the latter are limited to the particular acts authorized.

§7.51. Who may act under a power of attorney

As a general rule, any person who is competent to contract may execute or act under a power of attorney. However, a person who has interests adverse to those of the principal cannot act as an agent when the principal is without knowledge of such adverse interests.

§7.52. Recordation of power of attorney

For the purpose of dealing with real property, the power of attorney must be acknowledged and recorded. When a power of attorney is once recorded, a certified copy may be recorded in other counties with the same effect as if the original were recorded.

§7.53. Execution of instruments

When a deed or other instrument is executed by an attorney-in-fact pursuant to a power of attorney, the attorney-in-fact must sign the name of his principal, followed by his own name as attorney-in-fact.[41] The principal's name alone should appear in the body of the deed, and the deed then should be executed as follows: "A. B. by C. D., his attorney-in-fact." A signature in the following manner is not sufficient: "C. D., attorney-in-fact for A. B."

§7.54. Restrictions on authority

There are several restrictions on the authority of an attorney-in-fact. An attorney-in-fact is prohibited from (1) making a gift deed, or making a deed, mortgage, or release without a valuable consideration; (2) conveying or mortgaging property on which a declaration of homestead has been filed; (3) dealing with the principal's property for his own benefit; (4) deeding the principal's property to himself; (5) releasing a mortgage made by himself to the principal; (6) mortgaging the principal's property to himself; or (7) delegating his authority, unless properly authorized.

§7.55. Termination of power of attorney

A power of attorney may be terminated by an express revocation by the principal. The instrument of revocation must be recorded in the same office as the power of attorney. A power of attorney is also terminated by the death of the principal or, unless it is a durable power, by the incapacity of the principal to contract.[42] However, under the provisions of the Civil Code, the authority of an attorney-in-fact is not terminated as to any person entering into any bona fide transaction without actual knowledge of the death or incapacity of the principal.[43]

V. ESCROWS

§7.56. In general

In California, escrows have become an almost indispensable mechanism, not only in the consummation of real estate sales and exchanges and loan transactions, but also in a variety of other transactions covering the sale or encumbrance of personal property, sales or pledging of securities, sales of assets of a business (bulk sales), sales of promissory notes secured by trust deeds, transfers of liquor licenses, and many other types of transactions.

The most common use and purpose of escrow is to enable the buyer and seller to deal with each other without risk, because all responsibility for handling funds and documents is placed in the hands of the escrow holder. In a relatively simple transaction, the mechanics are these: The purchaser delivers to the escrow holder the funds required and agreed on by the parties for the purchase of a certain described piece of property. The purchaser's instructions, briefly, authorize the escrow holder to deliver to the seller the stated sum of money when the escrow holder can obtain from the seller, in the case of a sale, a deed, and can have issued or can procure a policy of title insurance vesting the title to the property in the name of the purchaser, the title to be subject only to the matters set forth in the escrow instructions. Concurrently, the seller deposits the deed and other documents with the escrow holder, authorizing their delivery when the purchaser has deposited the agreed-on purchase price. The escrow officer is the agent for both parties and is responsible for the interests of each.

§7.57. Definition of escrow

Escrow is generally defined as a deed, bond, or other type of written obligation, delivered to a third person, to be delivered by him or her to the grantee only on the performance or fulfillment of some conditions. The deposit of the escrow places it beyond the control of the grantor, but no title passes until the fulfillment of the condition.

The common law concept of escrow required a deed alone, and a contract was not essential. In California and many other jurisdictions, there must be a valid contract between the parties in addition to an instrument of conveyance.

§7.58. Code definition

The common law definition of escrow has been codified in California in the Civil Code, which provides: "A grant may be deposited by the grantor with a third person, to be delivered on performance of a condition, and, on delivery by the depositary, it will take effect. While in the possession of the third person, and subject to condition, it is called an escrow."[44] It has been held that the word *grant* as used in the code definition is not confined to deeds, but includes other instruments as well.[45]

§7.59. Scope of escrow

In California, escrow has developed into an expedient instrumentality in all real property transactions, sales or otherwise. It is an effective means of providing (1) a custodian who holds the funds and documents and makes concurrent delivery thereof at the exact moment when all of the terms and conditions of the transactions have been performed; (2) a clearinghouse for the payment of all demands; (3) an agency that provides the clerical details in making prorations and adjustments for settlement of accounts between the parties; and (4) a method that can be used and often is used to achieve a binding contract between the parties during the period of abeyance.

§7.60. Escrow as "stakeholder"

The word *stakeholder* is sometimes used to designate the escrow holder. The escrow holder is considered as the agent of the respective parties until such time as the escrow is closed, and then becomes a trustee for the money and documents until they are distributed in accordance with the escrow instructions.

§7.61. Requisites of a valid escrow holder

For an instrument to operate as an escrow holder, there must be a valid and enforceable contract between the parties. A contract sufficient to support an escrow holder must comply with the requirements of any valid contract, namely, competent parties, a valid consideration, a proper subject matter, and mutual assent as to the terms and conditions of the contract. It must be in writing when required under the Statute of Frauds, a rule that applies in all cases involving the sale of land. The contract may be evidenced by the purchase contract itself or by the escrow instructions prepared by the escrow holder pursuant to the direction of the parties, or by both.[46]

Additional requirements. The escrow agreement must also comply with the following requirements: (1) the escrow agreement must contain a condition; (2) the deed deposited in escrow must be a sufficient and valid deed; and (3) the escrow holder must be a stranger (neutral party) to the transaction.

§7.62. Agency status of escrow holder

The status of the escrow holder is that of an agent or trustee for both parties at the inception of the escrow and until the conditions have been performed. For example, if a deed is deposited in escrow, under a valid escrow contract for delivery to the grantee on payment by him or her of a specified sum of money, and the grantee deposits the funds in escrow for payment to the grantor in exchange for the deed when a policy of title insurance can be issued showing title as called for in the agreement, the escrow holder, as to the deed and money, is an agent or trustee for both parties. However, when the conditions of the escrow agreement have been performed, the nature of the dual agency changes to an agency not for both, but for each of the parties respecting those things placed in escrow to which each is entitled. In other words, the escrow holder becomes the agent or trustee for the seller as to the money, and the agent or trustee of the buyer as to the deed.[47]

§7.63. Nature of agency

Although an escrow holder is an agent for the parties to a transaction, it is generally considered to be a limited agency rather than a general agency. Since an escrow holder is an agent, it might seem to follow under the general rules of agency that it would be his duty to communicate to his principals any knowledge that he has or acquires concerning the subject matter of the escrow, and that any such knowledge would be imputed to each of the parties to the escrow agreement; however, it has been recognized in many cases that a general agency is not created, and that the agency is a limited agency only, under which the obligations of the escrow holder to each party in the escrow agreement are limited to those set forth in the instructions.[48]

EXAMPLE In one case, it was held that an escrow holder in an escrow for the sale of land was under no duty to disclose to the buyer that his seller was purchasing the land from the record owner in the same escrow arrangement and reselling it to the buyer at a profit, when the buyer's escrow instructions did not include any demand for such information.[49] However, later cases might support a contrary view.[50]

The doctrine of a limited agency appears to be the rational view of an escrow holder's status, but it is nonetheless generally concluded that an escrow holder, regardless of the absence of legal liability, should decline to handle an escrow agreement involving a secret profit by a person, such as the broker, standing in a fiduciary relationship to a principal to the escrow arrangement.

§7.64. Regulation of escrow agents

Since 1947, escrow agencies have been regulated by state law. An *escrow agent* is defined in the code as "any person engaged in the business of receiving escrows for deposit or delivery for compensation."[51] The provisions of the escrow law are reasonably related to the purpose of protecting the public from unfair, fraudulent, and incompetent service in the handling of escrows.[52]

The regulations originally provided that any person engaging in the business of an escrow agent must be licensed as such by the Commissioner of Corporations. Since 1953, individuals cannot be licensed as escrow holders; the license must be held by a corporation duly organized for the purpose of conducting an escrow business. The regulations do not apply, however, to banks, trust companies, building and loan associations, savings and loan associations, insurance companies, title companies, attorneys-at-law not actively engaged in conducting an escrow agency, brokers or others subject to the jurisdiction of the Real Estate Commissioner while performing acts in the course of or incidental to their real estate business, or to any transaction wherein a joint control agent disburses funds in payment for labor, materials, and other items of expense incurred in the construction of improvements on real property.

§7.65. Deposit and disbursement of funds

Escrow regulations as prescribed in the code require that all escrow funds must be deposited in a bank or a savings and loan association and kept separate, distinct, and apart from funds belonging to the escrow agent, and such funds when deposited are to be designated "trust funds," "escrow accounts," or some other appropriate name showing that the funds are not the funds of the escrow agent. Escrow funds are not subject to execution or attachment on any claim against the escrow agent individually. All officers and employees of an escrow agent having access to funds and having certain other responsibilities must be covered by a fidelity bond in such amount and form as the Corporation Commissioner shall prescribe.

As to release of escrow funds between buyer and seller, the Code was added in 1990 that allows damages of not less than $100 nor more than $1,000 that is not held to resolve a good faith dispute, if demand is made and the funds are not returned within 30 days.[53]

Regarding disbursements in escrow, the Insurance Code was amended in 1990,[54] to state that title insurance companies, controlled escrow companies, or underwritten companies may not disburse funds from an escrow account other than as specified.

Different escrow disbursement standards are provided for funds deposited by

1. Cash
2. Checks
3. Drafts
4. Electronic payments

Cashier's checks, certified checks, and teller's checks may be disbursed on the business day following the day of deposit because California law permits funds deposited by instruments accorded next day availability under Regulation CC (adopted by the Federal Reserve Board of Governors) to be disbursed in accordance with Regulation CC. Regulation CC permits next-day availability.

Drafts are treated differently from other kinds of deposits. Until the proceeds of the draft have become available for withdrawal from the financial institution to which the draft has been submitted for collection, disbursement may not be made. "Available for withdrawal" means the time when the draft has been submitted for collection and payment received.

Some other kinds of deposits are not accorded next-day availability under Regulation CC and hence under California law as well. For example, personal checks—whether written by individuals or firms—may not be disbursed until the day on which the funds must be made available to depositors under Regulation CC.

Regulation CC's temporary and permanent availability schedules change periodically. The schedules should be examined for applicable hold periods, which vary according to the location of the drawee bank.

The Insurance Code allows an exemption from disbursement standards. It permits disbursement on the business day following the business day of deposit *if* the depository financial institution informs the title company, for example, in writing, that final settlement has been had on the deposited item.

Recordation of documents prior to the time that funds are available for disbursement is not prohibited as long as all parties to the transaction give their prior written consent.

§7.66. Real estate brokers

The exemption permitting real estate brokers to handle escrows has been interpreted to mean that they may not hold escrows except in connection with some transaction wherein they are acting as a real estate broker, and that they may not hold escrows for compensation in connection with transactions by other brokers.[55] Also, a real estate licensee who acts as an escrow holder under this exemption provision of the escrow law must maintain all escrow funds in a trust account, subject to inspection by the Real Estate Commissioner, and must keep proper records.

§7.67. Escrow instructions

Escrow instructions are usually prepared on the escrow holder's printed form. Although an escrow holder cannot advise the parties as to their legal rights and obligations, he can and should ask such questions as are appropriate and essential to learn their intention concerning the terms and conditions of the sale, as a basis for drafting the escrow instructions.

When escrow instructions of buyer and seller are materially different, the instructions are not a contract between them. Their rights against each other depend upon their mutual agreement.[56] Further, if money is deposited in escrow with buyer's instructions and the conditions of the instructions are not complied with, the buyer retains ownership of the money.

§7.68. Procedural steps

Following the signing of the escrow instructions by both parties, the procedural steps that culminate in closing the escrow may be briefly described as follows:

1. A search of title is ordered and a preliminary report of title thereafter forwarded to the escrow office by the title company.

2. A Beneficiary's Statement is requested from the beneficiary under a trust deed shown on the title report. This is a statement of the unpaid balance and condition of the indebtedness.

3. Matters disclosed by the preliminary report of title that are not approved by the escrow instructions are reported to the seller for clearance, or to the buyer for approval.

4. When all documents and funds are in the hands of the escrow officer and the escrow is in a condition to close, the necessary adjustments and prorations

between the parties are made on a settlement sheet, and the instruments are forwarded to the title company with recording instructions.

5. The search of title is "run to date" as of the close of business of the escrow completion date. If no change of title is found, the deed is recorded the next morning, usually at 8 A.M., that is, at the moment the county recorder's office is open for business in many counties. If the documents are filed in the county recorder's office at that precise time, it is possible to issue a title policy and disburse funds in escrow with assurance that there are no intervening matters.

6. Immediately after the filing of the documents in the recorder's office, the escrow holder disburses the funds to the parties entitled thereto, causes any fire insurance policies to be transferred or amended, and presents a closing statement to the parties. The title policy is issued within a reasonable time thereafter.

§7.69. Duties and responsibilities of escrow holder

The duties and responsibilities of an escrow holder are many and varied. A fundamental rule is that the escrow holder may not deliver funds or documents unless there has been full compliance with the conditions of the escrow agreement. It is the duty of the escrow holder to see that funds or documents remain in its possession until the expiration of the time fixed by the instructions for performance. After the time limit has expired, the escrow holder does not have the authority to permit one of the parties to perform unless the escrow instructions contain appropriate extension provisions.

An escrow agent is liable to a principal for damages in the event of a failure to perform as directed or for negligence.

EXAMPLES
1. In one case, the escrow agent was held liable for failure to record a request for notice of default under a trust deed.[57]

2. In another case, the escrow agent was held liable for failure to deposit the vendee's check for collection or to advise the vendor that it was holding the undeposited check.[58]

Under the provisions of the Civil Code, escrow agents cannot pay anyone for referring to or soliciting business for them. Further, no commission can be paid by an escrow agent to a real estate broker prior to close of escrow.[59] Unwritten escrow instructions are binding on the escrow agent under principles of contract and agency law, and an escrow agent may be liable for failure to follow those instructions.[60]

Some escrow companies add a statement similar to the following to their escrow instructions to be sure the parties are aware of what they are signing and that legal assistance is usually necessary:

> *It is fully understood by the parties to this escrow agreement that the execution of instructions in this escrow and any related document may, and likely will, create or change existing legal rights or obligations relative to various matters, including, but not limited to, property taxes, interest deductions, rights under existing encumbrances, and/or homeowner's statutes. Therefore, each party hereto represents to escrow agent that they have either sought or waived the advice of competent counsel regarding any of the foregoing matters, it being fully understood that escrow/title company, as escrow agent, serves merely as an escrow agent and cannot give legal or financial advice to any party hereto.*

Further, the law now requires in an escrow agreement for the purchase or simultaneous exchange of real property, when a title policy will be issued to the buyer, that a notice be given in a separate document to the buyer advising that a new title policy should be obtained to insure the buyer's interest in the property.[61]

§7.70. Confidential nature of escrow

Escrow instructions are confidential. It is a primary rule that information concerning the existence or terms of an escrow agreement should not be given to persons who are not parties to the escrow. Each of the principals to an escrow has the right to see the instructions of the other party, which, when matched against his, constitute the escrow contract. This does not mean, however, that everyone in escrow has the right to see all the instructions of every other person. When the escrow additionally covers a resale by the original purchaser to a third party, the original seller is not entitled to see the instructions with respect to the resale, assuming, of course, that the original instructions do not expressly demand such information. When the escrow involves a resale, a responsible escrow holder will decline to act if it is apparent that the resale involves a breach of fiduciary relationship. This problem sometimes arises, for instance, when a broker has procured a "dummy" as purchaser and is making a secret profit on the resale.

§7.71. Title and possession during escrow

When a deed is placed in escrow for delivery to the grantee on payment of the purchase price, it has been stated that "the grantee does not acquire any title to the land" before the performance of the conditions.[62] However, if the escrow is supported by a valid contract of sale, whether created by the escrow instructions or by a separate instrument, a more accurate statement is that the grantor holds the legal title, and the grantee has the equitable title conditioned on performance of the contract.[63] As to possession of the property, this right remains in the grantor, unless the grantee is given possession by the terms of the contract. Unless the agreement provides otherwise, risk of loss is on the person who has the right of possession.

§7.72. Termite reports

Termite reports, technically designated as "Structural Pest Control Reports," can cause as much difficulty as anything else in escrow. They may be called many different names by the parties in escrow, such as termite clearance or termite statements. Actually, a termite clearance as such is not possible, since termite companies do not purport to furnish a clearance. It was their necessary practice to use qualifying words in their reports, such as *visible* or *accessible* areas; however, it is now required that the certification state either that (1) there is no infestation; (2) there is infestation, but all recommendations to remove infestation have been completed; or (3) there is infestation but all recommendations have not been completed. An acceptable way for the escrow holder to cover the matter, when the parties themselves have raised the question of termites, is to prepare instructions providing that a termite report be furnished at the expense of either the buyer or the seller, and that it is to be approved by the purchaser before close of escrow. Or a provision may be inserted that escrow is not to be closed until the buyer has been satisfied as to the question of termites and has so notified the escrow agent in writing.

Legislation regarding termite reports. Any person has a right on payment of the required fee to obtain from the Structural Pest Control Board a certified copy of all inspection reports and completion notices filed with the board by any pest control operator during the preceding two years.[64]

The real estate broker has the responsibility for delivering the report to the buyer, must make a record of the delivery, and must keep the record for a period of three years.[65] Also, a real estate licensee must disclose any knowledge he has regarding infestation or damage by wood destroying organisms.[66]

Liability of seller and termite company for negligence. In one case, the buyer purchased a house, and the termite report reflected that there were no infestations or indications of termites, dry rot, or fungus. In fact, there was a considerable amount of termite damage and dry rot, and the house was condemned. The court found both the seller and the termite company liable for the termite company's negligence. Even though there was no direct contract between the buyer and the termite company, the company did have a duty to properly inspect the property.[67]

Provision for termite statement. A suggested provision for inclusion in escrow instructions is the following:

> *The seller is to furnish a statement by a licensed Pest Control Operator, certifying the premises at [address of property] to be free from visible evidence of infestation by termites, dry rot, and fungi.*

Instructions for payment of corrective work. When the termite statement shows corrective work to be necessary, it is not safe for the escrow holder to assume that payment of the cost will automatically be borne by the seller. Specific instructions covering this obligation must be obtained.

EXAMPLE In one instance a purchaser called for a termite report subject to his approval. The report thereafter received by the escrow agent stated that several hundred dollars' worth of work should be done before the issuance of a clearance. The purchaser approved the report, with a proviso that the escrow agent hold the amount of money set forth in the report to do the necessary work. Several days after escrow closed, the seller demanded the money held in escrow for his account, contending that he authorized the holding of funds but never authorized payment of the termite bill. The escrow holder was obligated to return the funds to the seller, and paid the bill itself.

A distinction is made between corrective work and preventive work. Ordinarily, the seller becomes obligated for the cost of corrective work only.

§7.73. Performance of conditions

When an instrument is deposited in escrow for delivery on compliance with agreed conditions, the escrow holder is not authorized to make delivery, and the instrument cannot become operative until the conditions have been fully performed. Strict compliance with all the terms and conditions of the escrow is ordinarily essential. Performance must be made within the time limited by the terms of the agreement, unless a waiver is obtained.

§7.74. When title passes

When the conditions of an escrow agreement have been performed, a question may arise as to the time when title is deemed to have passed to the purchaser. It has been broadly stated that an instrument in the form of a deed deposited in escrow becomes effective to pass title as soon as the conditions of escrow are so far performed that the grantee is entitled to possession of the deed, although it is not then actually delivered to him.[68] However, this broad statement is subject to qualification, inasmuch as the moment at which the conditions of escrow are performed and the title passes is determined in a given case by the provisions of the particular escrow instructions, which vary according to the diverse forms in use by escrow holders.

§7.75. Doctrine of relation back

The doctrine of relation back is sometimes applied when an escrow has in fact closed in accordance with the conditions. Under this doctrine, to avoid hardship or to effectuate the intention of the parties, the delivery of the instrument to the grantee on performance of the conditions, that is, the second delivery of the deed, is considered to operate retroactively and to pass title by relation back to the date the instrument was delivered to the escrow holder, that is, the first delivery.[69] The doctrine of relation back has been applied to protect a purchaser in an escrow contract against an intervening grantee who took a conveyance from the grantor with knowledge of the pending escrow. In other cases, the doctrine has afforded protection to the buyer when an abstract of judgment was recorded against the grantor before close of escrow, but not until after escrow was in fact ready to close.

§7.76. Cancellation of escrow

An escrow agreement may be canceled voluntarily by the consent of all the parties. Ordinarily, the only parties necessary to the cancellation are the principals. Occasionally, however, third parties may have acquired rights that must be considered. If the seller has assigned in escrow all or a portion of the purchase price, as evidenced by an order to the escrow holder to pay the proceeds or a portion thereof to the third party on close of escrow, an escrow holder will usually require that the assignee consent to the cancellation. If the assignment or order to pay is contingent on the closing of escrow, the consent of the assignee to the cancellation of the escrow is not essential. Also, simply because escrow is canceled, such an act does not cancel the purchase contract.

EXAMPLES
1. S agreed to sell a home to B. During escrow a dispute arose and B filed suit for specific performance. Later, B and S agreed to, and did, cancel escrow. B continued to pursue his action for specific performance. The court held that canceling escrow was not intended as a rescission of the purchase contract or as an abandonment of B's suit for specific performance. If the parties wished to cancel the contract, they should have agreed in writing to cancel the escrow instructions as well as the purchase contract.[70]

2. If a broker, who also handles the escrow, cancels the escrow without the seller's permission, the broker is subject to discipline by the DRE, and his license may be suspended.[71]

§7.77. Payment of broker's commission

When the escrow instructions constitute an enforceable contract of sale and provide for payment of a commission to a real estate broker for the seller on "close of escrow," it has been held that the broker is entitled to recover the commission from his principal if the escrow is voluntarily canceled by the parties, but the broker cannot recover a commission if the escrow fails through no fault of the seller.[72]

§7.78. Change in instructions after escrow closes

Escrow officers must be careful to follow the exact terms of the escrow instructions.

EXAMPLE
In an action by seller to recover funds paid by the escrow agent to a real estate broker on the grounds that the agent had failed to comply with the escrow instructions, the trial court ruled in favor of the escrow agent. Four hours after close of escrow, seller sent the escrow agent new escrow instructions directing the agent to pay the broker a lesser amount. The escrow agent ignored the new instructions and paid the broker the full amount. On appeal, the court held that when an escrow agent agrees with a party to the escrow and with his creditor to pay the creditor from the proceeds of sale, the agent is required to disburse those funds to the creditor even though the party attempts to cancel the agent's authority. Once escrow closes, a party cannot unilaterally amend the instructions.[73]

On the other hand, until escrow is notified of an assignment to the broker of a commission out of the proceeds of the sale, an escrow agent is required to follow the instructions of its principals, both before and after close of escrow.[74]

QUESTIONS

Matching Terms

a. Quitclaim deed
b. Consideration
c. Acknowledgment
d. Notary public
e. Grant deed
f. Stockholder
g. Minor
f. Warranty
i. Power of attorney
j. Exception

1. Contains implied warranties and conveys after acquired title.
2. Anyone under 18 years of age.
3. Some part of a thing granted which is excluded and remains in the grantor.
4. Escrow agent.
5. An assurance or guarantee that certain defects do not exist in a title to property.
6. Written authorization to an agent to act on behalf of a principal.
7. Person authorized to take acknowledgments.
8. Declaration by a party executing an instrument that it is his act and deed.
9. Deed used to eliminate a cloud on title.
10. Anything of value.

True/False

T F   **11.** All deeds must be supported by consideration to be valid.

T F   **12.** Any person 18 years of age and over is qualified to execute a quitclaim deed.

T F   **13.** A deed may be valid even though not recorded.

T F   **14.** A sufficient description is essential to the validity of any deed.

T F   **15.** Any person may engage in the business of handling escrows in California.

T F   **16.** Escrow files are confidential and are not open for public inspection.

T F   **17.** A requisite of a valid deed is operative words of a conveyance.

T F   **18.** In some cases, acceptance of a deed will be presumed.

T F   **19.** As a general rule, any person who is competent to contract may execute or act under a power of attorney.

T F   **20.** There is no distinction between a fictitious name and a fictitious person.

Multiple Choice

21. Real property ownership may be transferred voluntarily by
   a. A quitclaim deed.
   b. A bill of sale.
   c. An assignment.
   d. Any of the above.

22. Which of the following is essential to any deed?
   a. Date.
   b. Consideration.
   c. Acknowledgment.
   d. Description.

23. A deed that conveys whatever present right, title, or interest the grantor has is a
   a. Warranty deed.
   b. Quitclaim deed.
   c. Trust deed.
   d. Grant deed.

24. A bona fide purchaser of real property is one who buys the property
   a. In good faith.
   b. For a fair value.
   c. Without notice of adverse claims.
   d. All of the above.

25. A deed
   a. Must contain words of a conveyance.
   b. Must be signed by a legally competent grantee.
   c. Both a and b are necessary.
   d. Neither a nor b is necessary.

26. That part of a thing granted which is excluded from a conveyance and remains in the grantor is called
   a. A reliction.
   b. An exception.
   c. Habendum.
   d. Riparian.

27. A deed to a person under an assumed or fictitious name is
   a. Void.
   b. Voidable.
   c. Permissible.
   d. Prohibited.

28. The requirements for taking an acknowledgment to a deed include the following:
   a. Grantor must personally appear before the notary.
   b. Grantor must be known to the notary for a minimum time of one year.
   c. Grantor must be vouched for by two acquaintances.
   d. All of the above.

29. If a notary neglects to comply with the requirements for taking an acknowledgment, he is
   a. Protected by his notary bond.
   b. Liable for damages, but not in excess of his bond.
   c. Not liable if he relied on the introduction by a mutual friend.
   d. Liable to the persons injured thereby for all damages sustained.

30. The instrument under which one person may convey title as agent for the owner of property is called
    a. Warranty deed.
    b. Power of attorney.
    c. Novation.
    d. Subordination.
31. The person who conveys title by deed is called the
    a. Testator.
    b. Grantor.
    c. Lessor.
    d. Grantee.
32. A forged deed is an example of a deed that is
    a. Void.
    b. Voidable.
    c. Authentic.
    d. Valid.
33. A conveyance to a minor
    a. May be taken in the name of the minor.
    b. Must be taken in the name of the guardian.
    c. Must be taken in the name of the parents.
    d. Is invalid.
34. A deed is not entitled to be recorded unless it is
    a. Witnessed.
    b. Acknowledged or proved.
    c. Supported by consideration.
    d. Verified by a notary.
35. The authority of an attorney-in-fact under an ordinary power of attorney is terminated by
    a. The death of the principal.
    b. The mental incapacity of the principal.
    c. An express revocation by the principal.
    d. Any of the above.
36. A deed and a land sales contract are similar in the requirement of
    a. Consideration.
    b. Description.
    c. Competent parties.
    d. Verification.
37. Escrow holders must be
    a. Impartial.
    b. Partial.
    c. Able to act without regard to instructions.
    d. One of the principals.
38. An escrow holder is ordinarily responsible for
    a. Ordering title report.
    b. Prorating taxes.
    c. Obtaining beneficiary statement.
    d. Any of the above.
39. If a dispute arises in a sales escrow, the escrow holder should
    a. Favor the buyer.
    b. Favor the seller.
    c. Favor the broker.
    d. Remain neutral.

40. When a deed is delivered into escrow
    a. Title immediately passes to the buyer.
    b. Title remains with the seller until all conditions have been performed.
    c. It must be recorded the same day.
    d. The buyer must immediately deposit the balance of the purchase price.
41. Payment of a broker's commission to an unlicensed person through escrow is
    a. Contrary to law.
    b. Permissible if seller approves.
    c. Permissible if in compliance with buyer's instructions.
    d. Permissible if authorized in writing.
42. If you are the escrow holder in a sales transaction, you should
    a. Advise buyer how to take title.
    b. Prepare subordination agreement if complicated.
    c. Record all documents as soon as received.
    d. None of the above.
43. If nothing is said about a termite report in the escrow instructions, the escrow holder should
    a. Explain its importance to the buyer.
    b. Order a copy of the last report from the Structural Pest Control Board.
    c. Tell the seller he may be guilty of fraud.
    d. Not get involved on his own.
44. Duties of an escrow holder include
    a. Skill.
    b. Care.
    c. Diligence.
    d. All of the above.
45. The word *diligence* has a meaning similar to
    a. Dilatory.
    b. Perseverance.
    c. Procrastination.
    d. Discrimination.
46. An escrow holder is under a duty to
    a. Exercise care in the preparation of documents.
    b. Maintain the confidential nature of the escrow arrangement.
    c. Exercise ordinary skill.
    d. All of the above.
47. Escrow instructions are
    a. Confidential.
    b. Open to public inspection.
    c. A matter of public record.
    d. Open for inspection by third-party claimants.
48. Adjustments or prorations in escrow may relate to
    a. Taxes.
    b. Interest.
    c. Fire insurance premiums.
    d. Any of the above.

49. Unless otherwise agreed, the primary responsibility for choosing the escrow holder is that of

   a. Buyer.

   b. Seller.

   c. Both a and b.

   d. Broker.

50. Escrow instructions for the sale of a residence and any amendments thereto

   a. Must be in writing to be enforceable.

   b. Can be modified by either party orally.

   c. Are subject to modification by the broker.

   d. None of the above.

NOTES

1. C.C. 1039.
2. I.R.C. 2515, *et al.*
3. C.C. 1113.
4. Pen. C. 115; Gemers v. Justice Court (1980) 106 C.A.3d 678.
5. C.C.1106; Schwenn v. Kaye (1984) 155 C.A.3d 949.
6. Govt. C. 27321.5.
7. C.C. 1045.
8. C.C. 1040; Odone v. Marzocchi (1949) 34 C.2d 431.
9. Kirkland v. Risso (1979) 98 C.A.3d 971.
10. C.C. 1055.
11. C.C. 1096.
12. C.C.P. 770.010 *et seq.*
13. Schade v. Stewart (1928) 205 C. 658.
14. The exception to this rule is the "Emancipated Minor" (C.C. 63).
15. C.C. 14.
16. Goodman v. Goodman (1913) 212 C. 730.
17. Kimbro v. Kimbro (1926) 199 C. 344.
18. Miller v. Brode (1921) 186 C. 409.
19. Johns v. Scobie (1939) 12 C.2d 618.
20. C.C. 1056.
21. C.C. 1058; Chaffe v. Sorensen (1951) 107 C.A.2d 284.
22. C.C. 711.
23. Govt. C. 27281.
24. Green v. Skinner (1921) 185 C. 435.
25. *See* 3 Witkin, Summary of California Law, 8th ed., p. 1885.
26. Willard v. First Church of Christ Scientist (1972) 7 C.3d 473.
27. Salmon v. Hoffman (1852) 2 C. 138.
28. C.C. 1198, 1199.
29. Govt. C. 27287.
30. C.C. 1180, *et seq. See also* Govt. C. 8203.1.
31. C.C. 1180.
32. Govt. C. 8206.
33. C.C. 1189.
34. C.C. 1189.
35. C.C. 1195, *et seq.*
36. C.C. 1195, 1198, *et seq.*
37. C.C. 1207.
38. Transamerica Title Insurance Co. v. Green (1970) 11 C.A.3d 693; McDonald v. Plumb (1970) 12 C.A.3d 374.
39. Iselin-Jefferson Financial Co. v. U.C.B. (1976) 16 C.3d 886. Other cases include: Bernd v. Eu (1979) 100 C.A.3d 511, involved a notary who was disciplined and her commission suspended, who was an escrow officer and who acknowledged the personal appearance of a man who had not appeared before her. *See also* Butterfield v. N. W. National Insurance Co. (1980) 100 C.A.3d 974 re statute of limitations against a notary on his bond. *See also* Govt. C. 8224, 8225 and Chapman v. Hicks (1919) 41 C.A. 158, 164 re a person acting

as an agent has no direct financial or beneficial interest in the transaction and thus is not precluded from taking the acknowledgment of the parties having such direct interest; Garton v. T. I. & T. Co. (1980) 106 C.A.3d 365, 376, *et seq.* re false taking of acknowledgment and liability and, therefore, liability of title abstractor.

40. Prob. Code 4000, *et seq.*; Drake v. Superior Court (1994) 21 C.A. 4th 1826.
41. C.C. 1095.
42. Prob. Code 4127, 4152, 4155. And *see* new Uniform Durable Power of Attorney Act, C.C. 2400-2407.
43. Prob. Code 4152(b).
44. C.C. 1057.
45. Rockefeller v. Smith (1930) 104 C.A. 544.
46. Escrow instructions can constitute a sufficient memorandum. Signed escrow instructions subscribed by the party to be charged and directed by him to the escrow agent have, when sufficient in content, been held to satisfy the statute of frauds. Beazell v. Schroder (1963) 59 C.2d 577, 580; Wilson v. Bidwell (1948) 88 C.A.2d 832. Escrow instructions do not supplant the actual agreement of sale, but instead surmount the barriers of the Statute of Frauds by constituting a written memorandum of that basic issue. Leiter v. Eltinge (1966) 246 C.A.2d 306, 314; Wolfe v. Price (1966) 244 C.A.2d 165.
47. Todd v. Vestermark (1956) 145 C.A.2d 374; Andover Land Co. v. Hoffman (1966) 264 C.A.2d 87.
48. Lee v. Title Insurance & Trust Co. (1968) 264 C.A.2d 160.
49. Blackburn v. McCoy (1934) 1 C.A.2d 648.
50. *See* Moe v. Transamerica Title Co. (1971) 21 C.A.3d 289; Akin v. Business Title Corp. (1968) 264 C.A.2d 153. The particular factual situation can be determinative rather than the application of a general rule.
51. Fin. C. 17000-17614.
52. Escrow Inst. of Calif. v. Pierno (1972) 24 C.A.3d 361, 363.
53. C.C. 1057.3.
54. Ins. C. 12413.1.
55. Escrow Owners Assoc. Inc. v. Taft Allen, Inc. (1967) 252 C.A.2d 506; Fin. C. 17006.
56. Vineland Homes, Inc. v. Bairch (1956) 138 C.A.2d 747; *see also* Angus v. London (1949) 92 C.A.2d 282.
57. Howe v. City Title Insurance Co. (1969) 255 C.A.2d 85. Escrow agent is also liable for its own fraud (Romo v. Steward Title of California [1995] 35 C.A. 4th 1609.
58. Wade v. Lake County Title Co. (1970) 6 C.A.3d 824; *see also* Gordon v. D & G Escrow Corp. (1975) 48 C.A.3d 616.
59. C.C. 1057.5. *See* Fin. C. 17420.
60. Zang v. Northwestern Title Co. (1982) 135 C.A.3d 159.
61. C.C. 1057.6.
62. Los Angeles City High School District v. Quinn (1925) 195 C. 377.
63. Estate of Erskine (1948) 84 C.A.2d 323.
64. B. & P. 8614. After four months, all subsequent inspections must be original and not reinspections (B. & P. 8516).
65. Comm. Regs. 2905; C.C. 1099, 2985.
66. Comm. Regs. 2903.
67. Hardy v. Carmichael (1962) 207 C.A.2d 218; *see also* Wice v. Schilling (1954) 124 C.A.2d 335.
68. Hagge v. Drew (1945) 27 C.2d 368.
69. Miller & Lux, Inc. v. Sparkman (1932) 128 C. 449.
70. Cohen v. Shearer (1980) 108 C.A.3d 939; C.C. 1057.3.
71. Mullen v. DRE (1988) 204 C.A.3d 245.
72. Wilson v. Security First National Bank (1948) 84 C.A.2d 427.
73. *See* Ogdahl v. Title Insurance & Trust Co. (1977) 72 C.A.3d Supp. 41, 44.
74. Contemporary Investments Inc. v. Safeco Title Insurance Co. (1983) 145 C.A.3d 999, 1005.

8

Ownership Forms and Implications

I. INTRODUCTION

§8.1. In general

In this chapter we consider not only various forms of real property ownership that may be used in the acquisition of a residence, but also ownership by entities for commercial or business purposes, and multiple ownership encountered in housing developments.

§8.2. Tax problems

How a person holds title to property can have drastic tax consequences.

EXAMPLE If a husband and wife hold property as joint tenants (real, personal, insurance, etc.) with an equity of $1,000,000 (rather than as community property, with an A–B living trust or will),[1] the total additional estate tax cost on their deaths is approximately $153,000, all of which could have gone to the couple's heirs! Therefore adequate estate planning (which includes how to hold title) not only should be considered—it is essential.

This presumes that title was held in a true joint tenancy, one of the common law estates. In Rev. Ruling 87-98 it was held that if property held in a common law estate is community property under state law, it is community property for purposes of relevant sections of the Internal Revenue Code, regardless of the form in which title was taken. In that case husband and wife purchased property as joint tenants and thereafter executed joint wills in which they declared the property to be a community asset.

Buyers and sellers (and licensees) seldom consider what their children (or other heirs) will lose as a result of their lack of knowledge. Unfortunately, this is often the result of an "advisor" improperly giving advice as to how to hold property without having the necessary information to do so. For example, what are *all* the assets in the potential estate of husband and wife, both community property and separate property, and property held in another fashion such as in a partnership or corporation? What complicates the situation is that a buyer or seller is often reluctant to disclose this information to a real estate licensee. Further, a given licensee will sometimes improperly give advice (or "hint" at it), at least as far as married couples are concerned,[2] and inform them that they should hold title to their real estate as joint tenants.

The reader will be given a better understanding of the various ways of holding title in this chapter. The chapter is by no means a treatise on the subject, for only the surface is touched upon. It is mandatory that the person consult a competent attorney or C.P.A., and be leery of many so-called tax advisors in determining how title should be held. Because of the potential damage to the buyer or seller, the licensee should have a good grasp of this topic in order to be aware of the potential damage if suit is brought for giving the wrong advice. The tax consequences should be borne in mind while reading this chapter and weighing one form of ownership with another.

§8.3. Sole owners and co-owners

Real property may be owned by a sole owner, or it may be owned jointly by two or more persons. A person who is the *sole owner* of a parcel of real property is said to be the owner thereof in *severalty*. When there is more than one owner, their ownership (referred to generally as co-ownership) may be in one of many ways.

§8.4. Types of joint ownership

Under the provisions of the Civil Code,[3] four types of joint ownership are recognized in California: joint tenancy, tenancy in common, tenancy in partnership, and community property. Each type of co-ownership has distinct characteristics, and a knowledge of the legal effects of the different forms of ownership is essential for anyone acquiring real property in California, particularly in case of acquisition of title by husband and wife.

§8.5. Ownership by married persons

Basically, a married person can own real property in California in two ways—either as separate property or as community property. *Separate property*, generally speaking, is property acquired before marriage, and property acquired after marriage by gift. *Community property* is defined in a negative way, as property that is not separate property.

Separate property may be owned either in severalty or in co-ownership. Co-ownership may be as tenants in common or in joint tenancy. The main difference between these latter two forms of co-ownership relates to the effect of ownership upon death.

§8.6. Change in ownership

Largely because of Proposition 13, a change in ownership from one person to another, one entity to another, *can* cause an increase in property taxes to the new owner. This area, too, must be explored before any change occurs to see if it will be financially advisable.[4] (See § 12.72 for further details.)

II. JOINT TENANCY OWNERSHIP

§8.7. In general

Joint tenancy is regarded as a single estate held by two or more persons jointly, such joint tenants holding as though they collectively constituted but one person, a fictitious unity. The main characteristic of a joint tenancy is the right of survivorship. When a joint tenant dies, his or her interest in the land is terminated and the estate continues in the survivor or survivors. When there is but one survivor, the estate becomes an estate in severalty, and on the death of this last survivor, title vests in his or her heirs or devisees.

§8.8. Statutory definition

A joint tenancy estate is defined as

> ... one owned by two or more persons in equal shares, by a title created by a single will or transfer, when expressly declared in the will or transfer to be a joint tenancy, or by transfer from a sole owner to himself and others, or from tenants in common or joint tenants to themselves or some of them, or to themselves or any of them and others, or from a husband and wife, when holding title as community property or otherwise to themselves or to themselves and others or to one of them and to another or others, when expressly declared in the transfer to be a joint tenancy, or when granted or devised to executors or trustees as joint tenants....[5]

§8.9. Creation of joint tenancy

The usual method of creation[6] of a joint tenancy is by a deed describing the grantee as follows: "to A and B, as joint tenants." The words *with right of survivorship* are often added, but are not a requisite, since this right is an incident of a joint tenancy, whether expressly recited or not. Although it has been held that the particular words of the statute, *in joint tenancy* or *as joint tenants*, are not essential when the words used show clearly an intent to create a joint tenancy, the cases are not in agreement as to what words are sufficient. To avoid any uncertainty, it is preferable that the words *as joint tenants* be expressed in the deed or other instruments of creation. The words *to A or B*, or *to A and B, jointly* are not considered sufficient to create a joint tenancy interest in real property.

Table 8–1

Comparison of co-ownership

	Joint Tenancy	Tenancy in Common	Community Property
Definition	Property held by two or more people, with right of survivorship	Property held by two or more people, without the right of survivorship	Property held only by by husband and wife
Creation	By meeting the four unities of title, time, interest, and possession, plus unequivocal intention	By expressly so stating; or any property acquired by unmarried persons that fails as joint tenancy or fails to state the nature of the tenancy	By expressly stating; may include any property acquired by married people that fails to state the nature of the tenancy
Unities	Time (created at the same time) Title (created by same deed) Interest (equal) Possession (undivided); modified in California	Possession (undivided)	Not applicable
Presumption	No	Yes, if not husband and wife	Yes, if married
Ownership	Each tenant is deemed the owner of the entire property	Each tenant owns a separate legal title to his or her interest	Each spouse owns one-half interest, although there is only one title
Transfer of Interest	Severs the joint tenancy as to that tenant's interest; does not affect the continuation of joint tenancy of any two other joint tenants	Each tenant has separate title that can be transferred separately by its owner	Title cannot be transferred separately; both spouses must join in the conveyance
Purchaser	Will be a tenant in common with the other owner(s)	Will be a tenant in common with the other owner(s)	Not applicable, as one spouse cannot convey separately
Death of One Party	Interest passes to the other joint tenant(s) outside of probate	Interest passes through probate per decedent's will or by intestacy	Interest passes according to will; otherwise all to surviving spouse. Passes through probate, except spouse may elect to take outside of probate
Tax Basis on Death	Deceased's interest only acquires stepped-up basis to fair market value	Deceased's interest acquires stepped-up basis to fair market value	Entire property receives stepped-up basis to fair market value
Amount Included in Decedent's Estate	Entire property, less percentage attributable to survivor's contribution. If community property held as joint tenancy or if between spouses only, may be treated as community property	Decedent's separate interest	Only half the property is included. It is assumed each contributed proportionately, so no tracing of amounts or percentages is involved

Effect when conveyance is insufficient to create a joint tenancy. When a conveyance is made purporting to create a joint tenancy in two or more persons, and the joint tenancy fails because it does not otherwise meet the requirements for creation of a joint tenancy, the conveyance, as a rule, is not wholly ineffective, but operates to pass title to the grantees as tenants in common.

Four unities essential. At common law, four unities were considered essential in the creation of a joint tenancy: unity of time, title, interest, and possession. This requirement was based on the concept that joint tenants take as one in a fictitious unity. Accordingly, they must have identical interests, acquired at the same time and by the same instrument. The code definition of a joint tenancy embraces the four unities, and the courts in California have frequently stated that the four unities are essential if a joint tenancy is to exist.[7]

Unity of title. The necessity for unity of title is expressed in the code requirement that a joint tenancy be created by a "single will or transfer."

EXAMPLE

If A conveys land to B, and B thereafter conveys to B and C as joint tenants, this would not create a valid joint tenancy at common law, because B's interest in the land arises under the deed from A, and C's interest arises under the later deed; thus the interests do not accrue by the same transfer.

Modification of rule in California. This rule has been modified in California to permit the creation of joint tenancies by direct transfer. A joint tenancy conveyance may be made from a "sole owner to himself and others," or from joint owners to themselves and others as specified in the code. Formerly, when one of the proposed joint tenants already owned an interest in the property, it was necessary for the purpose of creating a valid joint tenancy that the property be conveyed to a disinterested third party (a straw man), who then conveyed the title to the ultimate grantees as joint tenants. The statute has been liberalized with the result that few situations arise today in which the use of a straw man is essential.

Joint tenancy by a married person. When a married man contributes community funds to the purchase of real property, and takes title in joint tenancy with a person other than his wife, the attempted creation of a joint tenancy may be invalid. In such a case, the essential unity of interest is lacking. The interests created under the deed are considered to be a one-half interest in the married man and his wife as their community property, and a one-half interest in the other grantee. This results in an inequality of interest which defeats the joint tenancy. If a married woman uses community funds to acquire title in joint tenancy with a person other than her husband, the attempted joint tenancy may also be considered ineffective.

Special recitals. Before insuring the sufficiency of joint tenancies created between a married person and someone other than the spouse, title insurance companies usually require the written consent of the other spouse. This consent may be evidenced by the following recital in the joint tenancy deed: "John Doe and Jane Doe, husband and wife, consent to the creation of a joint tenancy in the grantees above named in the property herein described." Special recitals are also required in conveyances from a third person to husband and wife and one or more other persons as joint tenants.

Joint tenancies with persons under a disability. If one of the grantees in a joint tenancy deed is a minor or an incompetent person, and funds of the minor or incompetent person are used in the purchase of the property, the joint tenancy is questionable. An agreement by the minor or incompetent to take title in joint tenancy would be void or voidable under the usual rules governing contracts of persons under disability.[8] Insofar as guardianship proceedings are concerned, there is no statutory provision for a guardian to take title on behalf of his or her ward in joint tenancy with a third party. However, if the interest of the person under disability is based on a gift, such as a gift deed from a parent to a minor child and others as joint tenants, the joint tenancy appears to be unobjectionable.

Joint tenants must be natural persons. A question that sometimes arises is whether a valid joint tenancy may be created between a natural person and a corporation or between two corporations. The answer is no. A valid joint tenancy can be created only between natural persons primarily because of the survivorship aspect. Termination of a joint tenancy occurs when a joint tenant dies; a corporation does not "die" as does a natural person. Also, a joint tenancy between a natural person and a partnership is considered to be incompatible, at least for title insurance purposes.

§8.10. Nature of ownership as between husband and wife

Problems have frequently arisen regarding the true character of the ownership by husband and wife of property held of record as joint tenants. Frequently, such property, despite the record ownership, has been treated as community property for purposes of succession, transfer, disposition in marital dissolution proceedings, or seizure by creditors. Joint tenancy and community property are separate and distinct forms of ownership. It has been held that when husband and wife elect to take title as joint tenants, this is "tantamount to a binding agreement between them that the same shall not thereafter be held as community property but instead as a joint tenancy with all the characteristics of such an estate."[9]

Qualification of rule. The California Supreme Court has qualified the application of the foregoing rule to cases in which there is "an absence of any evidence to the contrary." This phrase is the foundation for a long line of decisions holding that evidence is admissible to show that husband and wife who took title as joint tenants actually intended it to be community property. This intention may be evidenced by an oral agreement at the time the property was acquired. Also, it may be shown that property taken in joint tenancy was thereafter converted into community property by either an oral or written agreement.[10] Thus, for many years the California courts recognized the right of spouses, by casual and informal agreement and understanding, to convert, to change, or to transmute, between them, the title to and the ownership of their community property and of their separate property. Over the years it became apparent that these decisions, based on a "fairness" doctrine, have done violence to the conventional application of the Statute of Frauds to real property transactions. That application requires, generally, that all real property transfers must be in writing. In an attempt to reconcile the problem, the legislature added new sections to what is now the Family Code.[11] Basically those laws provide that no transmutation of real property is valid unless made in writing by an express declaration that it is made by the spouse whose interest is adversely affected.

Effect when joint tenancy property is community property. The contention that joint tenancy property is in fact community property was often raised in divorce cases, and can be a point at issue in a marital dissolution proceeding. The court does not have the power to make an award of separate property, but if it is established that joint tenancy property is in fact community property, the court may award such property in accordance with the provisions of the Family Law Act. Under the act, there is a rebuttable presumption that all property acquired by husband and wife during marriage in joint form is presumed to be community property for the purpose of the division of such property upon dissolution of marriage or legal separation.[12]

Certain tax aspects. After December 31, 1976, under a "qualified" joint tenancy between husband and wife as to personal property[13] and real property,[14] joint tenancy is often treated as community property for tax purposes. As a result of the Economic Recovery Tax Act of 1981, after December 31, 1981, if property is held in joint tenancy, each spouse is deemed to be the owner of one-half of the property, even though there was not an equal contribution, and at the death of the first spouse, the property will pass tax free.[15]

Claim by creditors of either spouse. A claim that joint tenancy property is actually community property may also be raised by creditors of either spouse.[16] It was held in an earlier case that if it can be shown that joint tenancy property was acquired with community funds, a creditor could enforce the judgment against all of the purported joint tenancy property, rather than against the husband's interest alone.[17] Devisees of a deceased joint tenant may also be able to establish that the joint tenancy property is actually community property and therefore subject to testamentary disposition by the decedent.[18] This is, of course, a question of fact.

EXAMPLE   Husband and wife (H & W) purchased a residence and took title as joint tenants. W paid off the balance and H orally agreed that the residence was W's separate property. No change was made to the record title. After H moved out and the dissolution proceedings began, H borrowed $12,000 secured by a trust deed on the property. H represented that he and W were living together. W brought action to have the trust deed set aside. The court held that the lender was a bona fide lender without notice of W's unrecorded claim. W could have recorded a lis pendens at the time of the dissolution to protect her interest. She did not do so. (The wisdom of this case is questionable because unrecorded agreements often occur between co-owners, particularly joint tenants. This could lead to fraud by ex-spouses and some lenders.) [19]

---

§8.11. Survivorship aspect

The distinguishing characteristic of joint tenancy property is the right of survivorship. When a joint tenant dies, title to the property immediately vests in the survivor or surviving joint tenants. As a consequence, joint tenancy property ordinarily is not subject to testamentary disposition. Since title vests in the survivor immediately on death, there is no estate remaining on which the will of the deceased tenant can operate. The surviving joint tenant holds the whole estate free from debts and creditors' claims against the deceased joint tenant. This immunity from debts extends to liens, such as a trust deed, created by the deceased joint tenant alone on his interest.[20]

Proceedings to establish fact of death. Although conventional probate proceedings are unnecessary, court proceedings may be necessary for the purpose of determining the fact of death.[21] This procedure has fallen into disuse since the repeal of the California inheritance tax. However, the procedure can be used in an emergency when the issuance of a death certificate has been delayed, or a certified copy of the certificate cannot be obtained. It can also be used to terminate a legal life estate when the life estate tenant dies.

Affidavit method of establishing fact of death. An affidavit method of establishing the fact of death of record has been used in many areas in the state. An affidavit of death of joint tenant, with certified copy of the death certificate attached, is recorded in the office of the county recorder.

Effect of simultaneous death. The chief incident of and main reason for joint tenancy—survivorship—may be lost in a situation that sometimes occurs, namely, simultaneous death of the joint tenants. Under the provisions of the simultaneous death law, if there is no sufficient evidence that two joint tenants have died otherwise than simultaneously, the probate court may determine such fact by an order to that effect.[22] The property is then administered upon, and distributed or otherwise dealt with, one-half as if one had survived, and one-half as if the other had survived. If more than two joint tenants died simultaneously, the same procedure is applicable, with each tenant's estate having an interest in proportion to the whole number of joint tenants. The effect of simultaneous death on joint tenancy ownership, instead of avoiding probate, is to multiply the number of probate proceedings required. This is another reason to have a living trust, and properly place the real estate into the trust.

§8.12. Effect of murder or voluntary manslaughter

It has been held that a joint tenant who has caused the wrongful death of the other joint tenant, such as by murder or voluntary manslaughter, cannot succeed to the interest of the deceased joint tenants.[23] The wrongful death terminates the joint tenancy and creates a tenancy in common, with the interest of the deceased joint tenant vesting in the heirs or devisees.[24]

§8.13. Transfers by a joint tenant

During the lifetime of the joint tenants, either or any of them may voluntarily sever the joint tenancy as to his or her interest by a conveyance to a third party. If there are two joint tenants, the joint tenancy is terminated by such conveyance. If there are three or more joint tenants, the joint tenancy is severed as to the interest conveyed and continues between the other joint tenants as to the remaining interest.

EXAMPLES

1. If title is in A and B as joint tenants, and A conveys to C, B and C then own as tenants in common.

2. If title is in A, B, and C as joint tenants, and A conveys to D, then B and C continue as joint tenants as to a two-thirds interest, and D owns a one-third interest as tenant in common.[25]

The joint tenancy may be severed without the knowledge or consent of the other joint tenant. This sometimes occurs when a husband or wife wants to leave his or her interest by will. The usual procedure is to convey the interest to a third party, who in turn conveys the interest back to the party desiring to terminate the joint tenancy (sometimes referred to as a straw man device).[26]

EXAMPLES

1. In one case, a wife executed a power of attorney constituting her attorney as her attorney-in-fact to convey her interest in the property. The attorney-in-fact conveyed her interest by an unacknowledged and unrecorded deed to a third party, who later reconveyed the interest back to the wife. The wife then disposed of her interest by will. It was held that this was effective, even though the conveyance by the wife was done without the knowledge or consent of the husband.[27]

2. In another case, husband and wife owned a parcel of real property as joint tenants. The wife desired to leave her interest in the property to another person by will. She executed a deed for this purpose, but instead of using a straw man, she conveyed the property by deed to herself as grantee. After her death, her half-interest in the property was sought to be probated in her estate. This was the first knowledge her surviving husband had of the deed. He brought an action to quiet title against the representative of his wife's estate and prevailed in the action, not because he had not known about the deed, but because the deed was held to be ineffective, for the reason that to have a valid deed there must be a separate grantor and grantee. The case held that for a conveyance to be valid, the same person cannot be the sole grantor and grantee.[28]

3. On the other hand, a later case held contrary, stating, "common sense ... dictates that a joint tenant should be able to accomplish directly what he ... could otherwise achieve indirectly by use of elaborate legal fictions."[29]

In an attempt to make certain that which was uncertain, the legislature enacted a new section to the Civil Code to provide that a joint tenant may sever a joint tenancy by executing an intent to accomplish that purpose.[30] Joint tenants may agree in writing that a joint tenancy is not to be severable by the aforementioned methods. The Code was thereafter amended, to provide protection for a bona fide purchaser or encumbrancer for value against a severance contrary to a written agreement. (See also § 8.19, infra.)

§8.14. Lease by a joint tenant

Questions sometimes arise as to whether an act other than a conveyance of the fee by one joint tenant will sever the joint tenancy. One joint tenant has the right to lease his interest for a term of years, but whether the lease effects a severance of the joint tenancy was uncertain. However, in 1976 the California Supreme Court held that a lease by one joint tenant alone did not sever the joint tenancy, but the lease terminates upon the death of the joint tenant lessor.[31]

§8.15. Contracts of sale and encumbrances

A joint tenancy is severed by a contract of sale executed by one of the joint tenants, because the contract effects a transfer of the equitable title to the vendee. This is true whether the contract of sale is in favor of a third party or the other joint tenant.[32] However, a contract of sale executed by all the joint tenants in favor of a third party does not terminate the joint tenancy in the absence of such intent.[33] Also, the execution of a mortgage or trust deed on the interest of one joint tenant creates only a lien or charge, and does not in itself effect a severance of the joint tenancy.[34] If the mortgage or trust deed is foreclosed during the lifetime of the joint tenant executing the encumbrance, the transfer by foreclosure sale would result in a severance of the joint tenancy.

§8.16. Judgments against a joint tenant

The lien created by the recordation of an abstract of judgment against one of the joint tenants does not sever the joint tenancy, but an execution sale during the lifetime of the judgment debtor does effect a severance. It has been held that a judgment lien against one joint tenant ceases when the debtor dies before levy of a writ of execution, and before the 120-day grace period staying the sale of the property has expired, and therefore the surviving joint tenant holds the property free of the lien.[35]

§8.17. Bankruptcy of a joint tenant

If one joint tenant is adjudicated a bankrupt, the involuntary transfer of the interest to the trustee in bankruptcy operates to effect a severance of the joint tenancy, unless the interest is subject to a valid homestead.

§8.18. Action for partition

Filing an action for partition does not terminate the joint tenancy, but a judgment of partition will have such effect only if the action is tried during the lifetime of the joint tenants.[36] It should be noted, however, that the right to partition may be waived or modified by reason of an express or implied agreement between the parties.[37]

§8.19. Agreements affecting joint tenancy (including Marital Dissolution)

A joint tenancy may be terminated not only by an express agreement to that effect, but also by an agreement between the joint tenants that so operates on one or more of the elements of the joint tenancy as to cause a severance.[38] For example, an agreement that "if either joint tenant dies, the interest of that one shall go to a third party," destroys the element of survivorship, and terminates the joint tenancy. The title thereafter vests in the parties as tenants in common. The same rationale may hold true between husband and wife with respect to a property settlement agreement, but a "status only" dissolution will not sever the joint tenancy.[39] An agreement to sever operates to effect a severance and the intervening death of one of the joint tenants will not defeat the severance even though the agreement is not performed.[40]

§8.20. Severance by mutual wills
Although the attempt by one joint tenant alone to dispose of joint tenancy property by will does not sever the joint tenancy, the execution of a mutual will by two joint tenants can effect a severance.

EXAMPLE   In one case, the court stated that when title is in husband and wife as joint tenants, they may convert the tenancy into community property or into a tenancy in common by the execution of both of them of an agreement or a deed to themselves for that express purpose, and the joint tenancy may also be severed by mutual wills.[41]

---

§8.21. Agreements as to possession
A question sometimes arises in dissolution proceedings as to whether a property settlement agreement under which one spouse is given the exclusive right of occupancy of joint tenancy property, will terminate the joint tenancy. It has been held that this is primarily a question of intent. The right of possession, which must be an equal right at the time of creation of the joint tenancy, can be modified by an agreement entered into subsequent to the creation of the joint tenancy without severing the joint tenancy.[42]

§8.22. Advantages and disadvantages of joint tenancy
Joint tenancies have advantages and disadvantages, depending on the particular circumstances.

Advantages.

1.   The main advantage is, of course, the incident of survivorship, eliminating the time and expense of probate proceedings. Of course, the traditional advantage of joint tenancy over community property has been eliminated, allowing the surviving spouse to succeed (if taken outright) to the decedent's community property share without estate administration.[43]

2.   The fact that the surviving joint tenant holds title free from debts and claims solely against the deceased joint tenant, even when secured by trust deed or other encumbrance, is another distinct advantage of the survivor.[44]

Disadvantages.

1.   The possibility that the joint tenancy may be severed at any time by a transfer, voluntarily or by operation of law, of one cotenant's interest.

2.   The fact that the joint tenant who dies first ordinarily has no power of testamentary disposition over such property.[45]

3.   No provision exists for administering the estate of a joint tenant who has been missing for five years and who is presumed to be dead.[46]

4.   The tax consequences, both as to estate and income taxes, may be unfavorable,[47] e.g., loss of stepped-up basis to the surviving spouse. However, this disadvantage may have been eliminated or lessened under Revenue Ruling 87–98.

5.   If a husband and wife die, guardianship proceedings (and court supervision and expense) are necessary; plus, child gets entire estate at age 18.

6. Particularly with second marriages, children of first marriage are often unintentionally disinherited.

§8.23. Should a joint tenant make a will?

Even though joint tenancy property is ordinarily not subject to testamentary disposition by the joint tenant who is the first to die, the joint tenants should make a will for various reasons, including the following:

1. The will of the survivor will be effective.

2. If deaths are simultaneous, the property will be subject to probate.

3. If one joint tenant murders the other, the will of the murdered joint tenant will be effective as to his or her interest.

4. The joint tenancy may be terminated at any time by one of the joint tenants without the knowledge or consent of the other.

5. Tax savings for the heirs may be achieved.

6. The joint tenancy might be invalid for some technical or other reason.

III. TENANCY IN COMMON

§8.24. In general

A tenancy in common is characterized by only one unity, that of possession. The cotenants own undivided interests, but unlike a joint tenancy, these interests need not be equal in quantity or duration, and may arise from different conveyances and at different times. There is no right of survivorship; each tenant owns an interest that on his death vests in the heirs or devisees, subject to probate administration.

§8.25. Definition of a tenancy in common

A *tenancy in common* is defined in the code in a negative manner. The Civil Code provides that a tenancy in common arises whenever property, real or personal, or an interest therein, is transferred, whether by conveyance, devise, descent, or by operation of law, to several persons in their own right, unless acquired by them in partnership, for partnership purposes, or unless declared to be in joint tenancy, or unless acquired as community property.[48]

§8.26. Interest of cotenants

When title is acquired by two or more persons as tenants in common, the deed should recite the respective interest of each, by words such as the following: *to A and B, as tenants in common, each as to an undivided one-half interest.* If the respective interests are not set forth in the instrument of acquisition, or otherwise shown of record, there is a presumption that their interests are equal.[49] This presumption is not conclusive, however, and may be overcome by evidence showing that by virtue of unequal contributions to the purchase price or otherwise, the cotenants hold unequal interests.

§8.27. Right of possession

Cotenancy, whether as joint tenants or as tenants in common, involves mutual rights and obligations. Cotenants enjoy an equal right of possession. Each tenant may occupy the whole land, or any part thereof, but cannot exclude a cotenant from occupancy. When one cotenant is in the sole possession of land, he is not liable to a cotenant out of possession for the rental value of the land,[50] or for the products of his labor, such as crops. However, he must account to the cotenant for a share of rents and profits received from third persons, and for profits derived from a use of the land that removes something therefrom, such as extraction of oil or minerals.

§8.28. Adverse possession of cotenant

As a general rule, one cotenant cannot acquire title by adverse possession against another cotenant. Since each cotenant has a right to occupy the whole of the property owned in common, possession of one is deemed possession of all. However, one cotenant in possession may acquire title by adverse possession if there is first an "ouster" of the other cotenant, that is, an act that manifests an intention on his part to hold exclusively for himself, and if the tenant out of possession has notice of such hostile claim.

§8.29. Repairs and maintenance

A right of contribution exists in favor of one cotenant who pays taxes or other liens against the entire property. If the property is income-producing, he may deduct the expenditures from rents and profits of the property. In addition, he is entitled to an equitable lien on the shares of the cotenants for their proportional amount of such expenditures. A cotenant is also entitled to contribution for the cost of repairs. If one cotenant makes improvements on the common property, he cannot, as a rule, assert a lien for contribution on the share of the other cotenant, unless the latter assented to the improvements.

§8.30. Confidential relationship of owners

Cotenants, whether joint tenants or tenants in common, stand in a confidential relationship. One cotenant cannot take advantage of a defect in the common title by purchasing an outstanding title or encumbrance and asserting it against the cotenants. Accordingly, when a cotenant acquires a tax title under a sale for taxes on the common property, or takes an assignment of a certificate of sale issued to the purchaser at a foreclosure sale under a mortgage or trust deed on the common property, the title so acquired by the cotenant is deemed to be held in trust for the other cotenants if they choose within a reasonable time to claim the benefit of the purchase by contributing their share of the purchase price.[51]

§8.31. Transfer of interest of cotenant

As in the case of a joint tenancy, the interest of a tenant in common may be transferred, either voluntarily or by operation of law. A conveyance by a tenant in common of his undivided interest passes the identical interest of such grantor in the whole property.

EXAMPLE   If title is vested of record in A, as to an undivided one-third interest, and in B, as to an undivided two-thirds interest, a deed from A describing an undivided one-third interest in the common property passes all of his interest in the land, and his grantee becomes a tenant in common with B.

---

§8.32. Lease by cotenant

One cotenant cannot execute a lease of the whole property, or of a specific portion, that will bind the cotenants and give the lessee exclusive possession of the land. Such a lease is valid, however, as to the interest of the lessor-cotenant.

IV. COMMUNITY PROPERTY

§8.33. In general

The husband-and-wife relationship is essential to the community property type of co-ownership. In California, property of a married person is either separate property or community property. If separate property, it may be held in severalty, or in joint tenancy, or as tenants in common, or in partnership.[52]

§8.34. What is community property?

Community property is defined as property acquired by husband and wife, or either, during marriage, when not acquired as the separate property of either.[53]

The concept of community property is that both spouses contribute to the acquisition of property during marriage, and both should have an interest in such acquisition. The California Supreme Court has held that the military retirement pension of a spouse, whether vested or not, is community property if acquired during the marriage.[54] The Supreme Court of the United States held otherwise in 1981, but this was changed in 1982 by the Uniformed Services Former Spouses Support Act.[55]

Under provisions of the Family Code, *separate property* is defined as property owned before marriage, and that acquired afterward by gift, bequest, devise, or descent, and the rents, issues, and profits thereof.[56] Separate property also consists of: (1) the earnings and accumulations of a spouse while living separate and apart from the other spouse;[57] (2) the earnings or accumulations of each party after the rendition of a judgment decreeing legal separation of the parties; (3) under certain conditions, all money or other property received from a third party in satisfaction of a judgment for damages for personal injuries or pursuant to a settlement agreement;[58] (4) property conveyed by either husband or wife to the other with the intent of making it the grantee's separate property; and (5) disability benefits, if not accepted in lieu of retirement benefits that have matured and vested and would otherwise be community property.

§8.35. Agreements between spouses

Prior to marriage, a man and a woman can enter into a written contract (Prenuptial Agreement) agreeing as to the status of earnings after marriage (it cannot include an agreement regarding child or spousal support, however). The consideration for this contract is the actual marriage. After marriage, the parties can also enter into such an agreement (Postnuptial Agreement); however, this agreement cannot be entered into in contemplation of separation or dissolution. It is valid if there is no fraud, coercion, or undue influence.[59] The spouses can also enter into a Marital Separation Agreement and dispose of or divide the community property and agree upon what, if any, is separate property. In a separation agreement, it is important to be sure it contains numerous, necessary paragraphs. Often the agreement is 25 or more pages long. It should **never** be drafted by anyone who is not a competent attorney. Among other paragraphs, it should contain certain waivers set forth in the Probate Code.[60]

§8.36. Origin of community property in California

California owes the origin of the community property law to the Treaty of Guadalupe Hidalgo, referred to in Chapter 1, which expressly provided that the property rights of the inhabitants of the ceded territory were to be protected. The framers of the first state constitution in 1849 preserved the Mexican law as to marital property by adopting a provision that all property of the wife owned before marriage and that acquired afterward by gift, devise, or descent shall be her separate property, and directed that laws be passed more clearly defining the rights of the wife as to the property held in common with her husband. The first state legislature thereafter enacted a measure providing that all property acquired after marriage by either spouse, other than by gift, devise, or descent, shall be common property.

§8.37. Statutory changes

The community property law in California has been changed many times by amendments to the code, usually with the object of enlarging the rights of the wife. Before 1923 the interest of the wife was a mere expectancy, but this interest has been enlarged, and now the wife's interest in community property is defined as a present, equal, and existing interest. Prior to 1975, community property was under the management and control of the husband. Effective in 1975, the laws governing community property rights and obligations of a husband and wife were substantially revised, including an amendment granting equal management and control to husband and wife over community property whether acquired before or after 1975.[61]

However, in other instances in the past when the rights of the wife were increased and those of the husband limited, the statute cannot be applied retroactively so as to affect vested rights of the husband in property previously acquired. Accordingly, it is necessary to consider the date of acquisition of property to determine fully the rights of the parties.

§8.38. Quasi-community property

Several code changes were made in 1961 to create a classification of "quasi-community property"; consequently, *quasi-community property* is treated the same as *community property* in marital dissolution proceedings, under the homestead law, and for other purposes. It consists basically of real or personal property, wherever situated, acquired while the spouses were domiciled elsewhere but which would have been community property if the spouses had been domiciled in California.[62]

§8.39. Community rights of a putative spouse

Although there can be no "community property" when there has been no marriage, it has been held that a woman who lives with a man as his wife in the good-faith belief that a valid marriage exists is entitled, on termination of their relationship, to share in the property acquired by them during its existence. The Family Code now provides specifically that the division of the property is made in accordance with the rules for division of community property upon a marital dissolution.[63] A man who believes in good faith that he is the lawful husband of a woman is given the same rights. Such person believing in good faith that he or she is lawfully married is designated as a *putative spouse*. Their accumulated property is called "quasi-marital property."

§8.40. Meretricious relationships

In a meretricious relationship there is no marriage at all, and the couple knows it. They are merely living together. Although in a minority of states such an arrangement can ripen into a marriage (common law marriage), this has not been the case in California.[64] However, it has been held by the California Supreme Court that the courts

> *should enforce express contracts between nonmarital partners except to the extent that the contract is explicitly founded on the consideration of meretricious sexual services. Also, in the absence of an express contract, the courts will inquire into the conduct of the parties to determine whether that conduct demonstrates an implied contract, agreement of partnership or joint venture, or some other tacit understanding between the parties. The courts may also employ the doctrine of quantum meruit, or equitable remedies such as constructive or resulting trusts, when warranted by the facts of the case.[65]*

Because of this ruling, parties living together should seriously consider entering into a written "living together" contract with wording similar to a premarital agreement.

§8.41. Determining character of property

In determining whether property is separate or community, the condition of the record title is not necessarily controlling, at least as between the spouses. Property may be community property even though the record title stands in the names of the husband and wife as tenants in common or as joint tenants. Evidence may be admitted in appropriate proceedings to show that the parties intended to take property otherwise than as shown of record. Recitals in deeds do not determine the character of the property unless both spouses evidence their agreement to the truth of the recitals.

EXAMPLES

1. For example, the recital of a deed from a third party to a married woman that the property is conveyed to her "as her separate property" might be disproved by the husband.

2. Also, it may be shown that property originally acquired as separate property was subsequently converted into community property by agreement of the spouses.

§8.42. When purchase completed after marriage

If either husband or wife owns an incomplete right to property before marriage, but completes the acquisition during marriage, the property is classified in proportion to the separate and community funds expended. For instance, if the husband is the vendee under a land contract entered into before marriage, with a balance of the purchase price paid after marriage, the property is community property to the extent that community funds went into the purchase, and separate property to the extent that his separate funds were used.[66]

EXAMPLE When a home is purchased before the marriage by the wife, but community property was used to make some of the payments after the marriage, the husband obtains a community property interest in the home. The community has an interest in the ratio that the payments on the purchase price with community funds bear to the payments made with separate funds. If the fair market value has increased disproportionately to the increase in equity, the community is entitled to participate in that increase in a similar proportion.[67]

Statutory law has modified the above example and should be carefully considered.[68]

§8.43. Improvements on separate property with community funds (or vice versa)

Previously, when community funds were used to improve the wife's separate property, the improvements followed the title to the land, and were separate property. The husband, who formerly had management and control of community funds, was presumed to have intended a gift to the wife in such case, in the absence of any agreement to the contrary. He was not entitled to a lien on the property or to a right of reimbursement. Since the law now gives both spouses management and control, the former law is less certain. In the past, when community funds were used by the husband to improve or pay taxes or encumbrances on his own separate property, the wife was entitled to reimbursement to the extent of her share of the community funds so used. However, if she consented to the improvements, she may not be so entitled.[69]

§8.44. Commingling

In one case it was held that separate property may become community property by the process of commingling in such manner as to make segregation impossible, thus requiring application of the presumption that the property is community.[70] Mere commingling of separate funds with community funds in a bank account does not destroy the character of the former if the amount can be ascertained.[71] The presumption that property is community is controlling only when it is impossible to trace the source of the specific property.[72] From a practical standpoint, however, once commingled, it is often difficult to prove a gift was not made to the community.

§8.45. Important distinction between community and separate property

Determining whether property of husband and wife is separate property or community property is extremely important, as different rules apply in the various actions or proceedings affecting property of a married person. Joint tenancy property or property held as tenants in common is subject to a partition action, whereas an action for partition by a spouse (or spouses) or a putative spouse (or spouses) for division of community, quasi-community, or quasi-marital property is expressly excluded from the revised partition law.[73] If either the husband or wife was adjudged incompetent, special rules for property disposition formerly applied. Rights under the homestead law may depend on whether property is separate or community property.

In marital dissolution proceedings, the power of the court to award property depends on the character of the property. This power is limited to community property and homestead property, and does not extend to separate property. However, it is often difficult to prove what is separate property unless there are specific documents presented to the court sufficient to establish a separate property interest.

§8.46. Award of community property in marital dissolution proceedings

The adoption of the Family Law Act in California in 1970 had an important effect on community property rights in connection with a marriage dissolution.

The act includes changes in terminology. Instead of divorce, separate maintenance, and annulment, the terms now used are dissolution, legal separation, and nullity. The act reduces the grounds for dissolution of a marriage from seven to two, namely, irreconcilable differences and incurable insanity. What used to be called alimony is now called spousal support. Disposition of property on dissolution of a marriage has also been changed.

The Family Law Act requires an equal division in all but three specific instances, without regard to the reasons for the dissolution.

The first exception is that if the nature of the property is such that an equal division is not possible without impairment of a principal asset, then the court shall have the discretion to establish conditions that will result in a substantially equal division. For example, if a major asset is a going business, it could well be destructive to award each spouse a half-interest therein. Under the "substantially equal" requirement, however, the court could award the entire business to the husband and grant the wife her one-half interest in cash, or give her a greater share of other property or a greater support allowance.

The second exception is that if community funds have been deliberately squandered or misused by one spouse, the other may be granted a greater share of the remaining property. If most of the community property has been squandered, payments to compensate for the misappropriation may be ordered.

Under the third exception, the court may now award all the community property to one party if the other party cannot be located with reasonable diligence and if the net value of the property is less than $5,000. This amendment was added because in many cases the husband had deserted the wife, leaving her with little other than the family home, which could not be sold or refinanced without his signature.[74]

§8.47. Liability of community property for debts

The community property is made liable for contracts of either spouse after marriage.[75] Neither the separate property of a spouse nor the earnings of the spouse after marriage are liable for the debts of the other spouse contracted before marriage.[76]

Judgments. A money judgment against a spouse, when an abstract of judgment is duly recorded, is a lien on all community real property. However, both parties must consent to any encumbrance on the community real property.[77]

§8.48. Disposition of community property when death occurs

On the death of a spouse, one-half the community property belongs to the other spouse. This is so even though the community property is recorded in only one name.[78] The other half is subject to the testamentary disposition of the deceased spouse, and in the absence thereof, it all goes to the surviving spouse. However, the community property is subject to the deceased spouse's debts and to the administration of the estate. For this reason, it is sometimes advisable to go through probate in order to discharge creditors' claims.

As to property acquired before August 17, 1923, a wife's interest was an expectancy only and died with her. As to property acquired after that date, at which time the wife was given the right of testamentary disposition of one-half the community property, all of it goes to the husband without administration if the wife dies intestate. If she exercises her right to dispose of one-half, that half is subject to administration in her estate. After 40 days from the death of a spouse, the surviving spouse has power to convey, encumber, or otherwise deal with the property unless the claimants under the deceased spouse's will have recorded a notice that an interest in the property is claimed.[79] The right of the spouse depends on the community character of the property, and if the vesting of title does not disclose that the property is community property (e.g., held as joint tenants "for convenience" but intent was community property), a proceeding to establish the status of the property as community property may be essential.[80] Unfortunately, a community property determination in this proceeding is not binding on the I.R.S., and the spouse may lose the stepped-up basis advantage she would otherwise have gained.

If the deceased spouse owned separate property or community property and left it to someone other than the surviving spouse, the estate must be administered through probate; however, if all the property was community property and the deceased died intestate, or if separate property and the deceased left this estate to the surviving spouse, no probate is required.[81]

§8.49. Disposition of community property when spouse is incompetent

When either the husband or wife or both are incompetent, and community or homesteaded property is involved, the conventional guardianship proceedings to effect a sale, transfer, or other disposition of such property are applicable, or a special type of proceeding may be utilized. Under such procedures, the sane spouse (or if both spouses are incompetent, the guardian of the estate) can petition the court for an order permitting him or her to sell and convey, exchange, mortgage, lease, or execute a trust deed on the homestead or community property, or for an order permitting him or her to transfer such property in compromise, composition, or settlement of a mortgage or trust deed thereon.[82]

V. PARTNERSHIPS

§8.50. In general

The ownership of property by several persons, in addition to other forms such as joint tenancy and tenancy in common, may be of "partnership interests."[83] A *partnership interest* is defined as one "owned by several persons, in partnership for partnership purposes."[84] Since the Uniform Partnership Act was adopted in California years ago, title to real property may be taken in the name of the partnership. The partnership is considered an entity capable of acquiring title to real property. Property so held is impressed with certain characteristics that distinguish it from property owned in other forms of cotenancy.

Two forms of partnerships are provided for by law: general partnerships and limited partnerships. The basic difference between them is that in a *general partnership*, each partner is liable for the debts of the partnership, whereas in a *limited partnership*, a limited partner's liability is limited to the amount of the partner's investment and he is not otherwise liable for the debts of the partnership.

§8.51. Definition of a partnership

A *partnership* is defined as an association of two or more persons to carry on as co-owners a business for profit.[85] It is created by an agreement between two or more persons, either evidenced by an express contract, or implied from their acts and conduct, to carry on jointly a business and share the profits. A partnership may include individuals, another partnership, corporations, or other associations.[86]

§8.52. Certificate of fictitious name

A partnership or other person transacting business under a fictitious name, or a designation not showing the names of the persons interested in such business, is required to file with the clerk of the county in which its principal place of business is situated, a certificate stating the names in full and places of residence of all members of the partnership.[87] The certificate also must be published once a week for four weeks. If there is a change in the members of such partnership, a new certificate is required to be filed and a new publication made. Failure of the partnership to comply with this requirement penalizes it to the extent that it cannot maintain any action on contracts or transactions made under such fictitious name until the required certificate has been filed and publication completed. The purpose of the fictitious name statute is to make public the names of the members of the partnership so that those dealing with them may at all times know the identity of the persons to whom they are giving credit or becoming bound.[88]

§8.53. Statement of partnership

The Corporations Code provides that a partnership may file for record in the office of the county recorder of any county a statement of partnership that shall set forth the name of the partnership and the names of each of the partners, together with a statement that the partners named are all of the partners.[89] Such statement must be signed, verified, and acknowledged by two or more of the partners. If this is done, it is conclusively presumed in favor of any bona fide purchaser for value of partnership property in such county, that the persons named constitute all of the partners, unless a person claiming to be a partner shall, previous to such conveyance, record a statement showing the membership to be otherwise than as set forth in the original statement. Although filing the statement is optional, title insurers—as a rule of title practice—require that this statement be recorded before insuring a conveyance by a partnership.

§8.54. Title in name of partnership

A partnership may acquire title in the partnership name, such as "XYZ Company, a partnership composed of A and B, partners." Transfers of property so acquired are made in the name of the partnership, with the name appearing in the caption of the instrument. The instrument is executed in a manner similar to an instrument of a corporation. The spouses of married partners need not join in the execution of the instrument.[90] One partner, as a matter of law, may bind the partnership, because every partner is an agent of the partnership. However, it is a rule of title practice that conveyances of partnership real property must be executed on behalf of the partnership by all the partners, or by a partner, or partners less than all, who are expressly authorized, under the partnership agreement or otherwise, by all the partners to perform the particular act.

§8.55. Title in names of partners

Partnership property may be acquired not only in the partnership name, but also in the names of one or more of the individual partners, with or without a reference to the partnership. As between the partners themselves, it may be shown that property, vested of record in an individual partner or partners, is actually partnership property. However, when the rights of third parties are concerned, the record title may prevail. Thus a purchaser in good faith from an individual record owner would be protected against the claim of the partnership that the land was actually partnership property and that the partner holding the title was not authorized to make the conveyance. It is usually considered advisable that record title to property acquired by a partnership be taken in the name of the partnership itself, rather than in individual partners' names.

§8.56. Interest of partner in partnership property

The interest of a partner in specific partnership property[91] is not subject to attachment or to levy under execution on a judgment that is based on a claim exclusively against the individual.[92] A judgment against an individual partner is not a lien on the partnership property or the partner's interest.

§8.57. Effect of death of a partner

On the death of a partner, his or her right in specific partnership property vests in the surviving partner or partners. The representative of the estate of the deceased partner or the heirs has no interest in the property of the partnership as such. The interest of the deceased partner in the partnership is a right to an accounting and a share of the profits and surplus. This interest is personal property, and should be inventoried as such in the estate. The real property of the partnership is not properly inventoried in the estate of the deceased partner. The surviving partner has the title to the partnership property and the exclusive right of management of the partnership and accounting to the estate of the deceased partner.

§8.58. Adoption of Uniform Limited Partnership Act

In the ordinary partnership, each partner is liable for all of the firm's debts. The theory is that a person should not be allowed to share in the profits of a partnership and at the same time stipulate for a limitation of liability. A need arose, however, for some method of investment and profit sharing without partnership liability if the contributor of the capital did not permit his name to be used, and if there was absence of power or control over the business, other than a right to information and inspection of accounts. This purpose was achieved by the adoption of the Uniform Limited Partnership Act.[93]

Limited partnerships. A limited partnership is defined in the code as a partnership composed of one or more general partners and one or more limited partners, the latter having no control over the business and only a limited liability for debts. The maximum liability of the limited partners for losses is fixed at the amount of their contribution to the capital of the partnership. This type of partnership is entirely the creature of statute, and all requirements of the statute must be strictly complied with, including at one time the recordation of a certificate of partnership. However, since 1984, the county recorder can only accept limited partnership documents that have first been filed or registered with the Secretary of State on specified forms.

In recent years, there has been increased concern for investor protection, and with the adoption of a revised limited partnership law in 1984, a limited partner, under prescribed conditions, can exercise an increased amount of control without losing the limitation of liability benefits. The reader should be aware of the changes under the new act, including the necessity of filing the Certificate of Limited Partnership with the Secretary of State.

Under the revised act, two writings are essential to the formation of a limited partnership. The first writing is the agreement by which all of the persons who are general partners and all of the persons who are limited partners agree to become partners and to constitute collectively a limited partnership for the purpose of conducting a business. Such agreement must be executed by all the general partners and by all the limited partners.

The second of the writings essential to the formation of a domestic limited partnership is a certificate of limited partnership executed and acknowledged by all of the general partners. This certificate is required to be filed in the office of the Secretary of State and its acceptance for filing by that office marks the beginning of the life of the limited partnership.[94]

A copy of the certificate, duly certified by the Secretary of State, is conclusive evidence that the limited partnership was duly formed and is prima facie evidence of its existence.[95]

Tax advantage of limited partnership. One of the main reasons a person becomes involved in a limited partnership is because of the depreciation benefits. However, numerous limited partnerships are improperly drafted and do not meet the standards necessary to gain these benefits. The Internal Revenue Service has taken the position that if a partnership has the appearance of a corporation, the limited partners do not receive the depreciation.[96] In other words, an entity will be taxable as a corporation if it has three of the following four characteristics: (1) limited liability; (2) centralized management; (3) continuity of life; and (4) free transferability of interest. Since tax aspects are of major concern, the rulings of the I.R.S. are of considered significance.[97]

§8.59. Syndicates

A syndicate may consist of many types of entities, but usually a limited partnership ownership is utilized. The subject of syndication is considered further in Chapter 13.

VI. JOINT VENTURES

§8.60. In general

A *joint venture* (or joint adventure) results from an agreement of two or more persons to conduct jointly a business enterprise for profit. It has been defined as a joint association of persons in a single enterprise for profit but falling short of a partnership.[98] The principal difference in purpose between a *joint venture* and a *partnership* is that the former is ordinarily formed to conduct a single enterprise, whereas the latter is used to carry on a general line of business. It depends on the actual intention of the parties.

§8.61. Formation

The persons who may associate to form a joint venture are considered to be the same as those who may become partners: individuals, corporations, and other associations. A partnership may be a joint venturer. There are no statutory or legal requirements or authorization for filing or recording any certificate or statement to establish the existence of a joint venture. However, if the association is doing business under a fictitious name, compliance with the provisions of the fictitious name statute is a prerequisite to maintaining an action in court on behalf of the association.

§8.62. Acquiring title

When title or any other interest in real property is to be acquired by joint venturers, the preferred methods for title insurance purposes of naming the grantee are either: (1) "A and B, doing business as the X Company, a joint venture"; or (2) "X

Company, a joint venture, composed of A and B." Other designations, such as "X Company, a joint venture," or merely "X Company," do not create or describe an entity capable of acquiring title. However, if inquiry discloses that a joint venture in fact exists and that title is in fact the joint venturers' property, and their identity is established, a conveyance by the joint venturers may be considered sufficient. Conveyances should be captioned as title is held, including or adding the names of the joint venturers, together with the name of the spouse of any married person who is a joint venturer and is not dealing with separate property.

Since 1970, if the members of the organization identify and designate their organization as an unincorporated association, and if this is confirmed by the contract binding on the members (Articles of Association), they may qualify as an association capable of acquiring and transferring title to property necessary and convenient for its business purposes and objectives in the name of the unincorporated association. (See later sections of this chapter for a discussion of unincorporated associations.)

VII. CORPORATIONS

§8.63. In general
A corporation is a "person" but is referred to as an artificial being, existing only in contemplation of law. It has only those rights given by its charter and the laws authorizing its formation. A corporation is treated as an entity distinct from its members, with rights and liabilities of its own. A corporation, whether domestic or foreign, may own real property in its corporate name.

§8.64. Types of corporations
A domestic corporation is one formed under the laws of California. All others are foreign corporations.

Corporations are also classified according to the purposes for which they are formed. Several types of corporations that will be encountered in real estate and title work follow:

1.   Ordinary business corporation, organized to conduct a business for profit.
2.   Nonprofit corporation, organized as a legal entity to conduct a business, but not primarily for profit.
3.   Public utility corporation, organized to serve the public for profit, and operated under the jurisdiction of the state Public Utilities Commission. Such corporations are subject to rate regulation by the Commission.
4.   Public corporation, agency, or political subdivision, formed by some public body and limited to acts that are expressly provided for in the law under which it is formed. A municipality is an example.
5.   Corporation sole, consisting of a single person and his successor in office, incorporated by law to permit ownership of property in perpetuity. An example is the Roman Catholic Archbishop of Los Angeles.
6.   Professional corporations created pursuant to provisions of the income tax laws for the purpose of setting up an approved pension or retirement plan. A professional corporation may consist of one person only, such as a doctor, a dentist, or a lawyer.
7.   Close corporation, effective January 1, 1977.[99] Most corporate formalities can be dispensed with by agreement among the shareholders.

§8.65. Distinctions between corporations and partnerships
The chief differences between a corporation and a partnership follow:

1.   A corporation must be organized in compliance with statutory requirements, and operates under the charter or permission of the state, whereas a partnership may be formed by mere association of the members in a business.

2. A corporation is a legal entity for all purposes, whereas a partnership is considered a legal entity for certain purposes only.

3. A corporation, except when limited by statute, has an unlimited existence that is unaffected by change in the personnel of its shareholders or officers, whereas a partnership usually has a limited term and the death of a partner may result in a dissolution of the partnership.

4. Shareholders of a corporation, as such, have practically no direct control over its affairs, whereas partners are mutual agents and each can act for the firm in most matters.

5. Holders of fully paid shares in a corporation are not liable for the debts of the corporation, whereas partners are individually liable for the firm debts, with exceptions to this rule applying in the case of a limited partnership.

§8.66. Formation of corporation
Effective January 1, 1977, the corporation laws were extensively changed. A corporation is now formed by the execution and filing of articles of incorporation in the office of the Secretary of State in Sacramento. The articles must now set forth (1) the name of the corporation; (2) a short and general purpose clause; (3) name and address of the initial agent of the corporation; (4) the share structure of the corporation; and (5) the signature and date of signing by one or more of the incorporators.[100] Within 90 days after incorporation, the initial statement[101] must be filed with the Secretary of State. The minimum number of persons required to execute articles of incorporation is one, and the minimum number of directors is also one under prescribed conditions.[102]

§8.67. Filing articles of incorporation
Although a copy of the articles, certified by the Secretary of State and bearing the endorsement of the date of filing in that office, formerly was required to be filed with the county clerk of the county in which the corporation has its principal place of business, and with the county clerk of every county in the state in which the corporation holds real property, that procedure is no longer necessary.

§8.68. Powers of corporations
Every domestic corporation is given the power by law (1) to acquire, hold, lease, encumber, convey, or otherwise dispose of real and personal property; (2) to borrow money and execute mortgages or trust deeds; and (3) to enter into any contracts, or do any acts incidental to the transaction of its business or expedient for the attainment of its corporate purposes.

§8.69. Exercise of corporate powers
The corporate powers of a corporation are exercised by or under the authority of its board of directors. A corporation must have as officers a president, secretary, and chief financial officer, chosen by the board of directors, and it may have any other officers deemed expedient. Any number of offices, including those of president and secretary, may be held by the same person, unless the articles or bylaws provide to the contrary.[103]

Powers of office. Officers have only such powers as are set forth in the bylaws and those given them by the directors, expressly or by acquiescence. For instance, the president does not have authority merely by virtue of his office to purchase, sell, encumber, or otherwise contract on behalf of the corporation with respect to property.

§8.70. Resolutions of board of directors
The authority of an officer to execute a conveyance or contract affecting real property of a corporation must ordinarily be evidenced by a resolution of the board of

directors. Evidence of the existence of a resolution authorizing a conveyance by a corporation is required, as a general rule, by a title company for title insurance purposes, but may be waived when: (1) the instrument is executed and acknowledged on behalf of the corporation by the president or vice president, and the secretary or assistant secretary; (2) the corporate seal is affixed; (3) the act is not a conveyance of all the assets or other prohibited transaction; and (4) the certificate of acknowledgment recites that the instrument is duly executed pursuant to authority duly given by the board of directors.[104]

§8.71. Corporate seal

A corporation may, but is not required to, adopt and use a seal. The seal must show the name of the corporation and the state and date of its incorporation. When an instrument executed by a corporation bears the corporate seal, such seal is prima facie evidence that such instrument is the act of the corporation, and that the instrument is executed by duly authorized officers or agents. It makes it eligible for recording and presumes consideration has been given. Generally, failure to affix the corporate seal does not affect the validity of an instrument.[105]

§8.72. Transfer of all assets

A corporation may not sell, lease, convey, exchange, transfer, or otherwise dispose of all or substantially all of its property and assets unless authorized by resolution of its board of directors and with the approval by vote or written consent of the shareholders entitled to exercise a majority of the voting power of the corporation.

§8.73. Certificate annexed to deed

Pursuant to provisions of the Corporations Code, any deed or instrument conveying any assets of a corporation may have annexed to it the certificate of the secretary or an assistant secretary, setting forth the resolution of the board of directors, and (1) stating that the property described in the conveyance is less than substantially all of the assets of the corporation, if such be the case; or (2) if such property constitutes all or substantially all of the assets of the corporation, stating the fact of approval thereof by the vote or written consent of the shareholders. Such certificate is prima facie evidence of the existence of the facts authorizing such conveyance, and conclusive evidence in favor of any innocent purchaser or encumbrancer for value.

§8.74. Real estate corporations

Real estate corporations were examined in Chapter 4. A real estate corporation is a permissible vehicle used by many brokers, who, under prescribed conditions, can have salespeople and nonlicensees as shareholders of the corporation.

§8.75. Corporations other than private business corporations

Instruments executed by corporations other than private business corporations, such as churches and other religious corporations, public utilities, mutual water companies, municipal corporations, school districts, and agencies or instrumentalities of the United States or of the State of California, are subject to various limitations, and conveyances by such types of corporations require special consideration for title insurance purposes.

§8.76. Foreign corporations

A foreign corporation may acquire, dispose of, or otherwise contract with respect to property in California, subject to limitations on its powers contained in its charter or articles of incorporation, and the law of the state of its incorporation. A *foreign corporation* is one not incorporated under the laws of California, that is, a corporation organized under the laws of another country or of a state other than California. Its organization, existence, and dissolution are controlled by the law of the place of its incorporation. The validity and effect of corporate acts performed in California may, however, be determined by the law of this state. A foreign corporation is covered by the California law governing domestic corporations only when such law expressly so provides.

Jurisdiction over foreign corporations. Because a state, under its police power, may exclude foreign corporations, other than corporations created by an act of Congress, from the right to do intrastate business, it may, accordingly, permit them to do business within its borders only on such conditions as it may see fit to impose. Doing *intrastate business* means entering into repeated and successive transactions in California other than in interstate or foreign commerce.

Requirements for doing business in the state. The filing of articles of a foreign corporation with the Secretary of State and the county clerk has become unnecessary. In lieu of such filing, a foreign corporation must secure from the Secretary of State a Certificate of Qualification to do intrastate business in California. Failure to obtain such certificate subjects the delinquent corporation to a fine and, until it complies with the requirement, prohibits it from maintaining any action or proceeding in any court in this state on any intrastate business so transacted. The Corporations Code now provides for the filing of incorporation papers of foreign corporations in the county clerk's office of any county in which such corporation held or holds real property, and when so filed these papers are conclusive evidence of the incorporation and powers of the corporation in favor of any bona fide purchaser or encumbrancer of such property for value, whether or not the corporation does business in this state.

Title company requirements. A title company, when insuring the acts of a foreign corporation, will ordinarily need to determine whether it has qualified to do business in California by complying with statutory requirements, and also whether the corporation was in existence when it acquired title and in good standing in its own state at the date of any conveyance or encumbrance executed by it.

VIII. UNINCORPORATED ASSOCIATIONS

§8.77. In general

In California it was a general rule for a number of years that an unincorporated association could not hold or convey property in the name of the association. The property of an unincorporated association was generally recognized as belonging to the members of the association, subject to the right of the trustees or governing committee or other board of control to make such use or disposition of the property as the laws of the association provide.

§8.78. Associations that may hold title

Since 1970, any form of association can now acquire title and convey in the name of the association.[106] This includes such associations as real estate syndicates and real estate trusts (REITs). The amendment further provides that the association may record, in any county in which it has an interest in real property, a statement listing the name of the association, its officers, and the title or capacity of its officers and other persons authorized on its behalf to execute conveyances of its real property. A conclusive presumption thereupon exists in favor of any bona fide purchaser or encumbrancer for value of the association's real property situated in the county where the statement is recorded.

IX. MULTIPLE HOUSING DEVELOPMENTS

§8.79. In general

The enactment of a condominium statute in California in 1963 stimulated considerable interest in multifamily housing. Although a condominium plan of ownership was adaptable under existing law, the adoption of the new condominium legislation eliminated certain problems that could arise, particularly as to separate tax assessments and compliance with zoning and other government regulations.

§8.80. Condominiums

Condominium is defined as an estate in real property consisting of an undivided interest in common in a portion of a parcel of real property together with a separate interest in space, called a unit, in a residential, industrial, or commercial building on the real property, such as an apartment, office, or store.[107] A condominium may include, in addition, a separate interest in other portions of the real property. Such estate (as it relates to the duration of its enjoyment) may be either a fee, a life estate, an estate for years, or any combination of the estates. A *unit* is defined as being the elements of a condominium that are not owned in common with the owners of other condominiums, and the term *common areas* is defined as the entire project excepting units that are granted or reserved.[108]

Before offering condominium or community apartment projects for sale, it was at one time necessary to obtain a permit from the Division of Corporations and a public report from the Department of Real Estate. Beginning in 1965, the need to obtain the approval of the Corporations Commission for a condominium plan of development was eliminated in most cases.

The condominium statute is comprehensive. It sets forth, among other things, the requirement that a description or survey map, diagrammatic floor plan, and certificate of consent to the plan be recorded. A declaration of restrictions that shall establish equitable servitudes inuring to and binding on the owners of all condominiums in the project must also be recorded. Such declaration may establish a management body to manage the project. If the project complies with the statutory requirements, each condominium owned in fee shall be separately assessed to the owner thereof, and the tax on each condominium constitutes a lien solely thereon. A separate loan and a separate policy of title insurance are obtainable on the individual units.

Although the act may have contemplated a high-rise structure, it has been extended to cover cluster-type and row housing. The act is adaptable not only to new structures, but also to apartment houses already constructed. Since the federal securities laws may be applicable to the offer and sale of condominium units when they are made in conjunction with an offer or agreement to perform or arrange certain rental or other services for the purchaser, the real estate licensee must act with extreme caution. If found to be applicable, the offering must comply with strict registration and prospectus requirements.

Time-sharing is a recent concept in condominium and other forms of multiple ownership. In essence, the time-sharing concept involves communal ownership with term occupancy for a specified time interval each year, a period commonly amounting to one to four weeks, that is geared to the actual use of the unit by the buyers at a fraction of the whole unit cost. This form of ownership is most commonly used for a condominium in a resort area.

§8.81. Stock cooperatives

Another method of ownership is the *corporate method* or *stock plan*, under which title to the entire property is vested in a corporation, and the individual "owners" are issued shares of stock in the owner corporation, which sets forth their rights of occupancy and use. This type is referred to as a co-op. The owner's rights are usually established by lease, by which the shareholder receives a right of exclusive occupancy of a portion, which is transferable only concurrently with the transfer of the share of stock held by the person having the right of occupancy.[109]

Still another method is the trust plan, under which title is vested in a trustee, and the individual owners are issued certificates of beneficial interest under the trust.

§8.82. Community apartment project (own-your-own)

The condominium concept of ownership basically involves a *divided interest* in real property as opposed to an *undivided interest*. The latter is the characteristic of the "own-your-own" apartment, in use before the advent of the condominium method, under which the individual apartment owners acquired a conveyance of an undivided fractional interest in the entire property, together with the exclusive right to use and occupy a designated apartment and garage, and the common right to use with others the common areas such as hallways, parkways, elevators, laundry rooms, and the like.

§8.83. Planned developments

Frequently called a planned unit development or townhouse development, this program is also referred to as a postage stamp subdivision. Maps of such projects, to which reference is made in conveyances, usually depict a series of small lots, frequently abutting one another in the manner of the row houses that are common in some eastern cities. Because of the small size of the lots and absence of side-yard setbacks and for other reasons, special zoning ordinances or variations under existing regulations are necessary for this type of project. The lots and the improvements thereon are in separate ownership, and separate tax assessments may be available. The lot owners may also obtain undivided interests in the commonly owned "green area" lots or recreational areas.

§8.84. Disclosure in resales

The owner of a condominium or a lot or unit in a planned unit development, community apartment, or stock cooperative must furnish to the prospective purchaser a copy of the declarations of restrictions, bylaws, and articles of incorporation affecting rights to the property offered for transfer. The material is to be furnished as soon as practicable before transfer of title or execution of an installment sale contract.[110]

The subdivision governing body (owners' association) is required to furnish the owner, within ten days of a written request, with a copy of the latest version of these documents and may charge a reasonable fee to cover the cost.

The enactment applies only to resales. Under existing law, in the initial transfer of the unit, the developer-subdivider is required to furnish to a prospective buyer a copy of the public report issued by the Department of Real Estate.

§8.85. Homeowners' associations

Homeowners' associations, whether incorporated or not, face significant problems not only in their formation but also in their general operation.[111] To assist in this regard, the Department of Real Estate has set up a homeowners' association (HOA) desk to assist associations in their function and to work with the developer. In addition, the Commissioner's Regulations provide in part that there must be "special procedures to assure that at least one representative of the governing body is elected solely by the votes of owners other than the subdivider at any election."[112]

An unincorporated association is entitled to recognition as a separate entity and, as a consequence, a member of such association may maintain a tort action against the association.[113] A covenant in a deed requiring membership in a homeowners' association is enforceable as a covenant running with the land.[114]

Assessments chargeable against the owners for maintenance and other expenses are a matter of concern. In one case, homeowners in a subdivision brought an action for declaratory and injunctive relief challenging an assessment against them by a corporation authorized to enforce the provisions of a recorded declaration of protective restrictions and to assess residents for expenses incurred in connection with such enforcement. The assessment in question was for the purpose of financing an action against the city to abate noise emanating from a nearby airport. The court held in favor of the homeowners, agreeing with their contention that the declaration permitted legal action to be taken by the corporation only against noise sources located within the boundaries of the subdivision.[115] On the other hand, a reasonable assessment for other legitimate purposes is permissible and necessary to assure maintenance and other payments, and becomes a lien on the debtor's unit.[116]

A homeowners' association can limit its liability to its homeowners in the covenants, conditions and restrictions (CC&R's) except for its own negligence, which shifts the burden on the homeowner. However, it does not relieve the association from its duty to maintain the common areas.[117] A HOA has the right to record a Notice of Violation even if the document does not precisely fit into the realm of documents usually recorded.[118]

Under a new section of the Civil Code it is now a requirement that if a homeowner questions the validity of the CC&Rs of a HOA, he must first request mediation or arbitration before filing suit in court.[119]

QUESTIONS

Matching Terms

a. Severalty
b. Joint tenancy
c. Separate property
d. Partnership
e. Corporation
f. Condominium
g. Own-your-own
h. Stock cooperative
i. Survivorship
j. Unity of time

1. Main characteristic of joint tenancy ownership.
2. An artificial being organized in accordance with statutory law, with limited liability.
3. Ownership by a corporation of a multiple housing project, with shareholders having right of possession of individual units.
4. Co-ownership of undivided interests in a multiple housing or other project.
5. Essential to the creation of a joint tenancy.
6. Ownership by two or more persons with right of survivorship.
7. A voluntary association of two or more persons to carry on a business for profit as co-owners.
8. Property acquired before marriage or after marriage by gift.
9. Individual ownership of units in a multiple housing or other project.
10. Ownership by one person alone.

True/False

T F 11. Any two or more persons can own property as tenants in common.
T F 12. Any two or more persons can own property as community property.
T F 13. Any two or more persons can own property in joint tenancy.
T F 14. All property acquired after marriage is community property.
T F 15. A corporation is treated as an entity distinct from its members, with rights and liabilities of its own.

T F 16. Title to real property may be acquired in the name of a partnership.
T F 17. One joint tenant cannot sever the joint tenancy without the consent of the other joint tenant.
T F 18. Basically, four unities are essential to the creation of a tenancy in common.
T F 19. It is generally considered advisable that a joint tenant make a will.
T F 20. Basically, a condominium form of ownership encompasses the individual ownership of separate areas of space in a structure.

Multiple Choice

21. Severalty ownership of real estate means
    a. Ownership by several persons.
    b. There are several ways to own property.
    c. Sole ownership by one person.
    d. Property has been severed in condemnation proceedings.
22. A man and a woman each acquired title to property while they were single. After marriage this property
    a. Becomes community property.
    b. Becomes jointly owned property.
    c. Continues to be separate property, absent an agreement to the contrary.
    d. Requires the consent of the other if either one chooses to sell.
23. Community property law in California originates from
    a. Common law.
    b. Municipal law.
    c. Federal law.
    d. Spanish and Mexican law.
24. If three persons own property as tenants in common

a. Each has the same right of possession.
b. Each automatically owns one-third interest.
c. Upon the death of one, each one's interest will vest in the survivors.
d. All of the above.

25. Either husband or wife has the right of testamentary disposition over the following amount of community property
    a. All.
    b. One-half.
    c. One-third.
    d. None.

26. Upon the death of a married woman intestate, her interest in community property
    a. All goes to her husband.
    b. Is divided equally between her husband and children.
    c. Is divided as follows: one-third to her husband and two-thirds to her children.
    d. Vests in her parents.

27. Upon the death of a married man intestate, leaving a wife and three children, his separate property
    a. All goes to his wife.
    b. Is divided equally between his wife and children.
    c. Is divided as follows: one-third to his wife and two-thirds to his children.
    d. Vests in his parents.

28. If a joint tenant is adjudged a bankrupt, his or her interest
    a. Vests in the other joint tenant.
    b. Vests in the trustee in bankruptcy unless exempt.
    c. Vests in the bankruptcy referee.
    d. Is not affected by the bankruptcy.

29. A brother and his married sister purchased a parcel of real property and acquired title as joint tenants. Later the sister conveyed her interest to her husband without the knowledge or consent of her brother. Her deed
    a. Has no effect on the joint tenancy.
    b. Terminates the joint tenancy.
    c. Is void since one joint tenant alone cannot deal with the property.
    d. Creates a joint tenancy between her husband and brother.

30. A domestic corporation is one
    a. Created solely to perform municipal functions.
    b. Created between husband and wife.
    c. Organized under the laws of a contiguous state.
    d. Formed under California law.

31. The unity of tenancy in common includes which of the following?
    a. Time.

b. Title.
c. Possession.
d. All of the above.

32. Separate property consists of property acquired
    a. Before marriage.
    b. After marriage by gift.
    c. After marriage by devise.
    d. By any of the above.

33. A corporation can hold title to real property with another person in all except which of the following ways?
    a. Tenants in common.
    b. Joint tenancy.
    c. Partnership.
    d. None of the above.

34. The following property is ordinarily not subject to testamentary disposition:
    a. Community property.
    b. Joint tenancy property.
    c. Fee simple title.
    d. Property owned as a tenant in common.

35. Certain unities are necessary to create a joint tenancy. The unities include
    a. Marriage.
    b. Interest.
    c. Relationship.
    d. Freehold estate.

36. Which of the following is not a legal way to take title to real property in California?
    a. Joint tenancy.
    b. Community property.
    c. Tenancy by the entireties.
    d. Tenancy in common.

37. A and B are joint tenants. A conveys a one-fourth interest to C. This changes the ownership as follows:
    a. A, B, and C own as tenants in common.
    b. A, B, and C own as joint tenants.
    c. A owns one-half, and B and C each own one-fourth, all as joint tenants.
    d. B and C own the title as joint tenants.

38. A, B, and C are joint tenants. A conveys his interest to D. This changes the ownership as follows:
    a. B, C, and D are joint tenants.
    b. B, C, and D are tenants in common, each as to one-third.
    c. D owns one-third as a tenant in common with B and C who own two-thirds as joint tenants.
    d. None of the above.

39. All partners in a limited partnership, as compared with a general partnership, have
    a. Unlimited liability.
    b. Limited liability.
    c. No liability.
    d. None of the above.

40. Strictly speaking, only a husband and wife (married to each other) may own property as
    a. Joint tenants.
    b. Community property.
    c. Tenants in common.
    d. None of the above.
41. Corporations can be classified as either
    a. Profit or nonprofit.
    b. Private or public.
    c. Domestic or foreign.
    d. Any of the above.
42. Condominium ownership in a structure ordinarily includes ownership of
    a. Undivided interests.
    b. Divided interests.
    c. Both a and b.
    d. Neither a nor b.
43. *Unit*, *project*, and *common areas* are terms ordinarily associated with
    a. Severalty ownership.
    b. Community property.
    c. Condominiums.
    d. All of the above.
44. Ownership of an "own-your-own" apartment is basically
    a. In divided interests.
    b. In undivided interests.
    c. A restraint on alienation.
    d. None of the above.
45. The unit of a condominium may be owned
    a. As community property only.
    b. Only in joint tenancy.
    c. Only in severalty.
    d. In any fee estate.
46. Title to an individually owned unit in a multifamily structure is the characteristic of
    a. An "own-your-own" apartment.
    b. A condominium.
    c. A stock cooperative.
    d. A royalty interest.
47. If a condominium complies with statutory requirements, a unit owner may obtain a
    a. Separate encumbrance.
    b. Separate tax bill.
    c. Separate policy of title insurance.
    d. All of the above.
48. A condominium may be
    a. Residential property.
    b. Industrial property.
    c. Commercial property.
    d. Any of the above.
49. Which of the following is obligated to pay the real property taxes on a condominium unit?
    a. Project owner.
    b. Unit owner.
    c. Board of Directors.
    d. Auditor for the condominium.
50. A condominium unit may consist of
    a. An apartment.
    b. An office.
    c. A store.
    d. Any of the above.

NOTES

1. *See* §6.44, *et seq.* Because the law may change depending on the political climate, the reader should check current legislation.
2. This, basically, is true since the 1976 and 1978 Tax Reform Acts.
3. C.C. 682.
4. Cal. Const., Article XIIIA,§61-67; Rev. & Tax. C. 480, *et seq.* A change from joint tenancy to community property or tenants in common, between husband and wife, will not cause a gift tax to occur. Whether this would be advisable depends upon a number of factors. *See* Rev. and Tax. C. 60, *et seq.*
5. C.C. 683.
6. If it involves real estate between a husband and wife, and there is not an equal contribution, only one-half of the value of the property is included in the estate of the first to die. *See* I.R.C. 2040(a) and (b) and I.R.C. 403(c) re estate tax.
7. Yeoman v. Sawyer (1950) 99 C.A.2d 43.
8. *See* Pro. C. 1557.1.
9. Siberell v. Siberell (1932) 214 C. 767; in re Marriage of Lucas (1980) 27 C.3d 808; Abbett Electric Corp. v. Storek (1994) 22 C.A. 4th 1460.
10. Delaroy v. Delaroy (1932) 216 C. 23; Tomaier v. Tomaier (1944) 23 C2d 754.
11. Fam. Code 850-853.
12. Fam. Code 760, 2580-2581, 2640. *See also* in re Marriage of Hilke (1992) 4 C. 4th 215; in re Marriage of Allen (1992) 8 C.A. 4th 1125.
13. I.R.C. 2040(b).
14. If an I.R.C. 2515 election is made (regarding no immediate payment of gift tax).
15. The Marital Deduction under I.R.C. 2056, as to separate property, is usually of benefit to husband and wife upon death of one and, therefore, this too must be considered in an overall estate plan.
16. Fam. Code 2580.
17. Hulse v. Lawson (1931) 212 C. 614.
18. Huber v. Huber (1946) 27 C.2d 784.
19. Kane v. Huntley Financial (1983) 146 C.A.3d 1092.
20. Hammond v. McArthur (1947) 30 C.2d 512.
21. Pro. C. 200-204.
22. Pro. C. 296, *et seq.*
23. Abbey v. Lord (1959) 168 C.A.2d 499.
24. *See* Pro. C. 258; C.C. 2224; Estate of Hart (1982) 135 C.A.3d 684. Presumably, there would be a different result if the spouse did not intentionally cause the death of the other spouse. Estate of Kramme (1978) 20 C.3d 567.
25. In re Estate of Galletto (1946) 75 C.A.2d 580.
26. C.C. 683.2; Meyer v. Wall (1969) 270 C.A.2d 24; Estate of Dean (1980) 109 C.A.3d 156. Such a transfer would not affect any homestead, however (Estate of Grigsby [1982] 134 C.A.3d 611).
27. Burke v. Stevens (1968) 264 C.A.2d 30.
28. Clark v. Carter (1968) 265 C.A.2d 291; C.C. 1039.
29. Riddle v. Harmon (1980) 102 C.A.3d 524, 530; C.C. 683.2. But *see* Estate of Levine (1981) 125 C.A.3d 701, and Re v. Re (1995) 39 C.A. 4th 91 (severance by unrecorded joint tenancy deed).
30. C.C. 683.2; Estate of Englund (1991) 233 C.A. 3d 1.

31. Tenhet v. Boswell (1976) 18 C.3d 150.
32. Smith v. Morton (1972) 29 C.A.3d 616.
33. County of Fresno v. Kohn (1962) 207 C.A.2d 213.
34. People v. Nogarr (1958) 164 C.A.2d 591.
35. Grothe v. Cortlandt Corp. (1992) 10 C.A. 4th 1313; Ziegler v. Bonnell (1942) 52 C.A.2d 217.
36. Teutenberg v. Schiller (1955) 138 C.A.2d 18.
37. Williams v. Williams (1967) 255 C.A.2d 648, 651.
38. Wardlow v. Pozzi (1959) 170 C.A.2d 208.
39. Estate of Gerbert (1979) 95 C.A. 3d 370; Estate of Layton (1996) 44 C.A. 4th 1337.
40. Estate of Asvitt (1979) 92 C.A.3d 348.
41. Chase v. Leiter (1950) 96 C.A.2d 439; *see also* Estate of Levine (1981) 125 C.A.3d 701.
42. Cole v. Cole (1956) 139 C.A.2d 691.
43. Pro. C. 201-205.
44. But *see* Kane v. Huntley Financial (1983) 146 C.A.3d 1092.
45. *See* Estate of Levine (1981) 125 C.A.3d 701. In re Marriage of Hilke (1992) 4 C. 4th 215; in re Marriage of Allen (1992) 8 C.A. 4th 1225.
46. Evid. C. 667; Pro. C. 1350, *et seq.*
47. *See* §8.2 and IRC 1014 and Regs. 1.1014-2(b).
48. C.C. 686. As to bankruptcy problems with tenants in common, *see* Wilson v. S.L. Rey Inc. (1993) 17 C.A. 4th 234.
49. Caito v. U. C. B. (1978) 20 C.3d 694, 705.
50. Estate of Nughes (1992) 5 C.A. 4th 1607.
51. Smith v. Goethe (1911) 159 C. 628.
52. Fam Code 750; *see also* Estate of Newman (1994) 25 C.A. 4th 472.
53. C.C. 687; *see also* §8.10 and Fam. Code 760.
54. In re Marriage of Brown (1976) 15 C.3d 838.
55. 10 U.S.C. 1408.
56. Fam. Code 770.
57. In re Marriage of Berquet (1976) 16 C.3d 583; Fam. Code 771.
58. Fam. Code 781; in re Marriage of Devlin (1982) 138 C.A.3d 804. *See* in re Marriage of Fisk (1992) 2 C.A. 4th 1698 re personal injury damages for worker's comp.
59. Fam. Code 721.
60. Fam. Code 1620, 3580; Prob. Code 141, 143, 145; Estate of Gibson (1990) 219 C.A. 3d 1486. *See also* Prob. Code 78 regarding annulments.
61. Fam. Code 1100, 1102; and *see* Fam. Code 751 re fiduciary relationship between husband and wife and required disclosures. *See also* Fam. Code 2100-2113; Hyatt v. Mabie (1994) 24 C.A. 4th 841.
62. Fam. Code 125.
63. Fam. Code 2251-2252.
64. Vallera v. Vallera (1943) 21 C.2d 681; Keene v. Keene (1962) 57 C.2d 657.
65. Marvin v. Marvin (1976) 18 C.3d 660; Friedman v. Friedman (1993) 20 C.A. 4th 876; *see also* Beckman v. Mayhew (1975) 49 C.A.3d 529.
66. Vieux v. Vieux (1926) 80 C.A. 222.
67. In re Marriage of Moore (1980) 28 C.3d 366, 373-374.
68. Fam. Code 2580-2581, 2640.
69. In re Marriage of Jafeman (1972) 29 C.A.3d 244. For a case involving improving community property with wife's separate funds, *see* in re Marriage of Sparks (1979) 97 C.A.3d 353; in re Marriage of Rives (1982) 130 C.A.3d 138.
70. Estate of Hirschberg (1964) 224 C.A.2d 449.
71. In re Marriage of Mix (1975) 14 C.3d 604.
72. In re Marriage of Bjornstad (1974) 38 C.A.3d 801, 806.
73. C.C.P. 872.210(b).
74. Fam. Code 2604.
75. Fam. Code 910-911; Oyakawa v. Gillett (1992) 8 C.A. 4th 628.
76. Fam. Code 913; Lease First v. Borelli (1993) 13 C.A. 4th Supp. 28; but *see* Gunn v. United Air Lines, Inc. (1982) 138 C.A.3d 765. However, under Fam. Code 914, separate property of one spouse is liable for the debts incurred by the other spouse for the necesseties of life.
77. Draeger v. Friedman, Sloan & Ross (1991) 54 C.3d 26.
78. Horton v. Horton (1953) 115 C.A.2d 360; *see also* Carlston v. Coss (1984) 153 C.A.3d 1069.
79. Pro. C. 13540.
80. Pro. C. 13650, *et seq.*
81. Pro. C. 13500.
82. Pro. C. 3000, *et seq.*
83. C.C. 682.
84. C.C. 684.
85. Corp. C. 15006.
86. Corp. C. 15002. A LLC (Limited Liability Company), which has many of the aspects of a corporation, should be discussed as well (Corp. Code 17000-17705).
87. B. & P. 17900, *et seq.*
88. Levelon Builders, Inc. v. Lynn (1961) 194 C.A.2d 657.
89. Corp. C. 15010.5.
90. Corp. C. 15025 (e).
91. Corp. C. 15024.
92. Evans v. Galardi (1976) 16 C.3d 300.
93. Corp. C. 15501, *et seq.*
94. 15621(b) Corp. C.
95. 15621(c) Corp. C.
96. I.R.C. 301.7701-2(a).
97. *California Lawyer* (May 1984), p. 13. *See also* Corp. Code 17000-17705 regarding LLC's.
98. Fitzgerald v. Provines (1951) 102 C.A.2d 529.
99. Corp. C. 158.
100. Corp. C. 200, 202.
101. Corp. C. 1502.
102. Corp. C. 212(a).
103. Corp. C. 312(a).
104. *See* Corp. C. 900.
105. Corp. C. 207(a).
106. Corp. C. 20002.
107. C.C. 783 For a case re keeping a pet in violation of the CC&R's, *see* Nahrstedt v. Lakeside Village Condo. Assn. (1992) 9 C.A. 4th 1.
108. *See* C.C. 1350, *et seq.* as amended, now known as the Davis-Stirling Common Interest Development Act.
109. Calif. Coastal Commission v. Superior Court (1980) 104 C.A.3d 146.
110. C.C. 1360.
111. *See* Comm. Regs. 2792, *et seq.*
112. Comm. Regs. 2792.8(10). *See also* "Why You Should Incorporate a Homeowners' Association," 3 *Real Estate Law Journal* 311 (Spring 1975). A homeowners' association has standing to sue the developer for common damages without joining the individual owners (C.C.P. 374). Also, a homeowners' association may sue for enforcement of governing documents without joining individual owners.
113. White v. Cox (1971) 17 C.A.3d 824.
114. Anthony v. Brea Glenbrook Club (1976) 58 C.A.3d 506.
115. Spitser v. Kentwood Home Guardians (1972) 24 C.A.3d 215.
116. B. & P. 11003.3.
117. *See* Franklin v. Marie Antoinette Condo Owners Assoc. (1993) 19 C.A. 4th 824 re suit against HOA; Nahrstedt v. Lakeside Village Condo Assn. (1992) 20 C.A. 4th 539.
118. California Riviera HOA v. Superior Court (1994) 24 C.A. 4th 146 (HOA has the right to record a violation of the CC&R's against an owner's property); Park Place Estates HOA v. Nalser (1994) 29 C.A. 4th 427 re owner does not have right to set off against HOA assessment charge placed against the homeowner.
119. C.C. 1354.

Creation and Enforcement of Security Devices, Part I

I. INTRODUCTION

§9.1. In general

In California three principal types of instruments are employed to create a lien on real property as security for the payment of money or for the performance of some other obligation: (1) mortgages; (2) mortgages with power of sale; and (3) deeds of trust (or trust deeds, as they are commonly referred to). Occasionally, the long-term contract of sale has been utilized as a security instrument.

§9.2. Trust deeds prevalent in California

The trust deed is the type of real estate security transaction most widely used in this state, the real estate mortgage being little used by comparison. Nonetheless, consideration should be given to the nature and characteristics of mortgages, because the courts, in passing on the validity and effect of trust deeds, have drawn on the principles applying to mortgages as well as the principles applying to trusts, and features of each are contained in a trust deed.

§9.3. Lien theory

A *lien* is a charge, i.e., a financial burden, imposed on specific property by which it is made security for the performance of an act, usually the payment of money. Liens on real property may be created by a voluntary act of the landowner. For example, a trust deed or mortgage is a voluntary lien.

Involuntary liens, such as tax or judgment liens recorded by the creditor of the landowner, are discussed in Chapter 11. A *trust deed* is created to protect and secure a lender (beneficiary) against the possibility of the borrower (trustor) not paying the debt (promissory note) when due. To assure the lender, the trustor generally pledges his interest in the real estate to the beneficiary, up to the amount of the debt. The security (trust deed) and obligation (promissory note) are two separate things, although construed together. In other words, the *trust deed* is the security for the note, while the *note* is the underlying contract.

§9.4. Promissory note

A *promissory note* is a written instrument promising to repay a loan in accordance with stipulated terms. The note establishes a period of liability for payment on the part of the maker. A promissory note is generally a negotiable instrument.

Parties. The *payor* (also called maker, or trustor if secured by a trust deed) is the one who pays; the *payee* is the person who receives the payment.

Types of notes. The two types of notes considered are straight and installment notes. A *straight note* is one customarily used when interest only is paid at prescribed intervals, with the full amount of principal payable at the end of the term. An *installment note* is one on which periodic payments of both principal and interest are made. A form of installment note is illustrated by Figure 9-1. If the periodic payments are insufficient to amortize the note (i.e., when the installment payments do not pay off the loan in full by the due date), a "balloon payment" (lump sum) will be due at the end of the term.

Balloon payment. There are certain prohibitions against balloon payments. Essentially, installment notes with a term of less than three years must contain substantially equal installment payments, with no payment (including the final one) to be greater than twice the amount of the smallest installment. The latter requirement also applies to installment loans with a term of six years or less on an owner-occupied dwelling.[1] Effective January 1, 1984, in order to foreclose for non-payment when a trust deed contains a balloon payment, at least 90 days' notice must be given to the trustor.[2] These requirements do not apply to

DO NOT DESTROY THIS NOTE: When paid, this note, with Deed of Trust securing same, must be surrendered to Trustee for cancellation before reconveyance will be made.

NOTE SECURED BY DEED OF TRUST
(INSTALLMENT - INTEREST INCLUDED)

$ _____   _____, California_____, 19_____

In installments as herein stated, for value received, I promise to pay to_____

_____

_____

_____

_____

_____

_____or order

at_____the principal sum of

_____

_____dollars

with interest from_____ on unpaid principal at the rate of _____per cent

per annum; principal and interest payable in installments of_____

_____dollars or more on the_____day of

each_____month, beginning on the_____ day of _____, 19____

and continuing until

Each payment shall be credited first on interest then due; and the remainder on principal, and the interest shall thereupon cease upon the principal so credited. Should default be made in payment of any installment of principal and interest, the whole sum of principal and interest shall, at the option of the holder of this note, become immediately due. Principal and interest payable in lawful money of the United States. If action be instituted on this note, the undersigned promise_____to pay such sum as the Court may adjudge as attorney's fees. This note is secured by a DEED OF TRUST to **CHICAGO TITLE COMPANY, a California corporation, as Trustee.**

---   ---

---   ---

---   ---

THIS FORM FURNISHED BY CHICAGO TITLE COMPANY

FIGURE 9–1

Installment Note.

1. Institutional lenders

2. Purchase money trust deeds given back to the seller

3. First trust deeds of $20,000 or more, or second trust deeds of $10,000 or more[3]

§9.5. Negotiable instrument

A *negotiable instrument* is essentially a written *promise* or *order* to pay money. It can be in the form of a note, check, draft, or bill of exchange. Bank checks are the most common variety of negotiable instrument. A *check* is an *order* on a third party (the bank) to pay money to the person entitled to receive it, either the payee or an endorsee. Checks and drafts are referred to as three-party paper, whereas a note is two-party paper.

Negotiable instruments are freely transferable in commerce. If an instrument qualifies as a "negotiable instrument," certain benefits inure in favor of a subsequent holder, in that certain defenses that could be asserted against the original payee, such as fraud in the inducement or misrepresentation of facts, cannot be asserted against a *holder in due course.*

§9.6. Requirements for negotiability

To be regarded as a negotiable instrument,[4] the note or other document must conform strictly to the following requirements; that is, it must be

1. An unconditional promise

2. In writing

3. Made by one person to another

4. Agreeing to pay on demand or at a fixed or determinable future time

5. To order or to bearer

6. A sum certain in money

7. Signed by the maker

All the elements listed must be present if the instrument is to qualify as *negotiable.* If any of the listed elements is missing, the document may nonetheless be valid, but it will be transferable like any ordinary contract right. As such, the transferee receives no more than the transferor had, and defenses that were good against the original payee are good as against the assignees.

§9.7. Holder in due course

If the document is a valid negotiable instrument, then it may be possible that a transferee may receive more than the transferor had. A third-party transferee enjoys a favored position if he takes the note as a *holder in due course.*[5] A person is a holder in due course if he has taken a negotiable instrument under the following conditions:

1. In good faith

2. For a valuable consideration

3. Without notice of any defects

4. The note appears valid on its face

Defenses. The maker cannot use any of the following commonly recognized *personal defenses*[6] to refuse payment as against a holder in due course, but may use them against the original payee:

1. Lack or failure of consideration

2. Prior payment or cancellation

3. Fraud in the inducement

4. Setoff

5. Illegality that renders the obligation voidable only

6. Nondelivery

The following real defenses[7] are good against the payee, holder in due course, or anyone:

1. Forgery

2. Incapacity

3. Illegality that renders the obligation void

4. Material alterations

The negotiability of a promissory note is not affected by the fact that it is secured by a mortgage or a trust deed. Similarly, the negotiability of the note is not affected by the inclusion of a clause adding attorney's fees or court costs in the event litigation becomes necessary to collect, or by inclusion of an *acceleration clause* that provides that default in one of a series of payments makes the entire amount immediately due at the election of the holder.

II. TRUST DEEDS COMPARED WITH OTHER INSTRUMENTS

§9.8. Mortgage defined

A *mortgage* is a contract by which specific property is hypothecated for the performance of an act, without the necessity for a change of possession.[8] To *hypothecate* means to pledge a thing without delivering the possession of it to the pledgee. *Hypothecation* is a term of the civil law and, unlike a *pawn*, is that kind of pledge in which the possession of the thing pledged remains with the debtor.

In California the mortgage, by force of statute, creates merely a lien, with the legal title and right to possession remaining in the debtor until divested by foreclosure proceedings. The equitable right of redemption has been supplanted by a statutory right of redemption for a fixed period after sale of the mortgaged land under foreclosure proceedings.[9]

§9.9. Trust deed defined

A *trust deed* is a conveyance of property to an individual or a corporation *as trustee*, for the purpose of securing a debt or other obligation, with a power of sale in the trustee, exercisable on default, with the proceeds of the sale to be applied in payment of the obligation. Although title is conveyed to the trustee, it is a bare (or naked) title since the conveyance is for security purposes only; for all practical purposes, title remains in the trustor. The trustee not only has the power of sale, exercisable under prescribed conditions, but also the power to reconvey the property to the owner when the debt is paid or the obligation performed.

§9.10. Parties

Basically, both *mortgages* and *trust deeds* are forms of transactions involving land as security, but there are several distinguishing characteristics of each. As to *parties*, in a mortgage there are two parties, whereas in a trust deed there are usually three parties. The parties to a mortgage are the mortgagor (debtor) and the mortgagee (creditor). The parties to a trust deed are the trustor (debtor), the trustee, and the beneficiary (creditor).

§9.11. Title of debtor

In the case of a mortgage, title to the mortgaged property remains in the mortgagor, but subject to the lien in favor of the mortgagee. The mortgagor's title may be divested by foreclosure proceedings if the debt is not paid, but until such event occurs, the mortgagor has title. In the case of a trust deed, title passes to the trustee and remains there until the debt is paid or until transferred by the trustee to a purchaser under a sale based on a default. In the event of a default by the trustor (debtor), the trustee has the power to convey the legal title to a purchaser at a foreclosure sale. The trustee takes only such title as is necessary to the execution of the trust. Until the necessity of a sale actually arises, the trustee's title lies dormant. In the meantime, the trustor, like a mortgagor, may convey or encumber the property and exercise all the other usual rights of an owner subject, of course, to the effect of the encumbrance.

§9.12. Statute of Limitations

As to the Statute of Limitations, different rules apply to mortgages and to trust deeds. An action to foreclose a mortgage is barred when the Statute of Limitations has run on the obligation secured. In the case of a deed of trust, the Statute of Limitations is not a bar to a *trustee's sale* proceedings, which may be undertaken regardless of whether the statute has run on the principal obligation. The trustee has title, and for a long period of time the rule was followed that the trustee could always sell, with no limitation on the time when a default must be declared. However, regarding the laws relating to marketable titles, the California legislature has prescribed a procedure under which the lien of so-called ancient mortgages, trust deeds, and other real property security interests automatically expired on and after January 1, 1988.[10] Such expiration of the lien has the same effect as a recorded certificate of satisfaction, reconveyance, release, or other discharge of the security interest.

§9.13. Remedies

As to applicable remedies, there are material differences. Foreclosure by court proceedings is the only remedy for enforcement of the terms of an ordinary mortgage. Under a trust deed, alternative remedies are available, either (1) foreclosure by court proceedings, or (2) trustee's sale proceedings.

§9.14. Redemption rights

There are also differences with respect to the right of redemption and as to deficiency judgments. After foreclosure sale under a mortgage, the mortgagor has a statutory right to redeem within a prescribed period of time. In the case of a trust deed, although the owner has a right of reinstatement for a prescribed period before the sale, there is no right of redemption after a trustee's sale.

§9.15. Deficiency judgments

When a mortgage is foreclosed, a deficiency judgment may be entered unless the mortgage is a purchase money mortgage and the deficiency limitations do not apply.[11] There is no provision for a deficiency judgment after a trustee's sale under a trust deed. If a deficiency judgment is desired, it is necessary to foreclose the trust deed like a mortgage. An exception to this rule might apply, however, in the event of waste or conversion by the trustor that impairs the security.[12] However, a deficiency judgment can be had even on a purchase money trust deed if the rights of the United States are affected when, for instance, an FHA or VA loan is involved.[13]

§9.16. Mortgages with power of sale

The addition to a conventional mortgage with a power of sale whereby, on default, the mortgagee may effect a sale of the property without the necessity of judicial proceedings does not change its essential character from that of a lien. This power of sale in the mortgagee is similar to the exercise of a power of attorney, and in the absence of express provision in the mortgage, the mortgagee must execute his deed to the purchaser, after sale under the power, in the name of the mortgagor by himself as attorney-in-fact or as donee of the power. When the debt is outlawed by lapse of time, the power of sale under a mortgage is lost. This is a major difference between a mortgage with power of sale and a trust deed, because under the latter, the power of sale does not outlaw and can be undertaken even though judicial enforcement of the debt and security is barred, subject, however, to the prescribed limitations set forth in the Civil Code (see § 9.12).

§9.17. Extinguishment of lien

Pursuant to the provisions of the Civil Code, the lien of a mortgage is extinguished by lapse of the time within which an action can be brought on the obligation.[14] The only action that can be brought on an obligation secured by a mortgage is an action for foreclosure of the mortgage,[15] and when recourse to judicial foreclosure is barred by lapse of time, the lien ceases. However, it is still a matter of record until a release is recorded or a decree quieting title is obtained and recorded. That the debt is outlawed will not necessarily entitle the mortgagor or his successor to a quiet title decree against the holder of the obligation. A quiet title action is a proceeding in equity, and it is a principle of equity that the obligor or his successors in interest cannot obtain relief by clearing the property of such "outlawed" mortgage without "doing equity," i.e., paying the debt as a condition for obtaining a decree quieting title. As to the statute of limitations running on a trust deed, the beneficiary cannot collect by a judicial foreclosure. However, as in the case of a mortgage, the trustor cannot quiet title without discharging the debt, although he is entitled to remain in possession.[16]

§9.18. Comparison with contract of sale

The contract of sale, or installment land contract, is sometimes used in real estate transactions, but in the past was not considered to be a security instrument in the conventional sense. When a contract of sale is used, legal title to the real property is retained by the seller until the buyer (debtor) has paid the purchase price in accordance with the terms of the contract, at which time he or she is entitled to a conveyance of the property by deed. Contracts of sale and their presently limited use are discussed further in Chapter 10.

§9.19. Absolute deed intended as security

Sometimes parties intend to create a security device, but actually convey the property to the creditor by deed. The intent of the parties is determined at the time the transaction begins.[17] To show the intent, the courts will allow a broad exception to the parol evidence rule.[18]

EXAMPLE In one case, the court laid down the following factors to consider: (1) the continued existence of a debt or a promise to pay; (2) the fact that the amount to be paid for reconveyance is to be the same as the amount to be paid for the original deed; (3) a great inequality between the value of the property conveyed and the price alleged to have been paid for it; (4) the grantor remains in possession with the right to reconveyance on the payment of the debt; and (5) a declaration of the grantee that he would not take the mortgage.[19] If these criteria are not met, an actual conveyance may be established.[20]

III. NATURE AND CHARACTERISTICS OF A TRUST DEED

§9.20. In general

The trust deed is considered somewhat of an anomaly in the California legal system. Although California, at an early date, adopted the *lien theory* as to mortgages, it adopted the *title theory* as to deeds of trust. The title theory in reference to trust deeds is that bare legal title to the property is conveyed to the trustee, who retains title until the debt is satisfied or the property is sold to enforce payment of the obligation secured thereby. Most states regard trust deeds simply as mortgages with power of sale.

The *trust deed* is a more flexible security device than the *mortgage*, and the rules for foreclosure by trustee's sale have been firmly established, with the result that the trust deed is widely used in California in preference to the mortgage.

§9.21. Application of recording laws

The recording statutes apply to trust deeds the same as they do to a conveyance by deed. Before a trust deed can be recorded, it must be executed and acknowledged by the trustor or proved as required by law, and it must describe the property with common certainty. A trust deed, like a deed, should be filed for record with the recorder of the county in which the property is situated. On recordation, it obtains the same priority and protection from recordings as a deed.

The Government Code requires, as a condition to acceptance for recording, that every trust deed or mortgage with power of sale specify the address of one trustor or mortgagor and contain a request that a copy of any notice of default and any notice of sale be mailed to such trustor or mortgagor at such address.[21]

§9.22. Priority of trust deed

As a general rule, a trust deed, when duly recorded, is prior to any interest or lien subsequently attaching. It is also prior to any interest or lien previously created but not then of record unless the beneficiary had knowledge thereof at the time the trust deed was recorded. A trust deed does not have priority over the lien of federal, state, or local taxes or assessments if by statute such liens are accorded preference over private rights. Also, under some circumstances a trust deed may be inferior to a subsequently recorded mechanic's lien.[22]

§9.23. Form of trust deed

There is no standard form of trust deed prescribed by statute in California. However, standardized forms have been prescribed for FHA purposes, and through the efforts of the large lending institutions, basic forms have been adopted that are more or less standardized and are in general use by lenders. These printed forms contain substantially the same general provisions that the laws of this state, court decisions, and experience have shown to be essential for the creation of a valid and practical deed of trust. Figure 9-2 is a typical short form of trust deed used in many parts of California.

§9.24. Debt or obligation

The trust deed is an incident of the debt or obligation secured, and there can be no trust deed without such debt or obligation. When the obligation is satisfied, the trust deed ceases to be more than a cloud on the title, and the discharge of the trust deed of record can be compelled.[23]

§9.25. Obligation evidenced by promissory note

The obligation secured by a trust deed, when consisting of a debt of fixed amount, is ordinarily evidenced by a promissory note (or notes), payable to the lender or order. The note or notes are usually negotiable in form. If negotiable, they gain certain advantages under the Negotiable Instruments Law.

§9.26. Nature of obligation

It is not essential that the trust deed contain a full description of the obligation; it is necessary only that there be an obligation in fact, and that this be referred to in the trust deed sufficiently to put third persons on inquiry. The obligation may be a debt of fixed amount then owing to the beneficiary, or all existing indebtedness

RECORDING REQUESTED BY

AND WHEN RECORDED MAIL TO

Name
Street
Address
City &
State

SPACE ABOVE THIS LINE FOR RECORDER'S USE

SHORT FORM DEED OF TRUST AND ASSIGNMENT OF RENTS (CORPORATION)

THIS DEED OF TRUST made this _____ day of _____ , between

a corporation organized under the laws of the State of _____ , herein called TRUSTOR,
whose address is _____

(number and street) _____ (city) _____ (state) _____ (zip)

_____ , herein called TRUSTEE, and

_____ , herein called Beneficiary,

WITNESSETH: That Trustor IRREVOCABLY GRANTS, TRANSFERS AND ASSIGNS to TRUSTEE IN TRUST, WITH POWER OF SALE, that property in _____ County, California, described as:

TOGETHER WITH the rents, issues and profits thereof, SUBJECT, HOWEVER, to the right, power and authority given to and conferred upon Beneficiary by paragraph (10) of the provisions incorporated herein by reference to collect and apply such rents, issues and profits.

FOR THE PURPOSE OF SECURING: 1. Performance of each agreement of Trustor incorporated by reference or contained herein. 2. Payment of the indebtedness evidenced by one promissory note of even date herewith, and any extension or renewal thereof, in the principal sum of $_____ executed by Trustor in favor of Beneficiary or order. 3. Payment of such further sums as the then record owner of said property hereafter may borrow from Beneficiary, when evidenced by another note (or notes) reciting it is so secured.

TO PROTECT THE SECURITY OF THIS DEED OF TRUST TRUSTOR AGREES: By the execution and delivery of this Deed of Trust and the note secured hereby, that provisions (1) to (14), inclusive, of the fictitious deed of trust recorded in Santa Barbara County and Sonoma County October 18, 1961, and in all other counties October 23, 1961, in the book and at the page of Official Records in the office of the county recorder of the county where said property is located, noted below opposite the name of such county, viz:

COUNTY	BOOK	PAGE	COUNTY	BOOK	PAGE	COUNTY	BOOK	PAGE	COUNTY	BOOK	PAGE
Alameda	435	684	Kings	792	833	Placer	895	301	Sierra	29	335
Alpine	1	250	Lake	362	39	Plumas	151	5	Siskiyou	468	181
Amador	104	348	Lassen	171	471	Riverside	3005	523	Solano	1105	182
Butte	1145	1	Los Angeles	T2055	899	Sacramento	4331	62	Sonoma	1851	689
Calaveras	145	152	Madera	810	170	San Benito	271	383	Stanislaus	1715	456
Colusa	296	617	Marin	1508	339	San Bernardino	5567	61	Sutter	572	297
Contra Costa	3978	47	Mariposa	77	292	San Francisco	A332	905	Tehama	401	289
Del Norte	78	414	Mendocino	579	530	San Joaquin	2470	311	Trinity	93	366
El Dorado	568	456	Merced	1547	538	San Luis Obispo	1151	12	Tulare	2294	275
Fresno	4626	572	Modoc	184	851	San Mateo	4078	420	Tuolumne	135	47
Glenn	422	184	Mono	52	429	Santa Barbara	1878	860	Ventura	2062	386
Humboldt	657	527	Monterey	2194	538	Santa Clara	5336	341	Yolo	653	245
Imperial	1091	501	Napa	639	86	Santa Cruz	1431	494	Yuba	334	486
Inyo	147	598	Nevada	305	320	Shasta	684	528			
Kern	3427	60	Orange	5889	611	San Diego	Series 2 Book 1961, Page 183887				

(which provisions, identical in all counties, are printed on the reverse hereof) hereby are adopted and incorporated herein and made a part hereof as fully as though set forth herein at length; that he will observe and perform said provisions; and that the references to property, obligations, and parties in said provisions shall be construed to refer to the property, obligations, and parties set forth in this Deed of Trust.

The undersigned Trustor requests that a copy of any Notice of Default and of any Notice of Sale hereunder be mailed to him at his address hereinbefore set forth.

STATE OF CALIFORNIA } SS
COUNTY OF _____

On _____
before me, the undersigned, a Notary Public in and for said State, personally appeared _____

personally known to me or proved to me on the basis of satisfactory evidence to be the person who executed the within instrument as the _____ President
and _____
personally known to me or proved to me on the basis of satisfactory evidence to be the person who executed the within instrument as the _____ Secretary
of the Corporation that executed the within instrument and acknowledged to me that such corporation executed the within instrument pursuant to its by-laws or a resolution of its board of directors.

WITNESS my hand and official seal

Signature _____

Signature of Trustor

_____ (a corporation)

By _____ (President)

By _____ (Secretary)

(This area for official notarial seal)

Title Order No. _____ Escrow or Loan No _____

TO 1938 1 CA (8-83) (OPEN END)

CAT NO. NN01062

FIGURE 9–2

A short form of trust deed.

of the trustor to the beneficiary, or either of these and additionally all sums afterward advanced by the beneficiary to the trustor, either under an optional advance clause or under an obligatory advance clause (open-ended trust deed).

§9.27. Effect of payments

Unless the trust deed is expressly made security for future indebtedness or advances, it secures only the existing obligation, and once the obligation so secured is reduced, a further loan may not be made on the security of the trust deed, although within the amount of such reduction. As payments are made on the obligation, the security is automatically satisfied and cannot be revived or extended to cover additional loans unless the original agreement so provides, or unless the agreement is so amended. Intervening encumbrancers, however, are not bound by a subsequent amendment unless they consent thereto.

§9.28. Future advances

If a trust deed contains a future advance clause, its priority as to additional advances depends on whether the advances are *obligatory* or *optional*. As a general rule, to the extent that the trust deed expressly secures future advances, it takes the priority of its original date of recording as against liens arising between such date and the date of the additional advance. This general rule applies if such advances are obligatory, that is, if the beneficiary cannot properly refuse to make them on demand of the trustor. In this category are successive advances under a building loan that the beneficiary has agreed to make as the building progresses.[24] This rule now applies in the case of intervening United States tax liens. By statutory amendment in 1966, the lien of a previously recorded trust deed securing a construction loan may extend its priority to additional advances made subsequent to the filing of a federal tax lien.

Obligatory advances. An obligatory advance clause requires the lender to make advances, usually as a building progresses in construction. Under this situation, even though the entire amount has not been given to the trustor, any subsequent lien placed on the property is junior in nature.

EXAMPLE | Assume an owner-builder obtains a construction loan for $100,000 containing an obligatory advance clause. At a given point in time the builder has used only $75,000, but has borrowed an additional $10,000 from an outside source. He then receives the remaining $25,000 from the first loan. Because of unforeseen circumstances, the project fails, the builder does not make payments on the respective loans, and the building is worth only $100,000. Who has priority? Since the primary lender's trust deed contained an obligatory advance clause, that lender will be entitled to receive first the amounts due it.

An obligatory advance clause typically reads as follows:

> *In addition to the foregoing sum, this deed of trust also secures payment of such further sums, not to exceed..., which the beneficiary shall advance to the trustor upon request, to be evidenced by another note (or notes) reciting it is so secured.*

Optional advances. Except as to a United States tax lien, the general rule as to priority also applies when the advances are optional, that is, discretionary with the beneficiary, provided the beneficiary does not have *actual knowledge* of intervening rights of third parties at the time when he makes an additional advance. This knowledge of intervening rights is something more than the constructive notice afforded by the recording laws; it must be actual notice, or knowledge of facts sufficient to put a prudent person on inquiry.[25]

An optional advance clause typically reads as follows:

In addition to the foregoing sum, this trust deed also secures payment of such further sums as the beneficiary may lend to the trustor, when evidenced by another note (or notes) reciting it is so secured.

When junior lienholders should give notice. A junior encumbrancer, *before* making a loan, should inquire of the beneficiary under a prior trust deed containing an optional advance whether additional advances have been made. If advances have not been made and a new loan is thereupon made, the new lender should immediately give notice to the beneficiary under the prior trust deed of the new loan to be secured by a junior lien on the property. Thereafter, any further optional advances under the prior trust deed will be junior to the rights of such intervening lender. It is highly advisable to obtain a beneficiary statement before making a junior loan to be sure of the actual amount owed on the senior lien.

Advances to protect security. The types of advances referred to above—optional and obligatory—constitute additional loans, and should be distinguished from advances made under the terms and provisions of the trust deed to protect the security, such as payment of real property taxes, insurance premiums, or sums due under prior encumbrances. Such types of advances are normally entitled to the same priority as the trust deed under which such payments are made.

§9.29. "Dragnet" clause

Many trust deeds contain a "dragnet" clause in small print on the reverse side or in another recorded instrument. Such a provision provides that the trust deed secures the particular debt and all other debts of the trustor, whether they presently exist or are subsequent to the trust deed.[26] Such a clause is an "adhesion" contract; therefore the courts will carefully examine the facts to determine the intent of the parties before it will be enforced against the debtor. If the trustor is aware of the clause, he may be bound by it, but in the event of a conflict, the burden is placed on the lender to show clearly that the parties intended any other loans to be included.[27]

§9.30. Personal property security agreements

Personal property, as well as real property, may be mortgaged. Previously, a mortgage of personal property was called a chattel mortgage, and for the protection of creditors of the mortgagor, certain statutory requirements peculiar thereto had to be observed. Such a mortgage had to be in writing, executed and acknowledged in like manner as a grant of real property; had to be clearly entitled, on its face, and apart from and preceding all other terms of the mortgage, *a mortgage of crops and/or chattels*, as the case may be; had to be promptly recorded; and had to be rerecorded within four years of the original recording or a subsequent rerecording. Since January 1, 1965, a personal property security agreement has been used instead of a chattel mortgage, with a financing statement to be recorded or filed.[28]

§9.31. Obligations secured by real and personal property

Sometimes an obligation is secured by both real and personal property, in which case the lender should take a trust deed on the real property and a security instrument on the personal property, with a recital in each that it is also secured by the other; that in the event of default, the lender may resort to both, concurrently or in such order or manner as he may elect; and that the application of the proceeds of enforcement of one will not cure existing defaults or impair any pending proceedings for the enforcement of the other. However, when there is a single debt secured by both personal property and real estate and the creditor elects to judicially foreclose only on the personal property, the creditor loses the security interest in the real estate against all parties and cannot foreclose on the real property.[29]

§9.32. After-acquired title

The after-acquired title doctrine, which was first encountered in Chapter 7 in connection with deeds, also applies to trust deeds. Thus, after-acquired title of a trustor inures to the benefit of the beneficiary as security for the debt.[30] For example, a trust deed on land will cover permanent improvements constructed afterward on the property. Also, a trust deed by its terms may be made to cover after-acquired property as well as that specifically described. The so-called *county indigent mortgage* is an example of a mortgage expressly covering after-acquired property.

§9.33. Priority as to after-acquired property

A provision extending the lien of the trust deed to after-acquired property is valid and binding on the trustor and on third parties dealing with the property, after its acquisition, with knowledge of such trust deed. However, the recordation of the trust deed before the date of acquisition of title by the trustor will not constitute constructive notice to innocent purchasers or lenders dealing with the trustor in good faith and for value, since the trust deed is not in the trustor's chain of title. Persons dealing on the strength of the record title are not obligated to run the records as to the party they are dealing with before the date of acquisition of title by the latter on the chance that he might have encumbered the property before the date he acquired it.[31]

§9.34. Priority of purchase money trust deed

Under the provisions of the Civil Code,[32] a trust deed given by the purchaser of real property to secure any portion of the purchase price of the property covered thereby obtains a special priority: It is superior to all other liens created against the purchaser, subject to the operation of the recording laws. The deed and the trust deed back are considered as contemporaneous acts, and no lien or charge then existing against the purchaser can be prior to the rights of the vendor under his purchase money trust deed. Thus, the lien of a previously recorded abstract of judgment against the purchaser is subordinate to a purchase money trust deed.[33] Also, when a third party advances the purchase money with the understanding that the advance will be secured by the property, his security comes within the rule and will be accorded that same priority.[34] However, this is but a rule of law. In an actual situation in which a buyer has an abstract of judgment recorded against him or her, it may be necessary to obtain a subordination of the judgment lien to the lien of the purchase money trust deed in order to have priority established as a matter of record, or based on a judicial determination that the trust deed is, in fact, a purchase money encumbrance.

§9.35. More than one purchase money encumbrance may exist

There may be more than one purchase money encumbrance on the same property at a time. This may occur in cases when a third party advances funds to the buyer for the purpose of completing the purchase and obtains a first trust deed, and the seller takes back a second encumbrance. It has been held that with purchase money encumbrances, the character of the transaction must be determined at the time the encumbrance is executed, and its nature is then fixed for all time.[35]

EXAMPLES   1.   In one case, the holder of a second trust deed (a purchase money second) brought an action on the note after the first trust deed had been foreclosed, the beneficiary under the first having become the purchaser at a sale that brought only enough to pay off the first trust deed. The trial court held that the beneficiary under the second could maintain an action on the note, since the security was lost on foreclosure of the first. However, the judgment was reversed on appeal, the Supreme Court expressing the opinion that, since this was a purchase money trust deed, there could be no deficiency, even though the security later became valueless. The security alone must be looked to for payment of a debt secured by a purchase money trust deed.[36]

2. In another case, a third deed of trust in favor of the broker was considered to be purchase money, and a personal judgment against the borrower after foreclosure was not obtainable.[37]

§9.36. Additional provisions in trust deeds

As illustrated by Figure 9-3, a trust deed usually includes numerous provisions that, although not essential to the validity or enforceability of the trust deed, have been developed as necessary or proper to afford adequate protection to the lender. These include covenants (1) to maintain and repair the property; (2) to comply with health laws and police regulations; (3) to keep the property insured against fire and other hazards;[38] (4) to pay taxes, assessments, and encumbrances having priority, and authorizing the lender to pay them if they become delinquent; and (5) to prosecute or defend proceedings when necessary to safeguard the security.

Additionally, provisions are included authorizing the beneficiary to take protective or defensive measures if the trustor neglects them, and to add the costs to the debt. Also, provision is made for disposition of condemnation awards, for partial releases, for subordination agreements and the grant of easements and execution of subdivision maps, and so on.

Waste and repair. An act of waste, by act or omission, applies also to a nonassuming grantee.[39]

Taxes and assessments. The fictitious deed of trust generally calls for taxes and assessments to be paid ten days before they become delinquent, i.e., as to taxes, on or before December 1 and April 1 of each year.

Impound accounts. Since nonpayment of taxes reduces the value of the security, the lender is concerned that the taxes and assessments may not be paid, as well as fire insurance premiums, and therefore sometimes requires an impound account.[40] Impound accounts are not permissible on a single-family owner-occupied dwelling, except

1. When required by a state or federal regulatory authority
2. When a loan is made, guaranteed, or insured by a state or governmental lending or insuring agency
3. Upon failure to pay two consecutive tax installments before delinquency
4. When the original principal amount of the loan is 90 percent of sales price or appraisal

The law further requires that the mortgagee, beneficiary, or vendor under a mortgage, trust deed, or real property sales contract, respectively, furnish the mortgagor, trustor, or vendee with (1) an itemized accounting of his impound account; (2) a statement of the new monthly rate of payment; and (3) an explanation of the factors necessitating an increase, before any increase in the monthly rate of payment will be effective, *whether or not the mortgagor, trustor, or vendee requests such information.* Under the preexisting law, it was not a prerequisite to the effectiveness of any such increase to provide such information except upon written request by the mortgagor, trustor, or vendee. Further, it was held that a borrower may be able to obtain an accounting as to the use of his funds and determine the gain of the bank or savings and loan.[41]

The Civil Code provides that money in an impound account shall be retained in California and, if invested, shall be invested only with residents of California (in the case of individuals), or with partnerships, corporations, or other persons, or the branches or subsidiaries thereof, that are engaged in business within California.[42] Effective January 1, 1977, every institution making loans secured by real estate on one- to four-family residences that receives impounds is required

The following is a copy of provisions (1) to (14), inclusive, of the fictitious deed of trust, recorded in each county in California, as stated in the foregoing Deed of Trust and incorporated by reference in said Deed of Trust as being a part thereof as if set forth at length therein.

TO PROTECT THE SECURITY OF THIS DEED OF TRUST, TRUSTOR AGREES:

(1) To keep said property in good condition and repair; not to remove or demolish any building thereon; to complete or restore promptly and in good and workmanlike manner any building which may be constructed, damaged or destroyed thereon and to pay when due all claims for labor performed and materials furnished therefor; to comply with all laws affecting said property or requiring any alterations or improvements to be made thereon; not to commit or permit waste thereof; not to commit, suffer or permit any act upon said property in violation of law; to cultivate, irrigate, fertilize, fumigate, prune and do all other acts which from the character or use of said property may be reasonably necessary, the specific enumerations herein not excluding the general.

(2) To provide, maintain and deliver to Beneficiary fire insurance satisfactory to and with loss payable to Beneficiary. The amount collected under any fire or other insurance policy may be applied by Beneficiary upon any indebtedness secured hereby and in such order as Beneficiary may determine, or at option of Beneficiary the entire amount so collected or any part thereof may be released to Trustor. Such application or release shall not cure or waive any default or notice of default hereunder or invalidate any act done pursuant to such notice.

(3) To appear in and defend any action or proceeding purporting to affect the security hereof or the rights or powers of Beneficiary or Trustee; and to pay all costs and expenses, including cost of evidence of title and attorney's fees in a reasonable sum, in any such action or proceeding in which Beneficiary or Trustee may appear, and in any suit brought by Beneficiary to foreclose this Deed.

(4) To pay: at least ten days before delinquency all taxes and assessments affecting said property, including assessments on appurtenant water stock; when due, all incumbrances, charges and liens, with interest, on said property or any part thereof, which appear to be prior or superior hereto; all costs, fees and expenses of this Trust.

Should Trustor fail to make any payment or to do any act as herein provided, then Beneficiary or Trustee, but without obligation so to do and without notice to or demand upon Trustor and without releasing Trustor from any obligation hereof, may: make or do the same in such manner and to such extent as either may deem necessary to protect the security hereof, Beneficiary or Trustee being authorized to enter upon said property for such purpose; appear in and defend any action or proceeding purporting to affect the security hereof or the rights or powers of Beneficiary or Trustee; pay, purchase, contest or compromise any incumbrance, charge or lien which in the judgment of either appears to be prior or superior hereto; and, in exercising any such powers, pay necessary expenses, employ counsel and pay his reasonable fees.

(5) To pay immediately and without demand all sums so expended by Beneficiary or Trustee, with interest from date of expenditure at the amount allowed by law in effect at the date hereof, and to pay for any statement provided for by law in effect at the date hereof regarding the obligation secured hereby any amount demanded by the Beneficiary not to exceed the maximum allowed by law at the time when said statement is demanded.

(6) That any award of damages in connection with any condemnation for public use of or injury to said property or any part thereof is hereby assigned and shall be paid to Beneficiary who may apply or release such moneys received by him in the same manner and with the same effect as above provided for disposition of proceeds of fire or other insurance.

(7) That by accepting payment of any sum secured hereby after its due date, Beneficiary does not waive his right either to require prompt payment when due of all other sums so secured or to declare default for failure so to pay.

(8) That at any time or from time to time, without liability therefor and without notice, upon written request of Beneficiary and presentation of this Deed and said note for endorsement, and without affecting the personal liability of any person for payment of the indebtedness secured hereby, Trustee may: reconvey any part of said property; consent to the making of any map or plat thereof; join in granting any easement thereon; or join in any extension agreement or any agreement subordinating the lien or charge hereof.

(9) That upon written request of Beneficiary stating that all sums secured hereby have been paid, and upon surrender of this Deed and said note to Trustee for cancellation and retention and upon payment of its fees, Trustee shall reconvey, without warranty, the property then held hereunder. The recitals in such reconveyance of any matters or facts shall be conclusive proof of the truthfulness thereof. The grantee in such reconveyance may be described as "the person or persons legally entitled thereto." Five years after issuance of such full reconveyance, Trustee may destroy said note and this Deed (unless directed in such request to retain them).

(10) That as additional security, Trustor hereby gives to and confers upon Beneficiary the right, power and authority, during the continuance of these Trusts, to collect the rents, issues and profits of said property, reserving unto Trustor the right, prior to any default by Trustor in payment of any indebtedness secured hereby or in performance of any agreement hereunder, to collect and retain such rents, issues and profits as they become due and payable. Upon any such default, Beneficiary may at any time without notice, either in person, by agent, or by a receiver to be appointed by a court, and without regard to the adequacy of any security for the indebtedness hereby secured, enter upon and take possession of said property or any part thereof, in his own name sue for or otherwise collect such rents, issues and profits, including those past due and unpaid, and apply the same, less costs and expenses of operation and collection, including reasonable attorney's fees, upon any indebtedness secured hereby, and in such order as Beneficiary may determine. The entering upon and taking possession of said property, the collection of such rents, issues and profits and the application thereof as aforesaid, shall not cure or waive any default or notice of default hereunder or invalidate any act done pursuant to such notice.

(11) That upon default by Trustor in payment of any indebtedness secured hereby or in performance of any agreement hereunder, Beneficiary may declare all sums secured hereby immediately due and payable by delivery to Trustee of written declaration of default and demand for sale and of written notice of default and of election to cause to be sold said property, which notice Trustee shall cause to be filed for record. Beneficiary also shall deposit with Trustee this Deed, said note and all documents evidencing expenditures secured hereby.

After the lapse of such time as may then be required by law following the recordation of said notice of default, and notice of sale having been given as then required by law, Trustee, without demand on Trustor, shall sell said property at the time and place fixed by it in said notice of sale, either as a whole or in separate parcels, and in such order as it may determine, at public auction to the highest bidder for cash in lawful money of the United States, payable at time of sale. Trustee may postpone sale of all or any portion of said property by public announcement at such time and place of sale, and from time to time thereafter may postpone such sale by public announcement at the time fixed by the preceding postponement. Trustee shall deliver to such purchaser its deed conveying the property so sold, but without any covenant or warranty express or implied. The recitals in such deed of any matters or facts shall be conclusive proof of the truthfulness thereof. Any person, including Trustor, Trustee, or Beneficiary as hereinafter defined, may purchase at such sale.

After deducting all costs, fees and expenses of Trustee and of this Trust, including cost of evidence of title in connection with sale, Trustee shall apply the proceeds of sale to payment of: all sums expended under the terms hereof, not then repaid, with accrued interest at the amount allowed by law in effect at the date hereof; all other sums then secured hereby; and the remainder, if any, to the person or persons legally entitled thereto.

(12) Beneficiary, or any successor in ownership of any indebtedness secured hereby, may from time to time, by instrument in writing, substitute a successor or successors to any Trustee named herein or acting hereunder, which instrument, executed by the Beneficiary and duly acknowledged and recorded in the office of the recorder of the county or counties where said property is situated, shall be conclusive proof of proper substitution of such successor Trustee or Trustees, who shall, without conveyance from the Trustee predecessor, succeed to all its title, estate, rights, powers and duties. Said instrument must contain the name of the original Trustor, Trustee and Beneficiary hereunder, the book and page where this Deed is recorded and the name and address of the new Trustee.

(13) That this Deed applies to, inures to the benefit of, and binds all parties hereto, their heirs, legatees, devisees, administrators, executors, successors and assigns. The term Beneficiary shall mean the owner and holder, including pledgees, of the note secured hereby, whether or not named as Beneficiary herein. In this Deed, whenever the context so requires, the masculine gender includes the feminine and/or neuter, and the singular number includes the plural.

(14) That Trustee accepts this Trust when this Deed, duly executed and acknowledged, is made a public record as provided by law. Trustee is not obligated to notify any party hereto of pending sale under any other Deed of Trust or of any action or proceeding in which Trustor, Beneficiary or Trustee shall be a party unless brought by Trustee.

DO NOT RECORD

REQUEST FOR FULL RECONVEYANCE

To be used only when note has been paid.

TO, Trustee: Dated _____

The undersigned is the legal owner and holder of all indebtedness secured by the within Deed of Trust. All sums secured by said Deed of Trust have been fully paid and satisfied; and you are hereby requested and directed, on payment to you of any sums owing to you under the terms of said Deed of Trust, to cancel all evidences of indebtedness, secured by said Deed of Trust, delivered to you herewith together with said Deed of Trust, and to reconvey, without warranty, to the parties designated by the terms of said Deed of Trust, the estate now held by you under the same.

MAIL RECONVEYANCE TO:

_____

_____

_____

_____

Do not lose or destroy this Deed of Trust OR THE NOTE which it secures. Both must be delivered to the Trustee for cancellation before reconveyance will be made.

FIGURE 9–3
Additional provisions in a trust deed.

to pay interest of at least 2 percent per annum. The institutions cannot charge a fee in connection with impounds.[43]

A lender is prohibited from maintaining an impound account in excess of that permitted in connection with certain federally related mortgage laws. Any excess shall be refunded within 30 days. Also, no lender may use impounds so as to cause an insurance policy to be canceled or to cause property taxes to become delinquent.[44]

Assignment of rents. The trust deed may also contain an assignment-of-rents provision, as additional security assigning the rents then due or thereafter to accrue, either absolutely or effective on some future event, such as a default in payment or performance of the obligations secured by the trust deed. As an aid to the enforcement of such provision, a receiver may be appointed by the court to collect the rents. A receiver may also be appointed upon a showing of waste or inadequacy of the security.[45] An assignment of rents usually constitutes only a pledge, not an immediate assignment, and therefore a court-appointed receiver is generally necessary. However, good cause must be shown. Further, the rents and profits are limited to the property standing as security. On the other hand, if an absolute assignment is clearly indicated on the trust deed, the beneficiary is immediately entitled to the rents, issues, and profits.[46]

§9.37. Fictitious deed of trust
Fictitious mortgages and trust deeds may be recorded with the county recorder.[47] They need not be acknowledged, but they must note on the face that they are fictitious. After recording, any provision of a fictitious mortgage or trust deed may be incorporated by reference in any mortgage or trust deed affecting real property in the same county. This saves recording charges, because only the face page of a short form trust deed need be recorded. The general provisions still appear on the reverse side, but are not recorded in view of their inclusion in, and being made a matter of record by, the fictitious mortgage or trust deed.

§9.38. Trustee cannot be compelled to act
Although the acceptance of the appointment as trustee is generally automatic, the trustee nonetheless has the right to decline to act at the time he is called on to perform. A refusal to act might be based on an objectionable provision in the trust deed that is contrary to the policy or practices of the trustee, or a trustee may refuse to act because the beneficiary fails to furnish sufficient evidence of a default, or when the obligation secured by the trust deed is usurious or otherwise illegal. The beneficiary may act as his own trustee.[48]

§9.39. Substitution of trustee
Another trustee may be substituted for the trustee named in a trust deed. Depending on the special circumstances, the substitution may be accomplished in several ways, including the following: (1) in the manner, if any, provided in the instrument, when practicable; (2) in the manner provided by the Civil Code;[49] (3) by agreement of the trustor and the beneficiary, or their respective successors in interest; and (4) by the Superior Court.[50]

The Civil Code specifies that the statutory method for the substitution of a trustee under a trust deed authorized by this section shall be effective and operative notwithstanding any contrary provisions in any trust deed executed on or after January 1, 1968, to set forth other pertinent changes, and to declare void a sale conducted by a substituted trustee, unless a new notice of sale is published and posted setting forth the name, street address, and phone number of the substituted trustee.[51]

§9.40. Assumption of obligation versus taking "subject to"
A purchaser may prefer to keep the existing financing on a piece of real estate rather than obtain a new loan. It must, therefore, be decided whether to *assume* the

existing loan at the prevailing rate, pay points or an assumption fee, and be able to financially qualify for the loan. The buyer may prefer to take *subject to* the trust deed at the interest rate set forth on the promissory note, pay no points, and not be personally liable on the note. The distinctions between these two avenues is critical.

Assumption. If the buyer expressly assumes the loan, he agrees, in writing, with the beneficiary-lender to pay the existing loan and becomes primarily (personally) liable on the note for any possible deficiency.[52] He also agrees to indemnify the grantor (trustor-seller). However, the lender, upon a default, must first exhaust the security. The maker (original trustor) of the note becomes a surety and may ultimately be liable if the buyer becomes judgment-proof and there was no novation (and the trust deed was not a purchase money trust deed). It should be noted that if there is no due-on-sale clause, the beneficiary cannot require the buyer to assume the loan.

Subject to. If a property is purchased subject to the existing loan, the property is primarily liable for the debt. The maker of the note is still secondarily liable, but if the loan was a purchase money trust deed, there is no deficiency.[53] There is no personal liability to the buyer who receives title subject to existing encumbrances.

§9.41. Assignment of obligation

An assignment of the obligation secured by a trust deed carries the trust deed with it, whereas an assignment of the trust deed apart from the obligation is ineffective and transfers nothing. The obligation may be assigned by an endorsement (1) on the note, (2) on the trust deed, or (3) by a separate instrument. To obtain the benefit of the recording laws, the assignment must be executed in form sufficient to entitle it to be recorded. Also, notice of the assignment should be given to the obligor. If the obligor does not have actual notice of the assignment, payment to the assignor may discharge the obligation, and the assignee will then be compelled to look to the assignor for payment. An assignment by the beneficiary "for security" transfers the right but not the obligation.[54]

§9.42. All-inclusive trust deed

A form of trust deed that has become more prevalent throughout the state is the *all-inclusive trust deed*, sometimes used instead of an installment type sales contract in the sale of real property. This type of deed of trust, sometimes referred to as an AITD, hold harmless, overlapping, overriding, or wrap-around deed of trust, is a form of junior trust deed, that is, inferior or subordinate to another trust deed on the same property. Basically, it includes not only the obligation owing by the trustor to the beneficiary in the particular transaction that gives rise to the use of an all-inclusive trust deed, but also the obligation owing under another and prior trust deed or deeds of trust. This form of trust deed requires special care in its preparation, and it is unlikely that a standard form will work. It must be tailored to fit the facts of each particular case. A preprinted form can be dangerous for both buyer and seller. For the protection of both parties, the instrument should be recorded.

EXAMPLE A sells real estate to B for $300,000, subject to a first trust deed of $150,000 at 8.5 percent interest. B pays $70,000 cash as a down payment, and A takes back a $230,000 all-inclusive deed of trust at 9 percent interest, which includes the underlying $150,000 trust deed. Legal title is transferred to B.

Potential problem areas. Unless the all-inclusive trust deed is drafted in a competent manner, problems can arise for both the purchaser and seller. For example, are the payments on the all-inclusive trust deed greater than on the senior trust deed?

Does the new buyer have the right to pay the original beneficiary if the holder of the all-inclusive trust deed fails to do so? Who is responsible for prepayment penalties? If impounds are required in the underlying trust deed, has an increase in payments been provided for in the all-inclusive trust deed? Is a collection account to be set up? Does a senior trust deed contain an alienation clause? If so, do the parties understand the law in this area?

Despite one common preprinted form, the beneficiary of the AITD does not have the right to receive anything more than his delinquent payments and interest. He may not also receive the amounts he has advanced to keep the underlying senior trust deed current.[55]

Advantages and disadvantages. To the seller, there are no apparent disadvantages. The seller would generally receive a higher yield and better control than by merely selling the property "subject to" an existing trust deed. Even though the effective yield may be higher than 10 percent, it has been held not to be usurious. The buyer saves on "points" and assumption fees, and may be able to receive an interest rate lower than what is presently available. The main disadvantage is an alienation clause that may exist in a prior trust deed which could affect the sellers' credit rating because, upon a foreclosure for violation of the alienation clause, the foreclosure will be in the name of the seller.

IV. SPECIAL PROVISIONS IN TRUST DEEDS

§9.43. Renewal and extension

A *renewal* agreement substitutes a new obligation, while an *extension* continues the old obligation. If the statute of limitations has not run, the mutual agreement between the parties is sufficient consideration, since each has extended his legal rights. For example, the trustor's promise to pay a higher interest rate is sufficient consideration. To be effective, a renewal or extension must be in writing and signed by the person against whom it is to be enforced. Care should be taken to avoid usury in drafting a modification agreement.[56]

Such an agreement has no effect on a junior lienholder who acquired his status before the extension or renewal and who did not agree to it.[57] If the senior lienholder renews and the junior lienholder has knowledge, the latter must foreclose to protect his interest or else he may be deemed to have waived his rights.[58]

§9.44. Acceleration

An *acceleration* clause appearing in a note and trust deed requires payment of the total unpaid balance upon the occurrence of a specified event. An acceleration may occur as a result of a default, or it may be based on a transfer of the property. In the absence of such a provision, the beneficiary cannot accelerate. As to obligations secured by a trust deed after July 1, 1972, on property containing four or fewer residential units, a due-on-sale clause must be contained in its entirety in both the promissory note and deed of trust.[59]

Effective January 1, 1976, an obligee may not accelerate any loan secured by real property on one to four housing units, and any waiver is void, by any of the following transfers:[60]

1. A transfer resulting from the death of the obligor when transfer is to a surviving spouse who is also an obligor

2. A transfer by an obligor when the spouse becomes a co-owner

3. A transfer resulting from a decree of dissolution or legal separation or from a property settlement agreement that requires the obligor to continue to make loan payments, and the other spouse, who is also an obligor, becomes the sole owner

4. A transfer into an inter vivos trust on which the obligor(s) are beneficiaries

5. A transfer when real property is made subject to a junior encumbrance or lien

§9.45. Due-on-sale clause

As noted above, there are two common types of acceleration clauses. One type provides for all sums of principal and interest to be due and payable at the option of the beneficiary upon the failure to pay, for example, any installment of principal, interest, taxes, or insurance when due. This is subject to a statutory right of reinstatement. The second type is the *due-on-sale* or *alienation* clause which, if enforceable, will not be subject to any period of reinstatement.

Many trust deeds provide that in the event of a transfer of the property by the trustor, the lender may, at its discretion, accelerate the balance due. The trial court's judgment upholding the validity of a due-on-sale clause was formerly overruled by the California Supreme Court.[61] However, thereafter, the validity of a due-on-sale clause was upheld by the United States Supreme Court.[62]

A typical due-on-sale clause reads as follows:

> *Should trustor sell, convey, transfer, further encumber or alienate the property, or any part thereof, or any interest therein, or agree to do so, or be divested of his or her title or any interest therein in any manner or way, whether voluntarily or involuntarily, without the written consent of the beneficiary, the beneficiary may declare the entire indebtedness secured hereby at his option immediately due and payable. Consent of one such transaction shall not be deemed to be a waiver of the right to require such consent to future or successive transactions.*

Historically, the lender claimed the primary reason for such a clause was to enable it to examine the financial responsibility of the grantee. Further, the lender would require the grantee to assume the obligation, agree to an increase in interest rates, and pay an assumption fee.

The California Supreme Court's Wellencamp[63] decision in 1978 was originally thought to resolve the problem regarding state lenders (private or institutional) affecting residential or commercial real estate.[64] Since California does not have jurisdiction over federally chartered savings and loans, for some time the law in that regard was unclear. However, since 1982, when the federal Garn–St. Germain Act was passed, all lenders (state and federal) have rights to foreclose for violation of a due-on-sale clause after a prescribed window period elapsed (October 15, 1985).

§9.46. Due-on-encumbrance clause

Most due-on-sale clauses also include a *due-on-encumbrance* provision that appears to give the beneficiary the right to declare the entire obligation due in the event the trustor shall further encumber the property. However, the Supreme Court has held that such a clause is unenforceable unless reasonably necessary to avert danger to the lender's security.[65] Effective January 1, 1976, the Civil Code was modified to prohibit the enforcement of a due-on-encumbrance clause in mortgages and trust deeds on real property containing one to four housing units.[66]

§9.47. Locked-in loan

The ordinary form of secured promissory note contains an "or more" clause (see Figure 9-1). This allows the trustor to discharge the obligation by prepayment if desired. If no "or more" clause is set forth, the trustor is "locked in," thus restricting a payoff.[67] If the beneficiary decides to accept an early payoff, he can condition its acceptance by requiring some consideration, such as full payment of interest for the unexpired term. Such a case has not been deemed to be usurious.[68]

Quite often the trustor is unaware of the significance of the absence of an "or more" clause. Because of this, the legislature added a section to the Civil Code that states any loan on residential property of four or fewer units may be prepaid at any time. Beginning on January 1, 1980, this section does not apply, during the year of sale, to purchase money taken back by the seller, if the seller does not take back four or more trust deeds in such calendar year. Beyond the calendar year of the sale, this section *does* apply and a purchaser can repay. However, the beneficiary can condition an early payment upon a prepayment charge. This limitation is necessary to protect the seller's installment sale in the year of sale.[69]

EXAMPLE Seller sold his ranch under an installment sale. Not wanting to receive a balloon payment for five years, he included a clause in the contract providing for a 50 percent penalty on payments in excess of those negotiated. After the sale, the buyer brought suit for declaratory relief. The court held that such a penalty is valid if the penalty is reasonably related to the obligee's anticipated risk of incurring increased tax liability on the occurrence of the prepayment.[70]

§9.48. Prepayment fees

A question frequently arises as to whether the trustor has the right to prepay an installment note at any time. It has been held that there is no right to prepay an obligation if the promissory note does not create one. This is a matter of contract between the parties.[71] When the right to pay the obligation before maturity is to be expressed, a provision may be included in the note secured by the trust deed.

Many lenders require a prepayment fee if the trustor wants to pay the note in full before the due date.[72] A typical prepayment clause reads as follows:

> *Privilege is reserved to prepay this note without penalty, provided, however, that I promise to pay _____ months' advance interest on that part of the aggregate amount of all prepayments made on this note in any one year which exceeds _____ percent of the original principal amount of this note.*

EXAMPLES 1. The validity of a prepayment clause was sustained in a prior case. The court held that a reasonable recovery through a prepayment fee of the lender's costs and loss of profit incurred by reason of early payment is permissible. However, the court stated that "points" or assumption fees charged must bear some reasonable relationship to the loan; that is, the points must bear some justifiable interest to the lender's administrative costs, loss of profits, etc.[73]

2. The validity of a prepayment fee was also sustained in another case. The court found no merit in a contention that the prepayment fee was excessive in that it bore no reasonable relationship to any damage sustained by virtue of the prepayment.[74] On the other hand, the court said it would not tolerate an "unconscionable" prepayment penalty. In other words, any payment over and above the typical six months' interest in the year of payment will likely be construed as unconscionable. If avoidance of the usury law is not the intent, a prepayment clause is not usurious.[75]

Since January 1, 1976, principal and accrued interest secured by a single-family owner-occupied real property may be prepaid, but only such prepayment within five years of the date of execution of the loan may be subject to a prepayment charge. If prepayment is made within five years, an amount not exceeding 20 percent of the original principal amount may be prepaid without penalty. A prepayment privilege may be imposed on the amount in excess of the 20 percent, but shall not exceed six months' interest.[76] For loan brokers the prepayment period is seven years rather than five.[77]

EXCEPTION A beneficiary who accelerates a loan upon a conveyance by the trustor may not claim a prepayment penalty resulting from that acceleration. This law only applies to four or fewer residential units (and need not be owner-occupied), in which the trustor has expressly waived the right to prepay without penalty, or has expressly agreed to a prepayment upon acceleration. For any loan executed after January 1, 1984, any such waiver shall be separately signed by the obligor (trustor).[78]

§9.49. Late charges

The validity of late charges has been the subject of several California court decisions. Clauses providing for late charges were held to be enforceable in a number of cases.[79] However, the amount must be reasonably calculated merely to compensate the lender for actual damages caused by the delay in payment; otherwise, it will not be enforceable.[80] If imposed as a penalty, it is unenforceable.

The imposition of a late charge regarding a single-family owner-occupied dwelling must not exceed 6 percent of the installment due or $5, whichever is greater, but no charge may be imposed more than once on the same installment. A payment is not late until at least ten days following the due date. The present law applies only to loans made after January 1, 1976.[81] Before the first default, delinquency, or late payment charge may be assessed by any lender on a delinquent payment of a loan secured by real property, and before the borrower becomes obligated to pay such a charge, the borrower shall either (1) be notified in writing and given at least ten days from mailing of such notice in which to cure the delinquency; or (2) be informed, by a billing or notice sent for each payment due on the loan, of the date after which such a charge will be assessed. If a subsequent payment becomes delinquent, the borrower is entitled to notification as therein prescribed. This law applies only on loans made after January 1, 1976.[82]

In a noninstitutional loan involving a first trust deed of less than $20,000 or a junior trust deed of less than $8,000, no late charge can be imposed if the payment is made within ten days of the due date. The payment received thereafter cannot be subject to a late charge in excess of 10 percent of the installment due or a minimum of $5. The charge permitted may be assessed *only* as a percentage of the principal and interest past due.[83]

§9.50. Interest rates

Unconscionable interest. Although interests rates are generally legal, some are unconscionable.

EXAMPLE Arrospid, while under emotional distress, signed a promissory note and trust deed for $4,000 with a 200 percent interest rate all due in three months! The lender, Carboni, continued making cash advances of an additional $21,000, and within four months the principal amount of the note had ballooned to almost $100,000. Following the borrower's failure to make the payments, the broker, Carboni, brought suit for judicial foreclosure and a deficiency judgment. At the time of trial, one and one-half years later, the principal and accumulated interest amounted to nearly $390,000. The question was whether such an interest rate was unconscionable. The obvious conclusion was: yes. The court reduced the interest rate to 24 percent.[84] (Even that rate is questionable, in the authors' view.)

Variable interest rates. In a market in which interest rates may vary, many loans provide for an automatic increase in the rate, geared to the prime rate or some other, similar factor. Borrowers have often been unaware that the note or trust deed they executed contained a provision for an automatic increase in the interest rate. In 1970 the California legislature enacted legislation[85] to regulate the use in California of a variable interest rate in a mortgage contract, trust deed, real estate sales contract, or any note or negotiable instrument issued in connection therewith, when the purpose of such document is to finance the purchase or construction of real property containing four or fewer residential units or on which four or fewer such units are to be constructed.[86] This law requires that a statement in at least ten-point bold type be attached to the mortgage contract, trust deed, or real estate sales contract, *and* to the note or negotiable instrument issued in connection therewith, saying: **NOTICE TO BORROWER: THIS DOCUMENT CONTAINS PROVISIONS FOR A VARIABLE INTEREST RATE.** Also, among other things, the rate cannot change more often than semiannually, and the change can be no more than one-fourth of one percent in any semiannual period.

§9.51. Questions of usury

A question sometimes arises as to whether a real estate transaction involves usury. A usury law was enacted in California in 1918 and, as modified by constitutional amendments in 1934, 1978, and 1989, it limited the rate of interest to 10 percent per annum with certain exceptions, including banks, savings and loan associations, and other institutions and activities governed by other statutes. The trend has been to increase the number of exempt lenders. A purchase money trust deed (discussed further in Chapter 10) taken back by the seller is also exempt.[87]

For usury to exist, there must be a *loan* or *forbearance* of money. A *loan* of money is a contract by which one delivers a sum of money to another, and the latter agrees to return, at a future time, a sum equivalent to that which he borrowed.[88] *Interest* is the compensation allowed by law or fixed by the parties for the use, forbearance, or detention of money.[89] *Forbearance,* within the meaning of the usury law, is a waiting to collect the debt, the giving of further time to pay, or the release of personal liability.

Usury has been held to be the conscious and voluntary taking of more than the maximum rate of interest; beyond this, no specific intent to violate the statute is necessary. When the form of a transaction makes it appear to be nonusurious, it can nonetheless be held to be usurious, and a court will determine as a matter of fact whether a loan was intended. Substance is more important than form, and the label for excessive payments is immaterial.[90] For example, "points" are treated as interest,[91] as well as service charges, if the charges are paid to the lender. Payment of interest in the form of an option may be usurious.[92] On the other hand, purchase of a note at a discount is not affected by the usury laws.[93] But if the discount was used as a subterfuge to avoid the usury laws, the court could look behind the form and look to the intent of the parties and thus hold such a transaction to be usurious. Under certain circumstances, parties can avoid usury laws by agreeing to be governed by foreign law.[94]

Presumptions of the law are in favor of legality. If a transaction is open to two constructions, one making for legality and the other for illegality, then in the absence of evidence pointing clearly to usury, it is the duty of the court to adopt the construction in favor of lawfulness.[95] In general, the existence of usury depends upon the specific wording of the applicable statute and/or constitutional provision as applied to the particular transaction.

An intent to exact a usurious rate of interest is conclusively presumed from a note or other instrument that clearly shows on its face that it is usurious, and no evidence of intent or lack of such intent is required.[96]

When an instrument is usurious, no interest whatever is recoverable by the lender. Also, any person who pays interest at a usurious rate may recover treble the amount he paid. An action to recover such interest must be brought within one year from the date of payment.

In 1979 California's voters approved substantial amendments to the usury provisions of the California Constitution.[97] The new law provided for a 10 percent annual interest-rate limitation on most loans made primarily for personal, family, or household purposes.[98] It also established as the maximum rate on nonconsumer loans the greater of 10 percent per annum, or 5 percent per annum plus the rate established by the Federal Reserve Bank of San Francisco on advances to member banks. The 1979 amendments exempted several classes of loans, such as secured loans made or arranged by licensed real estate brokers, from these interest limitations, and empowered the legislature to create new exemptions.

In 1980 federal legislation went into effect that preempted much of the new California law. Much of this federal legislation expired by its own terms on April 1, 1983. However, federal preemption remains the rule with respect to loans made by certain types of lenders that are secured by first liens on residential property.

Since 1979 the state legislature has created at least ten classes of exempt lenders and loans, including insurance companies, banks and savings and loan associations, business and industrial development corporations, securities and brokers under the jurisdiction of the Department of Corporations, pension funds, consumer finance lenders, and others.

The Consumer Finance Lenders Law applies to "a loan, whether secured by real or personal property, or unsecured, the proceeds of which are intended by the borrower for use primarily for personal, family, or household purposes." Consumer loans greater than $5,000 made by licensed consumer finance lenders are exempt from all interest and rate limitations, and smaller loans are subject to a scale of interest-rate limits.

The Consumer Finance Lenders Law provides for a severe penalty in the case of intentional violations. If a loan contract "intentionally" sets forth a rate greater than the maximum, it is void and causes a complete forfeiture of principal.

Under the general usury law, the penalty for willful violations, in addition to loss of interest and possible treble damages, subjects the offender to a felony conviction for loan sharking.

The real estate broker's exemption has been held to be retroactive.[99]

As stated in a recent article, we have seen in California a legislative willingness to exercise the authority granted under the 1979 law to create new classes of exempt lenders, and a judicial willingness to apply that law retroactively. These two trends have significantly diminished the effect of California's usury law. Usury has been a problem since Biblical times, and is of ongoing concern. Constant changes can be anticipated in the future, based on what has occurred in the past.

§9.52. Maturity

The promissory note secured by a trust deed becomes payable according to its terms. If there is no provision for installment payments and no date of final payment, it is due on demand.[100]

§9.53. Statute of Limitations

If the obligation is barred because of the Statute of Limitations, it cannot be enforced by court foreclosure. An action to foreclose is barred when the statute has run on the obligation secured by the trust deed, i.e., it is barred within four years of delinquency or maturity. However, under the power of sale in a trust deed, a trustee's sale can take place even if the Statute of Limitations has run on the obligation, subject however, to the effect of the marketable record title statutes referred to in § 9.12.

V. DISCHARGE OF OBLIGATION AND RELATED PROBLEMS

§9.54. Obtaining reconveyance

When the trustor or trustor's successor in interest has paid the amount due on the obligation, he is entitled to a full *reconveyance* of the trust deed. On making the final payment, the beneficiary or his successor in interest is required to deliver the original note and the trust deed to the trustee, together with a request for full reconveyance. This is so whether or not the trustor has requested reconveyance.

A reconveyance should then be obtained on payment of the trustee's fees and then be recorded. The trustee is required to deliver the original note and trust deed to the trustor afterward, upon request of the trustor. The trustee may charge a fee to the trustor for this service.

<table>
<tr><td>EXAMPLES</td><td>1.</td><td>Escrow holder mistakenly recorded a reconveyance. The court held the reconveyance voidable as to the beneficiary and against the defendant who had subsequently recorded an abstract of judgment against the purchasers.[101]</td></tr>
<tr><td></td><td>2.</td><td>On the other hand, a forged deed of reconveyance is void and, therefore, any later trust deed is subordinate to the prior valid trust deed.[102]</td></tr>
</table>

Payment or satisfaction of the obligation extinguishes the trust deed, which thereon ceases to be a lien. The record thereafter reflects a mere cloud on the title, and the beneficiary can be compelled to execute and deliver, in form sufficient to entitle it to be recorded, a certificate that the trust deed has been paid, satisfied, or discharged, or cause satisfaction to be entered of record. The beneficiary, trustee, or assignee is liable for all damages occasioned by a failure to effect a discharge after payment, within 30 days of request, and he may also be subject to a penalty of $300.[103] Also, it is a misdemeanor to refuse to release the trust deed after payment, with a penalty of not less than $50 or more than $400 and/or six months in custody.[104]

Later statutory enactments to the Civil Code provide that upon execution of a full reconveyance by a trustee, upon the request of the beneficiary, the trustee shall record or cause to be recorded the full reconveyance unless (1) notified to the contrary by the trustor or owner, or (2) such full reconveyance is to be delivered to the trustor through an escrow agreement.[105]

Release of lien when beneficiary cannot be located. Effective January 1, 1981, when an obligation secured by a trust deed has been satisfied and the beneficiary cannot be located after a diligent search, or refuses to execute a proper certificate of discharge or request for reconveyance, the lien shall be released upon meeting the lienor's certain statutory requirements including obtaining and recording a corporate bond and declaration.[106] By amendment to the Code, on and after October 1, 1989, under specifically described circumstances, the recording by a title insurance company of a full release of obligation secured by a deed of trust is authorized.

Necessity that note be preserved. The original note should not be destroyed after payment, as it must be surrendered to the trustee before a reconveyance can be issued; otherwise, a surety bond may have to be obtained and filed with the trustee to take the place of the note. If the note becomes lost, a surety bond will also be required in most cases.

Partial reconveyances. It is common practice to provide for partial reconveyances of property covered by a trust deed, particularly when the instrument covers several lots or separate parcels of land, or when the property is to be subdivided and developed as separate parcels. When partial reconveyances are to be made, the trust deed should contain an express provision to that effect, and the exact terms and conditions should be specified with certainty. When executing a partial reconveyance, it is normally required that the note be submitted to the trustee for the purpose of noting on it the fact that a partial reconveyance has been issued.

§9.55. Partial release clause

A typical partial release clause reads as follows:

> *Provided the trustor is not then in default hereunder or with respect to the payments due on the promissory note secured by this deed of trust, a partial recon-*

veyance from the lien or charge hereof may be had and will be given of any one or more of the lots herein before described at any time, and from time to time, prior to the maturity of the note secured hereby, upon payment of an amount (to apply on the principal of said note) based on the rate of $_____ for each lot to be so reconveyed.

The promissory note will contain a corresponding provision such as the following: "The privilege is reserved of making partial payments to apply on the principal hereof in accordance with the provisions of the deed of trust by which this note is secured."

In the development of a subdivision in stages, either for sale as lots or for construction of improvements and subsequent sale of individual lots as improved, it is ordinarily essential that the developer be able to obtain a release of individual lots from the lien of the original seller's purchase money trust deed. Without a release clause, the trustor is not entitled to a partial release on partial payments. However, a valid release clause will afford a contractual basis for payment for a portion only of the property, and will require a reconveyance of a part of the land in accordance with the formula set forth in the trust deed, provided, however, that the release clause is prepared with sufficient certainty.[107]

§9.56. Beneficiary statements

When the property subject to a trust deed is to be sold or refinanced, the owner will need to know the exact amount due under the existing trust deed. This information is furnished in the form of a *beneficiary statement*.

The Civil Code requires the lender, or assignee, on the written request of the borrower or beneficiary under a junior trust deed, before foreclosure proceedings have been commenced, to furnish a written statement showing, among other things: (1) the amount of the unpaid balance of the obligation secured by the mortgage or trust deed and the interest rate; (2) the amounts of periodic payments, if any; (3) the date on which the obligation is due in whole or in part; (4) the date to which real estate taxes and special assessments have been paid, if known, and other relevant information.[108] The statement (known as a "demand statement") together with a copy of the note must be mailed within 21 days after receipt of the request, and a lender who for a period of 21 days willfully fails to prepare and deliver such statement is liable for any actual damages sustained and in any case for the sum of $300.

The lender may make a charge of not more than $60 for furnishing the statement, provided the provision for such charge is contained in the trust deed. However, no charge may be made in the case of FHA or VA loans whether or not there is any such provision in the deed of trust.[109]

In addition to the mortgagor or trustor or a successor in interest to all of the property, the Code includes the successor in interest as to any part of the mortgaged property, and any beneficiary under a subordinate trust deed and any other person having a subordinate lien or encumbrance of record. The Code also includes the following information required to be in the statement: (1) the total amount of all overdue installments of principal or interest, or both, and (2) the nature and amount of any additional charges, costs, or expenses paid or incurred by the beneficiary that have become liens on the property. Also, the time within which the demand could be made requires any time before or within two months after the recording of the notice of default in the case of a power-of-sale foreclosure, or more than 30 days before entry of the decree in the case of a judicial foreclosure. The amendment further provides that the 21 days' grace period allowed for compliance with the demand begins on beneficiary's receipt of reasonable proof that the person making the demand is entitled to the statement. The liability for the $300 penalty for noncompliance is on the "person entitled to the statement," rather than on the trustor of the first deed, as in the previous provisions.[110]

The Civil Code requires a beneficiary or mortgagee to render an annual accounting of funds received from the borrower on real property containing a one- to four-family residence. These sections are intended primarily to inform the owner of the property of the status of the impound account.[111]

§9.57. Federal Truth in Lending Act

The Federal Truth in Lending Act, which became effective in July 1969 as a portion of the Federal Consumer Credit Protection Act,[112] together with Regulation Z issued pursuant to the act,[113] may apply in transactions involving a real estate security instrument executed by a natural person encumbering a dwelling or agricultural land, and regarding advertisements.[114] The act also applies to refinancing an existing loan.

The application of the act is limited to the extension or arranging of credit to a natural person when the money, property, or service that is the subject of the transaction is primarily for personal, family, household, or agricultural purposes, i.e., it excludes credit for business or commercial purposes. The act further applies when either a finance charge is to be imposed *or* the amount of credit is payable in more than four installments. Further, it applies when credit is extended for real property transactions of *any amount*, or personal property of $25,000 or less. It does not apply to business loans or to straight notes if there is no finance charge. It also does not apply to a commercial investor who purchases existing trust deeds.

In general, the act requires creditors or one who is an "arranger of credit"[115] to disclose the cost of credit in a statement to the customer (Disclosure Statement) before the consummation of a loan transaction. It does not, however, establish or limit the cost of credit.

Additionally, the act includes a right of rescission applicable in certain situations. The act and regulations provide that if a security interest is or will be retained or acquired in any real property transaction that is used or is expected to be used as the principal residence of the customer, the customer shall have the right to rescind the transaction until midnight of the third business day following the date of consummation of the transaction to extend credit or the date of delivery of the disclosures required by the act, whichever is later, by notifying the creditor of his intention to rescind. Exceptions apply in the case of a purchase money first mortgage or construction loan on a home taken back by the seller. Upon rescission, the customer is not liable for any finance or other charge, and any security interest taken by the creditor becomes void. A broker who extends credit to a purchaser (for example, by taking back a purchase money second trust deed to secure payment of his commission) should be sure to comply with all applicable provisions of the act.[116]

§9.58. Creative Financing Disclosure

Because of the numerous creative financing abuses, the Civil Code requires certain disclosures to be made to buyers and sellers when the seller extends credit involving dwellings of four or fewer units in which a real estate licensee or other arranger of credit is involved.[117] There are a number of disclosure requirements including identification of the note and the property, description of the principal terms and conditions of each previously recorded instrument, certain warnings regarding financing, all-inclusive trust deeds, and balloon payments, etc.

§9.59. Fair Credit Reporting Act (FCRA)

The FCRA is designed to protect abuses of credit reports by vendors and credit reporting agencies. Basically the FCRA gives the consumer the right to (1) be notified when adverse action is taken against him on the basis of a credit report; (2) be told of the source of the report and/or agency compiling the report; (3) obtain the information contained in the report; (4) have the file kept confidential and used only for particular purposes; (5) have disputed entries reinvestigated; (6) have procedures to ensure reasonable accuracy, including the elimination of obsolete data; and (7) receive advance notification in the event an investigative report will be or may be made.[118]

The FCRA does not apply if the report is obtained to extend credit for business purposes or business organizations, such as a partnership or corporation.

Because it could give rise to the legal obligation set forth above, it may be better for the licensee to not get involved in credit reports, but rather, leave them to the clients.

VI. ADDITIONAL ASPECTS OF TRUST DEEDS
§9.60. Deed in lieu of foreclosure
To save the expense and delay of foreclosure proceedings, a beneficiary under a trust deed sometimes will obtain a *deed in lieu of foreclosure* from the trustor or his or her successor in interest. Although it is contrary to law to stipulate in the trust deed that on default the property shall be forfeited to the beneficiary without the necessity of foreclosure, it is nonetheless permissible at any subsequent time and on a sufficient consideration to transfer the property to the beneficiary in satisfaction of the obligation so secured.[119] Because of the superior economic position of the lender, however, such transactions are scrutinized by the courts with great care to be sure that the subsequent conveyance by the trustor represents a bona fide sale, for an adequate price, and without any advantage being taken by the lender.

Consideration. Although no additional consideration may be necessary when the grantor is personally liable for the debt and it approximates the reasonable value of the property, some additional consideration is required when a deed in lieu of foreclosure is given by a person who is not personally liable. This is true because such person would lose nothing by the foreclosure and normally would have the value of the use of the property during foreclosure.

Special recitals. As a consequence of the foregoing, title insurers usually require special recitals in a deed in lieu of foreclosure, or special assurances by way of affidavit, before undertaking to pass such deeds as sufficient to eliminate the interest of the trustor or his successor in interest. These special recitals provide substantially as follows:

If the grantor is personally liable:

> *This deed is an absolute conveyance, the grantor having sold the land to the grantee for a fair and adequate consideration, such consideration, in addition to the sum above described, being in full satisfaction of all obligations secured by the deed of trust executed by _____, recorded in book _____, page _____, Official Records of_____ county. Grantor declares that this conveyance is freely and fairly made, and that there are no agreements, oral or written, other than this deed between grantor and grantee with respect to the land.*

If the grantor is not personally liable:

> *Grantor declares that this conveyance is freely and fairly made, grantor having sold the land to the grantee for a consideration equal to the fair value of grantor's interest in said land; and grantor further declares that there are no agreements, oral or written, other than this deed between grantor and grantee with respect to the land.*

Continued possession by trustor. When the grantor is permitted to remain in possession under a lease or an option to purchase or otherwise, this circumstance casts doubt on the sufficiency of the deed in lieu of foreclosure, and it may deter a title insurer from treating such deed as an effective satisfaction of the trust deed.

Effect of junior liens. A deed in lieu of foreclosure is usually undesirable when there are junior liens. When such a deed is given, a merger of the legal title with the equitable interest under such trust deed ordinarily results, and junior liens and encumbrances are not eliminated. If the rule were otherwise, the beneficiary of the junior trust deed would lose his interest without the benefit of his statutory foreclosure rights, such as his right to reinstate.

§9.61. Questions of priority

Questions of priority arise frequently under trust deeds. *Priority* means the quality of being prior or preceding in the order of time. It gives superiority or seniority in position, and is opposite to *inferiority* or *subordination*.[120]

Priority, as far as real property rights are concerned, generally but not always depends on time of recording. The principal exceptions relate to the following:

1. *Real property taxes and assessments*—Real property taxes are afforded priority from year to year by law.

2. *Mechanics' liens*—Priority depends on the date when the work of improvement actually begins on the ground, not on the date of recording of the mechanic's lien.

3. *Subordination agreements*—Priority may be voluntarily changed by the execution of a subordination agreement.

4. *Actual notice of an unrecorded lien*—If the beneficiary under a trust deed has actual knowledge of an earlier but unrecorded interest, his lien will be junior even though recorded earlier in point of time.

5. *The lien in favor of a municipality or other agency for the cost of removal of an unsafe or hazardous structure, caused by fire, earthquake, neglect, or other reason*—Municipal ordinances in many communities provide for the manner in which a lien may be created for the cost of removal of a substandard or unsafe structure. If a structure is deemed substandard or unsafe, the government agency having jurisdiction may give notice to the owner and to holders of encumbrances, requiring them either to correct the situation or to remove the structure. If the owner or encumbrance holder fails to comply, the government agency may cause the removal of the structure, and the cost thereof becomes a lien and is on a parity of equal rank with the lien of state, county, and municipal taxes. A foreclosure of such lien would eliminate the lien of a previously recorded mortgage, trust deed, or abstract of judgment.

6. *Federal tax lien*—See §10.20.

§9.62. Subordination agreements

Subordination agreements have created numerous problems and have been the subject of much litigation.[121] Such an agreement subordinates a prior trust deed or other lien, that is, makes it junior to any other specific lien, charge, or encumbrance. These clauses are generally of two types, referred to as *specific* and *future* (or future automatic subordination clauses or agreements). A specific subordination clause subordinates to a present, existing encumbrance, whereas a future subordination clause obligates the beneficiary of an existing trust deed to subordinate his deed of trust to one to be placed on the property at some future time. The usual reason for subordination is that the buyer intends to improve the property at a later date and wants the seller's purchase money trust deed to be subordinated to a construction loan. In view of several court decisions in which a contract of sale was held to be unenforceable because the subordination clause was not fair and just to the seller, it is unlikely that the use of future subordination clauses will be effective as far as the title industry is concerned.[122] The usual requirement for title insurance purposes is a specific subordination.

Forms of subordination agreements, prepared by title companies as a guide, are often provided to assist counsel in the preparation of such agreements as will be satisfactory to the parties and at the same time satisfactory for title insurance purposes. However, an attorney using these forms should bear in mind that forms are merely drafts, and that it is obviously necessary that the facts in each case fit the form being used. A form alone is not enough—the facts and the form must go together. The forms have been revised frequently to keep them abreast of changes necessitated by new legislation and case law.

This is an area of real estate practice in which the services of an attorney are particularly needed. Even attorneys encounter problems in connection with subordination agreements, but when an attorney fails to exercise ordinary skill, he is liable in damages. The failure of an attorney to protect his client adequately in the preparation of a subordination agreement resulted in a judgment for damages against the attorney in one case. The court stated:

> The inadequacy of the escrow instructions to afford plaintiff the protection which the circumstances of the transaction involved in this case obviously required is undeniable and virtually conceded. No lawyer with knowledge of the most elementary rules of law governing such transactions would have failed to insist upon more adequate provisions to insure that all of the proceeds of the $30,000 loan, which was to be given security prior to that of his client's purchase money lien, would be used to improve the property.[123]

With a view to protecting sellers of property, particularly homeowners in rezoned areas, subordination agreements have been the subject of legislation requiring that subordination documents be so entitled and that notices of subordination be included in prescribed type size in those instruments, including mortgages and trust deeds, coming within the scope of the act.[124]

§9.63. Agreements affecting priority

The relative priorities of trust deeds over other liens and charges may be altered in various ways: (1) by recitals of priority contained in the trust deed; (2) by the execution and recordation of a *subordination agreement*; or (3) by provisions in the trust deed that a prior encumbrance may be renewed in a specified way and that the renewal instrument will then be prior and superior thereto.

§9.64. Agreements not to convey or encumber

On what would otherwise be an unsecured loan, many banks and other lenders require the borrower to execute an agreement not to convey or encumber real property owned by him. It has been held in California that an agreement not to encumber or transfer property, exacted by a lender to protect its security interest, is not an invalid restraint on alienation. This is so because the restraint is reasonably designed to protect the creditor's justifiable interest in maintaining the direct responsibility of the parties on whose credit the loan was made.[125] Such an agreement has been held to be an equitable mortgage and, dependent on the particular terms and provisions thereof, it may be subject to judicial foreclosure.

In one case, it was held that the assignment of rents and agreement not to sell or encumber used in that particular transaction could not reasonably be construed as a mortgage, and that it could not be the subject of foreclosure.[126]

§9.65. Advantage to seller of trust deed over land contract

The advantage of a trust deed over a land contract, as far as a seller is concerned, is illustrated in the following case.

EXAMPLE This was an action for damages for unjust enrichment in a transaction involving the sale of residential property. The buyer of the property brought the action against the seller after the buyer lost the property at a foreclosure sale under the purchase money trust deed. The original selling price of the property was $145,000. The buyer paid $30,000 cash and signed a note secured by a purchase money trust deed for $115,000, with monthly payments of $900. The buyer was in possession approximately 21 months, making additional payments for repairs, improvements, taxes, interest, and payments on the note totalling almost $33,000.

In this action, the buyers alleged: (1) that the value of the property at the time the seller reacquired it at the trustee's sale was not less than the contract price plus the cost of the repairs and improvements (a total of $164,679.16); (2) that the reasonable rental value for the period of the buyer's occupancy was $750 per month (a total of $16,140); (3) that the total expenditure of the buyer was $62,961.54; and (4) that the buyer therefore had been damaged and the seller had been unjustly enriched by the difference, or the amount of $46,821.14. The court was asked to rule on the following question: If a vendor of real property forecloses a trust deed given to secure the vendee's purchase money note, and bids on the property at the foreclosure sale, and the value of the property at that time is more than the unpaid balance of the underlying debt, is the vendee entitled to restitution of payments made toward the purchase price of the property and moneys expended for repairs and improvements, less the rental value of the property for the period of his occupancy? The court ruled that he was not; however, if the sale had been under a land sales contract, then the court's ruling would have been in the vendee's favor.

The court stated that in a case such as this the rights of the parties are determined by the statutory provisions respecting foreclosures of trust deeds, and that the case law relating to forfeiture of rights under land sales contracts was not applicable.[127]

From the above, it is clear that the legislature intended that a properly conducted foreclosure sale should constitute a final adjudication of the rights of the borrower and the lender.

§9.66. Liability of construction lender

In one case, it was held that a savings and loan association had a close enough connection with a tract development for a duty to arise on the part of the association toward purchasers of individual residence houses in the development. In view of this, the court ruled that the individual purchasers should not have been nonsuited in their action against the lending institution based on faulty construction of their houses.[128]

In 1969 the legislature added a provision to the Civil Code limiting the liability of a lender. This law provides that a lender lending money that is, or may be, used to finance the design, manufacture, construction, modification, or improvement of real or personal property for sale to others shall not be held liable to third persons for any loss or damage caused by any defect in the borrower's product or by the borrower's negligence. Under this law, the lender is not precluded from liability when such loss and damages result from an act of the lender outside the scope of the activities of the lender of money, or when the lender has been a party to misrepresentations with respect to the real or personal property involved in the loss or damage.[129]

QUESTIONS

Matching Terms

a. Mortgage
b. Hypothecate
c. Assume
d. Trust deed
e. Trustor
f. Beneficiary
g. Subordination
h. Satisfaction
i. Wrap-around mortgage
j. Take-out

1. Acceptance of a lower mortgage priority than one a creditor already has.
2. Discharge of a mortgage upon payment of the debt.
3. Permanent loan used to pay a construction loan.
4. A security instrument that encompasses an existing obligation.
5. Three-party security instrument.
6. Two-party instrument used to secure payment of a debt.
7. Agreeing to be responsible for the debt of another obligor.
8. Borrower under a trust deed.
9. Lender under a deed of trust.
10. To pledge property to secure a debt without giving up possession.

True/False

T F 11. A mortgage is a three-party instrument, whereas a deed of trust customarily has two parties.

T F 12. Acceleration clauses in notes secured by a trust deed are unenforceable.

T F 13. A promissory note, to be valid, must be negotiable.

T F 14. An amortized note can be either fully amortized or partially amortized.

T F 15. A holder in due course is comparable to a bona fide purchaser for value without notice of defect.

T F 16. Basically, both mortgages and trust deeds are security instruments.

T F 17. Priority of a mortgage or trust deed is generally determined by time of recording.

T F 18. Balloon payment provisions are illegal in California.

T F 19. An alienation clause is a form of acceleration clause.

T F 20. Usury is charging more interest than the law allows on a loan or forbearance.

Multiple Choice

21. A trust deed or mortgage is regarded as
    a. A lien.
    b. An encumbrance.
    c. Both a and b.
    d. Neither a nor b.

22. A mortgage customarily has the following number of parties:
    a. One.
    b. Two.
    c. Three.
    d. Four.

23. A trust deed customarily has the following number of parties:
    a. Two.
    b. Three.
    c. Four.
    d. Five.

24. The trustee under a deed of trust is the party who
    a. Lends the money.
    b. Holds the legal title as security.
    c. Signs the note.
    d. Executes the trust deed.

25. An instrument by which an earlier recorded deed of trust is made junior to a later recorded trust deed is called
    a. An acceleration clause.
    b. An alienation clause.
    c. A subordination agreement.
    d. A subrogation.

26. "To be on a parity" means that a lien is
    a. Of equal rank.
    b. Prior.
    c. Subordinate.
    d. Any of the above.

27. If a trust deed secures payment of future advances, it is
    a. Unenforceable as contrary to public policy.
    b. Enforceable in accordance with prescribed rules of priority.
    c. Subject to foreclosure only by court action.
    d. Unenforceable for uncertainty.

28. A clause in an installment note that permits the payee, in the event of default, to declare the entire amount immediately due is called
    a. An acceleration clause.
    b. An amortization clause.
    c. A priority clause.
    d. An open-end clause.

29. The document used to clear a trust deed from the records is called a
    a. Release of mortgage.
    b. Satisfaction of judgment.
    c. Deed of reconveyance.
    d. Notice of completion.

30. The party who has the right of possession under a trust deed is the
    a. Trustee.
    b. Beneficiary.
    c. Mortgagee.
    d. Trustor.

31. A real property mortgage is cleared from the records by
    a. Final payment.
    b. Default of the mortgage.
    c. A deed of reconveyance.
    d. A release of mortgage.
32. The mortgagor's right to redeem property after the foreclosure sale is called
    a. Unlawful detainer.
    b. Deficiency judgment.
    c. Equity of redemption.
    d. Satisfaction of mortgage.
33. When a note secured by a trust deed is paid, the note should be
    a. Recorded.
    b. Destroyed.
    c. Burned at a public ceremony.
    d. Delivered to trustee when reconveyance is requested.
34. It is advisable for the holder of a junior lien to record a
    a. Notice of nonresponsibility.
    b. Notice of interest in real property.
    c. Lis pendens (notice of action).
    d. Request for notice of default.
35. A fictitious deed of trust can be foreclosed
    a. Either by trustee's sale or by court action.
    b. By trustee's sale only.
    c. By court action only.
    d. It is not subject to foreclosure.
36. The word *obligatory* has a meaning opposite to
    a. Compulsory.
    b. Conditional.
    c. Optional.
    d. Qualified.
37. To be valid, a trust deed must be
    a. Acknowledged.
    b. In writing.
    c. Verified.
    d. Recorded.
38. A purchase money trust deed has which of the following characteristics?
    a. Has priority over judgment liens previously recorded against the buyer.
    b. Is not subject to foreclosure.
    c. Is subject to foreclosure by court action only.
    d. Seller, with few exceptions, is entitled to a deficiency judgment.
39. The instrument that is used to secure a loan of personal property is called a
    a. Security agreement.
    b. Bill of exchange.
    c. Bill of sale.
    d. Trust deed.
40. If a deed is in fact a mortgage, who is the mortgagor?
    a. Grantee.
    b. Grantor.
    c. Both a and b.
    d. Neither a nor b.
41. A deed in lieu of foreclosure
    a. Should be supported by adequate consideration.
    b. Automatically removes a trust deed from the records.
    c. Must be recorded to be effective.
    d. Is contrary to public policy.
42. Which of the following requires the signature of the trustee under a trust deed?
    a. The note.
    b. The trust deed.
    c. Request for partial reconveyance.
    d. Deed of reconveyance.
43. When you use real property as security for a loan, you
    a. Pledge it and give up possession.
    b. Hypothecate it.
    c. Devise it.
    d. Bequeath it.
44. Until final payment is made, a trust deed ordinarily is retained by the
    a. Landowner.
    b. Trustor.
    c. Beneficiary.
    d. Trustee.
45. A trust deed can be given to secure
    a. Only payment of a debt.
    b. Only performance of an obligation other than a debt.
    c. Payment of a debt or performance of any lawful obligation.
    d. None of the above.
46. Under a purchase money deed of trust, a power of sale is given by
    a. Beneficiary to seller.
    b. Buyer to trustor.
    c. Trustor to buyer.
    d. Trustor to trustee.
47. A "wrap-around" trust deed has which of the following characteristics?
    a. It is similar to an all-inclusive trust deed.
    b. It is junior to another trust deed.
    c. The note is for an amount greater than the new obligation.
    d. All of the above.
48. The Federal Truth in Lending Act
    a. Is primarily a regulatory act.
    b. Is primarily a disclosure act.
    c. Applies only to real property transactions.
    d. Applies only to personal property transactions.
49. The recording of a "Request for Notice of Default" is ordinarily done by the

a. Trustee on the first trust deed.

b. Trustor on the first trust deed.

c. Trustee on the second trust deed.

d. Beneficiary on the second trust deed.

50. An acceleration clause in a note and trust deed is one that provides for

a. Increasing interest rates.

b. Decreasing interest rates.

c. Extension of due date.

d. Entire debt to become due upon a specified happening.

NOTES

1. B. & P. 10244.1; B. & P. 10244. *See also* Harris v. Gallant (1960) 183 C.A.2d 94; 35 Ops. Cal. Atty. Gen. 168; 27 Ops. Cal. Atty. Gen. 374.

2. *See* C.C. 2924i. *See also* section 10.3.

3. B. & P. 10245. *See also* B. & P. 10242.1 re licensee providing credit life and disability insurance.

4. U.C.C. 3104.

5. U.C.C. 3302(1).

6. U.C.C. 3306.

7. U.C.C. 3304, 3305.

8. C.C. 2920, 2924.

9. C.C.P. 729.030.

10. C.C. 882.020 and related sections; Miller v. Provost (1994) 26 C.A. 4th 1703.

11. C.C.P. 580b; *see also* Chapter 10.

12. Weaver v. Bay (1963) 216 C.A.2d 559.

13. McKnight v. U.S. (1958) 259 Fed.2d 540.

14. C.C. 2911.

15. C.C.P. 726. *See* C.C.P. 726(f) regarding damages, including punitive damages, for fraudulent conduct by borrower in inducing lender to make loan.

16. Aguilar v. Bocci (1974) 39 C.A.3d 475; Mixx v. Sodd (1981) 126 C.A.3d 386.

17. C.C. 2888, 2924.

18. Shusett v. Home Savings & Loan (1964) 231 C.A.2d 146.

19. Ricklers v. Temple (1970) 4 C.A.3d 869.

20. Develop-Amatic Engineering v. Republic Mortgage Co. (1976) 12 C.A.3d 143.

21. Govt. C. 27321.5.

22. *See* Chapter 11 for discussion of mechanics' liens and their priority.

23. C.C. 2941; C.C. 2941.5.

24. Fickling v. Jackman (1928) 203 C. 657.

25. Atkinson v. Foote (1919) 44 C.A. 149.

26. Lomanto v. Bank of America (1972) 22 C.A.3d 663; Union Bank v. Wedland (1976) 54 C.A.3d 393.

27. Wong v. Beneficial Savings & Loan (1976) 56 C.A.3d 286.

28. *See* §1.47–§1.49.

29. Walker v. Community Bank (1974) 10 C.3d 729.

30. C.C. 2930.

31. Dobbins v. Economic Gas Co. (1920) 182 C. 616.

32. C.C. 2898; *see also* § 11.39; Goldsmith v. Powell (1984) 152 C.A.3d 746.

33. Walley v. P.M.C. Investment Co., Inc. 91968) 262 C.A.2d 218.

34. Van Loben Sels v. Bunnell (1898) 120 C. 680; Stockton Savings & Loan Bank v. Massanet (1941) 18 C.2d 200.

35. Brown v. Jensen (1953) 41 C.2d 193.

36. Brown v. Jensen, supra.

37. Bargioni v. Hill (1962) 59 C.2d 121.

38. Schoolcraft v. Ross (1978) 81 C.A.3d 75.

39. Cornelison v. Kornbluth (1975) 15 C.3d 590; Hickman v. Mulder (1976) 58 C.A.3d 900; C.C. 2929.

40. C.C. 2954; *see also* Fin. C. 865, *et seq.*; 6600, *et seq.*; 5300, *et seq.*; and 18330, *et seq.*

41. Abrams v. Crocker Citizens National Bank (1974) 40 C.A.3d 551. A class action suit regarding impounds was instituted in McGhee v. Bank of America (1976) 60 C.A.3d 442.

42. C.C. 2955.

43. C.C. 2954.8.

44. C.C. 2954.1.

45. *See* C.C.P. 564 and Barclays Bank of Calif. v. Superior Court (1977) 69 C.A.3d 593; Turner v. Superior Court (1977) 72 C.A.3d 804.

46. C.C. 2938; MDFC Loan Corp. v. Greenbrier Plaza Partners (1994) 21 C.A. 4th 1045.

47. C.C. 2952. For attorney's fees under C.C. 1717, *see* Melnyk v. Robledo (1976) 64 C.A.3d 618.

48. Bank of America v. Century Land & Water Co. (1937) 19 C.A.2d 194.

49. C.C. 2934(a).

50. C.C. 2287, *et seq.*

51. C.C. 2934(a).

52. An exception exists if the assumption is specifically provided for in the deed; in that event it can be enforced against the grantee even though he has not signed the deed; C.C.1624(7); Moss v. Minor Properties, Inc. (1968) 262 C.A.2d 847.

53. If a federal lender is involved, a problem exists. *See* §9.45.

54. Black v. Sullivan (1975) 48 C.A.3d 557.

55. C.C.P. 360.

56. Donahue v. Le Vesque (1985) 169 C.A. 3d 620.

57. Lakeview Meadow Ranch v. Bintliff (1973) 36 C.A.3d 418. *See* §9.51 for further discussion on usury. Flack v. Borlund (1938) 11 C.2d 102; but *see* Western F. G. v. Security Title Co. (1937) 20 C.A.2d 150.

58. Ekmann v. Plumas County Bank (1932) 215 C. 671; C.C. 2911.

59. C.C. 2924.5.

60. C.C. 2924.6.

61. Wellencamp. v. Bank of America (1978) 21 C.3d 943, a landmark case in its time.

62. Fidelity Federal Savings and Loan v. de la Cuesta (1982) 102 S.Ct. 1272.

63. Wellencamp v. Bank of America (1978) 21 C.3d 943.

64. Dawn Investment Co. v. Superior Court (1982) 30 C.3d 695.

65. La Sala v. American Savings & Loan (1971) 5 C.3d 864.

66. C.C. 2949; C.C. 2924.6(a) and (c).

67. C.C. 1490; Record, etc. Co. v. Pageman Holding Corp. (1954) 42 C.2d 227, 232.

68. Sharp v. Mortgage Security Corp. of America (1932) 215 C. 287; French v. Mortgage Guarantee Co. (1940) 16 C.2d 26.

69. C.C. 2954.9; Furesz v. Garcia (1981) 120C.A.3d743

70. Williams v. Fassler (1980) 110 C.A.3d 7; C.C. 2985.6; B.&P. 10242.6.

71. Federal law preempts the field of prepayment of real estate loans to federally chartered savings and loans, so that state law is inapplicable to federal savings and loans operating within California. Meyers v. Beverly Hills Federal Savings & Loan (1974) 499 Fed.2d 1145; 12 U.S.C. 1464(a). *See also* Sacramento S & L v. Superior Ct. (1982) 137 C.A.3d 142. *See also* Biancalana v. Fleming (1996) 45 C.A. 4th 698; Ridgley v. Topa Thrift & Loan Assn. (1997) 53 C.A. 4th 1177.

72. Federal savings and loans cannot collect a prepayment penalty if they exercise a due-on-sale clause. 12 C.F.R. 545.8 3(g) and 12 C.F.R. 556.9(b) (1); Chambreau v. Coughlan (1968) 263 C.A.2d 712.

73. Hellbaum v. Lyttan Savings & Loan (1969) 274 C.A.2d 456; disapproved, when inconsistent with Wellencamp v. Bank of America (1978) 21 C.3d 943.

74. Lazzareschi Investment Co. v. San Francisco Federal Savings & Loan (1971) 22 C.A.3d 303; *see also* Meyers v. Home Savings & Loan (1974) 38 C.A.3d 544.

75. Abbott v. Stevens (1955) 133 C.A.2d 242; Groll v. San Diego Building & Loan Assn. (1932) 127 C.A. 244, 250.

76. C.C. 2954.9(b); 12 C.F.R. 545.8 5(b); B. & P. 10242.6.

77. B. & P. 10242.6.

78. C.C. 2954.10.

79. O'Connor v. Richmond Savings & Loan (1968) 262 C.A.2d 253; Walsh v. Glendale Federal Savings & Loan (1969) 1 C.A.3d 578.

80. Garrett v. Coast & Southern Federal Savings & Loan (1971) 9 C.3d 731.

81. C.C. 2954.4.

82. C.C. 2954.5.

83. B. & P. 10242.5, 10245.

84. Carboni v. Arrospide (1991) 2 C.A. 4th 76.

85. C.C. 1916.5.

86. *See* Vanguard Investments v. Central California Savings & Loan (1977) 68 C.A.3d 950.

87. Verbeck v. Clymer (1927) 202 C. 557; Giometti v. Etienne (1933) 132 C.A. 602, 606; 62 Ops. Cal. Atty. Gen. 735 "Applicability of Usury Laws to Sale of Real Property" (1979).

88. C.C. 1912.

89. C.C. 1915. *See also* Ghirardo v. Antonioli (1993) 19 C.A. 4th 862.

90. Mission Hills Development Corp. v. Western Small Business Investment Co. (1968) 260 C.A.2d 923.

91. 59 Ops. Cal. Atty. Gen. 452 (1976).

92. Regents of U.C. v. Superior Court (1976) 17 C.3d 533.

93. Milana v. Credit Discount Co. (1945) 27 C.3d 335, 340; Forte v. Nal (1972) 25 C.A.3d 656; *see also* Moe v. Transamerica Title Insurance Co. (1971) 21 C.A.3d 289, 300.

94. Sarlot-Kantarjian v. First Penn Mortgage Trust (1979) 599 Fed.2d 915.

95. Moore v. Dealey (1953) 117 C.A.2d 89.

96. Denny v. Hartley (1957) 154 C.A.2d 304.

97. Proposition 2; Cal. Const. Article XV.

98. However, loans made for the purchase, construction, or improvement of real property are not considered personal loans. *See* Andersen v. Lee (1951) 103 C.A.2d 24; Baker v. Butcher (1930) 106 C.A. 358. But *see* Strike v. Trans-West Discount Corp. (1979) 92 C.A.3d 735, 745; Cambridge Development Co. v. U.S. Financial (1970) 11 C.A.3d 1025, 1031, which stated that a contract not usurious in its inception does not become usurious by subsequent events. Rather than run the risk of having a prearranged sale of a promissory note declared usurious, the nonexempt lender wishing to receive more than the statutory maximum rate of interest is advised to eliminate the middleman and have a real estate broker arrange the loan, secured by a lien on real property, to the borrower. The real estate broker exemption exempts the entire transaction from the interest limitations imposed by Article XV of the California Constitution.

99. Orden v. Crashaw Mortgage & Investment Co. (1980) 109 C.A.3d 141, 167.

100. C.C. 1657.

101. Daley v. Westinghouse Corp. (1979) 97 C.A.3d 430. In First Nationwide Savings v. Perry (1992) 11 C.A. 4th 1657, the trustee of a senior trust deed mistakenly reconveyed the senior trust deed, and the junior trust deed beneficiary sold the property. The court held that the junior trust deed beneficiary was unjustly enriched and was required to reimburse the senior trust deed beneficiary.

102. Witzke v. Bill Reid Painting Service Inc. (1984) 151 C.A.3d 36.

103. C.C. 2941(d).

104. C.C. 2941.5.

105. C.C. 2941.

106. C.C. 2941.7; Carter v. Continental Land Title Co. (1991) 233 C.A. 3d 1597. Also, the beneficiary could be substituted as the trustee and issue the reconveyance.

107. White Point Co. v. Herrington (1968) 268 C.A.2d 458; Lawrence v. Shutt (1969) 269 C.A.2d. 799.

108. C.C. 2943.

109. Therefore, under these circumstances, an assignee would not be obliged to follow the dictates of C.C. 2943. Black v. Sullivan (1975) 48 C.A.3d 557.

110. C.C. 2943.

111. C.C. 2954, 2954.2.

112. 15 U.S.C. 1601, *et seq.*

113. *See* 12 C.F.R. 226(1), *et seq.*

114. The act (and the Fair Credit Reporting Act, §9.59) is enforced by the Federal Trade Commission.

115. *See* Gerasta v. Hiberia National Bank (1975) 411 Fed. Supp. 176.

116. Eby v. Reb Realty, Inc. (1974) 495 Fed.2d 646.

117. C.C. 2956-2967.

118. *See* 15 U.S.C. 1681, *et seq.*

119. C.C. 2881.

120. In Brock v. First South Savings Assn. (1992) 8 C.A. 4th 661, the court held that a purchase money trust deed has priority over a vendor's lien that arose simultaneously with the trust deed.

121. C.C. 2953.1, *et seq.*

122. Handy v. Gordon (1967) 65 C.2d 578.

123. Starr v. Mooslin (1971) 14 C.A.3d 988; Protective Equity Trust #83, Ltd. v. Bybee (1992) 2 C.A. 4th 139.

124. C.C. 2953.1, *et seq.*

125. Coast Bank v. Minderhout (1964) 61 C.2d 311.

126. Tahoe National Bank v. Phillips (1971) 4 C.3d 11; Orange County Teachers Credit Union v. Peppard (1971) 21 C.A.3d 448.

127. Smith v. Allen (1967) 68 C.2d 93.

128. Connor v. Grant Western Savings & Loan (1968) 69 C.2d 850; Eden v. Van Tine (1976) 61 C.A.3d 839 (re Statute of Limitations on latent defects).

129. C.C. 3434.

10

Creation and Enforcement of Security Devices, Part II

I. INTRODUCTION

§10.1. In general

In Chapter 9, the nature and characteristics of promissory notes and trust deeds were discussed. In this chapter, foreclosure procedures, both nonjudicial (trustee's sale) and judicial, are explained. Deficiency judgments and purchase money trust deeds are also considered, as well as installment land sales contracts and their use as a security device.

Foreclosure is a procedure used to terminate the trustor's interest in real estate. The beneficiary has the dual remedy of either a court foreclosure or a trustee's sale that can be used alternatively or concurrently. Although mortgages are rarely used in California, mortgage rules apply when judicially foreclosing on trust deeds.

The beneficiary cannot sue the trustor for money, on a default, until the security has been exhausted by foreclosure. The only exception to this rule is the situation in which, for example, the security of a second trust deed is adequate at the beginning, but becomes valueless afterward without fault of the beneficiary. Personal liability may be permitted under certain circumstances, but this depends upon whether or not a deficiency judgment is permitted (discussed in more detail later in this chapter).

The reacquisition of title by mortgagors and trustors after foreclosure can become a problem if liens and encumbrances subordinate in priority to the lien of a foreclosed trust deed are ignored in issuing subsequent evidences of title. Special rules of title practice have been adopted by title insurers in this type of situation.

II. NONJUDICIAL FORECLOSURE UNDER POWER OF SALE (TRUSTEE'S SALE)

§10.2. Trustee's sale proceedings

The *power of sale in a trust deed* is largely a matter of contract. Until regulated by statute, it depended entirely on the terms of the instrument conferring the power. Nonetheless, regard must be had for the terms of the instrument as well as the requirements of law, because the contract provisions will also apply to the extent that they do not conflict with legal requirements. In every foreclosure sale, the provisions of the Bankruptcy Code must be considered.

Several procedural changes have been made in the law relating to trustee's sale proceedings.[1] One major change is the provision that a bid is irrevocable. A bid for a higher amount, however, will cancel a prior bid. The trustee also has the express right to qualify a bidder before the sale begins.

§10.3. Evidence of default

When the trustee is called on to act after a default has occurred, the trustee usually obtains from the beneficiary the trust deed and note.[2] These are obtained together with receipts evidencing advances made by the beneficiary for the protection of the security, such as taxes, fire insurance, and payments due under prior encumbrances. The trustee also obtains a statement of the account between the trustor and the beneficiary, including a statement showing the date of the original default, the date to which interest has been credited, and the unpaid balance of the obligation secured. It is then essential for the purpose of effecting a sale that a notice of default be recorded. The Civil Code provides that, before the power of sale in the trust deed is exercised, a notice of default must be recorded in the county where the property is situated at least three months before notice of sale is given.[3] In the event the default was other than nonpayment of money—for example, not maintaining the property—it would seem that the beneficiary must first request that the trustor cure the default before accelerating payment.[4]

EXAMPLE   One case raised a question as to the right of the beneficiary under a second trust deed to declare a default when taxes were not paid by the trustor, but were paid by the beneficiary under the first trust deed. Both trust deeds obligated the trustor to pay taxes, insurance, and other items. The court held that the beneficiary under the second trust deed had the right to declare a default since there could be an impairment of his security, pointing out that a beneficiary under a second trust deed should not be required to sit idly by while the first encumbrance is enlarged by the failure of the trustor to make required payments.[5]

Balloon payments. On loans executed on or after January 1, 1984, on four or fewer residential, owner-occupied units, when the loan is for a term in excess of one year, in order to exercise the power of sale upon a default in the payment of a balloon payment, the holder must first give the trustor at least 90 days' notice before the final payment is due, by first-class mail, regarding the person to whom the balloon payment is to be paid as well as other factual data. The law also provides for attorney's fees to the debtor from any person who willfully violates the provisions of this section of the law.[6]

§10.4. Contents of notice of default and election to sell

The *notice of default* may be executed by either the trustee or beneficiary.[7] It must identify the trust deed by giving the recorded data or the legal description of the property affected.[8] It must also recite the name of the trustor and that a breach of the obligation has occurred and the nature thereof, and that the person executing the notice of default has elected to sell or cause a sale of the property to satisfy the obligation secured.[9] The more common breaches are the failure to pay when due principal and interest, taxes, insurance, or prior encumbrances. To meet due process requirements, the notice of default should state that the trustor has a right to a court hearing if he wishes to contest the matter. All these requirements must be complied with in order to exercise the power of sale properly.

§10.5. Mailing copies of notice of default

Within ten days after the recordation of the notice of default, a copy must be mailed to each person who has requested notice of default, including the trustor named in the trust deed and the present owner who may not have assumed the trust deed being foreclosed.[10] The trustee must also notify the successor in interest of the trust deed being foreclosed, the beneficiary of any junior trust deed or assignee, and the vendee under a land contract or his assignee within one month after recording the notice of default.[11] When a trustee mails the notice of default to the trustor and it is returned unclaimed, the trustee has a nonstatutory duty to use reasonable efforts to locate the trustor.[12]

The trustee can obtain this information through a title company in a "Foreclosure Guarantee" policy. If a request for notice of default is not contained in the deed of trust or has not been subsequently recorded, the notice of default must be published once a week for four weeks, the first publication being within ten days after recordation, or it must be personally served on the trustor. The beneficiary of a junior trust deed must notify the trustee of his change of address and record such change. However, if the trustee had knowledge of the beneficiary's new address, it is charged with actual knowledge.[13]

§10.6. Right of reinstatement

If the maturity date of the note has been accelerated by virtue of a default in payment of interest or an installment or taxes when due, or similar obligations, then during the three-month period following the recordation of the notice of default, the trustor or any junior lienholder has the right to reinstate the obligation by paying to the beneficiary all sums then due, including statutory costs and trustee's fees or attorney's fees.[14] This cures the default, compels a discontinuance of the sale proceedings, and restores the obligation and security to their former position.[15]

§10.7. When payment in full is required (redemption)

After the expiration of the three-month period, plus a period of up to five days before the scheduled sale, the right of reinstatement is gone and the beneficiary is entitled to payment of the full amount of the obligation (redemption) plus costs and fees, including all reasonable attorney's fees *and* trustee's fees. If these are not paid, the property may be sold. If tender is made and the beneficiary does not object, he waives any objections he could have made.[16] Partial payment does not waive the election to continue the foreclosure.[17] However, the beneficiary should so notify the trustor; otherwise the beneficiary may be estopped. If a junior lienholder pays a senior obligation in default, he can add these amounts to his obligation and foreclose if the trustor fails to reimburse him.

§10.8. Notice of sale

If reinstatement has not occurred and the beneficiary or his successor in interest desires to proceed with the foreclosure, the trustee executes a *notice of sale*. A copy of the notice of sale must be mailed (registered or certified) to the persons requesting notice of default and those who are statutorily required to be given notice at least 20 days before the sale.[18] No other notice is required to be given the trustor. The notice sets forth the time and place of the sale, describing the property to be sold and the occasion for the sale. The law requires that the notice contain the street address or other common designation, if any exists.[19] However, the notice is not invalid by reason of the omission of the address. If the property has no street address or other common designation, the notice must contain the name and address of the beneficiary and a statement that directions may be obtained upon written request within ten days from the first publication. The notice must also contain a statement of any unpaid balance and estimated costs, expenses, and advances as of the time of the initial publication of the sale, as well as the name, street address, and telephone number of the trustee conducting the sale. The sale is scheduled to allow sufficient time, usually 22 or more days, for the required publications and posting of notice.

§10.9. Publishing and posting notice of sale

The notice of sale must be published in a newspaper of general circulation printed and published in the city in which the property, or any portion thereof, lies, if there is such a newspaper, otherwise in the judicial district or in the county; it must be published once a week for 20 days, that is, in three publications not more than seven days apart. The notice must be posted for the same period in at least one public place in the city or judicial district where the sale is to be made and in some conspicuous place on the property. It also should be recorded at least 20 days prior to the date of sale.[20]

§10.10. Soldiers' and Sailors' Civil Relief Act

The Soldiers' and Sailors' Civil Relief Act of 1940 suspends legal proceedings that would prejudice the rights of military personnel.[21] It also applies to foreclosures of trust deeds on the property owned by a person in the military service, but entered into *before* induction. In other words, no sale or foreclosure under a power of sale is valid if made during the period of military service or within three months thereafter, except when the sale is made on written agreement of the parties or on a court order. Whether or not a trustor is in the military service must be determined by the trustee. This is usually accomplished by the beneficiary filing an affidavit of nonmilitary service.

§10.11. Place of sale

The sale must be held in the county in which the property, or some part thereof, is situated; it should be held on a weekday, during business hours, and in a place sufficiently public so that all intending bidders may attend.[22]

§10.12. Conduct of sale by auction

The sale should be so conducted that the best cash price for the property will be obtained by the trustee. If the trustee has refused to act, the beneficiary can substitute himself as his own trustee. The better practice, however, is to obtain another trustee. At the designated time and place the person conducting the sale announces the purpose of the sale and identifies the property, and then the sale is open to bidding. Any person, including the debtor and the creditor, may bid. Bids must be in cash or the equivalent.

Only the holder of the debt under foreclosure can offset the amount owing to him. He can bid without a tender of cash, up to the amount of the debt plus interest and costs. The holder of a junior encumbrance who is not foreclosing may not offset his encumbrance even if the surplus would otherwise be paid to him. To hold otherwise, the trustee would be requested to determine the validity, priority, and proper amounts of junior liens. This is an unreasonable burden upon the trustee that could also expose him to liability.[23] When the highest responsible bid is announced, the property is declared sold to such bidder, who pays the amount of the bid, and a trustee's deed is thereafter issued to him.

Beneficiary's duty to prospective bidder. A beneficiary who has actual knowledge of facts materially affecting the value of the property has a duty to disclose those facts to prospective bidders at a trustee's sale.[24]

§10.13. Trustee's deed

The *trustee's deed*, under the power of sale, passes to the purchaser the title to the property held by the maker of the trust deed on the date he executed the same, and any title acquired afterward, without covenant or warranty of title. It is free from any right or period of redemption, except in favor of the United States under prescribed conditions when there is a junior federal tax lien, and entitles the purchaser to immediate possession.[25] Pursuant to provisions usually contained in trust deeds, the deed should contain full recitals of the several steps and proceedings leading to and including the sale. Title insurance companies usually rely on the truth of such recitals appearing in deeds made by responsible trustees under the trust deeds.

Cancellation of note. Following a nonjudicial foreclosure in California, the trustee has the duty to cancel the note whenever the laws of California are applicable to the transaction, but need not cancel the note when the beneficiary may seek a deficiency judgment in another jurisdiction.[26]

§10.14. Postponement of sale

The sale may be postponed, from time to time, at the time and place fixed by the notice of sale.[27] Such postponements may be made (1) by oral announcement at the discretion of the trustee; (2) upon instructions of the beneficiary; or (3) by order of the court.[28] Further, the sale may be postponed as a result of a court injunction or mutual agreement.[29]

Postponement based on a consideration. When the postponement of the sale is made in consideration of partial payment by the trustor, a formal agreement should be executed by the parties setting forth the trustor's consent to the postponement, which will overcome any subsequent claim by the trustor that acceptance of part payment constituted a waiver of the default necessitating a new notice of default.[30]

§10.15. Proceeds from sale

After a trustee's sale, there may be more than enough funds on hand to pay off the creditor. This occurs when the amount bid is in excess of the debt due on the obligation under foreclosure. The proceeds of the sale are applied first in payment of the costs, fees, and expenses of the sale, and then in satisfaction of the obligation under the trust deed that was foreclosed. If the net proceeds are more than sufficient to fully satisfy such obligation, the balance is called surplus, and subordinate liens and rights that were cut off by the sale attach to these surplus funds in their order of priority and are immediately payable therefrom, whether matured or not.[31] If there is a dispute concerning disposition of the surplus funds, the trustee may bring an action in interpleader, and the court will then determine the issue.

§10.16. Defects in proceedings

It is important, of course, that all the steps leading to the issuance of the trustee's deed be complied with. Irregularities in the proceedings, such as a failure to publish or post properly, will invalidate the sale.[32] The presumption, however, is that the sale was properly conducted. It has been held that a material misdescription of the property in the notice of sale invalidates the sale.[33] A misstatement of the amount due is not necessarily fatal. It has been held that a sale under a power of sale specifying a larger sum than the amount actually due is valid in the absence of proof of fraud, if property rights of the debtor were not injuriously affected, or if bidders were not deterred from attending the sale.[34] Also, in order for a junior lienholder to set aside a trustee's sale for irregularities, the junior lienor must first tender the full amount owing the senior obligation.[35]

§10.17. Status of trustor

The power of sale in a trust deed is not extinguished by the death, subsequent incompetency, or bankruptcy of the trustor; however, in the case of bankruptcy of the trustor, the consent of the bankruptcy court must be obtained before the sale; otherwise, the sale may be held to be void, or at least subject to the right of the trustee in bankruptcy to pay the indebtedness and take the property as an asset of the bankrupt's estate.[36]

§10.18. Effect of sale on junior liens and encumbrances

Most junior liens are eliminated by a trustee's sale and may be ignored for title insurance purposes, and include state tax liens having the "force, effect, and priority of a judgment lien."[37] Encumbrances recorded after the trust deed, such as equitable servitudes,[38] are eliminated after the trustee's sale.[39] However, certain junior liens are not automatically eliminated and, in the absence of a specific release, a judicial proceeding may be necessary before such liens will be eliminated from a title report. Included in this category are mechanics' liens, even though recorded after the recordation of the trust deed. (See "Deficiency Judgments," §10.31.)

§10.19. Protecting the holder of a junior lien

As indicated earlier, it is not uncommon for real property to be encumbered by more than one trust deed with different priorities, such as a first, a second, a third, and even a fourth. A first trust deed is, of course, in the paramount position, and a foreclosure of the first will eliminate the junior liens. The holder of a junior lien, to be promptly informed of a notice of default under a prior trust deed, will ordinarily record a request for notice of default in the office of the county recorder in the county where the real property is located. He will then be entitled by law to receive notice of default under the prior trust deed within ten days of the recording of the notice of default. When a notice of default is received by the holder of a junior lien, the latter may elect to cure the default and then proceed to foreclose his own lien, adding the amount paid to cure the default to the amount due under the junior trust deed. If the holder of the junior lien does not cure the default under a prior trust deed, but seeks to protect his interest by bidding at the fore-closure sale under such prior trust deed, he must be able to bid at the trustee's sale the full amount *in cash or the equivalent*. He does not get credit during the bidding for the amount due on the obligation held by him.

§10.20. Federal tax liens

The Federal Tax Lien Act of 1966[40] provides, among other things, that written notice of a nonjudicial sale be given to the Secretary of the Treasury or the Secretary's delegate as a requirement for the discharge of a federal tax lien record-ed more than 30 days before the sale or the divestment of any title of the United States,[41] and establishes a right in the United States to redeem the property with-in a period of 120 days from the date of such sale.[42]

When a federal tax lien inferior to the trust deed being foreclosed has been recorded more than 30 days before the sale date, notice must be given to the feder-al government in order that the lien be eliminated by the sale. If the lien was record-ed 30 days or less before the sale, no notice is required. Although the trustee's sale will eliminate such lien, the right of redemption must still be considered.

§10.21. Mechanics' liens

Mechanics' liens may not be automatically eliminated, although recorded after the recordation of the trust deed under foreclosure. A mechanic's lien will have priority if the work of improvement began before the date the deed of trust was recorded.[43]

§10.22. Taxes and assessments

Real property taxes and assessments against the property are not affected by the trustee's sale or by a judicial foreclosure of the trust deed. Also not affected are liens subsequently arising in connection with the removal of substandard or unsafe structures, which liens are on a parity with state, county, and city taxes.[44]

§10.23. No deficiency judgments

Under the Code of Civil Procedure, there is no deficiency as a result of a trustee's sale.[45] However, if waste was committed by the trustor in bad faith, and the ben-eficiary bids less than the full amount of the obligation and acquires the property at less than the full amount of his interest, the beneficiary may recover damages for waste in an amount not to exceed the difference between the amount of his bid and the full amount of the outstanding debt.[46]

EXAMPLE In one case, this rule was extended in favor of a guarantor, the court holding that there could be no deficiency against a guarantor following the creditor's nonjudi-cial sale of the security.[47]

This rule does not preclude an action against the guarantor when the guar-antor has waived rights under that section[48] or when the obligation was a pur-chase money security.[49]

III. JUDICIAL FORECLOSURE OF TRUST DEED

§10.24. In general

Until 1933 judicial foreclosure of trust deeds was not permitted in the absence of special grounds for resort to equity. Since 1933, however, foreclosure by court action has been allowed by law.[50] When court foreclosure is sought, all the mort-gage rules apply. Thus such an action must be instituted within the applicable period of the statute of limitations, and the sale is subject to the right of redemption. A judicial foreclosure and a trustee's sale can be instituted at the same time.[51]

There is only one form of action that may be brought for the recovery of any obligation secured by a mortgage or trust deed, and that is an *action to foreclose the trust deed*.[52] This is an action in equity by the beneficiary against the record owner of the property and the record holders of all interests and encumbrances that are junior or subordinate to the trust deed under foreclosure. It is unnecessary, insofar as resort to the security is concerned, to join as defendants the trustor or others personally liable but no longer having an interest in the property. However, to the extent that enforcement of their liability for any deficiency is sought, they must be made parties to the action. The United States, as the holder of a subsequent federal tax lien against the property, may be joined as a party defendant and a judgment obtained against it. In such case, the United States is given a one-year period within which to redeem.[53]

§10.25. Nature of the action

The object of the *foreclosure action* is to sell the right, title, and interest that the trustor had in the property at the time of the execution of the trust deed, or that was thereafter acquired. The action must be brought in the Superior Court in the county in which the property or some part thereof is situated, within four years after the maturity of the obligation secured by the trust deed or after the last payment, when payments have been made after maturity. The action is begun by the filing of a *complaint*. A *notice of action* (*lis pendens*) should then be recorded in the office of the county recorder. This will bind persons acquiring interests or liens during the pendency of the action. After jurisdiction has been obtained over the defendants, either by service of process or by their voluntary appearance, a trial is held and a judgment entered. The judgment is called a *decree of foreclosure and order of sale*.

§10.26. Right to reinstate

The trustor has the right to reinstate the trust deed by reason of default in payment of an installment or other money obligation, by paying the beneficiary, at any time before *the entry of the decree of foreclosure*, the entire amount that would then be due had there been no default, plus statutory attorney's fees.[54]

§10.27. Appoint receiver

When the property is in danger of being lost, removed, or injured, or is insufficient to discharge the debt, the court can appoint a receiver.[55] The beneficiary may also wish a receiver appointed under the "assignment of rents" provision of the trust deed. The rents collected by the receiver are used to pay the trust deed and other costs. The receiver's costs and fees are deducted first, however.

§10.28. Judicial sale

The judgment in the foreclosure action establishes the existence and validity of the trust deed, the amount due thereon, including interest together with costs *and* attorney's fees, and directs the sale of the property, either by the sheriff or by a commissioner named therein, in the manner provided by law. The sheriff or commissioner, as the case may be, holds a public auction sale of the property after giving notice of the time, place, and purpose of the sale by posting and publication. On receipt of the amount bid, the officer conducting the sale issues a *certificate of sale* to the purchaser, which certificate operates as a conveyance of title to the property, subject to redemption as provided by law. If no redemption is made within the time allowed, a *deed* is issued in favor of the purchaser or his assignee.

§10.29. Right of redemption

Although the certificate of sale on foreclosure passes title to the purchaser, it is a conditional title, subject to being defeated by redemption, and does not carry the right of possession before expiration of the period of redemption. The purchaser, however, does have the right to rents or the value of the use and occupation, unless the trustor later redeems. If redemption is made, rents collected by the purchaser are credited on the amount of redemption to be paid. The effect of the *right of redemption* is to remove any incentive on the part of the beneficiary to enter a low bid at the sale (since property could be redeemed for that amount), and to encourage the making of a bid approximating the fair market value of the security.[56]

Who may redeem. The right to redeem property sold under decree of foreclosure is now purely statutory. Only one class can redeem: the judgment debtor.

Effect of redemption by judgment debtor. Upon redemption by the judgment debtor, the effect of the sale is terminated, and he is restored to his estate.[57] By paying to the purchaser or to the officer making the sale the purchase price, plus the statutory percentage and any interim advances made by the purchaser for taxes, assessments, insurance, or upkeep on the property and any sum paid on a prior obligation secured by the property to the extent such payment was necessary for the protection of his interest, he "redeems" the property and thereby terminates the sale, regaining the title to the property for all purposes as fully as though he had paid the trust deed without foreclosure. However, if a deficiency judgment was entered against him and an abstract of the judgment recorded, the lien of the judgment attaches to the title so regained by him on redemption.

§10.30. Period of redemption

Redemption by the judgment debtor or his successor in interest must be effected within 12 months after the sale. This 12-month period is shortened to 3 months if a trust deed or a mortgage with power of sale is foreclosed, and if the full amount of the judgment is bid at the sale.[58]

IV. DEFICIENCY JUDGMENTS

§10.31. In general

Deficiency legislation was enacted during the Depression of the early 1930s to help eliminate the difficulties homeowners were having as a result of foreclosures. Before antideficiency legislation, a beneficiary was able to purchase real estate at a foreclosure sale at a depressed price, far below fair market value, and thereafter obtain a double recovery by holding the debtor for a larger deficiency.[59] Because this antideficiency legislation was enacted by the State of California, it is not applicable to FHA or VA financing. In the latter event, federal law controls.[60]

If the remedy is available, the beneficiary can apply to the court for a deficiency judgment within three months after the sale.[61] The court then grants judgment against the trustor personally for the difference between the total amount due the beneficiary and the fair market value or gross sales proceeds, whichever is greater. The purpose behind the latter clause is to prevent the beneficiary from obtaining the property for less than fair market value. In the event that a senior beneficiary has foreclosed, either under a private sale—held under the power of sale clause—or under judicial sale, a junior lienholder can bring an action against the trustor directly on the note[62] unless the security is a purchase money trust deed.[63] In other words, if the trust deed is not a purchase money trust deed, the beneficiary can sue for and collect the entire balance due or can pay up the senior trust deed and foreclose on his or her junior trust deed.

To further clarify the issue, see Figure 10-1.

V. PURCHASE MONEY TRUST DEED

§10.32. In general

A *purchase money* trust deed is a trust deed given by the buyer of real estate to a third-party lender or to the seller for the balance of the purchase price. As to the

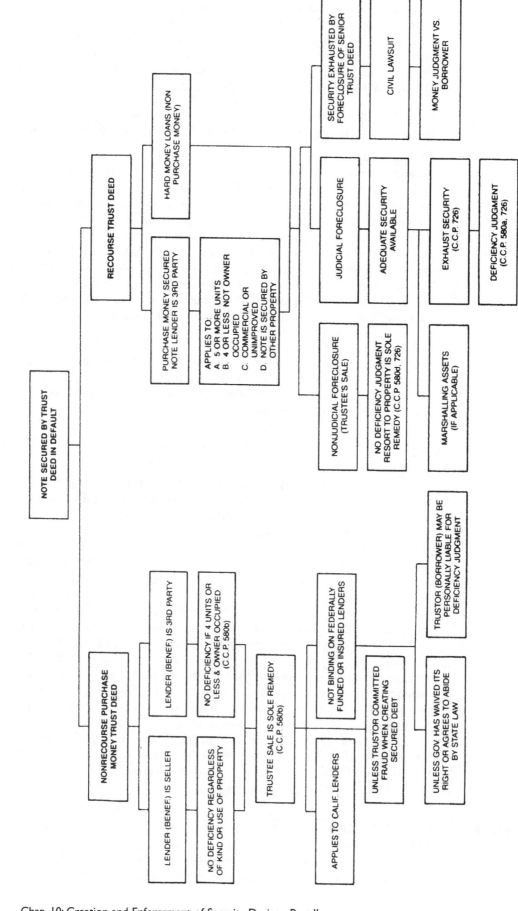

DEFICIENCY JUDGMENTS ON LOANS SECURED BY TRUST DEEDS

NOTE SECURED BY TRUST DEED IN DEFAULT

NONRECOURSE PURCHASE MONEY TRUST DEED

LENDER (BENEF.) IS SELLER

LENDER (BENEF.) IS 3RD PARTY

NO DEFICIENCY REGARDLESS OF KIND OR USE OF PROPERTY

NO DEFICIENCY IF 4 UNITS OR LESS & OWNER OCCUPIED (C.C.P. 580b)

TRUSTEE SALE IS SOLE REMEDY (C.C.P. 580b)

APPLIES TO CALIF. LENDERS

NOT BINDING ON FEDERALLY FUNDED OR INSURED LENDERS

UNLESS TRUSTOR COMMITTED FRAUD WHEN CREATING SECURED DEBT

UNLESS GOV. HAS WAIVED ITS RIGHT OR AGREES TO ABIDE BY STATE LAW

TRUSTOR (BORROWER) MAY BE PERSONALLY LIABLE FOR DEFICIENCY JUDGMENT

RECOURSE TRUST DEED

PURCHASE MONEY SECURED NOTE LENDER IS 3RD PARTY

APPLIES TO:
A. 5 OR MORE UNITS
B. 4 OR LESS NOT OWNER OCCUPIED
C. COMMERCIAL OR UNIMPROVED
D. NOTE IS SECURED BY OTHER PROPERTY

HARD MONEY LOANS (NON PURCHASE MONEY)

NONJUDICIAL FORECLOSURE (TRUSTEE'S SALE)

NO DEFICIENCY JUDGMENT RESORT TO PROPERTY IS SOLE REMEDY (C.C.P 580d. 726)

MARSHALLING ASSETS (IF APPLICABLE)

JUDICIAL FORECLOSURE

ADEQUATE SECURITY AVAILABLE

EXHAUST SECURITY (C.C.P. 726)

DEFICIENCY JUDGMENT (C.C.P. 580a. 726)

SECURITY EXHAUSTED BY FORECLOSURE OF SENIOR TRUST DEED

CIVIL LAWSUIT

MONEY JUDGMENT VS. BORROWER

Figure 10-1
An explanation of deficiency judgments. © 1982 W. D. Milligan All rights reserved

buyer, it is purchase money irrespective of the numbers of units or whether the property will be owner-occupied; however, it is not *treated* as purchase money, and a third-party lender (other than the seller) can obtain a deficiency judgment against the trustor if any of the following apply:

1. There are five or more units.

2. There are four or fewer units but not owner-occupied.

3. The property is commercial or unimproved.

4. Part of the purchase price is a note and trust deed secured by *another* parcel of land.[64]

(See Figure 10-1 for further explanation.)

It is necessary to distinguish the situation in which a builder, not intending to live in the house, purchases a vacant lot and then obtains a "construction loan" to have a house constructed; in that event, it is not purchase money.

EXAMPLES

1. In one case it was held that a construction loan obtained for the erection of a house on a lot owned by the borrower, who did not intend to live in the house, was not a purchase money trust deed. In a later action to foreclose the trust deed, the lender obtained a deficiency judgment. The defendant appealed, contending that the loan was actually purchase money, but the appellate court affirmed the judgment.[65]

2. On the other hand, in a later case, it was held that when an owner purchases a lot and later obtains a loan on the property to build a house he intends to live in, then this loan is a purchase money loan and not subject to a deficiency.[66]

3. The rule that there can be no deficiency on the foreclosure of a purchase money trust deed is subject to another exception, as declared by the Supreme Court.[67] In that case, the court held that the seller's agreement with the buyer to subordinate to a construction loan on a commercial development of the property was reason for applying an exception to the rule, and the seller could sue the buyer on the note given for the purchase price when the seller lost his security and the property by the foreclosure of the construction loan trust deed. On the other hand, rights under purchase money trust deeds can be waived after the loan has been made, but not at the time the loan is given.[68]

Special priority. A purchase money trust deed has a special priority. For example, if a trust deed is given for the price of real property *at the time of its conveyance*, it has priority over all liens created *against the purchaser*, subject to the operation of the recording laws.[69] Thus a previously recorded judgment against the purchaser would be subordinate to a purchase money trust deed.

VI. LAND CONTRACTS

§10.33. In general

Land contracts are contracts by which the seller of the land (the vendor) agrees to convey the land to a purchaser, called the vendee, on payment of the purchase price or performance of some other act at a future date, at which time the purchaser is entitled to a deed. Land contracts are variously designated as installment sales contracts, contracts of sale, agreements to convey, agreements for purchase and sale, or the like. There is no prescribed form for a contract for the sale of land, nor is the name by which the parties choose to call the contract controlling as to its true character. Thus when an instrument was called a lease but recited no term, and referred to *interest, payments,* and *purchase,* and contained other provisions showing its true character to be a contract for the sale and purchase of real property, it was so construed by the court.[70]

Except with Cal-Vet loans, land contracts are seldom used.

§10.34. Essential elements

The essential elements of a contract for the sale of land are those of any contract. In addition, there are certain specific requisites for this type of contract: (1) written agreement or note or memorandum thereof; (2) names and signatures of both parties; (3) sufficient description of the land; (4) a designated purchase price; and (5) the time and manner of payment.

Under the Civil Code[71] every real property sales contract entered into after January 1, 1966, shall contain a statement of (1) the number of years required to complete payment in accordance with the terms of the contract, and (2) the basis on which the tax estimate is made. A tax estimate is not required, but if it is made, the basis for the estimate must be set forth. Such contract is defined as one that does not require conveyance of title within one year from the date of formation of the contract.[72]

When the contract of sale contains a subordination clause, it has been held that such a clause must be "just and reasonable" in order that the contract be enforceable, and that such a clause must contain terms that will define and minimize the risk that the subordinating liens might impair or destroy the seller's security.[73]

Signature of the parties. The vendor's signature alone has been held sufficient in some cases, although the contract, as a rule, should be signed by both parties. It is mandatory that the contract be signed by the party against whom the contract is sought to be enforced, that is, the vendor, or agent duly authorized in writing.

Description of the property. The subject matter of the contract is the land, which must be described with certainty. However, contracts of sale are not held to the same degree of certainty in the description as are deeds.[74]

Prepayment privilege. The Civil Code requires that real estate contracts of sale affecting land subdivided into residential lots, or lots that contain a dwelling for not more than four families, must have a provision permitting the contract vendee to prepay all or part of the contract balance provided, however, that the seller, by an agreement in writing with the buyer, may prohibit prepayment for up to a 12-month period following the sale.[75] Waiver of such rights is expressly made contrary to public policy. On the other hand, there is no prohibition against charging a prepayment penalty.[76]

§10.35. Title or interest of vendor

In general. The contract passes the *equitable* ownership to the purchaser, leaving the legal title in the vendor for the purpose of securing the payments under the contract and the performance of the other conditions of the contract by the buyer. A vendor's lien is implied in favor of the vendor to secure payment of the unpaid portion of the purchase price.

Conveyances by vendor. The vendor may convey the land to a third party, which passes all of the vendor's rights, including the legal title to the land and the right to receive the unpaid purchase price. The grantee holds the legal title in trust for the purchaser under the contract, and will be bound to convey the title on completion of the terms of the contract by the buyer. The grantee from the vendor is under a duty to notify the contract buyer that the vendor has conveyed the legal title to him; otherwise, the contract buyer may continue to make payments to the original vendor. The contract buyer can compel a conveyance from the grantee of the vendor when the contract has been paid in full.

Assignment of contract interest by vendor. The law prohibits a transfer of the sales contract without a transfer of the real property; it also prohibits a transfer of the fee without an assignment of the contract.[77] However, the law permits the assignment of the contract for collection, or to the holder of a first lien as additional security, or a transfer of the fee in trust without the assignment of the contract.

Encumbrance by vendor. The vendor may encumber his interest by mortgage or trust deed. A trust deed executed by the vendor operates to transfer as security all of the vendor's interest in the property, including his interest under the contract. In such cases, arrangements may be made whereby the purchaser, after notice, will make payments to the lender, to be applied on the indebtedness.

Abuses in the use of land sales contracts resulted in legislation designed to give the purchaser a measure of protection from encumbrances by the vendor. The law was amended to provide that a person is guilty of a public offense punishable by up to $10,000 or five years in custody if a parcel of land is sold under a sales contract that is not recorded and thereafter causes the total encumbrances to exceed the amount due under the sales contract, or causes the aggregate amount in any periodic payment to exceed the periodic payment due under a sales contract, excluding the pro rata amount of insurance and taxes. A seller is guilty of a public offense with the same fine or imprisonment if he appropriates a payment from the buyer that is due to the seller, except to the extent that the payment received from the buyer exceeds the amount on such encumbrances.[78] In the definition of a sales contract, an exception is made for contracts that require the conveyance of title within a year from the date of formation of the contract.[79]

Other provisions to protect buyer. The Civil Code provides that when a seller of real property under a sales contract receives a pro rata payment for insurance and taxes, he must hold these amounts in trust for that purpose.[80] The Civil Code also provides that on a written request by the vendee, the vendor shall furnish an itemized statement of the moneys applied and disbursed by him.[81]

> *Buyers under such contracts should arrange with sellers to establish a neutral joint collection account wherein the collection agent is charged with making timely payment of taxes, or buyers should make an annual (or biannual) independent check with the tax collector to make sure taxes are being paid.*

Judgments against vendor. A *money judgment against the vendor* is a lien on the legal title and the vendor's interest in the payments due under the contract. If the vendor has been paid the full purchase price, a subsequent judgment against the vendor creates no lien. If there is an execution sale under a judgment against the vendor before payment of the contract in full, the execution purchaser stands in the place of the original vendor, and will be obligated to convey title to the vendee on full performance of the contract by the vendee.

Easements by vendor. Even though a vendor may transfer title or create a lien on the property in subordination of the vendee's interest, he cannot burden or charge the land with an easement or similar encumbrance that would be effective as against the purchaser when the contract is fulfilled.

Effect of death, disability, or bankruptcy of vendor. The death of the vendor will not terminate the contract of sale. An order may be obtained in probate proceedings directing the representative of the deceased vendor's estate to complete the terms of the contract on payment of the balance due under the contract. The same holds true in the event of a disability of the vendor. If the vendor becomes bankrupt, the bankruptcy trustee obtains the same interest as the vendor. Thus the trustee is obligated to convey title to the vendee upon full performance.

Liability of vendor for condition of premises. A vendor may be subjected to liability to the vendee, and to others on the land with the vendee's consent, for physical harm caused by a dangerous condition after the vendee has taken possession, if the vendor knows *or has reason to know* of an undisclosed dangerous condition, whether natural or artificial, and realizes *or should realize* the risk involved to those persons and has concealed or failed to disclose the condition to the vendee. Previously, liability was imposed only when the vendor actually knew of the condition and realized the risk involved.

As to persons outside the land who are physically harmed as a result of a dangerous condition of the premises, such as a structure in a state of disrepair, a vendor was previously liable when he had *created*, before the transfer of possession, such dangerous condition on the land. The liability has been expanded in scope by imposing liability when the vendor negligently permits such a structure or condition to remain on the land.

§10.36. Title or interest of vendee

In general. The vendee, as the equitable owner of the property, has many rights incident to the ownership of the fee. He may transfer his interest in the contract, either by an assignment of the contract or by a deed. Even though the contract contains a covenant against assignment without the vendor's consent, an assignment would nonetheless be valid as between the parties thereto, and passes the vendee's interest. A covenant against assignment is for the benefit of the vendor alone, who may waive it either expressly or by conduct, such as by accepting payments from the assignee. In order to transfer a Cal-Vet loan, written consent must first be obtained from the California Department of Veteran Affairs.[82] If the loan is assigned to a nonveteran, the department may wish to increase the interest rate. However, if, upon a marital dissolution, a spouse obtains the house and resides there with the veteran's children, the spouse may pay the original loan rate.[83]

Homestead by vendee. A homestead may be declared if the purchaser is in possession and if other conditions of the homestead law are complied with. The homestead on the purchaser's equitable interest under the contract protects the fee title acquired by the purchaser on fulfillment of the contract.[84]

Contracts by vendee. The purchaser may execute a contract of sale in favor of another purchaser, but such subcontract is not an assignment and creates no relationship between the original vendor and the second purchaser.

Encumbrance by vendee. The purchaser may mortgage or otherwise encumber the contract in the same manner as an encumbrance on real property, but the lien covers only the interest under the contract, which is generally considered not attractive security from a lender's viewpoint.

Judgments against vendee. The law provides that a recorded abstract of judgment against the vendee attaches as a lien on the equitable title of the vendee under an agreement of sale on the date the abstract is recorded. The lien of an abstract of an enforceable judgment against a vendee recorded prior to July 1, 1983 (although not then a lien) will attach as a lien on the vendee's equitable title on that date.[85]

No deficiency judgment against vendee. As in the case of a purchase money mortgage or deed of trust, there can be no deficiency judgment against the purchaser in proceedings to foreclose if a default occurs.

Effect of death, disability, or bankruptcy of vendee. The death of the purchaser will not terminate the contract of sale. If the purchaser dies, the executor or administrator has the right and the duty to perform the contract in accordance with its terms if it is in the best interests of the estate. Likewise, the disability or bankruptcy of the vendee does not terminate the contract.

Recording the contract. The purchaser is not entitled to record the contract unless it is acknowledged *by the vendor*. The vendor often prefers that the contract not be recorded, to avoid the necessity of obtaining a quitclaim deed from the buyer or a decree quieting title if the contract is not performed. A provision in the contract of sale that the contract is not to be recorded would doubtless be void.[86]

Contract interest disclosed by other matters. In cases in which the vendee does not take possession, it may be desirable for his protection that his contract interest appear of record. Although the contract itself may not be entitled to be recorded because it has not been acknowledged by the vendor, the effect of the contract is often disclosed of record indirectly. This may be accomplished by the recordation of various types of instruments executed and acknowledged by the vendee, such as a deed or assignment of his interest, a subcontract, a mortgage, a lease, or a property agreement. Further, an action to prove an instrument or other types of litigation may disclose the contract interest. If either the vendor or the vendee dies, is adjudged an incompetent, or becomes a bankrupt, the contract interest will usually be disclosed in the estate proceedings.

Recordation for purposes of veteran's exemption. For the purpose of qualifying the property for the veteran's exemption, the contract creating the buyer's interest must be recorded.[87] The mere reference to the contract in a recorded document is insufficient if the actual contract is not of record, either in an integrated form or by reference. Currently, the Revenue and Taxation Code permits a veteran who has an unrecorded interest in real property, consisting of a contract of sale, to qualify for exemption by filing a claim of a specified exemption.[88]

§10.37. Conveyance in fulfillment of the contract

In general. When the purchaser has fulfilled his obligations under the land contract, he is entitled to a conveyance in a form sufficient to pass the title, subject only to such encumbrances on the title as may have been provided for by the contract. Most contracts of sale contain stipulations regarding the condition of title and provide for a policy of title insurance showing title as required. In the absence of any express provisions as to title or encumbrances, there is an implied condition that the vendor will convey an unencumbered and marketable title.

The Civil Code restricts to $10 the fee that may be contracted for or charged by a vendor or lessor of a single-family residence property for signing or delivering a document in connection with the transfer, cancellation, or reconveyance of any title or instrument when the buyer or lessee exercises an option to buy or completes performance of the contract.[89]

Chain of title to vendee's interest. Problems of title are sometimes encountered in connection with the issuance of a deed by the original vendor. For instance, the deed may not be in favor of the original vendee, and the chain of title to the vendee's interest is thus broken, often because of an intervening assignment not being recorded. This omission may be corrected either by recording the assignments not of record when they are presently available for recordation, or by obtaining and recording a quitclaim deed from the original vendee or the last assignee of record. Otherwise, a quiet title action may be necessary.

Restrictions and reservations. A further problem may arise when the contract is made subject to certain restrictions or reservations, but the deed is silent as to these matters. Generally, a deed executed in consummation of a contract merges all prior agreements and, in the absence of fraud or mistake, the deed is the sole guide for measuring the rights of the parties. When restrictions in the contract have created rights in third parties—a general plan of restrictions, for instance—the mutual assent of the vendor and vendee eliminating such restrictions from the deed will not be effective insofar as the rights of third parties are concerned.

Procedure when vendor dies. When the decedent was bound by a contract in writing to convey real or personal property, a conveyance in fulfillment of such contract may be authorized. The procedure set forth in the Probate Code is not exclusive, but rather an alternative remedy to an action for specific performance. The Probate Code provides an effective means of completing a sale of real property in accordance with an escrow agreement executed by the decedent as vendor but not consummated before his death. The court may order such conveyance or transfer even though the obligation may not have arisen until *at* or *after* the death of the decedent. The amendment makes possible the enforcement of contracts when the decedent's obligation did not arise until his death, as in the case of an agreement for the purchase of a partnership interest when the right of the surviving partners to make the purchase does not arise until the death of the partner whose interest is to be purchased.

§10.38. Advantages and disadvantages of land sales contracts

In general. The installment contract for the purchase of land has certain advantages, particularly from the vendor's viewpoint, but it does have many disadvantages.

Use of land sales contracts. Traditionally, a primary purpose in using a land contract is to effect a sale to a buyer who can make only a small down payment plus small monthly payments over an extended period of time. The sale of real property under installment contracts when the vendor is a responsible corporation, such as a trust company, is a sound and recognized practice, especially in the disposal of unimproved lots held by a corporate trustee under a subdivision trust. The main disadvantage of the land contract from the buyer's viewpoint exists largely in case of sales by individual vendors or entities that do not prove to be financially sound.

Advantages to vendor. The advantages of such a contract from the standpoint of the vendor are the facility and economy in eliminating the purchaser's interest in the event of a default, provided that the contract interest is not disclosed of record. When a default occurs, the vendor may elect to terminate the purchaser's interest in accordance with the terms of the contract, a notice of termination often being all that is required. Less time may be consumed to regain possession after forfeiture than in the case of foreclosure of a mortgage or trust deed.

Disadvantages to vendor. The disadvantages from a vendor's standpoint usually arise if the contract is disclosed of record. The process of clearing the record title, such as by quiet title or other court action, may be involved, prolonged, and expensive, particularly if the purchaser or any of his assigns is under a legal disability—that is, is a minor or an incompetent person, is a nonresident or cannot be located, or is a bankrupt. Difficulties can also arise if the purchaser has suffered or created liens or other encumbrances or interests in favor of third persons whose rights must be adjudicated in a court action.

Advantages to vendee. Although the disadvantages to a vendee usually exceed the advantages, there is one situation in which a contract of sale does have an advantage over a deed to the vendee with a trust deed back to the vendor. The advantage arises in the event of a default by the vendee and an inability to perform the agreement. If a trust deed is foreclosed, the vendee is not entitled to a return of any of the money he has paid. If a contract of sale is in default, the vendee may be entitled to the return of a portion of the money he or she has paid. This rule is based on the theory of unjust enrichment.[90]

Disadvantages to vendee. The many disadvantages in the use of a land contract from the vendee's viewpoint include the following:

1. Transfers of the vendee's interest may be restricted or impeded because of covenants against assignment.

2. The vendee's interest is not considered an attractive security to lenders.

3. Unless the vendee is in possession or the contract interest is disclosed of record, rights in third parties may be created by the vendor and obtain priority over the interest of the contract purchaser.

4. The purchaser's rights might be prejudiced by liens against the vendor arising after the contract is made. For instance, installment payments made to the vendor after the vendee has notice of a judgment lien against the vendor may be at the vendee's peril.

5. There is a risk of loss of title by a declaration of forfeiture without redemption rights.

6. There is uncertainty that the purchaser, on completion of the terms of the contract, will get the title contracted for. Many forms of contracts provide for a policy of title insurance showing title as required, but not until the contract is performed. Before the time for performance, the vendor is not obligated to have good title, and the purchaser does not have the right to rescind for that reason alone, in the absence of fraud or incurable defects. The purchaser must continue to make installment payments in the hope that he can compel specific performance in accordance with the terms of the contract when he has paid the contract in full. If the vendor has no title or a defective title when the contract has been performed by the purchaser, the latter's sole remedy may be an action for damages against the vendor.

7. Regardless of the status of the title and the good intentions of the vendor at the time the contract is entered into, there is no assurance that the vendee will be able to obtain a deed without unanticipated court proceedings, arising, for instance, in cases when the vendor dies, becomes incompetent, or is adjudged a bankrupt.

§10.39. Remedies

Effect of forfeiture. The effect of a *declaration of forfeiture* is to terminate the contract. The vendor may, in a proper case, retain the money paid under the contract and thereafter deal with the land as if the contract had never been made; however, a purchaser in default may be relieved from a forfeiture on making full compensation to the vendor, except in the case of a grossly negligent, willful, or fraudulent default.[91]

Refund of purchase price. It was formerly the rule in California that the vendor had a right to declare the buyer's rights forfeited without refunding to the buyer any part of the purchase price paid.[92] However, later decisions have modified this rule, and the courts now permit even a willful defaulter to recover such portions of the payments as are in excess of the vendor's actual damages.[93] The basis of the decision in the later case is that to enforce a forfeiture would result in the unjust enrichment of the vendor. Also, the opinion has frequently been expressed that the courts "abhor a forfeiture."

Requirements for title insurance purposes. When the contract is disclosed of record, it normally cannot be ignored for title insurance purposes on the basis of an asserted breach and termination of the vendee's interest in accordance with the terms of the contract. A quiet title action is the customary and appropriate remedy to establish the fact of forfeiture and to eliminate the contract interest of record. A deed from the purchaser or a cancellation agreement between the vendor and the purchaser will, of course, be sufficient to eliminate the contract interest of the vendee. An election of a remedy by the buyer, such as an action of rescission and for damages, that is inconsistent with a further claim of interest under the contract, may be sufficient to eliminate the vendee's interest. Occasionally, contracts of sale may be disregarded for title insurance purposes on the basis of factors such as lapse of time, purchaser out of possession, small value of land, long-continued breach, relatively small equity, and similar considerations indicating little or no risk.

Election of remedies. As a general rule, the election by the vendor or vendee of any one of the available remedies is a waiver of another and inconsistent remedy.

§10.40. Implications of *Tucker V. Lassen Savings & Loan*

In 1974, the Supreme Court of California decided the case of *Tucker v. Lassen Savings & Loan,*[94] a significant case in its time. Prior to this case, there had been a question whether or not a lender could cause a foreclosure because of a breach of a due-on-sale clause. The California Supreme Court decided that the lender of an underlying trust deed could not *automatically* enforce the due-on-sale clause if a vendor contracts to sell the property under a land sales contract, subject to certain criteria. However, the law has since changed because of the federal Garn–St. Germain Act (see §9.45).

QUESTIONS

Matching Terms

a. Default
b. Power of sale
c. Foreclosure
d. Redemption
e. Prior
f. Surplus funds
g. Acceleration clause
h. Deficiency
i. Reinstatement
j. Junior

1. Right to cure a default for a limited time after notice of default and election to sell is recorded.
2. Sums derived from a distress sale in excess of obligation owing.
3. Allows a lender to demand immediate payment of an installment note under prescribed conditions.
4. Having a lower priority.
5. Authorization to a trustee under a trust deed to sell the security under prescribed conditions.
6. Regain ownership of property that is the subject of a foreclosure sale.
7. Failure to pay an obligation on time.
8. Superior in point of time.
9. Proceedings to effect a sale of secured property after default occurs.
10. Distress sale of property brings less than the amount owing.

True/False

T F 11. A trust deed can be foreclosed by trustee's sale or by court proceedings.
T F 12. A right of redemption applies to all foreclosure sales.
T F 13. The Statute of Limitations is a bar to a trustee's sale proceedings if the debt is outlawed.
T F 14. There is no right to a deficiency judgment after a foreclosure by trustee's sale.
T F 15. Surplus funds after a foreclosure sale are paid to the trustor in preference to junior lien claimants.
T F 16. Basically, a land sales contract is a security device.
T F 17. Mechanics' liens, if recorded after the trust deed, are automatically eliminated after a trustee's sale.
T F 18. Under a land sales contract, the vendee acquires an equitable title.
T F 19. Priority of a lien is extremely important in the event of foreclosure.
T F 20. A fully amortized loan is not subject to foreclosure.

Multiple Choice

21. If a trustor defaults on a trust deed, the lender can bring action in court or have the trustee sell the property. If he brings a court action, it is called
   a. Specific performance.
   b. Rescission action.
   c. Foreclosure.
   d. Action to compel reconveyance.
22. A second trust deed in the amount of $20,000 was foreclosed by trustee's sale. The property was encumbered by a purchase money third for $5,000. The property was sold by the trustee for $19,000, the amount due on the second. The holder of the third would be entitled to receive
   a. Nothing.
   b. $1,000.
   c. $5,000.
   d. One-fourth of the amount due.
23. A subordination provision in a contract of sale wherein a seller agrees to subordinate his security to a future construction loan means that
   a. Seller will lose priority.

b. Seller will gain priority.

c. Seller will be on a parity.

d. None of the above.

24. Surplus funds after a foreclosure sale under a trust deed are payable to

    a. Junior lienholders in order of their priority.

    b. Junior lienholders on a pro rata basis.

    c. The trustor in preference to junior lienholders.

    d. The beneficiary under the trust deed foreclosed.

25. Reasons for bringing a court foreclosure action rather than a trustee's sale under a trust deed include

    a. Deficiency judgment desired.

    b. To determine priority over mechanics' liens.

    c. Discrepancy between clauses of note and trust deed.

    d. All of the above.

26. Legal title to real property, under a contract of sale, is in the

    a. Vendor.

    b. Vendee.

    c. Beneficiary.

    d. Trustor.

27. After the foreclosure of a trust deed by power of sale, the trustor has a right of redemption for

    a. Three months.

    b. Six months

    c. One year.

    d. There is no right of redemption.

28. When a trust deed is to be foreclosed by trustee's sale, there is a right of reinstatement after notice of default is recorded for

    a. 30 days.

    b. 60 days.

    c. 90 days.

    d. 3 months.

29. A trust deed may be foreclosed

    a. Only by a trustee's sale.

    b. Either by a trustee's sale or by court proceedings.

    c. By the beneficiary selling under the power of sale.

    d. Only by court proceedings.

30. The time within which to reinstate a trust deed commences to run from the date

    a. Beneficiary directs the trustee to foreclose.

    b. The default first occurs.

    c. Notice of default is recorded.

    d. Request for notice of default is recorded.

31. A trustee's sale will eliminate

    a. Junior mortgages and judgment liens.

    b. Delinquent property taxes.

    c. Delinquent special assessments.

    d. Prior deeds of trust.

32. The Statute of Limitations does not apply to

    a. Judicial foreclosure of a trust deed.

    b. Power of sale under a trust deed.

    c. Court actions on a secured negotiable note.

    d. Any of the above.

33. In a court foreclosure of a trust deed, if the sale is for less than the amount of the debt, the redemption period is

    a. Eliminated.

    b. Three months.

    c. Six months.

    d. One year.

34. Which of the following is not subject to foreclosure?

    a. Purchase money mortgage.

    b. Fictitious deed of trust.

    c. Contract of sale.

    d. Purchase money trust deed.

35. A contract of sale, when recorded, transfers

    a. The full fee simple title to the purchaser.

    b. Equitable title.

    c. Legal title.

    d. An estate for years.

36. A contract for the sale of land, to be enforceable, must include which of the following?

    a. Consideration.

    b. Terms of the sale.

    c. Description of the property.

    d. All of the above.

37. After court foreclosure of a mortgage, there is a right of redemption for a period of

    a. Three months, if sale is for full amount of debt.

    b. Three months, if sale is for less than amount of debt.

    c. Six months in all cases.

    d. Twelve months in all cases.

38. A trustee's sale is held under a trust deed and the property is sold to the highest bidder. The trustor then has the following right:

    a. One year to redeem.

    b. 90-day equity of redemption.

    c. 21 days to pay off the loan balance.

    d. None of the above.

39. To be able to obtain a deficiency judgment in the foreclosure of a trust deed, the procedure for foreclosing must be

    a. Started within 30 days after default.

    b. By trustee's sale.

    c. By court action, the same as a mortgage.

    d. None of the above.

40. If the beneficiary on a second trust deed records a "Request for Notice of Default," this means that

    a. The first deed of trust cannot be foreclosed without his consent.

    b. He will be entitled to receive notice if a default is declared under the first.

c. He will be paid off if the first forecloses.

d. None of the above.

41. A foreclosure sale cannot legally proceed if
    a. Trustor dies.
    b. Trustor is adjudged incompetent.
    c. Trustor is adjudged a bankrupt.
    d. None of the above.

42. Default under a trust deed can be based on
    a. Failure to pay principal and interest when due.
    b. Failure to pay insurance premiums.
    c. Failure to pay real property taxes or assessments as they become due.
    d. Any of the above.

43. A notice of sale under a trust deed by trustee's sale must be
    a. Posted on the property.
    b. Published in a newspaper.
    c. Posted in a public place.
    d. All of the above.

44. Which of the following persons may offset the debt when bidding at a trustee's sale?
    a. Beneficiary under trust deed being foreclosed.
    b. Beneficiary under junior deed of trust.
    c. Judgment lien claimants that are junior.
    d. All of the above.

45. Which of the following persons has (have) a right to redeem from a mortgage foreclosure sale?
    a. Prior lien claimants.
    b. Any member of the public.
    c. Judgment debtor.
    d. All of the above.

46. Essential elements of a land sale contract include
    a. Competent parties.
    b. Consideration.
    c. Agreement in writing.
    d. All of the above.

47. If a vendee defaults under a land sales contract, vendor may
    a. Terminate vendee's interest by notice pursuant to terms of the contract.
    b. Institute a foreclosure action.
    c. Institute a quiet title action.
    d. Do any of the above.

48. Disadvantages of a contract from a vendee's point of view include
    a. Reluctance of some lenders to loan on equitable title.
    b. Possible difficulty in obtaining deed when contract paid.
    c. Transfer of vendee's interest may be restricted by terms of the contract.
    d. All of the above.

49. Disadvantages of a contract from a vendor's point of view include

a. Difficulty in regaining title if default occurs.

b. Liens imposed by vendee.

c. Unjust enrichment doctrine.

d. All of the above.

50. Contract interest of a defaulting vendee under a recorded contract may be eliminated from the records for title insurance purposes by
    a. Quitclaim deed from vendee.
    b. Election of remedies by vendee inconsistent with claim of title.
    c. Quiet title decree.
    d. Any of the above.

NOTES

1. A nonjudicial foreclosure sale constitutes private, not state action, and is therefore exempt from the constraints of the Fourteenth Amendment of the U.S. Constitution. Garfinkle v. Superior Court (1978) 21 C.3d 268. Whether a nonjudicial sale is constitutionally permitted under the Fifth Amendment regarding federally insured loans has not been finally determined. *See* Bank of America v. Daily (1984) 152 C.A. 3d 767.

2. The assignee of the beneficiary of a trust deed is also entitled to exercise the power of sale. Strike v. Trans West Discount Corp. (1972) 92 C.A.3d 735.

3. C.C. 2924.

4. There are new, strict rules for purchasing property in foreclosure. *See* C.C. 1695.1, *et seq.*; 2945.1, *et seq.*

5. Manning v. Queen (1968) 263 C.A.2d 672.

6. C.C. 2924i.

7. C.C. 2924. Only one need sign if there is more than one beneficiary. Perkins v. Chad Dev. Co. (1979) 95 C.A.3d 546. This section must be strictly complied with. Miller v. Cote (1982) 127 C.A.3d 888.

8. Includes a leasehold interest under C.C. 2924f(a).

9. Must be in Spanish if the trustor requested translation of the contract pursuant to C.C. 1632; *see also* B. & P. 7151.28, 7159. If it is a single-family, owner-occupied dwelling and involves a secured contract for goods or services, *see* additional requirements under C.C. 2924 f(c).

10. C.C. 2924b.

11. C.C. 2924b(3)(b).

12. I. E. Associates v. Safeco Title (1984) 158 C.A.3d 52.

13. Lupertino v. Carbahol (1973) 35 C.A.3d 742; C.C. 2924b(c), 2924b(3)(a).

14. C.C. 2924c; C.C. 2924d.

15. Burke v. CFS Service Corp. (1981) 119 C.A.3d 77.

16. C.C. 1501; C.C.P. 2076.

17. C.C. 1486.

18. C.C. 2924b; C.C. 2924f.

19. C.C. 2924f; C.C.P. 692. Under the Unruh Act, the requirements are different.

20. C.C.2924f. *See also* Bankruptcy Code 362 re automatic stay against lien enforcement.

21. 50 U.S.C. 501-591.

22. C.C. 2924g.

23. Nomellini Const. Co. v. Modesto (1969) 275 C.A.2d 114.

24. Karoutas v. Home Fed Bank (1991) 232 C.A. 3d 767.

25. However, the purchaser takes subject to pre-existing property taxes and senior trust deeds. Penziner v. West American Finance Co. (1937) 10 C.2d 160, 180.

26. Kerivan v. Title Insurance and Trust Co. (1983) 147 C.A.3d 225, 231.

27. C.C. 2924g(c).

28. There is a maximum of three postponements; otherwise a new notice of sale is required, but a postponement at the request of the trustor shall not be deemed a notice under this section. C.C. 2924g(c)(1) & (2).

29. *See* footnote 31. For damages for wrongfully enjoining a foreclosure sale, *see* Broccoli v. Golden Rule Church Assn. (1977) 73 C.A.3d 342.

30. Bechtel v. Wilson (1936) 18 C.A.2d 331.

31. Dockrey v. Gray (1959) 172 C.A.2d 388; Cuito v. U.C.B. (1978) 20 C.3d 694.

32. *See* Tut v. Van Voast (1939) 36 C.A.2d 282, 285 286.

33. Crist v. House & Osmonson, Inc. (1936) 7 C.2d 556.

34. Savings and Loan Society v. Burnett (1895) 106 C. 514; Alliance Mortgage Co. v. Rothwell (1995) 10 C. 4th 1226.

35. Arnolds Management Corp. v. Eischen (1984) 158 C.A.3d 575.

36. Cohen v. Nixon & Wright (1906) 236 Fed. 407.

37. Wayland v. State of California (1958) 161 C.A.2d 679. But a broker who has a commission secured by a junior trust deed can still sue escrow company for fraud regarding his commission even though the trust deed is eliminated by a trustee's sale (Romo v. Stewart Title of Calif. (1995) 35 C.A. 4th 1609.

38. *See* §12.13.

39. Sain v. Silvestre (1978) 78 C.A.3d 461.

40. Public Law 89 719.

41. I.R.C. 7425(b)(1); 7425(c)(1). *See also* I.R.C. 6232, 6323, 6334.

42. I.R.C. 7425(b) and (d).

43. *See* §11.20, *et seq.*

44. The latter type of lien is now found in the rules and regulations of the Department of Industrial Relations, Division of Housing. Title 8, California Administrative Codes, Section 1701.4.9.

45. C.C.P. 580d; Western Security Bank v. Beverly Hills Business Bank (1993) 16 C.A. 4th 974; Western Security Bank v. Superior Court (1993) 21 C.A. 4th 156; GN Mortgage Corp. v. Fidelity National Title Insurance Co. (1994) 21 C.A. 4th 1802.

46. Cornelison v. Kornbluth (1975) 15 C.3d 590; Krone v. Gaff (1975) 53 C.A.3d 191.

47. Union Bank v. Gradsky (1968) 265 C.A.2d 40.

48. Mariners Savings & Loan v. Neil (1971) 22 C.A.3d 232. But *see* Bank of Southern California v. Dombrow (1995) 39 C.A. 4th 1457.

49. Bauman v. Castle (1971) 15 C.A.3d 990.

50. C.C.P. 725a.

51. Flack v. Boland (1938) 11 C.2d 103.

52. C.C.P. 725a, 726; Ghirardo v. Antonioli (1995) 37 C.A. 4th 1551.

53. 28 U.S.C. 2410.

54. C.C. 2924.

55. C.C.P. 546 (2).

56. Cornelison v. Kornbluth (1975), 15 C.3d 590.

57. C.C.P. 703.

58. C.C.P. 725a.

59. C.C.P. 580b; Roseleaf Corp. v. Chierighin (1963) 59 C.2d 35; Western Security Bank v. Superior Court (1993) 21 C.A. 4th 156; Alliance Mortgage Co. v. Rothwell (1994) 27 C.A. 4th 218; Jack Erickson & Assoc. v. Hesselgessor (1996) 50 C.A. 4th 182.

60. U.S. v. Gish (1977) 559 Fed.2d 572.

61. C.C.P. 580a, 726; Bank of Southern Calif. v. Dombrow (1995) 39 C.A. 4th 1457. Even though the guarantors signed a waiver that would allow a deficiency judgment following a nonjudicial sale (trustee's sale), a deficiency judgment may not be permitted under certain circumstances. *See also* Bank of America (1996) 51 C.A.4th 607 re sold-out junior lienholder's right to recover after senior lien forecloses.

62. *See* Roseleaf Corp. v. Chierighin (1963) 59 C.2d 35.

63. Brown v. Jensen (1953) 41 C.2d 193.

64. Scott v. Fidelity Dev. Co. (1974) 39 C.A.3d 131.

65. Paramount Savings & Loan v. Barber (1968) 263 C.A.2d 166.

66. Prunty v. Bank of America (1974) 37 C.A.3d 430.

67. Spangler v. Memel (1972) 7 C.3d 603. But *see* Thompson v. Allert (1991) 233 C.A. 3d 1462.

68. Russell v. Roberts (1974) 39 C.A.3d 390.

69. C.C. 2898.

70. Losson v. Blodgett (1934) 1 C.A.2d 13.

71. C.C. 2985.5. *See also* C.C. 2985.51 re Subdivision Map compliance.

72. C.C. 2985.

73. Handy v. Gordon (1967) 65 C.2d 578; Spellman v. Dixon (1967) 256 C.A.2d 1.

74. Coleman v. Dawson (1930) 110 C.A.201.

75. C.C. 2985.6.

76. *See* 6 *San Francisco Law Review* 267, 291.

77. C.C. 2985.1.

78. C.C. 2985.2, 2985.3.

79. C.C. 2985.

80. C.C. 2985.4; Pen. C. 5066.

81. C.C. 2954; B. & P. 11010, 11018.2; C.C. 2985.4; People v. Thygesen (1979) 93 C.A.3d 895; *Real Estate Bulletin* (Summer 1980).

82. Mil and Vet 987.1.

83. Mil and Vet 987.02, 987.721, 986.35, 987.62.

84. Belieu v. Power (1921) 54 C.A. 244

85. C.C.P. 697.340.

86. Resh v. Pillsbury (1936) 12 C.A.2d 226.

87. 30 Ops. Cal. Atty. Gen. 201.

88. Rev. & Tax C. 261.

89. C.C. 1097.

90. Smith v. Allen (1968) 68 C.2d 93.

91. MacFadden v. Walker (1971) 5 C.3d 809.

92. Glock v. Howard & Wilson Colony Co. (1898) 123 C. 1.

93. Freedman v. Rector (1951) 37 C.2d 16.

94. (1974) 12 C.3d 624.

11

Involuntary Liens, Recording, Priorities, Homesteads, and Title Insurance

I. INTRODUCTION

§11.1. In general

In this chapter, a number of subjects are considered that, as we shall see, have an interrelationship, particularly as they relate to recorded liens. The subject of voluntary liens was discussed in Chapter 9. In this chapter, consideration is given to *involuntary liens*, i.e., those not created by a debtor who voluntarily executes a lien document, such as a mortgage or trust deed. The types discussed in this chapter are created in favor of a creditor by virtue of a statute, and include judgment liens, execution liens, attachment liens, and mechanics' liens. To obtain or enforce this type of lien, recording in the office of the county recorder in the county where the real property is located is the usual requirement. This often gives rise to questions of priority—i.e., as between two or more parties claiming a lien, who is in the favored position?

The *homestead law* is a right given to homeowners to protect the home from a forced sale in satisfaction of certain types of creditors' claims. For a number of years in California it was necessary to record a claim of exemption prior to the time a judgment was recorded; since 1975 a debtor may claim a homestead exemption under prescribed conditions after the levy of a writ of execution. There are many rules applying in the case of homestead exemptions that are reviewed in this chapter.

Regarding title insurance, much of the protection afforded to a property owner relates to the condition of the record title, i.e., the coverage is based on matters disclosed in the public records that give constructive notice. The use of title insurance policies in California is widespread. In fact, the requirement of a policy of title insurance is a condition of almost all real estate sale and loan transactions. The nature of title insurance and the forms and extent of coverage are considered in the last part of the chapter.

II. INVOLUNTARY LIENS

§11.2. Effect of lien on rights of landowner

A lien does not operate at the outset to transfer any title to, or estate in, the property subject to the lien. When a lien is created on real property, the ownership of the property, with the incidents of possession and right of transfer, remains in the landowner, subject, however, to the right of the lienholder to force a sale of the property, under judicial process or other prescribed methods, to satisfy the performance of the obligation secured by the lien. On a forced sale of the property, title then passes to the purchaser at the sale. Ordinarily, such transfer of title will relate back to the time when the lien arose and thereby convey the title held by the debtor at the date the lien attached, cutting off rights of third persons that accrued after the creation of the lien.

§11.3. Right to discharge the lien

The owner of the property subject to the lien, or certain other persons having an interest in the property, has the right, at any time after the claim is due and before the right of redemption has expired, to discharge the lien by satisfying the claim. Statutory provisions for enforcement of liens by judicial sale usually grant the owner of the property and other persons having interests under inferior liens the right to redeem the property within a specified time after the forced sale.

§11.4. Expiration of lien

Liens usually cease or become unenforceable after a lapse of time. The lien period of judgment liens and most statutory liens is fixed by the statute authorizing the lien.

III. JUDGMENT LIENS

§11.5. In general

The Code of Civil Procedure defines a *judgment* as the "final determination of the rights of the parties in an action or proceedings."[1] Judgments that may result in a lien on real property are of several types: (1) judgments (or decrees) that foreclose liens on specific property, ordering the sale of such property and the application of the proceeds of the sale to the amount found due in the judgment; (2) judgments that award money and impose a lien on specific property of the judgment debtor to secure payment of the award; and (3) judgments for money against a debtor that do not involve the imposition of a lien on specific property of the debtor, but that may result in a general lien on all property of the judgment debtor not exempt from execution when an abstract of the judgment is duly recorded. It is the last type that we consider in this chapter.

§11.6. Recording an abstract of judgment

Under the provisions of the Code of Civil Procedure,[2] an abstract of judgment may be recorded in the office of the recorder of any county, and from such recording the judgment, order, or decree becomes a lien on all the real property of the judgment debtor not exempt from execution in such county. The purpose of this provision is to give a judgment creditor a form of security for the enforcement of the judgment.[3] When the amount is paid, a satisfaction of judgment is recorded to release the lien.

Various statutes that impose a wide variety of taxes, assessments, and service charges also provide that the same shall have the force, effect, and priority of a judgment lien, when evidenced by the recording of a certificate, abstract, or notice of lien filed in the office of the county recorder. When recorded, they are treated the same as an abstract of judgment. The state income tax, the sales and use tax, and similar types of taxes can become liens on the property of the taxpayer in this manner.

§11.7. Duration and extinguishment of lien

Ordinarily, a judgment lien continues for ten years from the date of entry of the judgment or decree, unless enforcement of the judgment or decree is stayed on appeal, or unless the judgment or decree is previously satisfied, or the lien otherwise discharged.

A judgment lien may be extinguished in several ways besides lapse of time. The lien terminates on full satisfaction of the judgment either by an acknowledgment of satisfaction or by an execution returned fully satisfied. The judgment lien may also be released as to specific property by a partial release executed and acknowledged by the judgment creditor.

Demand for satisfaction of judgment. The Code of Civil Procedure provides that if a judgment creditor, without just cause, refuses to acknowledge a written demand for acknowledgement of satisfaction within 15 days after receipt, he is liable for damages plus $100. This is comparable to the right given an owner of real property to obtain a full reconveyance of a trust deed when the obligation has been paid.[4]

§11.8. Requisites of a judgment lien

For a judgment to constitute a lien, it must meet certain prerequisites, including the following:

1. It must be a judgment that money is owed.
2. It must establish a personal liability of the debtor for a definite specified sum.
3. It must be a valid judgment based on jurisdiction of the subject matter and the parties.

4. It must be a judgment rendered by a lawfully constituted court.

5. It must be an enforceable judgment; that is, its enforcement has not been stayed on appeal.

6. An abstract of the judgment containing the items required by the Civil Code of Procedure or a certified copy of the judgment must be recorded in the county in which the real property is situated.[5] If the judgment is lengthy, ordinarily an abstract is recorded to lessen recording fees.

Judgment for spousal, family, or child support. The Code of Civil Procedure provides that a certified copy of any judgment or order for spousal support, family support, or child support, when recorded, shall become a lien on all real property of the judgment debtor not exempt from execution in the county where recorded, for the respective amounts and installments as they mature.[6] The lien is effective for ten years from the date of recording. A certificate of the judgment debtor that all amounts and installments that have matured before the date of the certificate have been fully paid may be recorded to effect a release of the judgment from property sold to a bona fide purchaser.[7]

§11.9. Exempt property

The lien of a judgment does not attach to real property that is exempt from execution. If a valid declaration of homestead has been recorded before the recordation of an abstract of judgment, the judgment will not be a lien on the property subject to the homestead. (Homesteads are discussed further in Section IX of this chapter.) A recorded abstract of judgment becomes a lien on all real estate of the debtor if there is no prior recorded homestead. However, a writ of execution is prohibited against a dwelling unless it is first determined by the court that the dwelling is not exempt or, if exempt, that the creditor is entitled to reach the interest of the debtor in excess of the exemption.[8]

IV. EXECUTION LIENS

§11.10. In general

A *writ of execution* is a means of enforcing a judgment. In the case of the ordinary money judgment, an execution is a writ issued by the court directed to the sheriff or other officer to enforce the judgment against the property of a judgment debtor.[9] By its issuance, a sale of the property of the judgment debtor may be ultimately accomplished. The process involves several steps, namely, the issuance of the writ, the attachment of specific property (called the levy of the writ), the sale of the property after notice, the issuance of a certificate of sale to the purchaser, and the issuance of a deed if the property is not redeemed from the sale within the prescribed period of time allowed by law.

§11.11. Creation of lien

When a judgment is a lien on the debtor's real property, an execution does not extend the judgment lien or create a new lien. It is the method of enforcing such lien. However, when a judgment is not already a lien on the debtor's real property, the execution, when levied, not only provides the means for enforcement of the judgment but also creates a new and distinct lien as of the date of levy. An execution lien continues for a period of one year unless terminated sooner.

§11.12. Time when writ may issue

A writ of execution may be issued by the clerk of the court at any time within ten years from entry of the judgment, and thereafter by leave of court. A motion for issuance of a writ of execution after the lapse of ten years must be supported by an affidavit setting forth the reason for failure to have the execution issued within the ten-year period. It has been held that a creditor may show due diligence in pursuing a debtor's property within the period prescribed by statute, and that the debtor may show circumstances from which the court may conclude that the creditor is not entitled to collect the judgment.[10]

§11.13. Levy of writ

An execution is levied in the same manner as an attachment—that is, real property belonging to the debtor and not exempt from execution—and seized by filing for record with the county recorder a copy of the writ of execution, together with a description of the property and a notice of the levy, and by serving similar documents on the occupant of the property, or if there is no occupant by posting notice on the property.[11]

§11.14. Execution sale

Before a sale of real property on execution can be had, notice must be given by (1) posting written notice showing the time and place of the sale and describing the property, at least 20 days before the date of sale, in a prescribed public place and in some conspicuous place on the property to be sold; and (2) publishing a copy of the notice once a week for the same period in a prescribed newspaper of general circulation. Notice of sale must also be given by mailing to any person who has filed a request for notice with the clerk of the court.[12]

Time and place of sale. The sale must be held in the county where the property or some part thereof is situated, and must be made at public auction, to the highest bidder, at a designated time between 9 A.M. and 5 P.M.

Certificate of sale. The purchaser at the sale receives a certificate of sale from the officer conducting the sale, and a duplicate is recorded.[13] The certificate of sale is assignable. By the certificate of sale, the purchaser acquires legal title to the interest of the judgment debtor in the property sold.

§11.15. Right of redemption

The right of redemption from the sale in favor of the property owner or successor has been recognized in California for a long period of time. However, the right does not extend to junior lien claimants. Under the provisions of the Code of Civil Procedure,[14] real property sold on execution is no longer subject to such redemption. Except when a sale was improperly conducted, the sale is absolute and may not be set aside for any reason.

§11.16. Issuance of deed

The officer making the sale executes and delivers a deed to the purchaser or his assignee. This deed does not convey a new title, but evidences the fact that the sale has become absolute, and that the title by the certificate is no longer qualified by any rights of the judgment debtor.

V. ATTACHMENT LIENS

§11.17. In general

An *attachment* is defined as a seizure under legal process, called a writ of attachment, of the defendant's property as security for any judgment that the plaintiff may recover in the action. It is a proceeding auxiliary to the main action, and it enables the plaintiff to acquire a lien for the security of his claim by levy of process made before, instead of after, the entry of a judgment. The main purpose of an attachment is to hold property of the defendant for eventual sale under execution when the action has proceeded to judgment, thus assuring that the plaintiff will have something tangible to levy on in satisfaction of the claim.

§11.18. Actions in which attachment is available

In 1971 the validity of the attachment statutes was considered by the California Supreme Court in one specific case,[15] and it was held that various portions of the attachment law were unconstitutional and violated procedural due process of law by sanctioning attachment without notice and a court hearing. The legislature in 1972 substantially amended the attachment statutes to overcome the constitutional objections of that case by limiting the availability of the remedy to commercial cases basically, and by sharply circumscribing the situations in which there can be seizure without notice and hearing.

Types of claim against a resident. For a plaintiff to obtain a writ of attachment against a resident defendant, his claim must amount to $500 or more and be for a liquidated sum of money based on one of the following types of transactions: (1) money loaned; (2) a negotiable instrument; (3) the sale or lease of, or a license to use, real or personal property; or (4) services rendered.

As under the prior law, the claim must not be secured by any real or personal property unless the security has become valueless.

Type of claim against a nonresident. In the case of a nonresident defendant, the claim need only be for the recovery of money, whether or not the amount is liquidated and whether or not it is based on one of the types of transactions referred to above. The claim, however, must amount to $500 or more.

An attachment can thus be obtained against any nonresident who has property in California based on any claim for money, even a tort action for damages. However, the statute provides that such a defendant may have the attachment lifted merely by filing a general appearance in the action, unless the attachment would have been proper under the tests with respect to a resident defendant.

Resident defendants against whom attachment may be used. The statute restricts the remedy of attachment to the following types of resident defendants: (1) all business corporations (including professional corporations); (2) all general and limited partnerships; and (3) all individuals engaged in a trade or business.

The remedy is thus restricted to business defendants and is not available with respect to an action against a person on a consumer debt. Therefore, if a principal cancels a listing and refuses to pay a commission to the broker, the broker has no right to an attachment.

Property on which the writ of attachment may be levied. With respect to corporations and partnerships, all corporate or partnership property is subject to the levy of the writ of attachment. As to individuals engaged in a trade or business, the levy of the writ of attachment is restricted to the following types of property, subject to several limitations: (1) inventory; (2) accounts receivable; (3) bank accounts; (4) securities; (5) equipment; and (6) real estate. With respect to a nonresident defendant, any of his property located in California may be levied on.

§11.19. Attachment procedure

The main objection to the prior procedure for levy of a writ of attachment was that the defendant had no opportunity for a hearing before seizure of his assets. While the plaintiff was required to post a bond, the court considered that to be inadequate protection for a defendant whose assets might be tied up for years before he had any opportunity to contest the validity of the plaintiff's claim.

The new statute, to meet this constitutional requirement, provides for a hearing before a judicial officer prior to the levy of a writ of attachment, subject to some exceptions. However, to make some effort to prevent the defendant from removing or concealing his assets after receiving notice of such a hearing, the new statute provides that, on the filing of a verified application by the plaintiff, the court shall issue without any notice to the defendant a temporary restraining order, to be served on the defendant at the same time as the notice of hearing. The temporary restraining order restricts the defendant in the disposition of the property sought to be attached.

At the hearing, the court must determine on the basis of the affidavits and oral testimony offered by the parties whether grounds exist for the issuance of the attachment and whether the plaintiff has established the "probable validity" of his claim and the absence of any reasonable probability that a successful defense can be asserted by the defendant. If the court makes an affirmative finding with respect to these matters, it will direct the clerk to issue immediately a writ of attachment. If it is unable to make these findings, it will direct the dissolution of the temporary restraining order.

If the writ of attachment is issued by the court, it will be directed to the sheriff or other officer requiring him to attach all property of the defendant not exempt from execution, unless the defendant gives a sufficient undertaking or deposit of money in lieu of the property. If no undertaking is given by the defendant, the sheriff levies on real property by (1) filing for record with the county recorder a copy of the writ, together with a description of the property and a notice that it is attached; and (2) serving the occupant of the land with a copy of such writ, description, and notice, or posting the same if there is no occupant.

A sale of the property cannot be had pursuant to a writ of attachment; the attachment merely holds the property until a judgment is entered, at which time a sale of the property may be had under a writ of execution.

An attachment lien on real property continues for a period of three years after the date of levy unless sooner released or discharged, and it may be extended by the court for an additional period of two years.

VI. MECHANIC'S LIEN

§11.20. In general

A *mechanic's lien* is a statutory lien on real property to secure the compensation of persons whose labor or materials have contributed to the improvement of such property. The lien was unknown at common law or in equity. In California the right is based on a provision of the state constitution.[16] Most liens have priority from the date of recording, but the priority of a mechanic's lien relates back to the date when the work of improvement actually began on the ground.[17] The philosophy of construing the mechanic's lien law in favor of the classes benefited liberally is well settled. With respect to the requirements as to notices, the courts have declared that substance rather than form should prevail.

When policies of title insurance are issued that insure the priority of a lender's lien as superior to a mechanic's lien that might be recorded against a newly constructed building, or when the interest of an owner is insured free of the possibility of a mechanic's lien, the exposure to loss is greater than it is in cases involving judgment liens, attachment liens, and tax liens, for the following reasons:

1. The public records are not conclusive of the fact that a parcel of land is free from an unperfected claim of a mechanic's lien.

2. The priority of a mechanic's lien is not dependent upon the date it was recorded, but upon the date work commenced upon the work of improvement as a whole.

Thus, if commencement of work has occurred on a project prior to recordation of a trust deed, all mechanics' liens are prior to the recorded trust deed. Hence, the lender's "prior" right (prior to mechanics' lien claimants) can be defeated by a mechanic's lien claimant. The lender's margin of security for repayment of borrowed funds (construction funds, for example) is jeopardized by the commencement of work on the project prior to recordation of the trust deed, because if any lien claimant can show that commencement of work occurred prior to recordation of the lender's trust deed, *all* mechanics' lienors will take priority over the lender if the project real property is later sold at a sheriff's sale in a mechanics' lien foreclosure action.[18]

§11.21. Basis of claim

A mechanic's lien must be founded on a valid contract, express or implied. It is not essential, however, that the owner of the property personally enter into a binding contract for work or materials. A lien may arise from work done or materials furnished not only at the instance of the owner, but also at the instance of any person acting by his authority or under him as contractor, subcontractor, architect, or otherwise. It may also attach to the owner's interest when the work of improvement is contracted for by a lessee or a vendee, unless a notice of nonresponsibility is filed as required by statute. On the other hand, public property is not subject to a mechanic's lien.

§11.22. Persons who may claim liens

A mechanic's lien exists in favor of every person who contributes to a work of improvement—from the architect to the landscape gardener. The Civil Code[19] provides specifically for a lien in favor of "mechanics, materialmen, contractors, subcontractors, lessors of equipment, artisans, architects, registered engineers, licensed land surveyors, machinists, builders, teamsters, and draymen, and all persons and laborers of every class performing labor upon or bestowing skill or other necessary services on, or furnishing materials or leasing equipment to be used or consumed in or furnishing appliances, teams, or power contributing to a work of improvement."

§11.23. Work of improvement

A work of improvement includes not only new structures and alterations or additions to an existing structure, but also seeding, sodding, or planting of any lot or tract of land for landscaping purposes; the filling, leveling, or grading of any lot or tract of land; the demolition of buildings; and the removal of buildings.

EXAMPLES

1. In one case, it was held that the setting of permanent monuments by a civil engineer constituted a "work of improvement" even though nothing further was done on the subdivision.[20]

2. In the case of architects, it has been held that there must be work of a structural character for the architect to be entitled to a lien.[21] It was held that a trust deed had priority over a mechanic's lien for architectural services when no work had begun on the ground before the recordation of a trust deed.[22] This is true even in a case when the lender knew of the work of the architect and, in fact, used plans and specifications prepared by the architect in making its loan appraisal.[23]

The theory of the mechanic's lien law is that work must commence in order that persons dealing with the property will be made aware of the fact that construction has started as evidenced by a visual inspection of the property.

There is also a distinction between "on-site" work and "off-site" work when, for instance, a new subdivision will require the installation of streets, curbs, gutters, sewers, etc. (off-site) that will ultimately benefit the structures in the subdivision. Usually, separate contracts and contractors will be involved. Construction of the improvements on the lots in the subdivision is regarded as "on-site" work.

§11.24. What constitutes commencement of work

Not all acts are works of improvement. For example, one case involved an engineering company filing a mechanic's lien for nonpayment regarding aerial topographic maps. The court held that the placing of aerial markers and stakes was only a device to assist the company and not a work of improvement.[24] The question of what constitutes commencement of work for the purpose of determining relative priorities is a mixed question of law and fact. *Commencement of work of improvement* has been described as "some work and labor on the ground, the effects of which are apparent—easily seen by everybody; such as beginning to dig the foundation, or work of like description, which everyone can readily see and recognize as the commencement of a building."[25] The most difficult commencement problems concern operations that are preparatory to actual construction. The following evidence is usually regarded as commencement of work: (1) building materials or equipment deposited, whether on the property in question or on other property in the immediate vicinity, if intended for use on the property in question; (2) foundation stakes set by a surveyor; (3) test holes dug; (4) load of dirt deposited; (5) trees and weeds removed; (6) water meter set in parking place by contractor; (7) preliminary landscaping; (8) installation of sprinkling system; and (9) demolition of old buildings.

§11.25. Classes of claimants
Mechanic's lien claimants fall within certain classes—contractor, subcontractor, laborer, or materialman—and it is important to determine in a given case the particular classification of the claimant, as this will decide not only whether he is entitled to a lien, but also the time within which a claim must be filed.

Contractor. A contractor—or original contractor, as the term is used in the mechanic's lien law—is one who undertakes to furnish labor, materials, and superintendence under a direct contract with the owner or his agent, for all or some specific portion of the work of improvement.[26] An original contract is not limited to a contract for the entire work of improvement. For instance, an owner might enter into different original contracts for different phases of the work involved in the construction of a building. If he enters into a contract with A for all construction work except painting and a contract with B for painting, both A and B are classified as original contractors.

Subcontractor. A subcontractor is one who agrees with the original contractor to furnish similar services for some part of the original contract.

Laborer. A laborer is one who performs labor only on a building or other work of improvement. One who performs labor for a materialman is ordinarily not entitled to a lien.

Materialman. A materialman is one who furnishes materials only to the owner, contractor, or subcontractor, to be used and that are used in a building or other work of improvement. A person who merely sells materials to a materialman is not within the classification of those entitled to a lien.

EXAMPLE A furnished water softeners to B at an agreed price. B installed the water softeners in C's building under contract with C, and was paid the cost of the fixtures and installation by C. A was not paid, and claimed a lien asserting that he was a materialman who furnished materials to B as contractor. In the trial of the case, it was held that B was a materialman, and hence A, who furnished materials to a materialman, was not entitled to a mechanic's lien against C's building.[27]

---

§11.26. Notice of nonresponsibility
If the person who causes a building or other work of improvement to be constructed, altered, or repaired is not the owner in fee of the land, but has a lesser interest, such as a lessee's interest under a lease or a vendee's interest under a contract of sale, the fee owner may relieve his interest in the land from liability for

liens attaching to the structure by giving a notice of nonresponsibility as provided by law.[28]

When notice must be given. To relieve an owner of responsibility, a notice that the owner will not be responsible for the cost of construction, alterations, or repairs must be given within ten days after the owner obtains knowledge of the actual commencement of work. Notice is given by posting such notice in some conspicuous place on the property, and by filing a verified copy of such notice in the office of the county recorder of the county in which the land is situated. The notice must contain a description of the property sufficient for identification, together with the name and nature of the title or interest of the person giving the same, the name of the purchaser under contract, if any, or of the lessee, if known.

Notice must relate to specific work of improvement. The notice must refer to a work of improvement that has actually commenced. The law does not contemplate the giving of a general notice of nonresponsibility to be applied indiscriminately to all further improvements.

EXAMPLE In one case, it was held that an owner's notice of nonresponsibility, posted and recorded before the actual commencement of work, was ineffective to defeat the lien. The reason for this rule is that its object is to give notice to those actually engaged in work on, or furnishing materials to, a project. In other words, it is to require currency in the giving of notice.[29]

When notice ineffective. Under some circumstances, the giving of a notice of nonresponsibility will not relieve the noncontracting owner's interest from liability. Thus, if by the terms of a lease, a lessee is obligated to make the improvements, the entire interest or property will be subject to the lien for improvements by the lessee, despite a notice of nonresponsibility by the owner. In such a case, the lessee is regarded as the owner's agent in making the improvements.[30]

§11.27. Recording claim of lien

A mechanic's lien is not enforceable unless a *claim of lien* is recorded within the time and in the manner provided by law. This requirement has several purposes: (1) It gives notice of the claim to third parties dealing with the property; (2) it informs the owner of the amount of the claim, thus enabling him to protect himself against double payment by withholding from the contractor a sufficient amount to satisfy the claim; and (3) it fixes the time within which the claimant must sue to enforce the lien.

One of the requirements of a claim of lien is that it shall contain "a description of the property sought to be charged with the lien sufficient for identification." It has been held that errors in the description of property in a mechanic's lien claim may be disregarded if the identification of the property is otherwise sufficient, provided there is no fraud and no one is misled by the description.[31]

The *mechanic's lien law* provides that anyone entitled to assert a mechanic's lien claim or stop-notice right, except one under direct contract with the owner or one performing actual labor for wages, as a condition to filing a valid claim of lien and giving a stop notice, must give a preliminary written notice to the owner, to the original contractor, and to the construction lender not later than 20 days after the claimant has first furnished labor, services, equipment, or materials to the job site.[32] The notice can be given by personal delivery, left with a person in charge of the business or home, or by first class registered or certified mail.[33] If a claimant fails to give such notice within 20 days after first furnishing labor, services, or material, he is not precluded from giving such notice at a later date, but is then entitled to claim a lien and assert a stop-notice right only for such labor, services, or materials furnished within 20 days before giving such notice and at any time thereafter. The purpose of the notice is to inform the owner, original contractor, and construction lender, before the time of recording a claim of lien, that the improved property may be subject to liens arising from a contract to which they are not parties.

Since 1988, persons serving a preliminary 20-day notice may file that notice with the county recorder in which any portion of the real property is located.[34] The purpose of filing the preliminary 20-day notice is limited. It is intended to help those who filed the preliminary 20-day notice to obtain notice (from the county recorder by mail) of recorded (1) notices of completion, and (2) notices of cessation.

§11.28. When liens may be filed

If a valid notice of completion is recorded, a mechanic's lien may be recorded within the following periods: (1) by the original contractor within 60 days after the date of filing for record such notice; (2) by any claimant, other than the original contractor, within 30 days after the date of filing for record such notice.

In case a notice of completion is not recorded by the owner, then all persons have 90 days after the completion of the work of improvement within which to file a lien.[35]

Separate structures. Work of improvement means the entire structure or scheme of improvement as a whole. However, when the work consists of the construction of two or more separate residential units, each separate residential unit is considered a separate work of improvement, and the time for filing claims of lien commences to run on the completion of each unit.

Effect of recording notice of completion. The effect of the recording by an owner of a valid notice of completion is to shorten the time for filing liens from 90 days to 30 days by claimants other than the original contractor, and to 60 days by the original contractor.[36] The notice of completion, to be effective, must be recorded within ten days after the completion of the work of improvement.[37] Actual completion of a work of improvement means a substantial completion sufficient to enable the contractor to recover the contract price if he sued. Minor imperfections do not prevent completion. Occupation or use of a work of improvement by the owner or his agent, accompanied by cessation of labor thereon, constitute completion. The acceptance by the owner or his agent of the work of improvement is equivalent to actual completion.

Effect of a failure to record notice of completion. Although the code provides that the owner shall within ten days after completion of the work of improvement file for record a notice of completion, the only penalty for failure to do so is that the lien period is not shortened. A notice filed before the date of completion or more than ten days after such date is a defective notice, and will not shorten the lien period.

Cessation of labor. A cessation of labor may occur after commencement of a work of improvement. Such cessation may be tantamount to completion for the purpose of filing liens. A cessation of labor for a continuous period of 60 days is declared to be equivalent to a completion, and starts the lien period running just as actual completion sets it in motion.[38] Thus, if work has ceased for a period of 60 days, all claimants have 90 days thereafter within which to file a lien. However, the owner may record a notice of cessation within the time prescribed, in which event the original contractor has 60 days within which to file a lien, and all others have 30 days.[39]

§11.29. Time within which to file action

After a lien is duly recorded, the claimant has a limited time within which to bring an action to foreclose his lien. A mechanic's lien does not bind any property for a period longer than 90 days after the filing of the lien, unless foreclosure proceedings are commenced in a proper court within that time.[40] The 90-day period in which to file an action to enforce a claim of lien can be extended by a court order enjoining the foreclosure. The 90-day period will also be extended if bankruptcy proceedings for the owner are commenced within the 90-day period. If a credit is given, it can extend for no longer than one year from the time work was completed, and a notice of credit must be filed for record before the expiration of the 90-day lien period in order to bind good-faith purchasers and encumbrancers for value whose rights are acquired subsequent to the 90-day period.

§11.30. Nature of foreclosure action

An *action for the foreclosure* of a mechanic's lien is a proceeding in equity, and resembles an action to foreclose a mortgage. A complaint is filed, a summons issued, a *lis pendens* recorded, a foreclosure decree entered, a sale thereafter made by the sheriff or other officer pursuant to a writ of enforcement, and a certificate of sale issued to the purchaser at the sale, followed by a deed if no redemption is made within one year from the date of sale. In an action to foreclose a mechanic's lien, all parties claiming or having a subordinate interest in the property, whether an owner, mortgagee, lien claimant, or otherwise, are necessary defendants.

For the purpose of complying with the 90-day filing requirement, the action is deemed to have been commenced the day the complaint is filed with the clerk of the court.

§11.31. Bond to release lien

The mechanic's lien law authorizes the filing of a bond by the owner of the property or by the contractor or a subcontractor to effect a release of a mechanic's lien. On the recording of such bond, the real property described in the bond is freed from the claim of lien and any action brought to foreclose the lien.

§11.32. Stop notices

The mechanic's lien law also permits the filing of a *stop notice* as an additional remedy. Customarily, there is a construction lender on a private work of improvement who loans money to the owner of the project to finance the development, and who retains the money loaned to insure that such funds will be used for construction purposes under an agreed payout plan. A notice to withhold may be given to the construction lender by a person who furnishes labor, equipment, or material to the project. Such notice must be accompanied by a bond one and one-quarter times the claim. Such notice catches whatever funds are on hand at the time the notice is received, but no more than the amount of the demand. The general contractor may not file such a notice.

A notice to withhold may be given only for labor, equipment, or material already furnished. Such notice may be filed at any time before the expiration of the lien period. Further, a preliminary notice must be given to the construction lender within 20 days of first furnishing labor, equipment, or material.[41]

As pointed out in one case,[42] the provision for filing of stop notice claims is an additional remedy afforded to mechanics and materialmen that reaches the construction fund directly, whereas the mechanic's lien is against the property and could be extinguished by foreclosure of the construction lender's first trust deed that has obtained priority.

VII. RECORDING

§11.33. Purpose and effect of recording

Under the common law, if an owner of land conveyed property to A and later conveyed the same property to B, B acquired no title whatsoever. This common law rule has been changed by the recording acts that are in force in all of the states today. The distinctive features of the recording system in California, as applied to conveyances of land, may be summarized as follows: Conveyances of real property may be recorded in the office of the county recorder in the county where the property is situated, and from the time of recording impart constructive notice to subsequent purchasers and encumbrancers. Anyone thereafter dealing with the property is deemed to have notice of the record conveyance, even though he may not have inspected the public records and does not have actual notice of the conveyance.

If the conveyance is not recorded, it is considered void as against a subsequent purchaser of the same property in good faith and for a valuable consideration and without actual notice of the prior conveyance, once the subsequent purchaser records his deed. An unrecorded conveyance is valid, however, as between the parties and those who have actual notice.

The general purpose of recording statutes is to permit rather than to require the recordation of any instrument that affects title to real property, and to penalize the person who fails to take advantage of the privilege of recording. Although the recording statutes do not specify any particular time within which an instrument must be recorded, time of recording is, of course, very important in determining whether a person is bound by the constructive notice that recording imparts.

The practical effect of the recording laws is that an intending purchaser of land or a prospective lender may examine the public records and determine whether the reputed owner is the owner of record, and the date when and the person from whom he acquired his interest, and whether he has encumbered his interest. This determination may be made as to each of the owners in the "chain of title" back to the original source of title. Under the Civil Code, the conveyance, which must be recorded to give notice, includes any instrument in writing by which real property is mortgaged or otherwise affected, except wills.[43] An examination of the record title discloses the condition of the record title as well as the ownership of record. It is a felony to knowingly record a forged instrument.[44]

§11.34. Procedure to record

The Civil Code provides that an instrument is deemed to be recorded when, being duly acknowledged or proved and certified, it is deposited in the recorder's office, for recordation.[45] Technically, an instrument is said to be *filed for record* when it is deposited with the recorder under instructions to record and is actually not "recorded" until the recorder transcribes it into the record books. When the instrument is properly recorded, it operates to give constructive notice by relating back to the date it was filed for record.

Recordation of an instrument is accomplished by depositing it at the office of the county recorder in the county within which the property is located, with instructions to file for record. The recorder then endorses on the instrument the proper filing number in the order in which it is deposited, and the year, month, day, hour, and minute of its reception, and the amount of fees for recording. On payment of the recording fees and any documentary transfer tax that may be due, the instrument is entitled to be transcribed in the records. This is done by copying the instrument and retaining the copy in a separate book or a series of books called *official records*. The recorder notes in an appropriate place the instrument's filing number, the exact time of its receipt, and the name of the person at whose request it is recorded. Thereafter, the recorder endorses on the instrument the book and page of the official records in which it is recorded, and then returns the instrument to the party leaving it for record. Years ago, the instruments were transcribed in the official records by longhand; thereafter, typewriting replaced penmanship; and now photography is taking the place of typing as the means of reproducing the instruments. Microfilm is now being used as a means of conserving space.

The recorder is required to index the recorded instrument in alphabetically arranged grantor and grantee indices, showing the names of the parties, the title of the instrument, the date of filing, and the recording reference. These are called *name indices* and provide the only means by which the title to real property may be traced in the recorder's office.

EXAMPLE If a person is purchasing land from A, the alleged owner, he checks back in the grantee index until he finds the recording reference to the instrument by which A acquired title. He then runs A's grantor in the grantee index back to the instrument of acquisition, and in like manner each owner is traced to the source of original title, a government patent. In addition to a check of the grantee index, the name of each owner in the chain of title must be run in the grantor index subsequent to the date of his acquisition of ownership to determine whether he has executed a deed or encumbrance or other instrument, or whether he is a defendant in a court action affecting the title, or whether some other matter of record may be disclosed. At one time two index books were used, but since 1971 county recorders have been authorized to use a combined grantor-grantee index instead of two separate books.

§11.35. Lis pendens (notice of action)

As a general rule, a person not a party to a court action is not affected by any judgment that might be entered in such action. An exception was recognized at common law in the case of a person purchasing or otherwise acquiring an interest in land from another person who was a party to a pending action affecting the land. Such purchaser was conclusively presumed to have notice of the pending action, regardless of his lack of actual notice, and he acquired his interest subject to the final determination of the action. This rule, known as the doctrine of *lis pendens*, was established to prevent a party to pending litigation relating to land from transferring his interest in the land before judgment was entered against him, and thus rendering the judgment ineffectual.

The common law rule has been modified in California by statute, under which the plaintiff in any action concerning real property or affecting the title or right of possession of real property may file for record, in the recorder's office of the county where the property is located, a notice of the pendency of such action. Thereafter, a purchaser or encumbrancer of the property affected by the action is deemed to have constructive notice of the pendency of the action as it relates to the real property, and only of its pendency against parties designated by their real names.[46] A defendant who asks for affirmative relief may also record a notice of action. The code also allows recording in the county recorder's office of a notice of pendency of an action filed in the United States District Court, the same as in an action in a California court.

Actions to which the statute applies include specific performance, actions to quiet title, partition actions, actions to foreclose a lien on real property, actions to set aside conveyances of land, actions of ejectment, actions in eminent domain, and generally all conventional actions affecting the title or possession of real property, and now, as to fraudulent conveyances.[47] Additionally, failure to file a lis pendens in a McEnerney Action is jurisdictional.[48] Recent additions to the type of actions for which a lis pendens may be recorded include a real property forfeiture under the controlled substances law and criminal profiteering.[49] The notice of the pendency of an action must contain the names of the parties, the object of the action, and a sufficient description of the property affected by the action, and a copy must first be served on the other party and meet other criteria.[50]

Sometimes a lis pendens is recorded in an action that does not affect title or possession.

EXAMPLE In one case, it was held that the court was empowered to expunge such lis pendens from the record. In fact, the Code of Civil Procedure now expressly provides for expungement of such lis pendens.[51]

§11.36. Effective period of lis pendens

A lis pendens is effective only during the time that the action is pending, which is the period from the time of the commencement of the action until its final determination on appeal, or until the time for appeal has passed. Accordingly, the effect of a lis pendens as constructive notice ceases when the action is dismissed or when a judgment is rendered that has become final. If the successful party to an action desires to have constructive notice of his rights continue after final judgment, he must record a certified copy of the judgment.[52]

§11.37. Notice based on possession

When a vendee under a contract of sale or a grantee in a deed takes possession of the land, recording the instrument under which he claims his interest is not essential, insofar as rights of subsequent parties are concerned. The notice resulting from possession has the same effect as the notice imparted by recording. Thus, possession of land by a person other than the owner of record is notice to an intending purchaser or lender sufficient to be put on inquiry as to the right, title, or interest of the occupant, and the intending purchaser or lender is chargeable with knowledge of all that a reasonably diligent inquiry of the occupant would have disclosed.[53] The inquiry must be made directly to the person in possession, rather than merely to the vendor or to persons living in the neighborhood.

The possession by the third party must be of such character as to put the purchaser on inquiry, and must exist at the time of the purchase from and conveyance by the vendor out of possession. The purchaser is not chargeable with notice if he makes a diligent inquiry in good faith and fails to discover any adverse claim, as when the occupant refuses on inquiry to indicate the nature of his interest.

§11.38. Rights of persons in possession

Inquiry of a person in possession may disclose a claim of interest inconsistent with the record based, for instance, on rights under an unrecorded deed, or a contract of sale, or a lease containing an option to purchase, or the occupant may claim title based on adverse possession. Also, the continued exclusive possession of land by a grantor after he has conveyed the title is, like the possession of any other stranger to the title, regarded in California as sufficient to put a subsequent purchaser on inquiry as to any rights remaining in the grantor.

EXAMPLE   If A, the record owner, conveys the land to B by a deed that is recorded, but A continues in possession, a purchaser from B is charged with notice that A may still have an interest, such as an interest under an unrecorded instrument—for example, a deed back to A from B—or a possible right to avoid the deed from A to B for some reason—for instance, total failure of consideration.

VIII. PRIORITIES

§11.39. In general

The Civil Code provides that, other things being equal, different liens on the same property have priority according to their time of creation, subject to the operation of the recording laws and subject to the effect of statutes according special priority, as in the case of taxes and mechanics' liens.[54]

§11.40. Agreements affecting priority

Priority can also be determined by contact between the parties. This is often accomplished by use of a subordination agreement wherein one party, having priority of record, agrees that another instrument, later in point of time, can obtain priority under prescribed conditions.

§11.41. Priority of judgment lien

The lien of a judgment is subject to prior liens and conveyances, including those created by bona fide transfers that are unrecorded, and it takes precedence over all subsequent liens and conveyances, subject to exceptions in which other liens are given preference by statute, such as taxes and assessments. As to real property already owned by the judgment debtor, judgment liens rank in order of their creation, that is, according to the time of the recording of the respective abstracts. As to property acquired by the judgment debtor after the recording of the abstracts of two or more judgments, the judgment liens attach simultaneously at the moment of acquisition of title, and the liens all have equal rank. However, the creditor who first levies a writ of execution on specific property will obtain a superior lien.[55]

§11.42. Priority of attachment

The general rule covering priority among different liens on the same parcel of property applies in the case of attachments. Attachment liens rank in order of their date of creation, that is, the dates of the respective levies. A valid attachment lien on real property is prior to other liens accruing or conveyances made after the levy of attachment, except as to certain liens that are accorded priority by statute, such as property taxes and federal tax liens.

§11.43. Priority of mechanics' liens

Questions of priority are frequently encountered as between trust deeds and mechanics' liens. A mechanic's lien attaches as of the time the work of improvement began, and not at the time the lien was recorded or the time when the lien claimant performed his work or furnished materials. A mechanic's lien is declared to be superior to any mortgage, trust deed, or other lien or encumbrance that may have attached to the property subsequent to the time of commencement of the work of improvement in connection with which the lien claimant has done his work or furnished his materials.

EXAMPLE   In one case, it was held that obligatory advances under a loan agreement have priority over a mechanic's lien when the trust deed was recorded ahead of the mechanic's lien.[56]

---

§11.44. Priority not dependent on time of recording mechanics' liens

The time of recording or the sequence of recording does not necessarily determine priority. The mechanic's lien may be recorded after a trust deed but have priority by virtue of the earlier date of commencement of the work of improvement. Furthermore, a mechanic's lien is superior to a mortgage or trust deed or other lien of which the mechanic's lien claimant had no notice and which, although executed and delivered, was not recorded at the time of commencement of work. However, a mortgage or trust deed that is inferior to mechanics' liens because recorded after the work began, or for any other reason, may attain priority over such liens if a statutory bond is filed to protect lien claimants. Such bond must be in an amount not less than 75 percent of the principal amount of the mortgage or deed of trust.

§11.45. Prerequisites to priority of mortgage or trust deed over mechanics' liens

Generally, a mortgage or trust deed that is executed and recorded before the commencement of a work of improvement is superior to any mechanics' liens arising out of the work, and the priority thus attained extends to the building or other improvements, as well as to the land. However, there are certain prerequisites to priority besides recording the mortgage or trust deed. There must be a valid and existing debt or obligation in existence before commencement of the work of improvement. The proceeds of the loan evidenced by the mortgage or trust deed and the note secured thereby either must be paid to the borrower before commencement of the work, or the lender must be obligated to advance the funds. If the mortgagor or trustor does not acquire title until after the commencement of work, the mortgage or deed of trust, even though recorded before commencement of work, is subordinate to mechanics' liens arising out of the work. When optional rather than obligatory advances are made by the construction lender, there may be a priority of the mechanics' liens over the trust deed of the construction lender to the extent of the optional payments, if such optional payments were not used to pay labor and material claims on the project.

§11.46. Parity rule

The *parity rule* means that liens are of equal rank, i.e., that the foreclosure of one will not adversely affect the rights of the lien claimant whose lien is on a parity. For example, all mechanics' liens arising out of the same work of improvement are on a parity with each other, regardless of the time when the respective claimants performed labor or furnished materials. Such claimants are entitled to share pro rata in the proceeds of the foreclosure of the property under a mechanic's lien foreclosure decree.

IX. HOMESTEADS

§11.47. Nature of homestead rights

In California the importance of protecting the debtor's residence from the claims of creditors has been recognized since the adoption of the California Constitution, which requires the legislature to provide a statutory scheme to "protect, by law, from forced sale a certain portion of the homestead."[57] The governing statutes have changed over the years since the first provisions were created in 1841, the most recent major change being enacted as part of the "Enforcement of Judgments Law," effective July 1, 1983.[58]

Today there are two types of homesteads, the Declared Homestead and the Dwelling House Exemption, sometimes called the "automatic homestead." The Dwelling House Exemption came into being in the 1970s as a result of the legislature's feeling that unsophisticated persons were being deprived of homestead protection because of their unfamiliarity with the simple procedure involved in recording a Declaration of Homestead. The Dwelling House Exemption is now available to everyone, without having to have previously recorded any document or having taken any other procedural steps. The amounts of protection afforded by each type of homestead are the same, although there are differences between the two that have application in certain types of circumstances.

There are common misconceptions about homestead rights. A recorded Declaration of Homestead does not absolutely protect against sale of the homesteaded property. Neither does it totally "save" a person's equity or absolutely prevent suits to collect debts of a homeowner. What is protected is the amount of a homeowner's equity, over and above recorded liens on the property, up to the amount of the applicable exemption. In other words, a creditor may be able to force the sale of homesteaded property in an effort to reach the surplus equity in excess of liens and the amount of the exemption.

§11.48. Amount of exemption

The exemption amounts are presently $75,000 for a member of a family unit and $50,000 for other persons. The amounts refer to the actual cash value of equity of the claimant over and above all liens and encumbrances on the homestead at the time of the levy of a writ of execution.[59] The amount is increased to $125,000 if the person is 65 or older or is physically or mentally disabled and unable to work, or is a person 55 years of age or older with a gross income of not more than $15,000 (or if the judgment debtor is married, a gross annual income, including the gross annual income of the debtor's spouse, of not more than $20,000).[60]

The phrase "head of a family unit" includes the following:[61]

1. The judgment debtor and the judgment debtor's spouse if the spouses reside together in the homestead

2. The judgment debtor and at least one of the following persons whom the judgment debtor cares for or maintains in the homestead:

   a. The minor child or minor grandchild of the judgment debtor or the judgment debtor's spouse or the minor child or grandchild of a deceased spouse or former spouse

   b. The minor brother or sister of the judgment debtor or judgment debtor's spouse or the minor child of a deceased brother or sister of either spouse

   c. The father, mother, grandfather, or grandmother of the judgment debtor or the judgment debtor's spouse or the father, mother, grandfather, or grandmother of a deceased spouse

   d. An unmarried relative described in this paragraph who has attained the age of majority and is unable to take care of or support himself or herself

3. The judgment debtor's spouse and at least one of the persons listed in paragraph 2 whom the judgment debtor's spouse cares for or maintains in the homestead

§11.49. Declared homestead requirements

To declare a homestead, the claimant must record a signed and acknowledged declaration in the office of the county recorder in which the land is located.[62] The declarant must actually be residing on the property at the time the declaration is recorded, with the intent of making it a home.[63] The declaration must contain all of the following:[64]

1. Name of homestead owner

2. Description of declared homestead

3. A statement that the homestead is the principal dwelling of the claimant or claimant's spouse and that such person actually resides there on the date of recording

The declaration must include a statement that the facts stated are known to be true as of the personal knowledge of the person executing the declaration. The declaration may be executed by a person acting under a power of attorney.[65] The description may be either a street address or a legal description.[66]

The validity of a homestead cannot be assumed solely from the recordation of a Declaration of Homestead, even though it is in the proper form, because its validity also depends on certain off-record matters. For instance, the homestead may be invalid: (1) if the declarant was not actually residing on the property at the date of selection of the homestead; (2) if the property is not, in fact, a proper subject of homestead; or (3) in the case of a marital homestead, if the purported husband and wife were not legally married.

Courts have uniformly applied a strict construction of the homestead statutes. If any statutory element is missing, the Declaration of Homestead will be held to be invalid.

EXAMPLE A San Diego Superior Court Judge declared a Declaration of Homestead to be invalid when a judgment creditor pointed out that it had been recorded concurrently with the grant deed and trust deed at escrow closing, and the claimant didn't move in until three days later. Records of the moving company were introduced into evidence to prove the move-in date.

___

It is not necessary that the claimant be the sole owner of the homestead or that he be the owner in fee. The Civil Code of Procedure provides that any freehold title, interest, or estate that vests in the claimant the immediate right of possession, even though such right of possession is not exclusive, is sufficient. Thus a homestead may be declared on property on which the claimant has a life estate, or the right of possession under a contract of sale, or an interest as a joint tenant or a tenant in common with others. The homestead law permits a homestead on real property held under a long-term lease of 30 years or more.

§11.50. Type of structure selected for a homestead

Although the Civil Code of Procedure has for a number of years provided that the homestead consists of a "dwelling house," the structure selected does not necessarily have to be a single-family residence. Valid homesteads have been declared on a mobile home, a boat, or on multiple-unit residential structures when one unit was occupied by a claimant and the remaining units were rented to tenants. The Civil Code of Procedure provides specifically for the homesteading of a dwelling house that is in a condominium, a planned development, a stock cooperative, or a community apartment project. Such a homestead is expressly stated to include the interest in and right to use common areas and other appurtenances subject to the terms and conditions applicable thereto.[67]

That the premises are used partially for business purposes does not prevent selection as a homestead if the property is used primarily as a home.

§11.51. Effect of a declaration of homestead

Once the statutory requirements have been complied with, the homestead property is exempt from execution or forced sale except under two specific circumstances. But for these two statutory exceptions, a judgment lien will not attach to a Declared Homestead if (1) the declaration is recorded prior to the recording of the abstract of judgment; and (2) the declaration names the judgment debtor or debtor's spouse as a declared homestead owner.

The first exception is that a judgment for child or spousal support will attach to homesteaded property. The second exception is that a judgment lien attaches to a Declared Homestead in the amount of any surplus over the total of (1) all liens and encumbrances on the Declared Homestead at the time the abstract is recorded; and (2) the homestead exemption amount.

The homestead, however, will always remain subject to execution to satisfy judgments that became liens on the property prior to the recordation of the declaration, as well as to satisfy judgments on debts secured by recorded mechanics' liens and voluntary encumbrances such as trust deeds, whether recorded before or after the recording of the Declaration of Homestead. Further, a creditor can defeat a homestead claim if money obtained by fraud can be traced into the property.

§11.52. Abandonment of declared homestead

A Declared Homestead may be abandoned by recording a declaration of abandonment.[68] It will be abandoned by operation of law if the homestead owner records a new Declaration of Homestead on different property. A homestead may also be lost by adverse possession. The destruction of the original home and placing of a second home on the property, however, has been held not to be an abandonment.[69]

§11.53. Procedure to execute on homesteaded property

The procedure for reaching the surplus over liens and the homestead exemption amount is the same whether there is a recorded Declaration of Homestead or the owner is claiming the Dwelling House Exemption. The procedure is as follows:

1. Within 20 days after the owner is served with notice that a levy has been made, the judgment creditor must apply for an order of sale. If such an application is not filed with the levying officer within the allowed time, then the officer must release the dwelling.[70]

   The application must state whether or not the county tax assessor's records indicate a current homeowner's exemption and the persons who have claimed it, the reason the property is not subject to homestead protection, the value of the property, and the names and addresses of all persons with recorded liens on the property.[71]

2. The court then sets a time and place for a hearing, not later than 45 days after the application is filed, and issues an order to show cause why an order for sale should not issue.

3. At the hearing the court determines whether the property is exempt as a homestead and whether its value exceeds the amount of all liens and the exemption amount. The creditor must show nonexempt equity.[72]

4. If the debtor fails to appear, the order of sale is served along with a notice stating the debtor's right to another hearing. If the debtor requests a hearing, the sale must be postponed.

5. If the writ is issued at the first hearing, or if the defendant doesn't appear, after the second hearing, a sale date is scheduled. The sale is an auction-type sale.[73] The sale shall not take place if either no bid is received in excess of all liens and the exemption amount, or no bid exceeds 90 percent of the fair market value, as determined by the court, unless a new order is obtained. If a subsequent order is not obtained, then the creditor cannot seek to execute again for one year.

The procedure is expensive and time-consuming. When the 90 percent requirement is also considered, it is most difficult to attempt execution on homesteaded property.

§11.54. The dwelling house exemption

Effective July 1, 1975, the California Legislature enacted an exemption for dwelling houses that exempts a debtor's residence from execution to the same extent as the Declared Homestead.[74] This exemption is often called an *automatic homestead*, although it is not entirely automatic or equivalent to the recorded homestead.

The amounts of the Dwelling House Exemption are the same as under the recorded declaration. The procedure for reaching the surplus over liens and the homestead exemption amount is also identical. Thus, a person can obtain the protection afforded by the homestead laws without having to have previously recorded a Declaration of Homestead. The debtor still, however, must appear in court and claim the Dwelling House Exemption.

§11.55. Differences between the types of homesteads

1. If a married couple lives apart, each may record a Declaration of Homestead on their respective properties. When there is no recorded declaration, only the homestead of one of them may be claimed as a Dwelling House Exemption.[75]

2. Under the Dwelling House Exemption, the claimant must actually reside on the property when the exemption is claimed.[76] With a recorded declaration, however, the claimant may still claim the exemption even after moving from the property.[77]

3. Under the Dwelling House Exemption, judgment liens attach to the property. A judgment lien, however, attaches only to the excess value over and

above the existing liens and exemption amount when there is a Declaration of Homestead recorded.[78]

4. If a declared homestead is voluntarily sold, the proceeds of sale to the extent of the applicable homestead exemption amount are exempt from execution for six months after the sale date. If the proceeds are reinvested in a new dwelling and a new Declaration of Homestead is recorded within that time period, then the effect of the declaration is the same as if it had been recorded at the time the prior declaration was recorded.[79] This rule has no application when the debtor intends to rely on the Dwelling House Exemption.

5. If a debtor plans to file bankruptcy, there may be reasons for recording a Declaration of Homestead prior to filing the Petition in Bankruptcy. It may be advantageous to claim the state rather than the federal exemptions.

§11.56. Probate homestead
If a homestead was not recorded on property of a decedent before his death, or if a homestead was declared on decedent's separate property and the decedent had not joined in the declaration, the probate court is empowered to designate and set apart a probate homestead from suitable property of the estate, for the benefit of the surviving spouse and/or minor children, limited to the lifetime of the surviving spouse.[80]

X. TITLE INSURANCE

§11.57. Nature of title insurance
In general, a policy of *title insurance* insures the ownership of an estate or interest in land, or the priority and validity of an encumbrance on land. It is a contract to indemnify against loss through defects in the title, or against liens or encumbrances that may affect the title at the time the policy is issued.

As in other kinds of insurance, different types of title insurance coverage are offered. The usual form of a title insurance policy is a standard coverage policy, but an extended coverage type of policy is also available that insures against loss or damage from additional matters not included within the scope of coverage of the standard form. Although neither form of policy provides "full" coverage, the matters insured against afford invaluable protection to a buyer or lender, and it is considered essential in most types of real estate transactions that title insurance be obtained.

§11.58. Development of title insurance
In a small community, where land holdings are personal and become matters of common knowledge, the possession of real property by a family, passed on from generation to generation, usually constitutes sufficient proof of ownership, and will seldom be disputed. This was particularly true in past times. With the growth of communities, however, holdings are divided and contracted; strangers with no background of long and continuous occupancy acquire ownership; exact boundaries become important as land values rise. Documentary title becomes an essential proof of ownership, by which an owner can trace the right to the property in an unbroken chain of conveyance dating back to the original source of title, a land patent issued by the government.

§11.59. Necessity for recording laws
The danger, as time goes on, that important documents will be lost or destroyed, and the voluminous accumulation of documents resulting from a need to keep the originals over a long period of time, led to the establishment of a public repository for them—the county recorder's office—where authentic copies are preserved and may be examined. Documents are deposited with the recorder long enough

for the recorder to make copies and index them. Preservation of the originals, after recordation, becomes of minor importance.

§11.60. Reliance on public records
Formerly, the information readily available from the recorder's office, when considered with the known fact of occupancy, could be regarded as sufficient in most real estate transactions. Anyone dealing with a person who was recognized by his fellow citizens as the owner, and who had a good record chain of title, usually could rely with safety on such title. As time went on, more and more reliance came to be placed on the record title.

§11.61. Specialists in title searching
The increase in the number of documents affecting a particular parcel, and their distribution among various public offices, made it more difficult for the average person to search the public records for necessary information regarding property. As a result, the help of persons who began to specialize in title searching was enlisted. From merely helping to find the records relating to the property in question, these persons soon developed the business of furnishing summaries, called *abstracts*, of the pertinent documents. These searchers of title became known as *abstracters* and as their businesses grew, they formed abstract companies.

The work of the abstracter related only to the compilation of the "chain of title." It did not involve the construction, interpretation, or legal significance of the various items comprising such chain. This work called for the services of a lawyer versed in the intricacies of land law and having a knowledge of the laws relating to other matters affecting titles, such as corporation, probate, bankruptcy, and divorce laws. Only a qualified lawyer could construe authoritatively the instruments in the chain of title and form a conclusion, or "opinion," as to the current condition of the title. This system of abstract of title and an attorney's opinion developed to a high point of perfection and has afforded, and still affords, a reasonably satisfactory method of establishing a merchantable title in many areas of the United States.

§11.62. Liability based on negligence
Under an abstract of title, liability did not arise as to every mistake; it was limited to those types of omissions and errors of judgment that a qualified person should not have made, that is, to mistakes based on negligence. Liability was limited also to the actual loss occasioned by the error, and then only to the person for whom the work was done. As a practical matter, recourse was limited further to the financial responsibility of the abstracter or attorney.[81]

§11.63. Liability based on contract
As the need for evidence of title increased, *certificates of title* were issued, and then *guarantees of title*, which created a contractual liability rather than a liability based on negligence. However, such protection as they afford is limited to those matters that are disclosed by an examination of the public records. These records, particularly those in the county recorder's office, are merely transcribed copies of original instruments no longer available for inspection. Hidden defects that cannot be determined by an examination or study of such records alone may in fact exist. A deed may be forged, for instance, but this would not be detected solely by an examination of the recorded instruments. Defects arising from fraud, incompetency, identity, status, limitation of power, lack of delivery, or failure to comply with the law would not be detected from the record alone. None of the practices considered up to now—the abstract, the opinion, the certificate, or the guarantee of title—affords any protection against such matters. They are regarded as "off-record" risks, and as such are not within the contemplation of such evidence of title. Yet these off-record risks may result in a total failure of title.

§11.64. Coverage of a policy of title insurance

The policy of title insurance extends protection against the above-mentioned off-record risks. Its coverage may also be extended to other types of risks that are disclosed not from the public records, but from an inspection of the property. The scope of this coverage is continually expanding.

Need for greater coverage. The demand for wider coverage than that afforded by abstracts, certificates, and guarantees was first felt in the larger centers of population, where the rise of corporate ownership of land, the intensive improvement of land, and the use of land and improvements as security for the safe investment of trust funds and life insurance company reserves necessitated greater concern for and protection of the underlying title. The rapidly growing use of land in urban areas has created greater complexity in titles, including such things as complicated trusts, ground leases, new and novel easements above and below the surface, complete use of the surface necessitating close attention to boundaries, encroachments, party wall agreements, building restrictions, zoning laws, and police and fire regulations. Moreover, many substantial investors required additional protection at a time when the examination of titles was becoming increasingly complex. Title companies with extensive financial reserves and adequate facilities were called on to give such increased protection. The insurance of title to land has now become centered in established and progressive organizations.

§11.65. Regulation of title insurance companies

Under the provisions of the Insurance Code,[82] each title insurance company organized under the laws of California is required to make an initial deposit of $100,000 in cash or approved securities with the state treasurer. It must also set apart annually, as a "title insurance surplus fund," a sum equal to 10 percent of its premiums collected during the year until this fund equals 25 percent of the subscribed capital stock of the company. This fund, which is very substantial in the case of larger and older companies, is maintained constantly as a security to the owners of policies of title insurance. Title insurance companies are subject to various other provisions of the state insurance laws. Companies issuing policies of title insurance in substantial numbers and large amounts, and on the strength of which vast sums of money change hands, must necessarily be subjected to the same supervision and compliance with regulatory laws as other insurance companies.

§11.66. Basic coverage of title insurance

A title insurance policy represents the final results of three successive processes: (1) an examination or investigation of the title; (2) a determination of the amount of insurance required; and (3) the protection of the insured against possible title losses.

§11.67. Elements of risk

The elements of risk or chance in title insurance arise from three principal sources: (1) errors in searching the record; (2) errors in interpreting the legal effect of instruments found in the chain of title; and (3) facts external to the record. A title insurer meets the first two of these matters in much the same way as an abstract company. A title insurance company will have at its disposal a title plant from which most of the examination of the record title can be made, and will also have a corps of trained and experienced searchers and examiners, in addition to competent legal assistance. The added element of hazard—the risks that lie outside the public records—that is the distinctive coverage of the policy of title insurance requires additional cautions.

§11.68. Coverage of matters disclosed of record

The policy of title insurance affords the same protection as the guarantee of title insofar as coverage of the public records is concerned. The policy of title insurance provides that the public records so covered are those that impart constructive notice of matters relating to the land insured. These include not only the records in the county recorder's office, but additional public records as well, including the following: (1) federal land office records, both local and in Washington, D.C.; (2) records of the State of California, located in Sacramento; (3) tax records of every taxing agency whose levies constitute a lien on real property—cities, counties, and the state, as well as numerous districts, such as irrigation, reclamation, and drainage districts; (4) records of special assessment districts, which are filed in city and county treasurer's offices; (5) records of city and county clerks where government action relating to land is recorded; and (6) records in the office of the county clerk.

Court records. Other records are found in the offices of the clerks of the various courts, both state and federal. In these offices are maintained innumerable files of cases affecting titles to real property, or the status of persons having interests in real property. These actions include (1) foreclosure; (2) quiet title; (3) partition; (4) guardianship; (5) marital dissolution; (6) bankruptcy; and many other types of proceedings.

§11.69. Examination of public records
The files and records referred to above are examined, summarized, and classified by the title company at the time of filing, and a record made in the title company's plant. Absolute accuracy is essential to the proper performance of this function. Thereafter, when the title company is requested to issue a policy of title insurance, a search of title can be made from the records in its own title plant.

§11.70. Interpretation of instruments
After the title search is completed, the next important function in the examination of title is the interpretation of the instruments in the chain of title. Knowledge and experience are indispensable prerequisites in construing the validity and effect of the instruments in the chain of title. It must be determined that all necessary parties have joined in the execution of the instruments. Not only must they have signed their names, but they must have been correctly designated in the instrument and must have properly acknowledged its execution. To be effective, the instrument must be legally sufficient to accomplish its intended purpose, must identify the property correctly, and must be consistent with the prior title. If it is a lease or a declaration of trust, it must have a valid term and purpose. If it is a deed creating or reserving immediate or future interests, such interests must conform to the laws governing their nature and extent.

§11.71. Coverage against off-record risks
As mentioned above, the distinctive coverage of a policy of title insurance, as compared with a guarantee of title, is the extension of the coverage to certain off-record risks. These hazards, which the policy of title insurance was primarily developed to cover, relate to the identity and capacity of the parties. A policy of title insurance protects a bona fide purchaser or encumbrancer against forgery or false personation. Similar protection is afforded against loss due to lack of capacity on the part of any party to any transaction involving the title to the property.

§11.72. Types of policies
Two basic forms of policies of title insurance exist—the *standard coverage* and *extended coverage*. The standard coverage policy is the form customarily used by buyers and many lenders throughout California. This form is designated as the California Land Title Association Standard Coverage Policy Form, the approved form used by members of the California Land Title Association, the trade organization of the title companies doing business in the State of California. It is an

Owner's Policy if the owner only is insured; a Loan Policy if the lender only is insured; and a Joint Protection Policy when both an owner and a lender are insured. Land value with improvements is the basis of the charge for an owner's policy. The amount of the loan is the basis for a lender's policy.

For those desiring further information relating to the forms of policies of title insurance and their coverage, refer to *Escrows and Land Titles* by Arthur G. Bowman and John C. Hoag, published by the University of California Extension in Berkeley, California.

§11.73. Coverage of standard policy

The *standard coverage policy* insures the ownership of the land and the priority and validity of the insured mortgage or trust deed. In general, it insures the correctness of the information obtained from an examination of the public records, in addition to the off-record risks discussed above. It does not insure against types of off-record risks that are discoverable only from an inspection of the land or by making inquiry of persons in possession of the land. Nor does it necessarily insure that the property has access to a public street.

Most C.L.T.A. as well as A.L.T.A. policies exclude from their coverage environmental protection laws or the consequences of a violation of an environmental law, including ordinances and governmental regulations.

§11.74. Extended coverage policy

The protection afforded by the standard policy is limited by several exceptions, but these risks are primarily matters that the insured can assume as a result of an inspection of and familiarity with the property. Occasions arise, however, when the standard policy is not suited to the needs of the particular customer, and special extra-coverage, extra-premium policies have been devised to assume many of these risks. These policies are known as extended coverage policies. Most of the general exceptions contained in the standard coverage policy may be eliminated, provided, of course, that the title company's on-the-ground investigation of the title discloses no serious defect. Because of the additional work involved in making an inspection of the premises and the additional risks assumed, the cost of such policies is proportionately greater. Extended coverage policies are available to both owners and lenders, although the most prevalent use is by lenders in connection with loans made on recently completed structures.

The most common form of extended coverage policy is the American Land Title Association form of lender's policy (A.L.T.A. policy). This policy, which is used on a national basis, originated in the requirements of institutional lenders, such as the large eastern life insurance companies, which were not in a position to make local inspections of the land on which a loan was being requested. This policy, in addition to the usual coverage of the standard policy, eliminates when possible the standard exceptions pertaining to off-record easements and liens, rights of persons in possession, rights and claims that an inspection of the land or a correct survey would show, mining claims, reservations in patents, and water rights. This extended coverage is made possible by obtaining correct surveys and by the insurer's acceptance of the responsibility of inspecting the property in each case and determining whether any such rights or claims exist and, if so, their nature and extent. This form of policy also includes assurances that the property has access to a public street.

The American Land Title Association has also adopted an extended coverage policy form for owners, which affords basically the same protection to owners that the A.L.T.A. loan policy affords to lenders. Extended coverage policies lend themselves more readily to urban and subdivided land, although they can, of course, be written on rural property. Unimproved land may be covered, but the policies are more in demand when improvements have been made.

§11.75. Homeowner's policy

In 1975 title insurers expanded the coverage to homeowners beyond the standard coverage policy to cover possible title problems, which are not always disclosed by the examination of public records. Ordinarily, these title defects can be disclosed only by questioning the sellers, by obtaining a costly survey of the property, or by careful, personal inspection made by knowledgeable professionals. A new standard title insurance coverage program was then initiated.

The concept created provides the same standard coverage homeowners' protection that has been issued in the past, plus additional protection. Specifically, it gives the insured homeowner the following eight items of new protection:

1. *Encroachment*—Provides coverage against the enforced removal of the property improvements (excluding perimeter fences and plantings) that might extend onto your neighbor's land. Unless you paid for a costly survey, you wouldn't know about this until your neighbor notifies you. Correcting this situation can be costly to the homeowner.

2. *Lack of access to a public street or road*—The policy guarantees that your investment will not be a disaster due to an oversight of this nature.

3. *Unrecorded taxes and assessments*—There are times when taxes or assessments are not part of the ordinary tax records at the time of sale or close of escrow but are liens against the property. They can pop up at a most inopportune time, e.g., within a month or two of your moving into your new home.

4. *Unrecorded mechanics' or materialmen's liens*—These liens may be recorded after the homeowner has moved into a new home. There couldn't be a worse time to face an unknown expense authorized by the previous owner. While the previous owner is responsible for payment of the lien, there is usually legal expense in finding and serving papers on the seller. Sometimes the seller has left the state and cannot be found.

5. *Violations of covenants, conditions, or restrictions*—These C.C.&.R.s can limit the use of land, regulate the type and location of improvements, etc. If your residence or other improvements (again, excluding perimeter fences and plantings) should violate the C.C.&.R.s that are shown in your policy, and as a result you are prevented from using them, you will not sustain the loss.

6. *Violations of zoning ordinances*—As in the case of the C.C.&.R.s, property is sometimes found to be in violation of zoning ordinances. For example, if zoning requires that your house be set back ten feet from the property boundary, but in fact it is built closer to the street, the city might be able to require that it be moved back. The policy will protect you from sustaining this kind of loss to the same extent as if the C.C.&.R.s were violated.

7. *Damage from the exercise of mineral rights*—The policy will pay for damage to your property arising from a holder of reserved mineral rights in your land exploring for and removing minerals from your property.

8. *Inflation*—The appreciation of property values is an exciting fact of life to the homeowner. Not only does the homeowner receive the benefits of tax deductions and the establishment of equity, but he or she also realizes that a home represents an investment that can reasonably be expected to increase in value. The Inflation Indorsement will automatically increase the maximum amount of coverage each year by the same percentage of increase established by the U.S. Department of Commerce Construction Cost Index for the preceding year. These automatic increases are applied to your property up to a maximum insurance of 150 percent of the original face amount of the original policy. At one time an inflation indorsement was important when inflation could be categorized as "runaway," but presently inflation coverage is rarely issued.

§11.76. Use of special indorsements

Many of the risks that are not covered by the standard coverage policy of title insurance can be insured against by a title insurer by the use of a special indorsement and the undertaking of such additional coverage. Also, special indorsements can be used to expand the coverage of an extended coverage policy. (Traditionally, in the title industry the spelling of "indorsement" has been with an "i" instead of an "e" to distinguish between an endorsement on a check, for instance. For some inexplicable reason, the word "indorsement" is now spelled "endorsement" in various title insurer publications.)

Special indorsements are furnished, in proper cases, for various situations, such as protection to lenders against the assertion of priority by a mechanic's lien claimant; protection of the insured against forced removal of encroachments on adjoining land; and insurance against loss by reason of an existing violation of private building restrictions. The special indorsements can be adapted to numerous situations in which the insured desires special insurance against a particular risk, whether based on off-record matters or otherwise. An indorsement may be appropriate when a defect in the title appears of record and is known to the parties, but the insurer is reasonably satisfied that the defect will not result in a loss. Such defect is noted in the policy, but an indorsement is added, protecting the insured from any loss occasioned thereby. Following are two typical illustrations: (1) restrictions on the use of land, unlimited in duration but known or believed to be unenforceable; and (2) easements of record, but long in disuse and unlikely to be claimed in the future.

§11.77. Claims under a policy

Like other insurance companies, a title insurer is under a duty to act reasonably, promptly, and in good faith in the settlement of claims under an insurance policy.[83] If a valid claim arises, the insured is entitled to a fair and reasonable settlement without undue delay. The amount of insurance an insured obtains, in addition to the stated amount of liability in the policy, includes costs, attorney's fees, and expenses in connection with litigation arising under the policy.

The insurance policy should be clearly understandable to the insured. Although relatively few court cases in California have interpreted the language of a policy of title insurance, a number of cases involve other types of insurance policies. The rules of interpretation adopted in these other cases apply equally to a policy of title insurance. An insurance policy has been construed as a contract of adhesion. This is a standardized contract which, imposed and drafted by the party of superior bargaining strength, gives to the subscribing party only the opportunity to accept the contract or reject it. The following rules of interpretation apply to such contracts:

1. The contract must be interpreted in the light of the reasonable and normal expectations of the parties as to the extent of coverage.

2. Any noncoverage provisions must be conspicuous, plain, and clear.

3. Any ambiguity is construed in favor of the insured.

EXAMPLES 1. In one case, it was held that an exclusionary clause in a lengthy printed form of policy (described as containing an "ocean of words"), which was preceded and followed by clauses relating to promised benefits to the insured, was lost in a "sea of print" and was therefore inapplicable to bar a claim under the policy.[84]

2. In another case,[85] the court ignored an indorsement limiting the time in which to file a claim because the indorsement could not be read easily except by removing some staples by which it was attached to the balance of the policy. The court concluded that a condition contained in the second page of the rider to the policy did not become a part of the policy when the pages of the

rider were so stapled and taped together when delivered to the insured that the only way to read the second page without removing the staples was to press the two pages apart, forming a cylinder, and read the text sideways.[86]

§11.78. Duty to defend claims

In a recent case, it was held that a purchaser of property could state a cause of action against a title company for negligent infliction of emotional distress or for bad faith when the title company negligently failed to put recorded encumbrances in a preliminary title report, and refused to take affirmative action to remove the cloud on the insured's title.[87]

§11.79. Other title company services

Although the issuance of policies of title insurance represents a large proportion of the services of a title insurance company, a number of other services are available, including special reports furnished to attorneys in connection with litigation affecting title to real property, trustee's sale guarantees in connection with the foreclosure of a trust deed by trustee's sale, and subdivision guarantees in connection with land subdivisions.

In addition to policies for fee owners and lenders, numerous types of policies are available insuring other interests in real property. An *easement policy* insures the owner of a right of way or easement in land, such as might be required by an oil company or a public utility. In another type of policy, the fee title to the land and the easement appurtenant to the land are both insured. In several types of policies, the owner of a leasehold or the holder of a mortgage or trust deed on the leasehold is given assurance of title, as to both commercial leases and oil leases. Mineral estates, including oil and gas, are often the subject of title insurance.

Insurance of the title under a recorded contract of sale may also be obtained. The title is shown in the policy to be vested in the vendee as to the equitable title created by the specific contract of sale and purchase, and in the vendor as to the legal title. An option to purchase real property is also an insurable interest.

QUESTIONS

Matching terms

a. Lien
b. Judgment
c. Writ of execution
d. Mechanic's lien
e. Constructive notice
f. Priority
g. Homestead
h. Title insurance
i. Indorsement
j. Notice of nonresponsibility

1. An amendment to a policy of title insurance.
2. Superiority in position or rank.
3. Contract of indemnity.
4. A means whereby a landowner can relieve his land from mechanics' liens.
5. A dwelling that is protected from a forced sale in satisfaction of certain types of claims against the owner.
6. Statutory right given to laborers and materialmen who have contributed to a work of improvement.
7. A charge upon land to secure payment of a debt.
8. A means of satisfying a judgment by sale of the debtor's property.
9. Notice imparted to the public from matters properly recorded.
10. Final determination of the outcome of a lawsuit.

True/False

T F **11.** A judgment lien has priority based on date of entry of the judgment.

T F **12.** A judgment lien is a general lien rather than a specific lien.

T F **13.** A writ of execution when levied creates a specific lien.

T F **14.** Real property sold on execution is subject to redemption.

T F **15.** Real property sold to enforce a mechanic's lien for labor is not subject to redemption.

T F **16.** Attachment liens are available in all actions for money when the debtor is known to own real property.

T F **17.** The priority of a mechanic's lien is not based on the date of recording, but rather on the date the work of improvement first commenced on the ground.

T F **18.** The parity rule means that liens are of equal rank.

T F **19.** There are two types of homesteads under California law, identified as the Declared

Homestead and the Dwelling House Exemption.

T F 20. A policy of title insurance affords greater coverage than a guarantee of title.

Multiple Choice

21. A deed is not entitled to be recorded unless it is
    a. Acknowledged or proved.
    b. Witnessed.
    c. Verified.
    d. Supported by consideration.

22. A judgment lien can be obtained by recording an abstract of judgment in the county recorder's office. Priority is determined by the date of
    a. Entry of judgment.
    b. Recording.
    c. Filing the complaint.
    d. Satisfaction of judgment.

23. A writ of attachment permits property of a defendant to be seized
    a. Before an action is filed.
    b. After an action is filed but before judgment.
    c. After judgment is entered.
    d. After judgment is satisfied.

24. The priority of a mechanic's lien is ordinarily determined by the date when
    a. The work of improvement commences.
    b. The work of improvement is completed.
    c. The claim of lien is recorded.
    d. An action to foreclose the lien is filed.

25. A writ of execution permits property of a defendant to be sold
    a. Before an action is filed.
    b. Before judgment is entered.
    c. After judgment is entered.
    d. After judgment is satisfied.

26. The existence of a judgment lien is dependent upon
    a. Recording an abstract or certified copy of the judgment.
    b. Possession by the debtor.
    c. Ownership in severalty.
    d. All of the above.

27. The recording system was adopted in California and elsewhere in order to
    a. Collect evidence of title in a convenient central place.
    b. Inform prospective purchasers as to ownership and condition of title.
    c. Make property more readily transferable.
    d. All of the above.

28. Notice given by recording a deed or other document with the county recorder is called
    a. Actual.
    b. Constructive.
    c. Contingent.
    d. Conditioned.

29. Each county in California has a county recorder with whom documents relating to real property may be recorded. How many counties are there in California?
    a. 37.
    b. 49.
    c. 52.
    d. 58.

30. To give constructive notice, a deed must be recorded in the county where the
    a. Property is located.
    b. Seller resides.
    c. Buyer resides.
    d. All of the above.

31. Actual notice is that which consists of express information of a fact. Another type of notice is constructive notice. The latter is that which is
    a. Imputed by law.
    b. Inferred by law.
    c. Implied by law.
    d. All of the above.

32. When a deed is recorded it is indexed by the county recorder
    a. Alphabetically according to grantor and grantee.
    b. By street address.
    c. By legal description.
    d. According to the amount of consideration.

33. A Declared Homestead will protect a homeowner from
    a. Mechanic's lien foreclosure.
    b. Trust deed foreclosure.
    c. Federal income tax lien.
    d. None of the above.

34. In order to have a valid Declared Homestead, the declaration must
    a. Show the name of owner.
    b. Contain a description.
    c. State actual residence.
    d. All of the above.

35. A standard coverage policy of title insurance does not insure against
    a. Forgery.
    b. False personation.
    c. Zoning regulations.
    d. Competency of a grantor.

36. A standard coverage policy of title insurance does not insure
    a. Adequacy of consideration.
    b. Validity of a joint tenancy.
    c. Authority of a trustee.
    d. Authority of an attorney-in-fact.

37. Which of the following interests is insurable under a policy of title insurance?
    a. Vendee's interest under a contract of sale.
    b. Leasehold estate.

c. Fee interest.

d. Any of the above.

38. An extended coverage policy of title insurance does not include assurances as to

   a. Access.

   b. Market value.

   c. Mechanics' liens.

   d. Encroachment.

39. The elements of risk under a policy of title insurance include

   a. Errors in searching the public records.

   b. Errors in interpreting the effect of instruments of record.

   c. False personation.

   d. Any of the above.

40. You receive title by grant deed, record the deed, and obtain a standard coverage policy of title insurance. You then discover that a third party for a long time has been in possession under an unrecorded lease with option to buy. As against the party in possession, your deed is

   a. Subject to his rights.

   b. Superior to his rights since your deed is recorded.

   c. Void for all purposes.

   d. Invalid, but you would have recourse against the title company.

41. Of the following, which gives the greatest amount of protection to an owner?

   a. Abstract of title.

   b. Certificate of title.

   c. Guarantee of title.

   d. Policy of title insurance.

42. A policy of title insurance basically insures

   a. Bona fide purchasers and lenders.

   b. Improvident investors.

   c. Compliance with building codes.

   d. Personal property interests.

43. A policy of title insurance assures the sufficiency of

   a. Subordination agreements.

   b. Court decrees.

   c. Condominium procedures.

   d. All of the above.

44. Marketable title means a title

   a. Free from reasonable doubt in fact.

   b. Free from reasonable doubt in law.

   c. Deducible from the public records.

   d. All of the above.

45. Off-record risks not insured by a standard coverage policy of title insurance include

   a. Rights of a tenant under an unrecorded lease.

   b. Exact location of improvements on the property.

   c. Location of boundaries on the ground.

d. All of the above.

46. An extended coverage policy of title insurance insures the owner as to

   a. Off-record risks such as unrecorded easements.

   b. The effect of incorrect surveys.

   c. Rights of persons in possession.

   d. All of the above.

47. Special indorsements are used in title insurance in matters relating to

   a. Enforceability of deed restrictions.

   b. Encroachments.

   c. Exercise of rights under outstanding mineral interests.

   d. Any of the above.

48. A policy of title insurance does not protect against loss based on

   a. Invalidity of a joint tenancy.

   b. Defective execution of a deed.

   c. Insufficient description in a deed or mortgage.

   d. Facts known only to the insured and not disclosed of record.

49. A policy of title insurance includes coverage as to authority to execute instruments by

   a. Attorney-in-fact.

   b. Trustee under an inter vivos trust.

   c. One spouse without the other.

   d. Any of the above.

50. Which of the following documents must be properly executed and recorded in order to be effective?

   a. Declared Homestead.

   b. Notice of nonresponsibility.

   c. Mechanic's lien.

   d. All of the above.

NOTES

1. C.C.P. 577.
2. C.C.P. 674.
3. C.C.P. 681.010; Bulwash v. Davis (1977) 87 C.A.3d 8.
4. C.C.P. 697.410; C.C. 2941.
5. C.C.P. 674; Casey v. Gray (1993) 13 C.A. 4th 611.
6. C.C.P. 703.070; C.C.P. 683.120 *et seq.* Because of the number of dead-beat parents who don't pay child support, the laws are growing to punish the parents. *See* Fam. Code 4800, 5100, 5200, and others.
7. *See* Heller Properties. Inc. v. Rothschild (1970) 11 C.A.3d 705.
8. C.C.P. 704.710 *et seq.* It could be argued that the lien does attach to homestead property under section 704.710(c)(1), but sections 697.310 and 704.750, C.C.P. are to the contrary.
9. C.C.P. 699.510 *et seq.*
10. Butcher v. Brouwer (1942) 21 C.2d 354.
11. Under a similar procedure, a creditor can levy execution upon and sell a pending cause of action in which the judgment debtor was the plaintiff. C.C.P. 700.180; Abatti v. Eldridge (1980) 103 C.A.3d 484.
12. C.C.P. 701.540.
13. C.C.P. 701.660.
14. C.C.P. 701.680; Bateman v. Kellogg (1922) 59 C.A. 464.

15. Randone v. Appellate Dept. (1971) 5 C.3d 536.
16. Article XX, Section 15 (formerly); now in Article XIV, Section 3.
17. C.C. 3082, *et seq.*, especially C.C.3134 and 3137.
18. § 3134 Civ. Code.
19. C.C. 3110. Under B. & P. 7048, no contractor's license is required if the price is $200 or less; however, if over that amount, a contractor must have a license when the work was performed or he is denied recovery. Brown v. Solana County Business Development, Inc. (1979) 92 C.A.3d 192. And, if a person acting as a contractor is not a contractor, he is guilty of a misdemeanor (B&P 7028). Since the license laws do not apply to materialmen, if he sells materials to an unlicensed contractor, the materialman is still entitled to a mechanic's lien (E. A. Davis & Co. v. Richards [1953] 120 C.A. 2d 237, 240).
20. Nolte v. Smith (1961) 189 C.A.2d 140.
21. McDonald v. Filice (1967) 252 C.A.2d 613, citing Design Associates, Inc. v. Welch (1964) 224 C.A.2d 165.
22. Tracy Price Associates v. Hebard (1968) 266 C.A.2d 778.
23. Walker v. Lytton Savings & Loan (1970) 2 C.3d 152.
24. South Bay Engineering Co. v. Citizens Savings & Loan Assn. (1975) 51 C.A.3d 453.
25. Simons Brick Co. v. Hetzel (1925) 72 C.A. 1.
26. C.C. 3153 requires a contractor to defend any action brought on a mechanic's lien at his own expense, and when the owner incurs attorney's fees, the owner may recover from the contractor.
27. Harris v. Stunston, Inc. Ltd. v. Yorba Linda Citrus Assn. (1933) 135 C.A. 154. A mechanic's lien has been allowed for the lessor of rental equipment in Oil Too Exchange, Inc. v. Hasson (1935) 4 C.A. 2d 544, and in Rodini v. Harbor Engineers (1961) 191 C.A. 2d 560.
28. *See* Los Banos Grove Co. v. Freeman (1976) 58 C.A.3d 785.
29. Arthur B. Siri, Inc. v. Bridges (1961) 189 C.A.2d 599.
30. Ott Hardware Co., Inc. v. Yost (1945) 69 C.A.2d 593; but *see* Baker v. Hubbard (1980) 101 C.A.3d 226 and C.C. 3128.
31. Borello v. Eichler Homes, Inc. (1963) 221 C.A.2d 487.
32. C.C. 3097. If a contractor contracts with a lessee rather than the owner, he must file a preliminary notice (Kim v. J.F. Enterprise [1996] 42 C.A. 4th 849).
33. C.C. 3097.1.
34. C.C. 3097[o].
35. C.C. 3115, 3116.
36. C.C. 3117.
37. If filed before actual completion, it is invalid. Scott, Blake & Wynne v. Summit Ridge Estates, Inc. (1967) C.A.2d 347.
38. C.C. 3092, 3086(c).
39. C.C. 3115, 3116.
40. C.C. 3144.
41. C.C.P. 3907(b). If the lender is unknown, there are alternative methods to actual notice. Romak Iron Works v. Prudential Insurance Co. of America (1980) 104 C.A.3d 767.
42. Idaho Lumber Co. v. Northwestern Savings & Loan (1968) 265 C.A.3d 490.
43. C.C. 1215.
44. Pen. C. 115, 115.5; People v. Garfield (1984) 160 C.A.3d 1139.
45. C.C. 1170.
46. C.C.P. 405.20.
47. *See* Kendall-Brief Co. v. Superior Court (1976) 60 C.A.3d 462; Hunting World v. Superior Court (1994 22 C.A. 4th 67.
48. C.C.P. 751.13.
49. H&S Code 11488.4 and Pen. Code 186.4.
50. C.C.P. 405.20, except actions concerning eminent domain.
51. Allied Eastern Financial v. Gohren Enterprises (1968) 265 C.A.2d 131. *See also* United Professional Planning, Inc. v. Superior Court (1970) 9 C.A.3d 377; Empfield v. Superior Court (1973) 33 C.A. 3d 105; Markeley v. Superior Court (1992) 5 C.A. 4th 738.
52. F.D.I.C. v. Charlton (1993) 17 C.A. 4th 1066.
53. Three Sixty Five Club v. Shostak (1951) 104 C.A.2d 735.
54. C.C. 2897.
55. Hertweck v. Fearon (1919) 180 C. 71.
56. Rheem Mfg. Co. v. United States (1962) 57 C.2d 621; Lambert Steel Co. v. Heller Financial, Inc. (1993) 16 C.A. 4th 1034.
57. Cal. Const., Article XX, §1.5.
58. C.C.P. 704.710-704.990.
59. C.C.P. 704.730; Berhanu v. Metzger (1992) 12 C.A. 4th 445.
60. C.C.P. 704.730.
61. C.C.P. 704.710.
62. C.C.P. 704.920.
63. Tromans v. Mahlman (1981) 92 C. 1; Ellsworth v. Marshall (1961) 196 C.A.2d 471.
64. C.C.P. 704.930(a).
65. C.C.P. 704.930(b)(4).
66. Oktanski v. Brown (1956) 138 C.A.2d 419.
67. C.C.P. 704.710(a).
68. C.C.P. 704.980.
69. Rey v. Valdez (1959) 173 C.A.2d 502; Webb v. Trippet (1991) 235 C.A. 3d 647.
70. C.C.P. 704.750(a); *see also* Arighi v. Rule & Sons, Inc. (1940) 41 C.A.2d 852; Ortale v. Mulhern (1976) 58 C.A.3d 861.
71. C.C.P. 704.760.
72. C.C.P. 704.770; Rourke v. Troy (1993) 17 C.A. 4th 880.
73. C.C.P. 704.540, *et seq.*
74. C.C.P. 704.710.
75. C.C.P. 704.720(c).
76. C.C.P. 704.710(c).
77. C.C.P. 704.920.
78. C.C.P. 704.950(a).
79. C.C.P. 704.960(a); C.C.P. 704.960(b).
80. Estate of Murray (1982) 133 C.A.3d 601; C.C.P. 661. Estate of Dean (1980) 109 C.A.3d 156. *See also* Estate of Grigsby (1982) 134 C.A.3d 611, which held that one spouse can unilaterally terminate a joint tenancy that has been homesteaded by both spouses, but the homestead persists until the death of the second spouse; Pro. C. 6520, *et seq.*
81. Karl v. Commonwealth Title Insurance Co. (1993) 20 C.A. 4th 972.
82. Ins. C. 12340, *et seq.*
83. The Statute of Limitations on title insurance is two years [Tabachnick v. TICOR (1994) 24 C.A. 4th 70.]
84. Schmidt v. Pacific Mutual Life Ins. Co. (1969) 268 C.A.2d 735.
85. Rogers v. U.S. Fidelity & Guarantee Co. (1968) 260 C.A.2d 404.
86. Title insurance companies have been held liable in damages in the following illustrative cases: (1) failure to disclose easement (Overholtzer v. Northern Counties Title Ins. Co. [1953] 116 C.A.2d 113); (2) misdescription of an easement (H. Trisdale, Inc. v. Shasta County Title Co. [1956] 146 C.A.2d 831); (3) lack of access (Hawkins v. Oakland Title Ins. & Guaranty Co. [1958] 165 C.A.2d 116); (4) erroneous vesting of title in husband and wife as joint tenants (Hall v. San Jose Abstract & Title Co. [1959] 172 C.A.2d 421); (5) error in description of the property (Lagomarsino v. San Jose Abstract & Title Ins. Co. [1968] 261 C.A.2d 517); and (6) failure to show effect of bankruptcy proceedings (Moe v. Transamerica Title Ins. Co. [1971] 21 C.A.3d 289).
87. Jarchow v. Transamerica Title Insurance Co. (1975) 48 C.A. 3d 917. *See also* Southland Title Corp. v. Superior Court (1991) 231 C.A. 3d 530 which held that there is no liability to the title corporation for an error or omission in a preliminary title report. In 1119 Delaware v. Continental Land Title Co. (1993) 16 C.A. 4th 992, it was held that the title company is liable for its failure to include the conditional use permit in the abstract of title.

12

Limitations on Use, Including Tax Burden

I. INTRODUCTION

§12.1. In general

Limitations on the use of land fall into two general classifications: private restrictions and public restrictions. *Private restrictions* are those voluntarily imposed on land by the landowner. They usually constitute both a benefit and a burden. To the extent that land is restricted in the use that may be made of it, the restriction is considered a burden, but to the extent that the owner has a right of enforcement against other landowners, a benefit is obtained. One of the major objectives is to create a degree of uniformity in the development of a neighborhood, which in turn can help to maintain values.

Public restrictions are perhaps best exemplified by zoning ordinances. The trend today is toward more far-reaching control than local zoning ordinances, particularly in the need to preserve agricultural lands.

Other areas of concern relate to environmental quality and protection of the California landscape, especially in the coastal areas. These latter subjects are considered in Chapter 13.

Another subject of increasing concern to property owners is real property taxes. Although not limiting the use necessarily, taxes are a type of burden that property must bear, and in the event of nonpayment, a loss of the owner's title can result through foreclosure. These tax consequences are considered in the concluding part of this chapter.

II. CREATION AND VALIDITY OF RESTRICTIONS

§12.2. In general

As its name implies, an encumbrance in the form of a *restriction* in some way limits or restricts the use of the land by its owner. Restrictions are created by private agreement of property owners, typically by appropriate clauses in deeds, in agreements, or in a general plan affecting an entire subdivision. They are usually referred to as covenants, conditions, and restrictions (commonly shortened to CC&Rs), and are usually for the benefit of all future owners.

Although the imposition of restrictions on newly subdivided land is considered optional with the subdivider, it is mandatory under the common interest development law, previously known as the condominium law. Although the law doesn't define the nature of the restrictions, it does require that restrictions be imposed, essential to the concept of condominiums. One of the usual limitations in condominium projects is the exclusion of children. However, it has been held by the State Supreme Court that children may not be excluded from apartments and condominiums in most situations, bringing children under the protection of the Unruh Civil Rights Act.[1] On the other hand, senior citizen developments that impose restrictions on children are valid.[2]

§12.3. Permissible restrictions

Restrictions may be imposed on the use of property for any legitimate purpose. The right to acquire and possess property includes the right to dispose of all or any part of it and to impose on the grant whatever reservations or restrictions the grantor may see fit, provided that such restrictions are not contrary to prohibitions prescribed by law. Heretofore some municipalities have sought to prohibit owners from placing "For Sale" signs on their properties. Sections of the Civil Code declare void any restrictions on a fee owner of real property, or his agent, that would prohibit the display on the property of a sign of reasonable dimensions advertising the property for sale, lease, or rent, or any restrictions that prohibit or restrict the installation or use of a solar energy system.[3] Also, restrictions prohibiting the use of property by people of certain races are now not merely unenforceable—they are void. In an attempt to effectively eliminate such restrictions of record, a section was added to the Civil Code in 1987 to provide that a deed or other written instrument "which relates to title to real property" and contains a provision forbidding, restricting, or conditioning the right of any person to sell, buy, lease, rent, use, or occupy the real property because of the race or color of the person *is deemed revised* to omit the provision. The same is true of covenants, conditions, and restrictions of the same tenor.[4]

In contrast to zoning ordinances, private restrictions need not necessarily be promotive of public health, safety, morals, or public welfare. They may be intended to create a particular type of neighborhood deemed desirable to the individual tract owner, or they may be based solely on esthetic considerations. Regarding residential use, in a recent case it was held that a city cannot prohibit 12 unrelated persons from living together in a home in a single-family residence in violation of a City Ordinance.[5]

§12.4. Definition and enforcement

Private restrictions are classified generally as covenants and conditions. The distinction between those terms is based primarily on the right of enforcement in the event of a breach. Historically, restrictive provisions in deeds, if they did not fall into the category of conditions, were called *covenants*, promises or agreements to do or not to do certain things. The grantor could enforce the covenant only by suing for damages if the covenant was violated. Beginning over a hundred years ago, the courts began to enforce restrictive provisions in another method by enjoining or forbidding their violation. An injunction or a suit for damages is now a customary method of enforcing covenants.

A *condition* is a qualification annexed to an estate, on the happening of which the estate is enlarged or defeated. The outstanding characteristic of a condition in a deed is that the grantor has the power to terminate the interest conveyed in the event a violation of the condition occurs.

The term *restriction* is employed today as a general classification, embracing both covenants, whose enforcement may be by way of injunction or damages, and conditions, whose right of enforcement may additionally result in a loss of title.

§12.5. Methods of imposing restrictions

There are several methods of placing restrictions on property, including the following: (1) covenants or conditions imposed in a deed of a single parcel of land; (2) covenants contained in an agreement between two or more landowners; (3) covenants and conditions set forth in a recorded declaration of restrictions describing a general plan of restrictions for a tract, and thereafter imposed in deeds by reference to the recorded declaration; and (4) covenants and conditions imposed as part of a general plan for a tract by their inclusion in the deed for each lot or tract. The third method is customarily employed in connection with the imposition of restrictions on new subdivisions, and also in connection with condominium developments.

§12.6. Covenants and conditions construed

Covenants and conditions differ in two material respects: (1) in regard to the relief afforded; and (2) as to the persons by or against whom they may be enforced. Because a failure to comply with a condition may result in a loss of title, which is a harsh effect, the courts will construe the restrictive provisions of a deed as covenants only, unless the intent to create a condition is plainly expressed. The mere use of the word *condition* or *covenant* is not always controlling. The real test is whether the intention is expressed clearly that the enjoyment of the estate conveyed depends on the performance of the condition specified; otherwise, the limitation in use will be construed as a covenant only. Both covenants and conditions "run with the land" if they meet certain requirements.[6]

§12.7. Creation of covenant

Covenants are created for different reasons.

EXAMPLE A, the owner of adjoining lots 1 and 2, conveys lot 2 to B by agreement, contained in the deed, that B will not keep horses on any part of lot 2. If B breaches the agreement, A may sue B for damages or bring an action in equity to enjoin the violation.

§12.8. Creation of condition

A breach of a condition can have disastrous results.

EXAMPLE C conveys land to D on the express condition that D will not sell intoxicating liquors thereon, and further providing "that a breach of the foregoing condition shall cause the premises to revert to the grantor, his heirs, successors, or assigns, who shall have the right of immediate reentry upon the premises in the event of such a breach." If D breaches the condition, C or his successors may bring an action against D to have the title revert to C.

§12.9. When a covenant will be implied

As in the first illustration, a deed that merely recites that it is given on the agreement of the grantee to do or not to do certain things implies a covenant only and not a condition. Also, a recital in a deed that the land conveyed is or is not to be used for certain purposes, such as a clause "to be used for church purposes," or "that a schoolhouse be erected thereon," implies a covenant rather than a condition.

§12.10. Implied reversions

Although an express reentry or forfeiture clause is not essential if a condition in a deed is clearly expressed, it is the better practice to include such a clause so the intention will be plain. If the deed does not contain such a clause but it is clear that a condition was created, the deed will be construed as containing an *implied reversion*.

§12.11. Validity of restrictions

Regarding the legality of restrictions, it is a general rule that an owner of land can dispose of it as he sees fit, imposing such restrictions as he chooses. This right is limited, however, to the extent that the restrictions must not be unlawful or contrary to public policy. For example, a condition under which a party is to enjoy the use of property until he or she marries is not invalid.

Invalid restrictions. A restriction is invalid if it is repugnant to the estate granted, such as a restriction in a conveyance of the fee against alienation of the land to persons of a specified race or class, or against a sale of the land by the grantee without the grantor's consent or at a price to be fixed by the grantor. A restriction is void if it calls for the commission of an unlawful act or an illegal use of the land, such as the commission of a crime or the use of the land for immoral purposes.

Other types of invalid restrictions. A restriction that is unreasonable or capricious and not calculated to benefit any individual, such as a condition that there shall be no windows in a house to be constructed on the property, is of no effect. Although a grantor may lawfully impose restrictions forbidding certain types of activity on the property conveyed, such as a restriction against the sale of intoxicating liquors, such a restriction is void if the grantor imposed it solely for the purpose of reserving to himself a monopoly of such business.[7] A restriction is invalid if it is impossible of performance when created, such as a condition that title revert to the grantor if the grantee does not construct a perpetual motion machine within five years.

Conditions precedent. If the condition that is impossible of performance is a condition precedent—that is, a condition that must be performed before the title vests in the grantee—the condition is not void, but it operates to prevent the estate from vesting in the grantee.[8] In the other situations mentioned, when the condition is invalid, title nonetheless passes to the grantee, free of the restriction.

Effect of invalidity. Even though a restriction imposed in a deed may appear to be void because unlawful or contrary to public policy, the effect of such a restriction is generally shown for title insurance purposes because it is a matter of record, and generally can be eliminated only by a quitclaim deed from the grantor or a decree quieting title.

§12.12. Racial restrictions

In the past, the enforcement of racial restrictions has been the subject of considerable litigation. Although it was determined by the courts in California that restrictions against the sale of property to persons not of the Caucasian race were void as an unlawful restraint on alienation, no such decision was made with respect to restrictions that limited occupancy and use, and the latter types of racial restrictions were for a number of years considered to be valid and enforceable.[9]

Racial restrictions unenforceable. In 1948 the Supreme Court of the United States held that racial restrictions were unenforceable. In its decision, the Court declared that the judicial enforcement by state courts of covenants restricting the use or occupancy of real property to persons of the Caucasian race violated the equal protection clause of the Fourteenth Amendment. Following the decision in that case, the California courts have uniformly held that state court injunctive enforcement of a private racial restrictive covenant or condition as to occupancy of land is state action that denies persons of the excluded race their right to equal protection of the laws, and therefore violates the Fourteenth Amendment.[10]

Damages not recoverable for breach of racial restriction. Heretofore, the courts have declared that such a covenant is not itself invalid. No one would be punished for making it, and no one's constitutional rights are violated by the covenantor's voluntary adherence thereto, inasmuch as such voluntary adherence would constitute individual action only, as distinguished from state action. In a case decided in 1953, it was held that a property owner who is entitled to the benefit of a covenant restricting the use of land to Caucasians cannot recover damages from a vendor who sells real property subject to the restriction to a black purchaser, since an award of damages would result in the judicial enforcement of a discriminatory covenant by state action in violation of the equal protection clause of the Fourteenth Amendment.[11]

Open-Housing Law. In 1968 Congress enacted the Civil Rights Act of 1968 containing broad fair housing provisions.[12] As expressed in the act, it is the policy of the United States to provide, within constitutional limitations, for fair housing throughout the United States. The act affects all those connected with residential real estate: brokers, builders, lenders, buyers, sellers, and investors. It became effective on the date of enactment (April 11, 1968), and banned discrimination because of race, color, religion, or national origin, in the sale or rental of housing insured or guaranteed by the federal government and certain other housing. Effective January 1, 1969, the ban applies to all dwelling units, no matter how financed, with two exceptions: (1) single-family houses, provided the owner does not own more than three single-family houses at one time; and (2) one- to four-family dwellings, if the owner occupies one of the units. Banks, savings and loan associations, and other lenders are forbidden to discriminate in making loans on apartment buildings or houses, whether for purchase, repair, or construction. Also forbidden is discrimination in setting the terms of the loans. Real estate organizations and multiple listing services also cannot discriminate in their membership rules.

Since 1970, single-family homes are no longer exempt if they are sold or rented through a real estate broker or agent. In other words, under the act, the owner is permitted to choose any buyer he wishes only if he sells or rents the house himself. In addition, the owner loses the exemption if his advertising of the home for sale or rent has any discriminatory words or references.

The sale of vacant land is also covered if the land is offered for sale or lease for the construction of a dwelling.

The impact of a 1968 decision of the United States Supreme Court must be considered in any subsequent litigation relating to the Civil Rights Act of 1968.[13] An effect may be to eliminate the exemptions from the Act as they relate to racial discrimination.

EXAMPLE In one case, the plaintiff, suing for injunctive and other relief, alleged that the defendants had refused to sell him a home solely because he was a black, and that such refusal violated the provisions of an 1866 federal statute that all citizens shall have the same rights as are enjoyed by white citizens to purchase real property. The lower courts denied relief, but on appeal the U.S. Supreme Court reversed, holding that the statute was intended to bar all racial discrimination, private as well as public, in the sale or rental of property, and that the statute, thus construed, was a valid exercise of the power of Congress to enforce the Thirteenth Amendment prohibiting slavery and involuntary servitude.[14]

The court held that the 1866 statute stands independently of the Civil Rights Act of 1968, and it cannot be assumed that Congress, in enacting the 1968 act, intended to effect any change, either substantive or procedural, in the prior statute.

Race restrictions void in California. The Civil Code provides that any provision in any deed of real property in California that purports to restrict the right of any person to sell, lease, rent, use, or occupy the property to persons of a particular racial, national, or ethnic group by providing for payment of a penalty, forfeiture, reverter, or otherwise, is void. The impact of a section added to the Civil Code in 1987 must also be considered (see §12.3). This section adopts the "deemed revised to omit" concept in lieu of "void."[15]

§12.13. Equitable servitudes

Although a covenant may not fulfill the technical requirements of a covenant running with the land or may not in effect create a lien or legal easement, it may still be binding on successors of the covenantor under recognized rules of equity. A burden created in such manner is referred to as an *equitable servitude* or *equitable easement*. The principle is expressed in one case[16] as follows:

> *The marked tendency of our decisions seems to be to disregard the question of whether the covenant does or does not run with the land and to place the conclusion upon the broad ground that the assignee took with knowledge of the covenant and it was of such nature that when the intention of the parties coupled with the result of a failure to enforce it was considered, equity could not in conscience withhold relief.*

§12.14. Lien subordination clauses

When the grantor or his successor properly terminates the estate granted for breach of condition, title reverts to the grantor free from all rights, interests, and liens suffered or created by owners of the land after the creation of the condition, other than such paramount liens as taxes and assessments, unless the deed provides otherwise. Because of the drastic results that might occur, most lenders refuse to make loans to be secured by liens on land subject to a condition subsequent, unless the deed imposing the condition contains a *lien subordination* clause, preserving the lien of a lender in good faith and for value from the effect of any future reversion. It is common practice, then, for the instrument creating the condition to include a clause such as the following:

> *Provided, also, that a breach of any of the foregoing conditions, or any reentry by reason of such breach, shall not defeat or render invalid the lien of any mortgage or deed of trust made in good faith, and for value as to the property or any part thereof, but these conditions shall be binding on and effective against any owner of the property whose title is acquired by foreclosure, trustee's sale, or otherwise.*

III. GENERAL PLAN RESTRICTIONS

§12.15. In general

Modern subdivisions generally establish uniform restrictions as to the use and occupancy of all the lots and as to the character, cost, and location of structures to be built on the lots. It is desirable that each lot owner be able to protect his investment by having the power to enforce the restrictions as against every other lot owner in the tract. A deed from an owner imposing conditions or covenants in favor of the grantor does not give the grantee any right recognized at law to enforce the restrictions as against other land owned by the grantor or conveyed to other owners. But if the deeds from the subdivider properly express an intention that the tract restrictions are for the benefit of all lot owners, the restrictions then become enforceable by the grantees as between themselves.

§12.16. Subdivision restrictions

Most subdivision restrictions today are drafted in the form of covenants and conditions that are enforceable by the grantor and by all of the purchasers of lots in the subdivision as between themselves. These are known as *general plan restrictions,* as distinguished from *single plan restrictions.* The latter are in favor of the grantor alone or his successors, and are not for the benefit of other lot owners.

§12.17. Creation of general plan restrictions

The intention to create general plan restrictions must be expressed in the first deed of each lot in the tract. The existence of surrounding circumstances showing that the grantor actually intended the restrictions to be for the benefit of all lot owners is sufficient in some jurisdictions, but not in California. The first deed of each lot must expressly declare that the restrictions are for the benefit of lots in a designated area.[17]

§12.18. Rights acquired under general plan restrictions

The mutual servitudes created by general plan restrictions spring into existence at the time of the first conveyance by the tract owner. The grantee at that time acquires the right to enforce the restrictions against the grantor's remaining lots and the purchasers to whom the grantor later conveys such lots, and the grantee takes title to his or her lot subject to the right of enforcement in favor of the grantor and the subsequent purchasers.

§12.19. When enforcement may be denied

If some of the deeds of lots in a tract are silent as to restrictions, or if some deeds contain restrictions that differ in many respects from the restrictions contained in other deeds, such circumstances may be considered as showing a lack of a sufficiently uniform scheme of improvement to justify enforcement between the lot owners.

§ 12.20. Declaration of covenants, conditions, and restrictions

When a new subdivision map is recorded, the procedure is often followed by recording a "Declaration of Covenants, Conditions, and Restrictions" before the first deed out, and thereafter incorporating these restrictions in each of the deeds in language substantially as follows:

> *This deed is made and accepted upon the covenants and conditions set forth in "Declaration of Establishment of Restrictions" recorded [recording reference date], all of which are incorporated herein by reference to the declaration with the same effect as though fully set forth herein.*

Deed provisions. This practice has the advantages of reducing the recording fee for each deed and assuring that the restrictions in the deeds will be uniform. The deeds should use language specifically incorporating the recorded restrictions. The mere use of the phrase *subject to covenants, conditions, and restrictions* may be considered insufficient. The latter statement may be construed as no more than a recital of what the tract owner intends, and is not of itself an operative act of imposition of restrictions. The deed is the "final and exclusive memorial" of the rights of the parties.[18]

§12.21. Necessity of incorporating restrictions in deed

It is essential that restrictions be properly incorporated in the deed.

EXAMPLES
1. In one case, an action was brought against the owners of a lot in a subdivision to enjoin them from violating certain use restrictions. Plaintiff and defendants were the owners of adjoining lots in the subdivision and claimed under a common grantor. Certain restrictions stated as to all lots in the subdivision that "no noxious or offensive trade activity shall be carried on upon any lot, nor shall anything be done thereon which may be or become an annoyance or nuisance to the neighborhood." When the defendants began conducting a trucking business on their lot and on an adjacent lot, the noise was found to be offensive and this action was brought. The facts in the case disclosed that the original subdivider had prepared a map of the subdivision and recorded it, and at the same time recorded a document that described the entire parcel, and recited that the owners were declaring and establishing restrictions on the property and each part thereof. The document contained a list of the use restrictions, including the one quoted above. It stated that the tract should be known as a residential tract, and prescribed limitations on the types of residences that could be built and on the location of such residences on the lots with respect to front and side lines. It appeared that the owners had in mind a uniform plan of restrictions and read the defendant a copy of the restrictions. However, the deeds did not incorporate the restrictions. The trial court rendered judgment for the plaintiff, enjoining the defendants from violating the restrictions. The appellate court held that it was essential to incorporate the restrictions in the deed, by reference or otherwise, and this not being done, the restrictions sought to be imposed were therefore not enforceable.[19]

2.   In another case, the defendant sought to enforce building restrictions set forth in the CC&Rs recorded nine months after a conveyance to the plaintiff. The court held that the deed from the developers to the plaintiff, which did not contain the restrictions, was controlling.[20]

§12.22. Variations permitted

Although a general plan restriction implies uniformity, some variation is permissible. There must, of course, be a general plan of restrictions imposed on all of the lots in the tract, but it is not essential that all lots be restricted to the same uses or that all lot owners be given rights of enforcement as to each and every lot. The restrictive plan may provide that certain designated lots shall be used for residential purposes and other lots for business purposes. Rights of enforcement with respect to violations of restrictions in a specified area may be limited to the owners of lots in such area, for example, a specified block in the tract. Or the right to enforce restrictions as to any particular lot in the tract may be limited to the owners of lots immediately adjoining.

§12.23. Waiver by fewer than all lot owners

The right to waive, or cancel, the restrictions may be conferred on fewer than all of the lot owners, for instance, a stated percentage of the owners, or the owners in a specified area. A provision giving the grantor alone the right to modify the restrictions at any time may not in itself defeat the restrictive plan, although the exercise of such right might render the original restrictions unenforceable as between the lot owners.[21]

§12.24. Condominium requirements

The Condominium Act, now called the Davis-Sterling Common Interest Development Act, requires that, before the conveyance of any condominium, a declaration of restrictions relating to the project must be recorded. Although considerable latitude in the selection of appropriate language is permitted, the Act also establishes certain rights, benefits, and easements as statutory matters for the benefit and protection of all condominium owners. The Act provides that such restrictions shall be enforceable equitable servitudes and shall inure to and bind all owners of condominiums in the project. The law requires that an owner of a condominium shall furnish to a prospective purchaser a copy of the CC&Rs, by-laws, and articles of incorporation.[22] Further, on conversions, all substantial defects must be disclosed.[23]

IV. INTERPRETATION OF PARTICULAR RESTRICTIONS

§12.25. In general

Problems of interpretation of the exact meaning of provisions contained in deed restrictions often arise. They illustrate the importance of using precise language so that the intent and purpose of deed restrictions are fully accomplished.

§12.26. Residential purposes

A restriction that land "shall be used for residential purposes only" relates to the use or mode of occupancy to which a building may be put, and not to a type of building. Thus the restriction does not prohibit the construction of an apartment house, duplex, or any building used for residential purposes only, whether occupied by one family or a number of families. On the other hand, a restriction providing that "no buildings other than a first-class private residence shall be built" on the land relates to the type of structure and excludes any multiple residence as well as any business structure.

EXAMPLE   In one case, the deed restrictions provided that "no lot shall be used except for residential purposes." A cosmetologist was enjoined from the part-time operation of a beauty parlor in her home. Evidence disclosed that she averaged six customers a day. The court held that the use was detrimental to other owners in detracting from the residential character of the neighborhood.[24]

§12.27. Garages and outbuildings

A restriction limiting the use of land to "residential purposes," or prohibiting the erection of any structure other than a "residence" or "dwelling house," does not, as a rule, prohibit the erection of a private garage, whether or not attached to the main residence. When the restrictions provide that outbuildings must be in the rear of the premises or located on a specified portion of the lot, it is probable that a garage constructed as an integral part of a residence and in architectural harmony therewith is not an outbuilding, and would not violate the restriction.

EXAMPLE   In one case, it was held that a pad on which a house was to be built, consisting of 20,000 cubic yards of dirt, was not a "structure" separate from the house within a deed provision restricting construction to two one-story houses and garages and prohibiting "other structures." It was further held that the restriction did not require the buildings to be erected on the existing grade, slope, or level.[25]

§12.28. Obstruction of view

Restrictions against obstructing a view are enforceable.

EXAMPLE   In one case, it was held that a subdivision restriction forbidding the erection of a structure on any lot in such a location or in such height as to "unreasonably obstruct the view" from any other lot was not too vague to be enforceable, and, therefore, could be enforced by a lot owner whose view would be cut off by an addition to another lot owner's home.[26]

§12.29. Setback provisions

The application to a corner lot of a restriction that a building shall "face the front line," or shall not be nearer than a specified distance from the "front line," sometimes involves the question of which is the front and which is the side of the lot. Restrictions on the distance at which buildings shall be placed from the street or property lines, intended to secure unobstructed light, air, and vision for the benefit of adjoining lots and to preserve uniformity in the appearance of a tract, involve a problem as to what is meant by the term *building* and whether it includes eaves, steps, bay windows, awnings, and so forth.

§12.30. Use of the word *street*

When the restriction prohibits the construction of a building within a specified distance from a "street," a problem arises in the event the line of the street is changed by widening of the street. It is probable that the line of the street as it exists at the date of the imposition of restriction fixes the point.

§12.31. Cost of buildings

Restrictions against buildings costing less than a specified minimum price are enforceable, but when such restrictions are imposed in terms of fixed amounts without regard to the fluctuating purchasing power of the dollar, the purpose may be defeated. Thus, a $20,000 cost restriction imposed in 1930 would be complied with in 1999 by the construction of a residence far below the standard of a residence built at the date of the deed—a technical, but not a realistic, compliance.

§12.32. Approval of plans and specifications

Most modern tract restrictions provide that no structure shall be erected until the plans and specifications have been approved by an individual, usually the tract owner who imposed the restrictions, or by a group of persons, such as an architectural committee composed of representatives of the lot owners. Enforcement of such restriction is permitted when the refusal to approve plans is a reasonable determination made in good faith.[27] When the architectural committee has ceased to function or cannot be located, the lack of approval of plans by the committee may be unobjectionable if the improvements in fact comply with the restrictions in all other aspects and are in harmony with other improvements in the tract. Further, a committee cannot adopt rules that are contrary to the CC& Rs.[28]

V. TERMINATION OF RESTRICTIONS

§12.33. In general

Restrictions may be terminated in the following ways: (1) expiration of their prescribed period of duration; (2) voluntary cancellation; (3) merger of ownership; (4) change of conditions or other circumstances that cause the courts to deny enforcement; and (5) act of public authorities.

§12.34. Expiration date

Instruments creating restrictions usually provide for a date on which the restrictions will automatically expire. An expiration date is not essential, however, and there is no statutory provision limiting the duration of restrictions. When the duration is not expressly limited by the parties, it will usually be implied that the duration is such period as is reasonable under the particular circumstances.

§12.35. Voluntary cancellation or modification

A covenant or condition may be modified, waived, or released by mutual agreement between the parties affected, or by an instrument, such as a quitclaim deed, executed by the party entitled to enforce the restriction. When general plan restrictions are involved, the necessary parties to a completely effective modification or cancellation of the restrictions are all parties having a right to enforce the restrictions as to the land in question, which usually are all the lot owners in the tract. The restrictions may provide for a right of cancellation by less than all, however, and if the terms of the instrument establishing tract restrictions provide for modification or abrogation of the restrictions by specified persons or in a specified manner, such provisions are controlling.[29]

Effect of general plan restrictions on voluntary cancellation. General plan restrictions often create two separate rights that may be enforced independently.

EXAMPLE Thus when A, the tract owner, conveys all lots in the tract by general plan deeds that impose covenants and conditions giving a right of reentry to the grantor for breach of conditions, and mutual rights of enforcement in favor of all lot owners, A, as owner of the right of reentry, is the only person who can forfeit the title, but each of the lot owners has a right to enjoin a violation. The rights of A and of the lot owners are independent. Either may enforce or release the restrictions as to his or her interest without affecting the legal rights of the other. A complete cancellation and termination of the restrictions can be accomplished by unison of action by all of the holders of the right of enforcement.

§12.36. Termination by merger

Termination by merger is effected when the ownership of the land benefitted by a covenant and the ownership of the land burdened by the covenant come into a single ownership. When restrictions have been extinguished by merger, they do not revive on a subsequent severance of ownership. If the restrictions are to be effective on a subsequent severance of ownership, they must be newly created. Merger also results when the grantor in a deed containing a condition subsequent reacquires the ownership of the restricted land. However, merger of the right of reentry with the ownership of a parcel of land that is subject also to a general plan of restrictions will not affect the rights existing in favor of the other lot owners.

§12.37. Enforcement may be denied on equitable principles

Courts sometimes deny enforcement of restrictions on the ground that it would be inequitable or oppressive under the circumstances to give effect to the restrictions. Change in the character of the neighborhood; acts indicating an abandonment of the right of enforcement; prior violation of the restrictions by the party presently seeking to enforce the restriction—these and other circumstances may present hardships or unfairness that would justify denial of enforcement in a court of equity. Not only are equitable defenses available to the lot owner against whom enforcement of the restrictions is sought, but in a proper case the lot owner may obtain affirmative relief in an action for a declaration of rights and to quiet title as against persons claiming a right of enforcement.[30]

Effect of violations by party seeking enforcement. It appears to be well settled that general plan restrictions cannot be enforced if the owner is guilty of a substantial breach of the same restrictions. The breach must have been something more than trivial; it must be sufficiently material and of an adverse effect on the purposes sought to be achieved by the restriction. Thus an owner who builds a few inches beyond the prescribed setback line may not be precluded from enjoining another lot owner from building several feet beyond the line. A previous violation of one type of restriction will not necessarily preclude the complaining party from seeking relief to compel the observance of another restriction that is beneficial to his property. Thus a violation of setback lines will not estop the party from obtaining enforcement of another restriction limiting structures to private residences.[31]

Effect of acquiescence in violation. Acquiescence by the complainant, who may be the common grantor or an individual lot owner, in a substantial violation of general plan restrictions by one or more lot owners may preclude him from enforcing the restrictions as against others. However, the complainant's failure to object to minor violations, or to violations of which he has no actual knowledge, or that do not affect or injure him, such as a violation in a distant part of the tract, does not prevent him from objecting to violations that do cause him to be damaged. Also, acquiescence in the violation of one of several restrictions does not necessarily operate as a waiver of the right to object to a violation of other separate and distinct restrictions that are material and beneficial to him.

When uniform observance is lacking. The rule is set forth that when there has been no uniform observance of a general plan of restrictions, and substantially all the owners have so conducted themselves as to indicate an abandonment of the right to have the tract kept to the standard established by the original plan, and when enforcement will not tend materially to restore to the tract the character imposed on it by the general scheme, and the infraction complained of does not diminish the value of other estates, then it will be deemed to be inequitable and oppressive to compel at considerable loss compliance with the restrictions by another owner.[32]

Time limitations on right of enforcement. The law does not look with favor on persons who sleep on their rights.[33] A failure to proceed with reasonable promptness to secure relief against a violation of restrictions has the effect of precluding the one guilty of such neglect from securing relief. Thus in one case,[34] a delay of more than one year after a breach occurred, with knowledge that the owners of the restricted land were making valuable improvements thereon, was regarded as one of the factors barring relief. Apart from the period of time within which a court might hold that relief is barred because of laches or unwarranted delay in commencing an action, a statute of limitations[35] bars an action for forfeiture for breach of condition unless the action is brought within five years from the time the right accrued.

Change of conditions in area. Injunctive relief against violation of restrictions cannot be obtained if conditions in the area have so changed since the establishment of the restrictions that it is no longer possible to secure, in a substantial degree, the benefits intended to have been secured by observance of the restrictions. Forfeiture for breach of a condition may likewise be denied on a showing of change of conditions.

Changes affecting residential and minimum area requirements. Enforcement of residential restrictions has been denied when the character of the surrounding territory has changed to a business or commercial district.[36] Restrictions in the minimum area of parcels in a subdivision, often an acre or more, imposed 30 years ago when land was more plentiful, have been held unenforceable based on changed conditions.[37] The principle is stated in one case as follows:

> *Equity courts will not enforce restrictive covenants by injunction in a case where, by reason of a change in the character of the surrounding neighborhood, not resulting from a breach of the covenants, it would be oppressive and inequitable to give the restriction effect, as when the enforcement of the covenant would have no other result than to harass or injure the defendant, without benefiting the plaintiff.[38]*

When denial of enforcement is not warranted. The fact alone that the land subject to the restriction would be more valuable if used for a purpose not permitted, such as a use for business instead of residential purposes, does not warrant denial of enforcement when the original purpose of the restrictions can yet be realized.

Change of zoning. Although change of zoning by the city is not decisive, it has been recognized in many cases as evidence.[39] Also, some courts have declined to grant relief based on a change in the neighborhood unless zoning ordinances permit the contemplated use.

§12.38. Acts of public authorities

Lands acquired for public uses are released from private restrictions, at least during the time property is in public ownership. The state or any of its subdivisions may acquire land for public purposes by gift, purchase, or condemnation, and use it in violation of restrictions for public purposes inconsistent with the restrictions. Thus land restricted to residences has been acquired by school districts for school and playground purposes, free of the restriction.[40] In 1973 the California Supreme Court held that a building restriction enforceable by other owners in a subdivision constitutes *property* within the meaning of the eminent domain provision of the state constitution, and that such owners were entitled to compensation when the property taken by condemnation was to be used for purposes not permitted by the deed restrictions.[41] Before that ruling, the other lot owners were not entitled to compensation.

Redevelopment projects. The Health and Safety Code[42] provides for the elimination of any covenants, conditions, or restrictions (subject to some exceptions) existing on any real property acquired by a redevelopment agency within a redevelopment project area.

Effect of zoning ordinances. As a general rule, zoning ordinances do not affect private restrictions, and both may be effective with respect to the same land at the same time, with the private restrictions usually imposing additional limitations in the use.[43] However, when the private restrictions permit a use forbidden by zoning regulations, the latter will control. Conversely, if zoning regulations permit a use forbidden by deed restrictions, the latter will control. An exception to the latter is a residential care facility for six or fewer persons in a subdivision with a single-family residential restriction.[44]

§12.39. Effect of foreclosure of a lien

As a general rule, the foreclosure of a lien that is superior to the burden of restrictions will eliminate the restrictions. If the restrictions are part of a general plan, and only some of the restricted lots are released from a prior lien, the effect of the foreclosure as to the remaining lots is somewhat uncertain. There is no California case directly in point, but in other jurisdictions it has been held that if, through foreclosure under a prior lien, portions of the tract subject to the general plan of restrictions are sold free thereof, and if the effect of such sale is to render the enforcement of the restrictions unjust or inequitable as to the remainder of the tract, the restrictions will not be enforced as between the owners of such remaining portion.

VI. NATURE AND PURPOSE OF ZONING

§12.40. In general

Briefly, *zoning* is the governmental regulation of the use of land and buildings. It consists of the division of land into areas called zones, and the designation and control of the use made of the land in each of the zones. Zoning laws are enacted in the exercise of the police power, and ordinarily they do not constitute a taking of property for public use for which compensation must be paid.

§12.41. Types of zoning

Zoning is *comprehensive* when it is governed by a single plan for an entire municipality. It is *partial* or *limited* when it applies only to a certain part of the municipality or to certain uses. Fire, height, and building regulations are forms of partial or limited zoning that are antecedents of modern comprehensive zoning.

§12.42. Historical background

Partial or limited zoning and use regulations have long been government activities of United States municipalities. Use zoning to control the location of certain industries, potentially if not actually nuisances, such as distilleries, slaughterhouses, kilns, and the like, was established in the colonies as early as the last decade of the seventeenth century.

§12.43. Constitutional authority for zoning

In California local police regulations are authorized by the state constitution. It provides that any county, city, town, or township may make and enforce within its limits all such local, police, sanitary, and other regulations as are not in conflict with general laws.[45]

§12.44. Statutory authority for zoning

Zoning regulations are specifically authorized by the Government Code. It provides that pursuant to the provisions of that code, the legislative body of any county or city may by ordinance (1) regulate the use of buildings, structures, and land as among agriculture, industry, business, residence, and other purposes; (2) regulate location, height, bulk, number of stories, and size of buildings and structures, the size of yards, courts, and other open spaces, and the percentage of a lot that may be occupied by a building or structure; (3) establish and maintain building set-back lines along any street, highway, freeway, road, or alley; and (4) create civic districts around civic centers, public parks, and public buildings and grounds for the purpose of enabling a planning commission to review all plans for buildings or structures within the district before the issuance of a building permit to assure an orderly development in the vicinity of such public sites and buildings.[46]

§12.45. Charter provisions
Zoning may also be subject to provisions of city charters, and many cities have adopted various plans pursuant to their charters, rather than under the statutory authorization.

§12.46. Master plans for zoning
As elsewhere in the United States, master plans for zoning have been developed for many communities in California, covering the ultimate pattern for such things as freeways and recreational, airport, and shoreline development. These master plans or comprehensive zoning laws are of relatively modern origin, but their enactment has become widespread. The modern tendency is in the direction of extending the power of restriction in aid of city planning.[47]

Comprehensive zoning plan for a city. The Comprehensive Zoning Plan of the City of Los Angeles is an example of a master plan for a city. Before 1946, the city of Los Angeles had no comprehensive zoning ordinance. There existed a series of heterogeneous zoning ordinances applicable to various parts of the municipality, which were considered as stop-gap ordinances eventually to be absorbed by a single comprehensive zoning ordinance. The first such ordinance applying to every part of the city was adopted and became effective on June 1, 1946. The ordinance designates, regulates, and restricts the location and use of buildings, structures, and land for agriculture, residence, commerce, trade, industry, or other purposes. It regulates the height and size of buildings, regulates the open spaces, and limits the density of population. This comprehensive zoning ordinance has been held constitutional as a legitimate exercise of the police power.[48]

§12.47. Scope of city planning
Zoning is obviously a phase of city planning. Strictly speaking, however, zoning is exclusively concerned with use regulation, whereas planning is broader and connotes a systematic development of a municipality with the purpose of promoting the common interest not only with respect to uses of land and buildings, but also with respect to other matters of general concern, such as streets, parks, residential developments, industrial and commercial enterprises, civic beauty, public convenience, and the like. Urban renewal through redevelopment projects is another phase of government planning, designed to reclaim blighted and deteriorating areas.

§12.48. Justification for zoning
The justification for zoning ordinances is that they promote public health, safety, comfort, convenience, and general welfare. Like other laws of similar character, they must be reasonable and not discriminatory or oppressive. It has been held that a regulation for an esthetic purpose only is not a reasonable exercise of the police power.[49] However, if it also has for its purpose the protection of the public health, safety, or welfare, incidental esthetic considerations will not cause it to be invalid.[50] Recent cases indicate that esthetic considerations and preserving the beauty of the landscape have gradually become legitimate purposes of zoning.

EXAMPLES   1.   One case involved the validity of county zoning ordinances that would require the removal of billboards from specified areas in the county. The advertising signs were located along Highway 101, which had been designated on the state's master plan as a "scenic highway" requiring "special scenic conservation treatment." The defendant in the action asserted that these ordinances "bottom solely upon esthetics," and argued that zoning laws may be used only to protect the economic interests of a property owner and not "to preserve the priceless beauty of a countryside for all men." The court held that it was unnecessary to meet that argument directly, since the trial court had made a finding that in Santa Barbara County, scenic environment is commercial. The trial court had found that people came to the county because of its natural beauty, and that the maintenance of billboards along the highway may reasonably be believed to have an adverse effect on the economy.[51]

2. In another case, it was held that a city may regulate signs and billboards along freeways without adopting a zoning ordinance, provided that there is no substantial interference with land use. The Government Code[52] authorizes cities to regulate outdoor advertising, including billboards. The city of Escondido enacted an ordinance prohibiting the placement of billboards next to freeways, declaring them to be a nuisance. The court held that the statute constituted an exception to the general zoning statute, which made no reference to advertising signs and billboards.[53] In its decision, the court stated:

> City's ordinance does not purport to prohibit all signs and advertisements but only to regulate their location so that they do not constitute nuisances and for the obvious purposes of promoting highway safety as well as enhancing community aesthetic values.

Geological hazard zones. The Public Resources Code[54] provides for the adoption and administration by cities and counties of zoning provisions relating to the public safety in hazardous fault zones. The state geologist was required to prepare a map of "special studies zones" along known fault lines, within which zones the site of every proposed new real estate development or structure for human occupancy must be approved by the appropriate city or county in conformity with policies set by the State Mining and Geology Board and the findings of the state geologist. No such development or structure shall be approved in such a zone if "an undue hazard" would be created, and approval may be withheld pending geologic and engineering studies.[55]

Recent trends. Cities and developers are now able to enter into development agreements under state laws that, in effect, permit a city and developer to discard land use rules and start negotiating from scratch. It has been recognized that the development agreement and similar mechanisms have become the implementing tools of larger change. Large-scale development cannot readily be achieved without some joint public–private agreement.

EXAMPLE The city of San Diego adopted a practice of uniformly requiring landowners to pay for public improvements in urbanizing areas even if the owners had no immediate plans to build on the sites. When one landowner sued and obtained an injunction regarding the uniform policy, the city continued its practice by negotiating development agreements with landowners. On appeal the city won its right to impose a uniform requirement.[56]

Despite the novel nature of many negotiated zoning contracts, there are limits as to what cities will approve, even when developers are willing to mitigate the effects.

EXAMPLE In 1984, the city of San Francisco turned down a developer's request to construct a high-rise building that would have cast shadows over part of an existing public park, even though the developer offered compensation of added development of the park. The city had passed a law in June of that year that prohibited construction of buildings that would shade parks and playgrounds.

VII. OPERATION OF ZONING LAWS

§12.49. In general

As we have noted, the power of a municipality to enact zoning ordinances is expressly authorized by statutory and charter provisions, and by the general provisions contained in the state constitution. Zoning laws and ordinances, both for cities and for counties, usually provide for a zoning board or commission to administer the law, and usually require public notice for a specified length of time and the holding of a public hearing, either by the board or commission, before the submission of its report, or by the city council or other municipal legislative body before the adoption of the zoning ordinance, or a public hearing by both. Parties objecting have the right to appeal to the courts. However, every intendment is in favor of a zoning ordinance. The enactment of such an ordinance by a city is deemed to be a proper exercise of the police power and adopted to promote the public welfare.[57]

§12.50. Review by the courts

When a case is taken to court, the courts will inquire whether the scheme of classification and districting under a zoning ordinance is arbitrary or unreasonable, but a decision of the zoning authorities as to matters of opinion and policy will not be set aside unless the regulations have no reasonable relation to the public welfare, or unless the physical facts show that there has been an unreasonable, oppressive, or unwarranted interference with property rights and abuse in the exercise of the police power.[58]

§12.51. Basis for attack on zoning laws

The usual attack on zoning laws is on the ground of discrimination, that is, a denial of the right of equal protection. Although occasionally an ordinance has been held void in its application to a property owner by reason of arbitrary inclusions or exclusions, in most cases it is recognized that zoning necessarily results in some inequalities, particularly to persons on the boundaries of a zoned district. However, if the general scheme is reasonable and fair, individual hardship is not a basis for a constitutional attack on the legislative or administrative determination.[59]

§12.52. When zoning ordinances will be held invalid

The cases in which zoning ordinances have been held invalid and unreasonable as applied to particular property fall roughly into four categories: (1) when the zoning ordinance attempts to exclude and prohibit existing and established uses or businesses that are not nuisances; (2) when the restrictions create a monopoly; (3) when the use of the adjacent property renders the land entirely unsuited to or unusable for the only purpose permitted by the ordinance; and (4) when a small parcel is restricted and given fewer rights than the surrounding property when, for instance, a lot or parcel in the center of a business or commercial district is limited to use for residential purposes, thereby creating an "island" in the middle of a larger area devoted to other uses.[60] It has also been held that the location of school sites is not subject to municipal zoning ordinances.[61]

§12.53. Retroactive application

Zoning ordinances have generally been prospective in their application. In other words, they have not attempted to eradicate nonconforming uses immediately, but have sought to eliminate them gradually by prohibiting alteration or repair of nonconforming structures. A *retroactive application* may render the ordinance invalid. This rule is illustrated by one case[62] involving the validity of an ordinance restricting sanitariums to certain districts, which ordinance was expressly made retroactive. An action was brought to enjoin its enforcement, and the court held that nonconforming uses could not be summarily eliminated by a retroactive ordinance unless the uses were such as to amount to a nuisance.

§12.54. Right to change zoning

Zoning may be changed to the detriment of a property owner.

EXAMPLES

1. One case involved the validity of an ordinance amending the comprehensive zoning ordinance by rezoning vacant land in San Fernando Valley for light industrial in place of agricultural uses. Objections were made by owners of other property in the area, but the amendment was held to be valid.[63]

2. In another case, the city council rezoned a vacant piece of commercial real estate to R-1, thus substantially reducing its value. The court held that an inverse condemnation action did not lie. It stated that landowners have no vested right in existing or anticipated zoning ordinances, and that "some uncompensated hardships must be borne by individuals as the price for living in a modern enlightened and progressive community."[64]

§12.55. Examples

There are numerous cases reflecting the enforcement of zoning laws.

1. In one case, the court pointed out that a landowner's purpose in purchasing land must yield to the public interest in the enforcement of a comprehensive zoning plan.[65]

2. In a second case, the court upheld an ordinance prohibiting auction sales in a residential district on the theory that the assembling of curious crowds attracted by auctions furnished an opportunity for petty frauds and other crimes to be perpetrated.[66]

3. A third case presented a question relative to the effect of annexation on a zoning ordinance. It was held that when land that was subject to a county ordinance zoning it for single-family residences was thereafter annexed by a city having no such ordinance, the land left the territorial jurisdiction of the county and thereupon ceased to be subject to its zoning ordinance and was no longer limited to single-family residences.[67]

4. In a fourth case, it was held that an ordinance prohibiting real estate agents from placing their names and addresses or telephone numbers on "For Sale" or "For Rent" signs is a reasonable restriction to prevent advertising of commercial business in a residential zone.[68]

5. A fifth case held that a zoning ordinance enacted by the city of San Diego to regulate the architectural design of buildings and signs within public view in the area of "Old Town" was valid. In its decision, the court stated as follows:

   > Preservation of the image of Old Town as it existed prior to 1871, as reflected in the historical buildings in the area, as a visual story of the beginning of San Diego and as an educational exhibit of the State of California, contributes to the general welfare; gives the general public attendant educational and cultural advantages; and by its encouragement of tourism is of general economic

value. The purpose of the ordinance clearly is within an exercise of the police power.[69]

§12.56. Effect of zoning on deed restrictions

Deed restrictions are ordinarily not affected by zoning regulations. If a zoning law permits a use to be made of property that is restricted by construction and use limitations contained in a deed, the deed provisions will control. A zoning law cannot relieve land within the district covered by it from lawful restrictions affecting the use of the land imposed by deed or by a recorded declaration of covenants, conditions, and restrictions.

§12.57. Spot zoning

The problem of *spot zoning* is encountered when a large area, such as a zoning district for residential purposes, has small zones, sometimes no larger than a city lot, created within its confines permitting other uses, usually commercial in nature. By spot zoning, a specified parcel of property is thus placed in a different zone from that of neighboring property. This situation is usually accomplished by the amendment of a general zoning ordinance.

Spot zoning may result in the creation of two types of "islands." The legally objectionable type arises when the zoning authority improperly limits the use that may be made of a small parcel located in the center of an unrestricted area.[70] The second type of island results when most of a large district is devoted to a limited or restricted use, but additional uses are permitted in one or more "spots" in the district. The validity of the latter type depends on the basis for the difference in use.

Spot zoning is justified when it is in fact germane to an objective within the valid exercise of the police power. No hard and fast rule can be made that such zoning is or is not illegal. The question is dependent on what is reasonable under all of the circumstances. The zoning of shopping and business districts at convenient places within residential districts generally is sustainable as reasonable and valid.

VIII. EXCEPTIONS TO ZONING

§12.58. Nonconforming use

A comprehensive zoning ordinance places limitations on the use of land within certain areas in accordance with a general policy that has been adopted. Such ordinances ordinarily except from their operation any existing lawful uses that are in conflict (generally referred to as nonconforming uses), primarily because of the hardship or unusual difficulties as to certain properties, and also because of the questionable constitutionality of legislation that would terminate such uses immediately. Zoning legislation looks to the future; it may effect the eventual liquidation of nonconforming uses. As stated in one case, it is the purpose of zoning to crystallize present uses and conditions and to eliminate nonconforming uses as rapidly as is consistent with proper safeguards for those affected.[71] To this end, provisions that preclude the extension or enlargement of such uses, forbid resumption of a use when terminated, or provide a reasonable time within which the use must cease have been sustained as a valid exercise of the police power.

When the nonconforming use relates to the existence of a type of structure, provisions that look to the elimination thereof through obsolescence or destruction have been approved.[72] There is also a growing tendency to guard against the indefinite continuance of nonconforming uses by providing for their liquidation within a prescribed time.[73] The view was expressed in one case[74] that the adoption of a comprehensive plan of community development looking toward the containment and eventual elimination of nonconforming uses, including rock and gravel operations, accords with recognized zoning objectives under settled legal principles.

§12.59. Variances

Zoning ordinances generally provide for *variances* or exceptions from the strict rule or literal enforcement of zoning laws. Such provisions are designed to introduce a measure of elasticity in the administration of zoning, and are based on exceptional circumstances or hardships.

EXAMPLES

1. The granting of a variance for the construction of a swimming pool was held to be valid.[75]

2. A variance was granted for the installation of a service station.[76]

The granting or denial of petitions for variances from certain requirements of a zoning ordinance rests largely in the discretion of the administrative body designated by ordinance for such purpose. Once an exception has been granted, it cannot be summarily revoked. As stated in one case,[77] an exception under a zoning ordinance represents a valuable property right that cannot be revoked except on grounds and through procedure prescribed by the ordinance.

§12.60. Conditional use permits

Zoning ordinances usually authorize the administrative board or commission to grant a conditional use permit upon a finding of the existence of certain facts justifying the issuance of the permit, such as a finding that the permitted uses of the property are essential or desirable to the public convenience or welfare, and are in harmony with the various elements or objectives of the master plan.

EXAMPLE

A conditional use permit was granted to the defendant to excavate for the commercial production of rock, sand, and gravel in an area of land containing 105 acres in the San Fernando Valley area of the city of Los Angeles. The owners of properties within 3,000 feet of the defendant's property brought an action to have the permit declared void. The court denied relief to the adjoining property owners and sustained the action of the city in issuing the permit, but did impose additional conditions to the permit.[78]

In this case, the defendant's property had been classified in an R-A zone, which permitted residential and agricultural uses only, and excluded the excavation of rock, sand, or gravel. However, the ordinance provided for the granting of variances from its existing provisions, and also provided for the granting of conditional use permits by the planning commission or the city council to permit certain uses of public concern, including "the development of natural resources," in zones from which such uses would otherwise be excluded, "when it is found that such uses are deemed essential or desirable to the public convenience or welfare."

IX. TITLE INSURANCE COVERING ZONING

§12.61. In general

Policies of title insurance in their printed provisions specifically exclude zoning and other government regulations from their coverage, including environmental laws and regulations. Under its conditions and stipulations, a policy of title insurance does not insure against loss or damage by reason of any law, ordinance, or government regulation, including building and zoning ordinances, restricting, regulating, or prohibiting the occupancy, use, or enjoyment of the land, or regulating the character, dimensions, or location of any improvements on the land. However, assurances with respect to zoning have been given to lenders by special endorsement, respecting (1) the zone in which the land is situated; (2) the type of structure that may be erected; and (3) the minimum area measurements for a building site.

Zoning reports. Reports on zoning are also obtainable from title companies, which furnish information that the land may be used for a certain purpose, or that a certain type of building may be constructed thereon, or that the land is situated within a particular zone.

X. OTHER GOVERNMENT REGULATIONS AFFECTING USE

§12.62. In general

In addition to zoning ordinances, many other ordinances and laws restrict, prohibit, or affect the use that may be made of property. In many areas, building line ordinances have been enacted under which setback lines are established on certain streets. The general purpose of such ordinances is to keep buildings a required distance from streets, thereby affording more light and air, reducing the danger of the spread of fire, keeping dwellings farther from the dust, noise, and fumes of the street, and affording a better view at street intersections to lessen the risk of accidents. Ordinances may also provide for liens, as in the case of mosquito or weed abatement, for instance, or other types of nuisances.

§12.63. Ordinances regulating construction

A municipality in the exercise of its police powers may also enact ordinances regulating the construction, repair, or alteration of buildings.[79] It may provide for the summary abatement, destruction, or removal of unsafe structures and of unsightly or partially destroyed buildings. It may regulate the location and construction of drains and sewers, and the materials used in wiring structures for electricity and piping them for water, gas, or electric supply, and may prohibit structures not conforming to such regulations.[80]

EXAMPLE   A local ordinance may require that only a licensed electrical contractor perform work on a home, except that the property owner may perform such work subject to his passing the electrical homeowners' examination.[81]

§12.64. Building codes

Building codes have been adopted pursuant to the foregoing and other statutory authority, specifying in detail the various requirements as to the construction of buildings. Permits are required before construction can start on a work of improvement. An application for a building permit, with its accompanying plans and specifications, is examined not only for possible zoning ordinance violations but also for possible violations of the building code.

§12.65. Enforcement of building ordinances

Departments of Building and Safety, created in larger communities to enforce the city's building ordinances, issue permits for the building of new structures and inspect existing structures for all factors of safety, including plumbing, electrical, and heating installations.

§12.66. State Housing Law

The State Housing Law is designed to provide minimum construction and occupancy requirements for all apartment houses and hotels throughout the state and all dwellings located in cities.

In 1970 the legislature amended the State Housing Law by directing the State Housing Commission to adopt rules and regulations imposing the same requirements are contained in various uniform building codes, and required every city and county to adopt ordinances or regulations imposing the same requirements within one year after the effective date of the 1970 amendment. The state law does not preclude cities from adopting additional regulations on subjects not covered by the state regulations.

Low-income housing. Redevelopment agencies are authorized to loan monies to nonprofit firms to finance the acquisition of multifamily rental housing by the nonprofit firm within the agency's territory. The multifamily development must devote a certain percentage of that housing to lower-income households, as defined in the Health and Safety Code, and under certain conditions a specified percentage of housing must be for occupancy of very low-income households.[82]

As a condition of financing, the nonprofit firm is required to enter into a regulatory agreement with the redevelopment agency.[83] The regulatory agreement must

1. Be recorded in the office of the country recorder in which the housing is located

2. Be indexed to the nonprofit firm as grantor and to the redevelopment agency as grantee

3. Provide that the covenants and conditions of agreement are binding upon successors in interest of the nonprofit organization

4. Require, specifically, that the units be reserved for occupancy by lower-income households and shall remain available on a priority basis for occupancy for the term of the bonds issued to provide the monies or 30 years, whichever period is longer

Public health. Another state agency that exercises a degree of control over housing and construction is the State Department of Public Health. State law requires the appointment of a local health officer in every county and city. In most cases, the local health officer enforces both state and local health laws, using the State Department of Public Health as an advisory agency. Drainage, plumbing, sewage disposal, and water supply are under the jurisdiction of both the local health officer and the State Department of Public Health. These officers can require the halting of any proposed development that may result in contamination of the water supply or drainage system, or that may result in improper sewage disposal. The sanitary conditions of all housing are also subject to control by the health authorities.

Hazardous waste property. There are numerous California statutes relating to hazardous waste existing upon real property. For example, the law imposes restrictions and regulations on the use of land designated as "hazardous waste property" by the Department of Health and Safety upon, into, or under which hazardous waste materials have been received. The use of adjoining property within 2,000 feet of hazardous waste property, known as "border zone property," is also subject to use restrictions.[84]

After land has been determined by order of the department to be hazardous waste property or border zone property, notice of that determination is required to be recorded.

Unless a specific variance is granted, property determined to be hazardous waste property cannot be devoted to any new use unless it is an industrial or manufacturing facility in existence since 1981. Subdivision of the land is also generally prohibited.

Limitations also apply in the case of border zone property. Unless a specific variance is granted, property determined to be border zone property cannot be used as a residence, hospital for humans, day care center for children, or for any human habitation. Use for industrial purposes is not prohibited. Also, subdivision of the land is generally prohibited.

XI. TAXATION OF REAL PROPERTY

§12.67. In general

A *tax* is a burden or charge imposed on persons or property, or a proportional contribution levied by the sovereign, to raise money for the support of the government and to enable it to discharge its appropriate functions. It is not a *debt*, as that term is ordinarily used, but a *levy*, under authority of law, for government purposes, that creates a lien on the property subject to the tax.

Property taxes. These are the most important source of revenue at the local level. The property tax is the principal source of revenue for most government functions, such as police and fire protection, schools, roads, parks, and playgrounds. It is ordinarily paramount to all other claims and liens. It is the type of tax with which we are principally concerned in this chapter.

§12.68. Land as a basis of taxation

Land first drew the eyes of the tax assessor as a basis of taxation in England, over 600 years ago, on the assumption that taxes should be assessed in accordance with a person's ability to pay. In those times, the extent and quality of an individual's agricultural holdings were a dependable index of one's ability to pay taxes, because the income was derived almost entirely from agricultural products. It therefore followed that land that a person owned became a surface guide for determining the amount of tax to be levied. Another reason for taxation of land is that it is so easily assessable and cannot be concealed from the tax collector.

§12.69. Requisites of a valid tax

The exercise of the taxing power has long been a source of concern. "Taxation without representation" was a primary complaint in colonial times and a motivating factor in the Revolutionary War. Today, the validity of a tax depends on certain jurisdictional requirements that must be present to sustain the exercise of the tax power. The jurisdictional requisites of a valid tax are set forth in one case as follows: (1) a duly constituted taxing authority; (2) property to be taxed within the territorial jurisdiction of the taxing body; (3) property or subject matter legally subject to the tax, in other words, property that is not exempt; and (4) sufficient notice and opportunity for hearing to constitute compliance with due process of law.[85]

§12.70. Property subject to tax

Generally, all property within the jurisdiction of the taxing power is taxable, unless specially exempt, and exemption statutes are strictly construed. Further, the owner of the improvements can be taxed and assessed separately from the owner of the land.[86]

§12.71. Assessment and levy of property tax

Property taxes are levied annually by each county on the taxable property within its borders, and by each city on the taxable property within such city, except that most cities take advantage of the provisions of the Government Code[87] permitting cities to delegate the levy and collection of their taxes to the county.

    The first step in the taxing of property is the determination of its value, in relation to the value of all other property to be taxed, so that no substantial inequality or unfairness will result. This job is performed by the county tax *assessor*, an elected official whose legal responsibility requires him each year to discover, appraise, and list all taxable property in his jurisdiction. This *assessment* is made annually to the person owning, claiming, possessing, or controlling the property on the lien date (March 1).[88] All requests for changes in property description or property divisions must be made to the assessor before the lien date for entry on the assessment roll for the ensuing year. The assessor is not the tax collector and has nothing to do with the total amount of taxes collected. The assessor's primary function is to determine the fair market value of taxable property.

In the assessment of real property the assessor is not obliged to look any further than the records of the county recorder for the name of the property owner. Ordinarily this record owner will be the named assessee. However, the assessor is authorized to assess real property to unknown owners. In the event a person who claims title to real property, or who is in possession of it, or who is in control of it, presents written evidence of that interest to the assessor prior to the lien date, the assessor could no doubt be persuaded to assess the real property to someone other than the record owner. The law provides that when a person is assessed as either an (1) agent, (2) trustee, (3) bailee, (4) guardian, (5) conservator, (6) executor, or (7) administrator, that representative designation shall be added to that person's name and the assessment entered separately from that person's individual assessment.[89]

§12.72. Property taxes under Proposition 13

In 1978, Proposition 13 (known as the Jarvis-Gann initiative) was enacted, which amended the California Constitution. It imposed a maximum ad valorem tax on real property of one percent of its full cash value (determined by the 1975–1976 county assessor's valuation).[90] Real property can be reassessed either when it is newly constructed or when it changes ownership. What constitutes "change of ownership" is an important aspect that must be considered beforehand. The sales price of the property may be used as the full cash value. Increase in real property taxes may be made yearly, not to exceed two percent of the full cash value base to reflect inflation. Since 1986, under Proposition 58, transfers of a personal residence and additional real estate up to $1,000,000 between parents and their children do not constitute a change of ownership.[91]

§12.73. Equalization of assessments

The yardstick by which the assessed value is determined is not as important as is the *equalization* of the assessment, that is, the application to each assessment of an effective method of determining that no parcel is assessed on a different basis than any other parcel similarly situated. This is the function of each county board of supervisors, sitting as a *Board of Equalization* and as such, vested with the power and authority to adjust manifest inequalities in the assessments. The board of supervisors meets annually for this purpose in July. Acting as such Board of Equalization, it may increase or lower any assessment, but not the entire roll, and it may not lower any assessment unless the owner files an application for such reduction. Several counties have created assessment appeals boards to administer this function on behalf of the county. The *State Board of Equalization* performs a similar function respecting property subject to taxation by the state. Adjustment of valuations cannot be made after adjournment of the board.

§12.74. Levy of tax

After all taxable property has been assessed, the assessments equalized, the amount of revenue to be raised determined, and the tax rate established, the board of supervisors *levies the tax*, that is, formally determines that the taxes be collected and enforced. The county auditor thereupon extends the tax against each parcel or item subject to taxation by applying the rate fixed by the board against the assessed value of each such property. The assessment roll is then delivered for collection to the tax collector, who prepares and mails the tax bills.

The *tax base* is the total assessed value in a given taxing district. The sum of moneys needed each year by all the taxing agencies, as well as by the county, determines what is called the *tax rate*. This tax is a levy per each $100 of assessed value.

§12.75. Due date of taxes

Tax levies cover a fiscal-year period from July 1 to the following June 30. All taxes on personal property secured by specific real property, and one-half the tax on real property, are due November 1 and are delinquent after December 10, and a penalty thereafter attaches. The second half of the tax on real property is due on February 1 but may be paid sooner, either with payment of the first half or thereafter. The second half of real property taxes is delinquent after April 10. The second half cannot be paid unless the first half has been paid. Current taxes can be paid even though prior years' delinquencies exist.[92] In addition, a supplemental tax bill will be received and due on new construction and when property is sold.[93] Figure 12-1 illustrates important real property tax dates.

§12.76. Delinquent tax list

The property tax lien for current taxes remains on the property until the taxes are paid. After the delinquency date for the second half of the tax, the tax collector prepares and publishes a *delinquent list*, describing all property that is delinquent for the current fiscal year.

§12.77. Sale for delinquent taxes

Real property taxes, and also secured personal property taxes, are enforced by a sale of the property at a tax sale if payments become delinquent. The procedure involves two sales, one at the end of the fiscal year and another at the end of the fifth year thereafter.

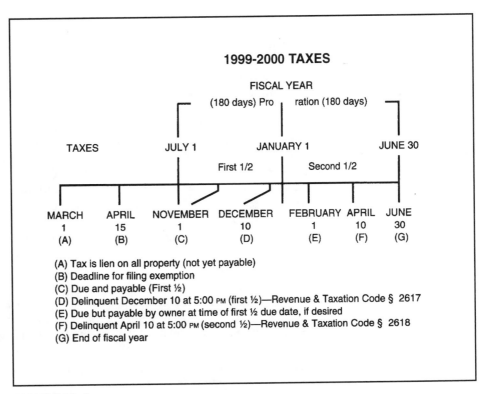

FIGURE 12–1
Chart showing important real property tax dates.

§12.78. First tax sale

On or before the end of the fiscal year (June 30), real property on which the tax for the year or either installment is delinquent is sold to the state at the time fixed in the publication of the notice of intent to sell to the state. Although referred to as the first tax sale, this is not a sale in the conventional sense, but is a so-called book transaction, with the fact of sale being noted on the tax rolls. It establishes the commencement of the statutory five-year period of redemption during which the owner has a right to redeem from the sale by paying all delinquent taxes together with the prescribed penalties. Taxes for ensuing years continue to be assessed, but no subsequent "sale" is entered on the tax rolls while a prior "sale" is still in effect.

§12.79. Second tax sale

At the end of the fifth year following the initial "sale" to the state, the property for the first time becomes available for sale to the State of California. This is an actual sale and in the absence of any fatal defects in the tax sale proceedings, the state acquires an absolute title, freed from all private rights, interests, encumbrances, and claims, except easements burdening the property, water rights held separately, restrictions, recorded offers of dedication of the property to the public, and recorded options in favor of any taxing agency.[94] It is not free, however, from special assessments or improvement bonds that are on a parity, or from municipal taxes separately assessed by a municipality and not included in the delinquent taxes satisfied by the sale.

§12.80. Effect of sale to the state

Once sold and conveyed to the state, the property is off the tax rolls. It belongs to the state, although it is actually held in trust for the county and other taxing authorities whose levies were included in the delinquent taxes for which it was sold.

§12.81. Tax sales to the public

Sales of tax-deeded property to the public are made at public auction by the county tax collector, on authorization of the board of supervisors and with the approval of the state controller, after notice by publication and mailing. An incorrect mailing of the notice of intent to sell does not void the sale.[95] Such sales may be at the request of prospective purchasers or on the initiative of the tax collector. A minimum bid usually is established, at least sufficient to cover expenses. If the real property is in fact not sold, the right of redemption will revive.[96] Any person, including the former owner, may be a purchaser at such tax sale. Formerly, no resale of tax-deeded property by the state could be made for less than the amount required to redeem, thus assuring ultimate payment of all delinquent taxes. However, sales may be made for less, that is, to the highest bidder. A tax deed is issued on payment of the amount of the bid, and the proceeds of the sale distributed pro rata among the taxing agencies having an interest in the delinquent taxes that were the basis of such sale. If any such taxing agency objects to the sale, it must elect to purchase in accordance with a prescribed procedure.

§12.82. Tax deed

The deed issued by the tax collector on completion of the sale of tax-deeded land should be promptly recorded by the purchaser. In the absence of fraud, this deed is declared to be conclusive evidence of the regularity of all proceedings, commencing with the assessment of the tax, to and including the execution of the tax deed.

§12.83. Redemption from tax sale

Real property that is sold to the state at the end of the fiscal year may be redeemed by paying the delinquent taxes that led to such sale, all similar taxes subsequently assessed thereon, and statutory penalties. This is an absolute right, which continues for five years.[97] The taxpayer's right of redemption is actually five years certain, plus any additional time until the right of redemption has been terminated. During the five-year redemption period, title to and possession of the real property is retained by the assessed owner.

Real property deeded to the state *after* five years from the first sale may also be redeemed by paying all delinquencies and statutory penalties at any time before the disposition of such property by the state. This is a *privilege*, however, and not a right, and can be curtailed by subsequent legislation. Upon the request by a redemptioner, the tax collector must issue a certificate of redemption.[98] If tax-defaulted property is redeemed, the tax collector records a rescission of the notice of delinquency.[99] There is no redemption after a tax sale to the public—it is then too late to redeem.

§12.84. Special assessments

In addition to annual taxes levied for the general support of state or local government, there are several ways in which property is assessed for its share of special levies: (1) for the support of schools, flood control, irrigation, drainage, and similar purposes; (2) for the cost of local improvements such as streets, sewers, and other public conveniences; or (3) for maintenance of publicly owned utilities, such as street lighting.

Special assessments differ from *property taxes* in that property taxes are levied for the support of the general functions of the government, whereas special assessments are levied for the cost of specific local improvements.

Special assessments are of three general types: (1) assessments at rates fixed annually and collected at the same time as the annual local taxes; (2) assessments for the maintenance of districts, such as irrigation districts, levied annually but collected separately and in the manner specified in the laws governing such districts; and (3) nonrecurring assessments, levied at the inception of work of special benefit to property in a limited area, called a special improvement district, and designed to cover the costs of installation of a particular local improvement, such as streets, sidewalks, or sewers. An adjunct of nonrecurring assessments is the levying of subsequent annual assessments to cover the cost of maintenance, such as street lighting.

§12.85. Improvement bonds

Assessments exceeding a stated amount (usually $25) may be allowed to "go to bond," that is, to stand as security for the amount due, which is made payable over a period of years in equal annual installments, with interest and evidenced by negotiable bonds, issued by the local government and sold either to the contractor or to the investing public. Such bonds are not, ordinarily, a general obligation of the local government, but are payable only out of collections on the underlying assessments by the city or county officials.

Bond foreclosures. Upon or at any time after default in the payment of an installment of principal or interest of an assessment securing a particular bond, and before the expiration of four years after the due date of the last installment, the holder of that bond may enforce the bond in either of two ways: (1) by treasurer's sale; or (2) by judicial foreclosure, provided such right existed at the date of issuance of the bond. Rights subsequently accorded bondholders by law do not extend to bonds then outstanding, because so to apply the law would be an unconstitutional impairment of the contract deemed to exist between bondholder and property owner.

§12.86. Relative priorities of taxes and assessments

A problem with which the taxing authorities and the court have frequently had to deal in the past is the *relative priorities of taxes and special assessments*. The rule now followed in this state is that they are on a parity of equal rank so that the enforcement of either one does not extinguish the other. This rule is stated in one case,[100] as follows:

> We may now safely conclude that under our system of taxation, liens, in favor of county and municipal corporations, and special assessments, under the authority of state agencies for public purposes, are all on an equality. By this is meant that, in case of delinquency, a deed to any one of these agencies for such taxes will not obliterate the existing liens on the property in favor of any or all of the others.

However, the parity rule does not apply when a tax deed is based on a tax levied at a time when the property was not subject to other taxes or assessments.[101] Liens relating to the cost of removal of substandard structures are also on a parity with the lien of state, county, and municipal taxes.[102]

§12.87. Impact of parity rule

When the title acquired by a purchaser of a tax title by deed from the state or other taxing agency, and the title acquired by a purchaser at a street bond foreclosure or by treasurer's deed pursuant to a sale for delinquent assessments, are on a parity, such purchasers become tenants in common, each owning an undivided one-half interest in the property, irrespective of the time when the liens arose on which their respective titles are based. The time when their respective deeds were executed with reference to each other is immaterial. Each party has an equitable lien against the property to the extent of the amount paid by him. In the event of a subsequent sale of the property, which may be effected through partition proceedings, each cotenant is entitled to reimbursement for the amount paid by him, and after such payments the parties are entitled to an equal division of the excess. The parity rule does not apply, however, as between successive special assessments and improvement bonds themselves. Numerous decisions by the courts have established intricate rules for determining the relative priority of successive liens.

§12.88. Other types of taxes

Waste disposal has become a serious problem in recent times, and has resulted in the enactment of new legislation imposing special taxes, including the hazardous substance tax law[103] and the solid waste disposal site cleanup and maintenance fee law.[104] Real property may be seized and sold under these acts if the person who is required to pay the tax or fee is delinquent.

After January 1, 1989, no right or redemption following sale of the real property is provided for under the hazardous substance tax law.

In 1989, the State Board of Equalization submitted a report on changes that might be needed to improve the due process procedure applicable to the seizure and sale of real property under the above-mentioned acts. The report was required to include changes that might be needed to meet the requirements set forth by the U.S. Supreme Court to assure adequate notice to the affected parties.[105]

As was seen in the preceding chapter, various types of state taxes may become liens on real property when a certificate of tax or an abstract of judgment is recorded. Such certificate or abstract creates a lien having the effect and priority of an ordinary money judgment. Included in such taxes are the sales tax, the use tax, the income tax, and the unemployment tax. Other taxes, such as the federal estate tax, become a lien on real property without the necessity of recording notice thereof in the county recorder's office. These latter taxes automatically become a lien on the date of the owner's death to secure payment of any death taxes that subsequently might be found due.

QUESTIONS

Matching Terms

a. Covenant
b. Ad valorem
c. Variance
d. Servitude
e. Tax
f. Merger of title
g. Assessments
h. Ordinances
i. Prospective
j. Zoning

1. Opposite of retroactive.
2. Legislative enactments of cities or counties.
3. Governmental regulations relating to use an owner can make of property.
4. Uniting of different interests in a parcel of property into one ownership.
5. Special charges on property to pay for local work of improvement.
6. According to value.
7. A promise to do or not to do a certain thing.
8. A right in another person's property in the nature of an easement.
9. A levy, under authority of law, for governmental purposes.
10. An exception or departure from the general rule.

True/False

T F 11. Zoning ordinances are generally prospective in their application.
T F 12. If zoning and deed restrictions are inconsistent with each other, neither is enforceable.
T F 13. Zoning is generally justified under the police power.
T F 14. Private deed restrictions usually constitute both a benefit and a burden.
T F 15. There is no limitation on what private deed restrictions can impose.
T F 16. Basically, private deed restrictions are either covenants or conditions.
T F 17. Taxes and special assessments are generally on a parity.
T F 18. There is no right of redemption after a tax sale.
T F 19. All property within the jurisdiction of a taxing authority is subject to tax.
T F 20. Private deed restrictions, to be valid, must be promotive of the public welfare.

Multiple Choice

21. The term "CC&Rs" generally relates to
    a. Zoning regulation.
    b. Building codes.
    c. City and county regulations.
    d. Private deed restrictions.
22. Police power is regarded as the power of the state to enact laws within constitutional limits to promote

a. Order.
b. Safety and health.
c. General welfare.
d. All of the above.

23. A subdivider may place restrictions on individual lots in a subdivision by
    a. Zoning ordinances.
    b. Covenants in a deed.
    c. Police power.
    d. Eminent domain.
24. Restrictions on the use of real property may be created by
    a. Deed.
    b. Agreement.
    c. Governmental regulations.
    d. Any of the above.
25. A deed restriction is considered to be primarily
    a. A lien.
    b. An encumbrance.
    c. Both a and b.
    d. Neither a nor b.
26. Limitations on the use of real property may be imposed by
    a. Deed restrictions.
    b. Zoning ordinances.
    c. Building codes.
    d. Any of the above.
27. Restrictions limiting the use of real property because of race, color, creed, ancestry, or national origin are
    a. Enforceable.
    b. Void.
    c. Voidable.
    d. Permissible if uniform.
28. Remedies for breach of a condition subsequent in a deed restriction include
    a. Loss of title.
    b. An action for damages.
    c. An action to enjoin.
    d. Any of the above.
29. Generally, zoning will not be enforceable if based solely on
    a. Aesthetic considerations.
    b. Public safety.
    c. Public welfare.
    d. Public health.
30. An owner who wants to place a 15-foot fence on his property should check
    a. Zoning ordinances.
    b. Deed restrictions.
    c. Both a and b.
    d. Neither a nor b.
31. Deed restrictions are considered to be
    a. A benefit.
    b. A burden.

c. Both a and b.

d. Neither a nor b.

32. Deed restrictions may be terminated or extinguished by

   a. Merger of ownership.

   b. Voluntary cancellation by all affected lot owners.

   c. Change in the character of the neighborhood.

   d. Any of the above.

33. If zoning prohibits a use permitted by deed restrictions,

   a. Deed restrictions control.

   b. Zoning controls.

   c. The zoning is unenforceable.

   d. The deed restrictions are enforceable.

34. If deed restrictions prohibit a use permitted by zoning, the

   a. Deed restrictions control.

   b. Zoning controls.

   c. Zoning is unconstitutional.

   d. Deed restrictions are invalid.

35. If exceptional circumstances arise or hardship may result from zoning regulations,

   a. No relief is available because zoning must be applied uniformly.

   b. A variance or exception may be granted.

   c. The zoning is invalid.

   d. None of the above.

36. Zoning ordinances are unenforceable if they are

   a. Arbitrary.

   b. Capricious.

   c. Unreasonable.

   d. All of the above.

37. Height limits can be restricted by

   a. Deed restrictions.

   b. Government regulations.

   c. Private agreement.

   d. Any of the above.

38. Zoning regulations are primarily sanctioned or permitted under the

   a. Police power.

   b. Negotiable instrumental laws.

   c. Fair housing laws.

   d. Penal code.

39. The remedy for breach of a covenant contained in a deed restriction may be

   a. Injunction.

   b. Loss of title.

   c. Specific performance.

   d. Condemnation by the state.

40. The remedy for or effect of a violation of a condition in a deed restriction includes

   a. Reformation.

   b. Criminal action.

   c. Condemnation by the state.

   d. Possible loss of title.

41. All of the following statements concerning restrictions are true except one. Which one is not true?

   a. Deed restrictions are enforced by the local building inspector.

   b. Deed restrictions are limitations on use created by private agreement.

   c. Deed restrictions are encumbrances on title.

   d. Deed restrictions are usually referred to in a deed but not set out at length.

42. Real property in California is taxed in

   a. Proportion to its area regardless of value.

   b. Proportion to its value.

   c. Accordance with the owner's ability to pay.

   d. Accordance with the rate prevailing in the United States.

43. Property taxes and special assessments are ordinarily

   a. On a parity.

   b. Subordinate liens.

   c. Inferior to a purchase money mortgage.

   d. Inferior to a construction loan.

44. A levy under authority of law for governmental purposes is known as a(n)

   a. Tax.

   b. Mechanic's lien.

   c. Judgment lien.

   d. Artisan's lien.

45. For a tax to be valid, the following requirements must be met:

   a. A duly constituted taxing authority.

   b. Property (nonexempt) within the jurisdiction of the taxing authority.

   c. Notice and opportunity for hearing.

   d. All of the above.

46. The tax assessor is charged with the duty of

   a. Collecting taxes.

   b. Determining value.

   c. Fixing the tax rate.

   d. Selling tax delinquent property.

47. The total assessed value in a taxing district is called the

   a. Tax rate.

   b. Tax base.

   c. Tax equalization.

   d. Tax deed.

48. The levy per each $100 of assessed value is known as the

   a. Tax rate.

   b. Tax base.

   c. Tax equalization.

   d. Tax deed.

49. Special assessments are charges against real property for the cost of local improvements such as

   a. Sidewalks.

   b. Curbs.

c. Street lighting.

d. Any of the above.

50. Taxes and special assessments are ordinarily on a parity, which means that they rank

a. Equally.

b. Unequally.

c. Differently.

d. None of the above.

NOTES

1. Marina Point Ltd. v. Wolfson (1982) 30 C.3d 721; O'Connor v. Village Green Owners Assn. (1983) 33 C.3d 790. In Nahrstedt v. Lakeside Village Condo Assn (1992) 25 C.A. 4th 473, it was decided that a condo owner has the right to challenge a pet restriction on the condo CC&Rs.

2. C.C. 1462 and 1468; Taflormina Theosophical Comm. Inc. v. Silver (1983) 140 C.A.3d 964. Further, CC&Rs excluding a nonresident owner from using common owner recreational facilities are valid and reasonable (Liebler v. Pt. Loma Tennis Club [1995] 40 C.A. 4th 1600).

3. C.C. 712, 713, 714.

4. Linmark Associates, Inc. v. Township of Willingboro (1977) 97 S. Ct. 1614; C.C. 782.5.

5. City of Santa Barbara v. Adamson (1980) 27 C.3d 123. *See also* City of Chula Vista v. Pagard (1981) 115 C.A.3d 785, which held that a city can prevent overcrowding by reference to a floor space ratio, rather than legal or biological relationships.

6. Soman Properties, Inc. v. Rikuo Corp. (1994) 24 C.A. 4th 471. As to a HOA's right to record a violation of CC&Rs, *see* California Riviera HOA v. Superior Court (1995) 37 C.A. 4th 1599; Citizens for Covenant Compliance v. Anderson (1995) 12 C. 4th 345 (CC&Rs not applicable to these types of situations).

7. Burdell v. Grandi (1907) 152 C. 376. *See also* Portola Hills Common Assn. v. James (1992) 4 C.A. 4th 289, which held that CC&Rs against satellite dishes, when they are not visible to other residents, are unreasonable as a matter of law. HOA recording a notice of noncompliance allegedly in violation of CC&Rs is invalid and homeowner has right to expunge the record (Ward v. Superior Court [1997] 55 C.A. 4th 60).

8. City of Stockton v. Weber (1893) 98 C. 433.

9. Los Angeles Investment Co. v. Gary (1919) 181 C. 680; C.C. 53(b).

10. Shelley v. Kraemer (1948) 334 U.S. 1; Coleman v. Stewart (1949) 33 C.2d 703.

11. Barrows v. Jackson (1952) 112 C.A.2d 534; affirmed by the United States Supreme Court, 346, U.S. 249.

12. Public Law 90-284.

13. Jones v. Mayer Co. (1968) 392 U.S. 409.

14. 42 U.S.C. 1982.

15. C.C. 782 & 782.5; *see also* C.C. 53.

16. Richardson v. Callahan (1931) 213 C. 683; *see also* Sain v. Silvestre (1978) 78 C.A.3d 461; Terry v. James (1977) 72 C.A.3d 438; MacDonald Properties, Inc. v. Bel-Air Country Club (1977) 72 C.A.3d 693; Soman Properties, Inc. v. Rikuo Corp. (1994) 24 C.A. 4th 471.

17. Werner v. Graham (1919) 181 C. 174; Martin v. Ray (1946) 76 C.A.2d 471.

18. Beran v. Harris (1949) 91 C.A.2d 562.

19. Murry v. Lovell (1955) 132 C.A.2d 30; Soman Properties, Inc. v. Rikuo Corp. (1994) 24 C.A. 4th 471. However, if CC&Rs are recorded before the execution of the contract of sale, merely because the restrictions are not mentioned in the deed, CC&Rs are still enforceable (Citizens for Covenant Compliance v. Anderson [1995] 12 C. 4th 345).

20. Riley v. Bear Creek Planning Comm. (1976) 17 C.3d 500; Soman Properties, Inc. v. Rikuo Corp. (1994) 24 C.A. 4th 471.

21. Burkhardt v. Lofton (1944) 63 C.A.2d 230.

22. C.C. 1368.

23. C.C. 1134.

24. Biagim v. Hyde (1970) 3 C.A.3d 877.

25. Howard Homes, Inc. v. Guttman (1961) 190 C.A.2d 526.

26. Seligman v. Tucker (1970) 6 C.A.3d 691; Ezer v. Fuchslock (1979) 99 C.A.3d 849.

27. Hannula v. Hacienda Homes, Inc. (1949) 34 C.2d 442.

28. Ticor Title Insurance Co. v. Rancho Santa Fe Assn. (1986) 177 C.A.3d 726.

29. Sharp v. Quinn (1931) 214 C. 194.

30. Downs v. Kroeger (1927) 200 C. 743.

31. Robertson v. Nichols (1949) 92 C.A.2d 201.

32. Bryant v. Whitney (1918) 178 C. 640.

33. C.C. 3527.

34. Hannah v. Rodea Vellejo Ferry Co. (1928) 89 C.A. 462.

35. C.C.P. 320. But the statute of limitations does not commence until a demand for performance is made (Cutujian v. Benedict Hills Estate Assn. [1996] 41 C.A. 4th 1379.

36. Wolff v. Fallon (1955) 44 C.2d 695.

37. Hirsch v. Hancock (1959) 173 C.A.2d 745; Key v. McCabe (1960) 54 C.2d 736.

38. Hurd v. Albert (1931) 214 C. 15. Effective January 1, 1983, C.C. 885.040 gives statutory recognition to the case law, under which real property titles can be freed from obsolete and outmoded conditions and restrictions.

39. Bard v. Rose (1962) 203 C.A.2d 232.

40. Sacket v. Los Angeles City School District (1931) 118 C.A. 254.

41. Southern California Edison Co. v. Bourgerie (1973) 9 C.3d 169.

42. H. & S. 33397.

43. Wilkman v. Banks (1954) 124 C.A.2d 451.

44. Welch v. Goswich (1982) 130 C.A.3d 398; H. & S. Code 1566 *et seq.*

45. Article XI, Section 11.

46. Govt. C. 65800.

47. In fact, it is necessary that each city and county adopt a comprehensive, long-term general plan for the physical development of the county or city. Govt. C. 65300.

48. Beverly Oil Co. v. City of Los Angeles (1953) 40 C.2d 552; Zahn v. Board of Public Works of the City of Los Angeles (1925) C. 497.

49. Varney & Green v. Williams (1909) 155 C. 318.

50. Brougher v. City & County of San Francisco (1930) 107 C.A.15.

51. County of Santa Barbara v. Purcell, Inc. (1967) 251 C.A.2d 169.

52. Govt. C. 38774.

53. City of Escondido v. Desert Outdoor Advertising, Inc. (1973) 8 C.3d 785.

54. Pub. Res. C. 2621, *et seq.*

55. *See* §5.26.

56. J. W. Jones Co. v. City of San Diego (1984) 157 C.A.3d 745; *California Lawyer* (December 1984).

57. Willett & Crane v. City of Palos Verdes Estates (1950) 96 C.A.3d 757.

58. Lockard v. City of Los Angeles (1949) 33 C.2d 453.

59. *See* Strumsky v. San Diego Employees' Retirement Assoc. (1974) 11 C.3d 38; Topango Assoc. for a scenic Community v. County of Los Angeles (1974) 11 C.3d 506.

60. Wilkins v. City of San Bernardino (1946) 29 C.2d 332; Kissinger v. City of Los Angeles (1958) 161 C.A.2d 454.

61. Town of Atherton v. Superior Court (1958) 159 C.A.2d 417.

62. Jones v. City of Los Angeles (1930) 211 C. 304.

63. Robinson v. City of Los Angeles (1956) 145 C.A.2d 810.
64. HFH Ltd. v. Superior Court (1975) 15 C.3d 508; *see also* Eldridge v. City of Palo Alto (1975) 51 C.A.3d 726.
65. County of San Diego v. McClurken (1951) 37 C.2d 683.
66. Hart v. Beverly Hills (1938) 11 C.2d 343.
67. City of South San Francisco v. Berry (1958) 120 C.A.2d 525.
68. Burk v. Municipal Court (1964) 229 C.A.2d 696.
69. Bohaman v. City of San Diego (1973) 30 C.A.3d 416.
70. Hamer v. Town of Ross (1963) 59 C.2d 776.
71. Orange County v. Goldring (1953) 121 C.A.2d 442.
72. Rehfeld v. San Francisco (1933) 218 C. 83.
73. County of San Diego v. McClurken (1951) 37 C.2d 683.
74. Consolidated Rock Production Co. v. City of Los Angeles (1962) 57 C.2d 515.
75. Ames v. City of Pasadena (1959) 167 C.A.2d 510.
76. Flagstad v. City of San Mateo (1957) 156 C.A.2d 138.
77. Ricciardi v. County of Los Angeles (1953) 115 C.A.2d 569.
78. Wheeler v. Gregg (1949) 90 C.A.2d 348.
79. H. & S. 15153.
80. Govt. C. 38660.
81. City & County of San Francisco v. Pace (1976) 60 C.A.2d 906.
82. H&S Code 50079.5; 50105.
83. H&S Code 33742.
84. H&S Code 25117.3 *et seq.*
85. Miller v. McKenna (1944) 23 C.2d 774.
86. Rev. & Tax. C. 4188.2. For exempt property (for example, churches), *see* Rev. & Tax. C. 2062; Regents of U.C. v. State Board of Equalization (1977) 73 C.A.3d 660.
87. Govt. C. 51500, *et seq.*
88. Rev & Tax. Code 405.
89. Rev. & Tax. Code 611, 612.
90. *See* Cal. Const. Article XIII A; Rev. & Tax. C. 50 100.5 & 110 110.5; McMillin-BCED/Miramar Ranch North v. County of San Diego (1995) 31 C.A. 4th 545; Munkdale v. Giannini (1995) 35 C.A. 4th 1104.
91. Rev. & Tax. Code 60, *et seq.*; R&T Code 63.1 regarding when the claim for exclusion must be filed. *See also Summary of California Law* (Witkin, 9th ed. Taxation §114, 115).
92. Rev. & Tax. Code 2607.
93. Rev. & Tax. Code 75, *et seq.*
94. Rev. & Tax. C. 3712.
95. Philbrick v. Huff (1976) 60 C.A.3d 633.
96. Rev. & Tax. Code 3707(d), added in 1986.
97. Rev. & Tax. C. 4101, *et seq.*
98. Rev. & Tax. Code 4105.2, effective on July 1, 1988.
99. Rev. & Tax. Code 4112.
100. Masa Lemon Grove & Spring Valley Irrigation District v. Hornbeck (1932) 216 C. 730.
101. Elbert, Ltd. v. Barnes (1951) 107 C.A.2d 659.
102. Rules & Regulations of the Department of Industrial Relations, Division of Housing.
103. Rev. & Tax. Code 43000 *et seq.*
104. Rev. & Tax. Code 45001.
105. Mennonite Board of Missions v. Abrams (1983) 462 U.S. 791.

13

Land Use, Descriptions, Subdivisions, and Investment Regulations

I. INTRODUCTION

§13.1. In general

California, as well as many other places in the United States, has been undergoing a metamorphosis in urban and suburban growth and development, and there is little prospect of any significant abatement over the next several decades. Consequently, the problem of how to contain this growth most effectively will increase in importance and complexity. It will necessitate a reorientation of land use controls from the narrow, locally based, single-lot concepts of the past to a basic philosophy of land development calculated to accommodate population increase and urbanization, and, at the same time, preserve open space areas for parks and recreational facilities, as well as to protect the natural beauty of the countryside. Also, greater concern is being expressed for the preservation of agricultural land as a source of food. The concern of the environmentalists must also be made compatible with the growing demand for the development of sufficient energy to meet the needs of today's society. What to do with our waste, particularly hazardous waste, is becoming of vital concern, not only in California but throughout the world. Dumping our garbage in so-called landfills hasn't proven to be a satisfactory solution.

In the past, relatively uncontrolled growth has led to a more or less haphazard unfolding of urban and suburban development. Zoning and other land use control techniques in the past have made an ambivalent contribution to the problem of the ease with which such controls lend themselves, through amendment and variance, to political and other pressures, and the somewhat fortuitous review given to them by the court on a case-by-case basis. These elements have contributed to disorderly development in many areas, what is commonly referred to as urban sprawl. It is generally considered that uncontrolled growth is inevitably destructive, and the modern view is promotive of the fully planned community as a substitute.

Another area of concern relates to airport expansion. Statewide zoning standards have been sought in recent years for compatible use of airport land. Until recently, the emphasis of zoning for airports has been restricted to the purpose of protecting landowners in the path of airplane takeoff and landing patterns. Of late, noise has been of considerable concern to homeowners and land developers. It is anticipated that in future planning for airports, communities will allow for adequate noise buffer zones as well as for the obstruction-clear zones required for safety purposes. One of the problems that arises with such zoning regulation is that more than one jurisdiction is often involved in the areas surrounding an airport, and coordination is sometimes difficult. Hence the proposal that a statewide policy for "compatible land use" around airports be considered when local governments are unable to establish suitable regulation.

In this chapter we briefly review numerous laws relating to land use and then consider the subject of how land is described. Subdivision controls, both as to local regulations and as to sales to the public, are reviewed. The chapter concludes with a consideration of investment regulations affecting real property, including the regulation of syndicates involving real property.[1]

II. LAND USE

§13.2. Environmental impact reports

Of increasing concern in the use and development of land in California is the protection of the environment. This concern has necessitated environmental impact reports in most new developments.

The adoption of a law in 1970 creating a new state office of planning and research[2] is illustrative of the increasing concern in the state with planning for the future. In that law, the legislature declared that recommendation, continuous evaluation, and execution of statewide environmental goals, policies, and plans are included within the scope of the executive functions of the governor.[3] Under the provisions of the Government Code,[4] the governor is required to prepare, and thereafter shall cause to be maintained, regularly reviewed, and revised, a comprehensive State Environmental Goals and Policy Report. The maximum public understanding and response to alternative statewide environmental goals, policies, and actions must be sought in the preparation and maintenance of such report.[5]

The Government Code[6] provides that the Office of Intergovernmental Management shall be the clearinghouse for requests from cities and counties that appropriate state agencies evaluate the environmental impact of any proposed subdivision within the purview of the Government Code, or any proposed land project within the purview of the Business and Professions Code.[7]

The new laws relating to environmental impact reports have been the subject of a number of court cases in which the validity of this type of legislation has been sustained. Other cases have related primarily to the application of the new laws to a particular development.

§13.3. National Environmental Policy Act

A federal National Environmental Policy Act was adopted by Congress in 1969 and became effective in 1970.[8] The act requires all agencies of the federal government to include in "every recommendation or report on proposals for legislation and other major federal actions significantly affecting the quality of the human environment" an environmental impact statement considering all adverse effects and possible alternatives.

The purpose of the act is to declare a national policy that will aid in accomplishing the following:

1. Fulfill the responsibilities of each generation as trustee of the environment for succeeding generations.

2. Assure for all Americans safe, healthful, productive, and esthetically and culturally pleasing surroundings.

3. Attain the widest range of beneficial uses of the environment without degradation, risk to health or safety, or other undesirable and unintended consequences.

4. Preserve important historic, cultural, and natural aspects of our national heritage, and maintain, wherever possible, an environment that supports diversity and variety of individual choice.

5. Achieve a balance between population and resource use that will permit high standards of living and a wide sharing of life's amenities.

6. Enhance the quality of renewable resources and approach the maximum attainable recycling of depletable resources.[9]

§13.4. California Environmental Quality Act (CEQA)

The California Environmental Quality Act was first adopted in 1970 and has since been substantially amended. The act provides that local government agencies "shall make an environmental impact report on any project they intend to carry out which may have a significant effect on the environment."[10] As the express legislative intent declares, the CEQA was designed to be a milestone in the campaign for "maintenance of a quality environment for the people of this state now and in the future."[11] CEQA requires various state and local governmental entities to submit environmental impact reports before undertaking specified activity. These reports compel state and local agencies to consider the possible adverse consequences to the environment of the proposed activity and to record such impact in writing.

Pursuant to the Code,[12] the environmental impact reports required by the act must set forth the following information:

(a)   The environmental impact of the proposed action

(b)   Any adverse environmental effects that cannot be avoided if the proposal is implemented

(c)   Mitigation measures proposed to minimize the impact

(d)   Alternatives to the proposed action

(e)   The relationship between local short-term uses of people's environment and the maintenance and enhancement of long-term productivity

(f)   Any irreversible environmental changes that would be involved if the proposed action should be implemented.

(g)   The growth-inducing impact of the proposed project[13]

As stated by the court in one landmark case:

> *In an era of commercial and industrial expansion in which the environment has been repeatedly violated by those who are oblivious to the ecological well-being of society, the significance of this legislative act cannot be understated. As section 21001, subdivision (g), clearly sets forth, the CEQA requires governmental agencies at all levels to consider qualitative factors as well as economic and technical factors and long-term benefits and costs and to consider alternatives to proposed actions affecting the environment.[14]*

In this case, the specific question presented was whether the CEQA applies to private activities for which a permit or other similar entitlement is required. The court held that the act did include private activities as well as public improvements for which a government permit is necessary.

§13.5. California Coastal Act of 1976

In 1972, the voters of California approved an initiative measure to establish a state coastal zone conservation commission and six regional commissions.[15]

The state commission was directed to prepare and submit to the legislature a coastal zone plan for the preservation, protection, restoration, and enhancement of the coastal zone environment, with recommendations for policies and powers required for implementation of the plan. Portions of the original act were repealed. The act is now known as the California Coastal Act of 1976. It has since been revised; revisions to the coastal zone boundary have been fairly numerous.

The *coastal zone* is defined as "that land and water area of California, from Oregon to Mexico, extending seaward to the outer limit of the state's jurisdiction (including islands) and inland to the highest elevation of the nearest coastal mountain range," except that in Los Angeles, Orange, and San Diego counties the inland boundary is to such highest elevation, as stated, or five miles from the mean high tide line, whichever is less. There have been revised boundaries of other counties and cities since the enactment of the Act.

The State Coastal Conservancy Act (Public Resources Code, §3100) is also designed to protect the coastal area. There have been many conservancy acquisitions for the protection of coastal resources.

§13.6. Other governmental controls

Numerous other controls on land use have been enacted by the legislature and will be considered briefly in the discussion that follows.

§13.7. Zoning and assessment lien reports

Intended largely as a protection to buyers of residential property, ordinances have been enacted by several cities and counties in California pursuant to sections of the Government Code,[16] providing that prior to the sale or exchange of any residential building, the owner or his authorized agent shall obtain from the city a report of the residential building record showing the regularly authorized use, occupancy, and zoning classifications of such property. The referred-to statutes require that (1) the report be delivered to the buyer or transferee prior to consummation of the sale or exchange; and (2) such ordinance declare it to be unlawful to sell or exchange a residential building without first having obtained and delivered the required report. An exemption from the above is provided for the first sale of a residential building located in a subdivision for which a final map has been approved and recorded within two years prior to such first sale. The statute further provides that no sale or exchange of residential property shall be invalid solely because of a failure to comply with such an ordinance unless such failure would be an act or omission that would constitute grounds for rescission in the absence of such an ordinance.

EXAMPLE Illustrative of the application of this law is an ordinance enacted by the City of Los Angeles in 1973 that requires such reports, originally on a voluntary basis and later on a mandatory one. In addition to a zoning and occupancy report, the ordinance also requires an assessment report disclosing pending assessments for local works of improvement and similar information.[17]

§13.8. Building inspection reports

An ordinance was also enacted by the City of Los Angeles in 1973 permitting an owner of residential property to obtain from the Department of Building and Safety a "Certificate of Housing Compliance." The owner may file an application for such a report and shall pay a fee in a prescribed amount, starting with a single-family dwelling or the first dwelling in a multiple-dwelling unit. After the application has been accepted, the Superintendent is required to cause an inspection to be made and a report prepared. If, after taking into account nonconforming rights, the inspection report indicates that any building or portion thereof does not conform to the requirements of the Los Angeles Municipal Code, that portion shall be made to conform.

When compliance has been secured, or if no corrections are required as a result of the inspection report, the Superintendent will issue to the owner a Certificate of Housing Compliance stating that the building is now in substantial compliance with the applicable provisions of the Los Angeles Municipal Code for existing buildings.

An obvious target of the ordinance is home improvement work done by unlicensed contractors or by owners without obtaining a building permit. The basic reason for the enactment of the ordinance was a ruling that from and after September 10, 1973, all Conditional Commitments on FHA loans would be conditioned on the submission of evidence that the property is in compliance with the applicable local housing code for existing dwellings. Comparable ordinances have been enacted in other communities.

§13.9. Land Conservation Act

Under the California Land Conservation Act of 1965 set forth in the Government Code, agricultural land may be restricted to agricultural purposes by means of contracts between cities or counties and private landowners. Such contracts may run for an initial period of ten years or more. The inclusion within an agricultural preserve of lands within a scenic highway corridor, a wildlife habitat area, a saltpond, a managed wetland area, or a submerged area is authorized.[18] Among the bases of this law is a legislative finding that in a rapidly urbanizing society, agricultural lands have a definite public value as open space, and the preservation in agricultural production of such lands—the use of which may be limited pursuant to the provisions of this new law—constitutes an important physical, social, esthetic, and economic asset to existing or pending urban or metropolitan development.

III. DESCRIPTIONS

§13.10. In general

Real property is identified in ordinary day-to-day transactions by street address or popular name, which is sufficient for many purposes, such as receiving mail and directing visitors. In conveyancing, however, a sufficient legal description is essential. Land is unique; no two parcels are exactly alike, since each is located in a different place on the earth. The particular location of any parcel of land may be described in such a way that it can be distinguished from all other land, and when this is accomplished the land can be identified by what is referred to as a good or sufficient legal description.

§13.11. How descriptions are obtained

As was learned in Chapter 7, one of the essential elements of a deed is a sufficient legal description of the property conveyed. Before such a description is written, some person, usually a land surveyor, locates on the ground the exact boundaries of the tract of land in question, and then puts into words the directions for locating the lines the surveyor has traced on the ground. By this method a legal description is obtained.

§13.12. Sufficiency of description

Any of several methods of describing land may be used, including metes and bounds descriptions, the government survey, and tract descriptions as contained in recorded maps. As a general rule, a description of land in a conveyance is *sufficient* if it identifies the land or furnishes the means of identifying the land. It has been held that if a competent surveyor can take the conveyance and locate the land on the ground from the description contained in the instrument, with or without the aid of extrinsic evidence, the description is legally sufficient.[19]

§13.13. Parol or extrinsic evidence

Parol or extrinsic evidence is sometimes admitted in a proper case as an aid in identifying the land. *Extrinsic evidence* is evidence that is not furnished by the document itself, but is obtained from outside sources. The circumstances under which an instrument was executed, statements made at the time, and informal writings, such as letters and memoranda, would be extrinsic evidence. The word *parol* refers to oral utterances, but the term *parol evidence*, within the meaning of the parol evidence rule, is often used in the same sense as extrinsic evidence. *Extrinsic evidence* generally cannot be used to explain the meaning of a written instrument, since the written instrument supersedes prior and contemporaneous negotiations. Its use is permitted, however, when the written instrument is ambiguous and its meaning cannot be determined from the instrument itself.[20]

§13.14. Effect when description is insufficient

If the conveyance has an insufficient description and does not furnish the means by which the description may be made definite and certain to locate the land readily, the conveyance is void. From the standpoint of a title insurer, a good description is important not only in determining whether the instruments describe the land with sufficient certainty to be valid and operative, but also in determining whether the successive instruments in the chain of title, which may vary greatly in form, in fact describe the same land. Generally, a title insurer in issuing a report of title will vest title in the last grantee under a conveyance containing a sufficient legal description and then show as an exception the effect of subsequent deeds (or other instruments) containing apparent defective descriptions.

§13.15. Metes and bounds

Land may be described by naming its boundaries in detail. These boundaries may be indicated in various ways, as follows: (1) by naming natural boundaries, such as rivers, streams, trees, or stones, or artificial monuments, such as walls, fences, stakes, or roadways, to, from, or along which the boundaries are to run; (2) by stating the courses and distances of the boundary lines; (3) by designating the lands of an adjoining owner as a boundary; or (4) by using two or more of these elements in the same description. All of these ways of describing land may be classed generally as descriptions by *metes and bounds*, that is, so many units of measurement along a stated boundary line, metes meaning measurements and bounds meaning boundaries. However, a metes and bounds description is more commonly thought of as a description that commences at a certain fixed point of beginning and goes on courses and distances to another point, and thence follows the boundary lines of the tract of land by successive courses and distances until the point of beginning is reached, with or without calls for monuments as tie points.

The first requisite of a metes and bounds description is a definite and stable starting point. Sometimes this point is marked by a monument, such as an iron pipe; often the point is described as the intersection of two streets, the corner of a lot shown on a recorded map, or a point located at a specified distance from such street or lot corner. The boundary line must then be run continuously from one point to another and return to the starting point so as to produce a closed area.

§13.16. Government Survey

After California became part of the United States, public lands, consisting of lands not embraced within the boundaries of pueblos and valid Mexican or Spanish grants, were subject to survey under the rectangular system of surveys adopted by Congress by an ordinance in 1785. This system provided for the division of the public land into townships six miles square. By running lines north and south at one-mile intervals and east and west at right angles, the townships were divided into 36 sections of 640 acres each. This system, known as the Government Survey, had been employed previously in vast areas of the United States, such as the Northwest Territory, created in 1787.

Describing sectional property. A legal description of a parcel of land in a government survey identifies the land by designating the township, range, and section of the principal meridian area involved as follows:

> The northwest quarter of the southwest quarter of section 10, Township 2 North, Range 3 West, San Bernardino Meridian.

Additional references in description. The names of the county and state are customarily added to the description, but omission thereof in this type of description does not make the description defective. It is desirable, especially when several government surveys have been made, to identify the land further by adding a reference to the particular government plat that controls the location of the land in question.

§13.17. Lot and block descriptions

From the earliest days of conveyancing in California, as elsewhere, it has been a recognized practice to deposit maps or plats in the office of the county recorder and to make sales or conveyances by reference to them. A description of land by mere reference to a lot or parcel number on the map is sufficient if the map can be produced and identified and if a surveyor, by applying the rules of surveying, can locate the land from the descriptive data.

Typically, a description making reference to a map refers to a designated lot in a block of a designated tract, followed by words comparable to the following:

> as shown on a map recorded in book _____, page ___ of Maps, in the Office of the _____ County Recorder, State of California.

The exact location of the property is shown on the recorded map of which the particular lot is a part. Various matters affecting the ownership of the lot, such as easements for street purposes, storm drains, or dedications for parks or other public uses, may also be shown on the map.

§13.18. Record of survey

A map showing the record of a survey by a surveyor or civil engineer may be filed with the county surveyor and, when approved, it must be filed with the county recorder and placed in a book entitled Record of Surveys. Such a map may be filed for the purpose of showing material evidence not appearing of record or material discrepancies with the record.[21] A description by reference to a record of survey map filed in the county recorder's office may be sufficient if the boundaries of the land described can be identified without question from the data shown on the map.

As a general rule, merely recording a record of survey does not necessarily provide constructive notice, because the record of survey may or may not be in the chain of title. Customarily, a title insurer will not rely upon a record of survey unless it is the primary control or reference for the grantee's title.

§13.19. Official maps

In addition to maps prepared by private individuals, official maps also may be referred to in legal descriptions. The law permits the filing with the county recorder of an "official map" of a city, town, or subdivision, showing lot and block numbers, prepared by the city engineer or county surveyor and approved by the governing body of the city or county, as the case may be.[22]

§13.20. Assessor's maps

The law also permits the county assessor to prepare and file in his or her office maps showing parcels of land designated by number or letter. Under the provisions of the Revenue and Taxation Code,[23] land may be described by a reference to such map for assessment purposes, but shall not be described in any deed or conveyance by a reference to any such map unless such map has been filed in the county recorder's office.

The Revenue and Taxation Code[24] authorizes a local entity, in its ordinance imposing a documentary transfer tax, to require every written instrument by which realty is conveyed to have noted on it the tax roll parcel number of such realty. It is expressly stated to be for administrative and procedural purposes only, and the stated legal description on the document governs in the event of any conflicts. The act further provides that an erroneous parcel number, or its omission altogether, shall not affect the validity of the document, and no liability shall attach to anyone for such an error or omission.

§13.21. State plane coordinate system

Another system of describing land, which has been growing in use, is provided for in the Public Resources Code[25] and is referred to as the California Coordinate System. This system is based on the theory, first advanced by Sir Isaac Newton, that the earth is an oblate spheroid (a sphere flattened at the poles); it had previously been considered to be a perfect sphere. Various government offices in California have adopted this system of describing land.

§13.22. Parcel maps

The Business and Professions Code provides for the preparation, approval, and filing with the county recorder, of *parcel maps*. Legislation was adopted providing that divisions of land that did not qualify as a subdivision under the Map Act would require the submission of a tentative map or parcel map to the governing body (local city or county). That governing body was not authorized to waive this requirement. In 1972 the law was amended to give discretionary authority to the governing body to waive the requirement of a map under prescribed conditions.

As a rule of title practice, a parcel map may be used for primary reference purposes in a legal description, provided the map is complete and sufficiently definite to identify conclusively the boundaries of the land.

§13.23. Assessment district maps

Various sections of the Streets and Highways Code provide that the map of a proposed assessment district, formerly filed with the county clerk, shall be filed with the county recorder in a book of maps of Assessment Districts. The use of such descriptions may be encountered in assessments, bonds, certificates of sale, and deeds on foreclosure of such liens, instead of using the record description. If the assessment district map as filed varies in dimensions or location from the record title and does not definitely and conclusively identify the land, remedial action may be necessary for title purposes, such as a quiet title action or corrective deeds.

§13.24. Unrecorded maps

An unrecorded map may be sufficient for purposes of direct reference in instruments, provided the map can be introduced and properly identified or otherwise established. But a title based on instruments containing such descriptions is not a good title of record and is not regarded as insurable.

When a lot conveyed by deed is described by reference to a map, such map is made a part of the deed and the conveyance is subject to all matters shown on the map.[26]

§13.25. Blanket descriptions

A conveyance of land by a *blanket* description, such as "all lands (of the grantor) wherever the same may be situated," or "all lands belonging to the grantor in _____ county," is sufficient to pass title to all of the grantor's land within the scope of the description.

§13.26. Description of a tract by common name

Another method of description sometimes used, though it was more common in the early days of conveyancing in California, is a description of a tract by a name by which it is known by and may be identified by. Extrinsic evidence may be admitted as an aid in locating the land and establishing the boundaries. Ordinarily, a conveyance by a descriptive name is not acceptable as sufficient unless the boundaries are shown of record. A deed to the "Rancho San Vicente," a well-known Mexican grant with recognized boundaries, is considered sufficient, but a deed to the "Johnson Ranch," which has reference to sectional land owned by Johnson, is not a sufficient description for title purposes until its exterior boundaries are clearly defined by court decree or other appropriate means of record.

§13.27. Use of street address

A street address may be sufficient under some circumstances; however, the use of a street address alone in most instruments of conveyance is not recommended. Although it is sometimes held that a conveyance of a house and lot that designates the property by reference to an established house number, naming the street and city, is a sufficient description of the house and lot upon which it is located,[27] the need for parol evidence to identify the boundaries and the uncertainty as to the extent of the land that would pass by the description usually result in a title that is unmarketable and uninsurable until the boundaries are definitely fixed.

In commercial leases covering a large structure consisting of numerous store areas, a designation of a smaller area by street number is not an uncommon practice and is generally considered sufficient for such purposes.

In the publication of notice of sale of real property in probate proceedings, adding the street address to the legal description by a phrase such as "which property is commonly known as 123 North Elm Street, San Diego, California," many times proved helpful when discrepancies or omissions in the legal description occurred. It was the practice to include the street address whenever possible. The Probate Code[28] provides that notices of sale shall give the street address or other common designation or, if none, a legal description of the real property to be sold. The legal description, of course, is essential in the instruments of conveyance following the sale. The same requirement now applies in notices of execution sales and notices of sale in trust deed foreclosure proceedings.

§13.28. Conveyance of fractional part of a lot

When a part only of a lot as shown on a recorded map, or a part of a quarter section or other subdivision of sectional land, is being conveyed, the division is sometimes made not by a metes and bounds description but by a description of a specific fractional part of the lot, such as the north one-half, or of a specific quantity of the lot, such as the north fifty feet or the north ten acres. When the lot to be divided is regular in shape, no problem usually develops; but when a lot is irregular, conflicts often arise.

EXAMPLE   If a deed conveys the "north half" or an irregular lot, a question may arise as to whether it describes the north half of the lot by area or by width. Figure 13-1 illustrates but one of many problems that are encountered in lot division descriptions.

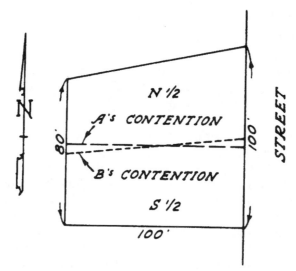

FIGURE 13–1.
Lot division description.

By deeds bearing the same date, assume that the owner of the lot shown in Figure 13-1 conveyed the "north half" to A and the "south half" to B. Two conflicting claims may thereafter arise. B may claim title to the portion of the lot lying south of a line extending from the middle point of the west boundary line, whereas A may claim title to one-half of the lot bounded by a straight line drawn east and west sufficiently north of the south line to embrace one-half of the lot area. Although under either contention the lot is equally divided, the location on the ground differs. This can be very material, particularly when street frontage is affected.

§13.29. Lines of division

The word *half*, used in a description without qualification, is given its usual meaning: one of two equal parts into which anything may be divided. A conveyance of "half" of a parcel is usually construed to mean a conveyance of a half in quantity. But when the location is not indicated by the context of the conveyance, there is no fixed formula for determining the location of the line that effects the equal division. Such location depends on the intent as shown by the surrounding circumstances, and these circumstances might be such that the division line determined will actually result in unequal portions.

§13.30. Rules of construction—basic principle

The cardinal rule for the construction of the description in a conveyance is to carry out the intent of the parties if by any possibility that intent can be gathered from the language employed. In determining this intention, the court will place itself as nearly as possible in the position of the parties at the time the instrument was executed and, taking it by its four corners, read the instrument. To determine what land was intended to be described when there is an ambiguity, as when part of the boundaries or calls is omitted, the description may be read by reversing the courses.

§13.31. Intention must be expressed

The intention must be expressed in the conveyance, not merely surmised. If the writing itself does not furnish the means whereby the description may be sufficiently definite and certain, then the instrument is considered void.

§13.32. Interpretation of a grant or reservation

To aid in determining the probable intent of the parties when the description is ambiguous, rules of construction have been established, some of which have been enacted into statutes. Under the provisions of the Civil Code,[29] a *grant*, other than a grant by a public officer or body, is to be interpreted in favor of the grantee. A *reservation*, however, is interpreted in favor of the grantor.

§13.33. Boundaries and monuments

The Code of Civil Procedure[30] provides that when permanent and visible or determined boundaries or monuments are inconsistent with the measurement, either of lines, angles, or surfaces, the boundaries or monuments are paramount.

EXAMPLE As an illustration of this rule, if a call in a deed is for a line running to a specified street, such line will be carried to that point, whether the distance required to do so be more or less than named in the deed. Or, if the call in a deed is for a line running along the center of a road on a certain bearing, the true boundary is the center of the road even though such line is in conflict with the bearing given in the deed. The rule of control of monument is not absolute and inflexible, however; like other rules, it is subject to qualifications and exceptions when necessary to carry out the true intent of the parties.

---

§13.34. Land adjoining a highway

The rule is also expressed in one case that a conveyance of land bounded by a highway, the fee title to which is owned by the grantor, carries the fee to the center of the highway even though the highway is not mentioned in the description.[31]

Presumption as to ownership to street center. The law favors the ownership of abutting owners in public ways and creates a presumption that a conveyance of land adjoining a public way transfers title to the center of the way. The Civil Code[32] provides that "an owner of land bounded by a road or street is presumed to own to the center of the way; but the contrary may be shown." The Civil Code[33] also provides that "a transfer of land, bounded by a highway, passes the title of the person whose estate is transferred to the soil of the highway in front to the center thereof, unless a different intent appears from the grant." These sections of the Civil Code state a presumption of law and rule of construction, but do not necessarily establish ownership of roads in the abutter, because ownership depends on matters shown in the chain of title, which may disclose the fact of ownership of the underlying fee in a person other than the abutting owner.

EXAMPLE
The application of the presumptions set forth in the Civil Code is illustrated by one case wherein it was held that a description of land as bounded by "the south side of Spring Street" carries the grantor's fee title to the center of the street. The court stated that the "south side of Spring Street is the south half thereof," and further stated that the presumption set forth in the Civil Code is highly favored in the law.[34]

Particular words used. The following words or terms in a description have also been held sufficient to carry title to the center of the street, provided the grantor in fact has title: "to the east line of Maple Street and thence along Maple Street"; "along Oak Street"; to or along "the street line"; to or along "the line of Elm Street."

Words or terms in a description may be such, however, that the description will not carry title to the center of the street. This is true if the description reads as follows: "to the east line of Maple Street, and thence along the east line of Maple Street." The rule that such a description excludes the street has been modified to the extent that it is held inapplicable to conveyances made by a referee in partition proceedings for the purpose of dividing all the land, including streets, of the parties to the partition action.[35]

IV. REGULATION OF SUBDIVISIONS

§13.35. In general

The laws governing the subdivision of real estate are now contained in two different Codes. One part, covering the sale of subdivided lands and known as the Subdivided Lands Act, is administered by the Real Estate Commissioner.[36] The other part, known as the Subdivision Map Act, regulates the filing of subdivision maps with the recorder in the county in which the land is located and enables cities and counties to pass ordinances governing subdivisions.[37]

V. SUBDIVISION MAP ACT

§13.36. In general

Frequently called the Map Act, this law prescribes a method for statewide subdivision filing procedures. Before 1929 there was no effective control over the filing of subdivision maps in California. As a result, subdivisions lacked any coordination with overall community development plans.

The Map Act gives local governing bodies direct jurisdiction over subdivisions in their areas. These local authorities have the right and the obligation to enact ordinances regulating the creation of subdivisions. Such ordinances must meet the limitations and scope set forth in the Map Act. The responsibility for the kind and type of subdivision improvements to be created is left to the control of the local city or county jurisdiction.

The Map Act now has three major objectives:

1. To coordinate subdivision plans and planning, including lot design, street patterns, right of way for drainage, sewers, and so on, with the community pattern and plan as laid out by the local planning authorities

2. To insure that the areas dedicated for public purposes by the filing of the subdivision maps, including public streets and other public areas, will be properly improved initially by the subdivider so that they will not become an undue burden in the future on the general taxpayers of the community

3. To identify in some orderly way taxable parcels of land, in order to create conditions for realizing the maximum amount of ad valorem real property taxes

By amendments in 1989, the Map Act provides that each local agency shall by ordinance regulate the initial design and improvement of common interest developments.[38]

Among the subjects of concern to the local governing authorities are the following: (1) location and boundaries of the property; (2) physical features of the property as disclosed by a topographic map; (3) availability of public utilities; (4) general features of the area as disclosed by a site location map; (5) natural features; (6) accessibility; (7) character of the neighborhood; (8) drainage; (9) flood hazard; (10) geological report; (11) sewage disposal; (12) water supply; (13) public park and recreational facilities; and (14) schools.

§13.37. Subdivisions under Map Act

In general and with certain exceptions, a *subdivision* is defined under the Subdivision Map Act as "any real property, improved or unimproved, or portion thereof shown on the last preceding tax roll as a unit or as contiguous units, which is divided for purpose of sale or lease, financing whether immediate or future, by any subdivider into five or more parcels." The act contains several exceptions, including, for example, any parcel or parcels divided into lots or parcels each of a gross area of 20 acres or more, and each of which has an approved access to a maintained public street or highway. In the enforcement of this act, local governing bodies are primarily interested in the physical aspects of the subdivision, such as lot size and design, road improvements, water mains, sewer lines, and drainage. Under this act, it is provided that conveyances of any part of a subdivision shall not be made by lot or block number, initial, or other designation unless and until a final map has been recorded pursuant to the provisions of such act.

§13.38. Recording of subdivision maps

The enforcement of the provisions of the Subdivision Map Act is vested in the governing body of each county and city. The enforcement of the act is delegated in many instances to the planning commission of either the city or county in which the land is located. Under the act, the procedure for recording a subdivision map encompasses the filing of a tentative map for approval of the governing body. If the tentative map is approved, the subdivider must file a final map with the county recorder within one year, or within any extension of time that may be permitted. The final map shows (1) lot numbers or lot and block numbers; (2) exterior boundaries of the tract; (3) all survey data as to monuments and so on; (4) street names; (5) dedication of any public easements required by the governing body; and (6) various certifications required by law, including a certificate signed and acknowledged by all parties having any record interest in the land subdivided, with certain exceptions, consenting to the preparation and recordation of the map. Condominium and community apartment projects are within the scope of the act if they contain five or more condominiums or five or more parcels, respectively.

The Government Code[39] provides that when a soils report has been prepared, this fact should be noted on the final map together with the date of the report and the name of the engineer making the report. Also, the Code provides that a waiver of direct access to any property dedicated for street or highway purposes may be required from the owner of an interest in abutting property as a condition precedent to the approval of a final map.[40]

§13.39. Access to ocean and other waters

Legislation has been enacted to prohibit the approval of a final subdivision map that does not provide or have available reasonable access from public highways to the ocean or bay within the subdivision.

§13.40. Environmental impact

Legislation also requires the submission of a tentative map under the Subdivision Map Act by the governing body to the Office of Intergovernmental Management for an evaluation of the environmental impact of the proposed subdivision. Also, the Government Code[41] prohibits approval of a tentative or final subdivision map unless the city or county finds that the proposed subdivision, including its provisions for design and improvement, is consistent with applicable general or specific plans of the city and county.

§13.41. Dedication of land for public purposes

Various provisions of the Subdivision Map Act require (1) a dedication of land for school purposes as a condition for final approval of a subdivision; (2) dedication of land or payment of fees in lieu thereof for park or recreational purposes; and (3) dedication or an offer of dedication for street opening or widening or for easements.[42]

The dedication of land for park or recreational purposes was considered by the California Supreme Court in one case. The court held that recreational facilities are sufficiently related to the health and welfare of a proposed subdivision to justify either the dedication or in lieu thereof payment of a fee.[43]

§13.42. Conversions to condominiums

The legislative body of a local community shall not approve a final map for a subdivision resulting from a conversion of residential real property to a condominium unless it finds both of the following: (1) each tenant has been given written notice 180 days prior to termination of the intent to convert; and (2) each tenant has been given a 90-day exclusive right to purchase his or her respective unit.[44]

§13.43. Conveyances in violation of Map Act

Conveyances of any part of a subdivision are not permitted to be made by lot or block number, initial, or other designation unless and until a final map has been recorded. If a conveyance is made by lot or block number or other designation in violation of the Subdivision Map Act, the conveyance is not void, but is voidable at the sole option of the grantee, his heirs or representatives, within one year following discovery of the violation.[45]

The Government Code prohibits any city or county from issuing any permit or granting any approval necessary to develop any real property that has been divided or that has resulted from a division of real property in violation of the Subdivision Map Act or ordinances adopted pursuant to the act, when it is found that development of the property is contrary to the public health or safety.[46] The prohibition applies whether the applicant was the owner of the property at the time of the violation or a subsequent owner who took with or without actual or constructive knowledge of the violation. In such cases, however, a permit or approval may be granted, but the local entity may impose such additional conditions as would have been applicable to the division of property at the time the current owner of record acquired the property.

The Government Code requires cities and counties, on request of a property owner, to determine whether the applicant's real property complies with the act and ordinances adopted pursuant to the act.[47]

The Government Code requires cities and counties having knowledge of a division in violation of the act or related local ordinances to record a notice of violation describing the real property, the owners of the property, and the violation.[48] Recordation is deemed to impart constructive notice of the violation to all successors in interest in the property.

§13.44. Regulation of lot splits

City and county ordinances may regulate the division into smaller parcels of land not covered by the state laws. An ordinance adopted by the City of Los Angeles in 1962 is illustrative of one that regulates lot splits. The ordinance defines a *lot split* as the division of land by separating its ownership or otherwise dividing into two, three, or four parcels. Such a lot split is intended not only to control the shape and size of the new lots, but also to provide sufficient land for street improvements or access to the newly created lots. Sales contrary to lot split regulations are voidable to the extent and in the same manner as sales in violation of the Subdivision Map Act.

§13.45. Other public controls

Other public controls relate to housing and construction and may have an effect on the subdivision of land. The State Housing Law is designed to provide minimum construction and occupancy requirements for all apartment houses and hotels throughout the state and all dwellings located in cities. Additionally, any city or county may supplement these requirements. The State Department of Public Health has the power to control and regulate the statewide enforcement of health measures. Drainage, plumbing, sewage disposal, and water supply are all under the jurisdiction of both the local health officer and the State Department of Public Health.

The Health and Safety Code[49] requires that each city and county enact ordinances requiring preliminary soil reports on land in subdivisions. Under certain conditions, waivers can be obtained. If the preliminary report shows the soil unstable, corrective action is to be recommended by a registered civil engineer.

VI. SALE OF SUBDIVIDED LANDS

§13.46. In general

The California Real Estate Law regulating the sale of subdivided lands defines a *subdivision* in general, as a division of lands, improved or unimproved, for purposes of sale or lease or financing into "five or more lots or parcels."[50] This law exempts land sold in parcels of more than 160 acres for other than oil or gas purposes when such parcels are described on current assessment rolls by government surveys. The Business and Professions Code also includes as subdivisions any of the following: (1) a planned development containing five or more lots; (2) a community apartment project containing two or more apartments; (3) a condominium project containing two or more condominiums; and (4) a stock cooperative having or intending to have two or more shareholders.[51]

The sections of the law administered by the Real Estate Commissioner are designed primarily to prevent fraud in the sale of subdivided lots. As stated in one case, the purpose of the Business and Professions Code relating to subdivided lands is to protect individual members of the public who purchase lots or houses from subdividers, and to make sure that all purchasers receive full information concerning public utility facilities and other essential facts with reference to the land.[52]

The Real Estate Commissioner investigates each tract and publishes a report of his findings, which is available to the public. In addition to matters pertaining to title, liens and encumbrances, restrictions, and method of sale, the report covers information about topography, drainage facilities, available fire protection, sanitation, public utilities (including water, gas, and telephone), streets and roads, public transportation, public schools, and shopping facilities.

EXAMPLE A husband and wife (unlicensed) were in the illegal business of selling subdivided land through their organization without first filing written notification with the Real Estate Commissioner and obtaining a public report.

Their practice was to acquire 30 or 40 acres of land and within a short time of acquisition solicit purchasers and sell off 5- or 10-acre parcels under real property sales contracts. From the date of purchase, the buyers paid monthly installments of principal, interest, and prorated tax amounts to the sellers. Postsale correspondence was carried on with buyers by the wife. However, the taxes were not paid by sellers and remained continuously delinquent, mostly for the years 1970–1975.

In the resultant Superior Court action, the sellers were convicted for violations of the Business and Professions Code (offer to sell or lease subdivided lands without filing notice of intention and offering and selling without public report) and nine counts of violations of the Civil Code (receipt of prorated payments for taxes under a real property sales contract and failure to place the amounts in a trust fund and for disbursing money without consent of payors). On appeal the judgments were affirmed.[53]

The law has been amended from time to time to impose additional requirements. For instance, in 1965 it was amended to require that a true statement on the maximum depth of fill used or proposed to be used on each lot, and a true statement of the soil conditions in the subdivision supported by engineering reports showing the soil has been or will be prepared in accordance with the recommendations of a registered civil engineer, be filed with the notice of intention filed with the Real Estate Commissioner.

The law was further amended to provide the Real Estate Commissioner with an additional ground for the denial of the public report if there is a failure to demonstrate that adequate financial arrangements have been made for any guaranty or warranty included in the offering.[54]

A copy of the public report, when issued, must be given to each purchaser before accepting a deposit for the execution of any agreement for the sale or lease of a subdivision lot or a unit in a community apartment, condominium, or stock cooperative project.

§13.47. Remote subdivisions (land projects)
Special public interest legislation has been enacted regarding the sale of lots in subdivisions located in sparsely populated areas in California on the basis of intensive promotional efforts tending to obscure the highly speculative nature of the offerings. Such *subdivisions* are referred to as land projects, and characteristically they contain 50 or more parcels. Purchasers of such lots originally were given two days to rescind the transaction if they so chose. By amendment, the period to rescind has been extended to 14 days.[55] This law allows the Real Estate Commissioner to prevent the sale of subdivisions in remote areas when promised improvements appear to be financially unfeasible. It also requires subdividers of large projects distant from population centers to report the names of defaulting purchasers to the Real Estate Commissioner.

§13.48. Sale of undivided interests
The law also includes "undivided interests" in the definition of a subdivision and subdivided lands, and to provide for jurisdiction by the Real Estate Commissioner in the sale of such interests. Exempt from this law are interests held or to be held by relatives, and interests to be sold solely to persons who present evidence that satisfies the Real Estate Commissioner that they are "knowledgeable and experienced investors who comprehend the nature and extent of the risks involved."

§13.49. Out-of-state lands
The sale or lease within California of lots or parcels in a subdivision situated outside the state is governed by the real property securities dealers section of the Real Estate Law, as well as by the regular subdivision law. The out-of-state subdivider must obtain a real property securities permit, in addition to the Real Estate Commissioner's public report, before offering such land for sale in California.

§13.50. Federal Interstate Land Sales Act
The Federal Interstate Land Sales Full Disclosure Act[56] became effective in 1969. The act and its implementing regulations require a full disclosure in the sales or leases of certain undeveloped land in interstate commerce or through the mails. The act requires developers who contemplate selling or leasing property in affect-

ed projects to file a registration statement with the Office of Interstate Land Sales Registration (OILSR). The act affects developers of 50 or more lots.

After the statement becomes effective, a property report must be submitted to the purchaser in advance of the signing of any contract or agreement for sale or lease. The contract or agreement for purchase or leasing is voidable at the option of the purchaser if the property report has not been given to the purchaser in advance or at the time of signing. Besides refunding the purchase price of the lot, the developer may be required to pay the reasonable costs of all improvements on the lot or lots.

The regulations adopted pursuant to the act provide that a copy of the material filed with the State of California under state law shall be an effective statement under federal law. Several exemptions apply, including "the sale or lease of lots where the offering is entirely or almost entirely intrastate."

Any developer subject to the act who sells lots by using the U.S. mails or any other instrument of interstate commerce, without first registering with OILSR and providing the purchaser in advance of sale with an approved property report, is in violation of the law and may be sentenced to a prison term of five years or a $5,000 fine or both.

VII. INVESTMENT REGULATIONS

§13.51. Real property securities transactions

The material in this section is based on that contained in the *Real Estate Reference Book*, published by California Department of Real Estate.

The Real Property Securities Dealers Law[57] was enacted as part of a legislative package designed to control those transactions that characterized "Ten Percenter" operations. This part of the Real Estate Law spells out the various requirements that must be met by any person before he can engage in the marketing of promissory notes and real property sales contracts that come within the definition of "real property securities."

The definition of a *real property securities dealer* is any person, acting as principal or agent, who engages in the business of

> *(a) Selling of real property securities as defined by Subdivision (a) of Section 10237.1 to the public, or (b) Offering to accept or accepting funds for continual reinvestment in real property securities, or for placement in an account, plan or program whereby the dealer implies that a return will be derived from a specific real property sales contract or promissory note secured directly or collaterally by a lien on real property which is not specifically stated to be based upon the contractual payments thereon.*

A special endorsement to a real estate broker license must be obtained by a licensee before he or she may engage in the business of dealing in "real property securities" either as a principal or as an agent. In addition to the license endorsement, the licensee must maintain on file with the Real Estate Commissioner a corporate surety bond of $5,000 or provide an alternative surety specified by statute.

In addition to the licensure requirement, a permit must be obtained from the Real Estate Commissioner by either the issuer or the real property securities dealer before real property securities can be sold to the public. Sales to corporations, institutional lenders, real estate brokers, general building contractors, attorneys, and to pension, retirement, or similar trust funds are not sales "to the public," and there is no licensing or permit requirement if sales of real property securities are confined to such entities. The law is intended to protect the less sophisticated members of the public.

§13.52. Permit requirements

A *permit* for the sale of real property securities to the public is quite similar to a permit that must be obtained from the Department of Corporations of the State of California to issue shares in a California corporation.

The statutory test for the issuance of a real property securities permit is also the same as that under the Corporate Securities Law. The Real Estate Commissioner must deny the application and refuse the permit unless it is determined that (1) the proposed plan of business of the applicant and the proposed sale of real property securities is fair, just, and equitable; (2) the applicant intends to transact business fairly and honestly; and (3) the real property securities to be sold are not such that they will work a fraud upon the purchaser.

The act also sets forth the elements of the disclosure statement that must be given to each prospective purchaser of a real property security. This statement serves the purpose of a prospectus or offering circular. Each purchaser of a real property security is required to sign a statement acknowledging receipt of the information, and the issuer of the securities must retain a copy executed by the purchaser for a period of four years. A purchaser must also be given a copy of an appraisal of the real property that secures the note or contract sold to him, unless the purchaser expressly waives this requirement by stating that he will obtain his own appraisal. An appraisal prepared by or on behalf of the real property securities dealer must be retained by him for a period of four years.

A dealer must annually file with the Real Estate Commissioner an audited financial statement containing the following information:

1. The total number of sales, as principal or agent, during the reporting period
2. The total dollar volume of such sales

Advertising material to be used in the offering of real property securities must be filed with the Real Estate Commissioner ten days prior to its use. The Real Estate Commissioner must notify the dealer within ten days after receipt if he determines that any of the advertising is false, misleading, or incomplete. If such notice is not given within ten days, the advertising is deemed to be "not disapproved."

§13.53. Syndicate Act

The jurisdiction of the Real Estate Syndicate Act is vested in the Department of Corporations. The Corporations Commissioner's jurisdiction applies to (1) general or limited partnerships or joint ventures; and (2) associations or other entities formed for the sole purpose of, and engaged solely in, investment in or gain from an interest in real property. The enactment exempts certain operations from the application of the act.[58]

The organizers of a real estate syndicate are required to file with the Corporations Commissioner a request to offer shares in the syndicate to the public. A "fair, just, and equitable" test is applied to the proposed offering, and if all appears to be in order, the permit will be forthcoming. The Commissioner is authorized to issue regulations to implement the legislation and define procedures that syndicate organizers will be required to follow.

§13.54. Nature of syndication

Real estate syndication offers opportunities to channel moneys into real estate investments that otherwise would not be possible, and it has become a popular method of financing the purchase and sale of properties in the higher price ranges.

The term *syndication* has no precise legal significance, and the responsibility, obligation, and relationship of the syndicator to the investment group, and the investors to each other, are determined principally by the form of entity utilized. It is a descriptive term for an organization or combination of investors pooling their capital for investment in real estate.

Real estate licensees are often active in the real estate syndication field as agents in purchase and sale transactions.[59] When confronted with a listing or other opportunity to sell property involving financing that could not be handled by a single purchaser, the established real estate broker turned to others on his client list for pooling of capital necessary to consummate the purchase.

§13.55. Reasons for use

By pooling limited financial resources with others who are similarly situated, a small-scale investor is afforded an opportunity to participate in ownership and operation of a piece of property that is too much for him to handle singly or in a joint venture with one or two others. It enables a small investor to obtain the benefit of a reduced cost per unit of income in a large project. It enables a small investor to own real estate and obtain a tax shelter. It also offers a degree of liquidity comparable to common stock ownership.

Syndication also offers professional management to the small investor that would not otherwise be economically available. Professional management is at the head of virtually every successful syndication. It is the basic commodity that the syndicator has to offer, and it is the ingredient lacking in the income property investment that is small enough to be owned by a single owner or by a joint venture of a few investors with limited resources.

From the syndication point of view, there are many advantages to a skilled syndicator, including (1) an equity position for services rendered; (2) management fees; (3) commissions on the purchase and resale; (4) a contractor's profit and, in some cases, a profit on the construction of improvements; and (5) tax advantages from the ownership of property.

When a permit is required, areas of concern to the promoter that must be taken into consideration when measuring the advantages include the following: (1) management experience; (2) avoidance of any conflict of interests; (3) limitation of fees, both as to the amount and time of payment; (4) disclosure of all relevant facts relating to the project; (5) the degree of sophistication of the investors; and (6) the application of the "fair, just, and equitable" doctrine.

In general, the expertise and knowledge required relate primarily to the syndicator's (1) ability to evaluate an investment; (2) ability to market the shares; and (3) having or obtaining management skills.

§13.56. Kinds of property

The kinds of property offered in real estate syndication are as varied as the nature of the real estate investment field. Initially the syndications concentrated almost entirely on income-producing properties, such as apartment houses, hotels, shopping centers, and professional office buildings. Later, and particularly in certain areas in the state, a considerable interest centered in the syndication of raw land. The particular type of property syndicated will, of course, greatly affect the specific benefits of the syndicate.

In the case of income-producing properties, areas of the greatest interest include the following: (1) tax shelter benefits of depreciation; (2) cash-flow return, i.e., the measure of cash generated from income and depreciation after debt-servicing expenses; and (3) leverage advantages inherent in real estate. Leverage generally means the use of borrowed funds to purchase real property in anticipation of a substantial increase in the value of the property in a relatively short period of time. Thus, it may produce a high return on a low down payment. In the case of raw land, the areas of greatest interest in addition to the leverage advantages include the anticipated appreciation in value and the security of the investment, which costs less to hold than improved property.

§13.57. Syndicate form

The entity selection involves practical as well as legal and tax considerations. Each of the available entities has advantages and disadvantages. The corporate form insures centralized management as well as limited liability for the investors, but is seldom utilized in modern syndication because of its negative tax features. The general partnership avoids the double taxation normally involved in a corporate entity, but the unlimited liability provision and lack of centralized management militate against its use. The limited partnership combines many of the advantages of the corporate and partnership forms. It has the corporate advantages of limited liability and centralized management and the tax advantages of the partnership. Consequently, the limited partnership form of organization is most frequently selected for real estate syndicates. Also, the Internal Revenue Code recognizes an ownership form called a Subchapter S Corporation, which is a recognized corporation under state law but for income tax purposes is treated similarly to a partnership. Since 1982 when new federal legislation became effective, the use of this type of entity as an investment tool has expanded.

§13.58. Federal regulation

Real estate interests in a syndicate may be subject to federal regulation under the Securities Exchange Act of 1934 and the Securities Act of 1933 if they have an interstate or public character and are not exempt. Basically, the Securities Act of 1933 prohibits the offer or sale of a security unless that security has been registered with the Securities and Exchange Commission (SEC) or unless it is exempt under the private offering exemption, the intrastate offering exemption, or the small offering exemption.

The failure to register a real estate interest that is deemed to be a security with the SEC carries severe civil and criminal penalties.

It is beyond the scope of this text to go into any greater detail about these laws, except to state that one must consider their applicability and that they must be considered if any of the people or property involved are located in more than one state.

QUESTIONS

Note: Some of the questions relating to condominiums are based, in part, on material appearing in Chapter 8.

Matching Terms

a. Starting point
b. Monument
c. Minimize
d. Base lines
e. Township
f. Syndication
g. Access right
h. Topography
i. Section
j. Meridians

1. Imaginary east–west lines that intersect meridians.
2. Having a way to get to a street or other public area.
3. An area of land containing 640 acres.
4. A group of investors who pool their resources in acquiring investment property.
5. Imaginary north–south lines that intersect a base line.
6. Requisite of a metes and bounds description.
7. Nature of the surface of land.
8. To lessen the impact of an environmental report.
9. An area of land containing 36 sections.
10. Objects used by land surveyors to establish a boundary.

True/False

T F **11.** Real property can be divided horizontally as well as vertically.

T F **12.** A condominium is basically a type of real estate subdivision.

T F **13.** Parol evidence cannot be used as an aid in identifying land.

T F **14.** Any valid real property description must contain a closed area.

T F **15.** A monument as used in descriptions can be either natural or manufactured.

T F **16.** Omission of the county will render a government survey description invalid.

T F **17.** A grant is ordinarily interpreted in favor of the grantee.

T F **18.** A reservation is ordinarily interpreted in favor of the grantor.

T F **19.** There is a presumption that a conveyance of land adjoining a public way transfers only to the side and not the center of the way.

T F **20.** Conveyances made in violation of the Subdivision Map Act are void.

Multiple Choice

21. Environmental quality laws, imposing restrictions on the use of land, are of
    a. Increasing concern.
    b. Decreasing concern.
    c. No consequence to a developer.
    d. None of the above.

22. Future planning and development in California include a consideration of

a. Coastal use.
b. Air pollution.
c. Mass transportation.
d. All of the above.

23. A subdivider and developer must be aware of many factors, both legal and economic, in developing new property. Which of the following would need to be considered?
    a. Topography.
    b. Environmental controls.
    c. Land conservation.
    d. All of the above.

24. There is a constantly increasing concern for which of the following as related to land development?
    a. Ecology.
    b. Access to coastal areas.
    c. Green belts.
    d. All of the above.

25. Subdivisions include which of the following?
    a. Surface divisions.
    b. Condominiums.
    c. Stock cooperative apartment projects.
    d. All of the above.

26. Real property may be described by
    a. Metes and bounds.
    b. Tract reference.
    c. Government Survey.
    d. Any of the above.

27. A deed or other document that refers to sections, townships, and ranges is using a legal description by
    a. Metes and bounds.
    b. Recorded map.
    c. U.S. Government Survey.
    d. None of the above.

28. In California the number of principal base and meridian monuments is
    a. Two.
    b. Three.
    c. Four.
    d. Five.

29. The description of land "as the NW of Sec. 10,T 2 N, R 3 E" is a description by
    a. Metes and bounds.
    b. Courses and distances.
    c. Government Survey.
    d. Reference to a recorded plat.

30. The description of land as "Lot 26 in Block 3 of the Ocean View Tract" indicates a description by
    a. Reference to a subdivision.
    b. Metes and bounds.
    c. Government Survey.
    d. State Plane Coordinate System.

31. The California Government Code provides that the legislative body of each city and county shall create a planning agency, a primary responsibility being the preparation and adoption of a comprehensive plan for the physical development of their area. Which of the following elements would be included in such a plan?
    a. Location and extent of land use.
    b. Location of thoroughfares.
    c. Population and building density.
    d. All of the above.

32. A subdivider obtained the Real Estate Commissioner's final public report on his subdivision and wants to use the report for advertising purposes. If he does, he
    a. May use whatever portions of the report he chooses.
    b. May use whatever portions he chooses, provided the D.R.E. approves.
    c. Must use it in its entirety.
    d. Must use it in its entirety but can underscore and emphasize portions of it.

33. Agencies of the state government concerned with subdivision development include, in addition to the D.R.E., the
    a. Division of Highways.
    b. State Water Pollution Control Board.
    c. Department of Public Health.
    d. All of the above.

34. Which of the following state agencies is concerned with subdivision development?
    a. Public Utilities Commission.
    b. Department of Veteran Affairs.
    c. Department of Corporations.
    d. All of the above.

35. In addition to a topographic map, which of the following types of maps would be used by a subdivider in planning a subdivision?
    a. Boundary survey map.
    b. Public utilities map.
    c. Site location map.
    d. All of the above.

36. Subdivision of land in California is governed by
    a. California Real Estate Law.
    b. Subdivision Map Act.
    c. Regulations of the D.R.E.
    d. All of the above.

37. Preliminary planning of a subdivision includes
    a. Economic analysis of feasibility.
    b. Location analysis.
    c. Ascertaining legal requirements.
    d. All of the above.

38. Unlike a surface subdivision, in a condominium subdivision a set of restrictions is
    a. Required by law.
    b. Optional.
    c. Discretionary.
    d. Not mandatory.

39. Under the Real Estate Law, which of the following are subdivisions subject to the rules and regulations of the Real Estate Commissioner?
    a. Planned Unit Developments.
    b. Community apartment projects.
    c. Condominiums.
    d. All of the above.

40. Title to an individually owned unit in a multi-family structure is the characteristic of
    a. An own-your-own apartment.
    b. A condominium.
    c. A stock cooperative.
    d. All of the above.

41. In order to have a valid statutory condominium, which of the following must be recorded?
    a. Description or survey map.
    b. Diagrammatic floor plan.
    c. Certificate consenting to the plan.
    d. All of the above.

42. The Real Estate Commissioner, under the subdivision laws, is responsible for the regulation of
    a. Sales of subdivided land.
    b. Lot design.
    c. Physical improvements on the property.
    d. All of the above.

43. When an out-of-state subdivision is offered for sale in California, the Real Estate Law requires which of the following?
    a. Current appraisal of lots.
    b. Bond in the amount of $5,000.
    c. Permit.
    d. All of the above.

44. An owner of land is classified as a subdivider if he divides a parcel of land into five or more parcels with the intention to
    a. Lease the individual parcels.
    b. Sell the individual parcels.
    c. Finance each parcel separately.
    d. All of the above.

45. The Real Estate Law requires certain minimum information concerning a new subdivision, and the D.R.E. has developed questionnaires to be used by subdividers for this purpose. Which of the following items must be included in the questionnaire?
    a. Condition of title.
    b. Type of financing.
    c. Handling of deposit money.
    d. All of the above.

46. In selling subdivided lands, the subdivider must furnish a prospective purchaser with a copy of
    a. Financial statement.
    b. Preliminary report of title.
    c. Notice of intention to subdivide.
    d. Public report.

47. The Subdivision Map Act is enforced by

a. Real Estate Commissioner.
b. Local governing bodies.
c. Corporations Commissioner.
d. State Department of Housing.

48. The main purpose of the Subdivided Lands Act is to protect the land-buying public from
    a. Fraud.
    b. Deceit.
    c. Misrepresentation.
    d. All of the above.

49. Before an apartment house can be converted to a condominium, tenants must be given written notice how many days prior to termination of the notice to convert?
    a. 60 days.
    b. 90 days.
    c. 150 days.
    d. 180 days.

50. Before an apartment house can be converted to a condominium, tenants must be given an exclusive right to purchase their units for a minimum period of
    a. 30 days.
    b. 60 days.
    c. 90 days.
    d. 120 days.

NOTES

1. Some of these subjects are considered in greater detail in Chapters 24 and 25 of *Ogden's Revised California Real Property Law* by Arthur G. Bowman, published by the California Continuing Education of the Bar (Vol 2).
2. Govt. C. 62025, *et seq.*
3. Govt. C. 65031.
4. Govt. C. 65041.
5. Govt. C. 65043.
6. Govt. C. 12037.
7. Govt. C. 66411, *et al.*; B. & P. 11000.5.
8. 2 U.S.C. 4321, *et seq.*
9. 42 U.S.C. 4331.
10. Pub. Res. C. 21151.
11. Pub. Res. C. 21100(a); Govt. C. 66474(e).
12. Pub. Res. C. 21100.
13. Public Resources Code 21100.
14. Friends of Mammoth v. Board of Supervisors (1972) 8 C.3d 247.
15. Pub. Res. C. 30000 *et seq. See also* Pub. Res. C. 30300, 30333, 30335, *et seq.*, and 30511, *et seq.*
16. Govt. C. 38780 relating to cities and Govt. C. 25846 relating to counties.
17. Ordinance No. 144942.
18. Gov. Code 51200, *et seq.* Under Fish and Game Code 3460, an owner of real property may enter into a contract with the Director of Fish and Game for conservation of waterfowl under the California Waterfowl Habitat Program.
19. Blume v. MacGregor (1944) 64 C.A.2d 244. Although most instruments contain the description as part of the instrument, it is possible to describe a parcel by reference to another instrument. In the older case of Harney v. Heller (1873) 47 C. 151, it was stated that land may be described by proper reference to another instrument that contains a sufficient description.

20. C.C.P. 1856.
21. B. & P. 8762.
22. B. & P. 11655.
23. Rev. & Tax. C. 327.
24. Rev. & Tax. C. 11911.1.
25. Pub. Res. C. 8801 8816.
26. Danielson v. Sykes (1910) 157 C. 686.
27. Estate of Wolf (1932) 128 C.A. 305.
28. Pro. C. 10304.
29. C.C. 1069.
30. C.C.P. 2077(2); *see also* §14.68, *et seq.*
31. Merchant v. Grant (1915) 26 C.A. 485.
32. C.C. 831; Besneatte v. Gourdin (1993) 16 C.A. 4th 1277.
33. C.C. 1112; Besneatte v. Gourdin (1993) 16 C.A. 4th 1277.
34. Brown v. Bachelder (1932) 214 C. 753; C.C. 1112.
35. Machado v. Title Guarantee and Trust Co. (1940) 15 C.2d 180.
36. B. & P. 11000, *et seq.*
37. Govt. C. 66410, *et seq.*
38. Govt. C. 66411.
39. Govt. C. 66434(f).
40. Govt. C. 66439, 66447, 66476.
41. Govt. C. 66473.5.
42. Govt. C. 66475, *et seq.*
43. Associated Home Builders v. City of Walnut Creek (1971) 4 C.3d 633. *See also* Norsco Enterprises v. City of Fremont (1976) 54 C.A. 3d 488, in which it was held that fees were properly assessed against an owner of an apartment building who had filed an application for approval of a subdivision map for conversion to a condominium.
44. *See* Pongputmong v. City of Santa Monica (1993) 15 C.A. 4th 99.
45. Govt. C. 66499.32; *see also* John Taft Corp. v. Advisory Agency (1984) 161 C.A.3d 749.
46. Govt. C. 66499.34.
47. Govt. C. 66499.35.
48. Govt. C. 6649936.
49. H. & S. 17953, *et seq.*
50. B. & P. 11000.
51. B. & P. 11004.5.
52. Barrett v. Hammer Builders, Inc. (1961) 195 C.A.2d 305.
53. People v. Thygesen (1979) 93 C.A. 3d 895; B.& P. 11010, 11018.2; C.C. 2985.4.
54. B. & P. 11018, *et seq.*
55. B. & P. 11000.5, *et seq.*
56. Public Law 90 448.
57. B. & P. 10237, *et seq.*
58. *See* Corp. C. 25102(f) & 15502(4); *see also* Corp. C. 25706.
59. A real estate broker is also exempt from obtaining a broker-dealer license from the Department of Corporations when the syndicate is owned by no more than 100 persons. Corp. C. 25206

14

Adjoining Owner Problems

I. INTRODUCTION

§14.1. In general

Most real property is affected by an easement, either as a benefit or as a burden. If the owner of Parcel A has an easement over Parcel B for ingress and egress, for instance, then Parcel A is benefitted by an easement and Parcel B is burdened by an easement. This would be an easement appurtenant (see §14.8).

A most common type of easement is one for public utility purposes, which ordinarily would be an easement in gross (see §14.9).

Easements are usually created for the benefit of adjoining land, which can give rise to problems for the adjoining owners unless the subject is properly understood. It is a fundamental rule that the right to use one's land is not absolute but is subject to rights of adjoining owners, such as the right to lateral support. All land will have a boundary, either adjoining land in private ownership or part of the public domain, or a body of water such as a lake or river or the ocean. This gives rise to certain reciprocal rights and obligations.

Because of the proximity of an owner's land to that owned by another person or persons, encroachment problems can arise, together with such other matters as the location and height of fences, the growth of trees and other vegetation, and lateral and subjacent support of land. This chapter considers these various subjects, emphasizing the practical aspects as well as legal responsibilities.

II. DEFINITION AND NATURE OF EASEMENTS

§14.2. In general

An *easement* is an interest in the land of another person that entitles the owner of such interest to a limited use or enjoyment of the land. It may be either an affirmative easement, involving the doing of some act on the land of another person, such as the right to cross over the other person's land, or it may be a negative easement, involving a right against another person to refrain from doing certain things with the land, such as the right to preclude the owner of adjoining land from constructing a building on the land that would obstruct light and air.

§14.3. Characteristics of an easement

The essential qualities and characteristics of an easement include the following:

1. It is an interest in land, being one of the elements of real property, and generally must be transferred and used subject to the rules governing real property.

2. It is an interest in the land of another person; an owner of land cannot, as a rule, have an easement on his own land.[1]

3. It is considered as a nonpossessory interest. The owner of the easement is not entitled to the same benefits that are given to those having possessory interests, such as a tenant under a lease. A tenant under a lease may exclude other persons from the use or possession of the land, including the landowner, but the holder of an easement, such as a right of way, has only such control of the land as is necessary for the purpose of using the easement. Ordinarily, the easement holder does not have such control as to enable him to exclude others from using the land as long as their use does not interfere with the enjoyment of the easement.

4. Ordinarily, it is essential that the right to use land, to be considered an easement rather than some lesser interest, must be one that, in accordance with common understanding, is capable of creation by a conveyance.

§14.4. Easements include "profits"

Easements also include profits. A *profit à prendre* is a right to take something from the land of another, either a part of the soil or something subsisting in the soil. A familiar example of a profit is the right to take minerals, including oil and gas, from the land of another person when such right has been obtained by grant, reservation, or some other means.

§14.5. Easement and license distinguished

A *license* is defined as a personal, revocable, and nonassignable permission or authority to enter the land of another person for a particular purpose, but without possessing any interest in the land.

EXAMPLE A theater ticket or a ticket to a sports event authorizes the purchaser of the ticket to enter the theater or sports arena solely for the purpose of viewing the performance.

---

§14.6. Characteristics of a license

It is often difficult to distinguish an easement from a license. The following are the usual distinguishing characteristics of a license:

1. It may be created by an oral agreement.

2. Being personal, it is usually incapable of assignment and does not pass to the licensee's heirs at death.

3. It does not give the licensee a right to sue third persons for interference with the exercise of the privilege given by the license.

4. It is of a temporary nature, and is revocable at any time at the will of the licensor.

§14.7. License may give rise to an easement

It has been held that a privilege to use another person's land is a license and not an easement if its creation lacks the formal requirements necessary to the creation of an easement, or if it is created to endure at the will of the owner of the land subject to the privilege.[2] However, there is an exception to this rule in cases in which a licensee, relying on a license, has made substantial expenditures of capital or labor in the exercise of the license under such circumstances that its termination would be inequitable. The licensor may be estopped to revoke the license, and in such case the privilege becomes, it is said, "in all essentials an easement."[3] The privilege has become a right, no longer revocable at the will of the landowner.

III. CLASSES OF EASEMENTS

§14.8. Easements appurtenant

Easements are generally divided into two classes: easements appurtenant and easements in gross.

Appurtenant means belonging to. An *easement appurtenant* is created for the benefit of and belongs to another tract of land. Consequently, for such an easement to exist, there must be at least two tracts of land in separate ownerships. One tract, called the *dominant tenement*, obtains the benefit of the easement, and the other tract, called the *servient tenement*, is subject to (or burdened by) the easement. The dominant tenement need not adjoin the servient tenement, although it usually does. An easement appurtenant attaches to the land of the owner of the easement, and passes with a transfer of the land as an incident or appurtenance thereto, even though not specifically mentioned. It cannot exist separate and apart from such land. Such an easement is said to "run with the land."

EXAMPLE A, the owner of Blackacre, grants to B, the owner of Whiteacre, the right to use a private road over a portion of Blackacre for the purpose of getting to and from Whiteacre. Such an easement is appurtenant to Whiteacre, the dominant tenement, and burdens Blackacre, the servient tenement.

---

§14.9. Easements in gross

Although an *easement in gross* is a right in another person's land, it is not created for the benefit of land owned by the easement holder, but rather is a personal right. It is a right attached to the person of the easement holder, and is not attached to any land owned by the easement holder. It is, however, as much an interest in the land of another person as an easement appurtenant. Since an easement in gross exists without a dominant tenement and cannot pass as an appurtenance to land, it must be expressly transferred.

EXAMPLES   Typical examples of easements in gross are public utility easements, such as a right granted to a telephone company or other utility company to install and maintain poles and wires on, across, or over the grantor's land. Another example is an easement for pipelines in favor of an oil company. A typical public utility easement created by reservation in a deed follows: "...excepting and reserving therefrom a right of way and easement with right of entry over the rear six feet of the property for the purpose of laying, constructing, erecting, operating, repairing, relaying, and maintaining conduits or pole lines for the transmission of electrical energy and for telephone lines."

§14.10. Determining the classification of an easement

A determination of whether an easement is appurtenant or in gross presents a problem if the instrument creating the easement fails to state that the easement is one appurtenant or one in gross, or if the dominant tenement is not identified.

EXAMPLE   A, the owner of Blackacre, conveys to B an easement for road purposes over the south 20 feet of Blackacre. A dominant tenement is not described, and nothing further is said as to the character or purpose of the easement.

   Thereafter, B executes a deed purporting to convey the easement to C. At the time of the creation of the easement, B was the owner of Whiteacre, an adjoining parcel of land, and it is determined that the easement was in fact created for the benefit of B in his use of Whiteacre. If B conveyed Whiteacre to D by a deed that did not expressly mention the easement, but that was executed before the deed to C, would C or D be determined to be the owner of the easement? Under the principles set forth above, D would prevail over C.

Rules of interpretation. In determining whether an easement is one appurtenant or one in gross, the following rules apply:

1.   The nature of the right and the intention of the parties creating it are of primary importance.

2.   An easement will not be presumed to attach to the grantee if it can be construed fairly to be appurtenant to land.

3.   When it cannot be determined from the instrument creating the easement whether the easement was intended to be in gross or appurtenant to land, evidence outside of the instrument of creation is admissible to determine the nature of the easement and to establish a dominant tenement.

IV. PURPOSES FOR WHICH EASEMENTS MAY BE CREATED

§14.11. In general

The Civil Code now lists 18 different land burdens, or servitudes on land, that may be attached to other land as incidents or appurtenances, including the right of: (1) pasture; (2) fishing; (3) taking game; (4) way; (5) taking water, wood, minerals, and other things; (6) transacting business on land; (7) conducting lawful sports on land; (8) receiving air, light, or heat from or over, or discharging the same on or over, land; (9) receiving water from or discharging the same on land; (10) flooding land; (11) having water flow without diminution or disturbance of any kind; (12) using a wall as a party wall; (13) receiving more than natural support from adjacent land or things affixed thereto; (14) having the whole of a division fence maintained by a coterminous owner, (15) having public conveyances stopped, or of stopping the same on land; (16) a seat in church; (17) burial,[4] and (18) receiving sunlight upon or over the land.[5]

§14.12. Statutory rights in gross
The Civil Code designates several types of land burdens that may be granted and held, though not attached to land, including the right: (1) to pasture, and of fishing and taking game; (2) of a seat in church; (3) of burial; (4) of taking rents and tolls; (5) of way; and (6) of taking water, wood, minerals, and other things.[6]

§14.13. Additional rights may be created
The foregoing lists of servitudes on land are not necessarily exclusive; other rights may also be created. As stated in an older case,[7] although the law may hesitate to increase the range of possible burdens on land by recognizing new easements, still the novelty of the incident is no bar to its recognition if its creation violates no principles of public policy.

EXAMPLE   Easements for the purpose of retrieving errant golf balls or permitting the flight of golf balls have been created;[8] also, vibration, noise, shadow, and navigation easements. The last includes more than the flight of aircraft across an owner's land; it also includes the right to cause such noise, fumes, dust, vibrations, or lights as are incident to the flight of aircraft. An illustration of an aviation easement follows:

> *Grantor grants and conveys to the grantee (an airport) the following easement:*
>
> *A right of flight for the passage of aircraft in the airspace above the surface of the premises above described, together with the right to cause in the airspace such noise as may be inherent in the operation of aircraft, now known or hereafter used for navigation of or flight in the air, using the airspace for landing at, or taking off from, or operating at or on the airport.*

---

§14.14. Right of way
A *right of way* is one of the most common types of easement, consisting of a privilege to pass over another person's land. The means of passage depends on the purpose and terms of the instrument of creation. It may be by foot, by motor vehicle, by a railroad, by pipelines, or by whatever other method is intended. A right of way may be private, existing for the benefit of a particular person or persons; or it may be public, existing for all members of the general public. An example of a right of way created in connection with a new subdivision follows:

> *… reserving a right of way for road purposes over the south 30 feet of the property, together with the right to dedicate the strip of land for public road purposes.*

A right of way easement may be both public and private. For example, a public easement for street purposes may also include private easement rights in each abutting owner to pass over that portion of the street in front of the adjoining owners' property. This private easement may survive a vacation of the street by the public authorities.

§14.15. Purpose should be stated
In creating a right of way, the mode of passage is usually expressed, for example: "right of way for railroad purposes"; "an easement for driveway purposes." Other

rights should also be designated with particularity.[9] In the creation of a party wall easement, for example, the following would sufficiently express the purpose:

A, owner of Lot 1, conveys the north half of Lot 1 to B, together with an easement consisting of the privilege of utilizing a division wall located equally on the north half and on the south half of Lot 1, reserving to A, for the benefit of the south half of Lot 1, an easement for party wall purposes over the portion of the wall located on the north half of Lot 1.

EXAMPLE In one case, a question arose with respect to the nature of the right to take water from the land of another person. The owner of a parcel of land conveyed a portion to X and, at the same time, agreed in writing to furnish X with water for his land from the water system on the land retained by the seller. Thereafter, the seller conveyed his remaining land to Y, who refused to furnish water to X, asserting that the water agreement was merely a contract to sell water as personal property, and consequently was not enforceable against him. The court held, however, that an easement appurtenant to X's land was created that constituted a burden on the seller's land, and was binding on subsequent purchasers of the land with notice of the agreement.[10]

§14.16. Light and air

An owner of land has no "natural right" to light and air, and cannot complain because the owner of adjoining land erects a building or other obstruction on his land that cuts off light and air. An easement for light and air may be created, however, but only by express grant or words of covenant, and cannot be acquired by use or by implication.

A recent problem originating from the need to develop new sources for heat and energy is this: Does a landowner have a right of access to the sun as a source of heat and power? Solar access zoning has been proposed in many areas, and the concept is being applied to commercial developments and urban centers. In Los Angeles, city planners stress solar access as a key factor in the city's redevelopment plans. Older rules may have to give way to needs that weren't visualized a few years ago. As noted in §14.11, the right of receiving sunlight upon or over the land is included in the list of appurtenant easements.

§14.17. Support of land

Certain natural rights are incident to the ownership of land, such as support for land, and these rights may be extended or diminished by agreements creating easements between the adjoining landowners. Generally, a landowner is entitled to have his soil remain in a natural position, and an adjoining owner cannot cause it to fall away by reason of excavation or other improvements on adjoining property. However, the right is that of support of the land in its natural state, without the added weight of a building on it. Although a prescriptive right or easement cannot be acquired for the support of buildings, an easement consisting of the right to receive the support of land together with the buildings thereon from adjoining land may be created by express grant.[11]

V. HOW EASEMENTS ARE CREATED

§14.18. In general

Easements may be created in a number of different ways, including the following: (1) express grant; (2) express reservation; (3) implied grant; (4) implied reservation; (5) necessity; (6) prescription; (7) condemnation; (8) open space procedure; (9) dedication; (10) conservation procedure; (11) estoppel; and (12) sale of land by reference to a plat.

§14.19. Express grant or reservation

An express grant or an express reservation in a deed is one of the most common means of creating an easement, although agreements between adjoining owners are often employed in lieu of deeds. Because an easement is an interest in land, the instrument creating the easement must contain the essential requirements of a voluntary conveyance of land, namely, the names of the grantor and grantee, operative words of conveyance or the equivalent, and a description of the easement and of the land that is subject to the easement with sufficient clearness to locate it. Execution of the instrument by the grantor and delivery of the instrument to the grantee are also essential to make it effective.

An important distinction applies, however, with respect to the description contained in an easement and a description contained in a deed. A deed conveying the fee title to an indefinite strip of land would be void for uncertainty, but a deed to an unlocated easement, sometimes referred to as a floating or a blanket easement, is valid.

EXAMPLE An easement for a roadway over and across Lot 1, without specifying the particular portion of Lot 1 affected, would be good. The exact location of the roadway may be determined subsequently, either by agreement of the parties or by use.

Reservation of easement by deed. When a landowner sells a part of his land only—for example, the portion fronting on a street—he may desire to reserve in the deed an easement in favor of the portion retained by him.[12] This can be accomplished by inserting, after the description of the land sold, a clause such as the following (when, for instance, the deed describes the east half of Lot I as the portion sold):

> *The grantor reserves to himself and his heirs and assigns, as an easement appurtenant to the west half of Lot 1, an easement for ingress and egress over and across the north 15 feet of the premises hereby conveyed.*

Who may create an easement. The only person who can grant a permanent easement is the fee owner of the servient tenement, or a person with the power of disposal of the fee (a life tenant with power of sale). The holder of an estate less than the fee may, however, grant an easement within the terms of his estate, but the easement ceases on the termination of such estate.

EXAMPLE A lessee of land for a term of ten years may create an easement in favor of a third party, but the easement would be terminated with the expiration of the lease.

Easements created by mortgage or trust deed. An easement may be created under a mortgage or trust deed, and upon a foreclosure the easement would be as effective as one created by a deed from the owner of the servient tenement.

EXAMPLE Assume that A, the owner of Lots 1 and 2, executes a deed of trust on Lot 1, together with an easement for a driveway over a designated portion of Lot 2. If the trust deed is foreclosed, the purchaser at the foreclosure sale acquires title to Lot 1 and the easement over Lot 2. If, however, the trust deed is reconveyed, the lien on the easement ceases, and the easement will no longer exist.

§14.20. Implied grant or reservation

EXAMPLE A, the owner of Lots 1 and 2, conveys Lot 1 to B. At the time the deed is executed and delivered, a driveway over a portion of Lot 2 is openly used and is reasonably necessary to the beneficial use of Lot l. An easement for driveway purposes over Lot 2 would ordinarily pass by implication with the deed of Lot 1.[13]

Statutory rule. The rule as to implied grants of easement is contained in the Civil Code, which provides that

> *A transfer of real property passes all easements attached thereto, and creates in favor thereof an easement to use other real property of the person whose estate is transferred in the same manner and to the same extent as such property was obviously and permanently used by the person whose estate is transferred, for the benefit thereof, at the time when the transfer was agreed upon and completed.*[14]

Certain conditions must exist. The courts have ruled that certain conditions must exist at the time of the conveyance before an easement by implied grant will be given effect. These conditions are as follows: (1) there must be a separation of titles; (2) the use that gives rise to the easement must have been so long continued and so obvious as to show that it was intended to be permanent; and (3) the easement must be reasonably necessary to the beneficial use of the land granted.[15]

Use must be apparent. The requirement that the use that gives rise to an implied easement be obvious or apparent does not necessarily mean that the use must be visible on inspection of the surface of the ground. For example, the use may consist of underground drains or sewers. If such use was known to the parties at the time of the conveyance, or could have been discovered by a reasonably prudent investigation, it is regarded as obvious or apparent.

Implied reservation. Implied easements by reservation are also recognized in California. If the owner conveys the portion of his land that is burdened by a use for the benefit of the land retained, an easement by implied reservation arises in favor of the grantor if all conditions that are indispensable to the creation of an implied easement are met.

Implied right of entry. A conveyance or reservation of the minerals carries with it an implied easement to enter and use the surface of the land for the purpose of extracting the minerals. This is known as the implied right of surface entry.

§14.21. Easement by necessity
An easement by necessity arises when a grantor conveys a part of the land that is entirely surrounded by the grantor's remaining lands, or by the land of the grantor and of third parties, and that has no means of access to a road.

EXAMPLE A, the owner of Lot 1, which consists of ten acres, conveys the north two acres thereof to B. The land conveyed has no access to a public road except over the remaining portion of Lot 1. B would have an easement of necessity over the land retained by A. Based on considerations of public policy favoring the full use of land and on the presumed intention of the parties that the grantee would have a means of access to his land, the courts have held in such cases that an implied way of necessity passes to the grantee as appurtenant to his land.[16]

There is no absolute right to access to a public street; it is possible to own property that is, in fact, landlocked. Thus in one case, the court refused to find that a way of necessity existed simply because the seller's land was landlocked.[17]

Easement in favor of grantor. A way of necessity may also arise by implied reservation in favor of a grantor who conveys part of his land in such manner as to leave the land retained inaccessible except over the land conveyed, but the courts might be less inclined to apply the doctrine in such a situation.

Distinguishing characteristic of easement by necessity. Although a way of necessity is considered an easement by implication, the requirements for its creation differ from those of the implied easements, primarily for the reason that the way of necessity does not depend on the existence, at the time of severance, of a way obviously and permanently in use over the servient tenement.

Strict necessity must exist. A way of necessity exists only in cases of strict necessity, that is, when the property would otherwise be landlocked, having no means whatsoever for passage to a public road.[18] The doctrine does not apply when the grantee has another means of access, even though it may be extremely inconvenient. The way of necessity ceases when the necessity ends, for instance, when the grantor dedicates another road for the grantee's use, or when the grantee acquires other land that gives him a means of access.

Creation by judicial proceedings. A way of necessity may occur not only as a result of a voluntary conveyance, but also when there is a severance of the land by judicial proceedings, such as a partition action in which an allotment of land is made and a portion is allotted without access; or when there is a sale on foreclosure of a mortgage or trust deed covering a parcel of inaccessible land.

Common ownership must have existed. A way of necessity does not arise indiscriminately over any land surrounding the grantee's land; it can be claimed only over other land owned by the grantor at the time of the conveyance and not over land owned by strangers. To establish such a way, the grantee must show that at some time in the past the land for which the benefit of the way is claimed and the land in which the way is claimed belonged to the same person.

§14.22. Easement by prescription

In California an easement by prescription may be acquired by adverse use for a continuous period of five years. As with adverse possession, a person can legally steal another's real property under this doctrine. The interest so acquired is as effectual as one obtained by conveyance, but it is not a marketable title until established of record by appropriate court proceedings against the owner of the record title to quiet title.[19] Most often an easement by prescription is for right of way purposes, but other uses have been recognized.

EXAMPLE   In one case, a defendant had fenced a backyard portion that belonged to plaintiff and used it for the statutory time. The trial court held that defendant had an exclusive easement over the fenced-in portion of plaintiff's property. However, the appellate court reversed, stating that an easement is not an ownership interest and does not amount to a fee simple. To permit the defendant's exclusive use "perverted the classical distinction in real property law between ownership and use."[20]

Elements of prescriptive easement. The essential elements that must be shown to establish an easement by prescription are: open and notorious use, continuous and uninterrupted for a period of five years, hostile to the true owner, exclusive, and under some claim of right.[21] Payment of taxes is not required to obtain an easement by prescription. The adverse user must so utilize the property that the intent to claim a prescriptive easement is obvious.

EXAMPLE   Defendants installed a sidewalk, sprinkler system, trees, and a lawn on a portion of plaintiff's lot because of an erroneously placed survey stake. The situation existed for more than five years. The court held that an easement by prescription had been established.[22]

A use cannot be the basis of a prescriptive easement if it is permissive. Thus, posted notices on land to the effect that the same is "private property" and "permission to pass is revocable at any time" have been held to be sufficient to rebut a claim of adverse use.[23] However, it has also been held that this is not conclusive, for posting of signs is only one of the many factors to be considered.[24]

Recording notice of consent. The Civil Code provides that the holder of record title to land may record a notice of consent to use his land for certain purposes.[25] Such notice of consent is evidence that the subsequent use of the land for such purposes is permissive and not adverse. Notice may be revoked by recording a notice of revocation. The advantage of the recorded notice is that it gives undisputed evidence of the date and scope of the permission. The Civil Code sets forth the form of such notice and provides that the notice of consent is conclusive evidence that the use is permissive.

Posting signs. The Civil Code also provides that no use shall ripen into an easement by prescription when the property owner posts signs, as required, stating in substance: "Right to pass by permission, and subject to control, of owner."[26]

§14.23. Easement by condemnation

Another method of creating an easement is by condemnation.[27] Although the fee title to land may be acquired for street and highway purposes by condemnation proceedings in the instances authorized by statutes—such as the taking of the fee title by the State of California for state highway purposes—the usual result when land is taken by condemnation for a street, a highway, a railroad right of way, or a telephone or power line is that the taker acquires only an easement. Most city streets and alleys are owned by adjoining lot owners, subject to an easement in favor of the public, and many of these easement rights were obtained through condemnation proceedings.[28]

§14.24. Open space easements

Open space easements, which may be acquired by condemnation, are granted to counties and cities that have adopted a general plan.[29] Such an easement restricts the property to open space for the public benefit and entitles the property to special tax consideration. Granted for a minimum of 20 years, an open space easement must be accepted by a resolution of the governing body that is endorsed on the face of the instrument.

§14.25. Easement by dedication

An easement may also be created by dedication, either statutory or common law. In California a statutory dedication is effected when, in accordance with a map act then in force, a map is recorded expressly dedicating areas shown thereon to public use. The Subdivision Map Act requires that the map bear a certificate signed and acknowledged by all parties having a record interest in the land, offering certain parcels of land for dedication for the specified public uses. The map must also bear a certificate evidencing acceptance by the governing body of such offer of dedication.

Common-law dedication. A common law dedication, which embraces all forms of dedication other than statutory, requires no written conveyance or particular form. It results from an intention of the owner, clearly indicated by words or acts, to dedicate the land to public use, and an acceptance of the offer by the public, either by formal act of the proper authorities (a resolution of acceptance by the city council, for instance), or by public use. For example, the owner of land conveys portions thereof by deeds that reserve connecting strips of land "for road purpose," such strips at the time being used by the public as a street. It has been held that such reservations constitute a dedication of the street.[30]

A common law dedication is generally regarded as conveying merely an easement to the public, with the fee title remaining in the original owner or his successors in interest. This rule has been clearly established in California as to dedicated streets and highways.

An easement by "implied dedication" is also discussed in Chapter 6. In those cases, however, the use must be great enough to clearly indicate to the owner that the property is in danger of being dedicated.[31]

In an interesting case, the plaintiff sought a judicial determination that it had acquired a prescriptive easement in, and there had been an implied dedication to, the defendant's land for over ten years. However, the court held that the plaintiff's use was not hostile or adverse.[32]

§14.26. Conservation easement

A *conservation easement* means any limitation in a deed, will, or other instrument in the form of an easement, restriction, covenant, or condition, executed by or on behalf of the owner, and binding on successive owners, the purpose of which is to retain land predominantly in its natural, scenic, historical, agricultural, forested, or open-space condition.[33] Only certain tax-exempt nonprofit organizations may acquire and hold conservation easements.[34] Actual or threatened injury to or impairment of this easement may be prohibited or restrained; in addition, the holder is also entitled to recover money damages for the cost of restoration, or loss of scenic, authentic, or environmental value. The court may award the prevailing party reasonable attorney's fees for costs of litigation.[35]

§14.27. Easement by estoppel

The creation of an easement by estoppel has been recognized by the courts in this state. For instance, when an owner, in conveying land, describes it as bounded on a street or way that he owns but that is in fact not dedicated as a street or way, he is estopped to deny the existence of the way for the benefit of the grantee. In effect, he thereby grants an easement for ingress and egress over the supposed street. Also, in the case of an attempted oral grant of an easement, when the grantee makes improvements for the purpose of exercising the easement right, the courts have recognized and enforced the easement on the theory of estoppel.

§14.28. Easement created by reference to maps

Still another method of creating an easement is by the sale of property by reference to a map or plat. When a landowner subdivides land into lots, blocks, streets, and alleys, and thereafter sells lots in the subdivision, each purchaser of a lot automatically acquires an easement of passage over the streets and alleys shown on the plat or map of the subdivision, even though the deed to the lot makes no mention whatever of such right.[36]

VI. EXTENT OF USE

§14.29. In general

An easement appurtenant can be used only for the benefit of the dominant tenement. It may not be used for the benefit of any other parcel of land without the consent of the owner of the servient tenement. Because of this rule, it is advisable to include a description of the dominant tenement in the instrument creating the easement. This may avoid a claim by the owner of the servient tenement that the easement was not intended to benefit all portions of the land allegedly included in the dominant tenement.

§14.30. Lands to be acquired in the future

When there is the possibility of the owner of the dominant tenement acquiring other lands in the vicinity that may need the benefit of the easement, such as commercial property for anticipated future expansion of plant facilities, the instrument creating the easement should provide that such subsequently acquired property shall enjoy the benefit of the easement.

§14.31. Right of way

It is not essential that a right of way be described by metes and bounds or otherwise specifically located, as long as the description of the servient tenement is sufficient. When a general right of way is granted or reserved, the owner of the servient tenement may in the first instance designate a suitable way, and if he fails to do so, the owner of the dominant tenement may designate it. If the parties are unable to agree, a court of equity has the power to fix a location.

Location of right of way. If the location of a right of way is not defined by the grant, a reasonably convenient and suitable way is presumed to be intended, and the right cannot be exercised over the whole of the land.[37] Once the location of an easement has been established, whether by express terms of the grant or by use and acquiescence, it cannot be substantially changed without the consent of both parties.

EXAMPLE In one case it was held that the grant of an easement for aerial wires was fixed as to location by wires installed for 17 years at a height of 51 1/2 feet from the ground, precluding a later increase in the height of the wires without the consent of both parties.[38]

When the easement is acquired by an implied grant, the scope of the easement is measured by the extent the property was obviously and permanently used at the time when the transfer was completed.[39] A purchaser of real estate is bound to take notice of all easements or servitudes that are apparent upon inspection of the property.[40]

EXAMPLE One case raised a question as to whether the adoption of a different method of transportation over rights of way would result in a loss of the easement. It was held that the paving and use, for motor coach transportation, of rights of way originally granted and used for electric railway services sufficiently complied with the purpose of the grantor to permit survival of the easement.[41]

§14.32. Reasonable use
When an easement for ingress and egress is created by grant, it may be used for all reasonable purposes and the use is not necessarily restricted to such purposes as were reasonable at the date of the grant. Accordingly, the use of an easement by motor vehicles will be permitted even though the easement was created at a time when horse-drawn vehicles were in use. However, when an easement is acquired by prescription, the extent of the right is fixed and determined by the use in which it originates, and it cannot be extended or increased so as to enlarge the burden. Under this rule, it has been held[42] that a prescriptive easement acquired for access to a farm and house could not be used to reach a pleasure resort thereafter established on the farm.[43]

§14.33. Incidental rights
A grant of an easement carries with it by implication certain secondary rights essential to its enjoyment, such as the right to make repairs, renewals, and replacements. Such incidental rights may be exercised so long as the easement holder uses reasonable care and does not increase the burden on, or go beyond the boundaries of, the servient estate, or make any material changes therein.

§14.34. Duty to maintain
It is the duty of the owner of an easement to maintain it.[44] If the easement is owned by more than one person, then the cost of repair shall be apportioned.

§14.35. Use by owner of servient tenement
The owner of the land subject to the easement has every right or incident of ownership not inconsistent with the easement and enjoyment and use of the same. The

servient owner has been permitted, for instance, to make use of the land beneath a power line; to maintain a fence across a drainage canal when no interference with the use of the canal resulted; and to grant another easement over land subject to a previous grant of a similar easement, such as a pipeline easement.

§14.36. Exclusive and nonexclusive easements

When an easement has been granted for a roadway across a portion of land, the owner may also use the road or grant the right of use to others if the easement owner's use is not interfered with.

EXAMPLE   In one case,[45] it was held that the grant of an easement to the city power company for electrical transmission lines did not prohibit the grantor's use for parking which did not interfere with the power company's easement.[46] These rights of the servient owner may be restricted, however, by the terms of the instrument creating the easement, as in a case in which the easement is such as to make it obvious that an exclusive easement was intended. When it is intended that the easement be nonexclusive, it is customary to specifically so recite in the instrument creating the easement.

VII. TRANSFER OF EASEMENT

§14.37. In general

Easements are property rights, and as such are transferable and inheritable in the same manner and subject to the same requirements as other interests in real property.[47] Under California law, an easement in gross is assignable unless expressly or by necessary implication made personal to a particular individual. Such an easement cannot, of course, pass as an incident or appurtenance to a dominant tenement, but must be expressly conveyed.

§14.38. Limitation on right of transfer

An important limitation on the transfer of an easement in gross exists: It cannot be apportioned so as to increase the burden on the servient tenement. In the case of easements appurtenant, this rule has been codified, the Civil Code providing that the dominant tenement cannot be partitioned in such a way as to increase the burden on the servient tenement.[48]

§14.39. Effect of transfer of dominant tenement

In the case of easements appurtenant, the easement passes as an incident of the transfer of the dominant tenement, even though the easement is not expressly mentioned and the conveyance does not expressly purport to transfer the appurtenances.[49] The type of transfer that will pass an appurtenant easement is not restricted to a deed; it can be a contract of sale of the dominant tenement, or a mortgage or trust deed on the dominant tenement, or a transfer by operation of law, such as an execution sale.

§14.40. Transfer of servient tenement

Insofar as a transfer of the servient tenement is concerned, the owner of the land subject to the easement may, of course, convey his interest in the land, and the grantee takes title to the servient tenement subject to the easement. If the grantee is a purchaser for value, this rule is modified by the further requirement that the purchaser have actual or constructive notice of the easement. If the grantee does not pay value for the property, he takes subject to the easement even if he has no notice. If the easement has been recorded, the purchaser is deemed to have constructive notice. If there is an unrecorded easement affecting the land, the purchaser will take subject to such an easement only if he has actual notice, or the easement is indicated by something visible or apparent from an inspection of the land.[50]

VIII. TERMINATION OR EXTINGUISHMENT OF EASEMENTS

§14.41. In general

Easements may be terminated or extinguished in several ways, including the following: (1) by express release; (2) by legal proceedings; (3) by merger of the servient tenement and the easement in the same person; (4) by nonuse for five years of an easement by prescription; (5) by abandonment; (6) by adverse possession by the owner of the servient tenement; (7) by the destruction of the servient tenement; or (8) in some cases, by excessive use.

§14.42. Express release

An easement, whether appurtenant or in gross, may be extinguished by an express release in favor of the owner of the servient tenement. The customary method of such express release is a quitclaim deed from the easement holder to the owner of the servient tenement.

§14.43. Legal proceedings

An easement may be extinguished by appropriate legal proceedings against the easement holder, such as a decree in a quiet title action against the easement holder in favor of the owner of the servient tenement. The owner of the servient tenement would have to have evidence to support the claim that he is entitled to a decree of the court finding that the easement no longer exists. In other words, an easement cannot be extinguished by legal proceedings unless there is a valid basis, such as foreclosure of a trust deed that was earlier than the rights of the easement holder.

§14.44. Merger of estates

An easement is extinguished by merger when the same person becomes the owner of the easement and the owner of the fee title to the servient tenement. The rule is fundamental that a person cannot have an easement over his own property.[51]

§14.45. Nonuse for five years

An easement acquired by prescription is extinguishable by nonuse for a period of five years; however, an easement founded on a grant or an agreement is not lost by mere nonuse for any length of time. At the most, such nonuse would be one of the facts from which an intention to abandon the easement might be inferred.

§14.46. Abandonment

An easement may be extinguished by abandonment, that is, an intentional relinquishment of the easement as indicated by conduct inconsistent with a continuance of the use. Intent to abandon is the essential factor in such cases.[52]

§14.47. Adverse possession

An easement may also be extinguished by the use of the servient tenement, by the owner thereof, in a manner adverse to the exercise of the easement, for a continuous period of five years or more.

EXAMPLE In one case, it was held that a 30-foot easement for a private road was extinguished as to a portion of the road on which the owner of the servient tenement maintained buildings for over five years with the knowledge of the owner of the easement.[53]

§14.48. Destruction of servient tenement

An easement is extinguished by the destruction of the servient tenement. The application of this rule usually occurs in connection with easements in buildings that are destroyed.

EXAMPLES 1. In one case, involving the destruction of a building without fault of the owner, it was held that the previous grant of the right to use a hall or stairway of the building, although constituting an easement, conferred no interest in the soil and did not survive the destruction of the building.[54]

2. Another case held that an easement in a building for a particular purpose (support for floor and ceiling joists) carries with it no interest in the land, and when the building is destroyed, the easement ceases.[55]

§14.49. Excessive use
An easement can also be lost by excessive use.

EXAMPLE In one case, it was held that an easement by grant for ingress and egress over private land became subject to extinguishment for misuse when the owner of the servitude greatly increased the servient burden by extending and connecting the lane with two public roads, making its use available not only to nondominant property owners but also to the general public.[56] In holding that the easement was extinguished, the court stated:

> The general rule is that misuse or excessive use is not sufficient for abandonment or forfeiture, but an injunction is the proper remedy. But where the burden of the servient estate is increased through changes in the dominant estate which increase the use and subject it to use of nondominant property, a forfeiture will be justified if the unauthorized use may not be severed and prohibited.[57]

IX. ENCROACHMENTS

§14.50. In general
An *encroachment* is described as a projection of a building or other structure on one parcel of land onto, or into the airspace of, an adjoining parcel of land. An encroachment by a building or other structure that rests in part on the adjoining land constitutes a trespass, whereas an encroachment in the airspace above the land of an adjoining owner constitutes a nuisance. This distinction is of particular importance with respect to the time within which to maintain an action for injunction or other appropriate relief.

§14.51. When an encroachment constitutes a trespass
The Statute of Limitations may bar relief if the encroachment amounts to a trespass.

EXAMPLE As stated in one case,[58] the encroachment of a building obviously intended to be permanent on the soil of another is a permanent trespass, and the cause of action based on such trespass is barred in three years under the applicable statute of limitations.[59]

Relief against encroachments has been granted in actions of ejectment, actions to quiet title, and for an injunction and damages, but such actions must be commenced within the prescribed three-year period. The usual type of action is one for the removal of *the encroachment and for damages*. However, if the defendant is a "good faith improver,"[60] the court may realign the boundary and award the plaintiff reasonable compensation.[61]

§14.52. When an encroachment constitutes a nuisance
When the encroachment is on the space above the land, it is considered a nuisance rather than a permanent trespass, and the cause of action is not barred by the lapse

of time. The maintenance of such an encroachment is considered to be a continuing trespass or nuisance, and every continuance thereof amounts to a new nuisance for which successive actions will lie until the nuisance is abated. Nuisances that consist of acts done or of particular uses of property are properly termed *continuing* when they are of such a character that they may continue indefinitely or, on the other hand, may be discontinued at any time.[62]

§14.53. Relief obtainable through judicial proceedings

A mandatory injunction will ordinarily issue at the instance of a landowner to compel the removal of the encroachment when the action is filed within the required time.[63] However, even though the right to an injunction may be firmly established, its issuance is largely discretionary with the court and depends on a consideration of all the facts, circumstances, and relative equities as between the parties. Consequently, an injunction will not be issued if the encroachment is slight, was unintentional, and if the harm to be suffered by the owner of the encroaching structure by its compulsory removal would be greatly disproportionate to the injury sustained by the owner of the land encroached on. In such cases, damages only will be awarded in lieu of an injunction.

EXAMPLE   In one case, the sum of $10 damages was awarded for an encroachment of between $\frac{1}{2}$ and $\frac{5}{8}$ of an inch, with no evidence of actual damages to the owner; and in another case, $200 was awarded when the encroachment was only $3\frac{5}{8}$ inches, and it would have cost $6,875 to remove the portion of the wall encroaching on the adjoining property.

---

§14.54. When an encroachment is intentional

If it appears that the encroachment was intentional, as distinguished from an innocent mistake, an injunction may be granted even in the absence of present damage to the land encroached on, and even though it appears that the encroachment is slight and the cost of removal is great. This rule was recognized in one case[64] involving an encroachment of $4\frac{1}{2}$ inches.

The rule is otherwise in the case of an unintentional encroachment.

EXAMPLE   One case[65] involved an encroachment of 15/100 acre of land worth $150 an acre. The encroaching structure was a reservoir that cost $7,000 to construct and served 500 people. The court awarded damages in the sum of $762.41. In denying a mandatory injunction, the court emphasized the serious harm to the defendant if the injunction were granted, the defendant's inadvertence and innocent mistake in constructing the reservoir, the fully compensatory nature of the damage awarded, and the serious injury to the public if the reservoir were ordered removed.

X. NUISANCES

§14.55. In general

The Civil Code provides that (1) anything that is injurious to health; or (2) is indecent or offensive to the senses; or (3) is an obstruction to the free use of property, so as to interfere with the comfortable enjoyment of life or property; or (4) unlawfully obstructs the free passage or use, in the customary manner, of any navigable lake, river, bay, stream, canal, or basin, or any public park, square, street, or highway, is a *nuisance*.[66] A *public nuisance* is one that affects any considerable number of persons. Any other is a *private nuisance*.[67] An injured person may abate a nuisance by removing or destroying it if he can do so without committing a breach of the peace or doing unnecessary injury.[68] However, reasonable notice must be given.[69]

§14.56. Interference with use and enjoyment of property

A nuisance consists of the unlawful interference with a person's interest in the use and enjoyment of his or her property. It is ordinarily immaterial whether the defendant acts intentionally, negligently, or with due care. The act or thing may affect the use of property, as in the case of an obstruction of a right of way, or it may affect the senses, as in the case of smoke or noxious odors.

§14.57. Examples of nuisances

Cases decided by the courts in California furnish innumerable examples of nuisances, including the obstruction of an abutting owner's access to a street, which is a private as well as a public nuisance; allowing illegal drug activity in an apartment building; pollution of water in a stream or an irrigation ditch; poisonous dust, sprayed to kill plant pests, carried by the wind to adjoining land, killing the owner's bees; chickens scratching in dry dust, which sent up clouds of dust and polluted the neighbor's vineyards;[70] and airport noise and vibration.[71]

§14.58. Acts offensive to esthetic sense

Where the act complained of merely offends the esthetic sense, it has been held that it cannot be enjoined as a nuisance.

EXAMPLE   In one case, the plaintiff sought to compel the removal of a wooden fence, $6\frac{1}{2}$ feet high, which the defendant had built within 3 inches of the boundary line between the property of plaintiff and defendant, but entirely on defendant's property. The plaintiff claimed, among other things, that the fence created an ugly and untidy appearance. The court stated that in the absence of some legislative action, the courts cannot set up esthetic standards to which builders must conform. The court, in quoting from another case, stated:

> No case has been cited, nor are we aware of any case, which holds that a man must be deprived of his property because his tastes are not those of his neighbors. Esthetic considerations are a matter of luxury and indulgence rather than a necessity, and it is necessity alone which justifies the exercise of police power to take private property without compensation.[72]

---

§14.59. Mental and emotional factors

EXAMPLES   1.   In an earlier case involving an undertaking establishment in a residential district, it was held that the resulting mental depression to a property owner could not be the basis for an injunction.[73]

2.   However, in a later case, the trial court held that the establishment of a mortuary and funeral parlor in a residential district should be enjoined as a nuisance, on evidence that it would be a constant mental irritant to the plaintiff and his family and would thereby cause them to suffer physical disturbances. The judgment was affirmed by the appellate court.[74] The opinion reviewed authorities from other states, which disclosed a trend in that direction. New weight has thus been given to mental and emotional factors in determining what constitutes a nuisance, thereby accomplishing, by actions to abate a nuisance, some of the purposes of modern zoning legislation.

XI. FENCES

§14.60. In general

A *fence* is a visible, tangible obstruction, made of wood, iron, stone, or other suitable material, interposed between two portions of land so as to separate and shut in land and set it off as private property. Unless they are portable, fences are fixtures, and thus become part of the real estate to which they are attached.

§14.61. Fencing largely a matter of discretion

In determining what constitutes a nuisance, the court may consider mental and emotional factors. Except for any duty to construct and maintain fences imposed by agreement, easement, or prescription, and the duty to keep domestic animals off the land of others, and other statutory duties imposed under special circumstances, as in the case of dangerous premises (for example, a fence surrounding a swimming pool), the land of the owner may be left unfenced. On the other hand, if so desired, the owner may build fences on his property where he pleases, provided they are not in violation of the spite fence law, are not a nuisance, are not constructed negligently so as to cause harm, and do not violate zoning regulations or deed restrictions.

§14.62. Spite fences

The statute provides that a fence unnecessarily over ten feet high, and maliciously erected or maintained for the purpose of annoying the occupant of adjoining property, is deemed a private nuisance and may be abated as such.[75]

§14.63. Maintaining division fences

The Civil Code provides that coterminous owners (adjoining owners) are mutually bound to maintain the fence between them, unless one of them chooses to let his land lie unfenced. If he afterward encloses his land, however, he must then contribute to the other owner a just proportion of the value of the fence dividing their property.[76]

§14.64. Interference with gates

Under the Penal Code, it is a misdemeanor to willfully open, tear down, or otherwise destroy or leave open the gate or bars of any fence on the enclosed lands of another.[77]

XII. TREES AND OTHER VEGETATION

§14.65. In general

Trees or hedges standing partly on the land of adjoining owners belong to them in common.[78] Neither owner can cut or injure them, except that one owner can cut limbs that cause damage to his property if such action does not injure the other owner's windbreak.

§14.66. Overhanging branches, and roots

Trees whose trunks stand wholly on the land of one owner belong exclusively to him although their roots grow into the land of another.[79] However, the adjoining owner has the right to cut limbs or roots overhanging or extending into his property, but only to the boundary line. An adjoining landowner does not have a cause of action from the mere fact that the branches of an innoxious tree on his neighbor's land overhang his premises. He has the right to cut off the overhanging branches, which is considered a sufficient remedy; however, if the encroaching roots are noxious, an action to abate a nuisance is maintainable, and, although he may have a right to cut the roots, he must do so in a nonnegligent manner (though determining what may be nonnegligent may be a problem for the adjoining landowner).[80] The landowner also has a duty to maintain the trees properly.

EXAMPLE
One case involved the liability of a landowner for injuries resulting from a fallen eucalyptus limb. The owner had planted a row of trees along the edge of the highway bordering his property, and the fallen limb injured a motorist on the highway. The owner was held liable for the resulting injuries. The court ruled that an owner must take reasonable precautions to guard against such an occurrence.[81]

§14.67. Control of weeds

In the absence of a statute or ordinance, a landowner owes no duty to an adjoining proprietor to prevent seeds (from vegetation) naturally growing on his land from maturing and being blown by the wind onto the adjoining land. Accordingly, a landowner has been held not entitled to the abatement of arrow weeds growing on the banks of a ditch that crosses his property.[82] However, weeds are subject to pest control, and may also be declared a public nuisance when dangerous to public health or safety.

XIII. BOUNDARIES

§14.68. In general

All land has its boundaries. The location of the boundary is largely a surveying problem. In the sale and purchase of real property, the parties should ascertain the exact location of the boundaries. An owner is presumed to know the location of the boundary, and any error in pointing out the boundary to a prospective purchaser, either by the seller or his broker, can result in a liability for damages. When the true location of the boundary is uncertain, adjoining landowners can establish it by agreement.[83]

§14.69. Land adjoining a highway

As mentioned in Chapter 13, when land is bounded by a monument such as a street or other way, a conveyance of the land usually carries to the center of the monument. The monument rule in the law of boundaries was expressed in one case[84] as follows:

> In the absence of any qualifying term the designation in a conveyance of any physical object or monument as a boundary implies the middle or central point of such boundary; as, for example, if the boundary be a road or highway, or a stream, the thread of the road or stream will be intended; if a rock, a heap of stones, or a tree be the boundary, the central point of such tree or rock or heap of stones will be intended.

This rule can have particular significance in cases in which a portion only of a large parcel fronting on a street is sold. In establishing the boundary line on the rear portion, a question will often arise as to whether the measurement is from the center of the street or from the side of the street, making, in some cases, a substantial difference in the usable area, with resulting controversies.

§14.70. Boundaries by water

The Civil Code sets forth the following rules with respect to land bordering on water: Except when the grant under which the land is held indicates a different intent, the owner of the upland, when it borders on tidewater, takes to the ordinary high-water mark. When it borders on a navigable lake or stream where there is no tide, the owner takes to the edge of the lake or stream, at low-water mark; when it borders on any other water, the owner takes to the middle of the lake or stream.[85]

§14.71. Boundaries after earth movement

The Code of Civil Procedure[86] provides for an action in the Superior Court to reestablish land boundaries and quiet title following "earth movements" (defined as including, but not limited to, "slides, subsidence, lateral or vertical displacements or similar disasters caused by man, or by earthquake or other acts of nature"[erroneously referred to as acts of "God"]).

A certified copy of the judgment in any such action shall be recorded in the county where the affected land is situated, and is constructive notice of the findings and of the plat(s) referred to therein; such findings and plats will supersede and control all prior plats, maps, and documents to the extent they are inconsistent.

XIV. WATER

§14.72. In general

Traditionally in California there have been two primary problems with water—either too much or too little. The latter situation relates primarily to value of land; the former situation will affect the rights and duties of adjoining owners.

§14.73. Diversion of waters

Before 1966, cases held that an owner cannot without liability divert surface or storm waters onto the lands of another over which they would not naturally have flowed nor can he accumulate surface waters on his land and precipitate them on a neighbor's land in larger quantities than, or in different amounts from, those which they would have taken in the course of nature. The rule regarding surface waters is relaxed somewhat as to city lots, and the owner may make changes in the surface of his land, but he may not cause an accumulation of storm waters that would injure adjoining property.

EXAMPLE

In one case, the California Supreme Court modified the rule followed since 1876 regarding the liability of an upper owner for discharge of water in an unnatural manner. In reviewing the California law with respect to surface waters, the court recognized that California had followed the so-called civil law rule to the effect that there exists a "servitude" of natural drainage between adjoining parcels, so that the lower owner must accept the surface waters that naturally drain onto his land. Correlatively, the rule denies to the upper owner any privilege to alter the natural system of drainage so as to increase the burden. Recognizing that the civil law rule had a tendency to discourage the improvement of land, since almost any use of property is likely to cause a change in drainage, the court abandoned the strict civil law rule and adopted what it calls a "modified civil law rule." Not every interference with natural drainage injurious to the land of another is now actionable. It must also be unreasonable. In its decision, the court stated:

What is, in any particular case, reasonable use or management has been held to be a mixed question of law and fact to be submitted to the jury under proper instructions.

> *Failure to exercise reasonable care may result in liability by an upper to a lower landowner. It is equally the duty of any person threatened with injury to his property by the flow of surface waters to take reasonable precautions to avoid or reduce any actual or potential injury.*
>
> *On the other hand, if both the upper and lower landowners are reasonable, then the injury must necessarily be borne by the upper landowner who changes a natural system of drainage, in accordance with our traditional civil law rule.*[87]

XV. LATERAL AND SUBJACENT SUPPORT

§14.74. In general

Lateral support is the support one tract of land receives from an adjoining tract separated from it by a vertical plane. At common law, an owner of land was entitled to have it supported in its natural condition by the adjoining land. Liability for infringing this right was not dependent on any lack of care or skill by a person who removed the natural support of land, but was absolute. Although a landowner may excavate his own ground for any lawful purpose, he must do so in such a manner that the land of an adjoining owner will not, either by its own weight or through the action of the elements, fall into the excavation.

§14.75. Statutory rule in California

This common law doctrine has been modified in California, which has been declared to be a relaxation of the rule of absolute liability.[88] Although the statute restates the common law concept that an owner of land is entitled to the lateral and subjacent support that his land receives from adjoining land, if the conditions specified in the statute are complied with, it permits a landowner to excavate his land freed from the absolute right of lateral support in the owner of adjoining land.

§14.76. Notice to adjoining owners

The statute permits an owner to make proper and usual excavations on his land for purposes of construction or improvement but requires him to give reasonable notice to adjoining owners. It also requires that ordinary care and skill be used in making an excavation, and that reasonable precaution be taken to sustain adjoining land.

§14.77. Duties of excavator

With respect to support for land alone, the owner making excavations must state in the notice to the adjoining owner the time the excavation is to begin and its intended depth. In actions against excavators for negligence, it is necessary to show that the negligent excavating was the proximate cause of the collapse of the adjoining land. However, heavy rainfall and saturation of soil may be a hazard reasonably foreseeable, and against which the excavator, in the exercise of ordinary care, should take due precautions. When an excavation is carefully made and substitute support is furnished, such as a bulkhead, and the land nonetheless subsides as a result of negligence in permitting weakening of the substituted support, the excavator is liable in the same manner as if the original support had been withdrawn.

§14.78. Support of buildings

At common law, the rule of absolute liability did not extend to the support of buildings, but only to the support of land. Hence, an excavator was not liable for damage to the building unless he was negligent, in which case the ordinary rules of tort liability applied.

Statutory rule. In California, liability for support of buildings exists under general tort principles for negligence in excavation, and the requirement of notice under the statute is applicable so that the excavator is also liable for failure to give notice. In these respects, the rule on damage to buildings is the same as that governing damage to the land itself. The statute additionally makes specific provision for liability when the excavation is deeper than the foundations of the adjoining building, or deeper than the standard depth of nine feet. If the excavation is to go deeper than the walls or foundations of the adjoining building and is to be so close as to endanger it, the excavator must give the owner of the building at least 30 days to protect it, and must for that purpose permit him to go on the land that is being excavated. If the excavation is to go to or deeper than the standard depth of foundations (defined as nine feet below curb level) and the foundations of the adjoining structure also go to such depths, then the excavator must support the land and building or other structure, without cost to the owner. The excavator is made absolutely liable for any damage except "minor settlement cracks" if he fails to do so.

§14.79. Slide damage

A landowner in a hillside area may be obligated to stabilize the land to prevent it from sliding onto adjoining property.

EXAMPLE In one case, the plaintiff brought an action for an injunction and for damages caused by excavation on adjoining property. The plaintiff's land was on a hillside, adjoining that of the defendant. The defendant made excavations on its property that resulted in slides creeping toward the plaintiff's land. At the time of the trial, this slide area was moving closer to the plaintiff's property but had not actually encroached on it, and no physical damage had actually occurred to the plaintiff's land. The court denied relief as to damages, but issued a permanent injunction, requiring the defendant to stabilize the hillside so as to prevent slides from encroaching on or damaging the plaintiff's property. Regarding damages, the court stated that if the defendant's land is stabilized so as to prevent slides from encroaching on or damaging the plaintiff's property, mere buyer fear of future slides or other psychological effect on prospective buyers of the use by the defendant of its property could not be the basis for an award of damages.[89]

§14.80. Subjacent support

Subjacent support is the support the surface of the earth receives from underlying strata. The general rule is that a landowner is entitled to the perpendicular support that is afforded by subjacent strata. Since the subject of subjacent support is closely related to that of lateral support, it is governed by similar rules.

EXAMPLE A city in constructing a tunnel beneath a street owes a duty similar to that imposed by statute on coterminous owners to use ordinary care and skill and to take reasonable precautions to avoid injury to the fee owner of a part of the street.[90]

XVI. LIABILITY TO PERSONS ON OR NEAR THE LAND

§14.81. In general

An owner of land, or the person in lawful possession thereof, owes to persons who come on the land certain affirmative duties of care with respect to activities or conditions on the land. The extent of the duty used to depend on the status of the person who enters on the land. A distinction was made as to the duties owed to three classes of persons: (1) trespassers; (2) licensees; and (3) invitees. A higher degree of care was owed to invitees than to licensees, and the least duty was that owed to a trespasser. However, the California Supreme Court abolished these distinctions, thereby increasing the landowner's liability.[91]

New concept of liability. In the cited case, the court formulated new tests to be applied to the liability of the owner or possessor of land for negligence and want of ordinary care or skill in the management of property. The court ruled that the status of the injured party as a trespasser, licensee, or invitee is not determinative of liability. The court held that actions involving liability of the possessor of land are governed by the Civil Code, which provides that everyone is responsible, not only for the result of one's willful acts, but also for an injury occasioned to another by reason of one's want of ordinary care or skill in the management of one's property.[92]

Test. The court concluded that the proper test to be applied to the liability of the possessor of land for injury to another is whether, in the management of his property, the owner has acted as a reasonable person in view of the probability of injury to others. Although the injured party's status as a trespasser, licensee, or invitee may, in the light of the facts giving rise to such status, have some bearing on the question of liability, the status is not solely determinative.[93]

QUESTIONS

Matching Terms

a.	Easement	**f.**	Nuisance
b.	Encroachment	**g.**	Subjacent
c.	Lateral	**h.**	*Profit à prendre*
d.	Appurtenant	**i.**	License
e.	Right of way	**j.**	Dominant tenement

1. Right to cross or pass over a parcel of land.
2. Land that obtains the benefit of an appurtenant easement.
3. Anything that is offensive and works an injury or harm to property.
4. Support below the surface of a parcel of land.
5. The right to take something from the land of another person.
6. A revocable right to enter upon another person's property.
7. A right to use the land of another for a limited purpose; an interest but not an estate in land.
8. Pertaining to the side.
9. The extension of an improvement onto the land of another person.
10. Belonging to.

True/False

T F 11. Easements and licenses are indistinguishable.

T F 12. Easements may be classified as either affirmative or negative.

T F 13. Easement rights are insurable under a policy of title insurance.

T F 14. Easements may be classified as easements appurtenant or easements in gross.

T F 15. A party wall agreement ordinarily will create reciprocal easements.

T F 16. Easements must be created by express agreement; they cannot be implied.

T F 17. There is an absolute right of a landowner to access to a public street.

T F 18. To acquire an easement by prescription, the claimant must pay real property taxes for the statutory period, but not thereafter.

T F 19. Easements may be either exclusive or nonexclusive.

T F 20. An owner of land is entitled to the lateral and subjacent support that his land receives from adjoining land.

Multiple Choice

21. The lawful term of an easement appurtenant is
    a. 25 years.
    b. 50 years.
    c. 99 years.
    d. There is no time limitation.

22. Encumbrances that affect the physical condition or use of property include which of the following?
    a. Building restrictions.
    b. Zoning requirements.
    c. Encroachments.
    d. All of the above.

23. In the use of real property, a landowner is subject to which of the following limitations?
    a. Police power of the state.
    b. Rights of his neighbor.
    c. Rights of the public.
    d. All of the above.

24. Limitations on the use of real property may also be imposed by such factors as
    a. Easements.
    b. Encroachments.
    c. Access.
    d. Any of the above.

25. Physical limitations in the use of real property may be based on
    a. Contour.
    b. Size and shape.
    c. Location.
    d. Any of the above.

26. The extension of an improvement onto the land of an adjoining owner is referred to as
    a. An abatement.
    b. A redemption.
    c. An encroachment.
    d. A preemption.

27. Thomas used a path across Robert's property for a continuous period of five years without permission. He then claimed an easement upon Robert's property. This is an example of an easement by
    a. Grant or reservation.
    b. Dedication.
    c. Prescription.
    d. Necessity.

28. An easement in gross
    a. Does not benefit any specific parcel of land.
    b. Is a right in another's land.
    c. Is a personal right, not created for the benefit of land owned by the easement holder.
    d. Any of the above.

29. The description of land as "the NW of Sec. 10, T 2 N, R 3 E" is a description by
    a. Express grant.
    b. Implied grant.
    c. Condemnation.
    d. Any of the above.

30. Easements may also be acquired by
    a. Express reservation.

b. Implied reservation.

c. Prescription.

d. Any of the above.

31. Easements may also be acquired by

   a. Dedication.

   b. Abatement.

   c. Unlawful detainer.

   d. Any of the above.

32. The right of a utility company to the use of a strip of land over a number of adjoining parcels is generally regarded as

   a. An encroachment.

   b. An easement in gross.

   c. A lien.

   d. A riparian right.

33. The purchaser of a theater ticket obtains

   a. An easement.

   b. A profit.

   c. A license.

   d. A lien right.

34. The land obtaining the benefit of an easement appurtenant is called the

   a. Dominant tenement.

   b. Servient tenement.

   c. Remainder.

   d. Reversion.

35. The land burdened by an easement is called the

   a. Dominant tenement.

   b. Servient tenement.

   c. Habendum.

   d. Hereditament.

36. When the same person becomes the owner of an appurtenant easement and the owner of the servient tenement, the easement is extinguished by

   a. Estoppel.

   b. Merger.

   c. Attornment.

   d. Subordination.

37. An encroachment is generally described as

   a. An extension of a structure onto the property of an adjoining owner.

   b. An overimprovement of property.

   c. A plottage increment.

   d. All of the above.

38. The height of fences can be limited by

   a. Deed restrictions.

   b. Zoning ordinances.

   c. Agreement between adjoining owners.

   d. Any of the above.

39. If branches of a pear tree extend from an owner's property into the airspace of his neighbor, the latter has the right to

   a. Cut down the tree.

   b. Trim the branches to the property line.

   c. Harvest the crop.

d. Claim the tree as his after five years.

40. Generally, the responsibility for maintenance of a party wall is that of

   a. The city.

   b. Owner on the north or west.

   c. Owner on the north or east.

   d. Both parties.

41. An aviation easement is one created for the benefit of

   a. Small boats.

   b. Kite flying.

   c. Flight of aircraft.

   d. Power lines.

42. Easements may be terminated or extinguished by

   a. Abandonment.

   b. Quitclaim deed.

   c. Merger of estates.

   d. Any of the above.

43. An easement that has been acquired by prescription may be terminated by

   a. Merger of ownership.

   b. Nonuse for five years.

   c. Written agreement.

   d. Any of the above.

44. A permanent easement for light and air may be acquired by

   a. Adverse use for five years.

   b. Prescription.

   c. Oral agreement.

   d. Grant deed.

45. If a person mistakenly builds a home on a lot he doesn't own,

   a. The lot owner obtains ownership of the home.

   b. He is entitled to purchase the lot for a fair price.

   c. He can condemn the land for his use.

   d. He can remove the home under prescribed conditions.

46. The one who has the duty to maintain an easement for ingress and egress is the

   a. Owner of the easement.

   b. Owner of the servient tenement.

   c. City, if land is within city.

   d. County, if land is outside city limits.

47. An easement for storm drain purposes on a recorded subdivision map is an illustration of an easement by

   a. Reservation.

   b. Grant.

   c. Dedication.

   d. Condemnation.

48. The main difference between an easement by prescription and title by adverse possession relates to

a. Continuous use.
   b. Hostile use.
   c. Open and notorious use.
   d. Payment of taxes.

49. An easement by prescription may be acquired by adverse use for the minimum period of
   a. Two years.
   b. Three years.
   c. Four years.
   d. Five years.

50. A community driveway is ordinarily one in favor of
   a. All residents of a city.
   b. Husband and wife exclusively.
   c. Adjoining landowners.
   d. Noncontiguous owners.

NOTES

1. C.C. 805; C.C. 802.
2. County of Alameda v. Ross (1939) 32 C.A.2d 134.
3. This principle was recognized in Stover v. Zucker (1906) 143 C. 516; Cooke v. Ramponi (1952) 38 C.2d 282.
4. For a classic case, *see* Cushman v. Davis (1978) 80 C.A.3d 731.
5. C.C. 801; C.C. 801.5.
6. C.C. 802
7. Wright v. Best (1942) 19 C.2d 368.
8. If it is not an easement, it may be a nuisance. Discussed in §14.55, *et seq.*, Sierra Screw Products v. Azusa Greens, Inc. (1979) 88 C.A.3d 358.
9. In determining the scope of the easement, extrinsic evidence may be used as an aid to interpretation unless such evidence imparts a meaning to which the instrument is not reasonably susceptible. Brechler v. Oregon-Washington Plywood Corp. (1976) 17 C.3d 520.
10. Relovich v. Stuart (1931) 211 C. 422.
11. *See* §14.74, *et seq.*
12. C.C. 1069. Although a grantor may reserve an interest in property to a stranger, that intent must be clearly shown, which may be done by extrinsic evidence. Willard v. First Church of Christ Science (1972) 7 C.3d 473; Continental Baking Co. v. Katz (1968) 68 C.2d 512, 513.
13. Vargas v. Maderos (1923) 191 C.1; Kytasty v. Godwin (1980) 102 C.A.3d 762; but *see* Leonard v. Haydon (1980) 110 C.A.3d 263.
14. C.C. 1104; George v. Goshgarian (1983) 139 C.A.3d 856.
15. Piazza v. Schaefer (1967) 225 C.A.2d 328. No easement by implication or necessity on landlocked real estate once owned by federal government and later transferred to privated owners (Moorce v. Walsh [1995] 38 C.A. 4th 104.
16. Taylor v. Warnaky (1880) 55 C. 350.
17. Daywalt v. Walker (1963) 214 C.A.2d 669. *See also* Lincoln Savings & Loan Assn. v. Rivera Estate Assn. (1970) 7 C.A.3d 449, 459.
18. Tarr v. Watkins (1960) 180 C.A.2d 362; Moorce v. Walsh (1995) 38 C.. 4th 104.
19. *See* C.C. 1006. As to who has the burden of proving a prescriptive easement, the cases are conflicting. McDonald Properties Inc. v. Bel-Air Country Club (1977) 72 C.A.3d 693, 701-702; Jordan v. Worthen (1977) 68 C.A.3d 310, 319. Although perhaps unusual, at least one court has indicated that there is no logical reason why a grantor cannot acquire a prescriptive easement from his or her grantee. McDonald Properties, Inc. v. Bel-Air Country Club, supra, 704. Parties

also have a right to a jury in these types of cases—Arciero Ranches v. Meza (1993) 17 C.A. 4th 114.

20. Silacci v. Abramson (1996) 45 C.A. 4th 558. In one case a *profit à prendre* in growing nut trees was obtained by prescription. In determining the rights of the parties, the court held that the easement holder had the basic right to harvest and retain the annual crops from the trees and, as secondary easements, the right to enter the land at appropriate times to care for the trees during their life span, but not the right to replant any that might die. (Costa v. Fawcett [1962] 202 C.A.2d 695); Cieterich International Truck Sales, Inc. v. J.S.&J. Service Inc. (1994) 3 C.A. 4th 1601.
21. Zimmer v. Dykstra (1974) 39 C.A.3d 422; Otay Water District v. Beckwith (1991) 1 C.A. 4th 1601.
22. Gilardi v. Hallam (1981) 30 C.3d 317; Mesnick v. Caton (1986) 183 C.A. 3d 1248; *see also* Sorensen v. Costa (1948) 3 C.2d 453; Raab v. Casper (1975) 51 C.A.3d 866; Cleary v. Trimble (1964) 229 C.A.2d 1, 11.
23. Jones v. Tierney-Sinclair (1945) 71 C.A.2d 366.
24. Pratt v. Hodgsen (1949) 91 C.A.2d 401.
25. C.C. 813.
26. C.C. 1008; 1009.
27. For a private owner's right to acquire property by condemnation for utilities, *see* C.C. 1001.
28. For a case involving an inverse condemnation action that discussed the possibility of an aviation easement by prescription, *see* Drennan v. County of Ventura (1974) 38 C.A.3d 84.
29. Govt. C. 5105, *et seq.*
30. City of Santa Ana v. Santa Ana Valley Irrigation Co. (1912) 163 C. 211.
31. County of Orange v. Chandler-Sherman Corp. (1976) 54 C.A.3d 561.
32. Richmond Rambling Motorcycle Club v. Western Title Guarantee Co. (1975) 47 C.A.3d 747.
33. C.C. 815.1.
34. C.C. 815.3.
35. C.C. 815.7.
36. This principle is well illustrated in the case of Bradley v. Frazier Park Playgrounds (1952) 110 C.A.2d 436, in which property owners in a subdivision located in a mountainous area just south of Lebec, in Kern County, were held to be entitled to a so-called equitable easement for the use of recreational facilities in a portion of the subdivision.
37. C.C. 806.
38. Youngstown Steel Products Co. v. City of Los Angeles (1952) 38 C.2d 407.
39. C.C. 1104.
40. Kytasty v. Godwin (1980) 102 C.A.3d 762.
41. Faus v. City of Los Angeles (1967) 67 C.2d 350.
42. Bartholomew v. Staheli (1948) 86 C.A.2d 844. This case has been modified. *See* Cushman v. Davis (1978) 80 C.A.3d 731, 736.
43. *See* Jordon v. Worthen (1977) 68 C.A.3d 310; Pipkin v. Der Torasian (1973) 35 C.A.3d 722; Buckler v. Oregon-Washington Plywood Corp. (1976) 19 C.3d 520.
44. C.C. 845.
45. City of Los Angeles v. Ingerrolt Road Co. (1976) 57 C.A.3d 889.
46. *See also* Keeler v. Hoky (1958) 160 C.A.2d 471.
47. C.C. 1044.
48. C.C. 807.
49. C.C. 1084, 1104.
50. C.C. 1214; *see* Pettis v. General Telephone Co. (1967) 66 C.2d 503. This also holds true for a purchase at a trustee's sale. Hamburger & Sons, Inc. v. Lemboeck (1937) 20 C.A.2d 565, 570.
51. C.C. 805.
52. Worthington v. Alcala (1992) 10 C.A. 4th 1404.

53. Glatts v. Henson (1948) 31 C.2d 368; Masin v. Marche (1982) 136 C.A.3d 687.
54. Rothschild v. Wolf (1942) 20 C.2d 17.
55. Walner v. City of Turlock (1964) 230 C.A.2d 399.
56. Crimmons v. Gould (1957) 149 C.A.2d 383; Scruby v. Vintage Grapevine, Inc. (1995) 37 C.A. 4th 697.
57. *See also* Hill v. Allan (1968) 259 C.A. 2d 470.
58. Bertram v. Orlando (1951) 102 C.A.2d 506.
59. C.C.P. 338.2.
60. C.C.P. 871.1, *et seq.; see also* Powell v. Mayo (1981) 123 C.A.3d 994.
61. Raab v. Casper (1975) 51 C.A.3d 866; *see also* Southern Pacific Transp. Co. v. Superior Court (1976) 58 C.A.3d 433.
62. Kafka v. Bozio (1923) 191 C. 746.
63. C.C. 3501; C.C.P. 731.
64. Agmar v. Soloman (1948) 87 C.A. 127.
65. Ukhtomski v. Tioga Mutual Water Co. (1936) 12 C.A.2d 726.
66. C.C. 3479.
67. C.C. 3480.
68. C.C. 3502.
69. C.C. 3503.
70. Lew v. Superior Court (1993) 20 C.A. 4th 866; Mangini v. Aerojet-General Corp. (1994) 26 C.A. 4th 760; McIntosh v. Brimmer (1924) 68 C.A. 770.
71. Baker v. Burbank-Pasadena Airport Authority (1983) 149 C.A.3d 872.
72. Haehlen v. Wilson (1936) 11 C.A.2d 437.
73. Dean v. Powell Undertaking Co. (1921) 55 C.A. 545.
74. Brown v. Arbuckle (1948) 88 C.A.2d 258.
75. C.C. 841.4.
76. C.C. 841.
77. Pen. C. 602(h).
78. C.C. 834.
79. C.C. 833.
80. Booska v. Patel (1994) 24 C.A. 4th 1786; Bonde v. Bishop (1952) 112 C.A.2d 1.
81. Coates v. China (1951) C.A.2d 304.
82. Boarts v. Imperial Irrigation Dist. (1947) 80 C.A.2d 574.
83. The requisites for an agreed boundary are: (1) uncertainty as to the true boundary; (2) agreement between coterminous owners as to the true boundary; (3) acquiescence to the line so fixed for a period equal to the statute of limitations; and (4) boundary so fixed must be identifiable on the ground. Berry v. Sbrogia (1978) 76 C.A.3d 876; Joaquin v. Shiloh Orchards (1978) 84 C.A.3d 192; Bryant v. Blevins (1993) 22 C.A. 4th 574.
84. Freeman v. Bellegarde (1895) 108 C. 179.
85. C.C. 830.
86. C.C.P. 751.50, *et seq.*
87. Keys v. Romley (1966) 64 C.2d 396; Ektelon v. City of San Diego (1988) 200 C.A. 3d 804, 810; Mehdizadeh v. Mincer (1996) 46 C.A. 4th 1296.
88. C.C. 832.
89. Rhodes v. San Mateo Investment Co. (1955) 130 C.A.2d 116.
90. Porter v. City of Los Angeles (1920) 182 C. 515.
91. Rowland v. Christian (1968) 69 C.2d 108.
92. C.C. 1714.
93. *See* Nga Li v. Yellow Cab (1975) 13 C.3d 804, regarding comparative negligence, which was adopted to ameliorate against the inequitable consequences of contributory negligence; but *see* American Motorcycle Assn. v. Superior Court (1978) 20 C.3d 578, wherein joint and severable liability is still in effect. *See also* Harris v. De La Chapelle (1976) 55 C.A.3d 644, as to liability of owners for allowing a hedge to overhang into a street; and Ornelas v. Randolph (1993) 4 C.A. 4th 1095.

15

Leases and the Landlord–Tenant Relationship

422

I. INTRODUCTION

§15.1. In general

The long history of the landlord–tenant relationship covers many situations, ranging from the rental of a furnished room in a private residence, to a single-family residence, to an apartment in a multiple housing development, to a suite of offices in a high-rise office building, to a retail store in a modern shopping center, to an industrial complex, and so on. The relationship can be created orally, as in the case of a month-to-month tenancy. If it is for a period longer than one year, a lease must be in writing to be enforceable.[1]

The law has undergone a number of changes, mostly favoring the tenant or lessee. The relationship between landlord and tenant, particularly with respect to living accommodations, can be an extremely personal one, giving rise to conflicts and misunderstandings. A landlord seeks to maximize his income through minimizing his expenses. The tenant pays rent not only for the right to occupy the premises, but also for quiet possession, goods and services, and a definite quality of housing. As in other areas of the law, when a dispute arises, practical considerations can be more important than strict legal rules in attempting to resolve a controversy.

The purpose of the law is to simplify, clarify, modernize, and revise the law governing landlord–tenant relations. It attempts to balance the bargaining positions of the residential landlord and tenant. It imposes a duty of good faith on both parties to a rental agreement, seeks to eliminate or render unenforceable any unconscionable provisions of leases, and sets forth the obligations of both parties with greater particularity. Rent control bills have likewise been given consideration in some municipalities.[2]

The relationship created under a lease involves the law of property, of contracts, and of torts. The principal types of leases that are used are (1) residential; (2) business and commercial; (3) farm or ranch; and (4) oil and gas leases. California is one of the largest oil-producing states, and the use of oil and gas leases has been widespread in this state. Because they are sometimes encountered in real estate transactions, a brief discussion of oil and gas leases is included in this chapter.

A lease of nonresidential land together with buildings and improvements on the land is usually referred to as a business and commercial lease. Leases of this type are not ordinarily written in contemplation of the lessee constructing new improvements or adding improvements to existing structures. A ground lease includes a lease of vacant land, or improved land upon which existing improvements are to be torn down and new improvements constructed by the lessee. Title to the improvements constructed by the lessee usually belongs to the lessee during the term of the lease but passes to the lessor when the lease is terminated. Such leases are generally referred to as being "net to the lessor" or "triple net." This means that lessee pays for the construction, the cost of repairs and maintenance of the improvements, real estate taxes, and insurance.

§15.2. Relationship between landlord and tenant

The relationship between landlord and tenant arises when there is a hiring of real property. The Civil Code defines a *hiring* as a contract by which one person gives to another the temporary possession and use of property (other than money), for reward (rent), with an agreement that it shall be returned at a future time.[3] The person who lets real property is known as the landlord or lessor, and the person who receives possession of the property is designated the tenant or lessee. The landlord–tenant relationship may exist without a formal lease, and sometimes does when the term is only of short duration—although this often gives rise to costly litigation expenses in the event of a dispute. The landlord's interest is divided into a present and future (reversionary) interest.

§15.3. Nature of a lease

Although the terms *landlord* and *lessor*, or *tenant* and *lessee*, are often used interchangeably without any distinction, in the strict sense the words *lessor* and *lessee* are more properly used to designate the parties to a formal lease. A *lease* is the designation given to the contract by which the possession and profits of land are exchanged for rent. It conveys an interest in the land to the lessee for a period of time, measured by the life of a party or for years or at will. The word *term* designates the time and period of the enjoyment of the estate. *Rent* is the return or compensation for the use of property.

A number of matters affecting the rights of the landlord and the tenant (or lessor and lessee) are normally considered before the parties enter into a lease agreement. Often these matters may be relatively unimportant in the oral, short-term, month-to-month tenancy, but they become increasingly important in the case of written leases for a longer period of time. Some of these matters ordinarily covered even in simple leases are the following:

1. Duration of the lease and any extensions
2. Rent, including any adjustment on renewals
3. Possession, repairs and maintenance, and improvements
4. Liability of the parties for injuries resulting from the condition of the premises
5. Transfer or assignment by the lessee, including approval by the lessor
6. Option to purchase in favor of the lessee
7. Special covenants, conditions, and provisions, such as the rights of the parties in the event of destruction of the premises by fire or other casualty
8. Termination, including notice requirements

There is no such thing as a standard lease, but "forms" of leases are in common use, both as to residential and commercial properties. Figure 15-1 is illustrative of a residential lease. Their formal preparation and analysis, however, should be entrusted to an attorney.

§15.4. Landlord–tenant relationship is based on contract

A tenancy may be created without a formal agreement. A person may become a tenant by mere occupancy with the consent of the owner, such as a tenant at will or a periodic tenant. However, the relationship between landlord and tenant presupposes a contract, express or implied, from which the intention to create the relationship must appear. There must be a permission to occupy, conferring on the lessee a legal estate and the right of possession. The relationship may be created by, or implied from, the promise of the occupant to pay rent and the acceptance of the promise by the owner.

§15.5. Application of fair housing laws

Like any other business establishment, a landlord is subject to the antidiscrimination laws. The California Fair Housing Act, also known as the Rumford Act, and the Unruh Civil Rights Act both apply to the furnishing of housing accommodations. The federal Civil Rights Act of 1968 also applies to the landlord–tenant relationship. A landlord may set up certain requirements for tenants, provided the same requirements and standards are equally applied to everyone.[4] A landlord may not refuse to rent to people with children under many circumstances.[5] However, he may, with some exceptions, refuse to rent to people with pets. He may require a certain income and credit references. However, he must apply the same rules to everyone, regardless of race, religion, age, sex, or national origin. Recent cases have held that a landlord cannot discriminate by applying different financial criteria to married and unmarried couples when renting apartments. If a landlord's religious beliefs dictate that he should not rent to an unmarried couple, he is in violation of the law.[6]

CALIFORNIA
ASSOCIATION
OF REALTORS®

RESIDENTIAL LEASE OR
MONTH-TO-MONTH RENTAL AGREEMENT

_____ ("Landlord") and
_____, ("Tenant") agree as follows:

1. **PROPERTY:**
   A. Landlord rents to Tenant and Tenant rents from Landlord, the real property and improvements described as: _____
   _____ ("Premises").
   B. The following personal property is included: _____
2. **TERM:** The term begins on (date) _____ ("Commencement Date"), **(Check A or B):**
   ☐ **A. Month-to-month:** and continues as a month-to-month tenancy. Either party may terminate the tenancy by giving written notice to the other at least 30 days prior to the intended termination date, subject to any applicable local laws. Such notice may be given on any date.
   ☐ **B. Lease:** and shall terminate on (date) _____ at _____ AM/PM.
   Any holding over after the term of this Agreement expires, with Landlord's consent, shall create a month-to-month tenancy which either party may terminate as specified in paragraph 2A. Rent shall be at a rate equal to the rent for the immediately preceding month, unless otherwise notified by Landlord, payable in advance. All other terms and conditions of this Agreement shall remain in full force and effect.
3. **RENT:**
   A. Tenant agrees to pay rent at the rate of $ _____ per month for the term of the Agreement.
   B. Rent is payable in advance on the **1st (or ☐ _____) day** of each calendar month, and is delinquent on the next day.
   C. If Commencement Date falls on any day other than the first day of the month, rent shall be prorated based on a 30-day period. If Tenant has paid one full month's rent in advance of Commencement Date, rent for the second calendar month shall be prorated based on a 30-day period.
   D. PAYMENT: The rent shall be paid to (name) _____, at (address) _____
   _____, or at any other location specified by Landlord in writing to Tenant.
4. **SECURITY DEPOSIT:**
   A. Tenant agrees to pay $ _____ as a security deposit. Security deposit will be ☐ given to the Owner of the Premises; or ☐ held in Owner's Broker's trust account.
   B. All or any portion of the security deposit may be used, as reasonably necessary, to: (1) cure Tenant's default in payment of rent, Late Charges, NSF fees, or other sums due; (2) repair damage, excluding ordinary wear and tear, caused by Tenant or by a guest or licensee of Tenant; (3) clean Premises, if necessary, upon termination of tenancy; and (4) replace or return personal property or appurtenances. **SECURITY DEPOSIT SHALL NOT BE USED BY TENANT IN LIEU OF PAYMENT OF LAST MONTH'S RENT.** If all or any portion of the security deposit is used during tenancy, Tenant agrees to reinstate the total security deposit within five days after written notice is delivered to Tenant. Within three weeks after Tenant vacates the Premises, Landlord shall (1) furnish Tenant an itemized statement indicating the amount of any security deposit received and the basis for its disposition, and (2) return any remaining portion of security deposit to Tenant.
   C. No interest will be paid on security deposit, unless required by local ordinance.
   D. If security deposit is held by Owner, Tenant agrees not to hold Broker responsible for its return. If security deposit is held in Owner's Broker's trust account, **and** Broker's authority is terminated before expiration of this Agreement, **and** security deposits are released to someone other than Tenant, **then** Broker shall notify Tenant, in writing, where and to whom security deposit has been released. Once Tenant has been provided such notice, Tenant agrees not to hold Broker responsible for security deposit.
5. **MOVE-IN COSTS RECEIVED/DUE:**

Category	Total Due	Payment Received	Balance Due	Date Due
Rent from _____ to _____ (date)				
*Security Deposit				
Other _____				
Other _____				
Total				

*The maximum amount that Landlord may receive as security deposit, however designated, cannot exceed two month's rent for an unfurnished premises, and three month's rent for a furnished premises.

6. **PARKING: (Check A or B)**
   ☐ **A.** Parking is permitted as follows: _____
   The right to parking ☐ is, ☐ is not, included in the rent charged pursuant to paragraph 3. If not included in the rent, the parking rental fee shall be an additional $ _____ per month. Parking space(s) are to be used for parking operable motor vehicles, except for trailers, boats, campers, buses or trucks (other than pick-up trucks). Tenant shall park in assigned space(s) only. Parking space(s) are to be kept clean. Vehicles leaking oil, gas or other motor vehicle fluids shall not be parked on the Premises. Mechanical work or storage of inoperable vehicles is not allowed in parking space(s) or elsewhere on the Premises.
   OR ☐ **B.** Parking is not permitted on the Premises.
7. **STORAGE: (Check A or B)**
   ☐ **A.** Storage is permitted as follows: _____
   The right to storage space ☐ is, ☐ is not, included in the rent charged pursuant to paragraph 3. If not included in rent, storage space shall be an additional $ _____ per month. Tenant shall store only personal property that Tenant owns, and shall not store property that is claimed by another or in which another has any right, title, or interest. Tenant shall not store any improperly packaged food or perishable goods, flammable materials, explosives, or other inherently dangerous material.
   OR ☐ **B.** Storage is not permitted on the Premises.
8. **LATE CHARGE/NSF CHECKS:** Tenant acknowledges that either late payment of rent or issuance of a non-sufficient funds ("NSF") check may cause Landlord to incur costs and expenses, the exact amount of which are extremely difficult and impractical to determine. These costs may include, but are not limited to, processing, enforcement and accounting expenses, and late charges imposed on Landlord. If any installment of rent due from Tenant is not received by Landlord within **5 (or ☐ _____) calendar days** after date due, or if a check is returned NSF, Tenant shall pay to Landlord, respectively, an additional sum of $ _____ as Late Charge and $25.00 as a NSF fee, either or both of which shall be deemed additional rent. Landlord and Tenant agree that these charges represent a fair and reasonable estimate of the costs Landlord may incur by reason of Tenant's late or NSF payment. Any Late Charge or NSF fee due shall be paid with the current installment of rent. Landlord's acceptance of any Late Charge or NSF fee shall not constitute a waiver as to any default of Tenant. Landlord's right to collect a Late Charge or NSF fee shall not be deemed an extension of the date rent is due under paragraph 3, or prevent Landlord from exercising any other rights and remedies under this Agreement, and as provided by law.

Tenant and Landlord acknowledge receipt of copy of this page, which constitutes Page 1 of _____ Pages.
Tenant's Initials (_____) (_____)   Landlord's Initials (_____) (_____)

THIS FORM HAS BEEN APPROVED BY THE CALIFORNIA ASSOCIATION OF REALTORS® (C.A.R.). NO REPRESENTATION IS MADE AS TO THE LEGAL VALIDITY OR ADEQUACY OF ANY PROVISION IN ANY SPECIFIC TRANSACTION. A REAL ESTATE BROKER IS THE PERSON QUALIFIED TO ADVISE ON REAL ESTATE TRANSACTIONS. IF YOU DESIRE LEGAL OR TAX ADVICE, CONSULT AN APPROPRIATE PROFESSIONAL.

The copyright laws of the United States (Title 17 U.S. Code) forbid the unauthorized reproduction of this form, or any portion thereof, by photocopy machine or any other means, including facsimile or computerized formats. Copyright © 1994-1997, CALIFORNIA ASSOCIATION OF REALTORS®, INC. ALL RIGHTS RESERVED.

Published and Distributed by:
REAL ESTATE BUSINESS SERVICES, INC.
a subsidiary of the CALIFORNIA ASSOCIATION OF REALTORS®
525 South Virgil Avenue, Los Angeles, California 90020

OFFICE USE ONLY
Reviewed by Broker
or Designee _____
Date _____

EQUAL HOUSING
OPPORTUNITY

RESIDENTIAL LEASE OR MONTH-TO-MONTH RENTAL AGREEMENT (LR-14 PAGE 1 OF 3) REVISED 10/97

FIGURE 15-1
A residential lease.

Premises: _____ Date _____

9. **CONDITION OF PREMISES:** Tenant has examined Premises, all furniture, furnishings, appliances and landscaping, if any, and fixtures, including smoke detector(s).
(Check one:)
- ☐ **A.** Tenant acknowledges that these items are clean and in operative condition, with the following exceptions _____
- OR ☐ **B.** Tenant's acknowledgement of the condition of these items is contained in an attached statement of condition, (such as C.A.R.'s MIMO-11).
- OR ☐ **C.** Tenant will provide Landlord a list of items which are damaged or not in operable condition within **3 (or ☐ _____) days after** Commencement Date, not as a contingency of this Agreement but rather as an acknowledgement of the condition of the Premises.
- OR ☐ **D.** Other: _____

10. **NEIGHBORHOOD CONDITIONS:** Tenant is advised to satisfy him or herself as to neighborhood or area conditions, including schools, proximity and adequacy of law enforcement, crime statistics, registered felons or offenders, fire protection, other governmental services, proximity to commercial, industrial or agricultural activities, existing and proposed transportation, construction and development which may affect noise, view, or traffic, airport noise, noise or odor from any source, wild and domestic animals, other nuisances, hazards, or circumstances, facilities and condition of common areas, conditions and influences of significance to certain cultures and/or religions, and personal needs, requirements and preferences of Tenant.

11. **UTILITIES:** Tenant agrees to pay for all utilities and services, and the following charges: _____
except _____ , which shall be paid for by Landlord. If any utilities are not separately metered, Tenant shall pay Tenant's proportional share, as reasonably determined by Landlord.

12. **OCCUPANTS:** The Premises are for the sole use as a personal residence by the following named persons **only:** _____

13. **PETS:** No animal or pet shall be kept on or about the Premises without Landlord's prior written consent, except _____

14. **RULES/REGULATIONS:** Tenant agrees to comply with all rules and regulations of Landlord which are at any time posted on the Premises or delivered to Tenant. Tenant shall not, and shall ensure that guests and licensees of Tenant shall not, disturb, annoy, endanger, or interfere with other tenants of the building or neighbors, or use the Premises for any unlawful purposes, including, but not limited to, using, manufacturing, selling, storing, or transporting illicit drugs or other contraband, or violate any law or ordinance, or commit a waste or nuisance on or about the Premises.

15. **CONDOMINIUM/PLANNED UNIT DEVELOPMENT:** ☐ (If checked) The Premises is a unit in a condominium, planned unit, or other development governed by an owner's association. The name of the owner's association is _____
Tenant agrees to comply with all covenants, conditions and restrictions, by-laws, rules and regulations and decisions of owner's association. Landlord shall provide Tenant copies of rules and regulations, if any. Tenant shall reimburse Landlord for any fines or charges imposed by owner's association or other authorities, due to any violation by Tenant, or the guests or licensees of Tenant.

16. **MAINTENANCE:**
A. Tenant shall properly use, operate, and safeguard Premises, including if applicable, any landscaping, furniture, furnishings, and appliances, and all mechanical, electrical, gas and plumbing fixtures, and keep them clean and sanitary. Tenant shall immediately notify Landlord, in writing, of any problem, malfunction or damage. Tenant shall pay for all repairs or replacements caused by Tenant, or guests or invitees of Tenant, excluding ordinary wear and tear. Tenant shall pay for all damage to Premises as a result of failure to report a problem in a timely manner. Tenant shall pay for repair of drain blockages or stoppages, unless caused by defective plumbing parts or tree roots invading sewer lines.
B. ☐ Landlord, ☐ Tenant, shall water the garden, landscaping, trees and shrubs, except _____

17. **ALTERATIONS:** Tenant shall not make any alterations in or about the Premises, without Landlord's prior written consent, including: painting, wallpapering, adding or changing locks, installing antenna or satellite dish, placing signs, displays or exhibits, or using screws, fastening devices, large nails or adhesive materials.

18. **KEYS/LOCKS:**
A. Tenant acknowledges receipt of (or Tenant will receive ☐ prior to the Commencement Date, or ☐ _____):
- ☐ _____ key(s) to Premises,
- ☐ _____ key(s) to mailbox,
- ☐ _____ key(s) to common area(s),
- ☐ _____ remote control device(s) for garage door/gate opener(s).
- ☐ _____
- ☐ _____
B. Tenant acknowledges that locks to the Premises ☐ have, ☐ have not, been re-keyed.
C. If Tenant re-keys existing locks or opening devices, Tenant shall immediately deliver copies of all keys to Landlord. Tenant shall pay all costs and charges related to loss of any keys or opening devices. Tenant may not remove locks, even if installed by Tenant.

19. **ENTRY:** Tenant shall make Premises available to Landlord or representative for the purpose of entering to make necessary or agreed repairs, decorations, alterations, or improvements, or to supply necessary or agreed services, or to show Premises to prospective or actual purchasers, tenants, mortgagees, lenders, appraisers, or contractors. Landlord and Tenant agree that twenty-four hours notice (oral or written) shall be reasonable and sufficient notice. In an emergency, Landlord or representative may enter Premises at any time without prior notice.

20. **SIGNS:** Tenant authorizes Landlord to place For Sale/Lease signs on the Premises.

21. **ASSIGNMENT/SUBLETTING:** Tenant shall not sublet all or any part of Premises, or assign or transfer this Agreement or any interest in it, without prior written consent of Landlord. Unless such consent is obtained, any assignment, transfer or subletting of Premises or this Agreement or tenancy, by voluntary act of Tenant, operation of law, or otherwise, shall be null and void, and, at the option of Landlord, terminate this Agreement. Any proposed assignee, transferee or sublessee shall submit to Landlord an application and credit information for Landlord's approval, and, if approved, sign a separate written agreement with Landlord and Tenant. Landlord's consent to any one assignment, transfer, or sublease, shall not be construed as consent to any subsequent assignment, transfer or sublease, and does not release Tenant of Tenant's obligation under this Agreement.

22. ☐ **LEAD PAINT (CHECK IF APPLICABLE):** Premises was constructed prior to 1978. In accordance with federal law, Landlord gives, and Tenant acknowledges receipt of, the disclosures on the attached form (such as C.A.R. Form FLD-14) and a federally approved lead pamphlet.

23. **POSSESSION:** If Landlord is unable to deliver possession of Premises on Commencement Date, such Date shall be extended to date on which possession is made available to Tenant. If Landlord is unable to deliver possession within **5 (or ☐ _____) calendar days** after agreed Commencement Date, Tenant may terminate this Agreement by giving written notice to Landlord, and shall be refunded all rent and security deposit paid.

24. **TENANT'S OBLIGATIONS UPON VACATING PREMISES:** Upon termination of Agreement, Tenant shall: (a) give Landlord all copies of all keys or opening devices to Premises, including any common areas; (b) vacate Premises and surrender it to Landlord empty of all persons; (c) vacate any/all parking and/or storage space; (d) deliver Premises to Landlord in the same condition as referenced in paragraph 9; (e) clean Premises, including professional cleaning of carpet and drapes; (f) give written notice to Landlord of Tenant's forwarding address, and (g) _____

_____
All improvements installed by Tenant, with or without Landlord's consent, become the property of Landlord upon termination.

25. **BREACH OF CONTRACT/EARLY TERMINATION:** In addition to any obligations established by paragraph 24, in event of termination by Tenant prior to completion of the original term of Agreement, Tenant shall also be responsible for lost rent, rental commissions, advertising expenses, and painting costs necessary to ready Premises for re-rental.

26. **TEMPORARY RELOCATION:** Tenant agrees, upon demand of Landlord, to temporarily vacate Premises for a reasonable period, to allow for fumigation, or other methods, to control wood destroying pests or organisms, or other repairs to Premises. Tenant agrees to comply with all instructions and requirements necessary to prepare Premises to accommodate pest control, fumigation or other work, including bagging or storage of food and medicine, and removal of perishables and valuables. Tenant shall only be entitled to a credit of rent equal to the per diem rent for the period of time Tenant is required to vacate Premises.

27. **DAMAGE TO PREMISES:** If, by no fault of Tenant, Premises are totally or partially damaged or destroyed by fire, earthquake, accident or other casualty, which render Premises uninhabitable, either Landlord or Tenant may terminate Agreement by giving the other written notice. Rent shall be abated as of date of damage. The abated amount shall be the current monthly rent prorated on a 30-day basis. If Agreement is not terminated, Landlord shall promptly repair the damage, and rent shall be reduced based on the extent to which the damage interferes with Tenant's reasonable use of Premises. If damage occurs as a result of an act of Tenant or Tenant's guests, only Landlord shall have the right of termination, and no reduction in rent shall be made.

Tenant and Landlord acknowledge receipt of copy of this page, which constitutes Page 2 of _____ Pages.
Tenant's Initials (_____) (_____) Landlord's Initials (_____) (_____)

OFFICE USE ONLY
Reviewed by Broker
or Designee _____
Date _____

EQUAL HOUSING OPPORTUNITY

RESIDENTIAL LEASE OR MONTH-TO-MONTH RENTAL AGREEMENT (LR-14 PAGE 2 OF 3) REVISED 10/97

FIGURE 15-1 (*Cont.*)
A residential lease.

28. **INSURANCE:** Tenant's personal property and vehicles are not insured by Landlord or, if applicable, owner's association, against loss or damage due to fire, theft, vandalism, rain, water, criminal or negligent acts of others, or any other cause. Tenant is to carry Tenant's own insurance (Renter's Insurance) to protect Tenant from any such loss.

29. **WATERBEDS:** Tenant shall not use or have waterbeds on the Premises unless: (a) Tenant obtains a valid waterbed insurance policy; (b) Tenant increases the security deposit in an amount equal to one-half of one month's rent; and (c) the bed conforms to the floor load capacity of Premises.

30. **WAIVER:** The waiver of any breach shall not be construed as a continuing waiver of the same or any subsequent breach.

31. **NOTICE:** Notices may be served at the following address, or at any other location subsequently designated:
    Landlord: _____   Tenant: _____
    _____   _____
    _____   _____

32. **TENANCY STATEMENT (ESTOPPEL CERTIFICATE):** Tenant shall execute and return a tenancy statement (estoppel certificate) delivered to Tenant by Landlord or Landlord's agent within 3 days after its receipt. The tenancy statement acknowledges that this Agreement is unmodified and in full force, or in full force as modified, and states the modifications. Failure to comply with this requirement shall be deemed Tenant's acknowledgment that the tenancy statement is true and correct, and may be relied upon by a lender or purchaser.

33. **JOINT AND INDIVIDUAL OBLIGATIONS:** If there is more than one Tenant, each one shall be individually and completely responsible for the performance of all obligations of Tenant under this Agreement, jointly with every other Tenant, and individually, whether or not in possession.

34. ☐ **MILITARY ORDNANCE DISCLOSURE:** (If applicable and known to Landlord) Premises is located within one mile of an area once used for military training, and which may contain potentially explosive munitions.

35. **TENANT REPRESENTATIONS; CREDIT:** Tenant warrants that all statements in Tenant's rental application are accurate. Tenant authorizes Landlord and Broker(s) to obtain Tenant's credit report at time of application and periodically during tenancy in connection with approval, modification, or enforcement of this Agreement. Landlord may cancel this Agreement, (a) before occupancy begins, upon disapproval of the credit report(s), or (b) at any time, upon discovering that information in Tenant's application is false. A negative credit report reflecting on Tenant's record may be submitted to a credit reporting agency if Tenant fails to fulfill the terms of payment and other obligations under this Agreement.

36. **OTHER TERMS AND CONDITIONS/SUPPLEMENTS:** _____
    _____
    _____
    The following ATTACHED supplements are incorporated in this Agreement: _____

37. **ATTORNEY'S FEES:** In any action or proceeding arising out of this Agreement, the prevailing party between Landlord and Tenant shall be entitled to reasonable attorney's fees and costs.

38. **ENTIRE CONTRACT:** Time is of the essence. All prior agreements between Landlord and Tenant are incorporated in this Agreement which constitutes the entire contract. It is intended as a final expression of the parties' agreement, and may not be contradicted by evidence of any prior agreement or contemporaneous oral agreement. The parties further intend that this Agreement constitutes the complete and exclusive statement of its terms, and that no extrinsic evidence whatsoever may be introduced in any judicial or other proceeding, if any, involving this Agreement. Any provision of this Agreement which is held to be invalid shall not affect the validity or enforceability of any other provision in this Agreement.

39. **AGENCY:**

    A. **Confirmation:** The following agency relationship(s) are hereby confirmed for this transaction:
       Listing Agent: (Print firm name) _____ is the agent of
       (check one): ☐ the Landlord exclusively; or ☐ both the Landlord and Tenant.
       Leasing Agent: (Print firm name) _____ (if not same as Listing Agent) is the agent of
       (check one): ☐ the Tenant exclusively; or ☐ the Landlord exclusively; or ☐ both the Tenant and Landlord.

    B. **Disclosure:** ☐ (If checked): The term of this lease exceeds one year. An agency disclosure form has been provided to Landlord and Tenant, who each acknowledge its receipt.

40. ☐ **INTERPRETER/TRANSLATOR:** The terms of this Agreement have been interpreted/translated for Tenant into the following language: _____. Interpretation/translation service has been provided by (print name) _____, who has the following Driver's License or other identification number: _____. Tenant has been advised to rely on, and has in fact solely relied on the interpretation/translation services of the above-named individual, and not on the Landlord or other person involved in negotiating the Agreement. If the Agreement has been negotiated primarily in Spanish, Tenant has been provided a Spanish language translation of this Agreement pursuant to California Civil Code. (C.A.R. Form LR-14-S fulfills this requirement.)

    Signature of interpreter/translator _____   Date _____

> Landlord and Tenant acknowledge and agree that Brokers: (a) Do not guarantee the condition of the Premises; (b) Cannot verify representations made by others; (c) Cannot provide legal or tax advice; (d) Will not provide other advice or information that exceeds the knowledge, education or experience required to obtain a real estate license. Furthermore, if Brokers are not also acting as Landlord in this Agreement, Brokers (e) Do not decide what rental rate a Tenant should pay or Landlord should accept; and (f) Do not decide upon the length or other terms of tenancy. Landlord and Tenant agree that they will seek legal, tax, insurance, and other desired assistance from appropriate professionals.

Tenant _____   Date _____
Tenant _____   Date _____
Landlord _____   Date _____
(owner or agent with authority to enter into this lease)

Landlord _____   Date _____
(owner or agent with authority to enter into this lease)

Agency relationships are confirmed as above. Real estate brokers who are not also Landlord in this Agreement are not a party to the Agreement between Landlord and Tenant.

Real Estate Broker _____   By _____   Date _____
(Leasing Firm Name)
Address _____   Telephone _____   Fax _____
Real Estate Broker _____   By _____   Date _____
(Listing Firm Name)
Address _____   Telephone _____   Fax _____

This form is available for use by the entire real estate industry. It is not intended to identify the user as a REALTOR®. REALTOR® is a registered collective membership mark which may be used only by members of the NATIONAL ASSOCIATION OF REALTORS® who subscribe to its Code of Ethics.

Page 3 of _____ Pages.

OFFICE USE ONLY
Reviewed by Broker
or Designee _____
Date _____

RESIDENTIAL LEASE OR MONTH-TO-MONTH RENTAL AGREEMENT (LR-14 PAGE 3 OF 3) REVISED 10/97

FIGURE 15-1 (Cont.)
A residential lease.

In 1976 the California Supreme Court stated that a landlord, subject to notice requirements, may normally terminate a tenancy for any reason or for no reason at all, but may not terminate for an improper reason.[7] Other cases have determined that a tenant cannot be evicted because of race.[8] As to violations of the Unruh Act, all arbitrary discrimination is prohibited including rejecting a tenant for long hair[9] or for being a homosexual.[10]

The Attorney General has determined that an apartment could justifiably be established to serve the elderly.[11] On the other hand, it probably would be arbitrary if denial were based on occupational or marital status. A termination of tenancy or refusal to rent housing based *solely* on the tenant applicant's eligibility for and receipt of public assistance benefits would be arbitrary discrimination and thus prohibited under the Unruh Act. But reasonable requirements for establishing a prospective tenant's ability to pay rent would appear to be proper under the act.

Recent legislation states that it is a denial of equal housing to refuse to rent to the blind or deaf or physically handicapped on the basis that the person is dependent on a guide dog.[12] However, a person who has a right to be accompanied by a dog is liable for any damage done to the premises by that person's dog. Further, there can be no denial of housing on the basis that the person is dependent upon the income of the spouse if the spouse is a party to the agreement. However, the landlord can still consider the financial status of the person and his or her spouse. If a landlord discriminates without a valid reason, the landlord is liable for each such offense for the actual damages and for any amount that may be determined by a jury, or the court sitting without a jury, up to a maximum of three times the amount of actual damages but in no case less than $250, and in addition such attorney's fees as may be determined by the court.[13]

I. TYPES OF TENANCIES

§15.6. Tenancy at sufferance

Although not a trespasser, a tenant at sufferance lacks some of the protection afforded other classes of tenants. The relationship is not by express consent of the landlord, but arises by implication; hence, the difference in the rights of the tenant. A tenant at sufferance is one who goes into possession lawfully, but whose right to remain in possession has expired, such as a tenant holding over after the expiration of a lease, or a tenant at will whose right to possession has expired by virtue of the death of the landlord.

Status of tenant at sufferance. Technically, a tenant at sufferance is not a tenant of anyone, but is an occupant against the reversioner; the phrase is used merely for convenience. A tenant at sufferance is nevertheless entitled to notice before ejection by the owner, and is liable for the reasonable value of the use and occupation of the property until the tenancy is terminated. If the owner of the property elects to treat him as a tenant, as by accepting rent at the rate previously paid during the term, the tenancy at sufferance ceases and the occupant becomes a tenant at will or a periodic tenant.

§15.7. Tenancy at will

A *tenancy at will* is created by agreement of the parties but has no fixed term and is terminable at the will of either party. Tenancies at will are now uncommon because of their conversion to periodic tenancies through acceptance of periodic rents.[14] Although the tenancy is terminable at the will of either party, both landlord and tenant are required to give 30 days' notice.[15]

Creation of tenancy at will. A tenancy at will is created when a person goes into possession with the consent of the owner to remain for a specified purpose without payment of rent, or when a tenant enters, with permission of the landlord, under an invalid lease or contract.

EXAMPLES

1. In one case, the court pointed out that a person who enters on land by permission of the owner under a void parol contract, or a void lease, or pending negotiations for a written lease, is a tenant at will. A tenant at will has no transferable interest, and an attempted assignment will terminate the tenancy. On acceptance of a periodic rental by the owner of the property, the tenant at will becomes a periodic tenant.[16]

2. In another case, a contract for the sale of real property provided that the purchaser should give the seller "free and full use of the premises from the time of passage of title until the last day specified in a written notice to move" given by the purchaser, and that there should be a 90-day written notice to move. It was held that such agreement should be construed as a tenancy at will, terminable on condition subsequent.[17]

§15.8. Periodic tenancy

A periodic tenancy is created by the parties to continue for successive periods of the same length, unless terminated sooner by notice. Examples are tenancies from year to year and tenancies from month to month. This type of tenancy does not terminate by mere lapse of time. It is deemed to be renewed at the end of each of the periods by which the payment of rent is determined, unless terminated by notice.

Tenancy may be created by implication. A *periodic tenancy* may be created by implication when a tenant under a lease for a fixed term holds over after expiration of the term, and pays rent periodically thereafter. In such a case, the tenancy is not renewed for a term equal to the term of the original lease, but a periodic tenancy is created, either from month to month or from year to year, whichever mode of payment of rent is adopted. It is presumed in such cases that the parties have renewed the hiring on the same terms and for the same time, not exceeding one month when the rent is payable monthly, and in any case not exceeding one year.[18]

Tenancy for an indefinite period. A tenancy for an indefinite period under which the rent is payable or is paid monthly is a tenancy from month to month. A tenancy of property other than a lodging or dwelling house, in the absence of contrary local usage, and unless a contrary intention is expressed in writing, is presumed to be a month-to-month tenancy. In the case of property used for agricultural or grazing purposes, the tenancy is presumed to be for one year.[19] When the possession under such a tenancy is continued beyond the year and rent is accepted monthly, the hiring is presumed to have been continued on a month-to-month basis on the same terms as before. A hiring of lodgings or a dwelling house for an unspecified length of time is presumed to be for such period as the parties adopt for the estimation of rent. Thus, a hiring at a monthly rate of rent is presumed to be for one month, and a hiring at a weekly rate is presumed to be for one week. In the absence of an agreement respecting the length of time or the rent, the hiring is presumed to be monthly.[20]

§15.9. Tenancy for a fixed term (estate for years)

A *tenancy for a fixed term* is the most common type of leasehold estate in commercial properties. Such an interest is possessed by a tenant having the right to the exclusive possession for a fixed period, whether for more or less than one year. The estate is often referred to as an estate for years, although as long as the period is definite, it may be for years, for a single year, or for a fixed period shorter than a year for example, for a specified month, specified weeks, or even for a specified day, as in the case of the rental of an auditorium for a concert, a lecture, or other specified event.

III. NATURE AND DURATION OF A LEASE

§15.10. In general

A *lease*, as it pertains to real property, is a *grant* or *conveyance* by the owner of an estate to another person of a portion of his interest therein for a term less than his own. It is also a contract in which temporary possession is given up in exchange for rent. On breach of any covenant contained in the lease the injured party has a right of action the same as he has with respect to other contracts.

§15.11. Two sets of rights

A lease has two sets of rights and obligations, one comprising those growing out of the relation between landlord and tenant and based on *privity of estate*, and the other comprising those growing out of the express stipulations of the lease and based on *privity of contract*.

§15.12. Reversionary interest

It is essential to the relationship between landlord and tenant, whether created by lease or otherwise, that the occupancy of the tenant be in subordination of the rights of the landlord, and that a *reversionary interest*, referred to as the reversion, remain in the landlord.

§15.13. Nature of estate

The interest or estate of the lessee under a lease is called a leasehold or leasehold estate. Leases for a definite period are considered to be personal property and classified as a *chattel real*,[21] whereas an oil and gas lease for an indefinite period is regarded as *real property*.[22]

§15.14. Statutory restrictions on term of lease

At common law, there was no limitation of the term for which a leasehold estate could be created. Whether the fixed term was for one year or for 500 years, the interest created was considered to be personal property and legally inferior to a life estate or other freehold estate. The incongruity of a lease for 500 years being less as a matter of law than a life estate led to the enactment at an early date of a statute in Massachusetts that converted every lease for 100 years or more into a fee simple ownership. Several states, including California, now have statutes providing that a lease for a term longer than 99 years is invalid.

§15.15. Duration of estates

There are several limitations on the duration of leasehold estates in California. Land for agricultural and horticultural purposes cannot be leased for a term in excess of 51 years.[23] Town or city lots may not be leased for a period in excess of 99 years.[24] A lease of a city lot for a permissible term, but with an option for renewal that, if exercised, would extend the lease beyond the term allowed, has been held to violate the statute.[25]

EXAMPLE In one case, the court held invalid a 15-year lease of agricultural lands containing an option to extend the same indefinitely for additional terms of one year each.[26]

---

§15.16. Leases for mineral production

A lease of land for the purpose of effecting the production of oil, gas, or other minerals from other parcels may be made for a period certain or determinable by any future event prescribed by the parties, but no such lease is enforceable after 99 years from the commencement of the term thereof,[27] which also covers drill site agreements, usually encompassing slant drilling.

§15.17. Government leases

With respect to leases by government bodies, there are various limitations on the permitted terms. The statutes must be examined to determine the particular limitation that applies, as to both the purpose of the lease and the lawful term. In the case of chartered cities, the provisions of the charter must also be examined to determine the authority of the city to enter into a lease. Statutory provisions limiting the lawful term of a lease of city property include limitations of 55 years for general purposes, with other periods permitted for certain designated purposes, such as 99 years for recreational purposes, 66 years for tide and submerged lands for waterfront and harbor development, and 35 years for mineral leases.

IV. REQUISITES OF A VALID LEASE

§15.18. In general

A lease for a term exceeding one year must (1) be in writing; (2) contain the names of the parties who must be competent to enter into a contract; (3) include a sufficient description of the property leased; (4) contain an agreement for the rental to be paid, and the time and manner of such payment; and (5) state the term of the lease. As in the case of all contracts, there must also be a meeting of the minds, that is, *mutual assent* of the parties to the creation of a binding lease, and a *consideration*, which is usually the undertaking to pay rent. The rent may consist of a fixed rental, a percentage of the business done by the lessee, or a combination of both a fixed rental and a percentage.

It is required by statute that an estate in real property, other than an estate at will or for a term not exceeding one year, may be *transferred* only by operation of law or by an instrument in writing signed by the lessor or his agent having written authorization.[28] Statutes also provide that an agreement to lease for longer than one year is invalid unless in writing and signed by the party sought to be charged.[29] This section has been construed to require that a one-year lease to commence at a future date must be in writing. An oral lease for one year to commence one day after the agreement is made has been held to be invalid. But there are conflicting cases as to whether the Statute of Frauds applies to leases of a year or longer if there is a provision for early termination.[30]

§15.19. Operative words

Leases should contain operative words, such as *let*, *lease*, or *demise*, expressed in the present tense, but otherwise no particular form of words is necessary. An agreement whereby one party obtains the right of enjoyment of the property of another, with the latter's consent and in subordination to his right, may create the relation of landlord and tenant.

§15.20. Description of premises

The requirement that a deed must describe the premises with certainty applies equally to leases. A street address may meet minimum requirements in many cases, but a careful draftsman will also describe the premises by a sufficient legal description. This requirement is of particular importance if a parking lot adjacent to a restaurant or store is involved. In such case, the use of a street address alone should be avoided. When only part of a building other than an entire floor is being leased, blueprints or other suitable sketches attached as exhibits to the lease may be used to show the exact space to be leased.

§15.21. Status of parties

In the preparation of a lease, it is important to have not only the correct names of the lessor and lessee, but also an accurate statement in the lease of the capacities of the parties and the nature of the equities. The marital status of the parties is of particular concern. Under the provisions of the Family Code, both spouses must join in executing any instrument by which community property is leased for a longer period than one year.[31]

§15.22. Parties acting in a representative capacity

If either party to a lease is acting in a representative or fiduciary capacity, the power to act should be determined by both parties; as to the one, to avoid breach of implied warranty of authority, and as to the other, to make certain of a valid lease. In the case of a trustee, the power to lease is not necessarily implied from the power to sell or the power to dispose of land. However, even though the trust instrument does not expressly authorize a lease, such power is sometimes regarded as implied from the purpose of the trust or as justified by the trustee's duty to keep the land productive. For title insurance purposes, though, the power to lease must be specifically conferred, or appropriate proceedings undertaken to raise a power or to determine that such power exists.

§15.23. Leases beyond term of a trust

The Probate Code provides that a lease for a reasonable period is not impaired by termination of the trust when (1) the term of the trust is of uncertain or indefinite duration, or is terminable at the death of one or more persons; (2) the trustee has power to lease; and (3) the instrument creating the trust contains no provision to the contrary.[32] In the case of a testamentary trust, an order of the probate court is required to establish the reasonableness of the term of such lease.

§15.24. Signature of parties

It is essential that the lessor sign the lease, but the lessee need not sign provided he accepts the lease and acts thereunder. Taking possession and paying rent is sufficient evidence of acceptance by the lessee. It is, of course, better practice to require the lessee's signature, to be certain that he or she will be bound under the covenants contained in the lease, for example, recovery of attorney's fees in the event of default by the lessee.

§15.25. Execution and delivery of lease

Like a *deed*, a *lease*, to be operative, must be executed by the lessor and delivered to the lessee. The instrument must pass into the control of the lessee to constitute an effective delivery. Under some circumstances, acceptance of the leased premises by the lessee may be regarded as delivery.

§15.26. Recordation

If the lease is to be recorded, it must be acknowledged by the lessor. It is sometimes the practice of lessees, particularly under oil and gas leases, to record a so-called short form of lease (or Memorandum of Lease) in lieu of the original lease with its many terms, conditions, and provisions, and to incorporate the terms and conditions of the unrecorded lease by reference. Such a *short-form lease* should give the names of the lessor and lessee, contain the necessary words to create a lease, and include a description of the property leased. If the short-form lease includes a provision that it is made

> *subject to the terms, conditions and provisions of that certain unrecorded instrument between the parties hereto, dated _____ ,*

it may be considered sufficient without the necessity of setting forth any other provisions of the lease, including the term and rental.

It has been found that many of the recorded short forms are deficient for title insurance purposes because they don't have present operative words of conveyance. Nonetheless, even though they are not insurable, they are sufficient to disclose the existence of an unrecorded lease.

§15.27. Extension and renewal

The Civil Code provides that printed lease provisions for automatic renewal or extension of a residence lease (if the lessee remains in possession after the expiration of the lease, or fails to give notice of intention not to renew or extend the lease) are required to be in at least eight-point bold type, otherwise such a provision is voidable by the party who did not prepare the lease.[33] There must also be reference to such provisions in eight-point bold type above the place for the lessee's signature. This requirement is similar to the requirements concerning the printing of certain types of subordination agreements, and is intended to protect a party from hidden clauses in printed document forms.

§15.28. Alteration of the lease

Any *alteration of the lease* must be in writing. The lease cannot be changed by mutual oral agreement, unless these agreements have been fully performed and thereby become an executed modification of the lease.

EXAMPLE In one case it was held that when the lessor accepts monthly rental payments less than called for by a written lease, in accordance with an oral agreement between the parties reducing rental, such payments constitute an executed oral agreement, but as to monthly payments subsequently due and unpaid, the oral agreement is not executed and the lessor is entitled to the amount named in the written lease.[34]

§15.29. Restrictive covenants

Under the provisions of the Civil Code, a lessor may covenant not to use land contiguous to leased property contrary to the terms of the lease (*negative covenant*). This agreement is binding on the lessor's successors in interest when, among other things, the lease is recorded. Frequently, only a memorandum of the lease is recorded which may not contain a description of the contiguous property. The Code also requires that the recorded lease include a description of any contiguous land described in an unrecorded instrument incorporated by reference in the lease.[35]

Under the provisions of the Civil Code relating to *affirmative covenants* (covenants of a lessor to do any act or acts on other real property that is owned by the lessor and is contiguous to the leased property), the recorded lease, for the covenants to bind successive owners, must include a description of the contiguous land described in any unrecorded instrument incorporated by reference in the lease.[36]

§15.30. Change in terms

The landlord is required to give the tenant 30 days' written notice of the change in terms if the rental period is for one month or less; or not less than seven days' notice if the parties agree, in writing, at the time of entering into such agreement.[37]

V. INTERPRETATION OF PARTICULAR LEASE PROVISIONS

§15.31. In general

The provisions of a lease must be construed according to the intent of the parties, which is gathered from the language of the lease and in accordance with the general rules of interpretation of contracts. To show the intention of the parties, it is often advisable to include a statement in the preamble to the document reciting that fact. For purposes of discussion in this chapter, the word *lease* likewise refers to and means *rental agreement*, whether month to month or otherwise.

§15.32. Rights of possession

When a tenant's term commences, he succeeds to all the rights of the landlord with respect to possession and enjoyment of the premises, unless special reservations are made. As a general rule, everything that belongs to the demised premises or is used with or appurtenant to them, and is reasonably essential to their enjoyment, passes as incident to them unless specifically reserved. In that event, the landlord does not have the right to enter the premises unless specified in the agreement or in emergency situations. Recent legislation sanctions entry by a landlord only under specified circumstances, e.g., in an emergency or when the tenant has abandoned the premises.[38] In all other instances (making repairs, showing the premises to prospective purchasers, tenants, or workmen), 24 hours' notice must be given the tenant.

§15.33. Use of premises

Unless restricted by agreement or zoning, the tenant can make use of the premises for any lawful purpose for which they were let, or for any purpose not materially different from that for which they are usually employed or adapted.[39] Under this rule, the tenant of a building or part thereof for business purposes has the exclusive right, in the absence of an agreement providing otherwise, to use for advertising purposes that portion of the outside walls included in the rental agreement, and may enjoin others from interfering with that right. If, in the use of the premises, certain designated tenants commit waste, they are liable to the landlord, and treble damages may be awarded.[40]

In connection with the use of the premises, a tenant may desire to make installations for his comfort or convenience that could fall into the category of fixtures. He should cover the subject by agreement with the landlord, otherwise the fixtures might be claimed by the owner of the land.[41]

§15.34. Payment of rent landlord's lien

Rent is payable at the *termination* of the successive periods of the holding either weekly, monthly, or yearly, as the case may be in the absence of usage or an agreement to the contrary. Generally, a landlord does not have a lien for the rent, unless provided for by agreement. However, keepers of furnished and unfurnished houses and apartments, innkeepers, hotel and motel proprietors, and keepers of boarding houses, lodging houses, and bungalow courts have statutory liens on the baggage and other property of the tenant or lodger for rents and charges. Certain items of property are exempt, which encompasses most of a tenant's furniture and furnishings.[42] Also, before a tenant's property can be sold, he or she must be notified and have the opportunity to present a defense.[43]

§15.35. Deposits or other security

It is common practice in the preparation of leases to require a *security deposit* or to provide for advance rental payments of a sufficient amount to ensure compensation in the event the lessor is unable to collect from the tenant. The agreement may specify the purpose of the deposit: (1) security for default in payment of rent, including costs of recovery of possession and for repairing damages; (2) return of keys; and (3) cleaning the premises.[44]

Four categories. The common characterization of all such payments as "security deposits" is often misleading.[45] In the past, the courts have broken down such deposits or advance payments into four categories, as follows: (1) advance payment of rent, usually for the last month of the term; (2) payment that is expressly stipulated to be a bonus or consideration for the execution of the lease; (3) payment of an amount as liquidated damages; and (4) payment as a deposit to secure faithful performance of the terms of the lease. If the deposit under the lease falls within the first three classes, it is invalid as such and may be able to be recovered by the lessee.[46] If it falls within the fourth class, it may be retained by the lessor only to the extent of the amount of damages actually suffered by him.[47]

Liquidated damages. When a lease contains a provision for liquidated damages in the event of a breach, such provision is valid only if it complies with certain requirements of the Civil Code relating to liquidated damages in contract cases.[48]

Cleaning deposits. In addition to security deposits covering payment of rent, a landlord often requires a deposit covering cleaning fees, or a key deposit.

EXAMPLE In one case,[49] a tenant brought a class action to determine rights in "cleaning fees" collected by the landlord and not returned to the tenant on termination of the tenancy. The court held that the "cleaning fee" had no possible purpose but to protect the landlord against costs of restoring an apartment not maintained as required by the rental agreement. Whether the landlord could retain it was a question of fact.[50]

Return or retention of deposit. Deposit payments shall be held by the landlord for the benefit of the tenant. The tenant's claim to the funds has priority over the claim of any creditor of the landlord other than a trustee in bankruptcy.[51] The landlord may retain only such amounts from the deposits as are necessary to remedy rent payment defaults, repair damages caused by the tenant, or clean the premises on termination of the tenancy *if* the deposit was expressly made for these purposes. That portion of the deposit that has not been so used by the landlord must be returned to the tenant not later than three weeks for residential property and 30 days for nonresidential property if necessary to repair, after termination. The landlord shall furnish the tenant with an itemized written statement of the security received and the disbursement of the security.[52] If the landlord retains any portion of the deposit in *bad faith* in violation of the Civil Code he may be subject to the assessment of damages not exceeding $600 ($200 for nonresidential property) in addition to any actual damages sustained by the tenant.[53] Further, the landlord has the burden of proof as to the reasonableness of the amounts claimed.

Status of deposit upon sale of property. If the owner's interest is terminated by death, sale, or assignment, in order to be relieved of further liability with respect to the deposit, he must, within a reasonable time, transfer the deposit to the successor in interest, *and* notify the tenant by personal delivery or certified mail, and notify the tenant of the new owner's name and address.[54]

If the notice is made by personal delivery, the landlord is required to obtain the tenant's signature on a receipt of the notice or a copy of the landlord's notice. Upon receipt of any portion of the security, the transferee shall have all the rights and obligations with respect to such security.[55]

Increased rent for holding over. A provision fixing rent in an amount greater than the amount otherwise specified, if the tenant remains after a certain time period, is valid and not treated as a penalty.[56]

§15.36. Attorney's fees provision

Even though a lease or rental agreement provides for the right to attorney's fees and costs to the lessor only, the law gives the court the right to award attorney's fees and costs to the prevailing party.[57]

EXAMPLE In one case the court held that even though there was no valid or enforceable lease, the lessee as the prevailing party was still entitled to reasonable attorney's fees.[58] The lessee may also recover attorney's fees from a sublessee if the lease provisions so provide.[59]

---

§15.37. Maintenance and repair

The lessor has the duty to keep a building intended for human occupancy in a fit condition, and to repair dilapidations that render it untenable, except that caused by the tenant.[60] However, by agreement, the tenant can undertake to make these repairs.[61] The landlord has no duty to repair if the tenant is in substantial violation of the following obligations:[62]

1.   Keep the premises clean and sanitary.

2.   Dispose of garbage and waste.

3.   Properly use all electrical, gas, and plumbing fixtures, and keep them clean and sanitary.

4.   Do not permit any person to willfully destroy, deface, damage, or remove any part of the structure or equipment.

5.   Occupy the premises only for the intended purpose.[63]

If the tenant has a legitimate complaint, he must notify the landlord or his agent, in writing or orally, to make repairs. In fact, notice to the landlord is a condition precedent to the lessor's duty to repair.[64] If the tenant does notify the landlord, he has certain remedies if the landlord fails to act within a reasonable time. He may abandon the premises[65] or spend up to one month's rent and make repairs.[66] The option to make repairs is available twice in any 12-month period. The lessor and lessee can agree, in writing, to arbitrate any controversy relating to a condition of the premises.[67]

§15.38. Implied warranty of habitability

In addition to the legal duty placed upon a lessor to maintain a property, there is also an implied duty to keep the premises safe and healthy. This duty is called the implied warranty of habitability, which is implied by law in residential leases.[68] This warranty cannot be waived.[69]

If the tenant decides not to make repairs but still wishes to remain, it is possible that he need not pay the full amount of the rent due, but only pay the rent corresponding to the relative reduction in the usefulness of the premises.[70] In fact, this warranty can be used as a defense to an unlawful detainer proceeding (discussed later in this chapter). It would seem, however, that in order to use this defense, and for the protection of the lessor, and in the interest of fairness, the tenant should be required to deposit in court the actual rental payment that is due, or the portion of rent he refuses to pay once an unlawful detainer is filed.

EXAMPLES   1.   It is a landlord's duty to provide security measures to protect tenants against crime, because his control of the areas of common use in an apartment complex can be a part of the implied warranty of habitability.[71]

2.   In one case it was held that a breach of implied warranty of habitability gives rise to an affirmative cause of action for damages, including retroactive rent abatement, even though the tenant subsequently vacated the premises. The court held that a cause of action for this type of breach should include the following: (1) the existence of a materially defective condition was affecting habitability; (2) the defective condition was unknown to the tenant at the time of occupancy; (3) the condition was not apparent from a reasonable inspection; (4) notice was given to the landlord within a reasonable time after tenant discovered or should have discovered the breach of warranty; (5) the landlord was given a reasonable time to correct the defect while the tenant remained in possession.[72]

§15.39. Retaliatory eviction

A landlord is prohibited from recovering possession, raising the rent, or decreasing services if the dominant purpose is retaliation against the tenant for exercising a right to repair or reporting the landlord for housing code violations.[73] If the lessor retaliates because the lessee exercises these rights, and if the lessee is not in default in rent, the lessor, for 180 days, may not (1) recover possession; (2) cause the lessee to quit voluntarily; (3) increase the rent; or (4) decrease any services.[74] This protection can be invoked only once in any 12-month period. In other words, a tenant cannot be deprived of his home because he is exercising a statutory right.[75]

§15.40. Interrupting utilities
The landlord is expressly prohibited from willfully interrupting a utility service of a tenant, changing locks, and removing doors or personal property.[76] All actual damages for such willful interruption can be awarded to the occupants of each unit, plus an amount not to exceed $100 and attorney's fees, for each day each unit is deprived of the service. However, penalties will be exacted only so long as the tenant lacks practical access to any residential utility. If the tenant succeeds in restoring it, or could have done so, the tenant cannot be considered to have been "deprived" of it.[77]

EXAMPLE Although the penalties cannot be constitutionally excessive, in one case the occupants of six rental units were awarded $36,000 in penalties for interruption of utility service (and compensating damages of $7,901, attorney's fees of $5,600, and punitive damages of $1,750).[78]

§15.41. Mental distress
In addition to other remedies, a tenant may recover damages from the landlord for an intentional infliction of mental distress. The elements of this cause of action are (1) outrageous conduct on the part of the landlord; (2) intention to cause, or reckless disregard of the probability of causing, emotional distress; (3) severe emotional distress; (4) actual and proximate causation.[79]

EXAMPLE In one case it was held that allegations in a complaint filed by a tenant that a process server was banging on the door in the middle of the night constituted a cause of action for mental distress.[80] The same holds true for changing the lock and removing the tenant's belongings.[81]

§15.42. Waiver
If the lease prohibits, e.g., an assignment, and contains a clause that a waiver by the lessor of any term shall not be deemed a waiver of subsequent breaches, and also that acceptance of rental payments would not constitute a waiver of breach other than the nonpayment of *that particular rent*, then there is no continuing waiver on the part of the lessor.[82]

VI. TRANSFER OF LESSOR'S OR LESSEE'S INTEREST
§15.43. In general
As a general rule, the landlord may sell the land during an unexpired leasehold term, in which event the purchaser becomes the landlord by operation of law. The purchaser succeeds to all the rights of the original lessor, and in the absence of a contrary stipulation, is entitled to all the rents that fall due on the next rent day. Exceptions to this rule apply, as in the case in which the lease contains a provision that a sale of the land before the expiration of the leasehold term shall terminate the lease.

§15.44. Assignment of rents
The owner of leased premises may convey the reversion and retain the rents, or may assign the rents and the covenant for rent under the lease without conveying

the reversion or the lease itself. When the rent is assigned, the assignee becomes chargeable with notice of any express or implied covenants of the lease. The right to receive future rents is an interest in land, called an *incorporeal hereditament*, and a grant of such right is a conveyance within the statutory definition.

§15.45. Transfer of lessee's interest

A lessee may assign or sublease all or a part of the leased premises, subject to any restrictions in the lease against assignment or subletting.[83] Whether a transfer by a lessee is an assignment or a sublease is of importance, since the respective rights and liabilities of the parties depend on the nature of the instrument of transfer.

§15.46. Assignment of lease

If there is to be an assignment of a lease, the assignee must take precisely the same estate that the assignor has in the property. A lessee who has not obligated himself personally to pay rent is relieved of any further obligation to pay rent when he transfers his interest to an assignee with the consent of the lessor. Such obligation is thereafter on the assignee, who has come into privity of estate with the landlord. However, when the lessee has expressly agreed to pay rent, his liability under his contract remains, notwithstanding an assignment with the consent of the lessor. The lessee is liable as surety in the event the assignee fails to perform the covenant to pay rent, unless the lessor specifically intended to release him from further liability by virtue of a novation.[84]

Unless a nonresidential lease of real property includes a restriction on assignment or sublease, a tenant may transfer the tenant's interest in the lease.[85]

"Transfer" is defined in the statute. A *transfer* of a tenant's interest in a lease means an (1) assignment, (2) a sublease, (3) or other voluntary or involuntary transfer or encumbrance of all or part of a tenant's interest in the lease.

Unless the lease includes a restriction on transfer (as defined), statutory rights/concepts under the Civil Code[86] include the following:

1. Ambiguities in the lease should be resolved in favor of transferability.

2. Absolute restriction on transfer is permissible.

3. Transfers may be made subject to express standards or conditions.

4. Transfers may be made subject to landlord's consent, which in turn may be subject to any explicit standards or conditions.

5. Leases that require landlord's consent to transfer but provide no standard for giving or withholding that consent are deemed to include an implied standard that consent may not be unreasonably withheld.

§15.47. Obligation of assignee

When the assignee takes possession under an assignment and pays rent without an express assumption of the obligation of the lessee and thereafter abandons the premises, liability, based only on privity of estate, is limited solely to the period of his occupancy and does not continue after his abandonment of the premises. When the assignee by express terms in writing covenants and agrees to pay the rent in the lease, the result is two sets of obligations and rights, one comprising those due to the relation of landlord and tenant based on *privity of estate*, and the other due to *privity of contract*. The *obligation of the assignee* is identical with that of the original lessee upon his or her express covenants. If the assignee repudiates the lease and abandons the premises, the lessor may sue to recover the rent to the same extent as though the assignee had been the original lessee.

§15.48. Effect of assignment without lessor's consent

An assignment of the lessee's interest made without the consent of the lessor, when the lease provides that his consent is necessary, does not of itself terminate the lease or render the assignment void, but merely gives the lessor certain rights provided by law, such as an election to declare a forfeiture of the lease or to sue for breach of the covenant. If the lessor ignores the breach, the lease is valid and subsisting as to all other parties. Acceptance of rent from the assignee constitutes a waiver of the lessor's right to declare a forfeiture, but only if he had *actual* knowledge of the assignment.[87]

Although the cases are conflicting, the better view is that a landlord cannot unreasonably withhold a consent to assign or sublet as long as the assignee or subtenant is financially responsible and stable. The law implies in each contract a covenant of good faith. If a landlord arbitrarily withholds consent, the tenant can establish an unreasonable restraint on alienation, which sufficiently establishes a cause of action for breach of contract and bad faith.[88]

§15.49. Distinction between assignment and sublease

The generally stated distinction between an *assignment* and a *sublease* is that an assignment transfers the entire unexpired term, whereas a sublease transfers only a part of such term, reserving some right, e.g., a right of reentry. If the transferring instrument gives the transferor a right of reentry, the transfer operates as a sublease and not an assignment. A lease that contains a provision against assignment but none against subletting does not prevent a sublease. A sublessee ordinarily is liable only to the *sublessor* and not to the original lessor, since the original lessor does not acquire the whole estate but only a portion of the unexpired term.

§15.50. Subtenant charged with knowledge

A subtenant is charged with notice of the provisions of the master lease and may not exert any greater rights under the sublease. This is true even if the subtenant was negligent by not reading the master lease before agreeing to the sublease.[89] The subtenant does not acquire any right to enforce the covenants contained in the master lease merely by virtue of the sublease.[90] Since the subtenancy is subordinate to the covenants of the master lease, if those covenants are breached by the subtenant, the landlord can terminate the master lease and thereby terminate the subtenant's right of possession.[91]

§15.51. Rights of sublessor

When a lease does not prohibit a sublease, and a tenant is in possession under a valid sublease, a voluntary surrender by the original lessee to the original lessor does not affect the right of the sublessee in possession, and the anomalous situation may arise when the sublessee may legally remain in possession without paying rent, although the original lessee is still liable. However, if the sublessee expressly assumes the obligations of the lease, he too is liable.[92]

The lessor can protect himself against such contingency, either by refusing to consent to such cancellation, unless it is accompanied by a surrender of possession by the sublessee, or by taking an assignment of the rentals under the sublease.[93]

§15.52. Option to purchase

An *option to purchase* contained in a lease is a covenant running with the land and, in the absence of restrictive language in the lease, an assignment of the lease includes the option. The general consideration of the lease, such as the covenant to pay rent or do other acts, supports the option to purchase, but such option does not normally exist beyond the fixed term of the lease. In the absence of a provision making the exercise of the option personal to the lessee, the option to purchase is severable from the other provisions of the lease and may be transferred without assigning the lease.[94]

An option to purchase is, of course, to be distinguished from a right of first refusal, which doesn't obligate the landowner to sell, but if he chooses to sell, does obligate him to offer the land to the person holding the right on terms set forth in their agreement.

If the lease does contain an option to purchase and the lessee's interest under the lease is to be subordinated to a trust deed, the option should be expressly subordinated to avoid any future dispute.

VII. LIABILITY OF LESSOR AND LESSEE FOR CONDITION OF PREMISES

§15.53. In general

As a general rule, a lessor of land is not liable for injuries resulting from a defective condition of the land.[95] In the absence of fraud, concealment, or a covenant in the lease, a landlord is not liable to a tenant or his invitee for defective conditions or faulty construction on leased property. Liability for injuries is placed on the one who is in control of the land, namely the lessee.[96]

There are several exceptions to this rule. When injuries result from a defective condition of that part of the land over which the lessor retains control—stairs, common hallways, and the like—the lessor and not the lessee is liable.[97] However, a liability does not arise when the structural defects are obvious. Also, in such cases the only duty of the lessor is to use reasonable care. Another exception to the general rule applies when injuries result from a latent defect that was not capable of discovery by a reasonable inspection made by the tenant, provided the lessor knew or should have known of the condition. A lessor is also liable for personal injuries resulting from a defective condition if he undertakes to make repairs and does so in a negligent manner.[98] In other words, in some respects, the policy of the law has been to expand rather than to limit the liability of the landowner.

EXAMPLES

1. In one case it was pointed out that subject to certain exceptions, a lessor is not exposed to common law liability to persons injured on the demised premises by reason of conditions that develop after possession has been transferred to the tenant. However, when an owner leases a building knowing it is to be used for a purpose that would require structural changes to comply with safety regulations, the duty to comply with these regulations is on the owner. When a tenant makes a structural change that violates safety regulations and the owner has knowledge of the change, a duty is imposed on the owner to terminate the tenancy or compel the tenant to comply with the regulation.[99]

2. In another case it was held that when a city ordinance imposed on a landlord a duty to repair a railing, that duty involved the obligation to inspect the railing. The duty is not restricted to the repair of defects of which the landlord knew, or as to which he received notice. He has the affirmative duty to inspect to determine if there are defects. The violation of this duty inures to the protection of the tenant, affording to the tenant a cause of action for injuries resulting from the defect.[100]

3. In a commercial lease, the lessor has a duty to prospective tenants to disclose material facts affecting the value or desirability of the leased premises when the prospective tenant was a jewelry store, and the premises had been burglarized in the past, and the premises were vulnerable to easy penetration.[101]

4. A case of first impression concerned an action by a minor against a landlord for injuries received when she was bitten by a vicious dog owned by a tenant. The court held that if a landlord has such a degree of control over the premises that it can fairly be concluded that he can obviate the presence of a dangerous animal, and has actual knowledge of the presence of the animal, and knew of its dangerous propensities, then public policy requires the imposition of a duty of ordinary care. Although the court held that the landlord was

under no duty to inspect the premises for the purpose of discovering the existence of a tenant's dangerous animal, a later case held that he was.[102]

5. It has also been held that a landlord owes a duty to take reasonable steps to protect a tenant from foreseeable criminal acts committed by third persons.[103]

6. The landlord is also liable when he has actual knowledge of defects that are not apparent to the tenant and fails to disclose them to the tenant, or when a nuisance exists on the land when the lease is made or renewed,[104] but may not be liable for asbestos removal in certain cases although the landlord or tenant may be liable to notify the other of hazardous waste.[105]

7. In another case action was brought by a tenant against a landlord for personal injury and property damage based on negligence of the landlord. The record indicated that the bottom unit of a double-plug electrical receptacle malfunctioned. Because there was no other outlet for the freezer and the refrigerator in the kitchen, the tenant purchased a lightweight extension cord and attached both freezer and refrigerator into two of the prongs, and plugged the cord into the top unit of the receptacle. The landlord had been repeatedly advised by the tenant of the condition, and had actually seen the extension cord, but had made no repair. The court found the landlord liable.[106]

8. As to liability on the part of the lessee, it has been held that the lessee is responsible for his own negligence and that of his independent contractor for negligent repairs or modifications.[107] Further, the lessee is criminally responsible for defrauding a lessor[108] or for writing a check with insufficient funds.[109]

Exculpatory clause. An exculpatory clause in a lease will not relieve a landlord of liability for the personal injury of a tenant in a fall on a common stairway in an apartment building.[110] Even though such a clause may violate public policy, if the clause is worded so that it gives the tenant the alternative of paying an additional fee to obtain such extra protection, but the tenant chooses not to do so, the landlord may still be protected.

VIII. TERMINATION OF THE LEASE

§15.54. In general

The expiration of the express term of the lease will, of course, effect a termination. Additionally, a lease may be lawfully terminated before the expiration of the term on several grounds. A lease may be terminated by the tenant for violation of the landlord's duty to place him in quiet possession, or for violation of the landlord's duty to repair, or on eviction by the landlord. The lease may be terminated by the landlord if the premises are used by the tenant for an unauthorized or illegal purpose. Either party may terminate the lease on breach of a condition of the lease by the other party, or on the destruction of the premises if there is no covenant to repair.

Upon the termination of a lease, disputes often arise between landlord and tenant regarding the ownership of items installed by the tenant. Are these items affixed in such a way that they become the property of the landlord under the rules regarding fixtures? This subject is discussed at length in Chapter One (in particular, §1.65).

§15.55. Surrender or abandonment of premises

A lease may also be terminated by the surrender or abandonment of the leased premises by the lessee and the unqualified acceptance thereof by the lessor. In such case, the lessee is released from all further liabilities under the lease. If there is no acceptance by the lessor, the lease continues in effect provided the lessor does not terminate the lessee's right of possession *and* the lease provides for this remedy and allows the lessee to sublet or assign.[111] In any event, the lessor is under a duty to mitigate damages by attempting to find another tenant. If the tenant wrongfully abandons the premises, the lessor may still recover damages.[112]

A difficult question arises in the situation in which the landlord believes the tenant has abandoned, but some of the tenant's belongings are still in the premises. In order to comply with the law, it is necessary for the lessor to follow a prescribed procedure.[113] If the tenant has left personal property and the landlord reasonably believes the value is more than $300, he must follow an additional procedure to sell the property.[114]

§15.56. Covenant of quiet enjoyment

In every lease there is an implied covenant by the lessor of quiet enjoyment and possession by the lessee during the term of the lease.[115] This warranty is breached by an eviction, whether actual or constructive. An *eviction* occurs, of course, when the landlord ousts the tenant. There does not have to be an actual *ouster* (forcible entry and detainer) to have an eviction. As a general rule, any disturbance of the tenant's possession whereby the premises are rendered unfit or unsuitable for occupancy, in whole or in a major part, for the purpose for which they were leased, or any interference with the beneficial enjoyment of the premises, such as threats of expulsion or an attempt to lease to others, may amount to a *constructive eviction*. When this occurs, the tenant has the right, if he so elects, to abandon the premises and pay no further rent. The courts have held that the tenant must actually surrender possession. If the tenant stays on, there is no eviction and he cannot escape the obligation to pay rent.[116]

EXAMPLES

1. In one case it was held that conditions allowed to exist in portions of a building other than the tenant's apartment may cause a constructive eviction.[117]

2. On the other hand, in another case it was held that there was no constructive eviction even though a cotenant made loud noises. The lease provided that the "lessor shall not be responsible for any damages arising from the acts or neglects of cotenants, or other occupants of the same building, or any owners or occupants of adjacent or contiguous property."[118]

In many cases a tenant will not have much choice but to move when the landlord's conduct or failure to perform amounts to a constructive eviction. This would be true in connection with maintenance of recreational areas, such as a swimming pool that was the tenant's primary purpose in renting the particular premises.

§15.57. Effect of condemnation action

If the entire premises are condemned in eminent domain proceedings, the lessee is released from his obligation to pay rent. However, if only a portion of the premises is taken by the condemnation proceedings, the lessee must pay the rent in full, but he, rather than the lessor, will be entitled to damages in the condemnation action.

§15.58. Destruction of the premises

In the event of destruction of the premises without the fault of the landlord, and the lease does not provide for an apportionment of rent, the tenant who has paid rent in advance cannot recover it.

§15.59. Doctrine of commercial frustration

The doctrine of *commercial frustration*, or "frustration of purpose" (discussed in Chapter 2), is sometimes invoked to allow termination of a lease by the tenant when the premises are leased for a specific purpose, and thereafter it becomes unlawful to use the premises for such purpose. A change in the laws forbidding the sale of liquor is an example. The doctrine has been approved in California, although some jurisdictions have refused to allow a termination of a lease on this theory because of the dual character of a lease as a conveyance of real property as well as a contract. If the premises may be used for other purposes to which the owner has consented, either in the lease or subsequently, the tenant will not be relieved of his obligations.

EXAMPLE   In one case it was held that the doctrine of commercial frustration was not applicable to a lease of property in Los Angeles for five years commencing September 15, 1941 for the purpose of conducting the sale of new automobiles, when the sale of new automobiles was subsequently prohibited by government wartime regulations adopted after the commencement of the term. The court stated that the doctrine is inapplicable when the frustrating event was reasonably foreseeable at the time of the execution of the lease.[119]

§15.60. Forfeiture of lease

A breach of a *condition* by the tenant gives the landlord a *right of forfeiture* of the estate, whereas a breach of a *covenant* ordinarily gives only an *action for damages*. However, if the lease provides for forfeiture for violation of conditions or covenants, the lessor may terminate the tenancy on either violation. A provision for forfeiture must be clear, and the courts will attempt to avoid it by judicial construction or interpretation if enforcement will lead to inequitable results.

§15.61. Title company practices

When a lease is terminated before the expiration of the term set forth in the lease, other than by judicial proceedings, and a title company is asked to ignore the effect of the lease for title insurance purposes, the company ordinarily will require either a cancellation agreement executed by both the lessor and the lessee or a quitclaim deed by the lessee with evidence of acceptance by the lessor as a cancellation of the lease.

§15.62. Termination of periodic tenancy

A *periodic tenancy* may be terminated by either party by giving 30 days' written notice.[120] Such notice in a month-to-month tenancy may be given at any time; it need not be given or expire only on the anniversary of the hiring. If the parties agree, in writing, at the time the agreement is entered into, a termination notice can be given for a period of not less than seven days, although such a provision is uncommon. If the tenant is in the military service, it is still necessary to give the landlord at least 30 days' written notice of termination.[121] Figure 15-2 is one form of a 30-day notice to quit.

§15.63. Failure to pay rent

Failure to pay rent does not ordinarily justify a forfeiture forthwith; a demand for payment is necessary and is usually made a part of a three-day notice to pay rent or quit.[122] Figure 15-3 is a typical three-day notice to quit.

EXAMPLES   1.   In one case it was held that when a lease does not work a forfeiture of the leasehold for failure of the lessee to pay rent, but only gives the lessor the right at his option to terminate, this amounts to no more than the right to terminate the lease in the manner provided by law and does not justify the lessor in reentering and dispossessing the lessee until he has been given the required three-day written notice to pay the rent or quit possession.[123]

2. The above rule was again expressed when the court held that no immediate right to possession of property can be obtained under a right of reentry until a proper three-day notice has been served on the lessee.[124]

3. It has also been held that the notice required to be given to a delinquent tenant, when the condition or covenant assertedly violated is capable of being performed, must be framed in the alternative, that is "pay the rent or quit" or "perform the covenant or quit"; a notice that merely directs the tenant to quit is insufficient.[125]

To

_____

_____

_____

    This is to give you notice that pursuant to California law which gives landlords the right to retake possession of their property on thirty days' written notice to a renter, whether or not the renter is in default in payment of rent, you are to vacate the premises at _____ on or before _____.

    Failure to vacate the premises by that date may lead to legal proceedings being commenced against you to recover possession, and to recover damages for the unlawful detention of the premises beyond the date.

    Dated: _____

                           _____

FIGURE 15–2
A 30-day notice to quit.

To

_____

_____

_____

NOTICE TO PAY RENT
OR SURRENDER POSSESSION

    NOTICE IS HEREBY GIVEN that, pursuant to the agreement by which you hold posession of the above-described premises there is now due and unpaid rent for the premises in the total sum of $_____, being the rent that became due on _____ for the period from _____ at a monthly rent of $_____.

    WITHIN THREE DAYS after service of this notice on you, you are required to pay the rent in full, or to deliver up possession of the premises to the undersigned, or legal proceedings will be commenced against you to recover possession of the premises, to declare the agreement forfeited, and to recover TREBLE RENTS AND DAMAGES for the unlawful detention of the premises.

    Dated: _____

                           _____

FIGURE 15–3
A three-day notice to quit

§15.64. Unlawful detainer

The remedy of *unlawful detainer* is available against a tenant who continued in possession after default in the payment of rent, or continued in possession after neglect or failure to perform other conditions or covenants of the lease, or holds over after the expiration of the term. Service of a notice, such as set forth in Figure 15-3, is the first step that must be taken by the landlord. This type of action is entitled to priority on the court's calendar. If the tenant vacated prior to the landlord's filing the complaint, no unlawful detainer lies.[126] Such an action in which the total claim does not exceed $25,000 may be brought in the Municipal Court.[127] Small Claims Courts are sometimes used to evict tenants. Unfortunately, when Small Claims Court is used the lessor is not entitled to preference on the trial calendar. In that event, a tenant will often remain, without paying rent, many more days than he would have been permitted to if the lessor had filed the action in the Municipal Court.

The second step, after the Notice to Pay Rent or Quit (or other notice), is to file the Complaint for Unlawful Detainer and have the tenant served with the Complaint and Summons.[128]

The following is a simplified outline of the procedure: Once served, the tenant has five days to file a written answer. If the tenant does not respond, the landlord can have a default entered. This is accomplished by filing certain documents and/or having a default hearing date set and heard, whereby the landlord will appear in court and testify to the facts and the breach by the tenant.

When judgment is entered against the tenant, a Writ of Possession can be obtained and given to the Sheriff or Marshall for service upon the tenant. The tenant has five days thereafter to vacate the premises or else the Sheriff or Marshall is empowered to physically evict the tenant. This procedure may take between 40 and 45 days (or longer) if the tenant does not answer the complaint and the case is heard as a default matter and assuming the landlord has complied with the legal process. Remember, many judges favor the tenants!

Because a tenant can unjustifiably refuse to pay rent and still remain in the premises until legally evicted, it would only seem fair that the law should require the tenant to pay the requested rent to the court within five days of being served with the Summons and Complaint for unlawful detainer, or else require immediate eviction of the tenant. To permit a willfully defaulting tenant to remain in the premises without paying rent is grossly inequitable to the landlord.

IX. PROPERTY MANAGEMENT
§15.65. In general

If the property is managed by a real estate licensee, the agent must comply with the same duties as all other licensees, as set forth in Chapters 4 and 5. For example, if a management contract with the owner includes an exclusive listing in the event the owner desires to sell the property, the contract must contain a definite termination date.[129] A resident manager of an apartment building does not need a real estate license. This also applies to his employees.[130] However, a nonresident manager who is not the owner must have a real estate broker's license.

A manager or some responsible person must reside on the premises and have charge of every apartment complex in which there are 16 or more units. If the complex has more than 4 but fewer than 16, a notice must be placed in a conspicuous place stating the owner's name and address.[131]

The owner or manager of every multiple residential dwelling in excess of two units is required to disclose to each tenant the name and usual address of the owner or agent and the manager. If the party who enters into a rental agreement on behalf of the owner fails to comply, he is deemed the agent of the owner for specified purposes, including service of process.[132] Notwithstanding the above, disclosure may be made by posting the information in at least two conspicuous places on the premises.[133]

Because a manager is an employee and not an independent contractor, the owner is bound to maintain worker's compensation insurance and to comply with the labor laws.

X. MOBILE HOME TENANCY

§15.66. In general

Since 1976, real estate licensees have been permitted to sell (and to lease) used mobile homes under prescribed conditions. Therefore, it is essential that the licensee be aware of the landlord–tenant laws affecting mobile homes.

§15.67. Rental agreement and rules and regulations

The mobile home rental agreement is required to be in writing and include a number of provisions, including the term of tenancy, rent, and the rules and regulations of the park.[134] A rule or regulation may be amended with the consent of the tenant at any time, or without his consent with six months' notice,[135] but must give a 60-day notice to increase the rent.[136] The owner or manager of the park shall have no right to enter the mobile home without the prior written consent of the occupant, except in an emergency or when the occupant has abandoned the mobile home.[137] No fees shall be charged to the tenant, except rent, utilities, and incidental reasonable charges for services actually rendered.[138] Tenant meetings relating to mobile home living are permitted to be held in the park or recreation hall, if the meeting is held at a reasonable hour and when the facility is not otherwise in use.[139] Tenant meetings are also permitted for social or educational purposes, including forums for or speeches by public officials or candidates for office. A person responsible for the operation and maintenance of the park shall be "available"; if the park has more than 50 units, a manager shall reside in the park.[140]

§15.68. Termination

Because of the high cost of many mobile homes and the cost of landscaping, the management may not terminate or refuse to renew a tenancy, except for specified reasons, and then shall give notice of not less than 60 days.[141] These reasons are as follows:

1. Failure to comply with state and local laws
2. Conduct that constitutes an annoyance to other tenants
3. Failure to comply with reasonable rules and regulations[142]
4. Nonpayment of rent and other charges
5. Condemnation or other change in use of park

The management is required to set forth *specific facts* as to the reason for termination, including the date, place, witnesses, and other circumstances. A tenancy cannot be terminated for the purpose of making the site available for a person who purchased a mobile home from the owner of the park or his agent.[143]

§15.69. Escrow accounts

Every new or used mobile home dealer shall put any deposit for the purchase of a new or used mobile home into an escrow account with an escrow agent, and no part of this deposit can be disbursed to the dealer until certain conditions have been fulfilled. Unless the parties agree to the contrary, the escrow account shall be terminated and the full refund shall be made to the buyer within 120 days from the date of the sales contract, unless delivery is made within this period. For a violation, the plaintiff shall be awarded actual damages and an amount not to exceed $2,000 and attorney's fees and costs.[144]

XI. OIL AND GAS LEASES

§15.70. In general

California is one of the large oil-producing states, and the use of oil and gas leases has been widespread. Oil and gas leases differ from the surface leases previously discussed; they are in effect something in addition to an ordinary lease. In a *surface lease*, the lessee generally has only the right to *use* the property; in an *oil and gas lease* he has, in addition, the right to *take* something from the ground (subsurface), namely, oil and gas. A surface lease generally runs for a definite period of time, whereas the usual form of oil and gas lease runs for a specified period of years and for an indefinite period thereafter, expressed "and so long thereafter as oil is produced in paying quantities."

Basically, there are two types of oil and gas leases, identified as follows:

Single ownership. In this type of lease, the owner of an individual lot or lots enters into an oil and gas lease with an oil company, in the same manner that any owner of land would enter into a lease. The lease is ordinarily executed by the mineral owner for the purpose of permitting the drilling for and extracting of oil and gas from beneath the land. Generally, there is no right of surface entry, and the drilling must be done at least 500 feet below the surface. A sale of the land by the lessor and the execution of a grant deed would result in a transfer of the lessor's interest in the lease.

Community oil and gas lease. This lease involves a number of property owners joining in the execution of one lease, all of them acting as lessors. Each owner-lessor assigns or conveys to the co-owner lessors an interest in all oil and gas, minerals, and so on, produced on his property by the lessee during the term of this particular lease. Reciprocal rights are created in that each lot owner has a percentage interest in the oil and gas produced from all of the lands subject to the lease, and not merely in the oil and gas produced from his individual parcel. A conveyance of a lot or parcel of land that composes part of a community oil and gas lease does not automatically carry with it the lessor's reciprocal right to the royalties from the other properties included in the lease. An assignment must be additionally drawn to transfer those rights, unless the oil and gas lease provides for a transfer of all the lessor's interest in the lease in the event of a sale of the land.

Oil and gas leases are often the subject of title insurance, which prudent lessees ordinarily require. Assurances as to the right of surface entry can be of vital concern. California recognizes the implied right of surface entry in the holder of the mineral estate. In this regard, the general custom of title insurers when insuring oil and gas interests can be set forth briefly as follows:

1. If the instrument creating an ownership in minerals neither grants nor excepts a right of entry, no reference to a right of entry is made in the evidence of title written on that mineral interest.

2. If the right of entry is included (or excluded) by express language in the grant of an interest in minerals, any evidence of title will disclose it as granted (or not) by using the precise language of the grant and by a reference to the public record of the conveyance.

§15.71. Nature of interest of lessee

In a *lease for a definite period*, the interest of the lessee is a chattel real and, as such, is *personal property*.[145] The interest of a lessee in an *oil lease for an indefinite period* is an interest in the real property in the nature of a *profit à prendre*.[146] This interest is an incorporeal hereditament and has been held to be real property. Accordingly, a judgment lien attaches to the interest of the lessee under an oil and gas lease for an indefinite period, but until recently did not attach to the interest of the lessee under an ordinary lease.

§15.72. Lease by co-owner

A co-owner can lease property for oil and gas purposes and if oil is produced, he is entitled to charge the interests of nonproducing co-owners for their proportionate share of drilling and operating expense.[147] If a lease is executed by one co-owner alone, the other co-owners may either recognize the lease and receive their share of the royalty thereunder, or reject the lease and receive their fractional part of the oil produced, less their proportionate part of the cost of discovery and production.

§15.73. Royalty interests

The term *landowner's royalty* (or *royalty*) is generally applied to fractional interests in the production of oil and gas created by the owner of the land, either by reservation when an oil and gas lease is entered into, or by a direct grant to a third person. When a lessor assigns to third persons the fractional interests in the royalties that he has reserved to himself, such persons acquire estates in real property and become tenants in common with the lessor. Such estates continue beyond the termination of the lease, unless the assignments specifically limit such estates to the term of the lease.

§15.74. Termination of oil leases

Termination by abandonment will more readily occur in the case of oil and gas leases than in other types of leases. The courts have declared that the rule that forfeitures are not favored in law does not apply to oil and gas leases.[148] However, an abandonment will not be inferred unless it can be shown that *nonuse* by the lessee is coupled with an intent to relinquish all rights in the premises.

§15.75. Distinction between "unless" and "drill or pay" leases

Oil and gas leases are sometimes referred to as unless leases and drill or pay leases. An *unless lease* is one that automatically terminates if the lessee does not commence drilling before a specified time, *unless* he or she pays a specified rental for the privilege of delaying commencement of drilling. Failure to drill or to pay the rent in the specified period terminates all rights of the lessee. A *drill or pay lease*, on the other hand, is one in which the lessee agrees to drill or, in lieu of drilling, to pay rental. Under such a lease, even when it contains a surrender clause, the payment of rentals is not necessary to keep it alive, nor does it automatically terminate. The landlord would be required to take some course of action to effect a termination.

§15.76. Termination by cancellation

A lease may be terminated by cancellation. A problem may then arise as to whether all necessary parties have consented to the cancellation. In the case of *single property leases*, as distinguished from *community leases*, a quitclaim deed by the lessee, which contains no reservations and is accepted by the owner, can be treated as a full cancellation. In the case of a *community oil and gas lease*, the usual form of lease provides in effect that the lessee may at any time quitclaim the lease in full, and thereupon the reciprocal rights of the lessors under the pooling agreement shall cease. If the lease does not contain such provisions, a cancellation of the lease and termination of the reciprocal rights requires consent of all the landowners.

QUESTIONS

Matching Terms

a. Rent
b. Term
c. Royalty
d. Assignment
e. Eviction
f. Unlawful detainer
g. Estate for years
h. Reversion
i. Periodic tenancy
j. Sublease

1. Court action to recover possession of premises from tenant for nonpayment of rent.
2. Lease for any specified period of time, with a beginning and an ending date.
3. Landlord's interest under a lease.
4. Occupancy of property for successive periods of time, such as weekly or monthly.
5. Transfer of a portion, but not all, of lessee's interest.
6. Ouster of possession of tenant.
7. Consideration for use of premises by a tenant.
8. Payments under an oil and gas lease, comparable to rent.
9. Specified period of time that a lease is effective.
10. Transfer of entire interest under a lease.

True/False

T F 11. A lease is both a contract and a conveyance.
T F 12. All real property leases must be in writing in order to be enforceable.
T F 13. A leasehold estate must be for a definite, fixed period of time.
T F 14. A court action by the landlord to regain possession of the premises is called a constructive eviction.
T F 15. Consideration for a lease must be payment of money.
T F 16. If a tenant fails to pay rent on time, he is entitled to receive a "Notice to Pay Rent or Quit" before an unlawful detainer action can be maintained.
T F 17. Oil and gas leases can be of indefinite duration.
T F 18. Leases of property owned by a city can be for any period of time.
T F 19. The leasehold interest of a tenant cannot be transferred unless the landlord approves the transfer in writing.
T F 20. Basically, both landlord and tenant have a responsibility for the condition of the premises.

Multiple Choice

21. Consideration for a lease can be
    a. Money.
    b. Services.
    c. Share of crops.
    d. Any of the above.
22. Landlord–tenant laws in general are intended to
    a. Protect the rights of the tenant exclusively.
    b. Protect the rights of the landlord exclusively.
    c. Define the rights and duties of both landlord and tenant.
    d. None of the above.
23. As compared with a single-family dwelling, the applicable period for notice of termination of a rental in a mobile home park is
    a. Longer.
    b. Shorter.
    c. The same.
    d. Notice is not required.
24. Which of the following is an example of an estate for years?
    a. A lease to start at 12:01 A.M. and terminate at 11:59 P.M. the same day.
    b. A lease to start at 7 A.M. on Monday and terminate at 9 P.M. on the following Sunday.
    c. A lease for a specified one-year period.
    d. All of the above.
25. A lease for real property must be in writing to be enforceable if for a period of
    a. One month.
    b. Six months.
    c. Ninety days.
    d. In excess of one year.
26. A leasehold gives the tenant a
    a. Remainder interest.
    b. Reversionary interest.
    c. Possessory interest.
    d. Nonpossessory interest.
27. Notice of a tenant's rights under a lease may be given by
    a. Recording the lease.
    b. Recording a memorandum of lease.
    c. Possession.
    d. Any of the above.
28. The landlord's interest under a lease is called the
    a. Reversion.
    b. Remainder.
    c. Reliction.
    d. None of the above.
29. When the landlord–tenant relationship is terminated, a question sometimes arises as to whether or not the tenant can remove fixtures he has installed. If a dispute arises, the court will ordinarily
    a. Favor the tenant because he paid for the fixtures.
    b. Favor the landlord because he owns the real property and everything affixed.

c. Apply the law strictly in favor of the landlord.

d. Require that the dispute be resolved by lot.

30. In order to be valid, a lease must contain
    a. Legal term.
    b. Property description.
    c. Lawful object.
    d. All of the above.

31. The validity of a lease is also dependent upon
    a. Competent parties.
    b. Consideration.
    c. Mutual assent.
    d. All of the above.

32. A lease for a term exceeding one year
    a. Must be in writing to be enforceable.
    b. Need not be based on consideration.
    c. Is legal regardless of the purpose, provided it is in writing.
    d. Must contain an option to purchase.

33. Rent payable under an oil and gas lease is called a
    a. Royalty.
    b. Security deposit.
    c. Reversion.
    d. *Profit à prendre.*

34. A commercial lease that provides for rental based upon the amount of gross business done by the lessee is called a
    a. Term lease.
    b. Percentage lease.
    c. Net lease.
    d. Open-end lease.

35. Which of the following is an example of a *profit à prendre*?
    a. Right to remove minerals from the land of another.
    b. Right to remove gravel from the land of another.
    c. Right to remove timber from the land of another.
    d. All of the above.

36. An assignment of a lease with option to purchase ordinarily
    a. Transfers the option to the assignee.
    b. Has no legal effect on the option, which remains in the original lessee.
    c. Is prohibited by statute.
    d. Cancels the lease.

37. The law that requires a lease for a period longer than one year to be in writing is the
    a. Statute of Frauds.
    b. Statute of Limitations.
    c. Statute of Uses.
    d. Statute of Descent.

38. A lease of real property is
    a. Both a contract and a conveyance.
    b. A contract but not a conveyance.
    c. A conveyance but not a contract.

d. Neither a contract nor a conveyance.

39. The doctrine of constructive eviction is based on
    a. Breach by landlord.
    b. Breach by tenant.
    c. Acts of public authorities.
    d. All of the above.

40. If a tenant fails to pay rent when due, the landlord has the right to
    a. Force the tenant to vacate the next day.
    b. Change the lock to the door.
    c. Serve a notice to pay rent or vacate.
    d. Turn off the utilities.

41. An action in court to evict a tenant for nonpayment of rent is known as
    a. Specific performance.
    b. Unlawful detainer.
    c. Abatement.
    d. Partition.

42. A tenant who continues in possession of real property after the end of the lease without an agreement to remain is known as a
    a. Life tenant.
    b. Tenant for years.
    c. Tenant by sufferance.
    d. Periodic tenant.

43. If Jones leased a mountain cabin from Smith for the period from June 1 to June 30, 1996, Jones would have
    a. A periodic tenancy.
    b. An estate for years.
    c. A reversion.
    d. A tenancy at will.

44. The party who executes a lease as owner of the property is called the
    a. Lessee.
    b. Lessor.
    c. Donor.
    d. Donee.

45. Tenants are afforded rights under the
    a. Condominium law.
    b. Mobile home tenancy law.
    c. Antidiscrimination law.
    d. All of the above.

46. A tenancy may be terminated by
    a. Lapse of time.
    b. Legal notice.
    c. Breach of conditions.
    d. All of the above.

47. A tenancy at will can be terminated
    a. Without notice.
    b. By landlord only.
    c. By tenant only.
    d. By either landlord or tenant upon notice.

48. To be entitled to be recorded, a lease must be acknowledged by
    a. Lessor.

b. Lessee.

c. Either a or b.

d. Neither a nor b.

49. A leasehold interest lying between the primary lease and a sublease is referred to as

   a. A percentage lease.

   b. A sandwich lease.

   c. A dormant lease.

   d. An inactive lease.

50. A landlord is not permitted to

   a. Intentionally shut off a tenant's utilities.

   b. Lock out a tenant for nonpayment of rent.

   c. Retain security deposits on termination of rental if tenant has complied with his obligations.

   d. Do any of the above.

NOTES

1. C.C. 1624.4.
2. *See* Birkenfeld v. City of Berkeley (1976) 17 C.3d 129.
3. C.C. 1925.
4. 56 Ops. Cal. Atty. Gen. 332 (1973); C.C. 51.2, 51.3; Roth v. Rhodes (1994) 25 C.A. 4th 530.
5. Marina Point Ltd. v. Wolfson (1982) 30 C.3d 721.
6. Smith v. FEHC (1996) 12 C.4th 1143.
7. S.P. Growers Assn. v. Rodriguez (1976) 17 C.3d 719.
8. Abstract Investment Co. v. Hutchinson (1962) 204 C.A.2d 242.
9. In re Cox (1970) 3 C.3d 204.
10. Stouman v. Reilly (1951) 37 C.3d 713; Flowers v. John Burham & Co. (1971) 21 C.A.3d 700.
11. 58 Ops. Cal. Atty. Gen. 608 (1975).
12. C.C. 54.1 54.6.
13. C.C. 54.3.
14. C.C. 1945.
15. C.C. 789, 1946.
16. Covina Manor, Inc. v. Hatch (1955) 133 C.A.2d Supp. 790.
17. First & C. Corp. v. Wencke (1967) 253 C.A.2d 719.
18. C.C. 1945.
19. C.C. 1943.
20. C.C. 1944.
21. C.C. 765.
22. Callahan v. Martin (1935) 3 C.2d 110.
23. C.C. 717.
24. C.C. 718; Shaver v. Clanton (1994) 26 C.A. 4th 568.
25. Epstein v. Zahloute (1950) 99 C.A.2d 738.
26. Coruccini v. Lambert (1952) 113 C.A.2d 48.
27. C.C. 718f.
28. C.C. 1091.
29. C.C. 1624(c).
30. *See* Fisher v. Parsons (1963) 213 C.A. 2d 829; Bed, Bath & Beyond of La Jolla Inc. v. La Jolla Village Square Venture Partners (1997) 52 C.A. 4th 867; Wickson v. Monarch Cycle Mfg. Co. (1900) 128 C. 156.
31. Fam. Code 1102.
32. Pro. C. 16231.
33. C.C. 1945.5.
34. Cirimele v. Shinazy (1954) 124 C.A.2d 46.
35. C.C. 1470.
36. C.C. 1469.
37. C.C. 827.
38. C.C. 1954.
39. C.C. 1930.
40. C.C.P. 732.
41. *See* §1.59, *et seq.*, in which the subject of fixtures is considered in detail.
42. C.C. 1861(a). To enforce such a lien, a landlord must obtain a court order.
43. Fuentes v. Shevin (1972) 407 U.S. 67.
44. Although the distinction was eliminated in 1978.
45. If the agreement is for residential purposes and for a period of less than six months (including month to month), the landlord cannot demand more than a total of two months' rent for an unfurnished dwelling and three months' rent for a furnished dwelling. C.C. 1950.5(c). As to security deposits for nonresidential property, *see* C.C. 1950.7.
46. People v. Sangiacomo (1982) 128 C.A.3d 942; CC 1950.5(b), 1750.7, which appear to eliminate any distinction. Therefore, all deposits may be subject to return.
47. Warming v. Shapiro (1953) 118 C.A.2d 72.
48. C.C. 1951.5, 1671. *See also* Feary v. Aaron Burglar Alarm (1973) 32 C.A.3d 553.
49. Bauman v. Islay Investments (1973) 30 C.A.3d 752; Granberry v. Islay Investments (1995) 9 C.4th 738.
50. No rental agreement or lease shall contain any provision characterizing any security as "nonrefundable." C.C. 1950.5(l).
51. C.C. 1950.5(d).
52. C.C. 1950.5(f), 1950.7(c) and must be returned in two weeks if not needed for cleaning or repair.
53. C.C. 1950.5(k), 1950.7(f) re nonresidential property. *See also* CCP 1174(b).
54. C.C. 1950.5(g), 1950.7(d); Trypucko v. Clark (1983) 142 C.A.3d Supp. 1.
55. C.C. 1950.5(g), 1950.7(e).
56. Vucinich v. Gordon (1942) 51 C.A.2d 434; Greenberg v. Koppelow (1946) 76 C.A.2d 631.
57. C.C. 1717.
58. Care Const. Inc. v. Century Convalescent Centers, Inc. (1976) 54 C.A.3d 701.
59. Iverson v. Sprang Industries, Inc. (1975) 45 C.A.3d 303.
60. C.C. 1941, 1941.1, 1927, 1928.
61. C.C. 1942.1.
62. Provided his violations contribute substantially to the existence of the dilapidation or interfere substantially with the landlord's obligations.
63. C.C. 1941.2.
64. Wal-Noon Corp. v. Hill (1975) 45 C.A.3d 605; C.C. 1942.
65. And be discharged from further payment as of the date of vacating.
66. C.C. 1942. The repairs cannot require an amount more than one month's rest.
67. C.C. 1942.1.
68. Green v. Superior Court (1974) 10 C.3d 616; Schulman v. Vera (1980) 108 C.A.3d 552.
69. But *see* Knight v. Hillsthanner (1981) 29 C.3d 46, 56 (dissent).
70. *See* Hinson v. Delis (1972) 26 C.A.3d 62; Robinson v. Diamond Housing Corp. (1972) 463 Fed.2d 853.
71. Secretary of Housing, etc. Development v. Longfield (1979) 88 C.A.3d Supp. 28; Kline v. 1500 Massachusetts Ave. Corp. (1970) 439 Fed.2d 477.
72. Quevedo v. Braga (1977) 72 C.A.3d Supp. 1.
73. C.C. 1942.5; Schweiger v. Superior Court (1970) 3 C.3d 507; Edwards v. Habib (1968) 397 Fed.3d 687.
74. C.C. 1942.5(a) For a violation, the lessor shall be liable to the lessee for all actual damages and punitive damages of not less than $100 nor more than $1,000 for each retaliatory act in which the lessor has been guilty of fraud, oppression, or malice. C.C. 1942.5(f). The court shall award attorney's fees to the prevailing party. C.C. 1942.5(g).
75. S. P. Growers Assn. v. Rodriguez (1976) 17 C.3d 719.

76. C.C. 789.3; Wolff v. Fox (1977) 68 C.A.3d 280.

77. Hale v. Morgan (1978) 22 C.3d 388.

78. Kinney v. Vaccari (1980) 27 C.3d 348.

79. Newby v. Alto Rivera Apts. (1976) 60 C.A.3d 288.

80. In Golden v. Dungan (1971) 20 C.A.3d 275.

81. Richardson v. Pridmore (1950) 97 C.A.2d 124.

82. Karbelnig v. Brothwell (1966) 244 C.A.2d 333.

83. *See* Meredith v. Dardarian (1978) 83 C.A.3d 248.

84. C.C. 1530 1531.

85. C.C. 1995.010, *et seq.*; C.C. 1995.21; C.C> 1951.4.

86. C.C. 1995.010-1995.03. *See also* R-Ranch Markets #2, Inc. v. Old Stone Bank (1993) 16 C.A.4th 1323.

87. German-American Savings Bank v. Gollmer (1909) 155 C. 683; Weisman vs Clark (1965) 232 C.A.2d 764. A landlord is liable in tort for wrongful refusal to assent to transfer of a lease. Richardson v. La Rancherita Inc. (1979) 98 C.A.3d 73.

88. Cohen v. Ratinoff (1983) 147 C.A.3d 321; Schweiss v. Williams (1984) 150 C.A.3d 883; Sade Shoe Co. v. Oschin and Snyder (1984) 162 C.A.3d 1174.

89. Pedro v. Potter (1926) 197 C. 751. But *see* Ilkhehooyi v. Best (1995) 37 C.A.4th 395.

90. Handleman v. Pickerill (1927) 84 C.A. 214.

91. Hartman Ranch Co. v. Associate Oil Co. (1937) 10 C.2d 232.

92. Western Camps Inc. v. Riverway Ranch Enterprises (1977) 70 C.A.3d 714; Wilson v. Gentile (1992) 8 C.A. 4th 759.

93. Buttner v. Kasser (1912) 19 C.A.755; Bailey v. Richardson (1885) 66 C. 416.

94. Mott v. Cline (1927) 200 C. 434. For the time within which to exercise an option to renew, *see* Simons v. Young (1979) 93 C.A.3d 170. The beginning time for an option cannot be ambiguous (WYDA Assn. v. Merner [1996] 42 C.A. 4th 1702.

95. *See* Andersen v. Souza (1952) 38 C.2d 825; C.C. 1668.

96. *See* Rowland v. Christian (1968) 69 C.2d 108, discussed further in §14.81.

97. Hennioulle v. Marin Ventures, Inc. (1978) 20 C.3d 512; Curties v. Hill Top Dev. Inc. (1993) 14 C.A. 4th 1651; C.C. 1953.

98. McCarthy v. Martinson (1996) 51 C.A.4th 632.Minoletti v. Sabini (1972) 27 C.A.3d 321. In Girard v. Delta Tarvers Joint Venture (1993) 20 C.A. 4th 1741.

99. Grant v. Hipsher (1967) 257 C.A.2d 375.

100. McNally v. Ward (1961) 192 C.A.2d 871; Fakhoury v. Magner (1972) 24 C.A.3d 58; Golden v. Conway (1976) 55 C.A.3d 948.

101. Moradzadch v. Antonio (1992) 5 C.A. 4th 1289.

102. Uccello v. Laudenslayer (1975) 44 C.A.3d 504; C.C. 1714. In the Uccellorcase, the tenancy was month to month. *See* Portillo v. Aiassa (1994) 22 C.A. 4th 1128; Donchin v. Guerreo (1995) 34 C.A.4th 1832.

103. Ann M. v. Pacific Plaza Shopping Center (1993) 6 C. 4th 666; Pamella B. v. Hayden (1994) 25 C.A. 4th 785; Pamela W. v. Millsom (1994) 25 C.A. 4th 950; O'Hara v. Western Seven Trees Corp. (1977) 75 C.A.3d 798 liability for rape of tenant; Kline v. 1500 Massachusetts Ave. Apt. Corp. (1970) 439 Fed.2d 477; Sherman v. Concourse Realty Corp. (1975) 365 N.Y.S.2d 239; Braitman v. Overloock Terrace Corp. (1974) 132 N.J. Super 51.

104. Shotwell v. Bloom (1943) 60 C.A.2d 303; Burroughs v. Bear's Auto Park, Inc. (1945) 27 C.2d 449; Alcaraz v. Vece (1995) 39 C.A.4th 1447—landlord may have a duty to warn tenant of dangerous condition of an adjoining property.

105. Braun v. Green (1993) 21 C.A. 4th 1172; H&S Code 25357.7.

106. Evans v. Thomason (1977) 72 C.A.3d 978.

107. Pappas v. Carsen (1975) 50 C.A.3d 261; Walfen v. Clinical Data Inc. (1993) 16 C.A. 4th 171. Further, a tenant may be liable for removal of asbestos even though it was present before the tenant rented the property—Braun v. Green (1993) 16 C.A. 4th 760. However, in the case in which a prior tenant installed a cabinet which, after he had vacated, fell on the new tenant and caused an injury, there is no liability on the part of the old tenant who engaged in minor remodeling (Lorenzen-Hughes v. MacElhenny & Co. [1994] 24 C.A. 4th 1684).

108. Pen. C. 537.

109. Pen. C. 476.

110. Hennioulle v. Marin Ventures, Inc. (1978) 20 C.3d 512.

111. C.C. 1951.4.

112. C.C. 1951.2.

113. C.C. 1951.3, 1951.7.

114. C.C. 1982, *et seq.*, 1988.

115. C.C. 1927.

116. Petroleum Collection, Inc. v. Swords (1975) 48 C.A.3d 841.

117. Buckner v. Azalai (1967) 257 C.A.2d Supp. 1013.

118. Cinterno v. Brown (1968) 263 C.A.2d 135.

119. Lloyd v. Murphy (1944) 25 C.2d 48.

120. C.C. 1946.

121. 50 U.S.C. App. 534. In one case it was held that a notice of termination of a tenancy from month to month that is insufficient under the Civil Code to terminate the tenancy as of the stated date because it is within the 30-day period, is not necessarily ineffective as a notice of termination after the lapse of 30 days from the date of the notice (Kingston v. Colburn [1956] 139 C.A.2d 623. Service can be accomplished by posting and mailing. *See* Highland Plastics, Inc. v. Enders [1980] 109 C.A.3d Supp. 1).

122. C.C. 791; C.C.P. 1161, 1162. It is 60 days for mobile home tenancies. Palmer v. Agee (1979) 87 C.A.3d 377.

123. Iguaye v. Howard (1952) 114 C.A.2d 122.

124. Jordan v. Talbot (1961) 55 C.2d 597.

125. Hinman v. Wagnon (1959) 172 C.A.2d 24.

126. Briggs v. Electronic Memories & Magnetic Corp. (1976) 53 C.A.3d 900.

127. C.C.P. 86.

128. *See* C.C.P. 1159, *et seq.* But the complaint cannot be filed until the three-day notice has legally expired (the three days excludes weekends and holidays); *see* Lamanna v. Vognar (1993) 17 C.A. 4th Supp. 4; WDT-Winchester v. Nilsson (1994) 27 C.A. 4th 694.

129. *See* Adams and Leonard Realtors v. Wheeler (1972) 493 P.2d 436 (Oklahoma case).

130. B. & P. 10131.01.

131. Admin. Code 17909.

132. C.C. 1962.

133. C.C. 1962.5.

134. C.C. 798.15-798.19. Discrimination is not allowed. C.C. 798.20.

135. C.C. 798.25. Notice re recreational facilities is 60 days.

136. C.C. 798.30; Rich v. Schwab (1984) 162 C.A.3d 739.

137. C.C. 798.26.

138. C.C. 798.31, 798.32, 798.36 798.38; B. & P. 10131.7(d). Fees for pets and guests, *see* C.C. 798.33, 798.34.

139. C.C. 798.50.

140. H. & S. 18603.

141. C.C. 798.55. The tenant must also give 60 days' notice to vacate. C.C. 798.59; Rancho Santa Paula Mobilehome Park Ltd. v. Evans (1994) 26 C.A. 4th 1139.

142. Must give the tenant written notice of violation and seven days to comply. C.C. 798.56(c).

143. C.C. 798.58. For information re transfer, advertising, actions, penalties, et al., *see* C.C. 798.70, *et seq. See* People v. McKale (1979) 25 C.3d 626 re right of D.A. to bring action against owner for violation.

144. H. & S. Code 18035.

145. Dabney v. Edwards (1935) 5 C.2d 1; Cassinos v. Union Oil Co. (1993) 14 C.A. 4th 1770.

146. Callahan v. Martin (1935) 3 C.2d 110.

147. Little v. Mountain View Dairies, Inc. (1950) 35 C.2d 232.

148. Wallace v. Imbertson (1961) 197 C.A.2d 392.

Glossary

This glossary includes most of the words and phrases the reader will encounter in the real estate field in addition to litigation involving real estate, including Latin phrases often encountered in court cases.

Abandonment. Giving up any further interest in a thing or a right.

Abate. To put an end to or terminate an offensive activity, such as a nuisance.

Abatement of nuisance. Termination or elimination of a nuisance.

Ab initio. From the beginning.

Abstract. Brief summary.

Abstract of judgment. A summary of the essential provisions of a money judgment. When recorded, it creates a general lien on real property of the judgment debtor in the county where the abstract is recorded.

Abstract of title. A summary of the condition of title based on an examination of public records.

Abut. To be adjacent to, touch, or border on other property.

Abutting. Touching or bordering a street or highway.

Abutting owner. Owner whose land touches a street or highway.

Acceleration clause. A clause commonly used in installment notes that permits the payee to declare the entire unpaid balance immediately due on default in payment. Such a clause contained in a note secured by deed of trust is subject to a statutory right of reinstatement. Cf. *alienation, due-on-sale clause.*

Acceptance. Consent to an offer to enter into a contract.

Access right. The right of an owner of land to have ingress and egress to and from his property via a public street.

Accession. Addition to property by natural increase or growth; also, by the installation of improvements.

Accommodation party. A person who, for the purpose of permitting another person to obtain credit, signs a note without receiving value.

Accretion. Increase of land on a shore or bank of a river by the gradual deposit of sand or soil by natural action of the water.

Accusation. A written statement of charges by the Department of Real Estate setting forth the acts or omissions with which a licensee is charged, delivered to the licensee before a hearing regarding a possible revocation or suspension of his or her license.

Acknowledgment. A declaration by the party executing an instrument that it is his act and deed. It is usually made before a notary public.

Acquisition. The act or process by which a person obtains title to property.

Acre. A measure of land equaling 43,560 square feet in area. An acre in the shape of a square measures approximately 209 feet by 209 feet.

Act of God. Any irresistible disaster, the result of natural causes, such as earthquakes, violent storms, lightning, or unprecedented floods.

Action. A court proceeding to enforce a right or redress (obtain satisfaction for) a wrong.

Action in personam. A court action that seeks a judgment against the person as distinguished from a judgment against property. An action for money against the maker of an unsecured note is an example.

Action in rem. A court action that seeks a judgment against property, such as an action to quiet title to real property.

Actual notice. Notice that a party has in fact or in reality, as compared to constructive notice (implied or inferred).

Adjoining. Contiguous; in contact with; touching.

Adjoining owners. Owners of two or more parcels of real property that are contiguous to each other, that is, touching.

Adjudication. Judicial determination of a case or controversy.

Ad litem. During the pendency of a court action or proceeding, e.g., a guardian ad litem.

Administrator. A person appointed by the Probate Court as the representative of a decedent's estate when the decedent left no will.

Administrator c.t.a. Administrator with will annexed (*cum testamento annexo*); the representative of a decedent's estate when no one is named as executor, or when the named person is unable or unwilling to act.

Ad valorem. According to the value.

Advances. Money advanced by the beneficiary under a trust deed to pay real estate taxes, hazard insurance premiums, and other items needed to protect the beneficiary's interest under the trust deed.

Adverse. Opposing one's interest in property; contrary; opposite.

Adverse possession. A method of acquisition of property based on an adverse or hostile and continued use of another person's property for a period of five years and payment of taxes thereon.

Affiant. A person who makes an affidavit.

Affidavit. A sworn statement or declaration in writing, made before an authorized official, such as a notary public.

Affirm. Confirm; verify; ratify.

Affirmation. A solemn statement or declaration in writing by a person who conscientiously declines taking an oath. It is made under penalty of perjury.

After-acquired title. Title acquired by a grantor who conveyed land before his ownership of it. The prior grantee automatically retains title to such land without the necessity of obtaining another deed from his grantor.

Agency. The relationship between a principal and an agent arising out of contract when an agent is employed to act on behalf of the principal in dealings with third parties.

Agenda. Things to be done; matters to be attended to.

Agent. A person who acts for another, called the *principal.*

Agreement of sale. A contract between a seller and a buyer in which they reach a meeting of the minds on the terms and conditions of the sale.

Alcalde. Chief magistrate or mayor (Spanish).

Alcoholic Beverage Control Act. A law (referred to as ABC) regulating the sale of alcoholic beverages.

Alias. Also known as.

Alien. An unnaturalized foreign resident.

Alienate. To transfer the title to real property from one person to another.

Alienation. The transfer of title to land from one person to another. It is voluntary if freely made; it is involuntary when contrary to the owner's desire, such as in bankruptcy or an execution or other judicial sale.

Alienation clause. A provision in a note and deed of trust calling for automatic maturity at the lender's option in the event of a sale or transfer of the real property to a third party. Also called *due-on-sale clause.*

Allegation. An assertion; a statement of a fact in a pleading.

All-inclusive deed of trust. A deed of trust that includes within the terms of the note the obligations owing under a prior deed of trust. See *wrap-around deed of trust.*

Alluvion. Soil deposited by accretion. Also called alluvium.

Ambulatory. Subject to being altered; changeable. A will is said to be ambulatory; that is, it can be changed at any time by the testator.

Amortization. Provision for the payment of a debt or obligation on an installment basis; also, recovery, over a period, of cost or value. Also, in zoning, the gradual elimination of a nonconforming use.

Amortized loan. A loan that is completely paid off, both as to principal and interest, by a series of regular payments that are equal or nearly equal.

Ancillary. Auxiliary.

Ancillary administrator. An administrator appointed in a state other than the decedent's domicile.

Annexation. The addition to property by adding or attaching other property to it, such as a fixture. Also, the addition of unincorporated territory in a county to a city or town.

Annuity. A series of assured equal or nearly equal payments to be made over a period of time, usually on a monthly basis.

Annul. To cancel or to make void and of no legal effect.

Ante. Before; prior. Opposite of *post*.

Antenuptial agreement. A contract by a man and a woman regarding their property, made in contemplation of their marriage. Also called prenuptial agreement.

Anti. Against.

Anti-deficiency legislation. Legislation originally enacted in the early thirties that prohibits a seller from obtaining a judgment for money against a defaulting buyer in foreclosure proceedings when the property is sold for less than the amount owing.

Appearance. The coming into court of a party to a lawsuit.

Appellant. A party appealing a court decision or ruling.

Appraisal. An opinion as to value of property; a conclusion resulting from an analysis of facts affecting fair market value.

A priori. From the past; from that which has previously transpired.

Appurtenance. Anything incidental or belonging to land that is considered part of the real property, such as an improvement on real property or an easement for ingress and egress (a way in and out).

Appurtenant. Belonging to.

Assessed value. Value placed on property as a basis for taxation.

Assessments. Special impositions on property to pay for the cost of a local work of improvement, such as sidewalks, curbs, sewers, or street lighting.

Assessor. County official who determines the assessed value of property for tax purposes.

Assign. Transfer a claim or other right in personal property to another person.

Assignee. The person to whom personal property is transferred.

Assignment. A transfer in writing of a person's interest in personal property, usually of a chose in action (intangible property).

Assignor. The person who assigns or transfers personal property.

Assume. Take over the obligation of another person; also, to suppose as a fact without further proof.

Assumption agreement. An undertaking or adoption of a debt or obligation primarily resting on another person.

Assumption of deed of trust. Agreement by buyer wherein he assumes liability for payment of an existing note secured by a mortgage or deed of trust against the property.

Assumption fee. A lender's charge for changing over and processing new records for a buyer who is assuming an existing loan.

Attachment. A seizure of property by judicial process during the pendency of an action, to have it available after a judgment is obtained.

Attest. Affirm to be true or genuine; an official act establishing authenticity.

Attestation clause. A clause added to a formal will reciting that the persons named have affixed their names as witnesses.

Attorn. Accept and acknowledge a new landlord.

Attorney-in-fact. A person who is authorized to perform certain acts for another person under a power of attorney.

Attractive nuisance. A potentially dangerous object or condition on an owner's property that is likely to attract young children who may become injured.

Avigation. Relating to the flight of aircraft, e.g., an avigation easement.

Avulsion. The sudden tearing away of land by the violent action of a river or other water course.

Balloon payment. The final payment on an installment note that is greater than the preceding payments and that pays the note in full.

Base lines. Imaginary east–west lines that intersect meridians to form a starting point for the measurement of land.

Bench marks. A location indicated on a durable marker by a land surveyor.

Beneficiary. One entitled to the benefit of a trust; as used in a trust deed, the lender is designated as the beneficiary, that is, he obtains the benefit of the security.

Beneficiary's statement. Statement of a lender giving the remaining principal balance due on a note and other information concerning the loan. It is usually obtained in escrow when the landowner wishes to sell or refinance.

Benevolent associations. Voluntary groups formed not for profit, but to render financial or other aid to their members.

Bequeath. Leave personal property to another person by will.

Bequest. A gift of personal property by will.

Bid. An offer made at a judicial or other sale.

Bilateral contract. A contract in which a promise is given in exchange for another promise. Cf. *unilateral contract*.

Bill of sale. A written instrument used to transfer title to tangible personal property. It is to personal property what a deed is to real property.

Binder. A notation of coverage on an insurance policy, issued by an agent, and given to the insured before issuance of the policy.

Blanket mortgage or trust deed. A mortgage or trust deed that covers more than one lot or parcel of real property; it often covers an entire subdivision. As individual lots are sold, a partial reconveyance from the blanket mortgage is ordinarily obtained.

Bona de. In good faith; without fraud.

Bona de purchaser. One who buys property in good faith, for a fair value, and without notice of any adverse claim or right of third parties.

Boot. Dissimilar property, such as money, given as part of the consideration in the exchange of properties having different values. Boot compensates for difference in value.

Breach. Inexcusable failure to perform a promise or a duty; the violation of an obligation.

Broker. A natural or legal person who, for compensation or in expectation of compensation, acts for another in the sale of real property or other transaction. A real estate broker must be licensed by the state.

Building code. A state, city, or county law that sets forth minimum construction standards.

Building line. A line set by law a certain distance from the street and beyond which an owner cannot build on his lot. Also called setback line.

Bulk Sales Law. Division 6 of the Uniform Commercial Code which regulates the sale of the inventory and stock in trade of a business; it is designed to protect the creditors of the seller.

Bundle of rights. Beneficial interests or rights an owner has in his property, including the right of use, the right of transfer, and the right to exclude others.

Business opportunity. The term used to describe a business or going concern; it includes the stock in trade, fixtures, and goodwill of a business.

Capacity. As used in contract law, it relates to mental state or age of a contracting party.

Caption. The heading or title of a document.

CAR. California Association of Realtors.

Case law. See *common law*.

Caveat. Let him beware.

Caveat emptor. Let the buyer beware. Places a duty on a buyer to examine the goods or property before purchasing in cases in which he buys at his own risk. Has little application today.

Certificate of sale. A certificate issued to the purchaser at an execution sale. It evidences ownership and will be exchanged for a deed if there is no redemption from the sale.

Certificate of title. A certified statement regarding the ownership of land, based on an examination of the record title.

Cestui que trust. The person for whose benefit property is held in trust.

Chain of title. A chronological list of recorded instruments affecting the title to land, beginning with the earliest in point of time and concluding with the latest evidence of ownership.

Chattel. Personal property.

Chattel mortgage. A mortgage on personal property. It has been replaced by a security agreement and financing statement under the Uniform Commercial Code.

Chattel real. Interest in real estate less than freehold, such as an estate for years.

Chose in action. A personal right not reduced to possession, but recoverable by an action at law. A creditor's right to money owed by a debtor is an example.

Circa. About; around; concerning.

Civil action. A court action involving the civil law and private rights of parties, rather than the criminal law.

Civil law. Law of the Roman Empire, based on the code of the Emperor Justinian. It is the basis of the law in many European countries today but not in England, where the common law applies.

Class action. A representative lawsuit in which the plaintiff files an action to recover money or redress a wrong not only on his individual behalf but also on behalf of all other persons similarly situated.

Client. The party represented by an attorney. It also refers to a real estate broker's principal, such as the seller of real property.

Closing statement. A financial statement given to the buyer and the seller at close of escrow. It gives an account of all funds received and expended by the escrow holder.

Cloud on title. A semblance of title or a claim appearing in some legal form but that is in fact invalid.

Code. A system of law.

Code of Ethics. The high standards of conduct established by the N.A.R. to which every Realtor and Realtor-Associate pledges observance; referred to as the "Golden Rule."

Codicil. A change or amendment to a will.

Collateral. Any property pledged as security for a debt, for example, the real estate pledged as security under a mortgage or trust deed.

Collateral assignment. An assignment of an interest in property, such as a note secured by trust deed, for security purposes; not an absolute assignment.

Collusion. An illegal agreement between two or more persons to defraud another of his rights or to obtain an object forbidden by law.

Color of title. That which gives the appearance of title, but is not title in fact.

Commercial acre. A term applied to the remainder of an acre of subdivided land after the area devoted to streets, sidewalks, curbs, and the like has been deducted from the acre.

Commingling. Unauthorized and improper mixing of one's funds with the funds of a client or customer.

Commission. An agent's compensation for performing the duties of his agency. In real estate practice this usually represents a percentage of the selling price of property, or a percentage of rentals, or the like.

Commissioner. An office created by the state legislature, such as the Real Estate Commissioner and the Corporations Commissioner, to carry out the responsibilities of various state agencies, including the enforcement of the law.

Commitment. A pledge, promise, or firm agreement. FHA commitments are of two types, conditional and firm. The former is a commitment of a definite loan amount on a parcel of property subject to the approval of a presently unknown borrower who will be required to have a satisfactory credit rating. The latter type is an agreement by FHA to insure a loan on specified property with a specified borrower.

Common law. Body of unwritten law, founded on general custom, usage, or common consent. It prevailed in England and most of the United States before the laws became codified.

Community property. Property acquired by husband and wife during marriage when not acquired as separate property. Generally includes earnings of each spouse after marriage and while living together.

Compensation. Money or equivalent in money received for services performed.

Competent. Legally qualified; capable of contracting.

Component. One of the features making up the whole property.

Con. In opposition to; against.

Conclusive presumption. An inference the law makes that cannot be contradicted.

Condemnation. The exercise of the power of eminent domain, that is, the taking of property for a public purpose on payment of just compensation. Also, declaration under the police power that a structure is unsafe or unfit for use. In the latter case, a structure can be condemned without payment of compensation.

Condition. A provision in a contract or other document providing that a right or interest in property depends on an uncertain future event that may or may not exist or happen.

Condition precedent. A condition that must be fulfilled before an estate can vest.

Condition subsequent. A condition by the failure or nonperformance of which an estate already vested may be defeated.

Conditional sale contract. A contract of sale in which title remains in the seller until the conditions of the contract have been performed.

Condominium. A system of individual ownership of units in a multifamily or other structure, combined with joint ownership of common areas of the structure and the land.

Confession of judgment. An entry of judgment on the debtor's voluntary admission of liability.

Confirmation of sale. Court approval of the sale of property by an executor, administrator, guardian, or conservator.

Consent. To agree to do something; to give permission, approval, or assent.

Conservator. A person appointed by the Probate Court to take care of the person or property of an adult person needing such care.

Conservatorship. Administration of a person or estate by a conservator.

Consideration. Anything of value to induce another person to enter into a contract. It may be money, services, or a promise, and consists of either a benefit to the promisor or a loss or detriment to the promisee.

Constructive. Inferred or implied.

Constructive eviction. Any disturbance of a tenant's possession by the landlord whereby the premises are rendered unfit or the tenant is deprived of the benefit of the premises.

Constructive notice. Notice given by the public records.

Constructive trust. A trust imposed by law to redress a wrong or to prevent unjust enrichment.

Contiguous. In actual or close contact; adjoining or touching on, such as parcels of land next to each other.

Contingent. Dependent on an uncertain future event. Cf. *vested interest*.

Continuation statement. Statement filed with the Secretary of State to extend the time on a previously filed financing statement.

Contour. The surface configuration of land.

Contract. An agreement by which a person undertakes to do or not to do a certain thing.

Conversion. Change from one character or use to another, such as converting an apartment house into a condominium; also, in criminal law, it is the wrongful appropriation of the property belonging to another person.

Convey. To transfer title to property from one person to another.

Conveyance. A written instrument transferring the title to land or an interest therein.

Cooperating broker. A broker who effects a sale for another broker with a listing. Shortened to "co-op broker."

Corporation. An artificial being, created by law, and possessing certain rights, privileges, and duties of natural persons. It may continue for any length of time the law prescribes.

Corporation sole. A corporation consisting of a single person and his successor in office, incorporated by law to permit ownership in perpetuity. An example is the Roman Catholic Archbishop of Los Angeles.

Cotenancy. Ownership of property by two or more persons.

Covenants. Agreements or promises contained in deeds and other instruments for the performance or nonperformance of certain acts, or the use or nonuse of property in a certain manner.

Damages. The amount of money recoverable by a person who has sustained an injury to either his person or property through the wrongful act or default of another.

dba. Doing business as.

Debtor. A person who owes a debt.

Declaration of Homestead. Document recorded by a homeowner to protect his home from a forced sale up to a prescribed amount in satisfaction of certain types of creditors' claims.

Declaratory judgment. A court decree determining the rights and obligations of parties to a dispute. The court action is called one for declaratory relief.

Decree. A type of court order.

Dedication. A donation of land by the owner for the use of the public.

Deed. Written instrument by which the ownership of land is transferred from one person to another.

Deed of trust. Written instrument by which title to land is transferred to a trustee as security for a debt or other obligation. Also called trust deed.

Default. Failure to perform a duty or to discharge an obligation.

Default judgment. A judgment taken against a defendant who fails to appear in a lawsuit.

Defeasance clause. The clause in a mortgage that gives the mortgagor the right to redeem his property on the payment of his obligation to the mortgagee.

Defeasible. Capable of being annulled or undone, such as a title.

Defendant. A party against whom a court action is brought.

Deficiency judgment. A personal judgment in a foreclosure action for the amount remaining due after a sale of the security.

Demise. A transfer to another person of an estate for years, for life, or at will.

Demurrer. An objection made by one party to his opponent's pleading, alleging that he should not be required to answer it because of some defect in the pleading.

Department of Real Estate. The government agency that administers the state Real Estate Law as contained in the Business and Professions Code.

Deponent. A person who gives testimony under oath or affirmation.

Deposit receipt. A document used when accepting "earnest money" to bind an offer for property by a prospective purchaser; also includes terms of a contract to purchase. Because the words may mislead a buyer into thinking the document is not a contract but merely a receipt, the better terminology is "Offer to Purchase and Receipt for Deposit."

Deraign. To trace or prove, such as a title.

Descent. Succession to property by an heir.

Desist and refrain order. The Real Estate Commissioner is empowered by law to issue an order directing a person to desist and refrain from committing an act in violation of the Real Estate Law.

Devise. A gift of real property by will.

Devisee. One who receives real property by will.

Dictum. An opinion of a judge on a point of law not essential to the decision on the main question.

Often mistakenly relied upon by persons appearing in *pro per* (*in propria persona*) as stating a rule of law of general application. Plural: dicta.

Discount. To sell a note for less than its face value or less than the unpaid balance.

Divest. To deprive of a right or title.

Doctrine. A rule, principle, theory, or tenet of the law.

Document. An original or official paper relied on as the basis, proof, or support of anything else; a more comprehensive word than *instrument*.

Documentary transfer tax. A tax on the transfer of real property located in any county in the state. Applies when the consideration exceeds $100. Tax is computed at the rate of $.55 for each $500 of consideration or fraction thereof.

Domicile. A person's legal residence.

Domiciliary administrator. The administrator of a decedent's estate appointed at the place of decedent's domicile.

Dominant tenement. The land obtaining the benefit of an easement appurtenant. Cf. *servient tenement*.

Donee. A person to whom a gift is made.

Donor. A person who makes a gift.

Double escrow. A procedure in which the closing of one escrow arrangement is dependent on closing of another; also known as *concurrent escrow*. The procedure is commonly used in exchanges of property as well as instances in which the buyer depends on funds he expects from the sale of another property.

Dragnet clause. A broad clause contained in many deeds of trust in favor of a lending institution to secure already existing loans. The clause extends the deed of trust to cover every past and present obligation between debtor and creditor.

Due-on-sale clause. A provision in a real estate loan calling for automatic maturity at the lender's option on a sale or transfer of the real property to a third party. Also called alienation clause.

Duress. Unlawful constraint (compulsion) exercised on a person to force him to do some act against his will.

Earnest money. Something given as a part of the purchase price to bind a bargain.

Easement. A limited right or interest in the land of another that entitles the holder of the right to some use, privilege, or benefit out of or over said land (such as to install pole lines, pipelines, roads, or driveways).

Easement appurtenant. An easement created for the benefit of a parcel of land. Such an easement belongs with the land.

Easement in gross. An easement created for the benefit of an individual apart from ownership of land. A public utility easement is an example.

E.g. For example. (From the Latin *exempli gratia*.)

Ejectment. Legal action by an owner of land for the return of his property and for damages when, for instance, a defaulting buyer under a land sales contract refuses to relinquish possession.

Eleemosynary. Charitable.

Emblements. Annual crops.

Eminent domain. The power of the government to take property for a public purpose upon payment of just compensation. See *condemnation*.

Encroachment. The extension of an improvement onto the land of another person.

Encumber. To place a lien or charge on land.

Encumbrance. A lien or charge on land. It includes anything that affects or limits the ownership of property, such as mortgages, easements, or restrictions. A lien is a form of encumbrance that makes the property security for the payment of a debt or obligation, such as mortgages and taxes.

Endorsement. Signature on the back of a promissory note or check, made for the purpose of transferring ownership.

Enforceable. That which can be made effective. A contract or agreement that either party can compel the other to perform.

Equitable lien. A lien recognized in a court of equity.

Equitable title. Title of the purchaser under a land sales contract.

Equity. State or quality of being equal or fair. A body of legal doctrines and rules developed to enlarge, supplement, or override a formal system of law that tends to become too narrow and rigid in its scope.

Equity in property. The amount or value of a person's interest in property above the total of liens or charges; the difference between the market value of the property and the amount of liens against it.

Equity of redemption. Right to redeem property after a judicial sale.

Erosion. Gradual eating away of the soil by the operation of currents or tides.

Escalation. The right reserved by the lender to increase the amount of the payments or interest on the happening of a certain event.

Escalator clause. A clause in a contract providing for the upward or downward adjustment of certain items of cost or expense to cover specified contingencies.

Escheat. The reverting of land to the state in cases in which there are no heirs, devisees, or legatees of a deceased owner.

Escrow. The deposit by contracting parties of a deed or other instruments and funds with a neutral third party for delivery to the respective parties on performance of a condition or conditions.

Estate. The degree, quantity, nature, and extent of the interest a person has in real property.

Estate of inheritance. An estate that may descend to heirs. A fee simple estate is an estate of inheritance.

Estate for life. An estate held by a person to continue during his life or for the life of any other designated person.

Estate at will. The occupation of lands and tenements by a tenant for an indefinite period, terminable by either party at any time after notice.

Estate for years. An interest in land based on a contract for the possession of the land by a tenant or lessee for a definite or fixed period of time. The period can be either more or less than a year.

Estoppel. A doctrine that bars one from asserting rights that are inconsistent with a previous position or representation.

et al. And others. (From the Latin *et alli.*)

Ethics. That branch of moral science, idealism, justness, and fairness that treats of the duties a member of a profession owes to the public, to his client, and to other members of his profession.

et ux. And wife. (From the Latin *et uxor.*)

Exception. Some part of a thing granted that is excluded from the conveyance and remains in the grantor.

Exclusive agency listing. A listing agreement giving one agent the right to sell property (find a buyer) during a specified time but reserving to the owner the right to sell the property himself and not be obligated to pay a commission.

Exclusive right to sell listing. A listing agreement giving the agent the right to sell property (find a buyer) during a specified time and to collect a commission if the property is sold by anyone, including the owner, during such period.

Exculpatory clause. Provision in a contract by which one party seeks to be absolved of liability for his negligent or other wrongful acts. An example is a clause in a contract providing that the buyer takes the property "as is," including defects not visible to him. Such clauses generally have only a limited effect.

Execute. To sign a deed or other document, or to perform a contract.

Execution. The act of completing; performance. In the real estate field, it particularly relates to the signing of a deed by the grantor.

Executor. A person who is designated in a will as the representative of a decedent's estate.

Executory. A contract or agreement that has not yet been performed.

Executrix. Feminine form of *executor.*

Exemption. An immunity from some burden or obligation.

Ex post facto. After the event.

Express. To state; to put into words or writing.

Extension agreement. A grant of further time within which to pay an obligation.

Facsimile. An exact and precise copy.

False personation. Assuming, without authority, the identity of another person for fraudulent purposes.

Fee. An estate of inheritance in real property. Also called fee simple.

Fee simple absolute. An estate in real property that gives the owner the greatest power over the title. It establishes the title of real property in the owner without limitation or end.

Fee simple defeasible. A fee simple estate that can be lost or defeated by the happening of some event subsequent to the initial grant, such as the breach of a condition contained in deed restrictions.

Fictitious deed of trust. A deed of trust recorded by a trustee that discloses all the general terms and provisions contained in the trust deed but does not relate to a specific transaction. It is used for reference only.

Fictitious name. A name used for business purposes that differs from the true name of the owner of the business.

Fiduciary. Held or founded in trust, or one who holds a thing in trust for another person.

Financing statement. Evidence of a personal property security agreement that may be filed with the Secretary of State or recorded with the county recorder under prescribed conditions. Has replaced the chattel mortgage. Affects real property if it relates to crops or timber to be secured.

Finder's fee. A sum payable to a person who introduces a prospective buyer to a seller and a sale is thereafter consummated.

Fixture. A thing that was originally personal property but has become attached to and is considered as part of the real property to which it is affixed.

Foreclosure. A proceeding to enforce a lien by the sale of the property given as security.

Foreclosure sale. The sale of property pledged as security for a debt, to pay the debt after a default occurs.

Forfeiture. A loss of some right, title, estate, or interest in property or of money in consequence of a default.

Forgery. Signing the name of another person to a document without authorization and with the intent to defraud.

Franchise. A right or privilege conferred by law, such as the right to operate a railroad or a bus service. Also, a contractual right to engage in a particular business using a trade name or designation owned by another person.

Fraud. Deception, deceit, trickery. A falsification or misrepresentation made to induce another person to part with some valuable thing belonging to him, or to surrender a legal right.

Freehold. An estate of inheritance (fee estate) or for life.

Future advance clause. A clause in a deed of trust permitting the lender to make additional advances in the future that will also be secured by the deed of trust. See *open-end mortgage*.

Garnishment. A statutory proceeding whereby property, money, or credits of a debtor in possession of a third party are seized and applied to payment of the debt.

General plan restrictions. Restrictions on the use of real property imposed for the benefit of all lots in a subdivision.

Gift deed. A deed given without any material consideration. Sometimes expressed as "love and affection," but is not, in fact, consideration.

Graduated lease. Lease that provides for a varying rental rate, often based on periodic future determinations; used largely in long-term commercial leases.

Grant. A transfer of real property.

Grant deed. A form of deed common in California that contains implied warranties to the effect that the grantor has not previously conveyed or encumbered the property.

Grantee. The person to whom a grant is made.

Grantor. The person who makes a grant.

Grazing rights. A right to pasture cattle or other livestock on the property of another person.

Ground lease. A lease covering the land only and not the improvements, which are to be installed by the lessee.

Ground rent. Earnings of improved property credited to the earnings of the land itself after allowance is made for earnings from the improvements.

Guarantee. An assurance or undertaking as to the performance, quality, or accuracy of a product.

Guaranty. A promise to answer for the payment of another person's debt or obligation.

Guardian. A person appointed by the Probate Court to care for the person or property of a minor or an incompetent person.

Habendum. The clause in a deed that repeats the name of the grantee thus: "to have and to hold unto the said _____," and describes the estate conveyed and to what use.

Heirs. The persons designated by the laws of succession to take the estate of a decedent who leaves no will. Heirs are relatives, but all relatives are not heirs.

Hereditaments. Any property that is capable of being inherited.

Holder in due course. The transferee of a promissory note or other negotiable instrument who takes it in good faith and for value before it is overdue and without notice of any defects at the time it was negotiated to him. Personal defenses that might have been available to the maker, such as fraud in the inducement or failure of consideration, are not available against a holder in due course.

Holographic will. A will entirely written, dated, and signed by the testator in his or her own handwriting. It requires no witnesses.

Homestead. A home on which the owner has recorded a Declaration of Homestead under California law.

Hypothecate. To give a thing as security without parting with possession.

i.e. That is; that is to say. (Latin *id est*.)

Implied. Presumed or inferred, rather than expressed.

Impound account. An account maintained by institutional lenders in which the borrower (trustor on a deed of trust) pays his real property taxes and hazard insurance premiums to the lender in monthly payments along with principal and interest. Required under certain types of FHA-insured loans.

Inchoate. Incomplete; not perfected, such as an attachment lien that is dependent upon a later judgment being entered before the property can be sold to satisfy the claim.

Incompetent. A person who is incapable of managing his or her affairs because of a mental disability.

Incorporeal. Intangible; without physical existence.

Indenture. Deeds or other documents that are executed by both parties.

Indorsement. The act of signing one's name on the back of a check or promissory note for the purpose of transferring it to a third party; see *endorsement*; also, a rider attached to an insurance policy to expand or limit the coverage.

Inherit. To receive property by the laws of inheritance or succession.

Injunction. An order or decree of a court of equity prohibiting some act or compelling an act to be done.

In personam. Against the person.

In propria persona. In his own person; acting for oneself in a lawsuit. Shortened to *pro per*.

In re. In the matter of.

In rem. Against a thing (property) and not against a person.

Installment land sales contract. A contract of sale in which the buyer receives possession but not legal title to the property. On completion of the installment payments, the buyer will be entitled to a deed.

Installment note. A promissory note providing for the repayment of a loan in monthly or other periodic payments over a stated period of time.

Instrument. A writing, such as a deed, made and executed as the expression of some act, contract, or proceeding.

Insurable interest. An interest in property of such a nature that the occurrence of the event insured against would cause financial loss to the insured. Such interest may be that of an owner, mortgagee, lessee, trustee, or the like.

Intangible. Incorporeal; something that does not have material or physical existence. An example is an asset such as the goodwill of a business, as compared with the stock in trade.

Inter alia. Among other things.

Inter vivos. Between living persons, e.g., an inter vivos trust.

Interest rate. The percentage of a sum of money charged for its use. In California the legal rate is 7 percent. The maximum rate for lenders subject to the usury law is basically 10 percent.

Interim loan. A short-term loan usually made during construction of a building. After completion of the structure, a permanent loan (take-out loan) is then customarily arranged.

Interlocutory decree. A court decree that does not finally dispose of a cause of action but requires that some further steps be taken. Two examples are eminent domain and marriage dissolution proceedings.

Intestate. Having made no will. A decedent who has left no will is said to have died intestate.

Inure. To accrue to the benefit of a person.

Involuntary lien. A lien not voluntarily created by the landowner, e.g., a judgment lien.

Ipso facto. Of itself, by the very fact.

Irrevocable. Not to be revoked or withdrawn, e.g., an irrevocable trust.

Joinder. Acting jointly with one or more persons; joining.

Joint note. A note signed by two or more persons who have equal liability for payment.

Joint tenancy. Title held by two or more natural persons in equal shares with right of survivorship.

Joint venture. A business undertaking by two or more persons to conduct a single enterprise for profit. Has characteristics of a partnership but relates to a single venture.

Judgment. The final determination by a court of competent jurisdiction of a matter presented to it.

Judgment lien. A statutory lien created by recording an abstract or certified copy of a judgment for money.

Junior lien. A subordinate or inferior lien, e.g., a second trust deed.

Jurat. A certificate evidencing the fact that an affidavit was properly made before an authorized officer.

Jurisdiction. The power of a court to hear and determine a matter.

Laches. Inexcusable delay in asserting a right; an equitable statute of limitations.

Landowner's royalty. Fractional interests in the production of oil and gas created by the owner of the land, either by reservation when an oil and gas lease is entered into or by a direct grant to a third person.

Land sales contract. A contract used in connection with the sale of real property whereby the seller retains legal title until all or a certain part of the purchase price is paid by the buyer. Often used when property is sold on a small down payment. See *installment land sales contract*.

Lands, tenements, and hereditaments. Inheritable lands or interests therein.

Latent. Hidden from view; concealed. Cf. *patent*.

Lateral. Pertaining to or directed toward the side.

Lateral support. The support that the soil of an adjoining owner gives to the neighbor's land.

Lawful object. An object of a contract that is permitted by law.

Lease. A contract for the possession of land in consideration of the payment of rent.

Legacy. A gift of personal property by will, usually money.

Legal description. A description by which property can be definitely located on the ground by reference to government surveys or approved recorded maps. Sometimes shortened to the word "legal."

Legatee. A person to whom personal property is given by will.

Lessee. The tenant under a lease.

Lessor. The landlord under a lease.

Levy. A seizure of property by judicial process.

License. A personal privilege to do some act on the land of another; also, authorization to engage in a business or profession on compliance with legal requirements.

Lien. A charge on property for the payment of a debt or performance of an obligation.

Life estate. An estate measured in duration by the life of a natural person.

Limited partnership. A partnership composed of one or more general partners together with one or more limited partners whose contribution, liability, and management authority are limited.

Lineal. In a direct line, e.g., a lineal descendant.

Liquidated damages. An agreed-to sum of money to be paid under a contract in the event of a breach when it would be difficult to prove the amount of actual damages.

Lis pendens. A recorded notice of the filing of an action affecting real property.

Listing agreement. A contract of employment between a real estate broker and a principal authorizing the broker as agent to perform specified services regarding the principal's property. Such contracts are entered into for the purpose of obtaining persons to buy, lease, or rent property. Shortened to "listing."

Littoral. Pertaining to the shore.

Lock-in clause. A loan provision specifying a period during which repayment is not allowed.

Lot split. The transfer of a part of a preexisting parcel of land. Lot splitting is generally regulated by local zoning ordinances.

L.S. The place of a seal. The letters sometimes appear on an instrument instead of an actual seal. (Latin *locus sigilli*).

Map Act. A law regulating subdivisions, administered by local governing authorities to control the physical aspects of the land division.

Market value. The price at which a willing seller would sell and a willing buyer would buy property, neither being under any undue pressure to sell or to buy; the highest price a property will bring if exposed for sale in the open market.

Marketable title. A merchantable title; a title free from reasonable doubt in law and in fact.

Material fact. Of consequence; important. In the field of agency, a fact is material if it is one that the agent should realize would be likely to affect the judgment of the principal in giving his consent to the agent to enter into the particular transaction on the specified terms.

Meander. To follow a winding course.

Mechanic's lien. A statutory lien in favor of contractors, subcontractors, laborers, and materialmen who have performed work or furnished materials or supplies to a work of improvement. If not paid, they have a right to record a lien within a prescribed period of time.

Merger of title. The absorption of one estate in another; a uniting of different interests in a parcel of property into one ownership.

Meridians. Imaginary north–south lines that intersect base lines to form a starting point for the measurement of land.

Mesne. Intermediate; intervening.

Metes and bounds. Measurements and boundaries. A method of describing real property.

Minor. Since March 4, 1972, a person under 18 years of age.

Misrepresentation. A false, incorrect, or misleading statement, account, or explanation.

Month-to-month tenancy. A lease of real property for the term of one month, renewable for each succeeding month at the option of either party.

Monuments. Objects or marks used by surveyors to fix or establish a boundary or land location.

Moratorium. Temporary suspension by statute of the enforcement of liability for a debt.

Mortgage. A written instrument by which land is given as security for the payment of a debt or performance of an obligation. In practice, the deed of trust has virtually replaced the mortgage in California.

Mortgagee. The party who obtains the benefit of a mortgage (the lender).

Mortgagor. The party who executes a mortgage (the borrower).

Multiple listing. A listing, usually an exclusive right to sell, taken by a real estate broker who is a member of an organized real estate listing service, with the provision that other members will have the opportunity to find an interested buyer and be able to share in the commission if they do. Basically, it involves an arrangement under which brokers pool their listings.

Muniments of title. Deeds and other original documents showing a chain of title to a parcel of real property.

Mutual consent. The approval or assent of both parties to the terms of a contract.

Mutual water company. A water company organized by or for the benefit of water users in a given district with the object of securing an ample water supply at a reasonable rate. Shares of stock are issued to the users.

N.A.R. National Association of Realtors.

Naturalization. The conferring of the rights of citizenship on a person who has been an alien.

Negotiable. Capable of being transferred by endorsement; assignable or transferable in the ordinary course of business.

Negotiable instrument. An instrument, such as a promissory note or check, meeting certain legal requirements which allow it to circulate freely in commerce.

Net listing agreement. A listing under which the broker is entitled to all proceeds of a sale in excess of a designated selling price.

Nominee. A party designated to act in place of the original buyer in a real estate transaction.

Non sequitur. It does not follow.

Nonjudicial foreclosure sale. A sale of property by the trustee or the mortgagee pursuant to the power of sale contained in the deed of trust or mortgage. Unlike a judicial sale, there is no right of redemption after the sale is made.

Notary public. A public officer who attests or certifies deeds and other writings to assure their authenticity.

Note. A paper, usually a printed form, acknowledging a debt and promising payment. A negotiable note gives transferees a favored position.

Notice of cessation. A notice that can be filed under the mechanic's lien law that will shorten the time to file a mechanic's lien when work has stopped on a construction project.

Notice of completion. A notice that can be filed under the mechanic's lien law within ten days after completion of a structure; it will shorten the time to file a mechanic's lien.

Notice of default. Recorded notice that a default has occurred under a deed of trust (usually entitled a Notice of Default and Election to Sell). It is the first step in the nonjudicial foreclosure of a deed of trust.

Notice of nonresponsibility. Notice that can be recorded under the mechanic's lien law by an owner to relieve the land from mechanics' liens when the land is in the possession of another party, such as a lessee or a vendee under a land sales contract.

Notice to pay rent or quit. Notice to a tenant in default either to pay the rent within three days or to vacate the property.

Novation. The substitution of a new obligation for an old one.

Nuisance. Anything that is offensive and works an injury or harm to a person or property. May be either a public nuisance (offends the general public) or a private nuisance (offends one property owner).

Nunc pro tunc. Now for then. A tardy act made retroactive so as to take effect as of the time when it should have been done.

Nuncupative will. An oral will made in contemplation of death; may dispose of a limited amount of personal property only.

Obiter dictum. That which is said in passing (plural: obiter dicta). Remarks in a court's decision that are not strictly essential but that contain meaningful observations.

Obligatory. That which must be done; binding; having no choice.

Obligor. One who places himself under a legal obligation, e.g., a mortgagor or other debtor.

Offer to purchase and receipt for deposit. See *deposit receipt*.

Offset statement. Statement customarily furnished to an escrow agent from a tenant regarding rent, security deposits, and other rights of possession in the sale of income property. Also, statement furnished by an owner of land subject to an encumbrance as to the amount due. Cf. *beneficiary's statement*.

Omnibus clause. A clause in a decree of distribution by which any property of the decedent, whether specifically described in the decree or not, passes to the distributees.

Open-end mortgage. A mortgage (or deed of trust) that, in addition to the original obligation, secures additional advances made by the lender after the date of execution of the mortgage. Additional advances may be either optional or obligatory. See *future advance clause*.

Open listing agreement. A nonexclusive listing. May be given to any number of agents without liability for payment of compensation except to the one who first obtains a buyer ready, willing, and able to buy on the seller's terms.

Option. A right given for a consideration to purchase or lease a parcel of property within a specified time and on specified terms.

Option listing agreement. A listing that gives the broker a right to buy the principal's property on specified terms.

Optional. Left to one's discretion or choice; not compulsory.

Oral. Spoken.

Oral contract. A contract not in writing; a verbal agreement.

Ordinance. A legislative enactment of a city or county.

Ostensible. Apparent; seeming to be. Sometimes encountered in the field of agency when a person may be regarded as an ostensible agent although not an agent in fact, with resulting liability on the part of a principal.

Outlawed. Describing a claim that can no longer be maintained because of the expiration of the period permitted by the statute of limitations within which to bring an action.

Overriding royalty. The interest in oil and gas to be produced that a lessee may retain when executing an assignment of an oil and gas lease.

Ownership. The right to the use and enjoyment of property to the exclusion of others.

Parcel. Any area of land contained within a single description.

Parol. Oral; verbal.

Parol evidence. Oral or verbal testimony of a witness; extrinsic evidence.

Partial reconveyance. The release of a portion of the property from the lien of a deed of trust.

Partial release clause. A provision in a land sales contract permitting the release to the purchaser of part of the property when certain conditions have been met, such as payment of a specified amount of the consideration.

Partition action. A court action by which co-owners can sever their joint ownership, either by a division of the land into separate parcels if practical, or by a sale of the property and a division of the proceeds in accordance with the respective interests of the owners.

Partnership. A voluntary association of two or more persons to carry on a business for profit as co-owners. May be either a general partnership or a limited partnership.

Party wall. A wall located on the boundary line for the common benefit of adjoining owners.

Patent. Noun: A conveyance by the federal government of title to a portion of the public land. Adjective: Apparent; obvious; open to view. Cf. *latent*.

Pendente lite. Pending suit.

Per capita. By the head. In the distribution of an estate, persons are said to take per capita when each one claims in his own right, based on an equal degree of kinship, an equal share of the estate; compared with the term *per stirpes*, which means by right of representation (according to the roots).

Per se. By itself; as such.

Percentage lease. A lease, usually in the case of commercial property, whereby the rental is determined by the amount of business done by the lessee. Customarily, this is a percentage of gross receipts from the business with provision for a minimum rental.

Periodic tenancy. A tenancy for successive periods of the same length (usually month to month) unless terminated sooner by proper notice of either party.

Perjury. The intentional making of a false statement under oath.

Personal property. Movable property; any property that is not real property.

Plaintiff. The party who brings a court action.

Pleadings. Papers filed in a court action by which the plaintiff sets forth his claim and the defendant sets forth his defense.

Pledge. The depositing of personal property by a debtor with a creditor as security for a debt or other obligation.

Pledgee. The one who is given a pledge or security.

Pledgor. The one who gives a pledge or security.

Police power. The power of the government to enact laws and regulations necessary for the common welfare.

Post. After; afterward; later. Opposite of *ante*.

Post mortem. Occurring after the end of something; after the event.

Power of attorney. A written authorization to an agent to act on behalf of a principal. It may be a special power, that is, limited to specified acts, or it may be a general power. A durable power of attorney is used more often nowadays.

Preamble. An introductory portion of a document.

Preemptive right. The right of the holder to buy property on the same terms as offered by a third party if an owner chooses to sell.

Prepayment clause. A provision in a loan agreement permitting the debtor, for a consideration, to pay part or all of the balance of the debt before its due date, thus saving interest.

Prepayment penalty. A charge imposed by a lender on a borrower who wants to pay all or part of the loan balance before its due date.

Prescribe. To set forth in writing, such as a statute, a rule, or a course to be followed.

Prescription. A method of obtaining an easement by adverse use of another person's property for a period of five years.

Presumption. That which may be assumed without proof.

Pretermit. To omit; to pass by. For example, a child who is not mentioned in his parent's will is referred to as a pretermitted heir.

Prima facie. Assumed correct until overcome by further proof.

Principal. A person who employs an agent to act on his behalf.

Prior. Earlier or previous in point of time or right.

Priority. Quality of being prior; superiority in position.

Privity. Closeness or mutuality of relationship; contractual relationship of original parties to an undertaking or agreement.

Probate Court. The branch of the Superior Court that administers the estates of decedents, incompetents, minors, missing persons, and so on.

Procuring cause. The cause originating a series of events that leads to the consummation of a real estate sale. Ordinarily, for a broker to be entitled to a commission, he must be the procuring cause of the sale.

Profit à prendre. The right to take part of the soil or produce of land.

Promissory note. A written paper promising to repay a loan in accordance with stipulated terms. The promissory note establishes a personal liability for payment on the part of the maker.

Property. Anything of which there may be ownership. Property is classified as either real property or personal property.

Prorate. To divide equally or proportionately to the time of use. In a sales escrow, it is the custom to prorate taxes, interest, rents, and hazard insurance premiums between buyer and seller in accordance with the respective periods of ownership.

Pro tanto. As far as it goes.

Public domain. Land to which title still vests in the United States of America.

Public Report. A report issued by the Real Estate Commissioner containing information of interest to a buyer about newly subdivided property.

Pur autre vie. During the life of another person.

Purchase money deed of trust. A deed of trust to secure payment of all or a portion of the purchase price of real property.

Quasi. Of similar nature; seemingly, but not actually.

Quasi contract. A contract implied by law, based on conduct.

Quiet enjoyment. Right of an owner to enjoy his property without disturbance or interference of possession.

Quiet title. A court action brought to establish title to property or to remove a cloud on the title.

Quitclaim deed. A deed that conveys whatever present right, title, or interest the grantor may have. Unlike a grant deed, it does not contain any warranties.

Q.V. (Quod Vide). Which see.

Range. As used in descriptions, a column of townships running north and south in a row parallel to, and east or west of, a principal meridian.

Ratable. Proportionate.

Ratification. The adoption or approval of an act performed on behalf of a person without previous authorization.

Ready, willing, and able buyer. A buyer who offers to purchase property on terms contained in the broker's listing or acceptable to the seller, and who has the legal capacity and financial resources to buy the property.

Real Estate Board. An organization whose members consist primarily of real estate brokers and salespersons.

Real Estate Investment Trust. A special formation authorized under federal law whereby, under prescribed conditions, investors may pool funds for investments in real estate and escape corporation taxes. Abbreviated to REIT.

Real property. Lands, buildings, and appurtenances (immovable property).

Realtist. A real estate broker holding active membership in a real estate board affiliated with the National Association of Real Estate Brokers.

Realtor. A real estate broker holding active membership in a real estate board affiliated with the National Association of Realtors.

Rebuttable presumption. A presumption that is not conclusive and may be contradicted by evidence.

Reconveyance. A conveyance to the landowner of the title held by a trustee under a deed of trust. May be full or partial.

Recordation. Filing for record in the office of the county recorder for the purpose of giving constructive notice of a title, claim, or interest in real property.

Redemption. Reacquiring (buying back) one's property after a judicial sale on payment of the amount of the sale plus expenses and other costs incurred by the purchaser.

Reformation. A court action to correct a mistake in a deed or other document.

Reinstatement. The curing of a default by a borrower and restoration of the loan to current status through payment of past due amounts.

Release clause. A clause in a mortgage or deed of trust providing for release of specified portions of the property on payment of a specific sum of money.

Reliction. Gradual recession of water from the usual watermark, exposing more dry land for productive use.

Remainder. A future interest in real property. It is an estate that takes effect after the termination of the prior estate, such as a life estate.

Request for notice of default. A notice recorded by the holder of a junior lien requesting that he be notified in the event that a notice of default is recorded under a prior deed of trust.

Rescind. To cancel a contract or other instrument.

Rescission. A court action brought to cancel or annul the effect of executing a contract or other document.

Reservation. A right or interest retained by a grantor in conveying property.

Residue. That part of a decedent's estate remaining after payment of debts and taxes and the distribution of specific bequests and devises.

Restraint on transfer. A limitation on an owner's right to transfer property.

Restrictions. Limitations on the use and enjoyment of property.

Resulting trust. A trust that is implied by law from the acts of the parties; for example, when money is furnished by one party but title is taken in the name of another party for convenience.

Reversion. A future interest in real property. It is the interest remaining in the grantor or his heirs after the termination of a lesser estate granted by him, such as a leasehold estate.

Reversionary interest. The interest a person has in lands or other property on the termination of a lesser estate, such as a leasehold estate.

Revocation. Withdrawal of an offer to contract. Also, the nullification or cancellation of a license to engage in a business or profession.

Rider. An addition, amendment, or endorsement to a document, such as an insurance contract.

Right of survivorship. The right to succeed to the interest of a deceased joint tenant. It is the distinguishing feature of a joint tenancy.

Right of way. A right to cross or pass over a parcel of land. It may be a right to use a roadway or a driveway, or a right to construct power lines through or over the land, or the right to place pipes underground.

Riparian. Pertaining to the bank of a river, a lake, or a tidewater.

Riparian rights. The right of a landowner to the water under or bordering on his land.

Rule against perpetuities. A rule that places a limitation on the time that property can be held in a private trust. The basic rule limits the time that property can be held in trust to lives in being plus 21 years. The rule has been modified by statute.

Sale and leaseback. A situation in which the owner of a parcel of property sells it to a third party and retains possession by simultaneously leasing it from the buyer.

Sales contract. A contract under which a buyer and seller agree to the terms of a sale of property.

Salesperson. In the real estate field, a person licensed to sell real property, but only if employed by a licensed real estate broker.

Sandwich lease. A leasehold interest that lies between the primary lease and the operating lease. It is created when the lessee enters into a sublease.

Sans. Without.

Satisfaction. Performance of the terms of an obligation, such as payment in full of a note secured by a deed of trust.

Satisfied. Paid in full.

Seal. An impression on a document that lends authenticity to its execution, such as affixing the corporate seal to a document executed by a corporation.

Secondary financing. A loan secured by a second mortgage or deed of trust on property.

Section. A measure of land. It is one of the divisions employed in a government survey. It measures one mile on each side and contains 640 acres of land (if regular in shape).

Secured party. The party having the security interest, such as the beneficiary under a deed of trust.

Security. Collateral; property pledged or hypothecated to secure payment of a debt or performance of an obligation.

Security agreement. Agreement between lender and borrower creating a security interest in property pledged or hypothecated.

Security deposit. A deposit of money made to assure performance of an obligation, such as by a tenant under a lease.

Security interest. The interest of the creditor in the property of the debtor pledged or hypothecated to secure payment of a debt or performance of an obligation.

Seizin. The possession of land under a claim of freehold. Also spelled seisin.

Separate property. Property of a husband or wife acquired before marriage and property acquired after marriage by gift, bequest, devise, or descent.

Servient tenement. An estate burdened by an easement. Cf. *dominant tenement.*

Servitude. A right in another person's property in the nature of an easement.

Setback ordinance. An ordinance prohibiting construction of a building between the curb and the setback line. It prevents improvements from being placed too close to the street.

Settlor. The person who creates a private trust. Sometimes referred to as the trustor, but settlor is preferable in order to distinguish the trustor under a deed of trust.

Severalty ownership. Ownership of property by one person alone; sole ownership.

Sheriff's deed. Deed given to the purchaser at an execution sale of real property after the redemption period has expired.

Sinking fund. A fund set aside from the income of property that, with accrued interest, will pay for the replacement of improvements.

Situs. Location of property.

Slander of title. False, unjustified statements regarding another person's title to property.

Soldiers' and Sailors' Civil Relief Act. A federal law, first enacted during World War II, that affords protection from foreclosure and other benefits to a person called into the military service when the obligation was incurred before entry into the service.

Special assessments. Charge on property for its proportionate share of the cost of a local work of improvement, such as street lights, curbing, or sidewalks. Distinguished from property taxes, which are levied for the general support of government.

Specific performance. A court action to compel performance of an agreement for the sale of land.

Spouse. A husband or wife.

Stare Decisis. The doctrine that the decisions of the court should stand as a precedent for future guidance.

State Housing Act. A state law that sets minimum building standards for certain types of construction in California.

Status. The standing of a person before the law; that is, whether an adult, a married person, and so on.

Statute. Laws enacted by a legislative body.

Statute of frauds. State law that requires that certain contracts, such as a contract for the sale of land, be in writing to be enforceable.

Statute of limitations. State law that prescribes various times within which court actions to enforce a right or for other relief must be filed.

Stock in trade. Merchandise held by a business for resale to the public.

Stop notice. A remedy under the mechanic's lien law for reaching unexpended construction funds in the hands of an owner or lender before payment to the general contractor.

Straight note. A note in which the entire principal is repaid in one sum, rather than in installments.

Street Improvement Act of 1911. The most frequently encountered of the state laws prescribing the method of payment for the cost of a local work of improvement.

Subdivision. A division of a tract of land into separate parcels, usually for residential purposes.

Subject to. A method of taking over a loan secured by trust deed without taking over the responsibility of a deficiency judgment if a foreclosure sale thereafter occurs. Cf. *assumption of deed of trust.*

Sublease. A transfer by a tenant of his interest in leased property for a term less than his own, the tenant retaining a reversion.

Subordinate. To make inferior or junior to another interest or lien.

Subordination agreement. An agreement under which a prior or superior lien is made inferior or subject to an otherwise junior lien.

Subpoena. A process issued by a court to cause a witness to appear at a hearing and give testimony.

Subpoena duces tecum. A subpoena that directs a witness to bring specified documents and files with him.

Subrogate. To substitute one person in the place of another with reference to an obligation.

Subsequent. Occurring or coming later in time.

Succession. The taking of property by inheritance.

Successor. One who succeeds to another person's ownership.

Summons. Court process that directs a defendant to make an appearance in an action filed against him.

Surety. A person who binds himself with another, called the principal, for the performance of an obligation; a guarantor.

Survey. The process by which a parcel of land is measured and its area and lines of possession are determined.

Syndicate. A pooling arrangement or association of persons who invest in real property by buying shares in some type of organization such as a partnership, joint venture, corporation, or other entity.

Take-out loan. A long-term, permanent loan that replaces a short-term, interim construction loan.

Tangible. Having a concrete or physical form; capable of being touched.

Tax. A levy, under authority of law, for government purposes.

Tax deed. A deed issued to the purchaser at a tax sale of real property.

Tax sale. Sale of property by the tax collector for nonpayment of taxes.

Tenancy in common. Ownership of property by any two or more persons in undivided interests (not necessarily equal), without right of survivorship.

Tenant. One who has the right of possession of another person's property under an agreement to pay rent.

Tender. An unconditional offer to pay a debt or perform a contract.

Tenements. All rights in land that pass with a conveyance of the land.

Tentative map. Under the Subdivision Map Act, a map submitted initially by a subdivider of land to the local planning authority for approval. After all conditions have been complied with, a final map is approved and recorded.

Tenure. The mode or manner in which title to land is held.

Term. The period of a lease, provisions of a loan, or any provision of a contract. Used variously in the real estate field.

Testament. The written declaration of a person's last will.

Testamentary trust. A trust created by will, effective when the testator dies, as distinguished from a living or inter vivos trust (which is effective during the lifetime of the trustor).

Testate. Having made a will. A decedent who made a will is said to have died testate.

Testator. A male person who makes a will.

Testatrix. A female person who makes a will.

Tier. As used in descriptions, a row of townships, running east and west, parallel to and north or south of a designated base line.

Time is of the essence. A clause in a contract that requires complete performance within the stated time limitations. It contemplates a punctual performance.

Title. Evidence of a person's right or the extent of his interest in property.

Title insurance. Assurances as to the condition of title. It protects the owner or other insured, such as a lender, against loss or impairment of title.

Toll. To bar; defeat.

Topography. Nature of the surface of land; for example, the topography may be level, rolling, mountainous, and so on.

Tort. A wrongful act; an intentional or negligent violation of another person's legal rights. A type of wrong not arising out of breach of contract.

Tortfeasor. A wrongdoer; a person who commits or is guilty of a tort.

Township. A part of a subdivision of the public lands of the United States. A township contains 36 sections, uniformly numbered starting with the northeast section, and each one mile square.

Tract. A real estate development in which one large parcel is divided into a number of smaller parcels called lots.

Trade fixtures. Articles of personal property, fastened to real property, that are necessary to the carrying on of a trade. When installed by a tenant, they are ordinarily removable on the expiration of the tenancy.

Trade name. The name or style under which a firm does business.

Transfer tax. A tax payable on the conveyance of real property, measured by the amount of consideration paid.

Trespass. An invasion of an owner's rights in his property; a wrongful entry on the land of another person.

Trust. A fiduciary relationship in which one party (trustee) holds the title to property for the benefit of another party (beneficiary).

Trust account. An account held in trust for another party as distinguished from one's own personal account.

Trust deed. Same as *deed of trust*.

Trust funds. Money or other thing of value received by a real estate broker or salesperson to be held for the benefit of other persons.

Trustee. The person who holds title in trust for the benefit of another person.

Trustee's deed. Deed given by the trustee under a deed of trust when the property is sold under the power of sale.

Trustee's sale. A foreclosure sale conducted by the trustee under a deed of trust after a default occurs.

Trustor. The person who conveys real property in trust to secure repayment of a loan.

U.C.C. Uniform Commercial Code, a state law effective January 1, 1965 that established a unified and comprehensive scheme or plan for the regulation of security transactions in personal property.

Ultra vires. Beyond their powers. A corporation is said to act ultra vires when it exceeds the authority given it by its charter and by-laws.

Undivided interests. The unsegregated interest of co-owners in the entire property owned in common.

Undue influence. Taking an unfair or fraudulent advantage of another person's weakness of mind, distress, or necessity.

Unenforceable. A contract or a law that cannot be legally enforced.

Unilateral contract. A contract that calls for an act in exchange for a promise. Cf. *bilateral contract*.

Unity. Oneness or singleness. As related to joint tenancy, four unities are necessary to create a valid joint tenancy: unity of time, title, interest, and possession.

Unjust enrichment. A legal doctrine designed to prevent a person from taking advantage of another person's mistake, such as an overpayment of an amount due. It is based on a rule of fairness.

Unlawful detainer. An action to recover possession of real property.

Unruh Act. State law that prohibits discrimination by real estate agents or business establishments because of race, color, creed, sex, or national origin.

Unsecured. Without security; that is, no property is put up as security for a debt.

Usury. The act of charging more interest than the law allows on a loan. The maximum rate of interest in California is 10 percent (unless exemptions are applicable).

Valid. Sufficient in law; effective.

Value. The worth of a thing in money or goods at a certain time.

Variable interest rate. Interest rate that fluctuates with the current cost of money. Subject to adjustment if the prevailing rate moves up or down.

Variance. A departure from the general rule; an exception.

Vendee. The buyer or purchaser under a contract of sale.

Vendor. The seller under a contract of sale.

Venue. The county in which a lawsuit is brought or tried, or the place in which an acknowledgment is taken.

Verification. Sworn statement before a duly qualified officer, such as a notary public, that the matters set forth in a pleading or other document are true.

Versus. Against. Abbreviated to *vs.* or *v.*

Vest. To give an immediate, fixed right in property, with either present or future enjoyment of possession.

Vested interest. An interest in property that is fixed or determined.

Viz. Namely; that is to say. (Latin *videlicet*)

Void. Having no legal effect; null.

Voidable. Describing an instrument that appears to be valid but is in fact lacking in some essential requirement.

Voluntary lien. A lien intentionally created by a debtor, such as a mortgage or deed of trust, as contrasted with a judgment lien.

Waive. To relinquish or abandon; to forego a right to enforce or require something.

Waiver. A giving up or abandonment of a right.

Warrant. To guarantee; assure.

Warranty. An assurance or guarantee that certain defects do not exist.

Warranty deed. A deed containing express warranties of title and quiet possession. Often used in other states but not in California, where assurances are customarily given by way of title insurance.

Waste. Destruction or injury to premises by a tenant, or impairment in value by a life tenant or by a mortgagor or trustor.

Water right. The right of a landowner to the use of the water bordering on or underneath his land.

Will. A disposition of property effective on the owner's death.

Witness. Verb: To see or know by personal presence and perception.

Wrap-around deed of trust. A method of refinancing in which a second lender assumes payment of the present trust deed and gives the borrower an increased trust deed at a higher interest rate. See *all-inclusive deed of trust*.

Writ. A process of the court directing that certain action be taken.

Writ of possession. A process by which an owner may be restored to possession of his land.

Zone. Area in a community set off by a zoning authority for specified uses, such as for single-family residences.

Zoning. Government regulations by a city or county relating to the use of property.

Answers to Textbook Questions

CHAPTER ONE

Matching Terms

1. f	2. j	3. h	4. i	5. b
6. a	7. c	8. d	9. g	10. e

True/False

11. T	12. T	13. F	14. T	15. F
16. T	17 .T	18. F	19. F	20. T

Multiple Choice

21. d	22. d	23. d	24. b	25. a
26. c	27. b	28. d	29. d	30. d
31. b	32. d	33. c	34. c	35. d
36. d	37. d	38. a	39. d	40. d
41. b	42. c	43. c	44. b	45. b
46. b	47. b	48. b	49. a	50. d

CHAPTER TWO

Matching Terms

1. d	2. g	3. f	4. i	5. a
6. h	7. j	8. b	9. e	10. c

True/False

11. T	12. T	13. F	14. T	15. T
16. F	17. F	18. F	19. T	20. T

Multiple Choice

21. a	22. b	23.d	24. d	25. d
26. c	27. d	28.d	29. a	30. d
31. d	32. a	33.b	34. d	35. a

36. b	37. d	38. d	39. d	40. b
41. d	42. b	43. c	44. b	45. c
46. c	47. d	48. d	49. d	50. c

CHAPTER THREE

Matching Terms

1. e	2. g	3. f	4. h	5. a
6. c	7. j	8. i	9. d	10. b

True/False

11. F	12. F	13. T	14. T	15. T
16. F	17. T	18. F	19. T	20. T

Multiple Choice

21. c	22. a	23. c	24. b	25. a
26. c	27. b	28. c	29. b	30. a
31. d	32. d	33. a	34. c	35. a
36. d	37. d	38. c	39. a	40. b
41. a	42. b	43. a	44. c	45. b
46. d	47. d	48. b	49. c	50. b

CHAPTER FOUR

Matching Terms

1. f	2. j	3. h	4. g	5. i
6. a	7. b	8. d	9. e	10. c

True/False

11. F	12. F	13. T	14. F	15. T
16. F	17. T	18. T	19. T	20. F

Multiple Choice

21. d	22. d	23. d	24. d	25. d
26. c	27. d	28. a	29. a	30. d
31. c	32. c	33. d	34. d	35. b
36. d	37. a	38. a	39. c	40. a
41. b	42. c	43. c	44. c	45. d
46. a	47. d	48. d	49. a	50. d

CHAPTER FIVE

Matching Terms

1. d	2. f	3. h	4. g	5. j
6. a	7. b	8. i	9. e	10. c

True/False

11. T	12. F	13. F	14. F	15. F
16. T	17. T	18. F	19. T	20. T

Multiple Choice

21. d	22. a	23. d	24. c	25. a
26. b	27. d	28. b	29. b	30. c
31. d	32. d	33. d	34. d	35. d
36. a	37. d	38. a	39. b	40. c
41. d	42. c	43. d	44. d	45. d
46. c	47. d	48. d	49. d	50. d

CHAPTER SIX

Matching Terms

1. e	2. h	3. f	4. j	5. b
6. i	7. a	8. d	9. g	10. c

True/False

11. T	12. F	13. T	14. F	15. F
16. F	17. F	18. F	19. F	20. T

Multiple Choice

21. b	22. c	23. c	24. d	25. b
26. d	27. d	28. d	29. b	30. d
31. a	32. b	33. b	34. a	35. b
36. a	37. c	38. a	39. c	40. d
41. b	42. d	43. a	44. c	45. d
46. a	47. d	48. b	49. d	50. d

CHAPTER SEVEN

Matching Terms

1. e	2. g	3. j	4. f	5. h
6. i	7. d	8. c	9. a	10. b

True/False

11. F	12. F	13. T	14. T	15. F
16. T	17. T	18. T	19. T	20. F

Multiple Choice

21. a	22. d	23. b	24. d	25. a
26. b	27. c	28. a	29. d	30. b
31. b	32. a	33. a	34. b	35. d
36. b	37. a	38. d	39. d	40. b
41. a	42. d	43. d	44. d	45. b
46. d	47. a	48. d	49. c	50. a

CHAPTER EIGHT

Matching Terms

1. i	2. e	3. h	4. g	5. j
6. b	7. d	8. c	9. f	10. a

True/False

11. T	12. F	13. F	14. F	15. T
16. T	17. F	18. F	19. T	20. T

Multiple Choice

21. c	22. c	23. d	24. a	25. b
26. a	27. c	28. b	29. b	30. d
31. c	32. d	33. b	34. b	35. b
36. c	37. a	38. c	39. d	40. b
41. d	42. c	43. c	44. b	45. d
46. b	47. d	48. d	49. b	50. d

CHAPTER NINE

Matching Terms

1. g	2. h	3. j	4. i	5. d
6. a	7. c	8. e	9. f	10. b

True/False

11. F	12. F	13. F	14. T	15. T
16. T	17. T	18. F	19. T	20. T

Multiple Choice

21. c	22. b	23. b	24. b	25. c
26. a	27. b	28. a	29. c	30. d
31. d	32. c	33. d	34. d	35. d
36. c	37. d	38. a	39. a	40. b
41. a	42. d	43. b	44. c	45. c
46. d	47. d	48. b	49. d	50. d

CHAPTER TEN

Matching Terms

1. i	2. f	3. g	4. j	5. b
6. d	7. a	8. e	9. c	10. h

True/False

11. T	12. F	13. F	14. T	15. F
16. T	17. F	18. T	19. T	20. F

Multiple Choice

21. c	22. a	23. a	24. a	25. d
26. a	27. d	28. d	29. b	30. c
31. a	32. b	33. d	34. b	35. b
36. d	37. a	38. d	39. c	40. b
41. d	42. d	43. d	44. a	45. c
46. d	47. d	48. d	49. d	50. d

CHAPTER ELEVEN

Matching Terms

1. i	2. f	3. h	4. j	5. g
6. d	7. a	8. c	9. e	10. b

True/False

11. F	12. T	13. T	14. T	15. F
16. T	17. T	18. T	19. T	20. T

Multiple Choice

21. a	22. b	23. b	24. a	25. c
26. a	27. d	28. b	29. d	30. a
31. d	32. a	33. d	34. d	35. c
36. a	37. d	38. b	39. d	40. a
41. d	42. a	43. d	44. d	45. d
46. d	47. d	48. d	49. d	50. d

CHAPTER TWELVE

Matching Terms

1. i	2. h	3. j	4. f	5. g
6. b	7. a	8. d	9. e	10. c

True/False

11. T	12. F	13. T	14. T	15. F
16. T	17. T	18. F	19. F	20. F

Multiple Choice

21. d	22. d	23. b	24. d	25. b
26. d	27. b	28. d	29. a	30. c
31. c	32. d	33. b	34. a	35. b
36. d	37. d	38. a	39. a	40. d
41. a	42. b	43. a	44. a	45. d
46. b	47. b	48. a	49. d	50. a

CHAPTER THIRTEEN

Matching Terms

1. d	2. g	3. i	4. f	5. j
6. a	7. h	8. c	9. e	10. b

True/False

11. T	12. T	13. F	14. T	15. T
16. F	17. T	18. T	19. F	20. F

Multiple Choice

21. a	22. d	23. d	24. d	25. d
26. d	27. c	28. b	29. c	30. a
31. d	32. c	33. d	34. d	35. d
36. d	37. d	38. a	39. d	40. b
41. d	42. a	43. d	44. d	45. d
46. d	47. b	48. d	49. d	50. c

CHAPTER FOURTEEN

Matching Terms

1. e	2. j	3. f	4. g	5. h
6. i	7. a	8. c	9. b	10. d

True/False

11. F	12. T	13. T	14. T	15. T
16. F	17. F	18. F	19. T	20. T

Multiple Choice

21. d	22. d	23. d	24. d	25. d
26. c	27. c	28. d	29. d	30. d
31. a	32. b	33. c	34. a	35. b
36. b	37. a	38. d	39. b	40. d
41. c	42. d	43. b	44. d	45. d
46. a	47. c	48. d	49. d	50. c

CHAPTER FIFTEEN

Matching Terms

1. f	2. g	3. h	4. i	5. j
6. e	7. a	8. c	9. b	10. d

True/False

11. T	12. F	13. F	14. F	15. F
16. T	17. T	18. F	19. F	20. T

Multiple Choice

21. d	22. c	23. a	24. d	25. d
26. c	27. d	28. a	29. a	30. d
31. d	32. a	33. a	34. b	35. d
36. a	37. a	38. a	39. a	40. c
41. b	42. c	43. b	44. b	45. d
46. d	47. d	48. a	49. b	50. d

Index

real estate purchase contract, 3.49-3.57

rescission of for economic duress, 2.43

retained by broker for 3 years, 3.1

reviewed by broker, 3.4

right to extend performance by broker, 3.52

revocation of authority and receipt for deposit, 3.17-3.18

right to compensation, 3.19-3.38

unconscionable contract, 2.3, 2.17

Conversion, 5.16

Conveyances. *See* Acquisition and conveyance of real property, methods of

Cooperating broker, duties and liabilities of, right to commission, 3.28

Corporate agent, liability, 5.20

Corporate Securities Law, 4.36

Corporation, broker as, 4.30

    liability of, 7.2

    suspension of license, 4.30

Corporations, ownership through, 8.63-8.76

    articles, filing of, 8.67

Counter offer, 2.7, 3.50

Court structure in California, 1.21-1.27

Covenant of good faith, 5.2

Covenants, 12.4

    in contracts, 2.24

    creation of, 12.7

    defined, 12.4

    distinguished from conditions, 12.4

    runs with the land, 12.6

Creative financing disclaimers, 9.58

Credit reports, 9.59

Curative act, re acknowledgments, 7.46

Damages, for breach of contract, 2.47-2.57, 5.2

    against landlord, 15.40

    benefit of bargain, doctrine of, 2.50, 5.22

    duty to mitigate, 2.55, 15.55

    out of pocket, 5.22

    trust deed, not disclosing, 2.49

Declaratory relief, 2.45

Dedication

    acquisition of real estate by, 6.21-6.27

    easements, 14.25

    implied dedication, 6.26

    limitation on use of land acquired by, 6.23

    under Map Act, 13.41

    nature of interest created, 6.22

    of public lands, 6.24

    subdivision dedication, 6.27

    subsurface use of park property, 6.25

    easement by, 14.25

Deed of trust. *See* Trust deeds

Deeds, conveyance of property through, 7.4-7.42

    acceptance, lack of, 7.33

    acknowledgments of, 7.43-7.47

    consideration in, 7.13-7.14

    defined, 7.5

    delivery of, 7.30

    form of, 7.7

    in lieu of foreclosure, 9.60

interests conveyed by, 7.12

requisites of, 7.11

security device intended as, 9.19

title, when passes, 7.30, 7.74

types of, 7.6

    gift deed, 7.6

    grant deed, 7.6-7.42

    quitclaim deed, 7.6, 7.8

    trust deed, 7.6, 9.9

    void, 7.41

    voidable, 7.42

    warranty deed, 7.9

Deficiency judgments, 9.15, 10.23, 10.31, 10.47

Department of Industrial Relations, 12.90

Department of Real Estate, California, 4.27, 4.38

Deposit

    cleaning, 15.35

    disposition of, 3.53, 4.41

    escrow, 7.65

    forfeiture of, 3.54

    promissory note as, 3.53, 5.4

    return of without authorization, 5.16

Description, 13.10-13.34

    assessment district maps, 13.23

    assessor's maps, 13.20

    blanket description, 13.25

    boundaries and monuments, 13.33

    conveyance of fractional part of lot, 13.28, Fig. 13ñ1

    government survey, 13.16

    how obtained, 13.11

    intention must be expressed, 13.31

    interpretation of grant or reservation, 13.32

    land adjoining a highway, 13.34

    lines of division, 13.29

    lot and block description, 13.17

    metes and bounds, 13.15

    official maps, 13.19

    parcel maps, 13.22

    parol or extrinsic evidence, 13.13

    record of survey, 13.18

    rules of construction, 13.30

    state plane coordinate system, 13.21

    sufficiency of, 13.12

    of tract by common name, 13.26

    unrecorded maps, 13.24

    use of street address, 13.27

Detrimental reliance, concept of, 2.8

Disability benefits, 8.34

Discharge of contracts, 2.28-2.37

Disciplinary proceedings, for violation of Real Estate Law, 5.44-5.47

Disclaimers, 5.28

Disclosing compensation from lender, 3.38

Disclosure, creative financing, 9.58

Disclosure and nondisclosure, 5.4

Discrimination, 4.42, 15.5

Disposition, right of, 1.30

Documentary transfer tax, 7.34, 13.20

Down payment. *See* Deposit

Dragnet clause, 9.29

Dual representation, 5.8, 5.14

    duty to disclose information received from one principal, 5.14

re escrow, 7.62

Due diligence, 3.18; Fig. 3ñ1; 5.51

Due-on-encumbrance clause, 9.46

Due-on-sale clause, 9.45

Durable power of attorney, 7.48

Duties owed to principal, 5.4-5.20

Duties owed to third parties, 5.21-5.38

Duty not to compete, 5.6

Duty not to disclose sales price, 5.19

Earnest money. *See* Deposit

Earth movements, boundaries after, 14.71

Earthquake faults. *See* Special Studies Zone Act

Easements

    cannot have on own land, 14.3

    classes of, 14.8-14.10

    condemnation, 14.23

    conservation, 14.26

    creation of, 14.18 et seq.

    dedication, 14.25

    definition and nature of, 14.2-14.7

    estoppel, 14.27

    express grant or reservation, 14.19

    extent of use, 14.29-14.36

    implied grant or reservation, 14.20

    necessity, 14.21

    open space easements, 14.25

    prescription, 14.22

    purposes of creation, 14.11-14.7

    solar easement, 14.16

    termination or extinguishment of, 14.41-14.49

    transfer of, 14.37-14.40

Education, continuing, 4.45

Eleemosynary, 6.46

Eminent domain, 6.11-6.20

Emotional distress, 2.53, 14.59, 15.41

Encroachments, 14.50-14.54

    good faith improver, 14.51

Encumbrances, 10.46

England, common law of, in California, 1.3, 1.60, 2.11, 7.2

Entry, right of by landlord, 15.32

Environmental impact reports, 13.2, 13.40

Equal dignity rule, 2.12, 4.9

Equitable mortgage, 9.64

Equitable servitudes, 10.18, 12.13

Equity, defined, 1.19

Errors and Omissions Insurance, 4.22

Escheat, property conveyed to state by, 6.55-6.56

Escrows, 7.56-7.78

    agency status of escrow holder, 7.62-7.63

    broker ownership of escrow company, 5.12

    cancellation of, 7.76

    confidential nature of, 7.70

    deposit & return of funds, 7.65

    double escrow, 7.63

    escrow holder, duties and responsibilities of, 7.69

    escrow instructions, 7.67

    estopped to terminate, 2.25

    mobile homes, 15.69

    ownership interest in, 5.12